HOW TO TEACH PIANO SUCCESSFULLY

SECOND EDITION

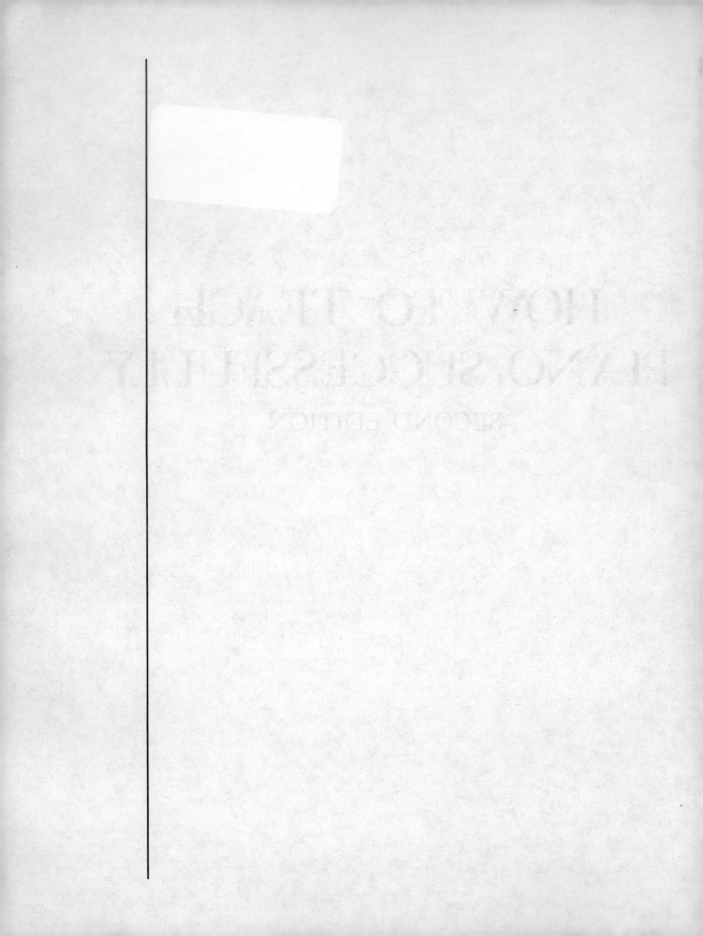

HOW TO TEACH PIANO SUCCESSFULLY

Second Edition

by

James W. Bastien

Kjos

General Words and Music Co. / Neil A. Kjos, Jr., Publishers
Park Ridge, Illinois and San Diego, California
Second Edition, 1977

Published by General Words and Music Co.

Distributed by Neil A. Kjos Music Company
National Order Desk, 4382 Jutland Drive, San Diego, California 92117

International Standard Book Number 0-8497-6109-3

Library of Congress Card Number 77-075481

Publisher's Edition Number GP40

Printed and Bound in the United States of America

For

Jane, Lisa and Lori

Preface

Piano teaching is an art which requires special study, aptitude, application and expertise. The purpose of this book is to present a program of study and a general survey of the teaching scene that will provide guidelines for the successful practice of piano teaching. Special emphasis is given to the important beginning stages of instruction. The book is designed to be used as a basic text for piano pedagogy classes and as a general reference book for the piano teacher.

The Second Edition incorporates over five hundred new teaching materials and books on music. In addition, a new chapter has been added, entire lists of music have been changed, and other chapters have been altered. It is the purpose of this edition to bring the materials as up-to-date as possible.

The four parts of *How to Teach Piano Successfully* deal with different areas of teaching. Part I discusses various organizational aspects of teaching and includes information on studio management, scheduling lessons, and business matters; a special feature of Part I is the survey of current teaching methods. Part II surveys the broad spectrum of teaching from the pre-school student through the intermediate student, and offers specific recommendations in the areas of repertoire, technique, theory, and materials. Part III includes a variety of subjects dealing with important specialized teaching matters; Chapters 12 through 17 were written by outstanding contributing authors who are recognized authorities in their fields. Part IV contains interviews with distinguished musicians and is included to provide insights into various aspects of teaching.

The lists of recommended materials in most of the chapters are intended to serve as guides to representative works at various levels. It is not the purpose of this text to provide exhaustive complete listings, but rather, selected choices. The approximate grading of works for the various chapters is intended to assist the busy teacher in the selection of materials. The grading is purposely intended for students of average ability who will comprise the majority of the average teacher's class. When surveying materials for pedagogy classes, it is helpful to have the recommended music available for thorough examination.

I have made an effort to keep this book flexible. Since each chapter is independent, the instructor or general reader can begin anywhere. Although the book was planned to permit a specific reading sequence, the reader should not feel bound to a page-by-page reading.

The extensive appendices are intended to provide the teacher with a variety of information. The lists were compiled during years of research and they include numerous recommendations from outstanding music educators.

Finally, I am especially grateful for the many helpful suggestions from my students and colleagues and to the many individuals who helped make this book possible. Special acknowledgments are made to the following musicians: to Joseph Banowetz, Louise Bianchi, Charles Braswell, Maurice Hinson, George Lucktenberg, and Ylda Novik for contributing chapters to the book; to Irl Allison, James Dick, Rosina Lhevinne, and Adele Marcus for their generosity in granting interviews; to Louise Bianchi, Dorothy Bishop, Rita Fuszek, William Gillock, Maurice Hinson, E. L. Lancaster, Frances Larimer, Clarice Lincoln, Ralph Pierce, Ylda Novik, and Jeanne Weisman for giving valuable lists for the appendices.

I wish to thank again all those who contributed their time and advice to the first edition. For assistance in preparing this Second Edition, special thanks go to the following publishers who were helpful in answering questions I had concerning their publications and who provided complimentary review copies of new publications: Alfred Music Co., Belwin-Mills, Boosey & Hawkes, Carl Fischer, Galaxy Music Corporation, Neil A. Kjos Music Co., Lorenz Publishing Co., Myklas Press, Theodore Presser Co., Lee Roberts Music Publications, G. Schirmer, Inc., Screen Gems – Columbia Publications, Stipes Publishing Co., Summy-Birchard Publishing Co., and the Willis Music Co.

James W. Bastien

Contents

General Teaching Considerations 1

What are the basic attributes of a successful teacher? Knowledge, personality, enthusiasm, self-confidence, leadership – the list could go on and on. Of course it is these qualities and many more that distinguish a brilliant teacher from a mediocre one.

Stop to reflect for a moment on your own background.

1. Who was the teacher who interested and inspired you the most?
2. Why was this person outstanding?
3. What were the most memorable characteristics of this person?

Instruction varies widely and is largely dependent on the teacher's personality. Although there are many instructional procedures, there is no one magic blueprint which can be described as *the method*. One teacher might be quite formal and another informal. One might be considered a taskmaster, another easygoing. One might be impatient, another quite patient. Since teachers work with people, not things, they must be searching constantly for new and effective lines of communication. Methods, goals and objectives must be periodically evaluated and reevaluated.

THE TEACHER'S CONCEPT OF TEACHING

If you are studying to become a teacher, why do you want to teach? If you are already teaching, what is your motivation?

The adage "Those who can, do; those who can't, teach," is at best a shoddy, inaccurate concept of teaching. This negative view must be rejected. The successful teacher usually is a positive person, concerned with others, who chooses the teaching profession as a career. Like other occupations this career has its share of rewards and frustrations. Financially, the teacher might achieve greater remuneration in another field, but he might not have the opportunity to observe living results of his abilities and efforts. The teacher usually derives a great deal of self-satisfaction from working with people rather than things, and often this is an important motivating factor in choosing teaching as a career.

Unfortunately for the profession, teaching is sometimes considered a stop-gap occupation: "I'll do this for a while until something better comes along." This idea is well stated by Adams:

> Some teachers from the very first consider themselves to be teachers-in-transit. These are the people who, for reasons of their own, need to work for a while before they enter professional schools, business, or matrimony. Many of the teachers-in-transit have been quite effective as teachers. However, too many of them never really identify with teaching, since their attention is constantly fixed upon noneducational goals.[1]

Many teachers think of themselves as pianists, scientists, or linguists first, and assign a secondary place to the teaching role. It does not necessarily follow that because one is an expert in a particular field he will likewise be a gifted teacher capable of making others learn.

The old saw "Teachers are born, not made," has been repeated all too often. This glaring generality is an inaccurate assumption. Although teaching is a personal art, it must be studied and not left to "doing what comes naturally." Highet discusses this concept when he says: "Most people are clumsy at learning and teaching, not because they are stupid, but because they have not thought about it."[2]

One's concept of teaching may be either positive or negative. For those who resort to teaching out of necessity, as a substitute for a concert career that did not materialize, it may be a frustrating occupation. However, for those who elect teaching as a career, it may be a satisfying experience which becomes increasingly more interesting. Positive, meaningful, effective teaching comes from individuals who are genuinely interested in others. In short, they *care* about their students.

THE TEACHER'S BACKGROUND AND TRAINING

Pre-College Training

A musician's career often is dependent on a chain of events which may date back to beginning instruction. If the training received as a child was solid both in pianistic and theoretical practices, then usually he has a firm foundation on which to build continued progress. However, if his training was sketchy, then it would be necessary for him to spend a considerable amount of time and effort trying to gain missing skills.

Consider your own training as a young student, and in retrospect evaluate your accomplishments. Answer the following questions "yes or no," and give yourself a rating.

1. Was your level of advancement carefully guided through thoughtful selection of materials which would insure steady, gradual progress?
2. Were you taught theory as a regular part of your basic instruction?

[1]Sam Adams and John L. Garrett, Jr., *To Be a Teacher* (Englewood Cliffs, N.J.: Prentice-Hall, Inc., 1969), p. 12. Reprinted by permission.

[2]Gilbert Highet, *The Art of Teaching* (New York: Vintage Books, 1950), p. 5.

3. Did your teacher stress such areas as ensemble playing, improvisation, ear-training, sight-reading, harmonization and transposition?
4. Were you assigned music written in a variety of keys, and did you, in time, play as well in one key as another?
5. Were you taught all key signatures, all major, minor, diminished, and augmented chords?
6. Were you taught to analyze music from a formalistic and harmonic standpoint?
7. Did you receive adequate technical instruction regarding posture at the piano; hand position; drills in scales, chords and inversions, arpeggios, and double notes?
8. Was your teacher particular about correct fingering, phrasing, balance between melody and accompaniment, dynamics, tempo, and the mood of the composition?
9. Did you learn the musical terminology used in the compositions studied, and did your teacher suggest that you use one of the music dictionaries?
10. Were you instructed to study the background of composers and the time in which they lived?

Rate yourself on a ten point basis. If your score is from 70 to 100, you had excellent beginning instruction! However, if your rating is below 70, then probably you had some serious gaps in your pre-college training.

Selection of the Pre-College Teacher

The musical training and development of a young pianist is entrusted almost exclusively to the private teacher. Since most schools ordinarily do not offer such courses as piano ensemble, theory, or chamber music, the private piano teacher is charged with the responsibility of providing a complete musical background for his students. It is, therefore, vitally important for a young student to have selected a competent and qualified teacher; for in a sense, the beginning teacher can "make or break" a young pianist.

The selection of a good private teacher is complicated by the fact that there is a lack of standardization among teachers. In other professions this is minimized. One would expect all doctors and dentists to have received similar, relevant training to prepare them for their careers. Unfortunately, this is *not* the case with the private piano teacher: some have college music degrees, others have only had a few years of training; some are professional artists who perform regularly; others can scarcely play at all and never perform. Credentials such as degrees, performance background, or recently acquired certification, are important criteria in determining professional standards. However, training and background alone will not assure competent teaching: other significant factors are the personality of the teacher, teaching experience, and the teacher's interest in teaching.

The instruction received during the pre-college period may be difficult to assess. Competent instruction is not always assured by the number of years one has taken lessons. For this reason a model program is offered as an insight by which personal evaluation may be measured.

Since pre-college backgrounds vary greatly among students because of various teachers one might have had, what would be an average, acceptable level of competence for a prospective piano major which would satisfy minimum requirements for college entrance?

Before listing specific requirements, several general considerations should be listed: (1) the length of study in the pre-college period, (2) the student's degree of application during this period, and (3) the quality of teaching received during this time.

Generally, young students begin formal piano lessons around the age of eight or nine; if lessons are continued without interruption throughout high school, the total length of pre-college study would be about eight years. However, it is not safe to assume that because a student has had eight or more years of lessons prior to college he will automatically be proficient. It is possible that the student used his time poorly during those years, was indolent, undisciplined, practiced little, and was not motivated towards serious piano study. Obviously he would have accomplished very little in relation to the time engaged in study.

Sometimes students begin a college degree program in music with very little piano background, possibly only two or three years of lessons. These students usually are weak in performance on their major instrument, and are often deficient in technique and sight-reading. In essence they are ill equipped, and would be seriously handicapped in a college music program where so much depends on what has been accomplished prior to college.

Consider the following exemplary student who is about to enter a college music department. He has had eight years of piano instruction, he was highly motivated by a gifted teacher, and he progressed satisfactorily during the pre-college period. What might be the extent of his accomplishments?

Repertoire and Performance Level

His repertoire should have consisted of four-period literature to give him a broad style background. His performance level upon entering college might consist of representative works from the following periods of piano literature.

1. **Baroque Period**

   Bach– *Two-* or *Three-Part Inventions*, preludes and fugues from *The Well-Tempered Clavier, French Suites*

   Scarlatti–any of the *Sonatas*

   Handel– *Aylesford Pieces,* any of the *Suites* or *Sonatas*

2. **Classical Period**

   Haydn–easier *Sonatas*

   Mozart– *Sonatas, Variations* or easier *Concertos*

   Beethoven– easier *Sonatas, Variations,* or *Concertos*

3. **Romantic Period**

   Representative works by Schubert, Schumann, Chopin, Liszt, Mendelssohn, Brahms, etc.

4. **Contemporary Period**

   Debussy– *Children's Corner Suite,* easier *Preludes* or either of the two *Arabesques*

   Bartók– *Roumanian Folk Dances, 3 Rondos,* later books of the *Mikrokosmos*

Poulenc– *Mouvements perpetuels*
Bloch– *Poems of the Sea*
Hindemith– *Sonata No. 2*
Dello Joio– *Suite for Piano*
Tcherepnin– *Bagatelles, Opus 5*
Muczynski– *Six Preludes*

Technique

He should have sufficient technique to play in a respectable manner using clean sound, good phrasing, tonal balance, clear pedaling, and appropriate dynamics. In addition to musical considerations, as part of a well-rounded technique, applied and pure technical studies might be selected from some of the following books.

1. **Applied Technique**
   Clementi– *Gradus ad Parnassum*
   Czerny– *The School of Velocity, Opus 299,* or *The Art of Finger Dexterity, Opus 740*
   Moszkowski– *15 Etudes de Virtuosité*
2. **Pure Technique**
   Dohnányi– *Essential Finger Exercises*
   Hanon– *The Virtuoso Pianist in 60 Exercises*
   Philipp– *Exercises for the Independence of the Fingers*
   Pischna– *Sixty Progressive Exercises*
   Major and minor scales, arpeggios, and broken chords in all keys

Sight-Reading Ability

It would be ludicrous for the student to be performing Haydn sonatas and not be able to read minuets from the *Anna Magdalena Notebook*! Unfortunately, the reading level of many students often is far below the performance level. Teachers should encourage their students not to neglect this important facet of musicianship. Therefore, to gain sight-reading skill, our model student should accompany his high school orchestra (band or chorus), or accompany various students when they audition for festivals and contests. In addition to accompanying, teachers should assign a variety of duets and two piano compositions, as ensemble material helps promote sight-reading skill. Emphasis on sight-reading over a period of years will enable the student to read music equivalent to: sonatinas (Clementi, Kuhlau, etc.), easier pieces from Schumann's *Scenes from Childhood*, pieces from Bartók's *Mikrokosmos*, and selections from Bach's four-part *Chorales.*

Theory Background

Too often piano students have received little or no training in theory before college. Even though they perform their repertoire competently, they may be hazy in such rudiments as key signatures, basic chords, and harmonic structure. This is analogous to pronouncing and reading a foreign language aloud without knowing the meaning of the words. The teacher should provide systematic theory instruction to all students (either privately or in a group situation). An understanding of keys, intervals, chords, and the like are important factors. In addition, students should receive ear training, improvisation, transposition, and harmonization as a basic part of the general theory program.

Music History and Literature

Although there is little time for formal music history classes, a private teacher can do much to develop concepts in this area. The teacher can encourage students to attend community musical events such as piano recitals, chamber music programs, symphonic and operatic performances, and other selected concerts. Lectures, workshops, master classes, and other informative presentations also should be suggested by the teacher. In addition to live performances or lectures, students should be encouraged to listen to recordings of works studied. These experiences will develop an awareness of basic information about music history and literature.

The model student who is knowledgeable in the five forementioned areas obviously would have received excellent pre-college training. He would have a fine potential as a musician, and he probably would be readily accepted in almost any college of his choice.

COLLEGE TRAINING FOR THE PIANO PEDAGOGY MAJOR

In a general sense the term "college" may imply any formalized training beyond high school and would include credits earned in a variety of schools: junior college, university, or conservatory. Titles of schools differ (Department of Music, School of Music, College of Fine Arts), and their curricula are often dissimilar. In addition, degrees offered in various music departments appear under such designations as Bachelor of Music, Bachelor of Music Education, Bachelor of Arts, Bachelor of Fine Arts, Bachelor of Science in Music, and many more. Therefore, the student should choose his school carefully, and try to choose the one which has the type of department and degree program which will best fit his special interest.

Before choosing a school one should also be aware of the type of accreditation various schools hold. Accreditation agencies such as the National Association of Schools of Music (NASM), North Central Association, Southern Association, etc., periodically review each school and pass judgment on the state of its curricula. Complete information regarding all the colleges in the United States may be easily found in numerous reference books; readily accessible references are *Barrons' Profiles of American Colleges,* Barron's Educational Series, Inc., Woodbury, New York; and *The College Handbook,* College Entrance Examination Board, New York.

Basic Course Offerings for the Pedagogy Major

Music Requirements

The degree program one would be seeking under this heading would be a Bachelor of Music degree, or a Bachelor of Music in Piano Pedagogy. In most schools of music general course offerings would be similar. Classes in theory, composition, music history and literature, ensemble, conducting, orchestration, and a heavy emphasis on the student's primary instrument would provide the basic courses. In addition, the piano pedagogy major would be required to elect specific courses in his area of specialization; courses may include piano literature, piano pedagogy, accompanying, and practice teaching.

Academic Requirements

Academic requirements vary greatly among colleges and it is difficult to make a composite picture of them. However, generally such courses as English, psychology, foreign languages, history, and philosophy provide some of the basic arts and science courses. It also would be beneficial for the pedagogy major to elect some of the general education courses such as introductory education, educational psychology, child psychology, or adolescent psychology.

Personal Accomplishments During the College Years

During the college years the student must build on the background he brought to college. If his background is weak, he must work harder than some of his peers. With a solid background the student can derive great personal satisfaction from further attainment.

Pertaining to the subject of accomplishment, Terwilliger asks:

> What makes Sammy run or Mary practice? Why do some students prosper while others fail? How important is talent? Do college pianists respond better to an authoritarian or a passive approach? What role should the college teacher play in motivating the college pianist?[3]

Because of variance in background and ability, each student must be evaluated on an individual basis. But regardless of background, talent, or other factors, some students achieve a great deal during college while others fall short of their potential. The determining factor in accomplishment is *motivation*.

A student may be motivated by such outside influences as (1) peer group pressures, (2) a desire to maintain a high grade point average, or (3) a desire to please an instructor (often an applied major teacher). Any or all of these factors might significantly influence and motivate the student.

While all these outside influences are necessary and often essential for a student's professional growth, the most beneficial and long lasting kind of motivation comes from the individual himself—self-motivation. After graduation, grades or a teacher's inspiration are no longer present. It is entirely up to the individual to produce. Therefore, during the college years the student must become highly motivated to accomplish and achieve for basically personal satisfaction, and he must become increasingly independent of his teachers by the time his college career comes to an end.

THE TEACHER'S PERSONALITY

What is this elusive and mysterious something called "personality" that is easy to recognize but difficult to define? Merriam-Webster defines personality as (1) "the totality of an individual's characteristics"; and (2) "an integrated group of emotional trends and behavior tendencies."

Personality is such a key factor in successful teaching that its study is of prime importance. The outward behavior of an individual's characteristics represents to others what kind of a person he is. He may be vivacious or dull, energetic or lethargic, optimistic or pessimistic, pleasant or unpleasant, enthusiastic or disparaging—the list could go on and on. An outward appearance certainly can be improved with constant analysis, thought, and effort. One's personality does not have to remain static year after year. Personality is what you are now and what you are *willing* to become.

[3]Gordon B. Terwilliger, *Piano Teacher's Professional Handbook* (Englewood Cliffs, N.J.: Prentice-Hall, Inc., 1965), p. 22. Reprinted by permission.

All of us, whether we teach or not, must be continually conscious of self-improvement. No one's personality is so ideal that he may go through life never bothering to change his image. The teacher especially must strive for a vital and pleasant personality.

The subject of self-improvement is so vast that volumes are devoted to its study. The numerous, well-known titles of best sellers attest to this fact. Many of us have read such books as *The Power of Positive Thinking* by Norman Vincent Peale (Prentice-Hall, 1952), and *How to Stop Worrying and Start Living* by Dale Carnegie (Simon and Schuster, 1948). These books and others like them are excellent and should be read by anyone interested in a more exciting and dynamic personality.

Consider for a moment someone who has an enviable personality. What kind of a person is he? What does he look like? What attracts you to this person?

Chances are he is "selling" himself in a very dynamic way. Salesmanship is frequently a key to success in dealing with people. John W. Newbern has written a very interesting and informative book on selling, and in the introduction he states:

> Everyone goes through life selling. The baby sells his mama on the idea that he needs food by screaming loudly. The little boy sells his daddy on giving him a nickel for an ice cream cone. The high school student sells his folks on raising his allowance, and letting him borrow the family car.
>
> The young man sells a pretty girl on the idea of marrying him—and then has to keep on selling her to get her to continue to live with him after she learns how imperfect he is.
>
> The doctor doesn't advertise; in fact, advertising is unethical for his profession, but his success, in part, is determined by his personality, and his attitude toward people. He has to sell his services to succeed.
>
> The school teacher is not a saleslady in the classroom, yet her attitudes, her personality, her outlook on life, the way she treats her students determine in a large measure how well she "sells" learning.[4]

A teacher wants to make a good impression on colleagues, students, and students' parents. Through conscious effort it is possible to build an effective personality and "sell" a good impression to others by specifically considering *personality needs.*

Personality Needs

Be Yourself

A self-confident teacher will reflect a positive image merely by being himself. He does not need to inflate the good qualities he already has. The student's confidence will be won by a forthright, honest approach. However, being yourself does not mean that your personal characteristics should remain the same forever.

[4]John W. Newbern, *How to Sell Your Way to Financial Freedom* (Fort Worth, Texas: Sales Research Institute, P.O. Box 8711, Fort Worth, Texas 76112, 1969), p. 5. Reprinted by permission.

Be Pleasant

A pleasant attitude is one of the most valuable attributes a teacher may possess. A genuine display of kindness and affection can often win even the most hostile and disagreeable child. Even though our moods vary greatly from day to day due to frustrations, personal problems, and life's vicissitudes in general, we must conduct ourselves with as much poise and self-control as possible when dealing with others. In a passage dealing with the influence of the teacher, Arthur Jersild says:

> . . . a teacher who is harsh and unsympathetic may interfere with the process of healthy development. In such an atmosphere the child can no longer be his forthright self, free to inquire and to develop. Instead, he must defend himself. Even the strongest beginner at school cannot be completely immune to the humiliation that may be inflicted on him by a sarcastic, punitive teacher.[5]

Be Enthusiastic

Norman Vincent Peale examines this topic thoroughly and effectively in his book, *Enthusiasm Makes the Difference* (Prentice-Hall, Inc., 1967). Some examples of subject headings in this book are: "Enthusiasm Rebuilds a Collapsed Personality," "Enthusiasm Will Improve Your Personality," "Keep the Fires of Enthusiasm Burning Under Your Goals." This book has a great deal to offer, and it should be read by anyone interested in revitalizing his personality. In essence Peale says: life is not always easy, and it has its share of difficulty, pain, and frustration. But with mental effort it is possible to maintain a positive, bright, enthusiastic outlook in our relationship with ourselves, and with others. Turn yourself on with optimism and enthusiastic action, and you will put new spirit and creative skill into your job and everything around you.

Be Encouraging

Realistic encouragement whenever possible is a sign of an outgoing personality. Rather than trying to get results by negative or sarcastic remarks, the positive teacher will bolster and encourage the student. This does not mean that the teacher should be unrealistic and promise a "concert career" for all students. Rather, by being encouraging the teacher is merely indicating that he is interested in his students and that he hopes his positive remarks will inspire them to higher attainment.

Be Patient

It is taken for granted that working with children either privately or in groups can be trying at times. However, a teacher with a wholesome outlook on life will be able to cope with frustrations which may arise. An understanding teacher will keep his patience and will not resort to sarcasm or temper fits. In teaching, a balanced position must be maintained in which the teacher is in control of the situation at all times.

[5] Arthur Jersild, *In Search of Self* (New York: Teachers College Press, Columbia University, 1952), p. 94. Reprinted by permission.

OPPORTUNITIES FOR THE TEACHER

What occupations are available for the young music graduate who has attained a Bachelor of Music degree in piano? Unless he is an unusually gifted pianist who can make a living from public performances, he will probably seek a teaching career, either as a private teacher, or as a college teacher.

Private Piano Teaching

The graduate may teach piano privately at home or at a studio. This is an ideal career for a young woman who is married. She can maintain a household and pursue an occupation at home (or outside the home). Private teaching is also an excellent career for any man or woman desiring to be self-employed.

The graduate may teach piano for someone else. Possibilities for employment would include: teaching piano in a music store or a private school, or teaching as an assistant to an established teacher who has more students than it would otherwise be possible to teach. Frequently, the young teacher does not feel quite ready to begin teaching on his own, to set up his own studio, and to assume all the responsibilities of having his own business. He may not have a large class of students waiting for him upon graduation, and he might feel more secure as an employee in a situation where he has a guaranteed number of students to teach. The novice teacher does not have the experience and reputation of his established colleagues, and his income might be limited for a few years until his name becomes known in the community. However, a young teacher need not feel that he *must* teach for someone else. An ambitious, self-confident person may have far more success teaching for himself.

The graduate may possibly teach piano in a college. College teaching today usually is limited to those with advanced training, advanced degrees, and some experience in their field. This is not always the case, and there are exceptions, but these qualifications are becoming more and more standard requirements.

The graduate should not be misled into thinking that a Bachelor of Music degree will entitle him to employment as a teacher in a public school. Public school teaching is limited to those who have majored in music education and have been certified by state authorities. Graduates with a Bachelor of Music degree would not qualify for this position because they would not have received credits in required education courses or received certification by state authorities.

College Piano Teaching

A teacher graduating from a college music department with a Master of Music degree or a doctorate may teach privately in any of the categories listed above or he may seek employment at the college level.

This is a position to which many young pianists aspire, but one which is becoming more and more crowded with talented, well-qualified applicants. Music schools all over the country are turning out well-trained graduates in the piano performance area, and the demand for employment is not as great as the supply. However, if you seek a college position you should understand the procedure for applying for employment.

The Degree is the Thing

Today, administrators are looking for applicants who have attained a terminal degree—the doctorate. This is not an absolute necessity for employment, but it adds to the attractiveness of an applicant's credentials. It often makes the difference between choosing one person over another.

> Not all colleges require the doctorate, and many of them do not expect it of beginning teachers. A few require the master's plus thirty additional hours to move from an instructor to the rank of assistant or associate professor. Others require sixty hours beyond the master's to be considered for a full professorship, and some colleges provide for exceptional cases by stating that one must have the doctorate or its equivalent.[6]

For the piano major the Doctor of Musical Arts degree (DMA) is specifically designed for the pianist interested in performance. He will be required to present numerous performances such as recitals, chamber music concerts, concerto performances, and lecture-recitals. In addition to performance requirements he will take advanced courses in theory, music history, research, and he may possibly have to write a dissertation.

Gathering Credentials

In applying for a college position, prepare credentials carefully and accurately. Credentials will consist of transcripts of course work, personal information, picture, performance record (recitals, accompaniments, appearances with orchestra and the like), and recommendations from former teachers or other prominent authorities who know your work.

It is difficult for faculty members to remember important information about the numerous students they teach, so be sure to ask them for letters of recommendation as soon as possible. Tell them what type of position you are seeking so they will know what areas of strength to list. Try to get a cross section of recommendations that will present a rounded picture of your attributes.

Graduates should file their biographical data with the Placement Bureau at their college or university, and with other professional placement agencies, preferably those holding membership in the National Association of Teacher Agencies, such as the Lutton Music Personnel Service (State National Bank Plaza, Suite 405, Evanston, Illinois 60201).

Graduates should also watch university bulletin boards for announcements of positions, and they should be encouraged to read professional magazines for possible job offerings. In addition, candidates may write letters to colleges throughout the country offering their services.

After a lead has been found, be prepared to offer yourself for examination in a personal interview. The employer will want to see first-

[6] Terwilliger, *op. cit.*, p. 50. Reprinted by permission.

hand how much poise and control the candidate demonstrates before others. Generally, the dean, with the help of other faculty members who act as advisors, chooses new faculty. Therefore, you can expect to be examined by others on the faculty as well as by the dean.

College Job Offerings for the Pianist

An applicant is more desirable if he is qualified to teach more than just piano. Frequently, an administrator is looking for a pianist who can perform, teach piano, and also teach either music appreciation, music history, or theory.

Because college enrollments have expanded greatly during the past few years, the necessity of class piano teaching has made job offerings available for qualified, experienced teachers in that special area. This is a growing field which should be given serious consideration for a pianist desiring to teach in a college.

Careers in Music

For a complete listing of music careers, see *Job Opportunities in Music,* published jointly by the Music Teachers National Association (408 Carew Tower, Cincinnati, Ohio 45202), the Music Educators National Conference (1902 Association Dr., Reston, Virginia 22091), and the National Association of Schools of Music (11250 Roger Bacon Dr., No. 5, Reston, Virginia 22090).

SUMMARY

Thus the total composite of one's training, background, personality, and motivation are combined to produce a skilled professional—in this case a teacher. The level and area in which the teacher will be working, whether private or employed teaching, will be determined largely by training and interest. Some may have a genuine desire to work with children, others may prefer working with adults at the college level. Whatever the level, the teacher must know the tricks of his trade, but he also must be an effective communicator capable of helping others to learn.

FOR DISCUSSION AND ASSIGNMENT

1. What is your view on teaching as a career?
2. Do you think you would enjoy working with children or adults? Describe your reasons.
3. Compare your pre-college training to the model student discussed in this chapter. How would you rate the teaching you received before college?
4. Describe the college program that you think would be the most advantageous as preparation for a private teaching career.
5. Do you have aspirations of teaching in a college? If so, in what capacity?

FOR FURTHER READING

Adams, Sam, and John L. Garrett, Jr. *To Be a Teacher.* Englewood Cliffs, N.J.: Prentice-Hall, Inc., 1969. PB. Designed as an introductory educational text, this refreshing book seeks to answer the vital question: Shall I be a teacher? Pertinent questions are asked which relate to such teaching decisions as what kind and what level, where would one want to teach, and many others. Specific suggested readings are: Chapter 1, "What is a Teacher?" Chapter 2, "Who Should Become a Teacher?" and Chapter 5, "What Are Some Decisions For the Teacher?"

Highet, Gilbert. *The Art of Teaching*. New York: Vintage Books, 1950. PB. A favorite since its publication, this warmly written book is a fine general treatise on the philosophy of teaching. The book begins by considering the character and abilities which make a good professional teacher, and then goes on to examine his methods. Readings of special interest are: I, "Introduction;" II, "The Teacher;" and V, "Teaching in Everyday Life."

Kuethe, James L. *The Teaching-Learning Process*. Glenview, Ill.; Scott, Foresman and Co., 1968. PB. Part of a series called *The Keystones of Education Series*, this well-written book discusses important problems in contemporary and historical education. Although somewhat academic, the book attempts to define the basic language of education, and it probes deeply such frequently used words as teaching, learning, intelligence, retention and forgetting, transfer of learning, and basic needs of the student. Practical chapters are: Introduction, "An Overview of the Process;" Chapter 5, "Motivation in the Classroom;" and Chapter 6, "Methods of Teaching."

Maltz, Maxwell. *Psycho-Cybernetics*. Englewood Cliffs, N.J.: Prentice-Hall, Inc., 1960. PB. Designed as a sort of do-it-yourself psychology kit for the layman, this book offers many important suggestions for creating a positive personality and a successful life. Forget Freud and the mysterious subconscious. In essence Dr. Maltz says: Self-image is the key to human personality and human behavior; the self-image can be changed consciously by repeated positive thoughts. The book is full of practical information. It is especially valuable for those interested in becoming teachers who will need all the help they can get in the personality department.

Schmitt, Sister Cecilia. *Rapport and Success: Human Relations in Music Education.* Ardmore, Pa.: Dorrance and Co., 1976. PB. The teacher's role is clearly stated in this well-written book. Numerous pro and con examples are given depicting the teacher as the catalyst in learning situations. The author discusses how to attain rapport with the students, how to raise students' self-concept, and how to attain success through rapport. The book provides food for thought for teachers desiring to improve their rapport in various teaching-learning situations. This book is a project of the National Consortium for Humanizing Education.

Aspects of Private Teaching 2

The piano teaching profession encompasses a vast panorama of multifarious areas. Since it is not possible to be all things to all people, the teacher will have to decide what to teach and to whom it will be taught. Few people can claim to be equally effective with all age groups. Consequently, the decision as to the level of teaching often makes the difference between satisfaction or frustration in a teaching situation.

Would you be interested in working with very young children of kindergarten age? Would you be interested in working with traditional age beginners, adult beginners, intermediate students, or advanced students? These questions should be given serious consideration before embarking on a private teaching career, because it is possible to work with all these various age groups, or specialize in one or more.

THE PRIVATE PIANO TEACHER

The private teacher referred to in this chapter is limited to one who teaches either at home or in a studio, and one who is independent of an educational institution. Also, since most teachers in this capacity are women, reference throughout will be in the feminine.[1]

Teaching Young Beginners

The prime consideration in this category is: Do you like children? "If we are not really fond of children, we shall never find happiness in teaching them, and it will be better to face up to it and change our profession before we become embittered."[2]

[1]In reference to the feminine private piano teacher, Angela Diller offers this amusing observation: "At the present time, in this country, more women than men are engaged in music teaching. Therefore, . . . the teacher is referred to as *she*. This does not imply any superiority of she's over he's, but merely recognizes that in point of numbers, the she's have it." From *The Splendor of Music*. Copyright © 1957 by G. Schirmer, Inc. Reprinted by permission.

[2]Hetty Bolton, *On Teaching the Piano* (London: Novello and Company Ltd, 1954), p. 22.

A second consideration in teaching children is: Would you enjoy teaching elementary music? In this regard college students are frequently apathetic, and they profess that they have neither the patience to teach youngsters nor an interest in teaching the elementary music young students would be playing.

If either of the preceding considerations is negative, a private teaching career almost surely is not for you. Consider the composition of an average teacher's class. Most of the students are children under twelve. "For every advanced student, there are probably a thousand beginners, most of whom want only to enjoy making music and to use their skill as a social asset."[3] There are more students taking lessons in this age group for several reasons. Youngsters usually are enthusiastic in the beginning, but after a few years many of them discontinue lessons. Some drop music entirely, some change instruments, and others become involved in the many curricular and extra-curricular activities that seem to be increasingly available to students today. Therefore, the private teacher is continually starting young students to fill vacancies.

Because the beginning years are critical, there is a decided advantage to starting beginners yourself rather than acquiring someone else's product. This is the time when students must learn such basic skills as correct hand position, correct phrasing, proper balancing of tone, and a feeling for melodic contours. In addition to technical considerations, a skillful beginning teacher who has a genuine enthusiasm for music can do much to stimulate interest and curiosity and instill a lasting love for music.

Teaching Adult Beginners

Traditionally, adult beginners represented a small portion of the teacher's class. But today, with increased leisure time, more and more people are looking for a creative, stimulating activity. Music lessons offer an important outlet to adults from the "teen" years to old age who are searching for some form of aesthetic fulfillment.

Teaching adult beginners can be a rewarding experience. Presumably adults study music because they are interested, whereas children often take lessons because of parental insistence. Adults are responsive, amenable to direction, and if taught properly, tend to progress at a rapid rate.

Adult beginners ordinarily do not reach astonishing heights in technical proficiency, since the development of finger facility should begin at an earlier age. Also the ability to read music fluently, which demands a complicated coordination of intellect, eyes, ears, and hands, probably will progress slowly. However, occasionally an adult will cover an amazing amount of material in a short time and become an accomplished musician.

A few teachers specialize in teaching adults. They enjoy the intellectual stimulation of working with adult terminology rather than the simple language often used in teaching children. Also they can make use of extra teaching time by giving lessons at times when children could not come.

Adult beginners can derive a great deal of satisfaction from piano playing and the study of music in general, and their accomplishments will be rewarding for teachers interested in working with this age group.

[3]Ruth Stevenson Alling, *How to Make Money Teaching Piano to Beginners* (private publication: Corpus Christi, Texas: Lo Kno Pla Music Institute, 1969), p.7.

Teaching Intermediate Students

A certain percentage of the students in a teacher's class will continue lessons for many years. While it is true that some pupils struggle along year after year with little progress, usually those continuing lessons are motivated, interested, and have a genuine desire to learn.

In age, the intermediate student usually is in junior high school (grades 7, 8, 9). Working with this age group can be a joy or a source of frustration. This transitional period from childhood to adulthood often produces behavioral anxieties. At this juncture adolescents are experiencing a newly awakened interest in sex. The need for acquiring status and independence is important. Peer recognition and acceptance assume increased importance. These developments, both physical and mental, keep them on edge for a number of years. Teen-agers often are moody and seemingly apathetic for no apparent reason. Due to these conflicts it takes a great deal of imagination and determination on the teacher's (and parents') part to keep them practicing and making progress.

However, working with this age group can be rewarding because signs of pianistic accomplishment are beginning to emerge. The rewards of early practice are now coming to fruition, and as a result, technique and musicianship are evolving into a more structured and unified whole.

Teaching Advanced Students

A small percentage of the students in a teacher's class will be continuing lessons in senior high school (grades 10, 11, 12). Their persistence is highly commendable. In spite of the demands of homework, dating, participation in sports and other extra-curricular activities, the possibility of holding part-time jobs, and myriad other duties that make extraordinary demands on this age group's time, they have persevered in their musical endeavors.

Some students are still taking piano lessons because their love of music is so strong that they are seriously considering a musical career. Most of them are beginning to think about vocational choices, and if the choice is music, this will directly involve the piano teacher. The teacher working with this age group must be prepared to act in an informal advisory role. Many students who cannot establish a close relationship with their parents will seek out adults, frequently their teachers, for consultations. This kind of rapport with teachers and the ability to communicate with them is of vital importance to high school students.

Teaching Private or Class Lessons

Before a teacher begins to organize a studio and purchase equipment for it, she will have to decide whether she wants to teach private lessons or class lessons, or a combination of the two. Therefore, the teacher should ask herself: (1) "Do I enjoy working with groups of children? (2) Am I confident that I can organize group activities, make classes interesting and appealing, and maintain discipline? (3) Am I convinced students will learn as much in group *lessons* as they would learn privately?"

It has always been possible to teach class *lessons* with two or more pianos, but since the advent of the electronic piano, class teaching has become increasingly popular. A number of private teachers now teach class piano, and they are very enthusiastic about the results. Most private teachers, however, still teach only privately and give little or no class work. This is due to a number of reasons–lack of teaching space, a general uneasiness about group work, lack of training and experience with group situations, and a general conviction that private lessons accomplish more and produce better results than group lessons.

Richard Chronister states that it is the *teacher* who is the determining factor in successful teaching, not the situation. "The problems in music education run far deeper than is suggested by those who would have us believe that the choice of group teaching or private teaching is anything but a superficial aspect of successful teaching."[4]

As an alternative to an "either-or" situation, Ylda Novik suggests that a combination of class and private work produces effective results.

> As the controversy rages between the proponents of private and group piano lessons, the almost obvious conclusion seems to be, "use the best of both for maximum results." There is no denying the demerits of each. The private student who goes to his lessons with the solo adult authority figure of his teacher and returns home to the solitude of his monastic cell to practice is indeed a creature to be pitied. But consider the plight of the ambitious or super-gifted group student whose needs are calling out for thirty or sixty minutes of individual attention which would allow him to go at his own pace, possibly many times faster than the group average rate of progress.
>
> Having experienced both methods, there was not the slightest doubt that eliminating many of the negative aspects of each and utilizing the positive would be a practical solution. How to eliminate the solitude was easy in principle: have each child attend a class weekly. . . . After seeing those who participated in classes progress at twice or thrice the rate of non-attenders, all parents now insist that their children be in the "theory class." "Theory" is in quotes because the class encompasses many other aspects of music training besides the study of basic theory.[5]

The preceding description is an attractive compromise which many teachers advocate, a combination of private and class teaching. The class lesson (approximately forty-five minutes long) would emphasize such basic skills as theory, keyboard harmony, ear training, sight-reading, and ensemble playing.

A few teachers advocate teaching entirely in groups. Two possible combinations of group lessons are: (1) two lessons per week, one being a small group of two to six for the "private" lesson, and a larger group of six or more for the class lesson; or (2) one or two lessons per week comprised of a large group of six or more students.

Because certain aspects of piano study can be presented easily to more than one student at a time, there are decided advantages in including

[4] Richard Chronister "The Irrelevant Controversy: Group Teaching vs. Private Teaching," *Keyboard Arts* (Spring, 1972), p. 17.

[5] Ylda Novik, "Class Work for the Private Student," *the American Music Teacher* (January, 1970), p. 23. Reprinted by permission of the author.

some group teaching. Theory, keyboard harmony, ear training, sight-reading, and ensemble playing can be presented more effectively in a class situation. Also, competition from peer groups can provide stimulating sessions which do a great deal to spark enthusiasm among the individual members as well as create class spirit.

While the many advantages of class lessons seem to be self-evident, there is little research available comparing the results of private piano lessons versus class instruction and, as far as we are aware, no statistical evidence available showing the advantages of one system of teaching over the other.

LEARNING HOW TO TEACH

How does a college piano major suddenly become a piano teacher? Are there teacher training programs available in colleges throughout the country for prospective piano teachers?

A number of colleges now offer programs designed to prepare students for private teaching. This area of the college music curriculum is called *piano pedagogy*. In such a program students are engaged in (1) examining beginning, intermediate, and advanced teaching materials; (2) preparing research papers based on topics relating to piano teaching; (3) observing private teachers and writing reports on the methodologies used; (4) presenting reports based on analytical study of various periodicals; and (5) garnering experience in practice teaching supervised by the instructor.

Unfortunately, not all colleges of music offer a complete teacher training program as just described. Angela Diller suggests an alternative for those who might not be able to experience such a program.

> If you cannot attend teacher training courses, your own piano teacher would perhaps be willing to have you serve as a sort of musical apprentice to her, by supervising the practicing of some of her young pupils. You can attend the pupil's lesson, observing experienced teaching, and the teacher will tell you what is to be stressed in the child's practice period. Since a young pupil's early lessons will be largely confined to learning how to work at home, it is helpful at the beginning for the child to have aid in organizing his time productively when he practices.[6]

By close association with an experienced teacher, either observing or working as an assistant teacher, students will have an insight into actual teaching situations. They will experience a wide range of ages and abilities in the teacher's class, and will be better able to assess the relative merits of teaching various age groups. Most importantly, the student will have an opportunity to discover if she really likes to teach.

Many professions require an in-service training period after graduation—music therapists have a pre-clinical training period before certification, and young doctors serve a long internship under supervision. It is logical to conclude that prospective piano teachers also need some supervised experience prior to beginning their own teaching careers.

[6]Diller, *op. cit.*, p. 10. Reprinted by permission.

THE TEACHER'S STUDIO

Unless a teacher gives itinerant lessons (traveling from one home to another), she will require a place of her own in which to teach. A teaching location should be in close proximity to students and may be either situated at home, which is most frequently the case, or at a studio. In either instance it is important that the physical accommodations be as pleasant as possible for optimum teaching results. Both the teacher and pupils are affected by adequate or inadequate facilities. A neat, attractive, well-equipped studio will provide a pleasant atmosphere in which to work, and students will look forward to their lessons in such surroundings.

A Studio in the Home

Teaching at home can be frustrating if there is not sufficient privacy—the phone rings, the dog barks, and children barge in on lessons. The teacher may be interrupted over and over again, and parents will complain that she is so busy with household duties that she is not devoting her full attention to teaching. It is not possible to be mother, cook, and teacher simultaneously. Therefore, if the teacher has small children of her own, she should hire a baby-sitter to look after them while she is teaching. It also would be advisable to hire part-time help to assist with some of the domestic chores. An understanding husband can offer a considerable amount of good help in the child care and homemaking departments if he is willing and if he has the patience for this kind of work.

In addition to privacy, sufficient teaching space and adequate equipment should be of prime consideration. Teaching in a small, cramped room on a small spinet for a number of hours each day will soon become tiresome and tedious.

If privacy and appropriate facilities can be insured, teaching at home does have some advantages—there is no need to invest in a second car to get to work; there are numerous tax deductions for the portion of the home used as a studio; and mother is there in case she is needed in an emergency.

A Studio Outside the Home

Very few teachers invest in teaching space apart from home. Since most of them are only teaching on a part-time basis for extra money, an impressive studio or studio location is not necessary. However, for a more commercial teacher who makes teaching a full-time career there are some advantages in studio rental.

If the teacher's home is not ideally located, an outside studio may be rented (or purchased) in a more convenient, commercial location such as a suburban shopping center or an outlying area where there are few teachers. Studio space may be rented in a music store, an office building, or even in another home which is more advantageously located than the teacher's residence. Additional advantages of studio rental are privacy, an opportunity to get away from home for a portion of the day, and a professional, business-like atmosphere.

Teaching Space

The studio should be large enough to accommodate pianos, blackboard area, tables and chairs, and other equipment. It should also be sufficiently large to accommodate some class teaching (class theory, kindergarten class, class piano, etc.). A utilitarian studio size is about 20' x 24'. At an estimated cost of $15.00 per square foot, a room of these dimensions would cost $7200, excluding equipment. While this price may be prohibitive for a beginning teacher, conversion of a double garage or basement area can provide the same space, if not more, at a fraction of the cost.

Two diagrams of class piano studios are offered here as guides to room sizes and arrangement of equipment for this special teaching situation. Norman Mehr's studios in Los Angeles, California (Ill. 2:1) is a large room with ample space for his eight pianos, blackboard, tables and chairs; the center of the room is cleared for classes in eurhythmics. Mrs. B. H. Kenna's studio in Jackson, Mississippi (Ill. 2:2) is smaller, but it has adequate space for her conventional piano, six electronic pianos, one projector and screen, and blackboard.

Ill. 2:1. Diagram of Norman Mehr's studio.[7]

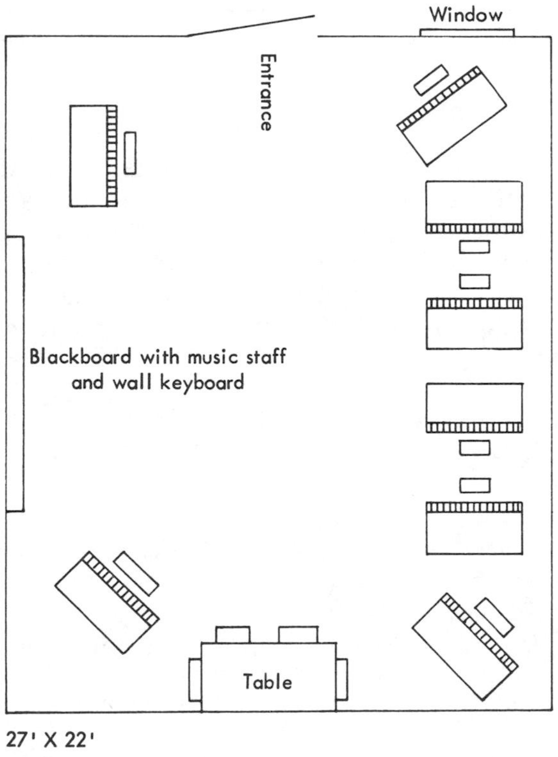

[7]From *Teaching Piano in Classroom and Studio*. Copyright © 1967 by the Music Educators National Conference. (Although Mr. Mehr has given up his studio since the publication of this book, he has given permission to use the diagram).

Ill. 2:2. Diagram of Mrs. B. H. Kenna's studio.[8]

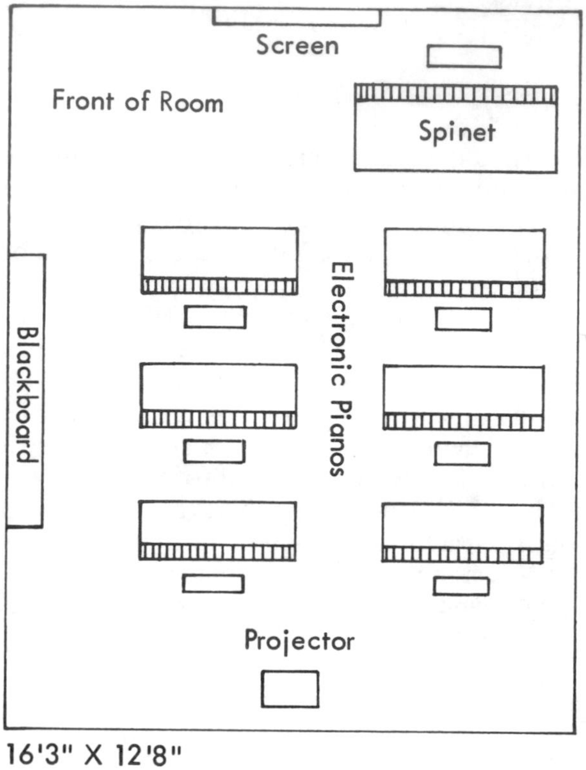

Studio Equipment[9]

Too often a teacher's studio and equipment consist of a room with one piano. Frequently the piano is a dilapidated relic of a spinet which may appropriately be called a "clunker." While it is entirely possible to teach under these circumstances, a more professional attitude should be taken toward the equipment which is utilized to make a living.

The following checklist is offered as a reference guide for the contemporary piano teacher.

A Checklist of Studio Equipment

a) Essentials

Pianos

A minimum number of two. The choice includes grands, uprights, studio uprights, spinets, and/or electronic pianos.

Electronic Pianos

(Optional) The electronic piano is designed especially for class use. Units range from 1 to 24, and are equipped with headphones for individual use. There may be an instructor's piano which may or may not be equipped with a communication device. Most makes have varying possibilities of audio play-through attachments (tapes and

[8] *Ibid*. Used by permission of Mrs. B. H. Kenna.

[9] For an interesting article on equipment, see: "Equipping the Music Studio for Piano Lessons" by Dorothy Bishop, *Clavier*, Vol. IV, No. 3 (May-June, 1965).

recordings). The best known makes are Baldwin (full 88 keys), Musitronic (68 keys), Rhodes (73 keys), and Wurlitzer (64 keys).[10]

Piano Seat

Adjustable piano-chairs are a solution to comfortable seating of all sizes of students. Two well-known makes are (1) The Sit-Rite Adjustable Piano-Chair (order from the company of that name, 6546 Bob-O-Link's Drive, Dallas, Texas 75214); and (2) the Yamaha adjustable Concert Chair (order from a Yamaha dealer).

Blackboard

Either stationary or portable board, or small individual slates. Substitutions for blackboards are flannel boards and magnetic boards (see a school supply store for various makes).

Telephone

(Optional) For those who do not like to be disturbed during lessons an answering service is a happy solution.

b) Audio-Visual Aids

Tape Recorder

Inexpensive models are the numerous cassettes (Craig, Sharp, Sony, Wollensak, etc.). Many students own cassettes, and lessons or ear training drills may be recorded and sent home for practice. For a listing of other standard tape recorder models (stereo and monaural), consult an electronics store.

Record Player

Models range from inexpensive portables to expensive, complex stereo equipment.

Overhead Projector

This projector comes in a compact, light-weight portable model. (Consult a school supply store for various makes.) Transparencies must be made from the original for projection onto a screen.

Opaque Projector

This projector reproduces the original and projects the image onto a screen. (Consult a school supply store for various makes.)

c) Special Equipment

Awards

Stickers, medals, trophies, statues, (cash!)—all are useful as incentives for work well done. (Consult a school supply store.)

Bulletin Board

(cork-type) Especially useful for listing items of special interest (concerts, contests, student recitals, etc.).

Charts

Great for student motivation—progress chart, honor roll, etc.

File Cabinet(s)

Myriad uses: music for reference, students' progress reports, business file, others.

Flash Cards

Notes, key signatures, intervals, chords, musical terms, rhythm patterns, melodic patterns. May be either home-made or store bought. (Consult a music store or a school supply store for various types.)

[10] For photos of these four makes, see Chapter 10, "Manufacturers of Electronic Pianos."

Metronome

Electric, transistor, wind-up (a practical wind-up model is the Taktell metronome). Consult a music store or a school supply store for various makes.

Silent Keyboard

Although class teaching should be done on actual pianos (electric or standard), silent keyboards are excellent for demonstration (see Ill. 5:10). One make is the Vandre Interlocking Keyboard which may be ordered from Belwin-Mills. It has raised black keys and is made of plastic in two octave sections; the sections may be fitted together to form a four or six octave length keyboard. (Consult a music store for other makes.)

Writing Equipment

Pencils, pens, markers (felt-tipped pens are very useful for writing attractive assignments and for correction; try using a different color marker each time mistakes are corrected), others.

The author has visited numerous private studios around the country. From those visited, the Keys of Melody Academy in Springfield, Illinois had some of the most creative equipment, made mostly by the teachers. The room was full of decorations for various holiday seasons (Halloween), wall charts, and other imaginative equipment (Ill. 2:3). Seven pianos, blackboard, file cabinet, desk, table and chairs, and other bought equipment was provided.

Ill. 2:3. A well-equipped studio.

Ill. 2:4. Blackboard work.

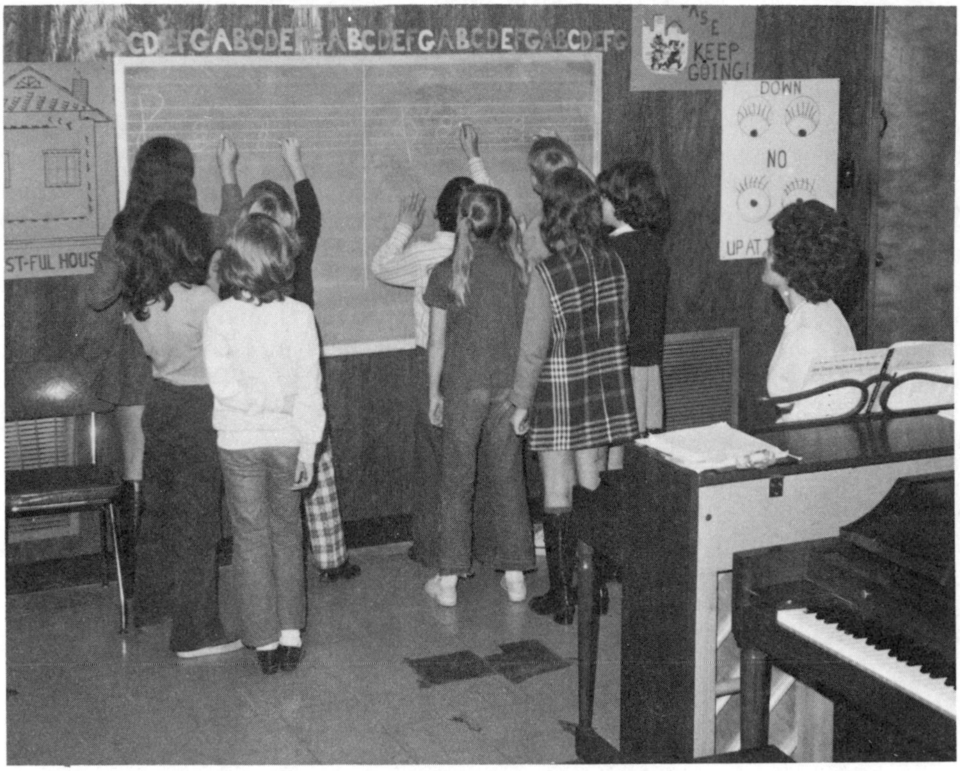

Through the equipment provided, a variety of class activities (Ill. 2:4) can be offered which will provide stimulation and motivation. A well-stocked studio such as this is a delightful working place for both teacher and students.

HOW TO OBTAIN STUDENTS[11]

Let us assume that a prospective teacher has had adequate preparation as a musician and sufficient training in piano pedagogy to prepare herself for a private teaching career. Even though she may be an excellent pianist, have an attractive personality, and hold one or more degrees in music, she will not automatically have an anxious class of pupils waiting for instruction. Where does a beginning teacher look for pupils, and how does she attract them?

Piano teachers attract students much the same way that doctors attract patients, by reputation and referral. Although this procedure works well for older established teachers, a beginning teacher must consider other methods.

[11]In her book, *How to Make Money Teaching Piano to Beginners*, Ruth Stevenson Alling offers several original, unusual methods of obtaining students. See Chapter 5, "Building Your Reputation and Enrollment Fast," pp. 23-28.

Locate in an Area of Children

Before opening a studio consider the community into which you are planning to settle. Are there numerous children in the area? Are there many or few piano teachers in that part of town? Since lesson fees are charged in relationship to the level of income in a given area, is it a lower, middle, or an upper class neighborhood?

A city suburb is often an ideal place in which to open a studio. Suburbia is exactly where prospective students live—great teeming numbers of them. The growth of the suburbs is often so rapid that there are not enough piano teachers offering lessons, and the demand for lessons is frequently greater than the supply of teachers. Even though a suburb is ideal in terms of numbers of students, beginning teachers are frequently reluctant to move to the suburban areas of a larger city. If they are not yet married, they feel isolated in outlying areas, and they are hesitant about leaving the conveniences of city life.

The studio location is equally important for both large and small communities. In a smaller town, however, it would not be as formidable for parents to bring their children to piano lessons from another neighborhood, even if they lived on the other side of town. Still, convenience is a factor in private lessons, and a beginning teacher should give careful consideration to the location of her studio.

Give Public Performances

Excellent publicity may be obtained from a recital, concert appearance, or some other type of public performance. Since the general public is invited, those sufficiently impressed by the performer's pianistic prowess might feel inclined to seek lessons. In addition, other teachers attending would learn of you and your abilities, and they might refer students to you when their classes became filled.

Newspapers will often run articles about public performances free of charge; information may be submitted to the music editor in sufficient time for printing the story. The article should contain information about the concert and about the performer. A sample news story is offered here.

> Miss Regina Chopin will present a piano recital on Sunday, November 19, at 4:00 P.M., in Confrontation Hall, 1330 W. 50th St. She will perform works by Bach, Beethoven, and Brahms.
>
> Miss Chopin recently graduated from the University of the Netherlands where she studied with Dr. Heinrich Ratskeller, famed pianist, composer, and teacher.
>
> Miss Chopin has given numerous concerts in this country and abroad. She has recently settled in Dallas and will divide her time between teaching and concertizing. This is Miss Chopin's debut in Dallas. The public is cordially invited.

Join Music Teacher Organizations

Membership in one or more music organizations is essential for professional standing. Although piano lessons may be given without a degree in music, without any advanced training, or without professional affiliations, teachers in this category usually belong to the less-trained, less-skilled group who are often teaching on a part-time basis.

Music teacher organizations are largely responsible for the improvement in teaching standards that have taken place in this country over the past three decades. These organizations are interested in the best means of training students, in establishing reasonable minimum lesson fees, in teacher certification, in sponsoring workshops and recitals for the benefit of both students and teachers, in sponsoring contests and auditions, and they are interested in providing a respectable membership list to offer the public as a reliable source for selecting music teachers.

By joining a local organization such as the *Dallas Music Teachers' Association*, or Boston's *New England Pianoforte Music Teachers' Association*, a beginning teacher would become known to the membership, and she might receive some referrals from well-established teachers who cannot take on additional pupils. Some organizations run a collective ad in their local newspaper listing all the teachers in their membership along with their addresses and telephone numbers. This often is of great benefit for a beginning teacher.

Since membership in local, state, and national music teacher organizations is so important for professional standing, a typical example of qualifications for membership is quoted here which covers general requirements for all three levels. This information is taken from the Constitution and By-Laws of the *Music Teachers Association* of Corpus Christi, Texas, which is affiliated with the *Texas Music Teachers Association* and the *Music Teachers National Association.*

ARTICLE III–MEMBERSHIP[12]

There shall be five classes of membership:

1. Active
2. Honorary
3. Provisional
4. Associate
5. Patron

Section 1. Active membership shall include music teachers whose qualifications are approved by the membership committee and whose professional fee shall be no less than three dollars ($3.00) for a thirty-minute lesson. To qualify as an active member, the teacher shall have:

(A) Earned a degree with a major in music or music education from an accredited institution or,

(B) Studied his instrument or singing privately with a qualified teacher a minimum of ten (10) years; and,

(1) Taught successfully for five consecutive years immediately prior to applying for membership; and,

(2) Presented three performing students before the membership committee as evidence of a high standard of teaching. Auditions shall be held after the first of May, with sufficient notice for interested teacher or,

(3) By certification by the Music Teachers National Association.

. . . Active members may vote, hold office, present pupils on recitals sponsored by the Association, and have their names printed in any advertising sponsored or approved by the Association. Active members are expected to accept responsibilities and support the organization with attendance at meetings

[12] Reprinted by permission of the Corpus Christi Music Teachers Association.

and participation in its activities. Those qualified for active membership must also belong to the *Texas Music Teachers Association* and the *Music Teachers National Association.*

National Professional Society Memberships

The following five professional society music teacher organizations are listed here as a reference guide.

1. *Music Educators National Conference* (MENC), 1902 Association Dr., Reston, Virginia 22091. This is the largest of all the music teacher organizations; membership is comprised largely of public school music teachers. This organization publishes an excellent magazine entitled *Music Educators Journal.*

2. *Music Teachers National Association* (MTNA), 408 Carew Tower, Cincinnati, Ohio 45202. This organization is closely associated with the needs and problems of private teachers, and it is responsible for private teacher certification. MTNA publishes a fine magazine, *the American Music Teacher.*

3. *National Catholic Music Educators Association* (NCMEA), Riggs Building Suite 228, 7411 Riggs Rd., Hyattsville, Maryland 20783. This organization is similar to MENC, but it is designed primarily for parochial school teachers. The NCMEA publication is entited, *Musart.*

4. *National Guild of Piano Teachers* (The Guild), Box 1807, Austin, Texas 78767. The Guild sponsors national student auditions, awards scholarships, and sponsors the prestigious Van Cliburn International Piano Competition quadrennially. The Guild's publication is the *Piano Guild Notes.*

5. *National Federation of Music Clubs* (the Federation), 310 S. Michigan Avenue, Room 1936, Chicago, Illinois 60604. The Federation sponsors national student auditions, awards scholarships, and sponsors the Young Artist Competition biennially. This organization publishes the *Junior Keynotes* magazine.

Advertise

In general, a beginning teacher starts with pupils recommended from among personal acquaintances—friends, relatives, and associates. Recommendations from this immediate source are known as "word-of-mouth" advertising, and this is often more valuable than the kind of advertising for which one pays. Nevertheless, publicity will probably be required to gain additional pupils to supplement referrals.

HOW TO ADVERTISE

Even the beginning teacher will quickly acquire a few students. Good or bad, motivated or indifferent, these must be nurtured and developed with all the skill and care that can be mustered, because these students will be the *best* source of advertising. Private teachers generally derive the main portion of their class from referrals, and referrals come most frequently from satisfied students and parents who are enthusiastic about the teacher and the teacher's work. Although parents may be highly complimentary about their children's accomplishments, others can best see and hear the results by a public performance—a recital.

Give Student Recitals

It is not necessary to rent the most elegant hall in town, fill it full of flowers, and send out engraved invitations to present an impressive recital. The musical quality of the performers is the determining factor in a successful program. Therefore, work to the fullest capacity with the few students you might have in the beginning of your teaching career (and thereafter also). Give extra lessons (for free), call the parents and encourage them to help their children practice, and do everything possible to stimulate an enthusiastic outlook toward the forthcoming recital.

The recital may be either informal or formal. An informal class recital which incorporates musical activities is often very effective. Parents are impressed by seeing what their children actually do at lessons, and various aspects of regular instruction may be presented—improvisation, harmonization, transposition, ear training games, etc. In addition, an informal recital may be especially advantageous for students who have only had lessons for a short time. They will have an opportunity to put their best foot forward and shine in class activities even though they are not yet accomplished performers. It is often an effective technique to invite *only* the parents to an informal recital. This can create an air of exclusiveness, and can be a good method of inducing parental support.

A formal recital is effective if (1) there are enough students for a thirty or forty-five minute program, and if (2) they have had lessons long enough to play their memorized pieces with assurance.

Thus the first and most important step in advertising is to show what you can produce. Requests for lessons should follow shortly thereafter.

Write Letters

This type of advertising is a real "shot in the dark," and it may or may not produce results. When advertising directly by letter, state your case plainly and concisely, and outline specifically what kind of a musical program you are offering. If you prefer working with beginners, advanced students, or adult beginners, say so. List any special features about your program such as class piano, class theory, private lesson class theory combination, and so on.

As a private teacher try to become known to school teachers and ministers in your area. Letters may be sent to parents of children in nearby schools and churches if these organizations will give out a list of names.

The following sample letter may serve as a general guide for direct mailing. It will be of special interest to teachers who are contemplating class piano lessons.

Dear Parents:

A new program for piano instruction is being offered in your area utilizing a piano laboratory. This approach is offered to groups of students, especially beginners.

Beginner classes meet once a week for a period of 50 minutes. Students of the same age level will learn such important basic keyboard skills as sight-reading, chord recognition, improvisation, harmonization, and transposition. In addition to learning to play the piano, students will learn about music in general through theory study, detailed piano technique building programs, blackboard work, and flash card drills.

Students are motivated by a natural sense of competitive spirit, and enthusiasm is generated by the pleasure of group instruction with friends. This program has been in operation in many parts of the country with great success.

At the end of one school year (September - May) beginners will be able to:

1. Sight-read
2. Play a variety of musical compositions from memory
3. Recognize chords, transpose, and harmonize melodies
4. Accompany

We believe this is an exciting new program, one which would give your child a solid foundation for further piano study, or even continued study in other instruments. This complete music background is of great value, especially for the beginning student.

We invite you to visit our new installation on Sunday, September 3, from 2:00 to 5:00 P.M. We will be happy to answer further questions you might have.

Our location is: 50 W. 25th St.
Sandpoint, Texas

Phone: 361-9425

Sincerely,

Sally Finch

Run Ads

Although it is not necessarily unethical, piano teachers ordinarily do not run ads in newspapers. Like doctors, lawyers, and other professional people, they are expected to operate their business by referrals. But newspaper advertising and ads in the Yellow Pages of the telephone directory may produce results. For those who wish to pursue this avenue of advertising, a general procedure is given.

To place an ad, it usually requires no more than an announcement of your name, address, telephone number, and your teaching services attractively arranged in a given space and submitted to the newspaper. You might want to list your qualifications as a teacher, your memberships in music associations, your picture, a picture of your studio, or any other information you think is necessary.

The cost of an ad is calculated by the column and number of lines used. Here is a sample of an ad that is one column by seventy lines.

Ill. 2:5 Sample newspaper ad.

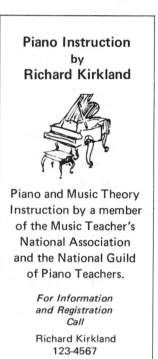

Piano Instruction
by
Richard Kirkland

Piano and Music Theory
Instruction by a member
of the Music Teacher's
National Association
and the National Guild
of Piano Teachers.

For Information
and Registration
Call

Richard Kirkland
123-4567
894 N. Melody Way
Tone, Fla.

Don'ts

As a safeguard for the novice teacher, here are some things *not* to do.

1. Do not seek out pupils who are already studying with another teacher. This is very unprofessional, and it reflects unfavorably on you as a person and upon your methods of operation.

2. Do not brag excessively about your abilities ("the world's greatest teacher"). Once it is known that you are in the market for pupils, you will be far more highly respected if you do not go overboard in appraising your worth. Time will tell eventually, because your students will reflect your teaching abilities. If you blow your own horn at every opportunity you will be suspected of having to do so because no one else does.

3. Do not bill yourself as a magician who can turn out fantastic pianists in a short time with little or no effort on the student's part. Learning to play the piano well is a skill that requires both time and effort, and this cannot be accomplished by a magic touch, no matter how inspiring and skilled the teacher may be.

4. Do not make extravagant claims that you will not be able to live up to. Nothing kills a teacher's reputation more severely than having great expectations disappointed. It is always more profitable to let people find out that you are better than you claim to be rather than not being able to live up to what you have led them to expect.

HOW TO INTERVIEW PROSPECTIVE STUDENTS

The purpose of an interview is for a discussion of various aspects of study: lesson time, fees, best times for practice, amount of practice, etc. A meeting of minds from the three concerned parties, the child, parents, and the teacher, must be accomplished and accord must be reached by this triumvirate before embarking on lessons. Since mutual cooperation is essential for optimum results, a good rapport must be established at the initial meeting and maintained throughout lessons.

To gain the confidence of the child and parents, the teacher should explain what she hopes to accomplish and explain what will be expected from the parents. The teacher should define her objectives and outline her program regarding (1) the type of teaching methods that will be used, (2) participation in theory classes (obligatory or optional), (3) length of lessons, (4) lesson attendance—others. The teaching program being explained may be quite different from the one with which the parents are familiar, and the interview should be used to clarify any misgivings that either the child or the parents might have. In short, the three parties need to understand each other. Both the child and parents should know exactly what they are getting into *before* enrolling for lessons.

Interview the Child, Not the Parents

Generally, the mother brings her child for an interview, and it is interesting to see whether the child talks for himself or whether the mother does all the talking. One sure way to get the child's view is to ask the mother to leave the room for a short time. Answers from the child alone are more apt to be a true indication of his feelings than if the mother is sitting there putting the words into his mouth. Remember, the child is the one taking lessons, not the mother (parents). Therefore, ask more questions of the child than you ask of his mother.

Another factor of importance is that of responsibility. Often if the parent does the talking and makes the arrangements, the student will feel that progress in lessons, outside practice, and punctuality in attendance are the parent's responsibility. The student needs to understand that this is *his* activity and that results obtained are in direct ratio to the amount of effort invested.

When interviewing a new student the teacher should learn as many facts about the child as possible. The more information the teacher has, the better she is able to assess the child's abilities and build a musical program to fit his needs.

Since different situations require different questions, we will divide the following sample questions into three sets. The first series of questions is designed for beginners, the second for the parents, and the third for transfer students.

Sample Questions to Ask Beginners (Ages 7-11)

1. *Name*? (for correct spelling)
2. *Address*?
3. *Telephone*?
4. *Father's name*? (for billing)

These first four items are simple questions that can be answered easily by the child, and this should help put him at ease. Sometimes a young child might not be sure of his address or telephone number; if he is unable to give this information, he probably has had very little parental help at home.

5. *What grade are you in*? Generally, it is not advisable to take beginners until they are at least in the second grade. For best teaching conditions they should be able to read words rather well; otherwise, they will have to have parental supervision during practice sessions.

6. *What school do you attend*? This knowledge is important because some schools are more demanding and require more homework than others. However, homework should not be much of a problem for the first few grades.

7. *Do you like school*? Most young children like school. A child who does not like school (1) may be having personal problems of adjustment to being away from home, to the teacher, or to group situations; or (2) he may not dislike "school," only school work. Therefore, ask him what subjects he likes best. If he answers "recess" rather than reading or math, he is probably not mature enough to begin the intricacies of piano study.

8. *Do you enjoy reading books*? Ask the child to read the directions from the method book he will be using. If his reading is slow and his comprehension is poor, he may also have a difficult time learning to read music. A poor reader will definitely need parental help during practice sessions.

9. (*How talented is the child*?) Talent is almost impossible to assess, especially for children with no previous musical training. Indeed, few authorities can agree on what talent is. Important indications, however, are accurate senses of pitch and rhythm. Perfect pitch is often mentioned as an infallible sign of talent, but this usually cannot be measured until the child has had some musical training and has become tone conscious. Most children, and many musicians for that matter, do not have absolute pitch—the ability to identify sounds "perfectly." More importantly, learning to play the piano well requires a high degree of physical coordination and mental acuity.

Even though the parents may have informed you that their child was "fantastically talented," do a little testing yourself. (1) Have the child sing a simple melody (*Mary Had a Little Lamb*) while you play and sing the tune along with him; about half-way through, drop out and let him finish the song alone. (2) Ask the child to sing a few pitches that are played in his singing range on the piano. A child who cannot match a single tone is probably not very musical. (3) If you have more than one piano in the room, have the child match tones that you play. Show him the groups of two and three black keys, and ask him to cover the three black keys with his first, second, and third fingers. Play some simple patterns on your piano using only the three black keys to discover if he can match the tones you play. (4) Ask the child to clap some rhythms back to you, the same as you give him, such as: long, short-short, long (quarter, two-eighths, quarter); or have him clap the rhythm to a familiar song (*Row, Row, Row Your Boat*). (5) Tell the child that the musical alphabet consists of seven letters, A through G. Then ask him to say the alphabet backwards from G. This will give you a clue to how the child thinks, and it will provide an insight to whether he can reason or whether he has learned things by rote.

10. *Do you want to take piano lessons*? It might be assumed that since the child has come for an interview he is indeed anxious to begin lessons. This is not always the case. Of course the answer to this question is crucial and can only be answered candidly from a child who does not fear retaliation from his parents. Most children are forthright and honest, and if they really do not want to take lessons, they will tell you so. Sometimes it is the parent who wants lessons for the child, rather than the child who wants lessons.

The teacher may incorporate additional questions, but this ten-point program covers general information rather completely. At this point invite the mother back into the room so a few more questions may be asked with both parties present.

Questions and Discussions for Parents

1. *Do either of you* (mother or father) *play the piano or another musical instrument*? This information is helpful, because beginners should have some parental supervision during the early stages of lessons.

2. *Does your child have many outside activities*? A child who has ballet lessons on Monday, swimming lessons on Tuesday, horseback riding lessons on Wednesday, Girl Scouts on Thursday, religious instruction on Friday, and is trying to squeeze in piano lessons on Saturday, will certainly not have time to do justice to it all!

3. Discuss the amount of daily practice that will be required with both the child and mother. Beginners should practice at least thirty minutes a day, six days of the week. Make sure this is clear to the child and mother, and ask them if there is time in their schedule for this daily routine. Piano lessons are fun, especially if steady progress is maintained. This can only be accomplished by sustained effort from the child assisted by parental encouragement.

4. Explain about the scheduling of lessons, and give the mother a printed brochure which lists the *calendar* (regular lesson days plus holiday interruptions), *tuition, payment of fees, policy on missed lessons, how to cancel lessons,* and the *lesson times* (both private and/or group). The policy statement insures against any misunderstandings that might arise later. It may be printed in letter or brochure form. A sample brochure is given here that could be adapted to any teaching situation (Ill. 2:6).

Ill. 2:6. Lesson brochure of the Preparatory Department, Newcomb College/Tulane University.

CALENDAR:

FALL SEMESTER

September 13—Monday—Classes begin

November 25-28--Thursday through Sunday—Thanksgiving recess

December 19—Sunday — Christmas holidays begin

January 3—Monday—Classes resume

January 15—Saturday—Last day of the Fall Semester

SPRING SEMESTER

January 17—Monday—Classes continue

February 14-16—Monday through Wednesday—Mardi Gras recess

March 30-April 15 — Thursday through Wednesday—Spring recess

May 20-Saturday—Last day of the Spring Semester

TUITION:

Based on 32 weeks of lessons, tuition is $270 for the school year. This includes one 30 minute private and one 45 minute group lesson each week.

For those students taking the 30 minute private lesson only, tuition is the same, $270.

PAYMENT OF FEES:

Fees, payable in advance of lessons, are to be made on the basis of $135.00 per semester; or, if you prefer are payable in nine equal payments of $30 each. Checks are payable to (   ).

MISSED LESSONS:

Missed lessons will be made up at the teacher's discretion depending on the student's need and the time available. Lessons missed by the teacher will definitely be made up.

CANCELLED LESSONS:

If you wish to cancel a lesson please call ________, before noon the day of the lesson.

LESSON TIMES:

Private________________________
Day   Date   Time

Place: (   ).

Group________________________
Day   Date   Time

Place: (   ).

5. Explain very clearly about your policy concerning payment of fees. Fees should be paid in advance at the beginning of the month on receipt of your statement. Also explain about the acquisition of music and how it should be paid for. If the teacher buys the music and re-sells it to her students, the price should be added to the monthly statement; if parents are required to purchase the music, suggest the best sheet music store(s) in town.

6. Parents will often have many more general questions about music lessons. They are frequently uncertain about various aspects of lessons such as the ideal age to begin lessons, selection of a teacher, selection of a piano, where to place a piano, how to help their child practice, etc. Therefore, a booklet is recommended for parents who are interested in helping their child achieve maximum results. The title of this booklet is, *A Parent's Guide to Piano Lessons,* by James Bastien (Kjos West, 1976).

Sample Questions to Ask Transfer Students

1. *Name*?
2. *Address*?
3. *Telephone*?
4. *Father's name*?
5. *Grade in school*?
6. *Name of the school*?
7. *How long have you had piano lessons*?
8. *Why do you want to change teachers*? His former teacher may have reduced her class or she may have moved to another neighborhood or city. Sometimes, however, the child will inform you that he really does not want to change teachers, his mother wants him to change. Moving from one teacher to another can be a little traumatic for a child, especially if he is satisfied where he is.

9. *What does he know*? A transfer student coming from another teacher either in your town or a different city should be asked some general questions about his background: what kind of music has he been studying; how long did he practice each day; does he like to practice; what recitals, auditions, or contests did he participate in, and what ratings did he receive; was he taught theory; was sight-reading stressed in his lessons; what were some of his memorized pieces; what did his teacher assign for technique. Many of these questions will be answered by hearing him play a few of the pieces he has prepared for the interview, however, test some of these things yourself. Ask him to read some music on his level. Some students are unable to read new music even after several years of study; students who have been taught entirely by rote often cannot name the notes. Ask the student to define the musical terms that are used in the piece he is reading. Also ask what the key signature is and what chords are used. How is his rhythm, fingering, and dynamics? Ask him to play some scales, chords and inversions, and arpeggios. Test his ear by playing various intervals for him to identify (have him stand so he cannot see the keyboard). Also play major and minor chords to discover if he can discern the difference between them.

Invite the parent (parents) back into the room and discuss the same general things that were mentioned previously for beginners' parents—explain about the lessons schedule, payment of fees, etc. In addition, be sure to suggest *A Parent's Guide to Piano Lessons*, because this book is just as valuable for transfer students as it is for beginners.

When the interview has been completed (for either beginners or transfer students), the next step is to decide whether or not to accept the child for lessons. Do not accept a student with the idea that you can get rid of him later if things do not work out! This method is unprofessional and it causes unnecessary emotional adjustments—the child feels rejected and frustrated and the parents may be intimidated. Therefore, carefully consider the pros and cons *before* enrolling a new student.

If the child seems willing and cooperative and if the parents are enthusiastic, all signals are "go," and a new student may be added to your class. However, if the child is either apathetic about beginning piano lessons, or if he seems too immature to handle the complexities of lessons at this time, it would probably be better not to get into a losing situation. Discuss problems such as these with the parents, with the child out of the room, and explain why you would not advise piano lessons. Do not use a transparent excuse like: "I don't have time in my schedule now for another student." Presumably you had room for a new student or the interview would not have been granted.

Once a new student has been accepted, the next consideration is how to arrange a suitable lesson time.

HOW TO SCHEDULE LESSONS

The hours available for private teaching include early morning hours (before school) and after-school hours. This schedule is a direct contrast to the normal 9:00 to 5:00 routine in which most other professional women are occupied. This irregular schedule has built-in advantages, however, such as being free during the day to look after small children and being able to attend to household duties. School hours are available for teaching in some cases. If the teacher's studio is located adjacent to a school, often the principal will allow students to take lessons during the noon hour or during normal class hours. (Some states even allow school credit for the private music lesson.)

The time available for teaching varies depending on how much the teacher is willing to work. Some teachers give 7:30 and 8:00 a.m. lessons five days of the week; some give two noon-time lessons; some organize pre-school music classes and adult classes during the day; and some teach until 10:00 p.m.! Only a few teachers are fortunate enough to have released time from school for teaching. However, an increasing number of schools are now so crowded that they must operate in two shifts. While one platoon is going to school, the other is at home, and these children are available for piano lessons during the day.

Since the average teacher's class is comprised of students of all ages, careful consideration should be given to the most advantageous times of the day and week for scheduling lessons. The following brief outline and discussion of various age groups is offered which may serve as a general guide for scheduling all types of lessons.

Kindergarten students — Kindergarten age children usually go to school in the mornings. Since some of them still take daily naps, a good time to schedule their lessons is about 2:45 during week days and at any time on Saturday morning.

Beginners — Average beginners are in the 2nd, 3rd, and 4th grades. They are relatively free from homework, and they get home earlier than older students. They may be given an early afternoon time or a Saturday time.

2nd, 3rd, and 4th year students — This age group is still young enough to escape rigorous homework. In addition, they have not yet become seriously involved in outside school activities (games, cheer-leading, baton-twirling, etc.). They may be given afternoon times and Saturday times.

Intermediate students — Intermediate students are usually about junior high age, and these students are generally more involved with after-school activities than younger children. Frequently there is a school game on Friday afternoon, so it is better to avoid lessons on Fridays if possible. Also, students of this age often spend Friday nights at a friend's home; therefore, Saturdays are also undesirable for lessons. Try to schedule lessons for intermediate students during the early part of the week—some conflicts will be avoided.

Advanced students — Advanced students usually are senior high age, and there are numerous considerations for this age group. Homework, dating, sports, and many other activities pose conflicts in scheduling. Because high school students often have exams on Friday, Thursday afternoons should be left free for studying if possible. Also, late Friday afternoon times are objectionable because students of this age are concerned with dating. Lesson times for this group should be scheduled during the early part of the week if at all possible.

Transfer students Transfer students are of varying ages. Since the most desirous times will probably be taken by continuing students, transfer students must be satisfied with the times available. Often these are unwanted times—late Friday afternoon, early Saturday morning, etc.

Adult students Adults are the easiest of all groups to schedule. If they work during the day, they may be given a late evening time. If they do not work during the day, they may be given a morning or early afternoon time.

For the uninitiated, scheduling lesson times can be somewhat problematic. Therefore, to help alleviate a number of the typical pitfalls which may be confronted in scheduling, we will outline three different types of schedules: *private lessons, combination private and class lessons,* and *small and large group lessons.*

Private Lessons

Although teachers are becoming increasingly interested in group lessons, most teachers still teach individually on a one to one basis. Private lessons are easy to schedule and times may be worked out according to the general guidelines already listed.

Teachers giving only private lessons generally offer three types: half hour lessons, forty-five minute lessons, and one hour lessons. An hour lesson can become tedious if the student is young or in the beginning stages. Therefore, the teacher should consider giving two thirty minute lessons per week instead of one extended lesson. The two lessons may be evenly spaced during the week to allow some time in between for practice: Monday-Thursday, Tuesday-Friday, or Wednesday-Saturday.

The following schedule (Ex. 2:1) is based exclusively on private lessons that are either thirty minutes or one hour long; all hour lessons are divided into two thirty minute periods. The circles indicate students who are scheduled for one thirty minute lesson a week.

Analysis of Schedule A: Forty students are scheduled during the week. The class break-down is:

4 Kindergarten Students
6 Beginning Students
8 Second Year Students
6 Third Year Students
4 Fourth Year Students
5 Intermediate Students
4 Advanced Students
3 Transfer Students

Fifteen students receive two thirty minute lessons per week (all beginners, 2nd-1, 2nd-2, 2nd-3, 2nd-4, 4th-2, I-1, I-2, A-1, A-4).

Twenty-five students receive only one thirty minute lesson per week, indicated by the circles (all kindergarten students, transfer students, and other assorted levels).

Note that this schedule utilizes four 8:00 a.m. times (Tue., Wed., Thurs., Fri.). If this early time is objectionable, lessons can be scheduled at other times—later in the evening, Saturday afternoon, or noon-time.

Ex. 2:1. Schedule A: private lessons.

Monday	Tuesday	Wednesday	Thursday	Friday	Saturday
	8:00 2nd-2	8:00 (3rd-2)	8:00 (3rd-3)	8:00 2nd-2	8:00 (Tr.-3)
2:30 (K-1)	2:30 (K-2)	2:30 (K-3)	2:30 (K-4)	2:30	8:30 B-5
3:00 B-1	3:00 B-3	3:00 B-5	3:00 B-1	3:00 B-3	9:00 B-6
3:30 B-2	3:30 B-4	3:30 B-6	3:30 B-2	3:30 B-4	9:30 A-1
4:00 2nd-1	4:00 (3rd-1)	4:00 2nd-3	4:00 2nd-1	4:00 (3rd-5)	10:00 2nd-3
4:30 I-1	4:30 (A-3)	4:30 2nd-4	4:30 I-1	4:30 (4th-4)	10:30 2nd-4
5:00 A-1	5:00 (I-3)	5:00 A-4	5:00 (3rd-4)	5:00 (3rd-6)	11:00 A-4
5:30 I-2	5:30 (I-4)	5:30 (I-5)	5:30 I-2	5:30 (2nd-5)	11:30 4th-2
6:00 (A-2)	6:00 (4th-1)	6:00 4th-2	6:00 (4th-3)	6:00 (Tr.-2)	1:00 (2nd-6)
6:30 (Tr.-1)					1:30 (2nd-7)
					2:00 (2nd-8)

K = Kindergarten Students
(K1 = 1st K student;
K2 = 2nd K student, etc.)
B = Beginners
2nd = Second Year Students
3rd = Third Year Students
O (circle) indicates students scheduled for only *one* thirty minute lesson a week.

4 = Fourth Year Students
I = Intermediate Students
A = Advanced Students
Tr. = Transfer Students

Three additional private teaching schedules are given here to provide an insight into actual teaching situations. These three schedules differ greatly regarding the number of students taught, the various levels of students, and the various teaching times utilized.

The first schedule (Ex. 2:2) is from the studio of John Erickson, Biloxi, Mississippi. He teaches a standard full-time private teaching class of forty-two students. His class is comprised of the following assortment of students:

1 Kindergarten Student
10 Beginners
3 Second Year Students
5 Third Year Students
15 Transfer Students of assorted ages and levels
8 Adult Students of various levels

15 students receive one 30 minute lesson per week.
19 students receive one 45 minute lesson per week.
8 students receive one 60 minute lesson per week.

The second schedule (Ex. 2:3) is from the studio of Bernice Robe, Detroit Lakes, Minnesota. She has an unusually large class of ninety-six students. Her class is comprised of the following:

1 Kindergarten Student
10 Beginners
15 Second Year Students
20 Third Year Students

16 Fourth Year Students
1 (slow) Fifth Year Student
20 Intermediate Students
11 Advanced Students
2 Advanced Adult Students

93 students receive one 30 minute lesson per week.
2 students receive one 60 minute lesson bi-monthly.
1 student receives one 30 minute lesson bi-monthly.

The third schedule (Ex. 2:4) is from the studio of Leonard Gay, Pensacola, Florida. He has one of the largest private classes in the country, teaching a grand total of 111 students per week! His class is comprised of the following:

9 Beginners
28 Second Year Students
16 Third Year Students
32 Fourth Year Students
23 Intermediate Students
3 Advanced Students

107 students take one 30 minute lesson per week.
2 students take 60 minute lessons.
2 students take 45 minute lessons.

Ex. 2:2. Schedule A-1 (from the studio of John Erickson).

Monday	Tuesday	Wednesday	Thursday	Friday	Saturday
2:30-3:30 A (beginner)	3:15-4:00 2nd	2:00-2:45 A (2nd year)	2:15-3:00 A (2nd year)	3:10-3:55 2nd	1:30-2:15 Tr. (4th year)
4:00-5:00 Tr. (4th year)	4:00-4:30 3rd	2:45-3:30 A (4th year)	3:10-3:55 B	4:00-4:30 Tr. (3rd year)	2:30-3:30 Tr. (4th year)
5:05-5:50 Tr. (2nd year)	4:30-5:00 B	4:00-4:30 B	4:00-4:45 Tr. (3rd year)	4:30-5:00 B	3:30-4:15 A (2nd year)
6:15-7:00 3rd	5:05-5:50 3rd	4:30-5:00 B	4:45-5:30 3rd	4:00-5:45 Tr. (4th year)	4:30-5:30 2nd
7:30-8:15 Tr. (4th year)	5:50-6:35 B	5:15-5:45 K	5:30-6:00 A (3rd year)	6:00-6:30 Tr. (3rd year)	5:30-6:30 Tr. (4th year)
8:15-8:45 A (2nd year)	6:35-7:35 B	6:00-6:45 Tr. (3rd year)	6:10-6:55 Tr. (I. level)	6:30-7:00 Tr. (3rd year)	6:30-7:30 A (beginner)
	7:35-8:35 A (beginner)	7:00-7:30 3rd	7:00-7:30 B	7:15-8:00 Tr. (4th year)	
		7:30-8:00 B	7:30-8:00 B		

Ex. 2:3. Schedule A-2 (from the studio of Bernice Robe).

Monday	Tuesday	Wednesday	Thursday	Friday	Saturday
10:00-11:00 A (bi-monthly)	9:15-10:15 A (bi-monthly)		8:00 3rd	8:15 2nd	9:00 I
11:30 2nd	11:00 3rd	11:00 3rd	8:30 3rd	11:00 Ⓐ (2nd year)	9:30 B
12:00 3rd	11:30 2nd	11:30 B	10:30 Ⓐ (4th year)	11:30 2nd	10:00 B
12:30 B	12:00 3rd	12:00 I	11:00 2nd	12:00 3rd	10:30 3rd
3:00 3rd	12:30 2nd		11:30 2nd	12:30 B	11:00 A
3:30 4th	2:30 A		12:00 3rd		11:30 I
4:00 I	3:00 A	3:00 3rd	12:30 3rd	2:30 K	12:00 A
4:30 A	3:30 4th	3:30 4th	3:00 2nd	3:00 I	
5:00 3rd	4:00 I	4:00 4th	3:30 3rd	3:30 4th	1:00 4th
5:30 I	4:30 4th	4:30 I	4:00 4th	4:00 4th	1:30 4th
	5:00 A	5:00 4th	4:30 A	4:30 4th	2:00 3rd
6:30 I	5:30 2nd	5:30 B	5:00 2nd	5:00 2nd	2:30 3rd
7:00 2nd			5:30 I	5:30 4th	3:00 I
7:30 I	6:30 A	6:30 B			3:30 3rd
8:00 (slow) 5th	7:00 B	7:00 3rd	6:30 A	6:30 4th	4:00 B
8:30 B	7:30 I	7:30 2nd	7:00 I	7:00 I	
9:00 A	8:00 I	8:00 I	7:30 4th	7:30 2nd	
		8:30 A	8:00 I	8:00 3rd	
		9:00 3rd (bi-monthly)	8:30 I		
			9:00 I		

A = Advanced Students
Ⓐ = Adult Students

Ex. 2:4. Schedule A-3 (from the studio of Leonard Gay).

Monday	Tuesday	Wednesday	Thursday	Friday	Saturday	Sunday
8:00 I	7:00 3rd	7:00 2nd	7:30 4th	7:30 4th	7:30 B	
9:30 I	7:30 B	7:30 4th	8:00 4th	8:00 2nd	8:00 B	
	8:00 B	8:00 4th		8:30 4th	8:30 3rd	
	9:00 I		9:00 A	9:00 I (hour)	9:00 4th	
	9:30 4th				9:30 4th	
	10:00 I		10:00 3rd		10:00 2nd	
2:30 I	2:30 I		2:30 A	2:30 4th	10:30 I	
3:00 B	3:00 2nd	3:00 I	3:00 I	3:00 3rd	11:00 4th	1:30 2nd
	3:30 I	3:30 2nd	3:30 2nd	3:30 2nd	11:30 I (hour)	2:00 2nd
4:00 I (45 min.)	4:00 4th	4:00 2nd	4:00 2nd	4:00 3rd	12:00	2:30 3rd
4:30	4:30 3rd	4:30 I	4:30 4th	4:30 4th		3:00 2nd
4:45 A (45 min.)	5:00 4th	5:00 I	5:00 4th	5:00 4th	1:00 2nd	3:30 B
5:30 3rd	5:30 2nd	5:30 3rd	5:30 B	5:30 4th	1:30 2nd	4:00 2nd
6:00 3rd	6:00 I	6:00 4th	6:00 2nd	6:00 4th		4:30 2nd
6:30 4th	6:30 4th	6:30 2nd	6:30 3rd	6:30 4th	2:30 4th	5:00 3rd
7:00 A	7:00 3rd	7:00 4th	7:00 2nd	7:00 3rd	3:00 2nd	5:30 2nd
7:30 I	7:30 3rd	7:30 4th	7:30 4th	7:30 I	3:30 B	6:00 4th
8:00 2nd	8:00 B	8:00 I	8:00 2nd		4:00 I	
8:30 4th	8:30 I	8:30 I	8:30 2nd		4:30 3rd	7:00 2nd
	9:00 4th		9:00 4th		5:00 2nd	7:30 I
					5:30 4th	
					6:00 4th	
					6:30 2nd	

Combination Private and Class Lessons

The private-class combination is an effective compromise between (only) private lessons and (only) class lessons. The private lesson (thirty minutes) deals almost exclusively with repertoire, sight-reading, some technique, and individual problems. The class lesson (forty-five minutes) emphasizes theory, ensemble playing, sight-reading, technique, and general musicianship. There is sufficient time between these two weekly lessons to cover a great deal of material, and students are exposed to a complete musical program. The result is usually superior musicianship.

There are a number of advantages in the combination of private and class lessons:

1. Teaching time is used efficiently.
2. Possibilities are provided for varied, effective presentations of materials.
3. Incentive is stimulated among class members.
4. Contact is provided with peer groups.
5. Musicianship is promoted through an awareness of other students' work.

The following schedule (Ex. 2:5) is based on a combination of one thirty minute private lesson and one forty-five minute class lesson per week for each of the forty pupils. In this schedule economical use of teaching time is utilized by providing both private and group instruction rather than private instruction exclusively.

Ex. 2:5. Schedule B: combination private and class lessons.

Monday	Tuesday	Wednesday	Thursday	Friday	Saturday
2:45 K	2:45 K	2:45 K	2:45 K	2:45 A	8:00 Tr.
3:15 B	3:15 B	3:15 2nd	3:15 4th	3:15 2nd	8:30 2nd
3:45 A	3:45 B	3:45 I	3:45 4th	3:45 2nd	9:00 B
4:15 [A-4]	4:15 [2nd-8]	4:15 [I-5]	4:15 [B-6]	4:15 [3rd + 4th-10]	9:30 B
5:00 A	5:00 2nd	5:00 I	5:00 3rd	5:00 3rd	10:00 [K-4]
5:30 3rd	5:30 3rd	5:30 2nd	5:30 I	5:30 3rd	10:45 B
6:00 I	6:00 3rd	6:00 A	6:00 I	6:00 Tr.	11:15 2nd
6:30 4th	6:30 4th				11:45 2nd
					12:15 Tr.

K = Kindergarten Students
B = Beginners
2nd = Second Year Students
3rd = Third Year Students

4th = Fourth Year Students
I = Intermediate Students
A = Advanced Students
Tr. = Transfer Students

[ ] = Class Lessons

Analysis of Schedule B: Forty students are scheduled during the week; each student has two lessons a week. The class break-down is the same as Schedule A:

4 Kindergarten Students
6 Beginning Students
8 Second Year Students
6 Third Year Students
4 Fourth Year Students
5 Intermediate Students
4 Advanced Students
3 Transfer Students (fit into class of appropriate level)

Both *kindergarten students* and *beginners* are spaced away from the class lesson times. This allows sufficient time in between for practice.

In succeeding years, spacing is not as important and students who live far away often appreciate the convenience of having two lessons on the same day (note: Wednesday, 3:45 and 5:00—one *intermediate student* before and after class).

Third and *fourth year students* may be grouped together for their class lesson (note: Friday, 4:15).

The *advanced student* on Friday, 2:45, may be able to get out of school if the last period is study hall.

Transfer students may need two private lessons a week for a period of time before they are caught up and ready to go into their appropriate level.

The level of each group depends mainly on age, but sometimes a class may be further divided by ability: for example, a slow second year class and a fast second year class.

Comparison of Schedule A and B

1. There are no morning times or Saturday afternoon times in Schedule B.
2. All students receive two lessons per week in Schedule B, whereas only fifteen students out of forty received two lessons a week in Schedule A.
3. The teacher following Schedule B could charge more because each student receives two lessons a week: for example, using Schedule B, a monthly fee of $20 per pupil would produce a monthly total of $800; using Schedule A, a monthly fee of $20 for fifteen students and $12 for twenty-five students would produce a monthly total of $600—a difference of $200 between Schedule A and B.
4. Less teaching time is used in Schedule B and it produces a greater return than Schedule A.

Small and Large Group Lessons

A growing number of teachers are beginning to offer group instruction only. There are several possibilities for scheduling class piano lessons: (1) one large class lesson per week (group of six to eight); (2) two large class lessons per week; (3) one small class lesson (group of four to six) plus one large class lesson per week (group of eight to twelve). Although the first two possibilities may be effective, the best results are most often produced by two lessons per week—one small group lesson plus one large group lesson.

Many aspects of group teaching are discussed in the informative booklet, *Greater Rewards Through Creative Piano Teaching* printed by The National Piano Foundation. In this booklet Robert Pace offers an interesting arrangement of scheduling small groups and large groups (Ex. 2:6). He suggests teaching each student two lessons per week: one forty minute lesson with a partner (group of two) and one forty-five minute class lesson (group of eight to twelve). This teaching program makes very efficient use of teaching time.

If teachers do not have enough students to form large groups, an alternative may be considered. Combine "overlapping" groups in the following manner: Have two students come at 3:30 for their lesson. At 4:00 they may be joined by two more students for thirty minutes. At 4:30 the first two students leave and the second two continue for their small class lesson (punctuality is a must for this schedule!). Additional variations may be devised which will best fit the teacher's schedule.

Ex. 2:6. Schedule C: small and large group lessons.[14]

Monday	Tuesday	Wednesday	Thursday	Friday	Saturday
2:30 II Johnny Bradley	2:30 I Gary Dan	2:30 II Mary Chris	2:30 I Liz Debbie	2:30 II Nancy Amy	
3:10 CLASS II 12 students	3:10 I Louise Jamie	3:10 I Annie Janie	3:10 I Paul Jim	3:10 CLASS I 12 students	
3:55 II Ellen Jane	3:50 II Ted Dick	3:50 IIIA Pat Doris	3:50 IIIB Janet Edith	3:55 I Jerry Susan	
4:35 IV Anne Terry	4:30 IIIB Ginny Alicia	4:30 IV Betty Denice	4:30 CLASS IIIB 8 students	4:35 IIIA Jane Mary Lou	
5:30 CLASS IV 10 students	5:10 II Sue Dan	5:25 IV Kevin Al	5:10 IIIB Jim Bart	5:15 CLASS IIIA (remedial) 6 students	
6:15 (to 7:05) IV Mike Donald	5:50 II Julie Lisa	6:20 (to 7:15) IV Joe Mark	5:50 (to 6:45) IV Allyn Nancy	6:00 (to 6:40) IIIA Bobby Gerald	
	5:50 (to 6:30) Eileen Lois				

CLASS I – 7 and 8 years old
CLASS II – 9 and 10 years old
CLASS IIIA – 10 to 12 years old
CLASS IIIB – 10 to 12 years old
CLASS IV – 12 to 15 years old

*Notice that CLASS IIIA is "remedial." These are transfer students who lack fundamentals, yet next year might group well with CLASS IIIB. By combining them later, the teacher will have a good group of advanced students.

SUMMARY

A teaching career is generally built by a steady chain of events that are carefully planned. Self-preparation is the first step in obtaining the desired goal. Although college study culminating in one or more degrees is a basic necessity, learning does not end there. On the contrary, experience is one of the most important factors in successful teaching. A great deal of learning will come by doing.

It might be well to remember that many beginning professionals have to start slowly. Apprentice lawyers may struggle for a few years before achieving financial success; dentists, and to some extent, physicians often experience slow beginnings until their reputations have become known in the community. Private teaching usually follows this same path. However, the financial rewards eventually can be considerable for the well-trained, capable, ethical, conscientious teacher.

Matters of organizing a studio, obtaining students, interviewing students, and scheduling lessons should be given serious consideration before embarking on a private teaching career. Organization is the key factor in any successful business venture, and private teaching is no exception.

[14] This schedule is from the booklet, *Greater Rewards Through Creative Piano Teaching* printed by The National Piano Foundation (435 North Michigan Avenue, Chicago, Illinois 60611) p. 3. Used by permission of copyright owner, Lee Roberts Music Publications, Inc.

FOR DISCUSSION AND ASSIGNMENT

As a class project, interview three private piano teachers in your community and report on various aspects of their teaching situations. Make an oral or written report on the following questions.

1. How did these three teachers learn to teach? Do you think their training was adequate? If not, what should be done to up-grade their present condition?
2. What is the total number of students in each teacher's class? How many are beginners? Second year students? Transfer students? Advanced students? etc. Do you think you would enjoy teaching a class of this composition? If not, why?
3. Describe their studios. Are the studios in their homes? What are the studio dimensions (approximately)? How many pianos are in each studio? What additional equipment is used? Do you think the studios and equipment in them are adequate? If not, what would you do to improve the situation?
4. How did these teachers obtain students when they first began to teach? What additional advertising might have been employed? Do they presently have all the students they would like to have?
5. Describe the type of interview these teachers use. What reasons are given for accepting or rejecting students? Do you think these are reasonable?
6. Describe the schedules these teachers follow. Do any of the teachers give class lessons? If so, how are these scheduled? Could you offer any suggestions for economizing teaching time?

FOR FURTHER READING

Alling, Ruth Stevenson. *How to Make Money Teaching Piano to Beginners.* (private publication: Lo Kno Pla Music Institute, P.O. Box 6767, Corpus Christi, Texas), 1969. Paper. This 112 page spiral bound book contains a wealth of practical information. Chapter headings include "How Much Can You Earn," "Building Your Reputation and Enrollment Fast," and "Improving Your Efficiency." The ideas presented in this book are based on the author's many years of experience. The interesting and unusual methods of procedure will be of special value for the novice teacher.

Blair, Glenn Myers, and R. Stewart Jones. *Psychology of Adolescence for Teachers.* New York: The Macmillan Company, 1964. PB. This book and the one following (*Psychology of the Child in the Classroom*) are especially illuminating for the teacher desiring to have an understanding of children and adolescents. Both books are part of *The Psychological Foundations of Education Series*. Concise and direct, these books may be read in their entirety. Readings of special benefit are: Chapter 1, "The Adolescent Period;" and Chapter 7, "Intellectual Development."

Charles, Don C. *Psychology of the Child in the Classroom.* New York: The Macmillan Company, 1964. PB. Read especially Chapter 1, "Motivation, Why Children Learn;" and Chapter 3, "Children's Abilities."

Ginott, Haim G. *Between Parent and Child.* New York: The Macmillan Company, 1965. An Avon PB. Although written primarily for parents, this best-selling book offers practical suggestion for solutions to a variety of problems which will be of interest to teachers. Topics such as communication, praise and criticism, jealousy, and others are treated with skill. Readings of special interest to piano teachers are: Chapter 1, "Conversing with Children;" Chapter 2, "New Ways of Praise and Criticism;" Chapter 3, "Avoiding Self-Defeating Patterns;" and from Chapter 4, the portion on "Music Lessons."

Pace, Robert, ed. *Greater Rewards Through Creative Piano Teaching.* Chicago:

The National Piano Foundation. Booklet. This informative 16 page booklet offers numerous valuable suggestions on teaching class piano. Aspects of class organization, scheduling lessons, class procedure, and class activities are clearly and concisely discussed. An excellent selection of teaching repertoire is given at the end.

Robinson, Helene, and Richard L. Jarvis, eds. *Teaching Piano in Classroom and Studio.* Washington: Music Educators National Conference, 1967. Paper. Consisting of a collection of nineteen outstanding articles by nationally known music educators, this 176 page volume is an extremely valuable reference source. The book stresses primarily class teaching and creative theory.

Sandström, Carl Ivor. *The Psychology of Childhood and Adolescence,* translated by Albert Read. Baltimore, Md.: Penguin Books, 1968. A Pelican PB. From Sweden comes this intelligent, well-written book designed as an introductory textbook for teachers. The author speaks with authority on a broad spectrum of subjects ranging from growth and development to the development of language and thought. Chapters of special interest are Chapter 4, "Survey of Development;" Chapter 7, "Motivation and the Development of Learning;" and Chapter 12, "Development of Personality."

The Music Teachers' Guide to a Successful and Rewarding Career, Bulletin G-12. Ridgewood, N.J.: International Library of Music Service. Booklet. This 40 page booklet contains many useful and practical suggestions regarding building a class of pupils, organizing recitals, teaching beginners of all ages, and many other topics. (Hopefully, this booklet is still in print.)

The Business of Piano Teaching 3

Musicians, like doctors, lawyers, and other professional persons must attend to business matters in an organized fashion. Such practical procedures as sending bills and keeping accurate accounts are necessary *modi operandi*. The difference between musicians and other professional groups, however, is the size of their business and the amount of income received. Piano teachers generally run a small business, and they must, out of necessity, keep their own books rather than hire a secretary or an accountant to handle this for them.

No one will think less of you or your musical ability if you have some practical sense. On the contrary, competence in managing your financial affairs efficiently will gain you respect from your students and especially from their parents.

PROCEDURES OF PAYMENT

Money matters are best handled between the teacher and parents. The student should not be placed in the position of an intermediary courier. Payment at the lesson by the student is cumbersome and unbusiness-like, and it detracts from the normal course of the lesson. Therefore, send statements and encourage parents to mail payments back by check.

Charge by the Month

It is advisable to charge by the month rather than by the lesson. If payment is made by the lesson, pupils will feel free to cancel, and the teacher will be left with both teaching vacancies and a loss of income.

What About Payment for Missed Lessons?

Sometimes a parent will ask: "May I deduct payment for a missed lesson?" To avoid any misunderstandings about payment for missed lessons, it is advisable to have a lesson brochure which specifically outlines your policy in this matter (see Ill. 2:6, *Lesson Brochure* in Chapter 2, page 37). Lessons should be paid for in advance for the entire semester or for the month. Just as there is no tuition refund if a child misses school for which he is paying tuition (private school), there should be no refund for missed lessons if the reason is flimsy or frivolous–going to parties, spending the night out, etc. If the teacher makes allowances for these situations she will be making up lessons until the wee hours. However, since the lessons are paid for, the teacher should make up lessons due to illness and other unavoidable situations. Too, under these conditions, missed lessons by the teacher must be made up.

What About Months With Varying Weeks?

Concerning monthly payments, a parent may ask: "Should I pay less when there are fewer lessons in the month?" It is true that some months have four weeks, some five, and some months have fewer weeks of lessons due to holidays (mainly Thanksgiving, Christmas, and Easter). To avoid any misunderstandings about variances in lessons per month, your calendar should be printed on the lesson brochure with the holidays clearly stated. Since tuition is based on a fixed number of weeks in the school year, monthly payments should be the *same* regardless of the number of weeks in the month.

Payment for lessons may be either by the semester or by the month. Payment is based on the number of weeks of lessons given during the school year – about thirty-six weeks of lessons is a good average number. The number of teaching weeks will vary for teachers of different localities due to dissimilarities in the commencement of school, vacations, and the dismissal of school. Summer teaching would be figured separately.

LESSON FEES

The amount charged per lesson, month, semester, or school year varies tremendously throughout the country. An artist-teacher may command a fee of $60.00 an hour, while a part-time neighborhood teacher may ask only $5.00 an hour for lessons. While it is not possible to state categorically a certain amount that will be applicable to all teachers, some guidelines may be offered.

In their advice to parents seeking a music teacher, Wills and Manners discuss the subject of lesson fees.

> A teacher who is confident of his abilities will charge as much as he feels the area can afford. While a very small fee may indicate that the teacher is just starting, it may also mean that he places small value on his talent. On the whole, you will get what you pay for. A bargain is a rare phenomenon in music education.[1]

[1] Vera G. Wills and Andre Manners, *A Parent's Guide to Music Lessons* (New York: Harper and Row, 1967), p. 58. Reprinted by permission.

Lesson fees are dependent on five main points: (1) background and capability of the teacher, (2) income bracket of the community, (3) status of music in the community, (4) length of lessons, and (5) type of lessons—private and/or class.

Background and Capability of the Teacher

The teacher's training and background includes a variety of areas: pre-college training, college training, advanced study with artist-teachers, workshop attendance, and other educational or professional experiences. All are relevant to the background of the teacher, and they would be valid factors in determining lesson fees. One would expect to pay more for lessons from a teacher with a Master's degree than from a teacher with a Bachelor's degree or no degree at all.

The teacher's capability is determined mainly by well-trained students. The ability to produce first-rate students year after year is not necessarily dependent on the teacher's performance ability or even a college education. Success may depend just as much on a winning personality and years of self-learning and improvement from experience as on degrees and other measures of professionalism. An experienced, successful teacher may charge a proportionately higher fee than a less experienced teacher.

Income Bracket of the Community

The socio-economic status of the community or neighborhood may be determined by external factors such as homes, schools, and automobiles. However, unseen factors often dominate the financial position of the area. The cost of living is a main determining agent in various communities. While salaries may be similar in both large and small cities, living costs usually are not at all the same. The price of land, homes, taxes, piano lessons, and everything else ordinarily is much higher in a large city than in a small town. Monthly lessons costing $40.00 in New York may be a real bargain, but in Hutchinson, Kansas, this fee may seem expensive. Therefore, fees must be somewhat scaled to the community. Lesson fees in a ghetto area of Boston could not be compared to those charged in Grosse Point.

Status of Music in the Community

Where do piano teachers prosper most frequently in a large city? Success usually lies in the suburbs rather than in the inner core of a large metropolitan area. The reason is simple: the status of music is important to the inhabitants, and they can afford them. Piano lessons in suburban communities are as commonplace as children and pets. A value is placed on music lessons as part of the children's general education. In short, parents in certain communities have both the inclination and the means to pay for what they value. Lesson fees will be adjusted accordingly.

Length of Lessons

In addition to the preceding, the length of the lesson often determines the fee. Teachers frequently have rates for half hour lessons, forty-five minute lessons, and hour lessons. Sometimes teachers charge a proportionately higher rate for a half hour lesson and slightly less for an hour – for example: $4.00 for a half hour lesson, and $7.00 for an hour lesson. The reduced price is offered as an inducement to take a longer lesson. If the teacher does not have a full class of students, more income can be gained by teaching hour lessons at "bargain prices." This system is usually used by young teachers with few students; established teachers generally charge standard fees.

Type of Lessons–Private and/or Class

Private instruction is generally more expensive than class instruction, but not proportionately. Fees for private lessons may run about $8.00 to $12.00 an hour; however, a fee of $2.00 per pupil for a class of ten would net the teacher $20.00 for an hour of group instruction.

Group lessons are more demanding than private lessons. There is more work involved in group teaching–lesson planning, preparing extra materials for class, etc. Teachers are justified in charging proportionately higher fees for group instruction.

Suggested Lesson Fees[2]

Private Lessons Only	General prices for one half hour private lesson per week range from $16.00 to $24.00 per month, or a comparable amount paid by the semester. This rate is based on a per lesson fee of from $4.00 to $6.00. Some less established teachers charge $3.00 per half hour lesson. Some well-established teachers charge up to $8.00 or $10.00 for a half hour lesson (a monthly total of $32.00 to 40.00 per month!).
Combination Private and Group Lessons	Reasonable prices for one half hour private lesson and one forty-five minute group lesson per week range from $20.00 to $30.00 per month, or a comparable amount paid by the semester.
Combination Small and Large Groups	Fees are about the same as above: from $20.00 to $30.00 per month, or a comparable amount paid by the semester.
Large Classes	Fees for this type of instruction should be nominal. One hour per week ranges from $8.00 to $16.00 per month, or a comparable amount paid by the semester.

Summary

Professional teachers who must live on what they earn must charge adequate rates to insure a reasonable yearly income. Most full-time profes-

[2]Prices are based on fees charged by professional private teachers from around the country whom the author knows personally.

sional teachers teach between forty and fifty pupils per week. A yearly income can be easily computed by multiplying the number of students by hourly or monthly prices.

Private lessons based on fifty pupils at $16.00 per month each (one half hour private lesson per week) would produce a nine-month income of $7200.[3] (This figure could easily be increased by teaching some students hour lessons instead of only one half hour lesson per week.)

Combination private and group lessons would produce a nine-month income of $9000, based on forty pupils at $25.00 per month each. It would, therefore, be practical to conclude that the best return for teachers is made by giving some type of class lessons. It is, likewise, the best rate for parents who receive more time proportionately for their money.

ADDITIONAL SOURCES OF INCOME

The most obvious method of increasing income is to work (teach) more. Additional lessons may be given by utilizing other portions of the day. Pre-school children may be taught either in the morning or early afternoon. Adults may be taught either in the morning, early afternoon, or evening.

Although it may be possible to teach from early morning until late at night, quality lessons can only be given when one is mentally and physically alert. Teaching is strenuous work, and the teacher should not cram the entire day exclusively with teaching. Before enrolling additional pupils, plan your schedule carefully so there will be sufficient time for outside activities.

Raise Rates

One of the most logical sources of additional income is to increase tuition. Teachers often worry needlessly about adjusting fees. The cost of living goes up, inflation continues, and piano teachers must raise their prices from time to time as other costs rise. It is not necessary to apologize for an increase in tuition—parents have probably been expecting it for some time.

It is not advisable to have different rates for different pupils. Raise your tuition at the same time for everyone. Some teachers charge new students a higher fee and wait to raise the tuition for students of long standing. It is better to have a uniform fee to avoid comparisons among parents which may possibly result in embarrassing confrontations.

It is best to raise rates at the beginning of a new school term rather than in the middle of the year. The change to the higher fee will not be so abrupt, and parents will have time to adjust to the idea of more expensive lessons.

A letter or brief note (Ex. 3:1) should be sent to the parents sometime in the spring (May) before the next school term. You may or may not state that tuition will be raised; likewise, reasons for the tuition increase do not have to be spelled out in great detail. A simple statement will suffice.

[3]Although summer lessons are given by most teachers, they are sporadic and, therefore, income is more easily calculated on a nine month basis.

Ex. 3:1. Sample tuition note.

> Dear Parents:
>
> The tuition for the coming school year will be $__________ for the (month, semester, or whatever system of payment is used).
>
> Sincerely,

Even a small tuition increase will raise yearly income. A raise from $20.00 to $24.00 per month for thirty-five pupils would amount to an increase of $140.00 per month, or $1,260 for the school year.

Give Summer Lessons

Most private teachers give some summer lessons, at least for the months of June and July. However, lessons are apt to be sporadic due to out of town interruptions. Most students take vacations or go off to camp, and summer piano lessons are usually irregular.

Summer income may be obtained by (1) continuing regular lessons, (2) offering special programs for regular students, or (3) offering classes for new beginners (six or eight weeks).

A percentage of regular students will want to continue lessons during part of the summer. If you are teaching the private-class combination during the regular school year, it might be difficult to continue this same program during the summer due to a reduced number of students. In this case continuing students may be given two private lessons during the summer.

There are several possible summer programs that may be offered: high school theory, music appreciation classes, piano pedagogy for older high school students, and special ensemble classes.

Beginners may be started during the summer in small classes of four to six on a trial basis at a reduced rate (optional). Those who show interest and promise could continue in the fall.

BOOKKEEPING PROCEDURES

Since the private teacher is self-employed, careful records must be kept of income and expenses for tax purposes. Because bookkeeping can be both time consuming and frustrating, the following sample forms are offered in the hopes of simplifying this process.

Monthly fees are easy to keep track of by simply checking each time payment is received (Ex. 3:2). Individual lesson payment complicates this procedure, and if used, the teacher will have to record payment received at least four times per month instead of once a month.

Accounting (Ex. 3:3) is not difficult if the amount of each bill is entered on the form when it is received. If bookkeeping is not kept up to date, a number of deductible items may be overlooked. Be sure to keep all receipts and canceled checks during the year for Internal Revenue purposes.

Ex. 3:2. Record of student payment.

Student's Name	Sept.	Oct.	Nov.	Dec.	Jan.	Feb.	Mar.	April	May
(Jim Roberts)	X								

Ex. 3:3. Monthly accounting form.

EXPENSES FOR THE MONTH OF (September)

I. Music Purchased:	(total)
Music Sold:	(total)
Balance:	(carry forward each month)
II. Rewards, Favors, Incentives Purchased:	
III. Studio Rent: (if renting)	
IV. Portion of Utility Services:	
V. Reference Materials	
Books:	
Music:	
Records	
Tapes:	
Total:	
VI. Office Supplies	
Envelopes, Paper:	
Postage:	
Printing:	
Statements or Receipts Purchased:	
Other:	
Total:	
VII. Telephone:	
VIII. Additional Expenses:	
(membership dues, workshops, piano tuning, etc.)	
Grand Total:	

For an insight into exacting bookkeeping procedures, see Jane Smisor Bastien's *Music Teacher's Record Book* (Kjos West, 1976).

TAX DEDUCTIONS

Although the tax structure changes from time to time, general tax deductions remain fairly constant. Items such as studio rent and expenses, office expenses, professional association dues, depreciation on equipment, etc., are all readily acceptable tax deductions.

The following checklist of deductible expenses is offered as a handy reference guide.[4]

Ex. 3:4. Musician's checklist of deductible expenses.[5]

Instruments, Equipment, and Supplies
- Instruments: depreciation, rental, maintenance and repairs, loss on sale or by theft, junking, or destruction
- Insurance on instruments
- Depreciation on record player, tape recorder, typewriter, other major equipment
- Records and tapes
- Metronome, stop watch, batons, etc.
- Sheet music, music writing pen and paper
- Office supplies: stationery, business cards, signs, postage, etc.

Studio (or separate portion of home)
- Rent
- Depreciation, real estate tax, and interest on mortgage
- Maintenance and repair
- Cost of moving to new location
- Insurance on business property: fire, liability
- Overhead: heat, light, cleaning
- Magazines and newspapers for waiting room

Performance
- Recital expenses: hall rental, flowers, programs, refreshments, transportation
- Royalties paid
- Coaching expenses
- Costume or uniform (but not evening dress if it can be used on non-business occasions)
- Costume or uniform cleaning

Fees and Dues
- Dues in professional organizations (MTNA, MENC, NBA, NSOA, etc.)
- Union dues
- Fees to employment agency, booking agent, press agent
- Fees to lawyer for employment contract or other business purposes
- Fees for preparing tax return
- Fees for bookkeeping or accounting
- Fees to arranger / composer / accompanist

Maintenance of Professional Skills
- Professional magazines and periodicals
- Professional books
- Conventions: all expenses including travel
- Workshops and clinics
- Educational expenses (maybe: check first)

Miscellaneous
- Advertising: any expense to promote business
- Local transportation not commuting: include parking
- Travel away from home overnight
- Telephone and telegrams
- And maybe:
  - Entertainment and gifts
  - Child care expense
  - Part of vacation travel

See any income tax guide for deducting other expenses not specifically related to a music career: taxes, interest, etc.

[4] For a thorough discussion on tax savings for the musician, see: "Tax Savings–How the Musician Can Save on Income Tax" by John C. O'Byrne, *Clavier*, Vol. VII, No. 2 (February, 1968), p. 16.

[5] From *Clavier*, Vol. VII, No. 2 (February, 1968), p. 47. Reprinted by permission.

If lessons are given in the home the teacher may deduct part of the household expenses from the gross income. If one room is used exclusively for income-producing purposes, a portion of the household expenses may be deducted. This is figured on the basis of the room's percentage of the total floor space in the house. Thus, a studio 10 x 15 feet in a 2500 sq. ft. home would permit a 6% (150 ÷ 2500) deduction of household expenses – rent, heat, light, air conditioning, etc. However, if the room is also used for family purposes, then the deduction may be made only in proportion to the hours used for giving lessons. For example: if the room is used fourteen hours after school and four hours on Saturday for a total of 18 hours, approximately 10% (18 ÷ 168 hours in a week) of the household expenses may be deducted, as these can be allocated to that portion of the home.

Any special costs to this room such as acoustical treatment, special lighting, etc., also may be deductible, if they are not capital expenditures for permanent home improvement.

Although the above mentioned deductions are standard pertaining to the business of private teaching, it is advisable to seek professional advice from a tax accountant. The accountant will be able to assist you in itemizing all allowable deductions.

Yearly Expenditures

Records of income and expenses must be accurately noted from month to month. Otherwise it is extremely difficult to gather this information when income tax time approaches.

To quickly compile information for income tax, total the monthly expenditures (Ex. 3:3) for the entire year and deduct these from the yearly income. The profit and loss statement (Ex. 3:5) on page 60 presents a clear picture of how to subtract expenditures from income.

Ex. 3:5. Yearly profit and loss statement.[6]

Income		$________
Less cost of Music*	________	
Less cost of Incentives	________	
Total cost of sales	________	– ________
NET INCOME		$
Expenses		
Recitals	________	
Advertising	________	
Piano Tuning	________	
Recording Tapes	________	
Studio Rental or		
Home studio % of total	________	
Office expenses	________	
Amortized Reference Material**	________	
Depreciation expense***	________	
Own Study, Workshops, etc.	________	
Total expenses		– ________
NET PROFIT or LOSS		$

*Cost of music (if not reimbursed)

Music on hand Jan 1	________	
+ Music purchased during year	+ ________	
Total music	________	
– Music on hand Dec. 31	– ________	
Cost of music used		$________*

**Reference Material

	Cost	Life	Current Year % Balance
Books			________
Music			________
Recordings			________
Tapes			________
Amortization amount taken (total)			________**

***Depreciation

	Cost	Life	Current Year % Balance
Piano			________
Piano			________
Music Cabinet			________
Record Player			________
Tape Recorder			________
Typewriter			________
Furniture, etc. (list separately)			________
Depreciation taken (total)			________***

[6]From the *Blue Book* by Lora M. Benner. Copyright © 1969 by Benner Publishers. Used by permission.

FOR DISCUSSION AND ASSIGNMENT

Under this heading in Chapter 2, questions were to be asked from three private teachers in the community. Further information about studio management can be learned by asking the following questions from the same three teachers.

1. What method of payment does each teacher use (by the lesson, month, or semester)? Discuss briefly the merits or demerits of each teacher's method.
2. What policy is used for a missed lesson? Are students charged for missed lessons? Are missed lessons made up?
3. How is payment handled for months of varying teaching weeks?
4. What fees are charged for lessons? (Teachers usually will not object to this question for research purposes.)
5. Are summer lessons given? If so, are any additional summer programs offered? How are fees handled for summer lessons?
6. Did any of the teachers raise their rates during the past few years? If so, how was this handled?

FOR FURTHER READING

Anderson, Jr., Arthur H. "Taxes and the Music Teacher." *Clavier*, Vol. XVI, No. 9 (December, 1977). Since changing tax laws necessitate constant vigil, the article offers up-to-date information for the teacher in clearly stated language.

Benner, Lora. *Handbook for Piano Teaching.* Schenectady, New York: Benner Publishers, 1975. Paper. This excellent 108 page book contains a wealth of information on studio management and teaching materials. The book is a combination of previously published books *(Blue Book* and *Gold Book)* in revised form. Matters of finance, bookkeeping, income tax, and many other studio problems are discussed.

O'Byrne, John. "Tax Savings–How the Musician Can Save on Income Tax." *Clavier*, Vol. VII, No. 2 (February, 1968). Mr. O'Byrne, Professor at Northwestern University Law School, is a recognized authority in the field of taxation. Although tax matter change frequently, the teacher can get a good understanding of the situation from this article which is clear and specific. A reprint of the article may be purchased separately from *Clavier*.

Stone, Marion. "This Business of Teaching Music." *Clavier*, Vol. VII, No. 2 (February, 1968). Matters of policy, lesson fees, and other pertinent business information are clearly discussed in this article. The information from various teachers represents a cross section of the country.

Survey of Methods for Beginners 4

More than any other country, the United States has led the other nations of the world in training large numbers of recreational pianists. Piano lessons have become standard fare *per se*, and an acceptable social activity as a part of general childhood education. Regardless of talent or excessive motivation, millions of students are engaged in the pursuit of musical instruction as an extension of the general learning process. It is usually not the intent or purpose of those studying to become professional musicians. Rather, for the majority who study, the general philosophy is that music study will develop a special skill which will enrich and broaden their lives. Music becomes a satisfying experience that gives direction to the basic needs of self-expression, an appreciation for beauty, and an outlet for emotional release.

Due to the great popularity of piano instruction, this country has produced a large body of teaching materials over the past fifty years. The sheer bulk of this output is sufficient to overwhelm anyone who endeavors to become knowledgeable on the subject. Therefore, the purpose of this chapter is to sort a number of these methods into groups and to discuss briefly those which are used most frequently. Out of necessity, the methods surveyed will be limited to those published in the United States which are currently in print.

TEACHING GOALS OF METHOD BOOKS

The word "method" is defined by Merriam-Webster as "a systematic plan followed in presenting material for instruction." The word further connotes a procedure which develops one integrated system of learning. Since method books have planned objectives for systematic progression, one should consider the specific goals outlined by each book or series.

Without thought or reference to any particular method of instruction, list your own teaching objectives. Consider basic skills that your students should have attained after a few years of instruction. The following list of teaching objectives is offered as a guide. These ten points represent general goals which would be endorsed by most piano teachers—no doubt you will think of many more.

After a few years of instruction students should be able to:

1. Understand the entire keyboard, not just part of it
2. Recognize notes fluently, including ledger line notes above and below the staff
3. Recognize chords and be able to play them (major, minor, augmented, and diminished)
4. Understand tempo markings, meter signatures, key signatures, and generally used musical terms
5. Improvise
6. Transpose
7. Harmonize melodies
8. Sight-read
9. Accompany
10. Memorize a number of pieces each year

Educational Philosophies

Philosophical concepts in education have changed greatly during the past five decades. Years ago elementary education of all sorts was looked upon as being necessarily strict; learning was a bitter pill that had to be swallowed before any good resulted. Old-school disciplinarians did not spare the rod or the dunce cap.

Students were not given the opportunity to enjoy the subjects they were studying. They often were forced to memorize long poems and essays, and they were required to learn tedious rules and facts whether they understood them or not. They were required to recite, copy and practice for the sake of training and discipline.

Piano lessons, too, often tended to be difficult and tedious. The child was taught to sit stiffly on the piano bench, with his arms in a certain fixed position. His fingers and wrist had to be held just so, and if it took him months to learn these beginning essentials, it was for his own good. If he survived these basics, he was taught scales and exercises for a period of time before the playing of musical compositions was even considered.[1] Students were trained so precisely in strict fundamentals that the mortality rate of student drop-outs was considerable, and those who survived were surely destined for the concert stage.

Fortunately, much of this stern autocratic approach to teaching along with the famous "willow switch" and the well-known "rap on the knuckles" is gone. The majority of students today are learning to enjoy music. Lessons are presented in such a fascinating and challenging way that practically every pupil is intrigued with his lessons and with his progress.

Although teaching methods have progressed markedly in the past ten years, it is difficult for some teachers to adjust to today's methods because of the way in which they were taught.

[1] Actually many of the European piano methods still appear much the same today—primarily exercises, scales, and a stiff dose of the "classics." See: *Piano Method* by Bartók-Reschofsky (Boosey & Hawkes: English edition, 1968); and *Die Klavier Fibel* by Willy Schneider (Heinrichshafen's Verlag, 1960).

> The forces of tradition make it quite difficult to introduce new teaching methods. Besides the inertia of existing methods, there is the problem of avoiding threat to teachers using the traditional approach. It is understandable that experienced teachers will resist change if they are made to feel that the way they have been teaching is inferior or that they must learn new skills. They will insist that the old way is the best way and find fault with the innovation.
>
> Techniques that are now traditional were, of course, at one time new. And, naturally, no teaching method has failed to undergo subtle changes in response to changing values of the culture.[2]

Teaching methods employed today should reflect the general evolution that has occurred in all phases of instruction. The teacher's style and technique of presentation should be oriented toward today's youth. Teaching should be relevant. The teacher should focus on the needs and objectives of students today, not those used thirty years ago.

Middle C Versus Multiple Key

Although there are numerous method books available by many different authors, essentially there are two basic approaches to teaching beginners in this country at the present time: one is the traditional "middle 'C' method," and the other is the more recent "multiple key method." Most teachers who are presently instructing children in piano grew up on the first method of instruction. It has been only within the past ten years that the multiple key method has been used with any frequency.

The middle C approach has been firmly established in the United States for many years. It was popularized by John Thompson's *Teaching Little Fingers to Play*, published by the Willis Music Company in 1936. Thompson, and others before him, began a trend of teaching beginners which has persisted to the present, and the middle C method is still the most frequently used instructional procedure among teachers today. The popularity of this approach is evident; even a cursory glance at subsequent methods reveals that *most* books are patterned after Thompson's blueprint.

The basic procedure of the middle C approach is to learn facts one at a time and eventually develop a musical picture. Whereas, the basic procedure of the multiple key approach is to present whole concepts and then break them down into parts.

The instructional technique of the middle C method requires the student to place both thumbs on middle C and begin playing (Ex. 4:1).

Ex. 4:1. Example of a middle C method: single line melody.

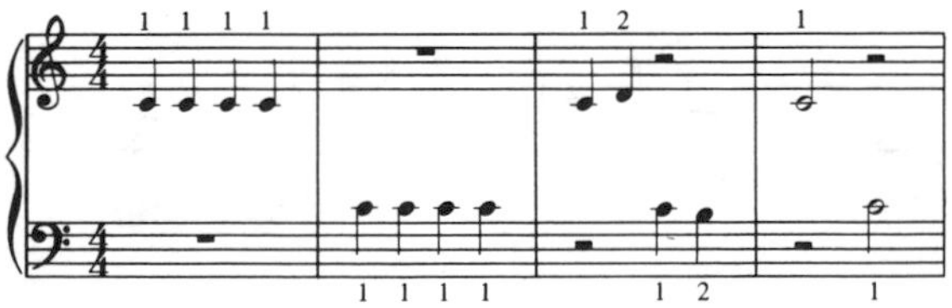

[2] James L. Kuethe, *The Teaching-Learning Process* (Glenview, Ill.: Scott, Foresman, 1968), p. 141. Reprinted by permission.

Without previous keyboard experience the student begins to play little melodies while simultaneously learning notation and rhythm. The method of instruction presents single line melodies divided between the hands. Later, melodies are written mostly in two parts (Ex. 4:2). Finger numbers are given

Ex. 4:2. Example of a middle C method: two-voice melodies.

for every note in most courses. The keys of the pieces are limited almost exclusively to C, G and F. Theoretical concepts such as intervals, chord structure and use, transposition, harmonization, the order of sharps and flats, key signatures, etc., may or may not be included; generally these presentations (if given) come later in the course.

The multiple key approach is a completely different concept of instruction, and is in direct contrast to the middle C method. Although not new, the multiple key method is only now beginning to find acceptance among an increasing number of teachers. A great deal of credit for the development and promulgation of this concept should be given to Raymond Burrows (*The Young Explorer at the Piano*, Willis Music Company, 1941), and to Robert Pace (*Music for Piano*, Lee Roberts Music Publications, Inc., 1961), both of Columbia University.

The procedure of the multiple key method is to learn all twelve major 5-finger positions (Ex. 4:3) within the first few months of instruction.[3]

Ex. 4:3. Example of a pre-notated multiple key pattern.

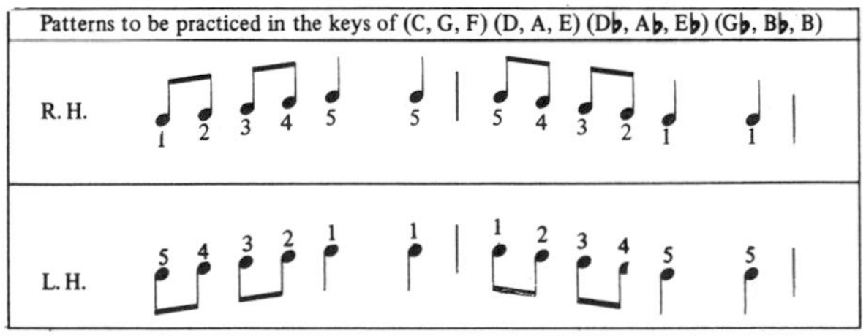

[3]The twelve major positions are most easily learned by dividing the keys into groups according to those which are related by both sight and touch–example: Group I Keys (C,G,F) have all white keys in the tonic chords; Group II Keys (D,A,E) have a white, black, white composition in their tonic chords; Group III Keys (Db,Ab,Eb) have a black, white, black composition in their tonic chords; Group IV Keys (Gb,Bb,B) are not related by sight or touch, because each is different.

Directional reading is developed by establishing the concept of intervallic elationships, mainly steps (seconds), skips (thirds), and repeated notes (Ex. 4:4). Later on, directional reading is further developed by continuing the

Ex. 4:4. Example of basic directional reading patterns.

expansion of intervals through the octave. Almost from the beginning, I and V7 chords are used, and melodies are harmonized with these two chords (Ex. 4:5). The following elements of theory are stressed throughout multi-

Ex. 4:5. Melody harmonized with I and V7 chords.

key courses: (1) intervals, (2) chords (tonic, sub-dominant, dominant, major, minor, diminished, augmented), (3) the order of sharps and flats, (4) key signatures, (5) transposition, and (6) harmonization.

A comparison of the middle C and multiple key methods is offered (Ex. 4:6) to discover areas of emphasis in these diverse approaches. The following comparisons are based on general areas of knowledge that a student may or may not have been exposed to after approximately two years of instruction.

From the following comparisons (Ex. 4:6) it might be concluded that the student would experience a greater variety of material using the multiple key method than with the middle C method. While this is basically true, the correct presentation of any material is essential; success cannot be guaranteed automatically by the materials chosen. The teacher, not a set of books, is the determining factor in quality results.

Ex. 4:6. Comparison of middle C and multiple key approaches.

	MIDDLE C METHOD	MULTIPLE KEY METHOD
Melodies	centering around middle C, especially at the onset of lessons	encompassing all 12 major five finger positions
Notation	largely confined to a two octave range and limited mainly to the white keys on the piano, with the exception of F#, Bb, and C#	four octave range including all the white and black (sharps and flats) keys, also ledger lines above, below and in between the staffs
Rhythm	somewhat restricted to 4/4, 3/4, 2/4, especially in the beginning stages of lessons, although within the first year, students would have been introduced to 6/8	similar, although 6/8 is usually introduced much earlier in this presentation
Theory	basically nonexistent "theory" is often nothing more than exercises in drawing the treble and bass clefs, note spelling, writing note values, writing counts, etc.	considerable intervals, chords, key signatures, and keyboard harmony are interwoven as basic ingredients in the general musical program
Chord usage	quite limited in this approach block chords are almost never used or explained, however, various types of broken chord basses are used as accompaniments to melodies	frequently used all major, minor, diminished and augmented chords are used in both block and broken form, and these are clearly explained and systematically used
Order of sharps and flats	excluded the order of #'s (F, C, G, D, A, E, B) and b's (B, E, A, D, G, C, F) is *not* used or explained in this approach	included students learn the order of sharps and flats in the first year of lessons and review these in subsequent years
Key signatures	quite limited the student is told that if there is an F# in the key signature, the piece is in G, but there is no attempt to systematically teach all the key signatures	emphasized continually all major (and later, minor) key signatures are explained and used; by frequent reference to "key," the student becomes aware of the tonal center

Transposition	some suggestions for transposition are sometimes given, but keys suggested usually are those of C, G, or F	considerable almost from the onset of lessons students are directed to transpose their pieces into a variety of keys
Harmonization	quite limited the harmonization of given melodies is virtually nonexistent in this approach	frequently used single line melodies are presented for students to harmonize in various keys
Improvisation	excluded	included students are given four measure *question* phrases and are told to improvise or create their own four measure *answer* phrases
Creative work	very limited, almost nonexistent	included, made a part of the general music program
Technique	included finger drills are used mostly in the key of C, and scales are presented early in this approach	included finger drills are used in all 12 keys in various ways: for legato and staccato touch, balancing of tone, phrase studies (down-up wrist motion), and for forearm rotation; scales are presented later in this approach
Sight reading	limited to the keys of C, G, and F (dependent on the student's ability)	reading facility is developed in many keys (dependent on the student's ability)
Comprehensive, inclusive musical program	somewhat limited confined mostly to the learning of pieces, technical studies, and scales	inclusive and challenging: repertoire, sight-reading, theory, technique, and creative work constitute the general music program

Gradual Multiple Key Approach

An alternative to learning all twelve keys at once (all 5-finger positions and tonic chords) is a gradual multi-key approach in which each group of keys is presented individually in depth. This approach may be beneficial for students who might have a difficult time handling all twelve keys simultaneously. Ylda Novik states: "A major premise [in this approach] is that the slower rate of key presentation might eliminate any possible confusion that could arise from the more rapid total twelve key presentation. Experience has indicated that this is especially true with very young students and those who get little parental guidance and assistance at home."[4]

The gradual multi-key approach is used in *The Bastien Piano Library* by James Bastien and Jane Smisor Bastien (Kjos West, 1976). Although not systematic, the gradual multi-key approach is used loosely in *Music Pathways* by Lynn Olson, Louise Bianchi, and Marvin Blickenstaff (Carl Fischer, 1974).

Landmark Reading Approach

An alternative to either the middle C or multiple key approach is reading by landmarks, first introduced in the Frances Clark *Library for Piano Students* (Summy-Birchard) in 1955. Directional reading is developed from given landmarks (Ex. 4:7) which are: bass clef F, middle C, and treble clef G. The student reads directionally by intervals up and down from these landmarks. Landmark reading is also used in *Creating Music at the Piano* by Willard Palmer and Amanda Vick Lethco (Alfred Music Co., Inc., 1971-72).

Ex. 4:7. Landmark reading: F-C-G.

The series *Music Pathways* by Lynn Olson, Louise Bianchi, and Marvin Blickenstaff (Carl Fischer, 1974) uses landmark reading from five C's on the staff (Ex. 4:8).

Ex. 4:8. Landmark reading: five C's. – where are they on piano?

[4]Ylda Novik, Review "The Bastien Library," *The Piano Quarterly* (Summer, 1976/Number 94).

AN ALPHABETICAL LISTING OF METHOD BOOK AUTHORS

It is difficult to produce a complete listing of method books – some are out of print; each music store carries different method books; and new method books are being written continually. Therefore, for this edition the author has relied chiefly on current listings in publishers' catalogs. In addition, a list titled "Music in Print" provided by Ralph Pierce of the Ralph Pierce Company in Pomona, California, has been most helpful. This listing has been recently compiled and contains most of the courses currently in print. Even this list, which is not entirely complete, is quite staggering when seen in its entirety displayed in the store. Mr. Pierce has conscientiously attempted to stock every beginning piano method. Unfortunately, most music stores are unable to carry a large inventory of piano music. This is especially true of the newer or as yet "unproven" piano courses. Because of the expense involved, most stores are somewhat justified in not stocking every method book in print. Due to the sheer bulk of piano instruction books, they are considered the anathema of the sheet music business.

An alphabetical list of better known and newer method book authors includes the following:

*Aaron, Michael
*Bastien, Jane Smisor
  and James Bastien
Bergenfield, Nathan
*Brimhall, John
*Burnam, Edna Mae
Burrows, Raymond
  and Ella Mason Ahearn
*Clark, Frances
*d'Auberge, Alfred
Davis, Jean Reynolds
  and Cameron McGraw
Diller-Quaile
*Duckworth, Guy
Eckstein, Maxwell
*Fletcher, Leila
Frisch, Fay
Frost, Bernice
*Gillock, William
*Glover, David Carr
Hirschberg, David
Kahn, Marvin
*Kasschau, Howard
Lyke, James B.
  and Maryland D. Blatter
*Marwick, Marion
  and Maryanne Nagy
Nelson, Harry
  and Allison Neal
*Nevin, Mark
*Noona, Walter
  and Carol Noona
*Olson, Lynn,
  Louise Bianchi,
  and Marvin Blickenstaff
*Oxford Piano Course
*Pace, Robert
*Palmer, Willard A.
  and Amanda Vick Lethco
*Pointer System
Quist, Bobbie Lee,
  Ruth Perdew,
  and Anne Demarest
*Richter, Ada
Ristad, Eloise
Sanucci, Frank
  and Virginia Lee Taylor
*Schaum, John W.
*Stecher, Melvin,
  Norman Horowitz,
  and Claire Gordon
Steiner, Eric
*Swenson, Lucile Burnhope
*Thompson, John
Wagness, Bernard
Werder-Paul
*Westmoreland, John
  and Marvin Kahn
*Weybright, June
Williams, John M.
*Zepp, Arthur

**indicates courses to be surveyed*

From this list of forty-five entries, how many names have you seen before? How many courses are familiar to you? There are probably only about ten names from this list which "ring a bell" – the others are apt to be unfamiliar.

Courses range in years from the very old (like the Williams, Thompson, and Oxford courses) to the very new (like the Bastien, Gillock, Glover, Noona, Olson, and Palmer courses). As a basis for comparison the teacher should have at least a working knowledge of the better known courses regardless of when they were written.

The courses which are used with some frequency will be found in music stores of any size. The teacher should make an effort to keep abreast of the new courses published by searching these out in the music store. If the store has a limited piano sheet music department and does not subscribe to new issues, information on new courses can be found in magazines such as *Clavier* and *Piano Quarterly*.

To acquaint students and teachers with methods that are used with some frequency, the author has chosen twenty-seven courses to survey.[5] The survey is purposely limited to American publications.

SURVEY OF TWENTY-SEVEN PIANO METHODS

AARON, MICHAEL *Piano Course* **Belwin-Mills**

Method Books	**Piano Primer** (1947); **Grades 1-5** (Grades 1 & 2, 1945; Grades 3 & 4, 1946; Grade 5, 1952).
Technic Books	**Piano Technic, Books 1 & 2** (1948).
Supplementary Books	**Note Reader** (1960); Duet Book; Note Spelling Game; others.
Adult Books	**Adult Piano Course, Books 1 & 2** (Bk. 1, 1947; Bk. 2, 1952).

METHOD BOOKS

Piano Primer is an introductory book designed especially for young beginners, ages five to eight. Elements of rhythm and notation are traditionally presented in a logical, systematic manner. The book is patterned on the middle C concept, and only single line melodies divided between the hands are used exclusively on the white keys.

Grade 1 presents attractive melodies mostly in the 5-finger positions of C, G, and F. Clear, concise explanations are given for such basic elements as 5-finger position, transposition, triads, and scales. Finger numbers are used liberally for almost every note.

Grades 2 through *5* become successively more difficult and reach approximately high school level difficulty. Original compositions and music by master composers comprise the bulk of the materials in these remaining four books.

[5]It is helpful to have most of these courses available for students enrolled in piano pedagogy. By actual examination of the books, students will gain useful information about each course and will be able to make meaningful evaluations. (Also, many teacher organizations have courses available for their members to survey.)

TECHNIC BOOKS

Piano Technic, Book 1 presents twenty-five original etudes designed to supplement first and second year study. *Book 2* contains twenty-one original studies at about late second year through early fourth year; included are studies for thumb crossing, wrist staccato, and rotary motion.

ADULT BOOKS

This two-book course is essentially a basic middle C approach for the older beginner. Compositions and arrangements are chosen from such old favorites as "Sweet and Low," "The Rose of Tralee," etc. Some elements of theory and technic are included.

BASTIEN, JANE SMISOR, and JAMES BASTIEN

Music Through the Piano	**General Words and Music Co.**
Kindergarten Books	**The Very Young Pianist, Books 1-3** (Bk. 1, 1970; Bks. 2 & 3, 1973); **The Very Young Pianist Workbook, Parts A & B** (1973); **Solos for the Very Young Pianist, Books 1 & 2** (Bk. 1, 1974; Bk. 2, 1976); **The Very Young Pianist Listens and Creates, Books 1-3** (1975); **Pre-Reading Duets, Books 1-3** (1977); **Pre-Reading Christmas Carols** (1977).
Method Books	**Pre-Reading Experiences** (1963); **First Reading Experiences** (1971); **Book 1 Reading** (1963); **Book 2 Reading** (1963); **Book 3 Reading** (1964).
Technic Books	**Magic Finger Technique, Books 1-3** (1966); **Major Scales & Pieces** (1966); **Minor Scales & Pieces** (1967); **Czerny and Hanon** (1970).
Theory Books	**Writing, Books 1-6** (Bks. 1 & 2, 1963; Bk. 3, 1964; Bks. 4-6, 1971).
Flash Cards	**Music Flashcards**–Notes, Key Signatures, Intervals (1969).
Stickers	**Helpful Hint Seals** (1974); **Honor Award Seals** (1974); **Lesson Award Seals** (1974); **Theory Award Seals** (1974).
Assignment Book	**Music Notebook** (1966).
Bookkeeping Book	**Music Teacher's Record Book** (1976).
Supplementary Books	**Pre-Reading Solos** (1971); **Folk Tunes for Fun** (1967); **More Folk Tunes for Fun** (1969); **Duets for Fun, Books 1 & 2** (Bk. 1, 1968; Bk. 2, 1971); **Hymns for Piano, Books 1 & 2** (1968); **Merry Christmas, Books 1-3** (Bk. 1, 1965; Bk. 2, 1966; Bk. 3, 1971); **Multi-Key Reading** (1970); **Playtime at the Piano, Books 1 & 2** (1967); **Christmas Carols for Multiple Pianos** (1971); **Walt Disney Favorites** (1969); **Pop, Rock 'n Blues, Books 1-3** (1971); **Rock 'n Blues for Fun** (1973); **Country Western 'n Folk, Books 1 & 2** (1974); **Scott Joplin Favorites** (1975); **Bastien Favorites, Levels 1-4** (1976); others.
Literature Books	**Piano Literature, Volumes 1-4** (Vols. 1 & 2, 1966; Vol. 3, 1968; Vol. 4, 1974). **Sonatina Favorites, Books 1-3** (1977).
Adult Book	**Beginning Piano for Adults** (1968).
Text Book (Piano Pedagogy)	**How to Teach Piano Successfully** (1973; Second Ed., 1977).

KINDERGARTEN BOOKS

The Very Young Pianist, Book 1 (seventy-two pages) is designed primarily for kindergarten age children or first graders. The book provides a knowledge of numbers (one through five), letters (A through G), and presents short pieces in the keys of C and G. All the pieces are presented in pre-staffed notation. A great deal of writing is incorporated (mainly number and letter drills). Rhythm is stressed throughout, both 4/4 and 6/8 meter. The teacher's notes at the back of the book offer many helpful suggestions for teaching young children.

Book 2 begins with pre-staffed melodies, but notation is introduced about halfway through. The Key of F (5-finger position) is introduced, and the student reads pieces in C, G, and F (the Group I Keys). Directional reading is first introduced by recognition of steps, skips, and repeats. Stick-on notes are provided for many of the pieces to promote note awareness. Some written work is included. The teacher's notes offer suggestions for teaching the book.

Book 3 introduces the remaining keys: Group II Keys (D,A,E); Group III Keys (Db,Ab,Eb); Group IV Keys (Gb,Bb,B). Pieces are written in these keys, as well as a number in the middle C position. Stick-on notes are provided. Some written work is included. The teacher's notes offer suggestions for teaching the book.

The Very Young Pianist Workbook A is designed to be used simultaneously with *The Very Young Pianist, Book 2.* Written exercises in the workbook provide reinforcement drills. *Workbook B* is to be used with *The Very Young Pianist, Book 3* for the same purpose.

The Very Young Pianist Listens and Creates (three books) is an ear-training course which may be used separately, or as a companion series to *The Very Young Pianist* course. The activities allow the child to listen to various sounds on the keyboard as well as to create his own music. Teacher's notes are provided for each book.

Pre-Reading Duets (three books) contains easy pre-staffed pieces for the student and notated teacher parts.

METHOD BOOKS

Pre-Reading Experiences is designed as an introductory keyboard orientation text; the book is based on the multiple key approach, as are subsequent books in the series. The book is divided into fourteen units which are presented as alternate playing and writing lessons. Approximately two units are to be covered per week (if two lessons are given per week); at that rate, the book should be completed in about seven to nine weeks. All melodies are in 5-finger positions and are presented in pre-staffed notation. The twelve major positions are taught by groups and are divided into those which are position-related by their tonic chords and 5-finger positions (Group I: C,G,F; Group II: D,A,E; Group III: Db,Ab,Eb; Group IV: Gb,Bb,B). Concepts of intervallic relationships are developed (mainly seconds and thirds) through step and skip drills. Directional reading is encouraged. Block chords (I and V7) are used to harmonize many of the melodies. Both 4/4 and 6/8 meter are used, and the student is directed to count note value names in the following manner: "quar-ter, quar-ter, half note" (equivalent to 1,2,3, 4). The staff is explained near the end of the book, and the following written work is presented: drawing line and space notes, drawing notes up and down from ones given, and naming all the line and space notes. Music note flash cards (*Music Flashcards*) should be introduced on page 62 for home and lesson drill. This book provides a foundation for subsequent books in the series, and it should be covered comprehensively before proceeding. (This book is also available in Spanish and Japanese.)

First Reading Experiences is designed to bridge the gap between pre-reading and reading. It is suggested that this book should be given before the completion of *Pre-Reading Experiences* (as early as page 62). Twenty-one specific daily assignments are provided for home drill. The drills consist mainly of naming all the lines and spaces (from bottom to top), naming individual notes (like traditional note spelling books), sorting out note flash cards to be learned, and playing short single line melodies. Naming notes and counting aloud while playing is stressed throughout. Extra material is provided in later units to reinforce concepts already covered.

Book 1 Reading is divided into nine lesson units and contains mostly single line melodies in all keys. Reading is developed by an eyes-on-the-page-approach through material purposely limited to 5-finger positions. Although some familiar melodies are used, the pieces are mostly originally composed to avoid playing "by ear." Materials include: minor positions (page 9); ledger line and space notes (page 11); the order of sharps and sharp key signatures (page 15); intervals of fourths and fifths (page 17); the order of flats and flat key signatures (page 22); and harmonization of melodies with I and V7 chords. The book is designed to be used simultaneously with *Book I Writing* which contains correlated materials. Supplementary books and solos are to be chosen from the listing on the back cover in Level One.

Book 2 Reading consists of a combination of well-known tunes and original compositions arranged in a step by step sequence. New presentations consist of: phrasing (page 5); dynamics (page 6); sub-dominant chord (page 15); extended finger positions (intervals of sixths, sevenths, octaves); and some shifting hand positions. The book is designed to be used simultaneously with *Book 2 Writing*. Supplementary books and solos are to be chosen from the listing on the back cover in Level Two.

Book 3 Reading provides material which serves as preparation for easier compositions by master composers. It is essentially a second year book containing a combination of folk song arrangements and original compositions. New materials consist of: broken chord accompaniment (page 7); triplets (page 15); waltz bass accompaniment (page 20); and Alberti bass accompaniment (page 28). The book is designed to be used simultaneously with *Book 3 Writing*. Supplementary books and solos are to be chosen from the listing on the back cover in Level Three.

TECHNIC BOOKS

Magic Finger Technique (three books) is designed to provide exercises in pure technic which reinforce concepts presented in the basic course books. These books are to be used simultaneously with *Reading, Books 1-3.* The desired objectives of *Book 1* are: good hand position, independent finger action, equal facility in both hands, and a thorough comprehension of all keys. The exercises are mostly in 5-finger positions. *Book 2* presents the following concepts: exercises for phrasing, touch (legato-staccato combinations), and balancing of tone. The exercises are in 5-finger positions and extended and contracted positions. *Book 3* stresses: finger independence, triads and inversions, scales, and wrist staccato.

Major Scales and Pieces and *Minor Scales and Pieces* are to be used after completion of the three technic books. All major and minor scales are presented as (1) scale exercises followed by (2) a piece in each key. Although each scale is presented in the same way, the related exercises are different, adding interest and providing additional opportunities to expand facility. Most of the compositions are originally composed, but there are some by Czerny and other well-known composers.

Czerny and Hanon contains study pieces on about the intermediate level. The Czerny studies are selected from the less difficult of the many that he wrote; included are studies from Opus 261, 821, and 599. The Hanon exercises are the first twenty from *The Virtuoso Pianist.*

THEORY BOOKS

Writing, Books 1-3, are to be used simultaneously with the three reading books, and they provide additional drills both in writing and playing (keyboard harmony). *Books 4-6* follow the same format and advance progressively to about the intermediate level. Materials include: note recognition, order of sharps and flats, key signatures, intervals, musical terms, scale writing and playing, chord spelling and playing, cadences, transposition, harmonization of melodies, and creative work.

SUPPLEMENTARY BOOKS

The basic course *(Reading, Books 1-3)* is intended to be supplemented with a choice of recreational books (folk tunes, duets, Christmas music, hymns, etc.) These books provide additional reading materials.

Multi-Key Reading serves a dual function as a second year review reader to this or any multiple key approach, and as a book which may be used for transfer students who have not been exposed to the multiple key approach. This sixty-four page book contains the following materials: all major and minor 5-finger positions, intervals through the octave, the order of sharps and flats, major key signatures, exercises for transposing and harmonizing, and numerous easy pieces in all keys. Written reviews are included in each of the four sections.

Playtime at the Piano (two books) contains varied pieces suitable for supplementary first, second and third year repertoire. Included are original compositions, folk song arrangements, and some of the easier works by master composers. Both books are designed as preparation for the literature series.

Bastien Favorites (four books) contains previously published solos in collection form. (Each solo is also available in sheet music.) These pieces may be used with either the *Music Through the Piano* course or *The Bastien Piano Library* (see page 77). Early elementary through upper elementary levels.

LITERATURE BOOKS

Piano Literature (four books) contains music from the Baroque to the Contemporary Periods. *Volume 1* includes compositions such as Bach and Mozart minuets; easier sonatinas by Spindler and Beethoven; "The Merry Farmer" and others by Schumann; and several of the easier pieces by Bartók, Shostakovich, and Kabalevsky. Included in *Volume 2* are sonatinas by Beethoven and Clementi; polonaises by Bach; and "Variation on a Russian Folksong, Op. 51, No. 1" by Kabalevsky. *Volume 3* consists of a collection of intermediate level pieces progressing to the difficulty of Bach Inventions (numbers 1,4,8) and sonatinas of medium difficulty by Spindler, Clementi, and Kuhlau. *Volume 4* is compiled for the early advanced student and contains such works as sonatas by Beethoven *(Op. 49, No. 2)* and Mozart *(K. 545);* easier pieces by Chopin; pieces from Schumann's "Scenes from Childhood;" and contemporary works by Kabalevsky, Khachaturian, Satie, Shostakovich, and Tcherepnin.

Sonatina Favorites (three books) contains representative sonatinas ranging in difficulty from early intermediate to upper intermediate. An explanation of sonatina form is provided, and themes are identified in the sonatinas. *Book 1* contains sonatinas by Duncombe, Bastien, Attwood, Spindler, Beethoven *(G Major),* Lynes, and Clementi *(Op. 36, No. 1). Book 2* contains works by Haslinger, Lichner, Beethoven *(F Major),* Clementi *(Op. 36, No. 2),* Kabalevsky *(Op. 27, No. 11),* and Bastien. *Book 3* contains works by Clementi, Kuhlau, and Bastien.

ADULT BOOK

Beginning Piano for Adults is designed primarily for students at the college level, either music major (piano minor) or non-music major. This 212 page volume is comprised of four main sections. Section I, *Pre-Reading,* is written in pre-staffed notation, is designed for keyboard orientation, and incorporates all twelve major 5-finger patterns, tonic chords, and dominant seventh chords. Section II, *Reading,* contains graded reading material and a variety of exercises for pianistic development. Section III, *Functional Piano,* contains a variety of "lead-sheet" melodies for harmonic improvisation. Section IV, *Piano Literature, Technique and Style,* provides an abundant selection of original piano literature and related exercises. The book is flexible and may be used for a two year period with supplement.

BASTIEN, JAMES, and JANE SMISOR BASTIEN
The Bastien Piano Library **Kjos West**

Method Books	**Piano Lessons, Primer-Level 4** (1976).
Technic Books	**Technic Lessons, Primer-Level 4** (1976); **First Hanon Studies** (1976).
Theory Books	**Theory Lessons, Primer-Level 4** (1976); **Note Speller, Level 1** (1976).
Supplementary Books	**Piano Solos, Primer-Level 4** (1976); **America '76** (1976); **Stephen Foster Favorites** (1976); Note: supplementary materials listed on page 73 may be used also with this course.
Sight Reading Books	**Sight Reading, Levels 1-4** (1976)
Book for Parents	**A Parent's Guide to Piano Lessons** (1976).
Adult Books	**Older Beginner Piano Course, Levels 1 & 2** (1977), **Musicianship for the Older Beginner, Levels 1 & 2** (1977); **Favorite Melodies the World Over, Levels 1 & 2** (1977).

METHOD BOOKS

The series *Piano Lessons* is multi-key oriented, but not in the usual way. Key presentations are introduced gradually in successive levels of the course. Each level contains original and selected folk materials. This series is to be used in conjunction with the technic, theory, sight reading, and piano solo series (plus other supplementary books). The result of this correlation of materials is a step by step method presented in an intelligent, enjoyable manner. The attractive illustrations, imaginative use of color, and interesting book design enhance this series.

Primer Level: Designed for beginners about seven to ten, this book contains six units divided into three units of pre-staffed music and three units of staffed music. The C, G, and middle C 5-finger positions are emphasized. The main materials introduced are: rhythm (♩ 𝅗𝅥 𝅝 𝅗𝅥. ♫), musical alphabet, intervals through the fifth, transposition, notation, tonic chord, legato-staccato touches, and music signs and terms. A written review page is included for each unit. Duet accompaniments are provided for many of the pieces.

Level 1: This book follows the *Primer Level* in sequence, but it could also be used as a first book for an older beginner (nine to twelve). Five-finger pieces are presented in the keys of C, F, and G. New materials include: the V7 chord (using only two notes: root and seventh), key signatures, upbeat, Group I Keys (C,G,F), dotted rhythm (♩. ♪), and pedal. Duet accompaniments are provided for some of the pieces.

Level 2: New concepts include: turning the thumb under; moving the thumb or little finger (to play out of 5-finger positions); and shifting hand positions. New materials include: half and whole steps; one-octave scales (C,G,F,D,A,E); interval of the sixth; I, IV_4^6, V_5^6 chords; 6/8 meter; the order of sharps; the Group II Keys (D,A,E); and minor chords. Transposition is suggested for many of the pieces.

Level 3: New materials include: various bass style accompaniments, triads of the scale, triplets, relative minor scales, minor key signatures, chromatic scale, inversions of triads, the order of flats, and the Group III Keys (Db,Ab,Eb).

Level 4: New materials include: overlapping pedal, intervals of sevenths and octaves, sixteenth notes, parallel major and minor scales, augmented and diminished triads, syncopation, and the Group IV Keys (Gb,Bb,B).

TECHNIC BOOKS

Technic Lessons provides additional materials to reinforce concepts presented in the basic course *(Piano Lessons).* A combination of pure and applied technic studies is presented in this series. The general goal of *Technic Lessons* is to develop hand and finger coordination and facility, and to develop ease and control at the keyboard.

The *Primer Level* contains six units divided into three units of pre-staffed music and three units of staffed music. Teacher's notes are included for the first three units which give student practice suggestions. Materials introduced in this volume include: playing clusters, playing intervals (seconds, thirds, fourths, fifths), playing the C and G 5-finger positions, playing chords (tonic chords), phrasing, legato and staccato touch, and the arpeggio. Imaginative use of illustrations enhances this volume.

Level 1 contains a variety of keyboard studies for 5-finger drills, chords (blocked and broken), touch (legato and staccato), phrasing, thumb crossings (scale preparation), moving hand positions, chromatics, pedal, and double notes. Imaginative illustrations brighten the pages in this volume.

The materials in *Levels 2-4* continue to expand the student's range and scope at the keyboard. Included in these three books are studies for scales, chords, finger extension, chromatic scale, double notes, phrasing, pedal, finger independence, triads and inversions, trill, and Alberti bass. A variety of rhythms, touches, and keys are utilized in the exercises and etudes in these books.

THEORY BOOKS

Theory Lessons is designed to be used simultaneously with *Piano Lessons* by level. The theory books contain a combination of written and playing work to reinforce concepts presented in the basic course.

Primer Level materials consist of: recognizing the sets of two and three black keys, direction on the keyboard, ear training drills, composition suggestions, rhythm work, the musical alphabet, intervals, tonic chords (C and G), the staff, notation, stemming notes, transposition, and music signs and terms.

Level 1 materials consist of: staff work, note spelling, rhythm drills, harmonizing melodies, key signature drills, drawing notes, intervals, transposition, the Group I Keys (C,G,F), and music signs and terms.

Level 2 materials consist of: recognizing half and whole steps, writing and playing major scales (C,G,F,D,A,E), question and answer phrases, harmonizing lead lines, rhythm drills, note drills (including leger line notes), intervals, the order of sharps, the Group II Keys (D,A,E), and music signs and terms.

Levels 3 and *4* provide expanded theoretical work to parallel the materials presented in *Levels 3* and *4* of *Piano Lessons.*

The *Note Speller, Level 1* is designed to introduce basic information about the staff, notes and rests, accidentals, and leger line notes. Materials are divided into twenty-seven written lessons plus one review lesson.

SUPPLEMENTARY BOOKS

The series *Piano Solos* (five books) contains additional repertoire and reading materials to supplement the basic course. Materials consist of a combination of original pieces and familiar songs and folk song arrangements. Attractive illustrations are used throughout this series.

SIGHT READING BOOKS

The series *Sight Reading* (four books) contains graded reading material ranging in difficulty from elementary to early intermediate. A variety of reading experiences is provided, such as legato and staccato touches, chords, and different styles and moods. Excerpts from familiar tunes are included also; some excerpts are not identified and are to be "discovered" by the student. The series may be used with this or any piano course to provide additional reading assignments.

BOOK FOR PARENTS

A Parent's Guide to Piano Lessons offers suggestions to parents who are about to start their child on piano lessons, as well as discusses problems which might be encountered during the first few years of study. The six brief chapters in this booklet consist of: (1) "First Considerations" (child's indication of wanting piano lessons, the piano as a first instrument, indication of musical ability, the best age to start lessons, etc.), (2) "Selecting a Teacher," (3) "Selecting a Piano," (4) "Hints for Beginners" (parent-teacher relationships, materials needed, how to help the beginner count time, etc.), (5) "On Practicing" (how long to practice, when and how often to practice, helping the child practice, etc.), and (6) "Recitals, Contests, Festivals and Auditions." Additional information is provided in the Appendices: (A) "Brief Outline of Music Facts" (for parents who have no knowledge of music), (B) "Brief Dictionary of Musical Terms," and (C) "Brief Reference Listing" (books on music and child psychology). This booklet will assist the busy teacher in dissemination of this practical information to parents.

ADULT BOOKS

The *Older Beginner Piano Course* (two books, ninety-six pages each) is designed for students from about age twelve and up. The course is designed functionally, allowing the student to play and harmonize melodies from the beginning (chord approach). Each book has ten units with a review page at the end of the unit. A combination of original and familiar music is used. Multi-key reading is introduced gradually through the course. Each method book is to be supplemented with the companion book *Musicianship for the Older Beginner* which contains additional theory, technic and sight reading materials.

Level 1 materials include: reading in the keys of C,G,F and D,A,E; I IV V7 chords; transposition; major scales; 4/4 and 6/8 meter; minor chords; and the pedal.

Level 2 materials include: bass styles; syncopated rhythm; minor scales and minor key signatures; triads of the scale; inversions of triads; the chromatic scale; augmented and diminished triads; sixteenth notes; and the keys of Db,Ab,Eb and Gb,Bb,B.

Musicianship for the Older Beginner (two books, forty-eight pages each) is designed to be used as a companion to the *Older Beginner Piano Course.* Each book is divided into ten units and each unit contains theory (written and keyboard), technic, and sight reading materials correlated to the basic course.

BRIMHALL, JOHN *Piano Method* **Charles Hansen**

Method Books	**Primer** (1970); **Books 1-5** (Bks. 1-4, 1968; Bk. 5, 1971).
Technic Books	**First Book of Hanon** (1970); **Hanon Through the Keys** (1970); **Encyclopedia of Scales and Arpeggios** (1968); **Complete Guide to Scales, Cadences and Arpeggios** (1972); others.
Theory Books	**Theory Notebooks, Books 1-3** (1969); **Keyboard Theory Papers: Notespeller** (1970); **Keyboard Theory Book: Notespeller** (1970); **3000 Chords for Piano or Organ** (1968); **It's About Time** (1976); others.
Flash Cards	**Instant Chord Cards** (1968); **The Ted Ross Music Flash Cards**, 4 Series (1968).
Supplementary Books	**Popular Chord Instructor** (1967); **Exercises in Rhythm** (1968); **Piano Blues** (1975); **Instant Chord Solos, Issues 1 & 2** (1976); numerous others.
Literature Books	**My Favorite Classics, Levels 1 & 2** (1969); others.
Class Piano Books	**Class Piano Method, Books 1 & 2** (1976).
Adult Books	**Young Adult Piano Course, Books 1 & 2** (Bk. 1, 1974; Bk. 2, 1975).

METHOD BOOKS

The *Brimhall Piano Method* offers a unique blend of the traditional middle C approach sprinkled through with pop hits. An attempt is made to bridge the gap between "classical" and "popular" lessons. The most appealing aspects of this course are the inclusions of pop favorites. The course *per se* offers nothing new, in fact, it seems to cling to the old fashioned manners of teaching reminiscent of Williams and Thompson. Nevertheless, used as "supplementary" books, the series is quite enjoyable and useful.

The *Primer* is intended for young beginners and contains mostly single line melodies divided between the hands in the middle C position. Some two-voice playing is presented near the end of the book. Compositions included are a combination of folk tune arrangements and original pieces. Duet accompaniments are provided for many of the pieces.

Book 1 is patterned in the traditional middle C concept and designed for average age beginners. Popular favorites include "King of the Road," "Guantanamera," and "Scarborough Fair."

Books 2-5 continue in the same fashion placing classical favorites and current popular songs side by side. Other popular songs within the series include "Born Free," "Tijuana Taxi," "Spanish Flea," "Theme From Romeo and Juliet," and many more.

TECHNIC BOOKS

The two Hanon books contain clever adaptations of the well-known original. *Encyclopedia of Scales and Arpeggios* is a fifty-six page volume that includes all major and minor scales (in octaves, thirds, and sixths) in both similar and contrary motion. Also included are all major and minor arpeggios, dominant seventh arpeggios, harmonic cadences, chromatic scales, diminished seventh arpeggios, and all modal scales.

THEORY BOOKS

Quite traditional in approach, the three *Theory Notebooks* contain written work exclusively (no keyboard harmony). Answer sheets are given at the back of all three books. The materials in *Book 1* include: naming notes, drawing notes, drawing clef signs, identifying rests, writing counts and time signatures, and writing a few scales. *Books 2* and *3* contain writing lessons in major key signatures, chromatic scale, intervals, chords, musical terms, and minor scales. (These books are also available in one complete volume.)

SUPPLEMENTARY BOOKS

Many piano teachers, and especially their students, have by now discovered Brimhall's numerous arrangements of current pop hits. Most of his supplementary books are comprised basically of piano arrangements of popular favorites. However, three books, the *Popular Chord Instructor* (first year level), *Exercises in Rhythm* (third or fourth year levels), and *Piano Blues* (third or fourth year levels) contain a number of original works. These books are excellently written and have instant appeal. *Instant Chord Solos* (two books – others planned) contain pop favorites in lead-line form to be harmonized from the chord symbols.

LITERATURE BOOKS

My Favorite Classics (two books) contains graded four-period literature ranging in difficulty from the upper elementary through upper intermediate levels.

CLASS PIANO BOOKS

Class Piano Method (two books, thirty-two pages each) is almost identical to the *Young Adult Piano Course* (see below), however some materials have been arranged for several players. Melody and accompaniment (chord approach) is the main feature of these books. Included are folk, traditional, original, and three pop tunes.

ADULT BOOKS

Young Adult Piano Course (two books, thirty-two pages each) provides instant music through melody and accompaniment (chord approach). Folk, traditional, original, and four pop tunes comprise the materials for playing. Theoretical explanations include principal chords in C,G, and F, major scales, inversions of triads, and explanations about various bass accompaniment patterns, rhythm patterns, and music terms. These books are almost in the do-it-yourself category.

BURNAM, EDNA MAE *Piano Course (Step by Step)* **Willis Music Co.**

Method Books	**Piano Course, Books 1-6** (Bks. 1-3, 1959; Bks. 4-6, 1960).
Technic Books	**Dozen a Day** series: **Mini Book** (1974); **Preparatory Book** (1957); **Books 1-4** (Bk. 1, 1950; Bk. 2, 1953; Bk. 4, 1964).
Theory Books	**Help Yourself to Harmony, Books 1 & 2** (1963); **Theory Papers, Books 1-3** (1970).
Supplementary Books	**A Dozen Piano Pieces in Various Styles, Books 1-4** (Bk. 1, 1959; Bk. 2, 1958; Bk. 3, 1961; Bk. 4, 1962); **A Dozen Folk Tunes From Various Lands** (1957); **For You Alone** (1958); **Play All The Time Signatures** (1966); **Mexico** (1970); **Echoes of Death Valley** (1975); **Abraham Lincoln** (1975); **Bicentennial Suite** (1975); **Sight Reading Short Shorts, Books 1 & 2** (1976); **Around the Tempo Circle** (1976); **Singles or Doubles, Books 1-3** (1976); **Two Piano Time** (1976); others.

METHOD BOOKS

A staunch supporter of the middle C concept, the author has written the entire *Book 1* in the middle C hand position without variance (no sharps and flats are used). The meter is confined to 2/4, 3/4, and 4/4. Duet accompaniments are provided for some of the pieces. *Book 2* has a note range of two octaves (C below middle C to C above middle C). The pieces are mostly in C (a few in F and G). Two-voice harmonizations are used primarily. Progress continues at a slow pace through the other four books. Very little explanation of theory is provided in this series.

TECHNIC BOOKS

The *Dozen a Day* six-book series contains short exercises in pure technic. The *Mini Book* contains very easy exercises in the middle C position. The *Preparatory Book* presents mostly 5-finger patterns utilizing the two basic touches, legato and staccato; other presentations include: scale passages, chords, crossing hands, holding one note while playing another in the same hand, slurs, chromatic scale, legato thirds, and arpeggios divided between the hands. All exercises are written in C, but the author suggests transposition in the preface.

New materials in *Books 1-4* include: scales in parallel and contrary motion, changing fingers on repeated notes, inversions of triads, wrist staccato studies (in thirds, sixths, and octaves), glissando runs, thumb studies, arpeggios, trills, four-note broken chords, and stretching exercises. *Book 4* reaches at least fourth or fifth year level difficulty.

THEORY BOOKS

Help Yourself to Harmony (two books) are not meant to be correlated with the method book series. The author states in the preface that these books would be helpful for a teen-ager or an adult beginner. Materials included in *Book 1* are: half steps and whole steps, scales, major key signatures, and intervals. Materials included in *Book 2* are: major and minor thirds, major and minor triads, inversions of triads, the dominant seventh chord, cadences, and some harmonization of melodies. Both books include original compositions emphasizing new theoretical presentations.

Theory Papers (three books) are compiled in loose leaf fashion to be handed out by the teacher one at a time. These books provide mostly written work. Materials are organized into reading (writing the note's name above or below it), writing (drawing the note's name), counting time, and note spelling. Also included are key signatures, music terms, and half and whole steps.

CLARK, FRANCES ***Frances Clark Library*** **Summy-Birchard Co.**

THE MUSIC TREE (New Course, 1973)

Method Books	**Time to Begin** by Frances Clark and Louise Goss (1955, 1960, 1973); **The Music Tree, Parts A, B, and C** by Clark and Goss (1973).
Teacher's Handbook	**Teaching the Music Tree** (1973).
Supplementary Books	**Playtime, Parts A-C** (ed.) Clark and Goss (1976); **Supplementary Solos** (ed.) Clark and Goss (1974); **The Riches of Rag** by Roger Grove (1976); **Couples Only** by Roger Grove (1976); **Two at One Piano, Books 1-3** by Jon George (Bk. 1, 1969; Bk. 2, 1972; Bk. 3, 1976); others.
Adult Book	**Keyboard Musician** by Clark, Goss, and Roger Grove (1976).

EARLIER EDITIONS (Second Series, 1962)

Method Books	**Look and Listen, Books A-D** by Clark, Goss, and David Kraehenbuehl (1962).
Technic Books	**Piano Technic, Books 1-3** by Marion McArtor (Bk. 1, 1954; Bks. 2 & 3, 1955); **Books 4-6** by Kraehenbuehl (1960).
Theory Books	**Pencil Play, Books A-D** by Clark, Goss, and Kraehenbuehl (1962); **Keyboard Theory, Books 1-6** by David Kraehenbuehl (Bks. 1-4, 1965; Bks. 5 & 6, 1966).
Supplementary Books	**Reader A** by Jon George, Louise Goss, and Lynn Olson (1969); **Reader B** by Jon George (1969); **Reader C & D** by Jon George (1970); **Jazz and Blues, Books 1-6** by David Kraehenbuehl (1963), (Bks. 3 & 4 are now incorporated in **Supplementary Solos Levels 3 & 4**).
Piano Literature	**Themes from Masterworks, Books 1-3** arr. by George and Kraehenbuehl (1963); **Piano Literature, Book 1** (1964); **Books 2&3** (1954); **Books 4A & 4B** (1957); **Book 5A** (1956); **Book 5B** (1957); **Book 6A** (1958); **Book 6B** (1956); **Contemporary Piano Literature, Books 1-6** (Bks. 1 & 2, 1955; Bks. 3-6, 1957).

EARLIER EDITIONS (First Series, 1957)

Method Books	**Write and Play Time, Parts A and B** by Clark and Goss in collaboration with John LaMontaine (1957, 1959).
Technic Books	**Technic Time, Parts A and B** by Clark and Goss (1957).
Theory Books	**Music Workbook, Books 1a, 1b, 2-3** by Clark and Goss in collaboration with John LaMontaine (1957).

As noted above, there are now three different elementary series in the *Frances Clark Library.* The original first book in each of the three series, *Time to Begin,* exists now only in the 1973 course.

Because the first series (1957) is little used now in comparison with the second series (1962) and *The Music Tree* series (1973), only the latter two will be discussed.

The Music Tree (New Course, 1973)

METHOD BOOKS

Time to Begin: Designed in an intelligent manner, this sixty-four page book develops a feel for the topography of the keyboard and teaches simple facts of direction (high and low), rhythm, key names, dynamics, intervals (through the fifth), and other basics. The book is divided into nine units; each unit has two basic parts: "Discoveries" (new concepts) and "Using What You Have Learned" (reinforcement material). In addition some rhythm drills, technical warm-ups, written and creative work are provided at the end of most of the units. Directional reading is introduced within pages 4-27 in a pre-staffed manner almost entirely on the black keys. From page 28 to the end of the book the staff is developed gradually from two lines; reading is limited to white keys only. Bass staff reading is introduced on page 58 stressing the F line (F clef). Treble staff reading is introduced on page 59 stressing the G line (G clef). The grand staff is introduced on page 61, and the reading on pages 61 and 62 emphasize the *landmarks* bass clef F, middle C, and treble clef G. Interesting duet accompaniments are provided for many of the pieces. Certainly not a middle C course, nor a multiple key course, this approach (reading by direction from given landmarks) offers teachers an alternative from either of these two systems.

The Music Tree, Part A: This sixty-four page book consists of ten units organized similarly to *Time to Begin.* Reading is developed from stressed landmarks (bass clef F, middle C, and treble clef G) by intervals up or down from these landmarks. Hand spans are limited to the interval of a fifth. New information includes: staccato touch (page 28), tied notes (page 34), up-beats (page 34), rests (page 40), sharps and flats (page 45), and letters (A and B) to show the parts of a piece (page 57). The music is limited to single-line melodies using quarter notes, half notes and whole notes. Useful technical warm-ups for all units are provided on pages 62-64.

Part B: New materials include: eighth notes, major and minor 5-finger positions, perfect fifths as accompaniments, note against note reading, new landmarks, and shifting hand positions.

Part C: New materials include: key signatures; intervals of sixths, sevenths, and octaves; triplets; other meter signatures (3/8, 6/8, 9/8, 12/8); crossing fingers over the thumb (scale preparation); and sliding the thumb under (also scale preparation).

TEACHER'S HANDBOOK

Teaching the Music Tree is a twenty-four page teacher guide for the four-volume series which gives helpful suggestions regarding pitch notation, other musical signs, rhythm, technic, theory, creativity and composing, and ear training.

SUPPLEMENTARY BOOKS

Playtime (three books) contains supplementary solos, many with optional accompaniment. The original music is by various composers such as Dittenhaver, George, Kraehenbuehl, and McArtor; in addition, some folk-tune arrangements are included.

Supplementary Solos is a sixty-four page collection of previously published materials from Jon George's *Students' Choice,* David Kraehenbuehl's *Jazz and Blues* (Books 3 and 4), and also includes five other solos. Materials are at levels 3 and 4.

ADULT BOOK

Keyboard Musician is designed to teach the older beginner similar concepts to those in *The Music Tree* series. Included are twelve units each containing five parts: (1) subjects (concepts), (2) repertoire (mostly original or folk-tune arrangements), (3) rote piece (slightly more complicated than the student's supposed reading ability), (4) technic-rhythm-improvisation, and (5) sight reading material. The reading in the beginning is the now familiar landmark system (directional reading from specified notes). Mostly single line melodies are used; some toward the end of the book have fifth or sixth intervals for accompaniments and a few have some triads. Many of the pieces have duet accompaniments.

Earlier Editions (Second Series)

METHOD BOOKS

Look and Listen, Part A: The organizational structure of this forty-eight page book is outlined in eight units, each representing a week of study. Directional reading is developed from given landmarks, which are: (1) bass clef F (fourth line), (2) middle C, and (3) treble clef G (second line). These three locations represent the bass clef (F clef), the treble clef (G clef), and middle C in between. The authors do not use any consistent hand positions. Students read directionally from these three landmarks either up or down by intervals, through the fifth. Colorful duet accompaniments are provided for many of the pieces. Only white-key melodies are used until page 38, and the tonality of some of the pieces is thereby affected in a somewhat distressing manner. Many of the melodies are in an F tonality and the use of B natural (tritone of an augmented fourth) in some of the pieces sounds unmusical.

Part B: New materials include: new landmarks with which to begin; major and minor 5-finger patterns; shifting hand positions.

Part C: New materials include: musical form (ABA, AA^1, others); major and minor triads (chordal playing is limited in this course and melody with block chord accompaniment is virtually non-existent); intervals of sixths, sevenths, and octaves; finger extensions; a sharp and flat at the beginning of the pieces (key signatures are not explained in this book, nor are they explained in the entire five-book course).

Part D: New materials include: other meter signs (3/8, 6/8, 9/8, 12/8), crossing over the thumb (scale preparation), turning the thumb under (also scale preparation).

TECHNIC BOOKS

The entire *Piano Technic* six-book series is a well-written *tour de force* encompassing several basic technical areas. Prime considerations throughout all six books are 5-finger positions, extensions, contractions, scale, and arpeggio crossings; these basic areas are explored in greater depth at each successive level. The studies are melodically conceived in applied technic form rather than as exercises in pure technic. *Book 1* begins at about second year level and *Book 6* reaches about late intermediate to early advanced difficulty. Although designed for technical purposes, these inventive compositions provide a wealth of material which may also improve the student's sight-reading level.

THEORY BOOKS

Pencil Play (four books) are to be used in conjunction with the *Look and Learn* series with which they are correlated by units. Concepts learned in the basic series are reinforced by written work dealing primarily with three areas of musicianship: note-reading, rhythm-reading, and musical terminology. Only a few aspects of theory are stressed: intervals, some major and minor 5-finger positions, and some major and minor triads. Although there is a great deal of writing activity, there is only a minimal amount of keyboard harmonization (harmonizations are limited to fifths and sixths rather than a I, IV, V chord approach).

The six-book *Keyboard Theory* series provides an intelligent, imaginative new approach to teaching "college-type" theory to students of any age or stage of development beyond the beginning. The main objectives of the course are: (1) learning good voice-leading technics, (2) acquiring facility in all major and minor keys through learning patterned groupings at the keyboard, (3) learning to make discriminating choices of harmonizations in a widening spectrum from tonic and dominant to seventh chords on any scale degree, (4) learning to modulate, and (5) learning to improvise and create short compositions.

SUPPLEMENTARY BOOKS

Readers A-D provide supplementary reading for the basic course. The materials are correlated to the *Look and Learn* series using the same landmarks, reading range, and rhythm patterns. Short pieces (mostly eight-measure length) are used, and words are included for many of the melodies.

The *Jazz and Blues* series is an excellent collection of imaginatively written pieces for recreational study on an elementary level. Written before the current pop-rock craze, this collection offers mostly boogie, blues, and traditional jazz styles, and these seem somewhat dated and a little behind today's "now" students. The composer, who is a first-rate pianist, has recorded selections from all six books on one 12-inch LP.

PIANO LITERATURE

Themes from Masterworks: This collection contains tasteful arrangements of themes from orchestral and vocal works on about second and third year levels. A few representative titles are: "Lullaby" by Brahms, "The Moldau" by Smetana, and "Musetta's Waltz" by Puccini.

Piano Literature: As a whole, this nine-book series offers an excellent array of tastefully chosen pieces from the seventeenth, eighteenth, and nineteenth centuries. *Book 1*, consisting primarily of folk song arrangements, serves as an introduction to the literature series proper and is designed for first and second year students who are not yet ready for the complexities of music by master composers. *Books 2-6B* survey three centuries of keyboard music at successive levels. Representative composers are: Couperin, Rameau, J.S. Bach, Handel, Scarlatti, C.P.E. Bach, Haydn, Clementi, Mozart, Beethoven, Schubert, Mendelssohn, Chopin, Schumann, Tchaikovsky, Grieg, and MacDowell. Short biographical sketches are also included.

Contemporary Piano Literature: Since its publication this important six-book series has maintained a prominent position in contemporary educational materials. In addition to such standard composers of children's music as Bartók, Kabalevsky, Shostakovich, and others, this collection also contains a wealth of music by the following commissioned composers: Finney, Kraehenbuehl, Moore, Siegmeister, Tansman, and Tcherepnin. Short biographical sketches are also included.

d'AUBERGE, ALFRED ***Piano Course*** **Alfred Publishing Co.**

Method Books	**Piano Course, Books 1-6** (Bk. 1, 1960; Bks. 2 & 3, 1961; Bk. 4, 1962; Bks. 5 & 6, 1964)
Supplementary Books	**Note Speller, Books 1 & 2** (Bk. 1, 1964; Bk. 2, 1966); **Recital Books, Books 1-3** (1966).

METHOD BOOKS

Book 1 presents the following traditional middle C concepts: single line melodies divided between the hands mostly on white keys (there are two pieces near the end of the book that use a Bb and an F#); meter confined to 2/4, 3/4, 4/4; a few note against note melodies near the end of the book. (One interesting observation is the explanation of staccato touch, but not legato.)

Book 2 contains mostly note against note harmonizations primarily in the 5-finger positions of C,G,F (a few in D and Bb). Some broken chord harmonizations are used. Some scale explanations are given.

A study of the other books in the series reveals that little explanation of theory, such as intervals, major and minor chords, etc., is incorporated into the course books. Although broken chord basses are used from *Book 2* on, the first block chord appears in *Book 3,* page 30. The books are lavishly illustrated.

DUCKWORTH, GUY ***Keyboard Series*** **The M-F Co.**

Method Books	**Keyboard Explorer** (1963); **Keyboard Discoverer** (1963); **Keyboard Builder** (1963); **Keyboard Musician** (1964); **Keyboard Performer** (1966)
Class Piano Book (for piano minors)	**Keyboard Musicianship** (Free Press, 1971).
Contemporary Series	**Library for Piano Performance, Volume I, Books 1-4** (M. M. Cole Co., 1974).

A fresh contemporary spirit pervades in this inventive series of five *Keyboard* piano books. These engaging books are based on the "discovery" learning system whereby students learn by doing, experimenting, and creating. Prime aspects of consideration throughout are rhythm and melody.

Keyboard Explorer (Book 1): This forty page introductory book is written primarily in pre-notated form and incorporates directional reading, recurring rhythm patterns, and creative work into a meaningful whole. All twelve major pentachord positions (a few in minor) are taught by discovering the correct sounds and adjusting to the corresponding keyboard patterns. Rhythm is taught by clapping and chanting long and short syllabic sounds that occur in nursery rhymes and folk melodies. Eurythmics play an important function in rhythm chants as the student is directed to "walk" and sway steadily to pulsating beats. Meter is limited to 2/4, 3/4, and 4/4. Direction is indicated by arrows, words, and hands at varying levels representing pitch degrees. Steps, skips, and repeats are emphasized as aids to directional reading. Transposition is suggested for most of the pieces. This book stresses rhythm and melody exclusively, harmonizations are omitted. An attractive little LP record accompanies the book. The student is directed to sing songs from the book along with Kathy (an arbitrary student) and the instructor.

Keyboard Discoverer (Book 2): Harmonization is the main feature of this book. I chords are introduced on page 23, V7 chords on page 25. Single line melodies are used in pentachord positions, and students choose their harmonizations at places indicated by an X. The tunes are a combination of nursery rhymes and folk tunes from many countries. Some of the melodies from Book 1 are repeated with indications for harmonizations. A record accompanies this book and the two that follow.

Keyboard Builder (Book 3); New presentations include: tetrachords, melodic extensions to sixths and sevenths, IV chord, grand staff (melodies on two staves on pages 32-35), turning the thumb under, and crossing fingers over the thumb (both for scale preparation).

Keyboard Musician (Book 4): New presentations include: major and minor scales, and counting with numbers (page 28).

Keyboard Performer (Book 5): This unique forty page volume consists mostly of solo and duet piano literature from the Baroque and Contemporary periods. The Baroque section, pages 5-18, leaves the choice of phrasing, fingering, touch, volume and tempo controls to the student. The music is presented in ultra-urtext form even including the soprano clef in several of the pieces. To avoid complete chaos some clues for the performer are provided. The Contemporary section, pages 19-33, is written by James Hopkins. The two-voice compositions employ such baroque devices as canon, ostinato bass, and the use of modality in many of the pieces. A short section, pages 34-40, contains melodies for harmonization and transposition similar to the preceding two books. The level of the book is a bit puzzling; is it for the college piano minor, or is it a continuation in this series? In any case, the book appears to be on the esoteric side.

CONTEMPORARY SERIES

This four-book series presents contemporary notation and sounds in a manner allowing the student to make some choices in pitches, fingerings, mood and tempo. Improvisation involves selecting indefinite pitches as well as some complete phrases to be improvised. Reading is begun in this series from the G line (treble clef), the F line (bass clef), and from middle C. The lines of the staves are expanded to the grand staff.

Book 1 by Guy Duckworth introduces the beginner to basic music facts, however, many aspects of the music are presented untraditionally: quarter notes and rests are used exclusively throughout the book, but more than one beat is given to many of the notes and rests; pitch is definite on the "landmarks" (bass F, middle C, and treble G), but notes farther away from these three tangibles are to be selected (improvised) by the student; a small vertical line by double notes indicates clusters; circled notes are to be played on the black keys. Explanations for using this book are given (pages 6 and 22).

Book 2 by Louise Guhl includes the following materials: rhythm drills (tapping, "knocking" on the closed fallboard of the piano, patting the music, snapping the fingers, etc.); playing and tapping pieces; accompaniments in fifths, clusters, and other intervals; traditional note values and rests; and mixed meters. The staff is developed to three lines. Suggestions for transposition and other ways of playing the music are given in the direction "Metamorphosis." A knowledge of the explanations in *Book 1* is necessary for use of *Book 2.*

Book 3 by Louise Guhl begins by presenting a number of pieces in contracted hand positions, mainly chromatic 5-finger positions. The five-line staff is introduced on page 17. Accompaniments use intervals through the fifth; a great deal of open fifth work is presented in this book. Some information about form is included.

Book 4 by James Hopkins contains melodies with tapping accompaniments, pieces in contemporary notation, and traditional looking, "Bartókish" sounding pieces.

Conclusion: The series thus far (other books are planned) contains a great deal of contemporary reading material plus a springboard for improvisation. Because this series is quite unique (for children) it will be useful for sophisticated, contemporary minded teachers and students.

FLETCHER, LEILA *Piano Course* **Montgomery Music Inc.**

Method Books — **Piano Course, Books 1-6** (Bks, 1-3, 1950; Bk. 4, 1952; Bk. 5, 1954; Bk. 6, 1956).

Theory Books — **Theory Papers, Books 1-3** (Boston Music Co.: Bk. 1, 1943; Bk. 2, 1945; Bk. 3, 1947).

METHOD BOOKS

Book 1 of this middle C course consists of original melodies, folk song arrangements, and a few nursery rhymes which are presented in single line fashion divided between the hands. Finger numbers are used for almost every note. Duet accompaniments are provided.

Book 2 contains many note against note melodies. Scales in tetrachords are presented for the keys of C,F,G,D. A few block chords are used in this book but are not explained. An attractive presentation of phrasing (two-note slur) is shown in a picture. Transposition is explained near the end of the book.

The other books in the series offer original and arranged pieces and elements of theory and technic as needed.

THEORY BOOKS

Designed primarily for very young children, these three books are not intended to be used conjunctively with the method books. The books are printed in loose leaf form and contain writing exercises covering the following musical elements: keyboard recognition, note recognition, clef signs, counts, rests, accidentals, major scale formulas (tones and semitones), and major key signatures. Information about the instruments of the orchestra is also included.

GILLOCK, WILLIAM ***Piano all the Way*** **Willis Music Co.**

Method Books	**Piano all the Way, Levels 1A-4** (1969); **Level 1-B** (1971).
Technic Books	**Technic all the Way, Levels 1A & 1B** by Ruth Burr and Gillock (1976); **Accent on Majors** (1964); **Accent on Majors and Minors** (1963); **Accent on the Black Keys** (1964).
Theory Books	**Theory all the Way, Levels 1A & 1B** by Gillock and Kenneth Newsome (1972); **Levels 2A & 2B** (1974).
Supplementary Books	**Accent on Solos, Levels 1-3** (Level 1, 1971; Levels 2 & 3, 1969); **A Young Pianist's First Christmas at the Piano** (1966); **Big Note Solos** (1970); **Folk Songs and Rhythmic Dances** (1969); **Favorite Hymns at the Piano** (1969); **A Young Pianist's First Hymnal** (1976); others.
Literature Books (original)	**Accent on Rhythm and Style** (1962); **Accent on Analytical Sonatinas** (1964); **New Orleans Jazz Styles** (1965); **More New Orleans Jazz Styles** (1966); **Still More New Orleans Jazz Styles** (1977); **Fanfare** (Summy-Birchard Co., 1957); **Lyric Preludes in Romantic Style** (Summy-Birchard Co., 1958).

METHOD BOOKS

Piano all the Way is an attractive multiple key course which presents fundamental keyboard concepts through a wide style-variety of original literature. Some written work is also included.

Level 1A consists of miniature pre-notated pieces for young beginners. The beginning of the book concentrates on playing two- and three-group black key melodies (much like Frances Clark's *Time to Begin).* The main elements of musical emphasis include: learning the geography of the keyboard (high-low-middle, and the patterns of black and white keys); learning rhythm (exclusively 4/4 and 3/4 meter) through a concept of pulse (counting '1' for every quarter note, and '1-2' for half notes similar to Clark's presentation); and learning steps, skips, and repeats on the keyboard. Some duet accompaniments are included.

Level 1B is designed to give first note reading experience. The book may be used after *Level 1A*, or it may be used as a first book for the teacher who desires to teach note reading from the beginning. Reading begins in the middle C position and expands to other starting places on the keyboard. Beginning elements of notation and rhythm are the basic considerations. Duet accompaniments are provided for most of the pieces.

Level 2 first presents notation in the middle C position. New presentations in this book include: all major and minor triads in both blocked and broken form, scales in tetrachords for all twelve major keys, I and V7 chords used for harmonizing 5-finger melodies, and intervals. Key signatures are not used or explained; sharps and flats are written in as needed. The positions are not restricted exclusively to 5-finger patterns, and hand position changes occur in a number of the compositions.

Level 3 begins much like Hazel Cobb's *All Over the Keyboard* (Belwin-Mills) which relates an extended reading range to the five C's (from low to high) and the four G's on the staff. This book presents all twelve major and minor scales in a one octave range, key signatures, and offers compositions in a variety of major and minor keys. Cut-out note flash cards are included for added note recognition drills.

New materials in *Level 4* include: voicing used in chorale-style playing (a number of the pieces are in four parts), inversions of chords (chordal inversions are used in many of the compositions), the sub-dominant chord, sixteenth notes, 6/8 meter, and cadences (plagal, authentic, and complete). The pedal is used in many of the compositions.

Conclusion: Because this four-book series is comprised almost exclusively of original compositions, these books (especially levels 2-4) are uncommonly useful for additional reading and study material to supplement any course. Most method books contain a variety of arrangements and original literature, but it is seldom that one finds the abundance of well-written original pieces offered in the Gillock series.

TECHNIC BOOKS

Technic all the Way (two books) contains a variety of exercises for the young beginner to supplement the basic course. *Book 1-A* includes exercises for playing on the black keys using the third finger of each hand, playing 3-, 4-, and 5-finger patterns on the white keys. *Book 1-B* includes exercises in the middle C position, exercises for loose arm and wrist, exercises for the drop-lift used in phrasing, and exercises for legato-staccato touches. Stretches are limited to the fifth. Most of the melodies (exercises) have words. The "exercises" seem more like reading experiences than technical studies.

Accent on Majors is essentially a second or third year level scale book, but some fundamental theoretical concepts are also included. Only white key major scales are used (C,G,D,A,E,B,F), and these antecede compositions in these keys. Theoretical concepts include: the meaning of the word "key," an explanation of the major scale formula, an explanation of the triads built on scale tones, an explanation of cadence (plagal and authentic), and an explanation of key signatures.

Although both *Accent on Majors and Minors* and *Accent on the Black Keys* are more difficult than *Accent on Majors*, they follow the same format. Within these three books all the major and minor scales are presented and compositions are provided in corresponding scale keys.

THEORY BOOKS

Theory all the Way (four books) is designed to be used simultaneously with the basic course unit for unit. The books contain written and listening drills (ear-training work). Teacher's music is provided on the ear-training pages.

SUPPLEMENTARY BOOKS

Big Note Solos and *Accent on Solos* are designed as additional elementary repertoire and reading materials to supplement the basic course. The compositions in these books are suitable for recreation, study, audition, or recital. The Christmas and hymn collections present first-rate arrangements of well-known favorites.

LITERATURE BOOKS

Accent on Rhythm and Style is a superlative collection of seven original compositions written in the styles of the Baroque, Classic, Romantic, and Modern periods. A concise, informative description of these four periods is given at the back of the book. Outstanding compositions are "Sonatina" (three movements) and "Spanish Gypsies." All compositions are about third year level. First-rate study and recital material.

Accent on Analytical Sonatinas is a fine set of three original sonatinas each comprised of three movements. Formal analysis is provided for each movement regarding repetition, contrast, variation, exposition, development, and recapitulation. The sonatinas are expertly written in imitative Classic style. The level of difficulty of this collection is about third year—pre-Clementi and Kuhlau.

New Orleans Jazz Styles and its sequel, *More New Orleans Jazz Styles* are both patterned after the traditional Dixieland style emanating from Basin Street in the famous French Quarter of New Orleans. Mr. Gillock, a longtime resident of New Orleans, has captured the spirit and flavor of the Blues and Dixieland style in such compositions as "The Constant Bass," "Mardi Gras Combo," "Dixïeland Combo," "New Orleans Blues," and "Mister Trumpet Man." Most of the compositions are fairly difficult, about upper intermediate to moderately difficult levels. The difficulty in most of the pieces occurs in the "off-beat" jazz rhythms. These books are most effective for students of better than average rhythmic instinct.

Fanfare, written in Baroque style, points the way to later Bach playing. The short pieces are written in suite form, and each movement bears such descriptive, story-book titles as "Cuckoo in the Palace Garden," "Tapestry Weavers," "The Lute Player," and "Lullaby of an Old Nursemaid." The music (about third year level) is engaging and tasteful and can be used to advantage for study and recital.

Lyric Preludes, a teaching favorite since its publication, is a collection of descriptive mood pieces of about intermediate level difficulty. The music is suggestive of Romantic composers (Schumann and Chopin particularly), but it is entirely valid and original, not a mere copy. Correct voicing, pedaling, dynamics, mood and style, are the dominant teaching features of these excellently written compositions. The pieces follow a major, parallel minor sequence which is an aid in developing a sense for tonality and key relationships.

Method Books	**The Piano Student, Primer-Level 4** by David Carr Glover and Louise Garrow (1967); **Levels 5 & 6** by David Glover (1971).
Technic Books	**Piano Technic, Levels 1-4** by Glover and Garrow (1967); **Levels 5 & 6** by David Glover (1971); **Write and Play Major Scales** by Mary Elizabeth Clark and David Glover (1967); **Write and Play Minor Scales** by Clark and Glover (1967); **Piano Arpeggios** by Glover and Clark (1970).
Theory Books	**Piano Theory, Primer-Level 6** by Clark and Glover (Pr.-Lev. 4, 1967; Levs. 5 & 6, 1971).
Supplementary Books	**Piano Repertoire, Primer-Level 3** by Glover and Garrow (1967); **Christmas Music, Primer and Level 1** by Glover and Garrow (1968); **Levels 2 & 3** by Glover (Level 2, 1973; Level 3, 1975); **Chords and Keys, Levels 1 & 2** by Clark and Glover (1968); **Piano Duets, Levels 1 & 2** by Glover and Garrow (1970); **Levels 3 & 4** by Glover (1971); **Bach for Piano Ensemble** by George Lucktenberg and Glover (1971); **An Adventure in Jazz, Books 1-4** by Walter Noona and Glover (1972); **An Adventure in Ragtime** by Maurice Hinson and Glover (1975); **Jazz (etc.) on 88, Levels 1-3** by Glover (1975); others.
Sacred Music Books	**The Church Musician, Primer-Level 6** by Glover and Earl Ricker (1972); **Advanced Hymn Playing, Levels 7 & 8** by Phyllis Gunther and Glover (1972); **Keyboard Harmony Workbook, Level 7 & 8** by Gunther and Glover (1972); **Advanced Sacred Music Solos, Levels 7 & 8** by John Kraus and Glover (1972); **Advanced Sacred Music Duets, Levels 7 & 8** by Kraus and Glover (1972).
Group Piano Books	**Group Piano Student Programs, Primer and Level 1** by Glover and Bob L. Bennett (1975); **Teaching Piano in Groups** (manual) by Bennett and Glover (1975)
Literature Books	**Piano Repertoire, Levels 4-6**: Level 4 ed. by Glover and Garrow (1967), Level 5 ed. by Glover (1971), Level 6 ed. by Lucktenberg and Glover (1971); **Contemporary Piano Repertoire, Levels 5 & 6,** ed. by Hinson and Glover (1971); **Early American Music, Level 4** ed. by Anne McClenny and Hinson (1971).
Adult Books	**Adult Piano Student, Levels 1-3** (1970).

METHOD BOOKS

Pedagogical Considerations

The *Piano Student* course by Glover and Garrow is essentially middle C oriented, but not in the traditional sense. Emphasis on chords (major, minor, augmented, diminished), key signatures, scales and arpeggios provide adequate material for a basic foundation. The course books plus theory books, technic books, and repertoire books (plus other supplementary books) are interrelated in a simple, intelligent, enjoyable manner.

Primer Level: Designed for young beginners (about six to eight). Uses traditional note and meter presentation. Confines almost all the pieces to the middle C position. Provides duet accompaniments for many of the primarily eight-measure melodies.

Level 1: Although this book follows the *Primer Level* in sequence, it could also be used as a first book for an average age beginner (seven to eleven). Phrasing is well-defined, and the melodies are molded into logical phrase structures. Accompaniments in the entire book are comprised of tonic chords having only a root and fifth (rather than full three-note triads), and by dominant seventh chords having only a root and seventh (rather than the usual V^6_5 arrangement given in many course books). Key selections are limited to C, G, and F, but some other keys are suggested for transposition (D,E,A,B).

Level 2: New materials include: full chords (I, V^6_5, IV^6_4), some one octave scales (C,G,F,D), 6/8 meter, and the use of the damper pedal.

Level 3: New materials include: triads and inversion, relative minor scales, major and minor cadence chords, and key signatures.

Level 4: New materials include: sixteenth notes, the trill, augmented and diminished triads, the chromatic scale, syncopation, and major and minor arpeggios.

Levels 5 and *6* contain a combination of original compositions by Glover and a great deal of literature by composers from various periods.

TECHNIC BOOKS

The *Piano Technic* series by Glover and Garrow provides additional materials to reinforce concepts learned in the basic course. The types of exercises presented in *Levels 1-4* consist of slurred notes for down-up hand motion; legato and staccato 5-finger patterns; scale etudes; rhythmic patterns (dotted quarter followed by an eighth, triplets, etc.): and some arpeggio drills. *Levels 5* and *6* by Glover consist mainly of etudes by well-known composers (Czerny, Hanon, Streabbog, etc.) and some original etudes by Glover.

THEORY BOOKS

Piano Theory (six books) contains mostly written exercises correlated to the materials in the basic course. Programed instruction format is used; answers are given in the back of each book. Materials presented include: note and note value recognition, accidentals, music terms, key signatures, transposition, chords, scales, intervals, cadences, and information about form and style. The materials are well organized and easy to comprehend.

SUPPLEMENTARY BOOKS

Additional reading material to accompany the basic course is provided in the first three books of the *Piano Repertoire* series *(Primer-Level 2)* These books contain a combination of folk song arrangements and original solos. *Level 3* consists of arranged works by master composers, such as "Elegie" by Massenet, "Dance Macabre" by Saint-Saëns, etc.

Chords and Keys (two books) introduces the student to all fifteen enharmonic major keys using I and V7 chords in *Level 2,* and I, IV, V7 in *Level 3.* Mostly folk-tune arrangements are used, some are original.

Bach for Piano Ensemble is a collection of seven pieces from the *Anna Magdalena Notebook* arranged for multiple ensemble keyboard groups at about the late second or third year levels.

SACRED MUSIC BOOKS

The Church Musician (seven books) surveys sacred music as well as provides method explanations of basic concepts. The music is a combination of standard hymns and original music by Glover and Ricker. Duet parts are provided for many pieces. First year through upper intermediate level.

Advanced Hymn Playing (three books) teaches basic choral style in method book manner and prepares the student to play advanced hymns using informative explanations with musical examples. *Keyboard Harmony Workbook* (three books) contains written and keyboard theory to accompany the method books. *Advanced Sacred Music Solos* and *Advanced Sacred Music Duets* provide additional sacred music experiences to accompany the method books.

GROUP PIANO BOOKS

Group Piano Student Programs (two books) contains materials from Glover's *Piano Student* course (1967) which are organized in twenty-one segments (each comprising a program) punched with holes for a loose leaf binder. Each program consists of pieces and theory.

The manual, *Teaching Piano in Groups,* offers general suggestions on aspects of group teaching and specific suggestions for teaching each program in the course books.

LITERATURE BOOKS

Piano Repertoire, Levels 4-6, contains standard literature from the Baroque, Classic, and Romantic periods. *Contemporary Piano Repertoire* (two books) contains music by Bartók, Kabalevsky, Rebikov, Gretchaninoff, Prokofiev, Stravinsky, Shostakovich, and Khachaturian ranging in difficulty from about third year through intermediate levels.

ADULT BOOKS

Adult Piano Student (three books) is a basic course of study designed for an older beginner (anyone from about eleven and up). The books offer a logical, stepwise progression of materials for easy comprehension and steady progress. Based on 5-finger patterns the books progress through most of the positions, and incorporate the I, IV, V7 chords in various accompanying figures. Ensemble drills, some aspects of theory, scales, chords, arpeggios, technic drills, and a combination of original compositions and arrangements of famous melodies comprise this attractive three-book series.

KASSCHAU, HOWARD *Piano Course* G. Schirmer

Method Books	**Teach Me to Play** (1959, Rev. 1969); **Books 1-5** (Bks. 1 & 2, 1959, Rev. 1969; Bks. 3 & 4, 1960; Bk. 5, 1959).
Technic Books	**106 Greatest Piano Studies, Vols. 1 & 2** (1961).
Supplementary Books	**First Grade Pedal Book** (1959); **Note Speller** (1960); **Reading Through Intervals** (1968); **25 Adventures in Rock, Western and Blues** (1976); others.

METHOD BOOKS

Teach Me to Play: A forty-eight page preparatory level traditional ("John Thompsonish") middle C beginner's book. The middle C position is used for the first twenty-three pages; the remainder of the book uses 5-finger positions in C,G, and F. Single line melodies divided between the hands are used mostly (some note against note style is used). Some written work is included (drawing notes, clefs, rests, and accidentals).

Book 1: A sixty-four page book which may be used to follow *Teach Me to Play* or may be used as a first book for an older beginner. The book contains pieces in the keys of C, G, and F exclusively. Tetrachord scales are given for these keys. Clear explanations are given for the following: legato, phrase, chords (I and V7), intervals, triads of the major scale, the pedals, and 6/8 meter. Although numerous concepts are presented (chords, intervals, etc.), many of these elements are not systematically developed (for example: the Alberti Bass is used on page 30 and not used again).

Book 2: Pieces and studies up to three sharps and three flats are included in this book. Arrangements abound (Schubert's "March Militaire," Bizet's "Toreador Song" from *Carmen,* Strauss' "Tales from the Vienna Woods," etc.). New materials include: scales and arpeggios in extended form, major key signature identification, chromatic scale, and diminished chords.

Books 3, 4, 5 stress primarily repertoire (original and arranged literature) and technic. *Book 5* reaches high school level difficulty.

TECHNIC BOOKS

106 Greatest Piano Studies consists of selected works by such famous etude composers as Czerny, Burgmüller, Clementi, Bertini, Gurlitt, Heller, and many others. Arranged in two, sixty-four page volumes, these studies are presented in their original form and appear in a graded sequence ranging from elementary to moderately difficult. Although compiled to supplement the *Piano Course,* these studies may be used to advantage with any other method.

SUPPLEMENTARY BOOK

Reading Through Intervals is an eighty-six page volume designed for older beginners and/or college piano minors. As stated in the "Foreword," the premise that reading by intervals "eliminates the necessity for learning the letter names of the lines and spaces," is ill-founded. The book may be used to advantage to supplement a directional reading approach, but this should not displace note learning.

The book focuses on five C's which are used as register landmarks (middle C, and the two C's above and below it). Intervals are presented in a sequential pattern ranging from seconds through octaves. Reading exercises follow each new presentation. Interval presentations are limited to basic interval concepts: seconds, thirds, etc.; no attempt is made to teach various kinds of intervals such as scale intervals and altered intervals (*i.e.* major and minor thirds, minor sevenths, etc.). A majority of the 122 studies are contemporary sounding (Bartók-like) employing mixtures of major and minor, and a touch of modality.

MARWICK, MARION, and MARYANNE NAGY ***Creative Keyboard***
Screen Gems/Columbia Publications

Method Books	**Creative Keyboard, Levels 1 & 2** (1975).
Technic Books	**Practice in Progress, Levels 1 & 2** by Susan La Magra (Lev. 1, 1975; Lev. 2, 1976).
Supplementary Books	**Finger Frolics, Levels 1 & 2** by Nora Brandt (1975), **Folk Song Duets, Levels 1 & 2** by Marwick and Nagy (1975); **Christmas Carols, Level 1** arr. by John August (1975); **Miniatures, Level 1** by Nagy (1975); **Keyboard Capers, Level 2** by Nagy (1975); **Popular Solos, Level 2** arr. by John August (1975).
Literature Book	**Master Repertoire, Level 2, Volume 1** ed. by Anthony La Magra (1975).

METHOD BOOKS

Subtitled "A Modern Approach to Learning Piano" the two levels of *Creative Keyboard* present a comprehensive multi-key course for at least two years study.

Level 1: Numerous music factors are presented within the first ten pages: black keys, finger numbers, white keys, meter and counting, half and whole steps, sharp-flat-natural, key signatures, and all 5-finger positions. Within pages 11-21 single line melodies are presented in various 5-finger positions. Major I chords are introduced on page 23, V7 chords on page 28, and melody-harmony pieces follow on succeeding pages. Also included in this volume are explanations about question-answer phrases, minor chords, IV chord, 4/4 - 6/8 meters, sixteenth notes, and a glossary of terms. The music is a combination of original and folk-traditional materials. Some duets are included. Progress is rapid in this fifty page book, and perhaps the course would work best with bright beginners no younger than eight years old.

Level 2: New materials include: major scales in tetrachords, inversions of triads, diminished-augmented chords, triads of the scale, major scales, arpeggios, whole tone scale, and relative major-minor key signatures. Mostly music by master composers is used.

TECHNIC BOOKS

Subtitled "Piano Technique and Musicianship" the two levels of *Practice in Progress* are designed as companion books to the basic course. The materials are organized into sections containing such materials as 5-finger studies in all keys, chords, legato-staccato touches, phrasing, major scales, intervals, arpeggios, and inversions of triads.

SUPPLEMENTARY BOOKS

Finger Frolics (two books) contains original, somewhat contemporary sounding pieces and duets in many keys. The fingering is sparsely given; perhaps it is intended to be written in by the student or teacher where omitted.

Miniatures contains ten one-page pieces in ten keys written in a variety of styles utilizing the keys of C, G, and F Major; D and G minor; and one piece using whole tones. *Popular Solos* is a collection of arranged popular songs such as "Alley Cat," "Brian's Song," "The Candy Man," and seven others. (Fingering is omitted in this collection.)

LITERATURE BOOK

Master Repertoire, Level 2, Volume 1 contains fourteen easy pieces by master composers from four periods. In addition, explanations about the music and practice suggestions are provided. The compositions are by Bach, L. Mozart, Beethoven, Schumann, Kabalevsky, Bartók and Stravinsky.

NEVIN, MARK ***Piano Course*** **Belwin-Mills**

Method Books	**Preparatory Book** (1960); **Books 1-5** (Bks. 1-3, 1960; Bk. 4, 1962; Bk. 5, 1965).
Supplementary Books	**Solo Gallery** (1963); **Look! No Finger Numbers, Books 1 & 2** (1965); **Jazz Jamboree** (1964); **Top Pop Tunes** (1970); **Tunes You Like, Books 1-4** (Schroeder & Gunther, Bk. 1, 1953; Bk. 2, 1954; Bk. 3, 1955; Bk. 4, 1957); **Piano Classics You Like, Books 1 & 2** (Schroeder & Gunther, 1961); **Forever Favorite Tunes You Like** (Schroeder & Gunther, 1975); **Famous Jewish Songs You Like** (Schroeder & Gunther, 1975); **My Very First Piano Pieces** (Willis, 1976); others.
Adult Books	**Piano for Adults, Books 1 & 2** (Marks Music Corp., 1969).

METHOD BOOKS

This middle C course contains a combination of original pieces, folk song arrangements, master composer arrangements, and some original literature. The *Preparatory Book* consists of single line melodies divided between the hands and some note against note playing. Included in *Book 1* is a clear, concise explanation of phrasing; some block chord harmonizations are used in this book. Included in *Book 2* is an explanation of intervals; some broken chord harmonizations are used. Most of the pieces in this series are written in C, G, and F. Elements of theory are presented as needed. Some technical explanation and drill is interwoven throughout the course.

SUPPLEMENTARY BOOKS

Although the various supplementary books by Nevin are not correlated to the basic *Piano Course,* they may be used to advantage to supplement this or any other course. *Tunes You Like,* a Schroeder and Gunther publication, has been a longtime favorite. This four-book sequence consists of familiar melodies in easy arrangements (early elementary to advancing elementary levels). *Jazz Jamboree* contains nine attractive blues and boogie pieces at about the third and fourth year level. A few of the pieces have swing basses which tend to make them sound old-fashioned compared to today's pop sound.

ADULT BOOKS

Piano for Adults (two books) is basically a stepwise middle C course designed for an older beginner. Aspects of theory (intervals, chords, scales, etc.) are included and inserted as needed as preparation for pieces that follow. Compositions and arrangements are essentially chosen from well-known tunes, with a sprinkling of contemporary styles. There is a summary at the back of each book that reviews the materials included in each volume. This course presents familiar materials attractively in an up-to-date manner.

NOONA, WALTER, and CAROL NOONA ***Mainstreams in Music***
Heritage Music Press

Method Books	**The Pianist, Phases 1-4** (1973).
Technic Books	**Projects, Phases 1-4** (1973).
Theory Books	**Pencil and Paper, Phases 1-4** (1973).
Supplementary Books	**The Performer, Phases 1-4** (1973); **The Contemporary Performer, Phases 1-4** (Bk. 1, 1976; Bks. 2 & 3, 1975; Bk. 4, 1976); **The Improviser, A-C** (1975); **Improvisor Projects, A-C** (1975); others
(other books are planned in this series)	

METHOD BOOKS

The Pianist course is basically multi-key oriented, although *Phase 1* begins in the middle C hand position. The four phases (levels) range from beginner level through early intermediate. Additional books in each phase provide materials for reinforcement of concepts in a well-related manner.

Phase 1: The beginner is introduced to basic middle C reading using middle C as the first "guidepost." Explanations of directional reading (step, skip, repeated notes) assist in first reading experiences. The F and G guideposts are added (similar to the Clark "landmark" concept). Note against note playing (hands together) is introduced about halfway through the book. Reading is limited to the 5-finger span with occasional hand position shifts. Duet accompaniments and experimental suggestions are provided for many of the pieces.

Phase 2: After a brief review, the following new materials are introduced: intervals, I and V7 chords, multi-key presentation in groups of keys somewhat related to the circle of fifths, eighth notes, parallel major-minor chords, the order of sharps and flats, and pedaling.

Phase 3: New materials include: syncopated rhythm, major scales (one harmonic minor scale), dotted notes, inversions of triads, primary chords (use of the IV chord for the first time), 6/8 time, and triplet rhythm.

Phase 4: New materials include: minor scales (three forms), relative minor key signatures, parallel minor scales, primary chords in minor, chromatic scale, whole-tone scale, sixteenth notes, trills, augmented and diminished triads, arpeggios, and seventh chords.

Conclusion: The materials covered in these four levels are extensive, and it appears that the level reached becomes difficult rapidly. Therefore, perhaps this method could be handled better in sequence by a slightly older beginner (about nine to eleven) rather than a younger beginner (seven to nine).

TECHNIC BOOKS

Projects is an imaginative multi-purpose series containing three sections in each book: Exploring, Creating, and Technical Studies.

Phase 1: Exploring deals with experimentation in rhythms and sampling keys at the keyboard. Creating consists of improvising and composing activities at the elementary level. Technical Studies contains exercises in dropping and lifting, contrary motion, two-note slurs, and legato and staccato touches.

Phase 2: The Exploring section provides sight-reading material in all twelve keys with suggestions for transposition and pattern analysis. The Creating section stresses melodic variation, question and answer phrases, and harmonizing and improvising using I and V7 chords. Technical Studies contains 5-finger patterns in legato and staccato touches, hand over hand arpeggios, and phrasing and interval studies.

Phase 3: The Exploring section provides sight-reading material with suggestions for transposition and analysis. Included in the Creating section are improvising studies with scales and chords and with inversions of chords, twelve-measure blues, as well as composing a piece in binary and ternary form. Technical Studies contains exercises using triplets, thirds and sixths, scales and inversions of chords.

Phase 4: The Exploring section contains sight-reading studies using the materials presented in *The Pianist, Phase 4.* In the Creating section the student is directed to compose musical answers to question phrases, play cadences, and compose several pieces. The Technical Studies consist mainly of major and minor scales, and major and minor arpeggios.

THEORY BOOKS

The *Pencil and Paper* books are designed to be used in conjunction with *The Pianist* series. Answers are given in the back of each theory book. *Phase 1* contains written drills for naming keys on the keyboard, drawing music signs, and naming notes. *Phase 2* contains interval drills, harmonizing melodies with I and V7 chords, key signature drills, major-minor chords, and lead line melodies for harmonization. *Phase 3* contains drills in naming leger notes, building major scales, inversions of chords, 6/8 rhythm, primary chords, triplet rhythm, and reviews some materials from the previous level. *Phase 4* contains drills in writing minor scales, writing major-minor key signatures, cadences, altered intervals, sixteenth note rhythms, augmented and diminished chords, scale degree names, seventh chords, and arpeggios.

SUPPLEMENTARY BOOKS

The Performer series consists of supplementary original, folk and some well-known composer pieces to provide additional materials at each level (phase). *The Contemporary Performer* series is designed to introduce the student to idioms of twentieth-century style such as modes, polyrhythms, clusters, polytonalities, twelve-tone rows, and ostinato patterns. The materials are well-organized and provide an excellent introduction to contemporary sounds.

The Improviser series (three books) is designed to teach the intermediate level pianist the basics of jazz improvisation. Original music in popular style provides the impetus for supplying basses, fill-ins, and melodic variants. Information about chord structure is supplied as needed. The *Improviser Projects* (three books) are designed as workbooks to accompany *The Improviser* books. For those interested in jazz improvisation at an easy (intermediate) level, this series is one of the most instructive and best organized.

OLSON, LYNN, LOUISE BIANCHI, and MARVIN BLICKENSTAFF
Music Pathways **Carl Fischer**

Method Books	**Discovery 1A, 1B-1C, 2A-2B** (1974).
Technic Books	**Technique 3A-3B, 4A-4B, 5A-5B** (1974).
Theory Books	**Activity 1B, 1C, 2A-2B** (1974); **Musicianship 3A-3B, 4A-4B, 5A-5B** (1974).
Supplementary Books	**Performance 1C, 2A-2B** (1974); **Ensemble 3, 4, 5** (1975); **Something Light 3, 4, 5** (1975).
Literature Books	**Repertoire 3A-3B, 4A-4B, 5A-5B** (1974).

METHOD BOOKS

The series *Discovery* (five books) contains a synthesis of learning paths combining the landmark reading approach (five C's) and the multiple key approach. The music is originally composed. The first three books contain a vinyl record of some of the pieces. "Discovery" learning is a featured element of the learning process, and in many instances the student is asked to experiment and discover things on his own rather than being given facts for memorization. A guide book for teachers, *Introducing Music Pathways,* is recommended for sorting out the thorny organization of books in the program by numbers, letters and levels.

Book 1A: Designed for average age beginners (seven to ten). Contains thirteen chapters (sixty-four pages). The first eight chapters are written in pre-staffed notation; the remaining six chapters are written on the staff.

Directional reading from multiple C's is the main feature of the book. Main materials introduced are: rhythm (♩ 𝅗𝅥 𝅗𝅥.), skips and steps, intervals through the sixth, notation (all over the staff, including leger lines), legato-staccato touches, and music signs and terms. The counting system used is Hungarian or European: ♩ ♩ 𝅗𝅥 (tah tah tah-ah) Mostly single line melodies are used. A few duet accompaniments are provided.

Book 1B: New materials include: melodies accompanied by fifths, whole steps and half steps, sharps and flats, eighth notes, 5-finger positions in the Group I and II Keys.

Book 1C: New materials include: 5-finger position in the Group III Keys, intervals of the sixth, question-answer phrases, dotted quarter rhythm, and pedal.

Book 2A: New materials include: major key signatures, 6/8 meter, tonic-dominant relationships, major triads, and triplet rhythm.

Book 2B: New materials include: sixteenth notes, minor 5-finger patterns, I and V7 chords, some major scale practice, major-minor 5-finger patterns.

TECHNIC BOOKS

The series *Technique* (six books) begins in the Pathways program when the student has completed the "method" part of the course. At this point he is playing repertoire, technical studies, and is beginning a comprehensive theory program called *Musicianship.* Each *Technique* book is divided into three sections: "finger drills" (for finger independence and strength), "technical skills" (to develop scale, chord, arpeggio facility, hand independence, and pedaling), and "etudes" (studies from the repertoire). Each book has only sixteen pages.

THEORY BOOKS

The *Activity* series (four books) contains materials paralleling those in the *Discovery* books. The activities are to be written and played. The *Musicianship* series (six books) contains some of the best thought out materials in the Pathways program. Discussions of style, rhythm, melody, harmony, form, and expressive elements in each book are related to the repertoire pieces in a meaningful, intelligent, imaginative manner. These books are well organized, comprehensive, and of considerable merit.

SUPPLEMENTARY BOOKS

The *Performance* series (three books) contains supplementary pieces in the first and second levels of the Pathways program. Some of the pieces have duet accompaniments. Each book has only sixteen pages. The *Ensemble* series (three books) contains standard duet literature from great and lesser composers. The series *Something Light* (three books) contains a potpourri of styles such as blues, boogie, western, rock, arrangements of familiar tunes, and includes some pieces by other composers.

Oxford Piano Course **Written by Ernest Schelling, Gail Martin Haake, Charles J. Haake, and Osbourne McConathy. Oxford University Press, Inc.**

Method Books	**Preparatory Book A, Singing and Playing** (1928); **Preparatory Book B, Learning to Play the Piano** (1942); **First Book** (1927); **Second Book** (1929); **Third Book** (1931); **Fourth Book** (1932).
Supplementary Book	**Play Tunes** by Polly Gibbs (1971).
Adult Book	**Beginner's Book for Older Pupils** (1929).

METHOD BOOKS

This is the oldest multi-key course in print. Although somewhat dated (pictures and texts), it is interesting to survey from an historical view.

Within the first three books, major and minor pentachord positions and I chords are presented in an arbitrary sequence (G major, F major, A minor, A major, etc.). Melodies are accompanied mostly by block chord harmonizations (I, IV, V7). Rhythms are to be taught first by rote, then by clapping and counting. Some aspects of form (ABA, etc.) are included. Blank staves are included for writing 5-finger positions and chords as they are presented.

Books 2-4 include a variety of piano literature, numerous exercises, and etudes by well-known composers. Aspects of form are clearly indicated throughout.

Two teacher's manuals are provided which contain outlines and detailed instructions for conducting both group instruction and private lessons. The *First Teacher's Manual* covers *Singing and Playing, Learning to Play the Piano,* the *First Book,* and the first half of the *Beginner's Book for Older Pupils.* The *Second Teacher's Manual* furnishes outlines and detailed instructions for the *Second, Third* and *Fourth Books,* and the second half of the *Beginner's Book for Older Pupils.*

ADULT BOOK

Oxford's sixty page *Beginner's Book for Older Pupils* is essentially a compilation of materials drawn from the children's series. To make it more adult oriented, the pictures and some texts have been eliminated. After preliminary 5-finger studies and several pages of melodies harmonized with I and V7 chords, the progression develops at a very fast pace. Broken chord harmonization begins on page 15, four-part harmony on page 20, four-part harmony with syncopated pedal on page 29, etc. Because every few pages becomes increasingly more difficult and complex, the student is not given an opportunity to develop his sight-reading ability. Most adult beginners using this book find reading almost impossible and have to memorize page by page before progressing. Although some aspects of theory are offered (essentially I, IV, V7 chords and scales), other theoretical aspects, such as intervals and more advanced chords, are omitted. Numerous related exercises are provided throughout which serve as preliminary and supplementary drills for many of the pieces. Formal analyses are provided for most of the compositions.

Pedagogical Considerations

PACE, ROBERT *Music for Piano* **Lee Roberts Music Publications, Inc.** (distributed by G. Schirmer)

Kindergarten Books	**Music for Moppets** by Helen Pace (1971); **Teacher's Manual** (1972); **Moppets' Rhythms and Rhymes** (1974); **Teacher's Book** (1974); **Moppets' Flash Cards** (1974).
Method Books	**Music for Piano, Books 1-6** (Bks. 1-3, 1961; Bks. 4 & 5, 1962; Bk 6, 1969).
Theory Books	**Skills and Drills, Books 1-5** (Bks. 1-3 & 5, 1961; Bk. 4, 1962); **Theory Papers** by Pace and Patrick Doyle (1970); **Tricks with Triads, Sets 1-3** by Don Fornuto (Set 1, 1970; Set 2, 1971; Set 3, 1973).
Flash Cards	**Teaching Aids**: 6 sets (1) **Lines and Spaces**, (2) **Key Signatures**, (3) **Major Chords**, (4) **Minor Chords** (1961), (5) **Augmented Triads** (1972), (6) **Diminished Triads** (1972).
Supplementary Books	**Christmas Music, Book 1** (1961); **Christmas Music, Second Collection** by Helen Pace (1967); **Jazz for Piano, Books 1 & 2** by Bert Konowitz (1965); **Duets for Piano, Sets 1 and 2** (1964); **Improvising the Blues, Vol. 1** by Don Fornuto (1974); **Jazz is a Way of Playing** by Bert Konowitz (1976); others.
Classroom Music Books	**Music for the Classroom** (1967); **Music for the Classroom, Teacher's Manual** (1967).
Adult Book	**Music for Piano for the Older Beginner** (1967).

KINDERGARTEN BOOKS

Music for Moppets is specifically designed for pre-schoolers, and includes the following materials: recognition of the black key groups, ear training activities, question and answer phrases, and creative work. The *Teacher's Manual* gives a page by page account of suggested class activities, uses for rhythm and melody instruments, and generally offers helpful directions for the use of the student book.

Moppets' Rhythms and Rhymes is a supplementary book consisting of educational rhythmic songs and games for group participation. Explanations and suggestions are provided in the *Teacher's Book*.

METHOD BOOKS

This well-written series is a landmark in the field of piano education. Repertoire, technic, ear training, improvisation, transposition, and harmonization are interwoven in an intelligent manner. Creative thinking is encouraged on the part of both the student and teacher through numerous improvisational studies. Basic musicianship is the primary concern throughout the entire series.

Music for Piano, Book 1: Multi-key designed, this forty-eight page first reading volume is comprised of original pieces, folk song arrangements, and melodies by master composers. The book is intended to be used in conjunction with *Skills and Drills, Book 1,* which contains correlated materials. The first six pages, written in pre-staffed fashion, introduce the student to a sampling of 5-finger melodies in several keys. Directional reading is indicated by lines representing pitch levels. Rhythm is to be taught by rote in this introductory portion. The sequence of materials through the remainder of the book is presented in the following manner: grand staff, page 8; musical notation, page 10 (note flash cards should be introduced at this time for home and lesson drill); 5-finger melodies begin on page 12; I chord, page 28; V7 chord, page 29; minor triads, page 40. Although this sequence appears logical and natural, there are a great many facts confronting the beginner at the outset: (1) a variety of keys, (2) the entire staff, (3) notation and rhythm, and (4) all major key signatures. A very young beginner (age six or seven) often finds concepts in rapid sequence (without development) somewhat confusing. However, a beginner of at least average age (eight to eleven) will be better able to comprehend this *gestalt,* multi-concept approach.

Book 2: Intended to be used in conjunction with *Skills and Drills, Book 2,* this book presents a continued study program of sight-reading, transposition, harmonization, ear training, improvisation, repertoire, and technic. New presentations include: major sharp scales in tetrachord fashion, page 5; major flat scales in tetrachords, page 12; various bass styles for harmonizing single line melodies (block chord, broken chord, off-beat chord, and Alberti chord bass), page 13; the IV chord in major keys, page 14; and aspects of form (repetition and sequence), page 24. Three duets are included in this volume. Also included are excerpts from original piano literature and some arrangements for piano of orchestral music.

Book 3: A continued balance of original compositions, folk song arrangements, duets, and pieces by master composers comprise the basic elements of this volume. New presentations include: augmented chords, page 6, and two major scales (C scale, page 13; G scale, page 17).

Book 4: Piano literature is more prevalent in this volume; the level of difficulty ranges from Beethoven's "Ecossaise" (page 2) to Chopin's "F major Mazurka" (page 46). New materials include: inversions of chords, harmonic progressions using the ii6 chord, intervals, the vi chord, and secondary dominants.

Book 5: Consisting mainly of lower advanced level repertoire and technic, this volume presents the following theoretical materials: seven scale tone triads, diminished seventh chords, and modulation.

Book 6: In addition to the advanced piano literature by well-known composers, new materials include: explanations about impressionistic and twentieth-century compositional technics, and explanations about musical forms. Some duets are included.

THEORY BOOKS

Skills and Drills (five books) contains a wealth of musician-building materials. Written drills, keyboard harmony assignments, sight-reading studies, and technic drills comprise the basic elements in this series. All five books are to be used in conjunction with their companion method books, *Music for Piano, Books 1-5.* The materials in *Skills and Drills* provide an impetus for improvisation and functional chording and offer the student an opportunity for self-expression and original thinking.

Theory Papers is a single sixty-four page volume in tear-sheet format designed for the beginning level student. This book provides additional drill in notes, key signatures, creative work, and harmonization, and it parallels the materials in *Skills and Drills, Book 1.*

Tricks with Triads (three sets) provides numerous opportunities for triadic harmonization of mostly familiar tunes. An example is given, and the student is to continue to add a similar bass. Various accompaniment styles are presented. The materials encourage mildly contemporary harmonization and interesting improvisation.

SUPPLEMENTARY BOOKS

Jazz for Piano (two books) is an attractive collection of well-written jazz pieces for study, recreation and recital. *Book 1* contains pieces at about third year level. *Book 2* is slightly more difficult, and is especially designed to teach improvisation. Syncopation, jazz chords (major, minor, and dominant sevenths, and other jazz progressions), and "lead-sheet" type melody lines are the featured elements of this instructional book. Bouncy dotted rhythms abound throughout this two-book series, characteristic of the jazz style prior to the current pop-rock scene prevalent today.

CLASSROOM MUSIC BOOKS

Music for the Classroom is a forty-eight page volume designed to introduce school children (elementary or junior high age) to the following fundamentals: all 5-finger patterns on the keyboard, notation, key signatures, meter and rhythm, and chords (major and minor triads, V7 and IV chords). Improvisation is a featured element. Written work is included. The *Teacher's Manual* provides step by step lesson plans and assignments.

ADULT BOOK

Music for Piano for the Older Beginner, Book 1, is designed to teach the adolescent or adult student the following fundamentals: all 5-finger patterns on the keyboard, notation, key signatures, meter and rhythm, and chords (major and minor triads, V7 and IV chords). The book contains folk song arrangements, themes from orchestral compositions arranged for piano, and original literature. Improvisation, functional chording, and technic recur systematically throughout.

PALMER, WILLARD A., and AMANDA VICK LETHCO

Creating Music at the Piano **Alfred Publishing Co.**

Method Books	**Creating Music at the Piano, Books 1-6** (Bk. 1, 1971; Bks. 2 & 3, 1972; Bk. 4, 1973; Bk. 5, 1974; Bk. 6, 1976).
Theory Books	**Theory Papers, Books 1-4** (Bks. 1 & 2, 1973; Bk. 3, 1974; Bk. 4, 1975).
Teacher's Manual	**Creating Music Teacher's Manual, Book 1.**
Supplementary Books	**Recital Book, 1-3** (Bk. 1, 1972; Bk. 2, 1973; Bk. 3, 1974).

METHOD BOOKS

Creating Music at the Piano contains interesting, imaginative materials and provides detailed explanations of the concepts presented. Since the approach is neither middle C, nor multiple key, the teacher is offered an alternative to either of these familiar presentations.

Book 1 presents fundamentals to the beginner in an expanding manner. Dynamics, a prime aspect in this course, is presented right at the beginning by having the student play soft and loud sounds (one key at a time). After the preliminaries of finger numbers, musical alphabet, and names of the keys have been presented, the student begins to play pre-notated melodies using finger numbers for direction. Rhythm is introduced by counting '1' for quarter notes, '1-2' for half notes, '1-2-3' for dotted half notes, and '1-2-3-4' for whole notes (like the presentation in Clark's *Time to Begin*). Note reading is first initiated by relating notes to the F clef (bass staff) and the G clef (treble staff); this approach is also similar to Frances Clark's "landmarks." The student is further directed to read notes related to the A,C,E groups in various places on the keyboard. Intervals through the fifth are presented, and the student is encouraged to read by interval. Near the end of the book eighth notes, sharp and natural signs are introduced. The staff is developed from a single line. Duet accompaniments are provided for most of the pieces. A *Teacher's Manual* is available for the *Book 1* level; it contains page by page discussions and suggestions.

Book 2 introduces the student to the following new materials: intervals of sixths and sevenths, tempo marks, broken chord bass, the flat sign, dotted quarter rhythm, half and whole steps, the chromatic scale, tetrachords, and the scales of C and G.

Book 3 introduces the student to the following new materials: interval of the octave, the D major scale, modes (dorian, phrygian, lydian, mixolydian, aeolian), block triads and inversions, and the syncopated pedal. A puzzling aspect in this course is the use of broken chord basses (some in *Book 2*, and up to page 25 in *Book 3*); these are used first before the block chord triad is finally explained on page 26. The presentation of materials in this regard seems out of order. *Book 3* is comprised primarily of folk song arrangements, original works, and a few masterwork compositions.

Book 4 new materials include: F major scale, relative minor scales (A,D,E), aspects of form (binary, ternary), and seventh chords.

Book 5 new materials include: triplet rhythm, sixteenth notes, Bb major and G minor scales, dotted eighth note rhythm, appogiatura, trill, and 6/8 meter. The music is mostly by well-known composers.

Book 6 is titled *Introduction to the Masterworks* and surveys the major periods in text and music. Palmer's discussion of ornamentation is included for each period and is an excellent reference source. The music is intermediate level difficulty.

THEORY BOOKS

Theory Papers provides parallel materials to be used with the basic course. In addition some new theory materials are introduced which go beyond the scope of the companion method book. Included are written and playing exercises, flashcards for the student to make, and some creative work.

Book 1: In addition to parallel materials, new materials include: conducting basic meters, transposing (written transposition), stemming notes, and adding note values in arithmetic fashion. Aspects of composing original melodies are also included.

Book 2: New materials include: circle of fifths, writing major scales beyond those introduced in the course book, and writing key signatures.

Book 3: New materials include: explanations of scale degree names, altered intervals, and diminished triads.

Book 4: New materials include: chord progressions, minor scales, augmented triads, and seventh chords and inversions.

SUPPLEMENTARY BOOKS

The *Recital Book* series (three books) contains folk, traditional and original pieces to supplement the basic course. Some of the pieces in *Book 1* have duet parts.

The Pointer System — Pointer System, Inc.

Method Books	**Pointer System Series: Books 1-3** (1959); **Book 4** (1960); **Book 5** (1966). **Modern Pianist Series: Books 1-4** (1962).
Supplementary Books	numerous varied collections such as Hymns, Waltzes; Christmas collections, others.

This system of instruction is unique among the various methods surveyed. The primary purpose is to teach single line melodies ("lead-sheet" style) with chord accompaniments. Functional chording is the dominant feature throughout the *Pointer System*. Popular style chords are used (chord symbols: C, G7, etc.) rather than Roman numeral chord indications.

The "pointer chord" is produced by pointing with the index finger of the left hand to the key note of any chord; the other two tones of the chord are played with fingers 1 and 5. Using this system, the root tone of chords never appears in the bass, because the chords are always used in inverted form, usually in $\substack{6\\4}$ position. Continued usage of inverted chords produces an unstable effect which is quite unsatisfactory on the piano. Transferred to the organ, however, the pedals can supply the missing bass tone.

RICHTER, ADA — *Piano Course* — Witmark/Warner Bros. Publications

Kindergarten Book	**Pre-School and Kindergarten Book** (1954).
Method Book (for young beginners)	**Stepping Stones to the Piano** (1964).
Method Books	**Piano Course, Books 1-4** (1954).
Technic Books	**Keyboard Games** (1954); **Piano Warm-Ups** (1966); **Know Your Scales and Arpeggios** (1963); **Adventures at the Keyboard** (1955); **Keyboard Technic** (1956); **More Keyboard Technic** (1958).
Theory Books	**Stick-A-Note Book** (1960); **Spell-A-Note Book** (1960); **Theory Work Sheets, Sets 1 & 2** (1959).
Supplementary Books	**Tune Time** (1967); **Christmas Carol Book** (1962); **A Little Hymnal** (1959); **Sing With Me** (1960); **Victor Herbert Made Easy for Piano** (1947); others.
Adult Books	**The Older Student, Book 1** (1956); **Book 2** (1957); **Book 3** (1958).

METHOD BOOKS

This course offers three beginning books. From these, the teacher can choose the one which best fits a particular student's age and ability. The *Pre-School and Kindergarten Book* is designed for very young beginners who can neither read nor write (ages four to six). *Stepping Stones to the Piano* may be used either as a beginning book for children not quite ready for *Book 1* (ages five to seven), or as a second book following the pre-school book. *Book 1* of the basic *Piano Course* is designed for average age beginners (ages seven to ten).

Pre-School and Kindergarten Book: Although very little is developed in this book, youngsters are offered a micro-music-readiness program. The concept of pitch (low, middle, high) is explored in three registers on the keyboard: the C below middle C, middle C, and the C above middle C. Other concepts explored include: learning finger numbers, line and space notes (to distinguish between these), treble and bass clefs, and bar lines. The notes and rhythm are to be taught by rote. C 5-finger positions are used. Duet accompaniments are provided.

Stepping Stones to the Piano: This book is quite similar to the pre-school book, but notation is to be learned rather than only playing by rote. Only the C 5-finger position is used. Most of the tunes are originally composed. Meter is confined to 2/4, 3/4, and 4/4. Some duet accompaniments are provided.

Piano Course, Book 1: This book follows the same principles as the previous two—C 5-finger position, similar meter presentation, etc. However, concepts are expanded and new territories are explored. New presentations include: chords (both I and V7), staccato touch, slurs, and the F and G 5-finger positions.

Book 2: New materials include: phrasing, broken chord accompaniments, dotted quarter rhythm, 6/8 meter, scales. The pieces are a combination of original and folk tunes.

Book 3: New materials include: triplet rhythm, arpeggios (divided between the hands), the damper pedal, other 5-finger positions. A few compositions by master composers are included (Bartók, Burgmüller, others).

Book 4: New materials include: chromatic scale, discussion of intervals, double notes, syncopated rhythms, minor chords, inversions of chords. The compositions consist of a combination of original pieces, folk tune arrangements, and a few compositions by master composers. *Book 4* reaches about fourth year level difficulty.

TECHNIC BOOKS

Keyboard Games is an elementary technic book which contains the following basics: legato and staccato touch, passing the thumb under, two note slurred groupings (for down-up wrist motion), skips, and arpeggios. The exercises are presented as short little pieces.

Piano Warm-Ups is a first or second year collection of short, elementary exercises. Five-finger positions played in a variety of touches, chords, slurred groups, intervallic stretches, scales, and arpeggios comprise this volume. The exercises are all in C, but transposition is suggested.

Know Your Scales and Arpeggios presents all the major and minor scales in various rhythms. In addition to scales and arpeggios, cadences are also included in this forty page volume.

Adventures at the Keyboard is a forty-eight page collection of technical studies by various composers: Lemoine, Köhler, Gurlitt, Czerny, others. About third or fourth year levels.

Keyboard Technic and *More Keyboard Technic* are designed for older students. Exercises include: legato and staccato studies, finger extensions, slurred groups, passing the thumb under, chords, arpeggios, thirds, sixths, octaves, trills, and wrist staccato.

THEORY BOOKS

Stick-A-Note Book is designed for young beginners. It consists of tear-outs to be placed in the proper location in sticker book fashion. The book stresses numbers, alphabet letters, and notes; it may be used with any of the three beginning method books.

Spell-A-Note Book is essentially a note speller. Written work includes: writing line and space notes, writing treble and bass clefs, adding stems to notes, naming notes, drawing rests, and writing accidentals.

Theory Work Sheets, Sets 1 & 2 contain only written work (no keyboard harmony). They are published in perforated, tear-out form and include the following elements of notation and elementary theory: sharps and flats, note and rest values, time, rhythm, measure, intervals, major and minor scales, triads, and melody writing.

SCHAUM, JOHN W. *Piano Course* Belwin-Mills

Method Books	**Pre-A Book** (1945); **Books A-H** (1945).
Technic Books	**Technic Tricks, Books 1 & 2** (Bk. 1, 1949; Bk. 2, 1950); **Technic Through Melody, Books 1 & 2** (1952); **Progressive Piano Technic, Books 1 & 2** (1949); **Hanon-Schaum, Books 1 & 2** (1946); others.
Theory Books	**Theory Lessons, Books 1-3** (1946); **Harmony Lessons, Books 1 & 2** (1949); others.
Supplementary Books	Numerous books available (see the Belwin Catalog); Duet books, Christmas books, Pedal study books, Note spellers, Sight reading books, etc.–approximately 48 supplementary books are listed in the Belwin Catalog.
Literature Books	**Bach-Schaum, Books 1 & 2** (Bk. 1, 1945; Bk. 2, 1946); **Chopin-Schaum, Books 1 & 2** (Bk. 1, 1947; Bk. 2, 1948); others.
Adult Books	**Adult Piano Course, Books 1-3** (1946).

METHOD BOOKS

Beginning with the *Pre-A Book,* this series presents a typical middle C approach consisting of the following elements: single line melodies divided between the hands in the middle C position; rhythm confined (especially in the first few books) to 4/4, 3/4, 2/4; key selection confined primarily to C,G,F especially in the first few books; two-voice compositions appear early in the course; block chords are generally not used or explained, but later books use broken chord basses for harmonizations.

From a pedagogical viewpoint, a disturbing feature of this course is the lavish use of finger numbers given for almost every note throughout the course. The result is often "finger-number reading," rather than note reading.

THEORY BOOKS

Theory Lessons (three books) are written independently and are not necessarily intended to be used with the basic course. Printed in loose leaf form, this three-book series presents the following materials: recognition and drill on finger numbers; direction on the keyboard; alphabet practice (forward and backward); black key group drills; drawing clefs; drawing line and space notes; naming notes that correspond to the keys on the keyboard; writing note value names; recognizing sharps and flats; recognizing half steps and whole steps; drills on leger line notes; stem placement; drawing beams on a group of notes; playing mordents, trill performance.

Harmony Lessons (two books) present the following materials: *Book 1:* key signatures, building scales, melody transposition, intervals, and chords. *Book 2:* inversions of triads, cadences, dominant seventh chord, improvising bass accompaniments.

SCHAUM, JOHN W. ***Making Music at the Piano*** **Schaum Publications, Inc.**

Method Books	**Making Music at the Piano, Books 1-8** (Bks. 1 & 2, 1962); (Bks. 3 & 4, 1963; Bks. 5 & 6, 1964; Bks. 7 & 8, 1965).
Technic Books	**Fingerpower, Preparatory Book** (1970); **Books 1-5** (Bks. 1 & 2, 1963; Bks. 3 & 4, 1966); others.
Supplementary Books	**Rhythm & Blues, Books 1-3** by Wesley Schaum (Bks. 1 and 2, 1965; Bk. 3, 1971); Numerous other books are available (see the classified list of Schaum books listed on all the books in print)—available are: Christmas collections; Sacred albums (**Catholic Hymns, Jewish Folk & Holiday Songs**, etc.); others.
Literature Books	**American Sonatinas** 1963); **Best of Bach, Beethoven, Chopin, Mozart,** etc.; others.

METHOD BOOKS

Pedagogical Considerations

The progression of materials in this series is quite similar to the earlier Belwin publication (see previous). However, noticeable differences are (1) finger numbers used a bit more sparingly; (2) some block chords used and explained (I, V7, others); and (3) inclusion of key signatures, intervals, and some other theoretical information. This series appears more up-to-date (pictures and format) than the earlier 1945 Belwin publication.

STECHER, MELVIN, NORMAN HOROWITZ, and CLAIRE GORDON
Learning to Play **G. Schirmer**

Method Books	**Learning to Play, Books 1-4** (Bk. 1, 1962; Bks. 2-4, 1963).
Supplementary Books	**Playing to Learn, Books 1-4** (1965); **Rock with Jazz, Books 1-5** (1969); **In the Spirit of '76** (1973); others.

METHOD BOOKS

Both sets of books *(Learning to Play* and *Playing to Learn)* are patterned on the middle C concept. The presentation, however, is cast in a fresh, attractive style that is immediately appealing. The books include well-arranged familiar tunes, a sprinkling of duets, and a variety of original compositions. The open-page layout with attractive illustrations makes these eight books particularly inviting to children.

SUPPLEMENTARY BOOKS

Playing to Learn (see above). *Rock with Jazz* (five books) contains attractive solos redolent to today's pop sounds (mostly rock and blues). Each book becomes slightly more difficult, and each contains four appealing original compositions.

SWENSON, LUCILE BURNHOPE ***Discovering the Piano – The Multiple Key Approach*** **Theodore Presser Company**

Method Books	**Melody Rhymes Through All the Keys** (1970); **More Melody Rhymes Through All the Keys** (1973); **Melody Preludes Through the Keys** (1970); **Melody Modes and Moods Through All the Keys** (1970).
Supplementary Books	**Preludes and Nocturnes for Piano** (1973); **Piano Pieces Through All the Keys** (1975).
Study Book	**Study Guide and Goals for Teacher and Student** (1969, 1972).

METHOD BOOKS

The *Multiple Key Approach* books provide numerous reading experiences in all thirty major and minor keys. *Melody Rhymes Through All the Keys* contains single line melodies in 5-finger positions in all keys. Some suggestions are given for practice, harmonization and improvisation. *More Melody Rhymes Through All the Keys* is a companion book to *Melody Rhymes Through All the Keys* and includes thirty short melodies to read, harmonize and improvise. The cadence chord pattern I, IV, I, V7, I precedes each melody.

Melody Preludes Through the Keys contains sixty short preludes in all keys utilizing the 5-finger positions and cadence chords. *Melody Modes and Moods Through All the Keys* provides a study of scales (major and three forms of minor) which precede a piece in each key.

SUPPLEMENTARY BOOKS

Prelude and Nocturnes for the Piano consists of seven pieces in romantic style at about the intermediate level. *Piano Pieces Through All the Keys,* designed as a companion book to *Melody Modes and Moods Through All the Keys,* contains twenty-six solos and two duets for first and second year students.

STUDY BOOK

Valuable suggestions are offered in this ninety-six page book for teaching *The Multiple Key Approach.* Detailed lesson outlines show how to introduce reading, theory and keyboard harmony to beginners and transfer students through the use of the six books in this series. Lists of additional reading materials (by other publishers) covering a five-year study plan are included.

THOMPSON, JOHN ***Piano Course*** **Willis Music Co.**

Method Books	**MODERN PIANO COURSE: Teaching Little Fingers to Play** (1936); **The First Grade Book** (1936); **The Second Grade Book** (1937); **The Third Grade Book** (1938); **The Fourth Grade Book** (1940); **The Fifth Grade Book** (1942). **EASIEST PIANO COURSE: Parts 1-8** (Parts 1-3, 1955; Parts 4-6, 1956; • Part 7, 1957; Part 8, 1959). **MELODY ALL THE WAY: The Preparatory Book** (1949); **Book 1-A** (1949); **Book 1-B** (1949); **Book 2-A** (1949); **Book 2-B** (1949); **Book 3-A** (1951); **Book 3-B** (1951).
Technic Books	**Tiny Technics in Tuneful Form** (1958); **Very First Etudes** (1962); **First Grade Etudes** (1939); **Fifty Second Grade Studies** (1944); **Third Grade Velocity Studies** (1938); **Fourth Grade Etudes** (1941); **Keyboard Attacks** (1936); **Octave Book** (1947); **For the Left Hand Alone, Books 1 & 2** (Bk. 1, 1959; Bk. 2, 1962); **Thompson-Hanon, Books 1 & 2** (Bk. 1, 1937; Bk. 2, 1964); others.
Theory Books	**Theory Drill Games, Books 1-3** (Bks. 1 & 2, 1956; Bk. 3, 1957); **Note Speller** (1946); **Scale Speller** (1947); **Chord Speller** (1957).
Supplementary Books	**Chips from Other Blocks** (1965); **All on One Page, 24 Preludes in all Keys** (1960); Numerous other books are available (see the Willis Catalog) – available are: Christmas books, Hymn books, Duets, Recital collections, etc. – approximately 27 supplementary books are listed in the Willis Catalog.
Literature Books	**An Introduction to Bach** (1946); **Bach, Two-Part Inventions** (1927); **Themes from Piano Concertos** (1946); others.
Adult Books	**The Adult Preparatory Book** (1943); **Adult Piano Books 1 & 2** (1973).

Teaching Litle Fingers to Play: This model middle C course contains the following elements: introductory rote playing; step (interval of a second) and skip (interval of a third) concept; single line melodies divided between the hands for half the book; some note against note playing in the last half of the book; finger numbers for every note. Simple, tuneful melodies have made this book a longtime favorite.

The First Grade Book: The following elements are presented in this volume: primarily note against note pieces in 5-finger positions; a good explanation of phrasing two note slurred groups with an actual photo of the down-up wrist motion; scales in tetrachords; explanation of intervals; explanation of chords and inversions of chords; harmonizations confined essentially to broken chord accompaniments; tonality mostly in C,G,F (later also D, A, Bb, Eb, E, Ab); finger numbers given for almost every note.

The Second Grade Book: Consists of much more difficult pieces than the previous book, arrangements of some pieces by master composers, explanation of the pedals, explanation of major and minor scales, explanation of cadence chords, explanation of arpeggios, numerous technic drills.

The Third Grade Book: Consists of much more difficult pieces than the previous book; mostly arranged pieces by the following master composers: Bach, Bizet, Burgmüller, Clementi, Ellmenreich, Grieg, Handel, Liszt, others.

Books Four and *Five* are similar to *Book Three* being comprised primarily of piano literature.

WESTMORELAND, JOHN, and MARVIN KAHN ***Piano Course***
Belwin-Mills

Method Books	**Discovering the Keyboard, Books 1-3** (Bk. 1, 1963; Bks. 2 & 3, 1964).
Theory Books	**Theory Papers, Books 1-3** by Marvin Kahn (Bks. 1 & 2, 1955; Bk. 3, 1958).
Supplementary Books	**Note Speller and Ear Training Book** by Marvin Kahn (1959); others.

METHOD BOOKS

Designed either for private or group instruction, this three-book course incorporates many features similar to multi-key courses: 5-finger positions, melody with block chord harmonizations, key orientation, etc. The emphasis on rhythm, melody, and chording throughout this well-planned course is especially applicable to class teaching. A teacher's supplement for each book provides numerous helpful suggestions.

Book 1 (eighty pages) presents the following materials: rote experiences with 5-finger positions in block and broken chord fashion, directional reading drills (steps, skips, repeats), rhythm drills, chords (I, V7, IV), a variety of keys (both major and minor). Several written exercises are included.

Book 2 (sixty-four pages) presents the following materials: explanation of rests; continued emphasis on rhythm through a variety of rhythm drills; a variety of accompanying figures (broken chord bass, Alberti bass, etc.); scale fingering for the key of C; slur, phrase, tie indications; continued exploration of major and minor keys.

Book 3 (sixty-four pages) becomes progressively more difficult and reaches at least late third year level. New materials include: diminished and augmented triads; lead sheet type melodies to be accompanied with I, IV, and V7 chords; the chromatic scale; the whole tone scale; a sampling of major scales; major and minor key signatures; several of the easier classical standards (Bach's *Minuet in G,* Mozart's *Minuet in F,* etc.).

THEORY BOOKS

Printed in loose leaf form, *Theory Papers* (three books) offers a beginning through upper intermediate course in theory fundamentals. *Book 1,* for the beginning grade level student, presents such rudiments as: note reading, major and minor seconds and thirds, and accidentals. Directional reading is developed through several sight reading drills.

Book 2, for the lower intermediate grades, includes: chords and chord progressions, melodies for harmonizing, and various types of bass accompaniment patterns. Special emphasis is given to ear training and keyboard harmony drills.

Book 3, designed for the upper intermediate grades, includes drills in: normal chord progressions, harmonization of melodies, basic chords of the key and their function, altered chords, circle of fifths and dominant sevenths and other seventh chords, and major key signatures.

WEYBRIGHT, JUNE *Belwin Piano Method* **Belwin-Mills**

Method Books	**Piano Method, Books 1-5** (1964).
Technic Books	**Technic for Pianists, Books 1 & 2** (1947).
Theory Books	**Theory Worksheets, Sets 1-3** (Sets 1 & 2, 1964; Set 3, 1965).
Supplementary Books	**Mildly Contemporary, Books 1-3** (Bks. 1 & 2, 1964; Bk. 3, 1965); Christmas books; others (see the Belwin-Mills catalog).

METHOD BOOKS

This middle C course is written in a simple, attractive style for average beginners. One noticeable difference between this course and other middle C courses occurs in *Book 2*; the student is asked to write his own fingering in the boxes provided.

Key signatures in this course are referred to by the number of sharps or flats (Key Signature F sharp), rather than by the key name (Key of G). This presentation tends to confuse students and does not promote a feeling for key orientation.

Books 4 and *5* incorporate a great deal of simplified arrangements of master composers' works as well as some piano literature and technic drills.

TECHNIC BOOKS

Technic for Pianists, Book 1 consists of fifteen short etudes of first year level. Transposition is suggested for most of the 5-finger studies.

Book 2 contains twenty etudes of about second or third year levels. Broken chords, scale passages, extended positions and double thirds comprise the majority of the studies.

THEORY BOOKS

Theory Worksheets (three sets) consist of elementary through early intermediate music fundamental drills printed in loose leaf form. Writing note names, counts, intervals, chords, scales, key signatures, and various note values comprise the basic elements in the three books.

ZEPP, ARTHUR *Piano Course* **Pro Art Publications**

Kindergarten Books	**Musical Kindergarten Course, Books 1 & 2** by Zepp and Montague (1953).
Method Books	**Preparatory Book** (1965); **Books 1-5** (Bk. 1, 1965; Bk. 2, 1966; Bk. 3, 1967; Bk. 4, 1968; Bk. 5, 1971).
Technic Books	**Technic Patterns, Books 1-3** (Bk. 1, 1965; Bks. 2 & 3, 1971); **Let's Learn Major Scales and Chords** (1966); **Let's Get Technical** (1961).
Supplementary Books	**Little Songs and Solos** (1965); **Fun with Three Chords, Books 1 & 2** (1955); **Just Write** (1966); **Let's Transpose** (1960); **Fun with Four Chords** (1958); **Let's Learn Chords, Books 1 & 2** (1958); Christmas books; Duet books; Hymn books; others (see the Pro Art Catalog for a complete listing).

KINDERGARTEN BOOKS

The *Musical Kindergarten Course* (two books) offers only general rudiments of music and is not intended to be used solely for piano instruction. These two books are designed for children from four to six years old. The materials consist of songs, rhythmic activities, and elementary writing exercises. Some condensed suggestions to the teacher are included; however, two separate teacher books are also available: *Teacher's Books A* and *B*.

METHOD BOOKS

This series presents a basic middle C approach. Attractive features of this five-book series are: clear, logical presentations of new materials; numerous well-written duets; a good balance of original compositions and arrangements; and a practical inclusion of melody and chordal accompaniment (primarily I, IV, V7).

Explanations about theory (intervals, chords, etc.) are included and explained as needed; for a complete harmonic background, additional theory texts should be used.

TECHNIC BOOKS

Technic Patterns, Book 1, is a collection of first year 5-finger exercises using thirty-three different patterns. Most of the exercises are in C and move up the keyboard on the white keys. The book contains a useful combination of finger studies, chord drills, double note exercises, and some exercises for balance of tone. *Books 2* and *3* become progressively more difficult; many of the studies in these books are based on well-known tunes ("Swanee River," "Greensleeves," etc.).

Let's Learn Major Scales and Chords is a first year collection of easy studies mostly in 5-finger positions. *Let's Learn Minor Scales and Chords* is more difficult.

Let's Get Technical is about a fourth year collection of exercises for the development of arpeggios, octaves, double thirds, and other intermediate presentations.

SUPPLEMENTARY BOOKS

Little Songs and Solos is an attractive twenty page collection of supplementary first year reading pieces. The majority of the pieces are in 5-finger positions (mostly C, G, and F).

A number of the supplementary books appear under the title *Social Piano Course: Let's Learn Chords, Let's Improvise,* others. This title implies that the books in this series are for recreational use for the less serious student.

SPECIAL MATERIALS APART FROM A METHOD SERIES

Numerous teaching materials have been written on various subjects which are not part of a piano course. In many cases there are *special* subjects which are not dealt with in any depth in beginning piano courses. Therefore, these books have special merit and must be listed separately. Some of these books (and solos) are listed below, alphabetically, by the author's name.

BARRETT, MEREDITH — ***Note Speller, Theory Papers***
Edward Schuberth & Co.

Note Speller Books	**Note Speller for Keyboard, Books 1 & 2** (1971).
Theory Books	**Theory Papers, Levels 1-4** (1970).

NOTE SPELLER BOOKS

Most note spellers are part of a piano course (d'Auberge, Bastien, Kasschau, Schaum, Thompson, etc.); however, these two books are written independently and may be used with any piano course. *Book 1* materials include: grand staff and the keyboard, numbering lines and spaces, spelling words with note names, accidentals, spelling the notes used in well-known tunes, rhythm spelling, and some quizzes. *Book 2* materials include: ties and slurs, rests, rhythm spelling, leger line notes, key signatures, whole and half steps, intervals, dynamic and tempo terms, and some quizzes.

THEORY BOOKS

Compiled in loose leaf format, these *Theory Papers* are designed to be handed out one at a time by the teacher. The work is mostly written. Some information about instruments is given. Answer sheets are provided. *Level 1* materials include: the keyboard and staff, note spelling, rests, rhythm spelling, and accidentals. *Level 2* materials include: leger line notes, stemming notes, whole and half steps, and note spelling. *Level 3* materials include: note and rhythm spelling, intervals, major and minor chords, chord symbols, major scale formation, and key signatures. *Level 4* materials include: chord symbols, minor scale formation, diminished and dominant seventh chords, intervals, key signatures, and modal scales.

CANNEL, WARD, and FRED MARX ***How to Play the Piano Despite Years of Lessons*** **Crown & Bridge/Doubleday (1976)**

Designed as a do-it-yourself beginning or review book, the authors discuss beginning fundamentals as well as intermediate aspects such as chord structure, harmonic progressions, playing by ear, and playing various popular styles. Voluminous text is used and music examples are sprinkled throughout. The thrust seems to be given to explaining with minimal doing. The title of the book is catchy, and many copies will be sold because of it; however, one might expect more in the way of preparatory studies and complete pieces in course fashion rather than an extensive text encouraging the reader to employ the "think system" to learn how to play the piano.

CLARK, MARY ELIZABETH ***Now Hear This*** **Myklas Press**

Ear Training Books **Now Hear This: Student's Book, Books 1-4** (Bks. 1 & 2, 1972; Bks. 3 & 4, 1974).
Now Hear This: Teacher's Book, Books 1-4 (Bks. 1 & 2, 1972; Bks. 3 & 4, 1974).

EAR TRAINING BOOKS

This series may be used with students in any area of music (keyboard, vocal, instrumental). The activities include some simple theoretical explanations such as drawing notes, stems, note values, intervals, chords, etc. However, the main emphasis is in providing listening experiences for discernment such as high-low, steps-skips, intervals, rhythm patterns, same-different melodies, major-minor, modes, and augmented-diminished chords. Numerous excerpts from well-known tunes are used. Each book contains pre-test and post-test questions. An answer sheet for the entire book is given in the back of each book. This series is particularly useful in keyboard theory classes.

The *Teacher's Book* at each level includes the student page with written out musical examples for the teacher to play. In addition, suggestions and instructions for using the books are given.

CLARK, MARY ELIZABETH *Rhythm from Myklas* **Myklas Press**

Piano-Rhythm Books	**Rhythm from Myklas, Books 1-4** ed. by Mary Elizabeth Clark (1975).
Piano Ensemble-Rhythm Pieces	**Bom Bom Boogie** by Billie Ferrell, duet with rhythm parts (1975); **Leprechauns at Play** by Eloise Ristad, duet with rhythm parts (1975); **Ski Slope** by Barbara Ellen, duet with rhythm parts; **Carnival** by Streabbog, arr. by Clark, piano trio with rhythm parts (1975); **Schottische** by Klicker, arr. by Clark, piano quartet with rhythm parts.

PIANO-RHYTHM BOOKS

This four-book series contains graded pieces ranging from about first year through third year levels for piano solo with optional rhythm parts. A separate sheet is provided which contains such rhythm parts as sticks, triangle, tambourine, drum, wood block, bongos, sand blocks, and cymbals. The music is by various new composers. Especially useful for class teaching.

PIANO ENSEMBLE-RHYTHM PIECES

These five ensemble pieces are especially useful in class work. The grading for the three duets is approximately as follows: *Bom Bom Boogie,* upper intermediate; *Leprechauns at Play,* early intermediate; *Ski Slope,* early intermediate. The grading for *Carnival* (one piano, six hands) is approximately intermediate; *Schottische* (two pianos, eight hands), intermediate.

McINTOSH, EDITH *Theory and Musicianship* **Carl Fischer**

Theory Books	**Theory and Musicianship, Book 1** (1955); **Book 2, Part 1** (1956); **Book 2, Part 2** (1957); **Book 3, Part 1** (1967); **Book 3, Part 2** (1969).
Supplementary Theory Books	**Supplementary Work Sheets** (to *Book 2, Part 1)* **The Major Mode** (1966); **Supplementary Work Sheets** (to *Book 2, Part 2)* **The Minor Mode** (1966).

THEORY BOOKS

This series contains work sheets (lessons) in loose leaf form to give out at lessons.

Book 1 is designed for beginners presenting fundamentals such as the keyboard, staff, clefs, note values, note names, accidentals, half and whole steps, intervals, and music terms.

Book 2 (Parts 1 and 2) materials include: major scale formation, tetrachords, major key signatures, altered intervals, triads, arpeggios, minor scales, parallel scales, figured bass, inverted triads, and includes ear-training suggestions.

Book 3 (Parts 1 and 2) materials include: principles of four-part harmony, cadences, seventh chords, ninth chords, transposition, and modulation. The work approaches college level difficulty.

SUPPLEMENTARY THEORY BOOKS

Pedagogical Considerations

The *Supplementary Work Sheets* for *Book 2* (Parts 1 and 2) provides additional exercises for practical application.

McLEAN, EDWIN *Improvisation for the Pianist* **Myklas Press (1976)**

The pianist (intermediate or beyond) will enjoy making up his own music based on the examples given here such as ostinatos, concept pieces (using seconds, whole-tone scale, etc.), and jazz and blues. Explanations are concise and clear.

SHANNON, SUE *Composing at the Keys, Books 1 & 2* **Alfred Publishing Co. (1976)**

Although composition activities are suggested in some method books, usually these are to be made up, not notated. These excellent two books show the elementary student how to compose music and notate it using specific materials such as intervals, varieties of touch, motives, 5-finger patterns in various keys, triads, question-answer phrases, scales, and accompanying patterns. The materials are well organized and are useful in getting elementary students to think about how music is made and to begin learning how to make it themselves.

CRITERIA FOR THE EVALUATION OF PIANO COURSES

Upon close scrutiny it can be discovered that *all* method books have strong and weak features. No one series has a corner on the market containing a magic blueprint which will automatically produce first-rate pianists. However, there are some guidelines which may be used to determine quality features in method books and to help determine approaches that will assist the skilled teacher in developing knowledgeable young musicians. The following criteria are offered as general guidelines in evaluating beginning course books.[6]

Design and Format

1. Basic approach:
   a. Middle C?
   b. Multiple Key?
   c. Other?

2. Format:
   a. Is color used?
   b. Are pictures and/or drawings used?
   c. Is the music legible?
   d. Is the size of the printing realistic for younger students?
   e. Is the marginal material helpful without being cluttered, and is it written in children's language?
   f. Is the book long enough to be practical, but short enough to give the student a feeling of accomplishment?

[6]This material is based on a set of guidelines used by David Piersel, Black Hills State College, Spearfish, South Dakota. Used by Permission.

3. Sequence and progression of materials:
   a. Does the series as a whole keep the student advancing in a *steady* manner, not by spurts?

4. Purpose of the course:
   a. For individual study?
   b. For group study?
   c. For a combination of individual and group study?

5. Note range:
   a. Does the series encourage the student to gradually explore more and more of the keyboard?
   b. Is the range confined to a central portion of the keyboard?

6. Methods of counting:
   a. Numerically?
   b. Syllabically?
   c. Other?

7. Presentation of rhythm:
   a. What types of rhythms are encountered as the series progresses?

8. Chords and scales:
   a. How and when are these presented?
   b. Are both block and broken chords used?
   c. How many different types of chords are used?
   d. Are both major and minor scales presented?

9. Theory:
   a. Are intervals used?
   b. Are chords presented?
   c. Is keyboard harmony included?
   d. Is functional harmonization included?
   e. Is transposition emphasized?
   f. Is creative work included?
   g. If separate books are used, how well does it integrate with the basic course books?

10. Supplementary materials:
    a. What types and varieties are available as part of the course?
    b. Including all supplementary materials, does the course claim to be complete as is? (Few, if any, courses are "complete" in themselves.)

11. Form and structure:
    a. What opportunities are offered throughout the course to teach musical form?

12. Musicianship:
    a. Is the student given an opportunity to develop musicianship or creativeness?
    b. Is undue emphasis given merely to the mechanics of playing the piano?

Fundamental Features of Method Books

1. Is it a comprehensive course of study?
   a. Does it include a logical, practical *sight-reading program*?
   b. Does it include a sensible *theoretical program* based primarily on keyboard harmony?
   c. Does it include a practical *technical program* geared to basic keyboard fundamentals?

d. Does the course offer a variety of *supplementary books* for reinforced learning at different levels of advancement?

2. Does the music make sense to the student?
   a. Is the music tasteful and appealing to children?
   b. Is the rate of progression gradual rather than abrupt?

3. What will the student have learned upon completion of the course?
   a. Will he be able to sight-read fluently?
   b. Will he be musically literate in basic fundamentals?
   c. Will his technic be sufficient to allow him to perform various levels of repertoire accurately?

4. What length of study time will it take for the student to become musically literate?
   a. Two years?
   b. Three years?
   c. Never?

THE TEACHER'S ATTITUDE TOWARD NEW APPROACHES

It is immediately apparent that there are numerous ways of starting beginners. No one music educator or one set of books has all the answers. It is up to the teacher to produce knowledgeable students who become musically literate in fundamentals within a two- or three-year time span. To accomplish this task, the teacher now has an immense array of beginning materials (more so than at any other time) to devise an effective program for each student.

An open mind should be kept at all times toward new or innovative methods. However, this should in no way imply that one should blindly accept a new method simply because it is the latest publication available. The pros and cons should be weighed carefully before embarking on a new system merely for the sake of trying something new.

Materials are important, but in many instances teachers have produced skilled, finished pianists using what would appear to be almost any materials at hand. Conversely, other teachers appear to be using excellent materials, but unfortunately the results produced are consistently poor. Teachers should realize that a "method" alone will not do the job for them. Some teachers become so attached to one author's course that they will not consider using another method even for supplementary purposes. This is a very narrow view and unnecessarily limiting. Quality teaching is determined by the *results* the teacher achieves, not necessarily by the methods used. Nevertheless, a gifted teacher using superior materials will be most likely to produce outstanding results.

Times change, pupils' needs change, and basic goals need periodic reevaluation. Many teachers today accept the fact that the majority of their students will not play in Carnegie Hall or even become professional musicians. Therefore, a functional approach to teaching is a more practical path to follow at least for the first few years of a student's career. Elements of keyboard harmony, theory, improvisation, and creative work lay a better fundamental foundation than merely learning to play a few pieces each year. Many of the standard older methods simply do not include these elements of practical musicianship.

Teachers are not easily persuaded to change their basic approach to teaching, indeed many languish from "hardening of the attitudes." Part of the problem here is that of comfort. If the teacher is thoroughly familiar with one type of instruction, it takes work, study, and above all, experimentation and practice to learn another procedure. The good teacher continues to learn and experiment with new methods. Every "method" will have its day. The successful teacher will set realistic student goals and use every ounce of creativity and expertise available to achieve those goals.

FOR DISCUSSION AND ASSIGNMENT

1. List the goals you consider to be of prime importance which should be covered in a method series.
2. What basic function should a method series serve?
3. The two basic approaches to teaching beginners are the middle C method and the multiple key method. Describe these approaches. Alternatives to these two approaches are found in other methods; describe these.
4. A complete program consists of reading, repertoire, technique, and theory. Which of the method books surveyed provides these materials? Are these methods "complete," or should supplementary books be used?
5. Would you use one series exclusively, or would you use a variety of books by different authors?
6. Make a detailed survey of a piano method for a class report. Discuss presentations of notation, rhythm, intervals, chords, etc. Discuss basic concepts presented in the course and their development. Make a critical judgment as to the progression of materials. What will the student have learned upon completion of this course?
7. Using your knowledge gained from examination of numerous beginning methods, plan and write a first lesson presentation as it would appear in a printed course. Design it the way you would like to begin teaching. Teach it to another class member.

Part Two

Pedagogical Techniques

Very Young Beginners 5

Very Young Beginners

Ill. 5:1. Jane Smisor Bastien greeting a pre-school class.[1]

[1]A thirty minute pre-school demonstration by Jane Smisor Bastien is available on Super 8 film from the Neil A. Kjos Music Company.

Elementary instruction of all kinds is of inestimable value. TV programs such as *Sesame Street* and various Head Start programs have taught us the advantage of early learning. "It is only recently that research has shown that the first five years are the most important years for intellectual development . . ."[2] Introductory structured learning may aid the pre-school child to understand basic concepts and simple reasoning processes. In addition to introducing the youngster to music through piano study, the knowledge learned will transcend purely musical facts and may carry over into other learning experiences. Developmental sensory-motor skills assimilated through piano study will generally aid the child in coordination of his small and large muscles.

If the child is really talented he will have a head start and be playing interesting music by the time he is in the second or third grade. In contrast, by the time the average age beginner gets to this point, at about the fourth grade, he is already caught up in the homework, extracurricular activity syndrome.

One of the prime advantages of pre-school music instruction is that it will give the youngster a definite interest and activity aside from play and nursery school or kindergarten.

Teachers often are skeptical about pre-school piano instruction. Does a pre-school child have a sufficient concentration span to accomplish anything constructive at the piano? And, won't a child of seven or eight accomplish more, faster? These and other questions are sure to arise. However, if home conditions are conducive to learning, and if the youngster is *ready* to begin piano lessons, he will learn a great deal from early instruction.

When is a Child Ready for Lessons?

Not every pre-school child will be ready to begin piano instruction. The maturity level of four- and five-year-olds varies greatly. Girls generally are better coordinated and exhibit better dexterity than boys at an early age. Before rushing headlong into piano lessons, parents should ask themselves a number of questions concerning their child's readiness level:

1. Does he show an interest in learning to play the piano? Perhaps he tries to pick out melodies on the piano, or perhaps he sings well. He may also just enjoy listening to music.
2. Is his attention span long enough to practice ten minutes at a time?
3. Does he have fairly good coordination of his small muscles? If a parent has taught him to draw letters, numbers, or to write his name, is he able to handle a pencil fairly well? A parent who has taught a child any of these things probably will be willing to help him practice.
4. Does he take instruction well from the person who will be helping him at home? This could be a parent or an older sister or brother.
5. Does the child receive a great deal of satisfaction from learning new things? Is he eager to learn?

[2] Dr. Fitzhugh Dodson, *How to Parent* (New York: New American Library, Inc., 1970), p. 256. Reprinted by permission.

If a significant number of these prerequisites are missing, it is recommended that piano lessons be started later when conditions are more conducive for learning. The readiness age will vary with each individual child.

How Much Practice Assistance is Required for the Pre-school Child?

The parent who is interested in starting his young child in piano instruction often is not aware that the youngster will need supervised practice sessions. Since the pre-school child cannot read, the directions will have to be read to him. Even simple tasks will have to be organized, for probably this is the child's first experience in a structured learning situation, and he will need guidance, especially in the beginning. The following items are listed as a guide for efficient practice.

1. The pre-school child will need supervised practice periods every day for about ten or fifteen minutes. For a child whose attention span is shorter than average, two brief practice sessions are advised.
2. The person helping should sit near the youngster so he will not feel isolated while practicing.
3. It is ideal to set aside a specific time each day for practice when there will be no outside interference from family members, television, etc. Hopefully, this will establish the *habit* of practicing which is vital to the learning of any skill.
4. It is a good idea to keep a record of the practice time (in a music notebook), and explain to the child that his effort is enabling him to play well.

Piano lessons can and definitely should be an enjoyable experience for a young child, whenever he is ready for them. However, parents and teachers should be cautioned to begin formal instruction *only* when a child is able to absorb instruction and practice on a regular basis. Lessons will be enjoyable only with a certain amount of work on the part of both the child and parent(s).

PRIVATE OR GROUP INSTRUCTION?

Instruction on any level may be taught individually or as a group learning experience, and valid arguments may be made for either case. However, very young children function especially well in group activities, and they gain a great deal of satisfaction from friendly competition with their peers. The group provides impetus for numerous musical experiences such as rhythm drills, note flash card drills, creative work, listening games, and ensemble experience. Any or all of the experiences may be taught privately, but usually they are more effectively presented in a group situation. Children learn a great deal of information by observing a new idea passed from child to child as the new concept is repeated.

What is an Efficient Class Size for Pre-school Instruction?

Group lessons for young children should be limited to a small number of about four to six students to promote constructive achievement.

Youngsters have a way of changing the subject, interrupting, and losing concentrated thought. In working with smaller groups the teacher will have more flexibility in moving from one concept to another, and each child will have a better opportunity for individual participation and demonstration.

What General Activities Should be Presented in Group Lessons?

Young children will benefit from a combination of singing, playing, and writing activities. Singing games, singing finger numbers, and singing words to pieces will help train the ear and develop a sense of pitch. Playing the piano will be the main focal point of the lessons, but additional activities should be encouraged. Creative work, ensemble playing, and eurhythmics are beneficial for the pre-school child.

EQUIPMENT

Class interest and enthusiasm is heightened by employment of meaningful teaching aids. Flashcards, keyboards, musical games, and rhythm instruments have been standard fare for pre-school music classes for a number of years. However, numerous other class aids can be made by a creative teacher.

One of the most valuable reference sources for homemade materials is *The Carabo-Cone Method Series, Book 2* by Madeleine Carabo-Cone, MCA Music, 1971. Miss Carabo-Cone is an authority on teaching music to pre-school children, and she lists a quantity of imaginative, original class materials in this excellent book.

In addition to homemade equipment, inexpensive readymade materials may be purchased from a music store or school supply store. Some suggested classroom aids of both varieties are offered here.

Homemade Equipment

1. Letter flash cards (A,B,C,D,E,F,G) and number flash cards (1,2,3,4,5) are useful for playing games teaching recognition. The flash cards are made out of construction paper with white stenciled letters or numbers pasted on (Ill. 5:2).

Ill. 5:2. Alphabet letter flashcard recognition drill.

Ill. 5:3. Student arranging felt-backed cards in a rhythm sequence.

2. Felt-backed cards (letters, numbers, notes, rhythm patterns, etc.) may be made and placed on a large felt board to teach a variety of concepts (Ill. 5:3).

Ill. 5:4. Student throwing a note bean bag.

3. A Grand Staff may be drawn on a large piece of cardboard, or on the studio floor; and round felt bean bags may be made for throwing on the staff (Ills. 5:4 and 5:5).

Ill. 5:5. Students recognizing line and space notes on a cardboard staff.

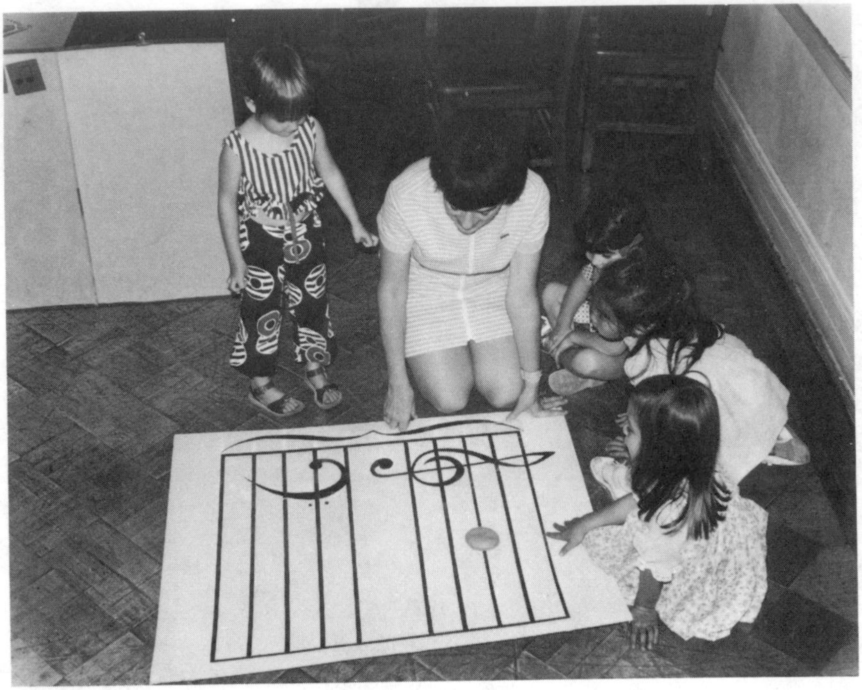

Ill. 5:6. Children walking on a homemade keyboard.[3]

[3] Photo courtesy of the Southern Methodist University, Dallas, Texas, pre-school department. Dorothy Brin Crocker, Director.

4. A large keyboard with letter names may be made (Ill. 5:6). Children can step on the keys and letters to create kinesthetic awareness for the topography of the keyboard. An even larger keyboard may be made (Ill. 5:7) which allows room for storage of rhythm instruments, musical games, etc.

Ill. 5:7. Large homemade keyboard.[4]

Ill. 5:8. Student arranging numbers on a magnetic board.

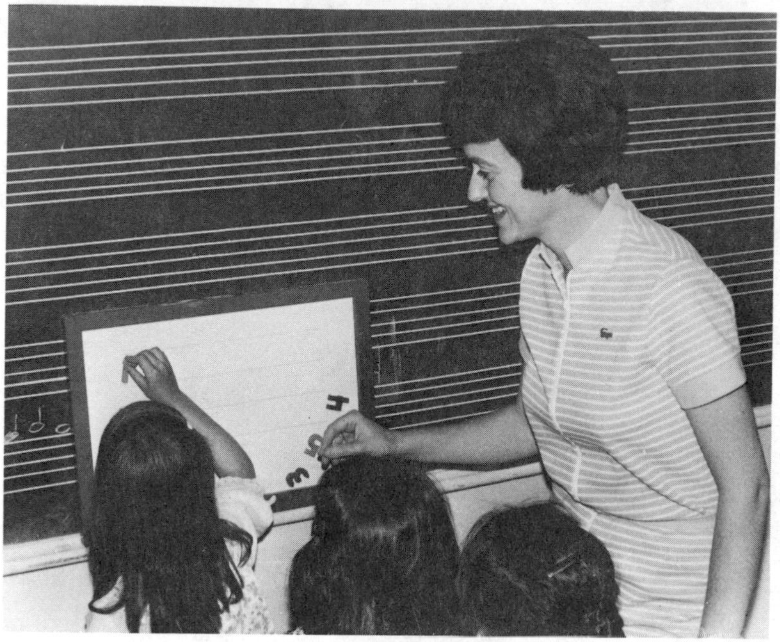

[4]Photo courtesy of the Keys of Melody Academy, Springfield, Illinois. Shirley Jo Trumper, Director.

1. A large felt board may be obtained at a toy store or a school supply store (Ill. 5:3).

2. A magnetic board may be obtained at a toy store or a school supply store (Ill. 5:8). Students may arrange letters or numbers in order on this board.

3. A blackboard of any size, portable or stationary, may be purchased from a toy store or a school supply store (Ill. 5:9).

Ill. 5:9. Students writing note values on a large blackboard.

Ill. 5:10. Plastic keyboard for demonstration.

4. A useful classroom aid is *Place a Note Magnetic Notefinder* which is distributed by G. Schirmer, Inc. It has moveable notes on a magnetic board. It may be obtained at a music store.

5. The *Magic Music Staff* is a helpful aid for individual staff work. It is a magic music slate with a wooden pencil. It may be obtained from Musicraft Industries, 2750 Stratford Road, Richmond, Virginia 23225.

6. Another useful aid is the *Wright-Way Note Finder* which is made by the Milo Wright Co. in Wichita, Kansas. It has a moveable note on a staff. It may be obtained at a music store.

7. For demonstration purposes a plastic keyboard is extremely useful. The one shown in Illustration 5:10 is distributed by Belwin-Mills and may be purchased at a music store.

8. Crayons, pencils, felt pens, etc. are necessary for class work (Ill. 5:11).

Ill. 5:11. Crayons for classwork.

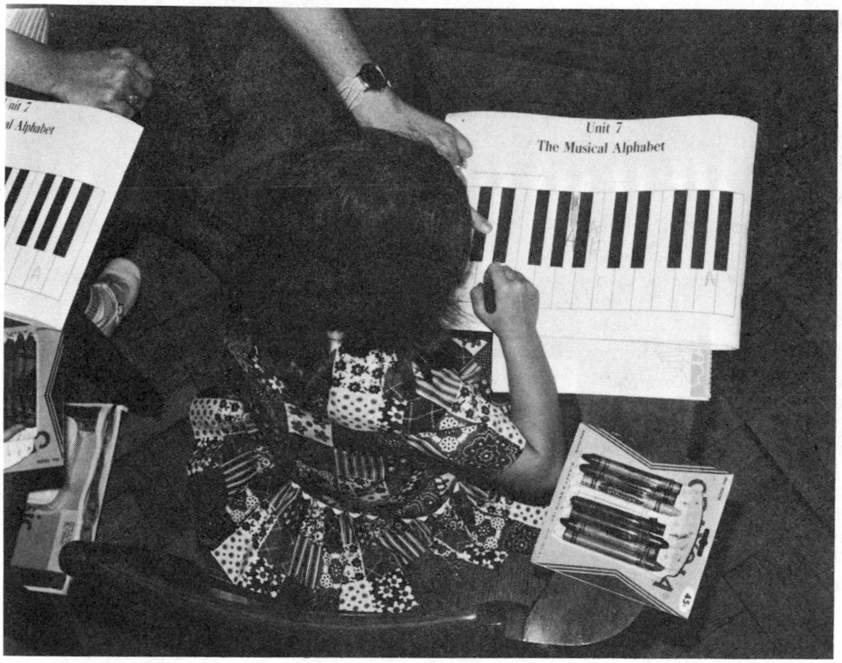

MUSIC READINESS PROGRAM

Lessons for young beginners (and average age beginners as well) should be a type of readiness program that will prepare children for the complete staff and its complexities.

Very Young Beginners

> Before any attempt is made to familiarize the child with the intricacies of printed music notation, it is absolutely essential that he experience a wide variety of musical activities. It is preposterous to expect a child to be interested in solving the printed score unless he has participated in and enjoyed many aspects of music. Programs of music reading are often begun too early, before the child has gained a sufficient variety and depth of musical experience.[5]

Numerous parallels may be drawn between the teaching of word reading and the teaching of music reading. An infant learns object names by imitating his parents, or his older brothers or sisters, and he expands his vocabulary as he matures. He is usually quite conversant before he begins to read. Kindergarten prepares him for reading by teaching him the alphabet, phonetic sounds, etc. Thus, he is using the language before actually reading the printed page. Conversely, children should be taught to play and make music before actually being confronted with the complexities of the printed page.

Contents of a Music Readiness Program

A number of exploratory conceptual experiences should be initiated in pre-school music classes. The following list represents specific items which provide a beneficial background towards the music reading goal.

1. Awareness of hands (right and left) and coordination between the two
2. Awareness of pitch—high and low sounds
3. Numbering of the fingers
4. The musical alphabet, both forward and backward
5. Rhythmic concepts
6. Pre-staffed notation
7. Creating simple melodies and rhythmic patterns
8. Listening to music and discovering fast and slow sounds, and loud and soft sounds

[5]Charles W. Heffernan, *Teaching Children to Read Music* (New York: Appleton-Century-Crofts, Educational Division, Meredith Corporation, 1968), p. 9. Reprinted by permission.

1. When first beginning to teach children right and left hands, do not face them, as this often confuses them. Turn your back to them, like a conductor, and say: "Right hand up, right hand down; left hand up, left hand down," etc. (Ill. 5:12).

2. Demonstrate high and low sounds on the piano. Then have the children come to the piano and play the following: a high key, a low key, a key in the middle of the piano, three high keys which go up, etc.

Ill. 5:12. Teacher demonstrating right hand with back to the group.

3. Have the children number their fingers by tracing their hands. Utilize different colors for perception growth—*i.e.*, color the third finger blue, the second finger red, etc.

Finger number games may be played by having the teacher hold up one or more fingers and having the children imitate (Ill. 5:13). Also, a cut-out hand is useful for demonstration (Ill. 5:14). Point to various fingers on the hand and ask the children to identify them.

Ill. 5:13. Children recognizing groups of two fingers.

Ill. 5:14. Children recognizing various fingers.[6]

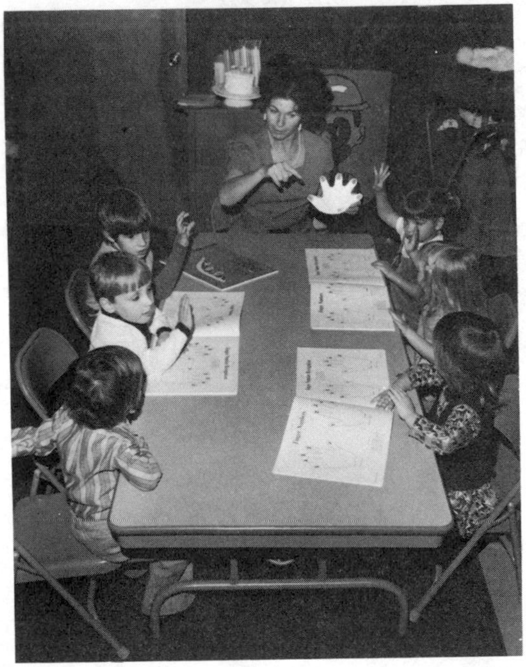

4. Tell the children that the musical alphabet names the white keys on the keyboard. At first let them trace the alphabet from an example given to them, as this will save time. Most youngsters have a good working knowledge of the alphabet (A-G), but often they are slow at drawing it. The teacher should move from student to student to assist when necessary (Ill. 5:15).

[6]Photo courtesy of the Keys of Melody Academy, Springfield, Illinois. Shirley Jo Trumper, Director.

Ill. 5:15. **Teacher helping the class write the musical alphabet.**

5. Rhythmic perception can be developed by clapping and counting note names (Ex. 5:1), and by stepping and counting note names (Ex. 5:2). Note names may be counted as follows:

Whole note, (looks like a football) count: "hold, that, whole, note."
Half note, (with a "clean face") count: "half note."
Quarter note, (with a "dirty face") count: "quar-ter."
Eighth notes, ("two quarters holding hands") count: "two-eighths."

Ex. 5:1. Counting and clapping note names.

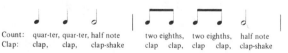

Count:	quar-ter,	quar-ter,	half note	two eighths,	two eighths,	half note
Clap:	clap,	clap,	clap-shake	clap clap,	clap clap,	clap-shake

Have the children count and step rhythms (Ex. 5:2). This will heighten their concept of long and short pulses.

Ex. 5:2. Counting and stepping note names.

Count:	quar-ter,	quar-ter,	half note	two eighths,	two eighths,	half note
Step:	step,	step,	step-slide	step step,	step step,	step-slide

Have one child play a note in rhythm at the piano and assist the others in class in chanting and clapping the counts (Ill. 5:16). If there is more than one piano in the room, allow one child to improvise a rhythm and ask the other students to imitate it on their piano.

Ill. 5:16. Playing and chanting rhythms.

Antiphonal response also is effective for teaching rhythm skills. In turn allow each child to be the leader. The leader "discovers" a rhythm, and the class responds in time:

Clapping and responding in rhythm can help teach the concept of continuity. Also, because the group activity is enjoyable, it can help lengthen attention span.

6. After the children know their finger numbers, know a few rhythms, and have been shown the groups of two and three black keys, they may play simple melodies in pre-staffed notation (Ex. 5:3).

Ex. 5:3. Pre-notated melody.[7]

[7]Example from *The Very Young Pianist, Book 1* by Jane Smisor Bastien (General Words and Music Co., 1970), p. 32.

From the beginning it is essential to develop an "eyes on the page" approach to reading (Ill. 5:17). This will establish the correct habit of watching the book and not looking down at the hands while playing.

Ill. 5:17. Student reading and watching only the book.

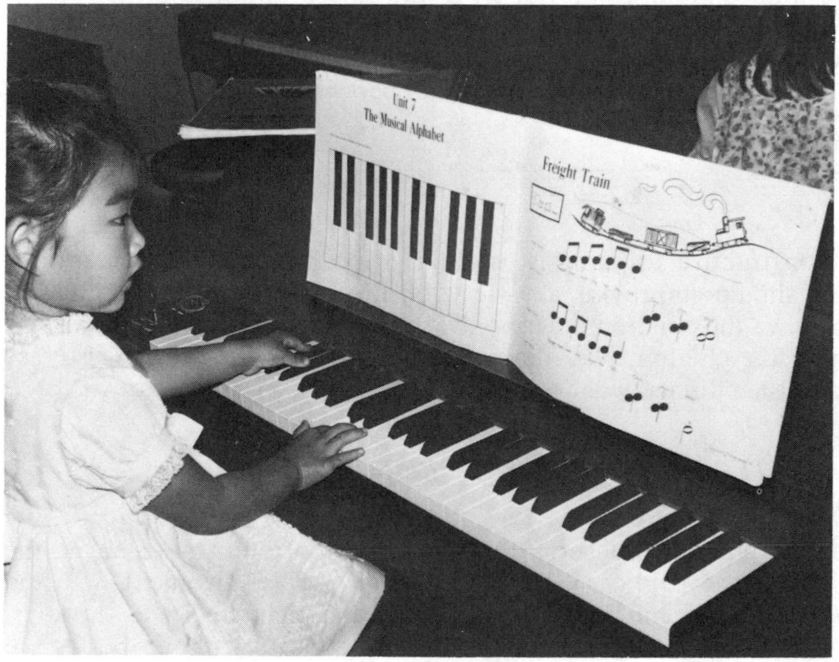

If the teacher has a piano for each student, the students may play their pre-reading pieces together for ensemble practice (Ill. 5:18). The teacher may move from student to student correcting hand position, notes, etc.

Ill. 5:18. Students playing in unison for ensemble practice.

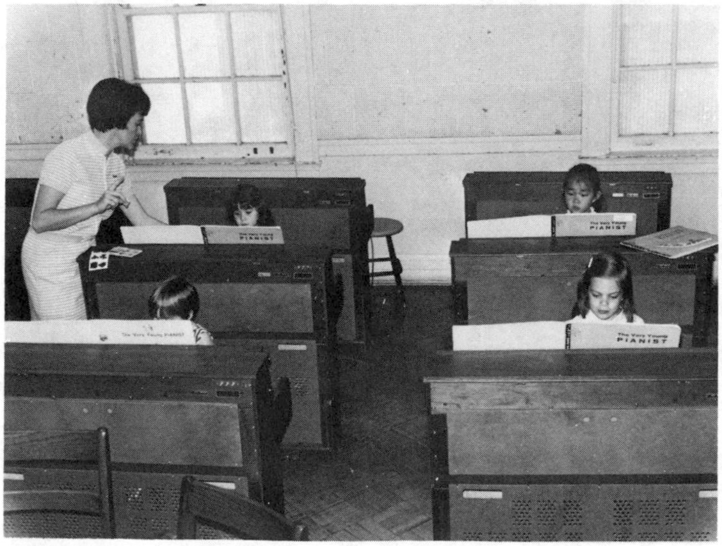

7. Most children are imaginative and inventive; generally, they gain a great deal of satisfaction from original experimentation. Learning by doing, or "discovery learning," is a methodology used today for beginning instruction. Children experiment with 5-finger positions, simple familiar melodies, and composed melodies until they arrive at the correct sound.

In the beginning the child may create his own melody to a nursery rhyme (Ex. 5:4). Improvisation such as this benefits the child both in the development of finger coordination and aural perception.

Ex. 5:4. A created melody.

Jack and Jill went up the hill to fetch a pail of wa - ter, etc.

8. Constructive listening is essential in promoting aural perception. The teacher should improvise a variety of pieces in various moods and tempos, and have the children describe the sound: thunder, raindrops, etc. In addition, have the children play their own heavy and light sounds (also fast and slow) and then discuss what they have played.

BASIC TECHNIQUE FOR THE PRE-SCHOOL CHILD

Height

One of the first concerns for the pre-school child is to sit at the proper height at the keyboard. He should be in proper alignment with the keys so that his hands and forearms will be in a straight line over the keys. An adjustable piano chair, cushions, or even several telephone books are recommended to raise the child to the correct level (Ill. 5:19).[8]

Ill. 5:19. Student using an adjustable chair with feet supported.

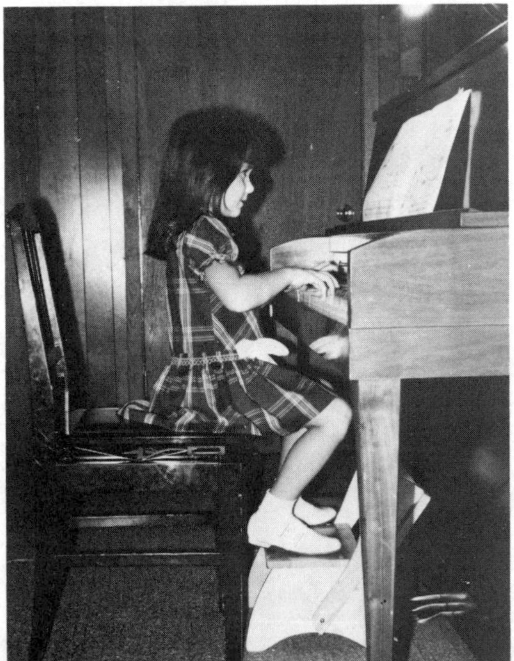

[8] An adjustable piano seat and footstool may be ordered from SMV Rogers Enp. (1731 Edenside Ave., Louisville, Kentucky 40204).

Once the child is raised to the correct height, a new problem arises. The child's feet are now swinging freely back and forth in the air unsupported. To balance the child, give him support, and give him assurance that he will not fall off the chair (bench), a footstool is recommended (Ill. 5:19).

Posture and Hand Position

Posture and hand position are prime concerns for students of all ages. The pre-school child must be shown how far to sit from the piano, to sit up "straight like a tree," and to hold his forearms in a straight line above the keys. Once these basics have been solved, the next consideration is hand position and finger placement. The hands, wrists, and forearms should be held in a straight line, and the fingers should be curved (Ill. 5:20). Tell the child to imagine he is holding a ball. This will give him a mental image of curved fingers. Flat fingers, wrists hanging down below the keys, and other unsatisfactory approaches should be discouraged from the beginning.

Ill. 5:20. Pre-school child with the correct hand position.

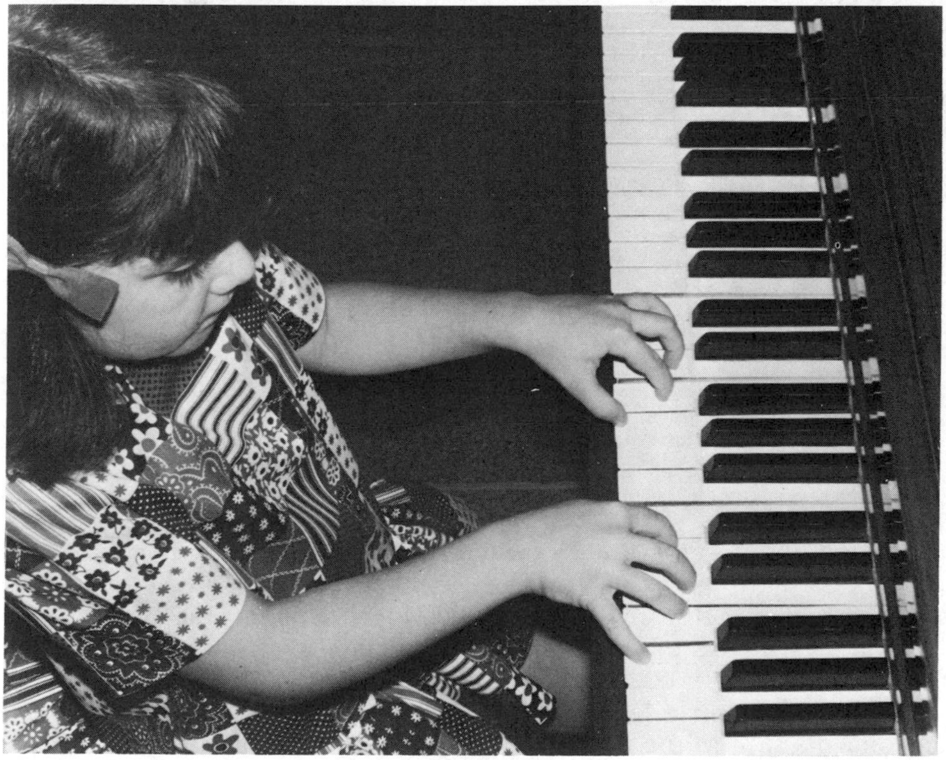

INCENTIVES AND REWARDS

Reward for work well done will produce a positive response from the members of a pre-school class. Praise is a necessary ingredient in the entire motivation factor. Young children respond to stars, stickers, candy, and prizes of all sorts (Ill. 5:21).

Ill. 5:21. Teacher awarding prizes to a pre-school class.

Many of the class activities often will be conducted as games; recognition and rewards for the winners will aid in promoting group spirit and enthusiasm. However, the teacher should be careful to measure the child on his own merits. If he receives a star for work well done, the award should be made on the basis of progress, not because he played better than another student.

Wall charts may be displayed listing various phases of the children's achievements such as the number of pieces learned and played for the class, the number of note names learned, etc.

A musical notebook is a valuable record of the child's progress. Achievement can be recorded in different colored markers in such areas as memorized pieces, recital participation, performances at the child's school, etc.

The pre-school program should be geared to reasonable goals. Class activities should be organized so that achievement of even the simplest tasks is possible. Incentives, rewards, praise, and encouragement will constitute a happy beginning.

METHOD BOOKS

Bastien, Jane Smisor The Very Young Pianist, Books 1-3 General Words and Music Co. (Bk. 1, 1970; Bks. 2 & 3, 1973), 72 pp. each

Book 1 in this series is designed primarily for kindergarten age children or first graders. The book provides a knowledge of numbers (one through five), letters (A through G), and presents short pieces in the keys of C and G. All the pieces are in pre-staffed notation. A great deal of writing is incorporated (mainly number and letter drills). Rhythm is stressed throughout, both 4/4 and 6/8 meter. The teacher's notes at the back of this book (and the other two books) offer many helpful suggestions for teaching young children. *Books 2* and *3* introduce notation and ten other keys, thus providing a basic introduction to the twelve 5-finger positions and tonic chords. The middle C position is also introduced in these two books, and duet accompaniments are provided for most of these pieces.

Clark, Frances, and Louise Goss The Music Tree: Time to Begin Summy-Birchard Co. (1973), 64 pp.

Although not specifically designed to be used for pre-school children, because of the pre-notated format in the first part of the book, it may be used for young beginners. Concepts include direction (high and low), rhythm, key names, dynamics, intervals, and other basics. The music staff is developed gradually from two lines. Duet accompaniments are provided for many of the brief pieces. A teacher's book is provided for the entire series: *Teaching the Music Tree.*

Crocker, Dorothy Brin Let's Discover Music: My First Piano Book and My First Writing Book Willis Music Co. (1971), 48 pp. each

These two companion books are specifically designed for pre-school children. Materials include recognition of the black key groups (two's and three's), rote songs, simple rhythms, finger numbers, the musical alphabet, and creating "discovery" pieces in the keys of C and G. The two books are to be used simultaneously and are to be correlated by the teacher according to the needs of the student. Some duet accompaniments are included.

Davidson, June, and Ardella Schaub Piano Progress, edited by Leo Podolsky Volkwein Bros, Inc. (1968), 32 pp.

Designed as a pre-primer for young beginners, the book presents the following materials: distinction between the two and three black key groups, finger numbers, rote songs, the musical alphabet, and elementary notation. Some written work is included.

Duckworth, Guy Keyboard Explorer M-F Co. (1963), 40 pp.

The book is presented primarily in pre-notated form and incorporates directional reading, recurring rhythm patterns, and creative work ("discovery" learning) into a meaningful whole. Rhythm is taught by clapping and chanting long and short syllabic sounds that occur in nursery rhymes and folk melodies. All twelve major pentachord positions (and a few minors) are taught by discovering the correct sounds and adjusting to the corresponding keyboard patterns. An attractive LP record accompanies the book which presents all the songs as they should sound so the student will have a guide to follow during practice periods.

Gillock, William Piano all the Way, Level 1-A Willis Music Co. (1969), 32 pp.

Although not written specifically for the pre-school beginner, the general format of this book is applicable to young beginners. Pre-notated melodies are used throughout. Materials include: learning the geography of the keyboard (high-low-middle, and the patterns of black and white keys); learning rhythm (exclusively 4/4 and 3/4) through a concept of pulse; and learning steps, skips, and repeated notes which are incorporated in the pre-notated songs. The melodies are played entirely on the two and three black key groups. Some duet accompaniments are included.

Kirby, Kelly The Kelly Kirby Kindergarten Piano Method, Books 1-4 The Frederick Harris Music Co., Ltd. (1939), 20 pp. each

This old-timer presents a basic middle C approach on oversized staffs. Some information about composers, some written work, and some cut-outs for pasting are provided. A teacher's manual named *The Key to Music Teaching* is available.

Pace, Helen Music for Moppets Lee Roberts/G. Schirmer, Inc. (1971), 48 pp.

Specifically designed for pre-schoolers, this book includes the following materials: recognition of the black key groups, ear training activities, question and answer phrases, and creative work. A study guide for teachers (*Teacher's Manual,* 1972, 68 pages) gives a page by page account of suggested class activities, uses for rhythm and melody instruments, and generally offers helpful directions for the use of the student book.

Richter, Ada Pre-School and Kindergarten Book Witmark/Warner Bros. Publications (1954), 32 pp.

This book develops only a few beginning concepts offering youngsters a micro-music-readiness program. The concept of pitch (low, middle, high) is explored in three registers on the keyboard: the C below middle C, middle C, and the C above middle C. Other concepts explored are: learning finger numbers, line and space notes (to distinguish between these), treble and bass clefs, and bar lines. The notes and rhythm are to be taught by rote. C 5-finger positions are used. Duet accompaniments are provided.

Steck, Sue Ann Music for the Mini, Lesson Book (Book 1) Heritage Music Press (1976), 32 pp.

The beginner is introduced to short melodies written at first on the staff with alphabet letters. Longer rhythmic values are indicated by numbers. At first the right hand 5-finger C position is used. Major key groups are shown on page 17, notation begins on page 19, and the remainder of the book contains pieces written in the middle C position. (Companion books are listed below).

Zepp, Arthur, and Montague Musical Kindergarten Course, Books 1 and 2 Pro Art Publications, Inc. (1953), 42 pp. each

These two books offer only general rudiments of music and are not intended to be used solely for piano instruction. They are designed for children from four to six years old. The materials consist of songs, rhythmic activities, and elementary writing exercises. Some condensed suggestions to the teacher are included; however, two separate teacher books are also available: *Teacher's Book A* and *Teacher's Book B.*

SUPPLEMENTARY BOOKS

Bastien, Jane Smisor Pre-Reading Christmas Carols General Words and Music Co. (1977), 16 pp.

The carols are in pre-staffed notation for the student, with notated teacher accompaniments.

Bastien, Jane Smisor Pre-Reading Duets, Books 1-3 General Words and Music Co. (1977), 16 pp. each

These books contain easy pre-staffed pieces for the student and notated teacher parts.

Bastien, Jane Smisor Pre-Reading Solos General Words and Music Co. (1971), 16 pp.

The twelve pre-notated solos contained in this collection are designed as supplementary reading material. The compositions are based on 5-finger positions and may be played in any key determined by the teacher or student. Notation is provided for the teacher on each page in the key of C; however, the student is encouraged to select other keys for study and performance. The songs incorporate 4/4 and 6/8 meter, chords (I and V7), and a variety of styles and moods.

Bastien, Jane Smisor Solos for the Very Young Pianist, Books 1 and 2 General Words and Music Co. (Bk. 1, 1974; Bk. 2, 1976), 16 pp. each

These books contain easy notated pieces in a variety of styles and moods which may be used for study and recital.

Bastien, Jane Smisor The Very Young Pianist Listens and Creates, Books 1-3 General Words and Music Co. (1975), 40 pp. each

These books provide an ear-training course which may be used separately or as a companion series to *The Very Young Pianist* course. The activities allow the child to listen to various sounds on the keyboard as well as to create his own music. Teacher's notes are provided for each book.

Bastien, Jane Smisor The Very Young Pianist Workbook, Parts A and B General Words and Music Co. (1973), 32 pp. each

These two books provide additional written drills and are correlated with the basic books in the following manner: *Workbook A* correlates with *The Very Young Pianist, Book 2; Workbook B* correlates with *The Very Young Pianist, Book 3.*

McCall, Adeline Timothy's Tunes Boston Music Co. (1943), 80 pp.

Designed especially for pre-school children, this attractive book presents right hand melodies printed in number form. The melodies are to be played from the numbers which correspond to scale degree tones (one through eight). Although dashes are given under the numbers to represent tone duration, the songs are meant to be taught by rote. Clever duet accompaniments are provided for all the songs.

Pace, Helen Moppets' Flash Cards Lee Roberts/G. Schirmer, Inc. (1974), 24 cards

These cards are designed to be used in group activity games. Included are steps-skips, note and rest values, and some music signs.

Pace, Helen Moppets' Rhythms and Rhymes Lee Roberts/G. Schirmer, Inc. (1974), 48 pp.

Educational rhythmic songs and games for group participation are provided in the student book. Explanations and suggestions are provided in the *Teacher's Book* (1974, 32 pages).

Richter, Ada Stick-a-Note Book Witmark/Warner Bros. Publications (1960), 28 pp.

Designed as an elementary workbook for children from pre-school age through second grade, the book presents drills in line and space notes. Notes and alphabet numbers are to be torn out from the back of the book and stuck on the corresponding pages. The notes are in stamp form to be moistened and stuck on. The C 5-finger position is stressed throughout, mostly in the middle register of the keyboard.

Schaum, John W. Keyboard Talent Hunt Schaum Publications, Inc. (1967), 24 pp.

This book is similar to *Timothy's Tunes* in that only right hand melodies are used. The melodies are to be taught by rote. The student reads alphabet letters. Dashes are given after letters which get an extra beat. Although the notation is given only for the right hand in the teacher's music, the directions suggest that each piece should be played first with the right hand, then with the left hand. Middle C position is used for most of the pieces. Duet accompaniments are provided for all the songs.

Steck, Sue Ann **Music for the Mini, Theory Book (Book 2);** **Just for Fun (Book 3);** **Teacher's Manual (Book 4)** **Heritage Music Press (1976)**

The *Theory Book* (40 pages) contains written studies correlated to materials in the *Lesson Book. Just for Fun* (32 pages) contains supplementary songs. The *Teacher's Manual* (32 pages) offers suggestions for coordinating and teaching the series.

SUMMARY

Evidence is increasing that a child's early years are the optimum period of intellectual growth in his lifetime. Jean Piaget, the noted Swiss psychologist, devoted thirty years to the study of children's thinking. He ascertained that children progress through specific learning stages in which critical thinking abilities advance in ordered sequence. He labeled the "sensory-motor" period, from birth to about two years, and the "pre-operational" period, from two to seven years. During the "pre-operational" period the child begins to think and respond to his environment through symbols such as language, drawings, dramatic play, and dreams. It is during this period that music instruction may be meaningful to the child who is ready for lessons. With proper assistance at home, the pre-school child can learn a number of important facts and basic skills which will form a foundation for further study.

FOR DISCUSSION AND ASSIGNMENT

1. Observe a pre-school class taught by someone in your area. Report on the following items: the type of instruction offered (readiness program or piano lessons); the size of the class; the equipment used; the type of class activities presented; the effectiveness of the program.
2. What advantages do pre-school beginners have over those who begin lessons later? Are there any disadvantages?
3. Should all pre-school children be exposed to music instruction?
4. Do you think you would like working with pre-school children? Give reasons pro and con.

FOR FURTHER READING

Arnoff, Frances Webber. *Music and Young Children.* New York: Holt, Rinehart, and Winston, Inc., 1969. Although directed to classroom teachers, there is an abundance of general information that would be helpful for piano teachers interested in this age group.Contains a useful bibliography.

Carabo-Cone, Madeleine. *A Sensory-Motor Approach to Music Learning, Book 1–Primary Concepts.* New York: MCA Music, 1969. Paper. Numerous helpful suggestions are offered in this book which will assist the teacher interested in learning new pre-school class activities.

———. *A Sensory-Motor Approach to Music Learning, Book 2–Materials.* New York: MCA Music, 1971. Paper. Various class materials are discussed and specific directions for their use are given in this valuable book on pre-school music activities.

———. *A Sensory-Motor Approach to Music Learning, Book 3 – Identification Activities.* New York: MCA Music, 1973. Paper. Specific class activities are described for identifying such music fundamentals as (1) landmarks (primarily: F-line, bass clef; middle C; and G-line, treble clef), (2) staff, and (3) time values. Photos of class activities and equipment enhance this useful book on pre-school activites.

Carabo-Cone, Madeleine, and Beatrice Royt. *How to Help Children Learn Music.* New York: Harper and Brothers, 1953. Although dated by the photos, many useful ideas are to be found in this book regarding pre-school materials and creative class activities.

Dodson, Dr. Fitzhugh. *How to Parent.* New York: Signet/The New American Library, Inc., 1970. PB. Although this book is directed to parents, it has direct application for teachers interested in pre-school children. The book deals only with children from infancy through pre-school age. Of special interest to the teacher are the extensive appendices dealing with selecting good books, educational toys, play equipment, and records for children. The book is direct and well written and is a valuable general reference source.

Findlay, Elsa. *Rhythm and Movement, Applications of Dalcroze Eurhythmics.* Evanston, Ill.: Summy-Birchard Co., 1971. Paper. Principles of the Dalcroze method are clearly described regarding "The Child and Rhythm." "Tempo," "Dynamics," "Phrase and Form," etc., through text, illustrations, and musical examples. Valuable suggestions for class activities relating movement to music.

Heffernan, Charles. *Teaching Children to Read Music.* New York: Appleton-Century-Crofts, 1968. PB. Teachers will find much useful information contained in this brief volume. For one interested in pre-school activities, Chapter 2, "The Readiness Program," is of special interest.

Nordoff, Paul, and Clive Robbins. *Music Therapy in Special Education.* New York: John Day Co., 1971. Although designed especially for handicapped children, this book offers numerous helpful suggestions for class activities. Various subjects include suggestions for singing games, uses of resonator bells, suggestions for instrumental activities, explanation of rhythm instruments and their use in class–all of which may be adapted to general pre-school music classes.

Nursery School Portfolio. James L. Hymes, Jr., *et al.* Association for Childhood Education International (3615 Wisconsin Avenue, N.W., Washington, D.C. 20016), 1969. Paper portfolio. The leaflets contained in this portfolio constitute important readings on various aspects of pre-school classes. Leaflets such as "How Young Children Learn," "The Arts," "Developing a Positive Self-Concept," and "Discipline," will be of interest to teachers working with very young children.

Average Age Beginners 6

Beginning piano instruction generally is given to children varying in age from about seven to eleven years old. The majority of beginners fall into this category for a number of reasons: children request lessons at different ages; parents purchase pianos at varying times; and parents and teachers have diverse opinions regarding an optimum beginning age.

Many of the same prerequisites for piano study discussed in the previous chapter apply to average age beginners regarding factors such as interest, concentration span, motivation, and musical aptitude. An interview is necessary to determine whether or not the child is ready for the structured lesson experience. Details of interviewing were discussed in Chapter 2—"How to Interview Prospective Students."

In the previous chapter advantages for very young beginners were discussed. No hard and fast rule can be given concerning the best age at which to begin. Some children may be ready to begin as early as five, others would do better to wait until they are nine or ten. Gifted children especially benefit from an early beginning. For children of average ability, however, the traditional starting age of seven to eleven will suffice.

PARENTAL SUPERVISION

Most children from the second grade on are proficient in reading. Although some of the younger ones (seven- or eight-year-olds) may be a little slow, most of them are beginning to be good readers, and they will be able to work at piano lessons on their own; hopefully they will be able to read the directions in their first piano book. However, beginners should not be left entirely on their own. Even a third, fourth, or fifth grade beginner should have some parental supervision in areas such as scheduling practice periods, checking on work in progress, creating an enthusiastic atmosphere for practice, and assisting when problems arise.

> In the case of smaller children the cooperation of the parents is essential. It is a good plan for the mother to attend an occasional lesson to see how the child should sit, and to get an idea of the work that is being done. These attendances

> should not be too frequent, as children are usually much easier to teach when mother is not there [amen!]. She can also have quite a paralyzing effect upon the child by chipping in at intervals during the lesson with such remarks as "He could play it perfectly well at home," or (to the child), "There, you see, I told you you were doing it all wrong."[1]

Parental cooperation and periodic supervision is extremely important in maintaining a healthy rapport between all parties concerned—the student, parents, and teacher. For an insight into specific solutions to many problems that often arise from this triangle, parents will profit by reading *A Parent's Guide to Piano Lessons* by James Bastien (Kjos West, 1976). Suggestions offered include "Helping Your Beginner," "Practice Suggestions," and the pros and cons of "Recitals, Contests, Festivals and Auditions."

GROUP OR PRIVATE INSTRUCTION?

Traditionally, average age beginners have been taught privately on a one to one basis. Students taught in this fashion, without any class participation, often lose interest after a year or two mainly because there is no external motivating force other than the teacher. True, the "yearly recital," plus auditions and competitions, do offer some goals throughout the school year, but these sparsely spaced activities cannot take the place of weekly class sessions.

A general lack of stimulation and motivation often experienced in the traditional piano lessons frequently has produced the following results: (1) some interest in practicing in the beginning, but sharply diminishing as lessons continue; (2) a reluctance to play for others because of shyness; (3) less over-all achievement compared to those who have benefited from some class participation; (4) quitting piano rather than going on, only to comment later in life, "I wish someone would have made me continue piano lessons."

Class lessons frequently motivate students in a positive manner. Group participation can be an effective means of generating enthusiasm for piano study. Students so motivated do continue to take lessons and enjoy them, are willing to play for others, and do not have to be forced to continue piano lessons.[2]

Since class sessions provide a significant degree of motivation, the teacher should make an effort to schedule some group meetings. Even infrequent get-togethers—once a month, bi-monthly, etc.—will provide incentive, enthusiasm, and lasting rewards. Whatever the combination of private and class lessons the teacher offers, over-all student achievement will be upgraded.

[1] Joan Last, *The Young Pianist* (London: Oxford University Press, 1954), pp. 5-6. Reprinted by permission.

[2] A number of dramatic photos of class activities are shown in an article by Barbara Weggeland Smith in *Clavier* (Vol. X, No. 9, December, 1971). The article is titled, "What Really is Going on in Class Piano?" The pictures tell the story and show some of the activities that occur in the piano class. The pictures also reveal the enthusiasm of the group while they are engaged in the activities.

It is impossible to prepare an exact blue print that would fit the needs of each student in the all-important first lesson. However, some general guidelines may be considered.

First, a congenial rapport should be established between the student and teacher. A positive attitude is: "We are both in this thing together, so let's make the most out of it and enjoy doing it." The well-known English pedagogue, Hetty Bolton, feels that "The principal thing is that we are getting to know a person, and that this person is beginning to form an impression of us. This personal contact is the most important thing in the first lesson."[3]

Begin by putting the child at ease by asking him some simple questions that he will be able to answer easily: "Where do you go to school? Does your mother play the piano?"–etc.

After the preliminaries, when the child is at ease, present him with his assignment book and his first piano book (some teachers prefer not to use a book for the first few lessons). Whatever method of instruction you are using, present the following concepts:

1. Explain right hand, left hand, and how the fingers are numbered.

2. Explain the pattern of keys on the keyboard (black keys in groups of two's and three's).

3. Show the correct posture and how the position of the hands should be at the keyboard (see Ill. 5:20 in the previous chapter).

4. Demonstrate how and why the fingers should be curved; show how the fingers should play on the fleshy part of the finger-tips (explain why fingernails must be kept cut short).

Each lesson, even the first, should contain a balanced program of varied activities. The student should be exposed to four basic categories: (1) *repertoire*, (2) *technique*, (3) *sight-reading*, and (4) *theory*.

1. The repertoire in the beginning will probably be in the form of pre-notated songs (Ex. 6:1). Pre-notated melodies allow the student to play and make music from the onset without the hindrance of learning notation simultaneously. Many teachers believe in "playing" first and learning to read later. Abby Whiteside "was firmly convinced that aural learning should be nurtured by every possible means–learning by rote, transposition, etc., at the beginning of music study. She even felt that, for this purpose, the teacher should postpone as long as possible learning to read music."[4] This manner of beginning is pedagogically sound and supported by several authors on child learning. Jean Piaget, the Swiss child psychologist, found in his studies with children that "There should be aural, kinesthetic, and visual imagery before the symbols of music are introduced . . . "[5]

[3]Hetty Bolton, *On Teaching the Piano* (London: Novello and Co., Ltd., 1954), p. 18.

[4]Abby Whiteside, *Mastering the Chopin Etudes and Other Essays* (New York: Charles Scribner's Sons, 1969), p. 197.

[5]Sister Cecilia Schmitt, "The Thought-Life of the Young Child," *Music Educators Journal*, Vol. 58, No. 4 (December, 1971), p. 24.

Ex. 6:1. Pre-notated melody.[6]

(Position: three black keys)

R.H. 3 2 1 3 2 1 1 1 1 1 2 2 2 2 3 2 1

Hot Cross Buns, Hot Cross Buns, One a pen - ny, Two a pen - ny, Hot Cross Buns!

2. Technique, in the beginning, should be given as an aid to developing finger coordination. The weak fingers of a beginner will benefit from simple exercises that may be devised by the teacher (Ex. 6:2).

Ex. 6:2. Beginning exercise.

3. Sight-reading is a skill that may be initiated at the first lesson. While reading, the student should maintain visual contact with the music. He should not be looking up and down between hands and music. Even at the onset an intellectual approach to reading should be established that will insure continuous playing without stumbling. The following items are listed to aid a child when reading a new piece.

a. Indicate the rhythm (slow and fast parts) before beginning to play; sing the words and clap the rhythm to the song.
b. "Play" the song in the air (or on a closed keyboard cover) singing the finger numbers aloud while moving the fingers.
c. Find the position for both hands before beginning to play.
d. Keep eyes on the book.
e. Play straight through singing the finger numbers or words while playing.

4. Theory, for the first lesson, may be no more than discovering that music is comprised of *melody* (the tune in "Hot Cross Buns"); *rhythm* (the slow and fast parts in "Hot Cross Buns"); and *harmony*. For this last item, harmony, have the student sample a number of triads; he may then sing a familiar song like "The Farmer in the Dell" and accompany himself by playing the tonic chord.

Much of the material presented at the first lesson will be based on whatever method book you are using. Hopefully, several concepts will be introduced. Since the material presented will be new to the student, make sure he understands clearly of what his lesson consists. Be specific in your lessons. Write down the assignment in a music notebook (one large enough

[6]Example from *Pre-Reading Experiences* by Jane Smisor Bastien (General Words and Music Co., 1963), p.8.

that will not get lost!). Tell him what you expect of him regarding practice time—about thirty minutes a day is sufficient in the beginning. Most importantly, tell him *how* you want him to practice; spell out practice suggestions. Describe clearly what you hope he will accomplish by the next lesson.

Throughout the first lesson be pleasant and encouraging. Ruth Edwards states: "The teacher's enthusiasm for the project in hand is first conveyed to the child through the channel of simple friendliness."[7] The beginner who senses that this is going to be great fun will be eager to return to his next lesson. The student, above all, needs reassurance. He needs to feel that the teacher *believes* that he will succeed. While this piano playing "game" requires serious application and responsibility, it can also be creative and pleasant.

FIRST YEAR MUSIC PROGRAM

The beginning piano student is faced with learning numerous concepts during the first year of lessons. Fundamentals of reading, rhythm, technique, and elementary theory must be assimilated during this period. Comprehension of these new skills will depend largely on an intelligent presentation which encourages the student to think and reason. Good habits well begun will form a solid foundation on which to build. Since first impressions are likely to be lasting, it is extremely important that the student *understands* what he is doing. Good or bad, the habits first learned are likely to be those which will endure.

Teaching Beginners to Read

Pre-reading

The student who has been exposed to a period of pre-reading, as discussed previously in the first lesson, will be more likely to comprehend the complexities of the staff when it is presented. The student will have already played and read directionally, he will have established an "eyes on the page" approach to reading, and he will have actually played the piano for a period of time without being confronted with the problem of learning notation concurrently. Most of the newer method books begin in this fashion—Bastien, Clark, Duckworth, Gillock, Olson, Pace, Palmer, Lyke and Blatter[8]—to name a few. The period of keyboard orientation varies with each of these publications. Some books require a pre-reading period as short as a week or two, others require up to two months or more. Whatever the duration, the time spent in the beginning to establish finger coordination and a feeling for the topography of the keyboard is well worth the effort.

Before beginning to read directionally on the staff, it is helpful to experience this sensation on the keyboard. To begin thinking directionally, have the student *play* skips and steps on the keyboard (Ex. 6:3). Explain to the student that a *skip* skips a finger and skips a letter in the musical

[7]Ruth Edwards, *The Compleat Music Teacher* (Los Altos, Calif.: Geron-X, Inc., 1970), p. 39.

[8]James B. Lyke and Marilyn D. Blatter, *Piano from A to G.* (Champaign, Ill.: Media Press, 1971).

alphabet; a *step* plays the next finger and is the next letter in the musical alphabet.

Ex. 6:3. Skip and step drill.[9]

Directions:

Find the position. Keep eyes on the book. Play the following skips and steps answering each question ALOUD. If you disagree with the answer given at the end of the exercise, repeat the exercise and correct your mistake.

Key of C

1. Play C
2. Up a skip?
3. Up a step?
4. Down a skip?
5. Up a step?

E

Drills of this sort may be taught easily without a book. The teacher can invent the drills and incorporate them into beginning lessons. If a book is not used, have the student watch you, not his hands; or he may close his eyes while hearing the directions. This study should be done by feel only. It is important for the student to have a mental picture of the keyboard, and this drill will help accomplish that desired goal.

Pre-reading experiences such as playing 5-finger positions, chords, and pre-reading solos in a variety of keys, prepares the student for reading notation. After a period of pre-reading, the student is ready to transfer his knowledge of keyboard relationships to the staff.

Directional Reading

Reading by shapes and contours is an important component in the mechanics of reading. Spatial relationships are difficult for a young student to perceive on the staff. However, with sufficient practice, the difficulties can be overcome. The student must perceive such relationships as up, down, same, equal distribution in the tonic chord, or unequal distribution in the dominant seventh chord (V^6_5). He must then make a judgement how far his fingers should move on the keyboard to match what he sees on the music. This process must become automatic, and the student must develop a quick reflex response to the printed symbol.

There are three basic movements possible on the staff: *up, down,* or *same*. Correspondingly, there are three types of distances possible on the staff: *steps* (seconds), *skips* (thirds, or larger intervals), or *repeats.*

When beginning to teach direction on the staff, it is advisable to start with just seconds, thirds, and repeated notes (Ex. 6:4).

Ex. 6:4. Steps, skips, and repeated notes.[10]

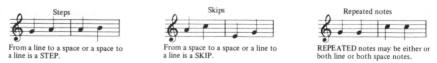

From a line to a space or a space to a line is a STEP. | From a space to a space or a line to a line is a SKIP. | REPEATED notes may be either or both line or both space notes.

[9]Example from *Pre-Reading Experiences* by Jane Smisor Bastien, p. 37.

[10]Example from *Pre-Reading Experiences,* p. 46.

Preliminary directional reading drills give the student basic concepts to follow. Devise a number of written drills (Ex. 6:5) which work with the concept of direction only. The names of the notes are not important at this stage.

Ex. 6:5. Skip and step practice.[11]

Directions: Write + for SKIP, o for STEP, and R for REPEATED NOTES.
Draw arrows to show whether the notes move UP or DOWN.

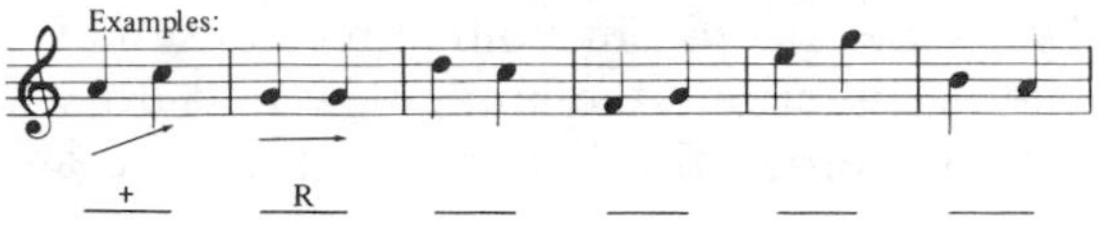

After the student has had some experience recognizing steps, skips and repeats on the staff, he is ready to name the notes. Some authors of method books prefer to use interval terminology from the beginning. The goal is the same–to teach the student to think and reason directionally from a given note.

Notation

Traditionally, notation has been taught to piano students by the middle C approach. In this system the student places both thumbs on middle C and begins reading up and down from C. Reading exclusively in this fashion limits the student to a part of the keyboard for a long time and works only in one key. Newer method books are moving away from this approach and presenting students with a more comprehensive view.

When teaching the names of the lines and spaces, it is helpful for the student to see how notes relate to each other on the *entire* staff, not just a part of it. Note names can be learned by relating all the lines or all the spaces on the staff. The student learns one landmark for each clef and relates the other notes from this point (Ex. 6:6a).

Ex. 6:6. Naming the lines.[12]

Directions:
G is on the bottom line of the bass clef. A SKIP up from G on the next line is B (skipping A in the space). Each line note is named by going UP A SKIP. Remember G, bottom line, bass clef; and E, first line, treble clef. You will be able to name any line note on the staff by thinking skips up from these notes.

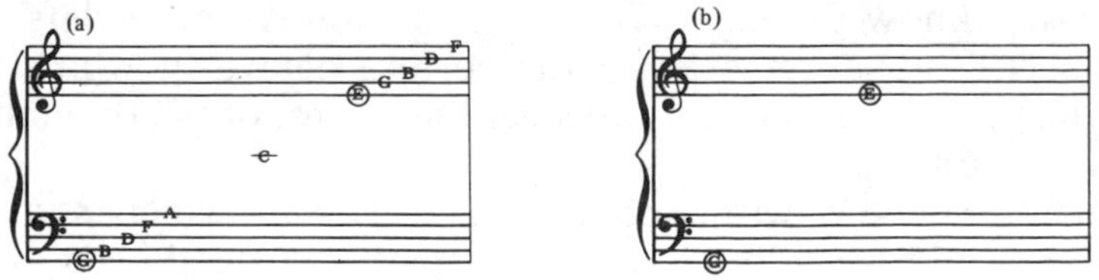

[11]Example from *Pre-Reading Experiences,* p. 47.

[12]Example from *Pre-Reading Experiences,* p. 54.

After much experimenting, the author has discovered that such jingles as "Every Good Boy Does Fine," or "George Brown Died Friday Afternoon," etc., are not lasting teaching devices. Cute though they may be, these jingles do not teach students to think and reason. If the jingles are forgotten, so are the notes along with them.

For thorough drill, direct the student to write the line notes four times a day as shown in Ex. 6:6b. The student may do this work on blank music paper. Organize the material so the student will know what to do. Write Monday on the first page, Tuesday on the second page, and so on for a week's work. Always be specific in your directions. This is a new concept. Without the teacher's directions the student would do what comes naturally—wait until the day before the lesson and try to cram in all the week's work at once.

After the student has worked with the line notes for a week or two, he may be given the space notes to write. Teach the space notes in the same manner as the line notes (Ex. 6:7).

Ex. 6:7. Naming the spaces.[13]

Directions:

F is the first space note in the bass clef. A SKIP up from F is A in the next space (skipping G on the line). Each space note is named by going UP A SKIP. Remember F, first space, bass clef; and D, first space, treble clef. You will be able to name any space note on the staff thinking skips up from these notes.

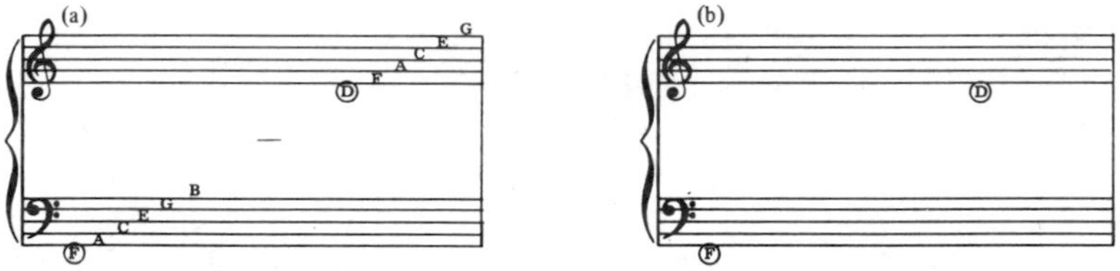

Individual Note Recognition

Fluency with note names requires patience and perseverance on the teacher's part over a period of time. A great deal of drill must be done in the first year of lessons on learning the notes. Often review in the second (and sometimes the third) year is necessary.

Too often upon interviewing transfer students one discovers that they (1) do not know the names of the notes in one or both clefs—frequently the bass clef, (2) do not know the correct octave in which the notes should be played, (3) do not know ledger line notes, or (4) only know a few notes around middle C.

The author has witnessed extreme cases in which students were playing (technically well) literature the difficulty of Beethoven's *Pathétique Sonata*, and they had difficulty naming the notes! These deficiencies may

[13]Example from *Pre-Reading Experiences,* p. 61.

have resulted from bad habits formed in the first few years of instruction.

There are several aids to learning individual note names:

1. Flash cards
2. Singing note names
3. Writing note names
4. Numbering the lines and spaces of both clefs

1. Note flash cards may be made by the teacher or pupil, or they may be purchased from a number of sources, for example: *Music Flashcards* by Jane Smisor Bastien, General Words and Music Co.; *Speed Drill Flash Cards* by Wallace and Winning, Gamble Hinged Music Co.; *Lines and Spaces* by Robert Pace, Lee Roberts Music Publications, Inc. Numerous other note flash card publications are available. Flash cards are sometimes included in method books, for example: *Piano All the Way, Level Three* by William Gillock, Willis Music Co.

Each student should have his *own* set of note flash cards for home drill. The cards should be sorted out by the teacher and divided into two piles, one containing line notes, and the other containing space notes. Each pile may be bound with a rubber band.

Line note flash cards should be given concurrently when first naming all the line notes as shown in Ex. 6:6. The same procedure should be followed when teaching the space notes.

When working at home, the student should *name* the note on the card and *play* it in the correct location on the keyboard. It is of little value to name the notes correctly, if he is unable to play them in the correct octave on the piano. After the line and space notes have been learned separately, they may be combined for study. Later, add the ledger notes below, in the middle, and above the staff.

Instruct the student to time himself and write down how long it takes to go through part, or all of the notes. Each week the time rate for naming a group of notes should decrease.

Flash cards also are useful in both private and group lessons. For first year students a few minutes of each lesson should be devoted to flash card drill. For class use a game can be made using the cards. Have the students form two lines; each may be given a name such as the Cubs and Jets (Ill. 6:1). Each group competes for the correct answers. Each student keeps the correctly answered card until all the cards have been used. The group with the most cards wins the game. Games such as this are stimulating and motivating. Other musical elements may be presented similarly such as chords, key signatures, intervals, etc.

2. Singing note names will aid in establishing good reading habits. The student should name each note aloud thinking directionally.

Unfortunately, many beginning courses have finger numbers given for each note with unfailing persistence. The unhappy result is often:

Teacher: "What is this note, Mary Sue?"
Mary Sue: "Three?"

Frequently the blame for this kind of answer should be placed where it belongs, not on the student, but on the teacher for not teaching the

Ill. 6:1. Group flash card drills.

student to think and reason in the first place. The teacher's function is to cause the student to learn. Mary Sue has not learned and has resorted to guessing.

Since most courses begin note reading with single line melodies, it will be possible to name each note until the music becomes too complex. Even when both hands play at the same time, the student can sing the notes of first one hand, then the other. Persist in having the student name the notes aloud until note reading (not finger reading) is secure.

3. Writing note names is helpful for thorough comprehension of the staff. Any phase of written work reinforces keyboard activity. Most writing books (or theory books) contain note drills. Note spellers provide additional work on individual note recognition. If a book is not used, the teacher may devise note drills as shown in the following two examples.

Ex. 6:8. Naming line notes.[14]

Directions:

Write the names of these line notes and play them in the correct place on the piano.

[14]Example from *Book 1 Writing* by Jane Smisor Bastien (General Words and Music Co., 1963), p. 6.

Ex. 6:9. Drawing notes.[15]

Directions:

Draw the following notes and play them in the correct place on the piano.

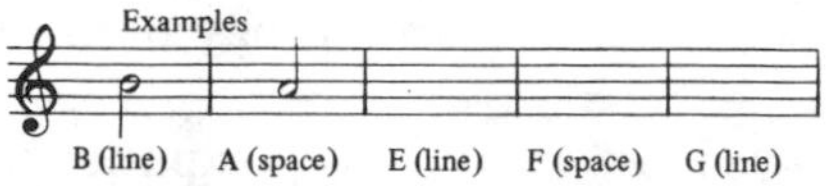

4. Numbering the lines and spaces aids in creating a mental image of the staff (Ex. 6:10). The exact placement of the notes can be instantly recalled. Some method books include this step, others do not.

Ex. 6:10 Line and space numbers.

The invention of the staff is ascribed to Guido of Arezzo (c. 1000). In addition to developing the staff, Guido used the human hand as an aid in memorizing the scale. Since the five fingers of the hand correspond to the five lines of the staff, the hand can be used effectively in teaching pitch location.

Hold up your hand in a horizontal position, and tell your students that the staff is related to the hand: five fingers, four spaces in between. Pointing to corresponding fingers, ask: "What note is on the first line, treble clef? What note is on the fifth line bass clef? What note is in the first space treble clef?" This physical, three dimensional representation of the staff makes a lasting impression on students, and it helps them remember pitch locations easily.

Beginning Technique

Technique is defined by Merriam-Webster as "the method or the details of procedure essential to expertness of execution in any art . . . " For the young pianist this would mean the ability to play adequately on a beginning level regarding clarity, evenness, and balance of tone.

Books on piano technique are ubiquitous. These books propose a variety of methods and approaches. Some titles chosen at random include: *The Physiological Mechanics of Piano Technique* by Ortmann (Dutton, 1962); *The Visible and Invisible in Piano Technique* by Mattay (Oxford University Press, 1932); and *The Riddle of the Pianist's Finger* by Schultz (Carl Fischer, 1949).

Plentiful as they are, most books on technique deal only with

[15] Example from *Book 1 Writing*, p. 15.

advanced levels. Terms like arm weight, forearm rotation, relaxation, etc., are encountered frequently. Although these terms apply to students of all levels, the beginner is confronted with more basic matters. Beginning technique should be pared down to simple concepts which relate to control and coordination at the keyboard. The terminology used should be easily understood by children.

Within the first year of lessons the beginner must learn many concepts. Matters of touch (legato and staccato), phrasing (two-note slur), and basic finger coordination will all be new. Although teachers may disagree on the order in which technical items should be given, most would agree that the following nine items are essential concepts for first year students.

1. Posture and hand position
2. Arm drops, large muscle motions
3. Legato touch
4. Staccato touch
5. Balance of melody and accompaniment
6. Down-up wrist motion for phrasing
7. Turning the thumb under or crossing over the thumb
8. Chromatic scale
9. Double notes

Posture and Hand Position

These considerations are as basic to good pianistic training as is the correct grip for golf. Matters of posture, hand position, height, distance from the keyboard, etc., were discussed in the previous chapter and the suggestions there apply equally to average age beginners. As mentioned in Chapter 5, posture and hand position are dependent on sitting at the correct height. Pillows or books placed on a music bench can be helpful in regulating height, but an adjustable chair is a better solution to this problem (see Ill. 5:19). József Gát is emphatic in his recommendations for posture:

> In teaching children it is a particularly difficult task to find the proper sitting posture. The feet of the child can usually only find support with the aid of a footstool. In the first years of study pedaling has no important part yet, and so the use of a footstool is not detrimental even from this point of view.[16]

Once the sitting level and feet problems have been solved, instruct the student to sit in the middle of the bench (not all the way back) and lean (not slouch) slightly forward over the keys. The hands, wrists, and forearms should be held in a straight line; the fingers should be well-curved.

Most standard method books begin in the middle C position and use single line melodies exclusively for an extended period. This procedure does little to shape the hand. Results of this method may be the following: thumbs hanging off the keyboard, flat fingers, or a low wrist (Ill. 6:2).

[16] József Gát, *The Technique of Piano Playing* (London: Collet's Holdings Ltd., 1965), p. 58.

Ill. 6:2. Incorrect fingers and wrist.

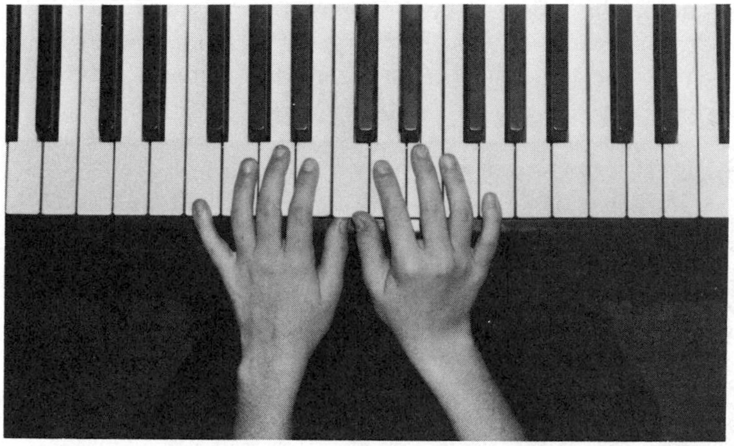

Rather than playing single line melodies exclusively in the beginning, triads and 5-finger positions are helpful for shaping the fingers and developing the correct hand position. Playing triads requires curved fingers. In addition, the hand easily forms the correct position with the bridge of the hand held up with the knuckles protruding (Ill. 6:3). In the beginning the

Ill. 6:3. Correct hand position used in playing a triad.

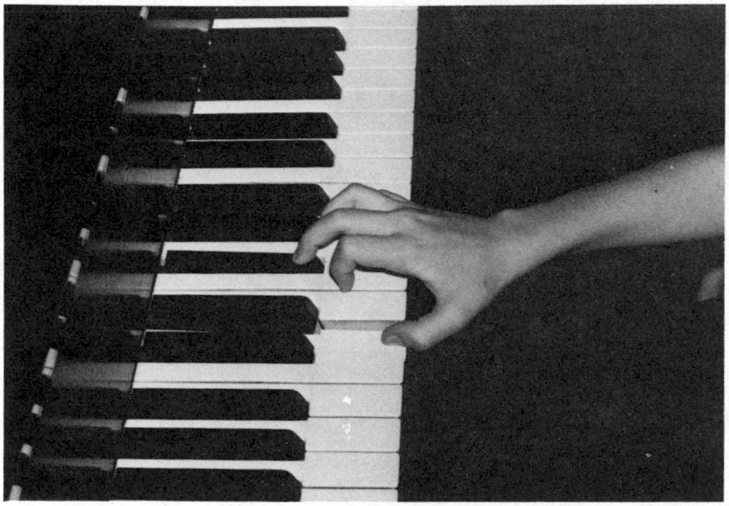

student will have to concentrate on the arched position of the hand, and he will have to work at maintaining firm, curved fingers. .

Young children especially have weak fingers. The tendency is to cave in at the first joint on the second, third, fourth, and fifth fingers (Ill. 6:4a).

Ill. 6:4a. Incorrect finger position.

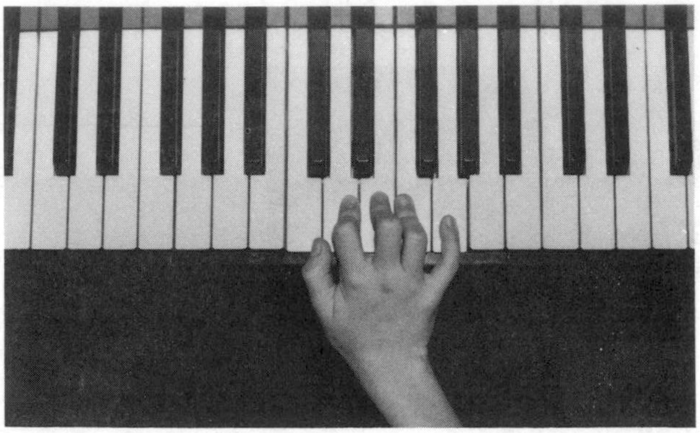

Ill. 6:4b. Correct finger position.

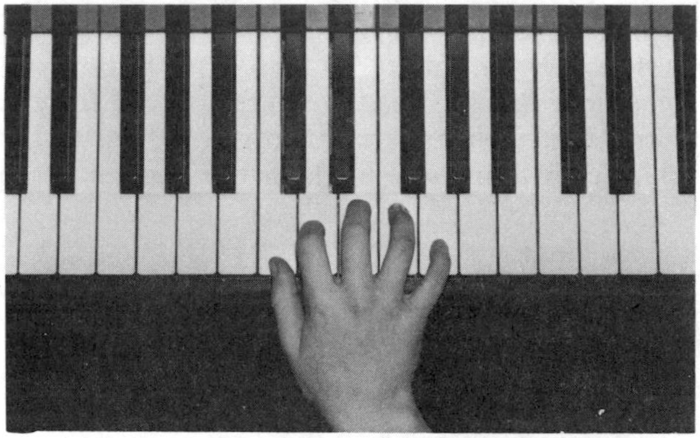

The little finger is particularly weak, and in addition to caving in, it often plays on the side, falling over (Ill. 6:5a).

Ill. 6:5a. Incorrect little finger.

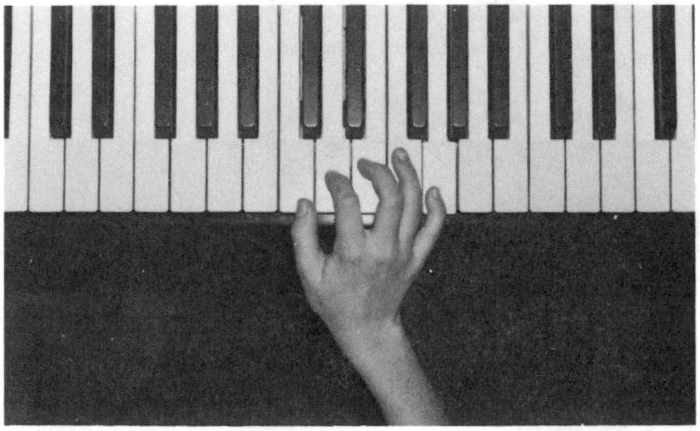

Ill. 6:5b. Correct little finger.

The beginner will not perfect these basics within the first year, perhaps not even in the second year. However, over a period of time matters of posture, hand position, curved fingers, etc. can be emphasized and repeatedly corrected by the teacher until these become natural to the student. The most important aspect of beginning lessons is to form correct habits.

Arm Drops

Some teachers like to begin by having the student use the large muscles first, then concentrate on the smaller motions used in coordinating finger action.

Arm drops may be taught in the beginning when key names are being learned. Tell the student to: (1) support his third finger with the thumb and raise his forearm in the air over a named key (Ill. 6:6a); (2) drop the finger onto the key (Ill. 6:6b), hold it for a short time, and lift off again. The teacher may direct the student to play a high key with the right hand, a low key with the left hand, three high keys that go up, etc. Other fingers may be supported and used in the same manner.

Supporting a finger and dropping with arm weight will give the student a feeling of security at impact, and it will give him the correct concept for holding his fingers in a curved position later when the support is not used.

Later, chords may be played in the same manner. Instruct the student to prepare the chord in the air and drop on the keys keeping the fingers well-curved. Fifths, sixths (octaves later) may also be played in this manner.

Ill. 6:6a. Supported finger raised over a key.

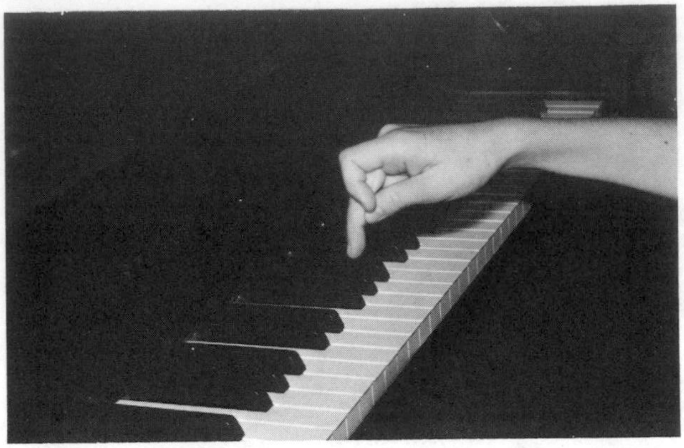

Ill. 6:6b. Supported finger on the key.

Legato Touch

The two basic touches, legato and staccato, should be taught during the first year. The execution of the legato principle requires the student to play a key, hold it, and release it when the next key is played. This concept comes easily to some students and is difficult for others. The process requires intricate finger coordination which may take some time to develop. However, it is vitally important for the beginner to understand this process and be able to do it easily. The importance of legato playing is emphasized by József Gát: "The basic task of teaching technique to the beginner is teaching legato playing."[16]

Legato may be explained to children by describing it in the following manner: as a person walks, one foot comes down, the other goes up, and the process is repeated over and over. This is analogous to "walking on the keys"—one key is played and held until the next key is played; the first key is released.

Two common errors in first attempts at legato playing are (1) blurring the tones by not releasing the keys after they have been depressed, or (2) bouncing the hand and arm up and down producing uneven, disconnected tones.

Studies for legato touch may be begun first with just two notes (see Ex. 6:2) by simply alternating fingers: (either hand) 1-2-1-2-1; 2-3-2-3-2, etc. Next, use 5-finger patterns up and down in a slow tempo (Ex. 6:11).

Ex. 6:11. Legato five-finger pattern.[17]

Staccato Touch

The beginner may be introduced to the staccato touch simply by having him separate the tones so that they sound short. Too often when directing young students to play staccato, the teacher says: "Jump off the keys as though they were red hot!" This may mislead the student into thinking that staccato tones are meant to be short, explosive, mini-sounds. The teacher should demonstrate the touch to the student so he will have an idea of what is expected when a dot appears over or under a note. Once the idea of staccato has been established in the student's mind, simple studies can be devised for staccato touch (Ex. 6:12).

Ex. 6:12. Staccato exercises.

[16]Gát, *op. cit.*, p. 269.

[17]Example from *Magic Finger Technique, Book 1* by James Bastien (General Words and Music Co.), p. 4.

For children, the technical means for producing staccato will be slightly different than for older students. Young children feel more secure if they prepare near the key and push up, rather than dropping from high and rebounding. Joan Last describes this action clearly:

> Many teachers liken a staccato action to that of a bouncing ball, but one must realize that the ball bounces *up*, not down, though here we are nearer the mark, because the upward bounce is the *result* of the downward movement. To produce this on the piano, however, the child will imitate the upward bounce *consciously.*[18]

Balance of Melody and Accompaniment

A well-trained student is easily recognized by his ability to play with sufficient control to balance voices. Voicing, or balancing tones, simply means playing one hand louder than the other. A simile may be used to explain this sensation to the child: play one hand as if it were weighted with lead; play the other hand as if it were weighted with feathers.

Coordination is a problem in balancing one hand against the other, because both hands "want" to do the same thing at the same time. Practice is required to overcome this problem. As a first exercise, instruct the student to play one hand louder than the other in 5-finger patterns (Ex. 6:11). Also, use a melody and chord study for this purpose (Ex. 6:13); instruct the student to play the melody louder than the chords.

Ex. 6:13. Melody and chords.[19]

Down-up Wrist Motion for Phrasing

Slurs and phrases produced on the piano are dependent on the correct motions of the hand, wrist, and arm. On other instruments slurs (or phrase endings) are produced by different means. The bow controls phrasing on stringed instruments, and the tongue is used for phrasing woodwind or brass instruments.

The mechanics of producing slurred groups can be taught to first year students when they have sufficient control to produce the proper motions (near the end of the first semester).

Demonstrate the motions used in playing a two-note slur to the student. Show him what it looks like to drop on the key with a slightly

[18] Last, *op. cit.*, p. 29. Reprinted by permission.

[19] Example from *Magic Finger Technique, Book 1*, p. 14.

lower wrist motion (Ill. 6:7a), and release the key with a higher wrist motion (Ill. 6:7b).[20] Several terms may be used to describe this process: (1) down-

Ill. 6:7a. Lower wrist.

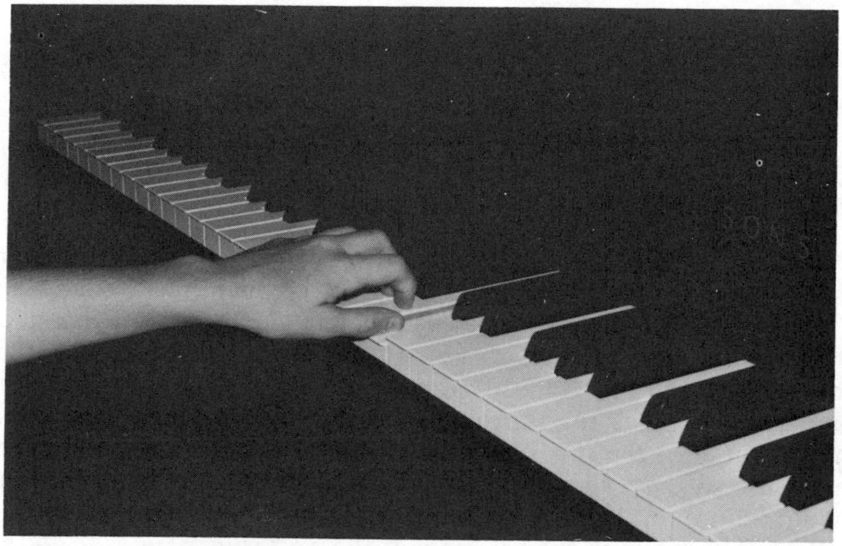

Ill. 6:7b. Higher wrist.

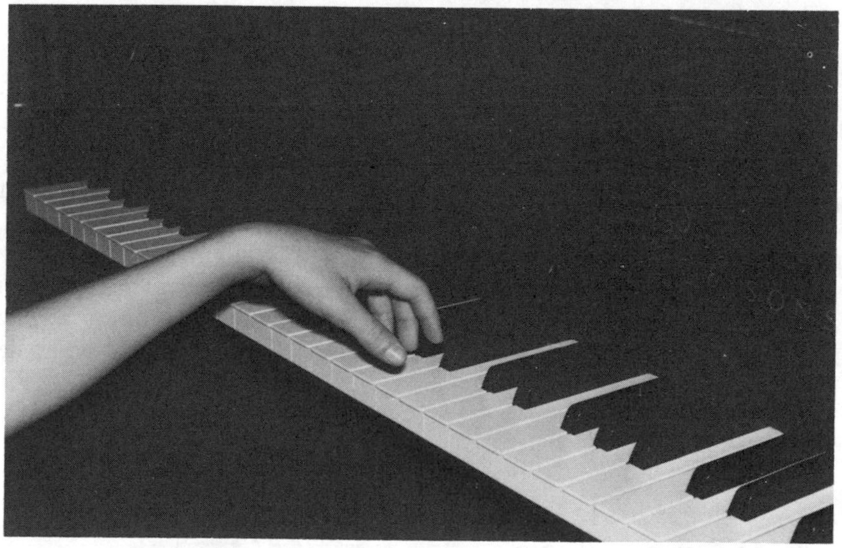

up wrist, (2) drop-release, or (3) drop-roll (rolling inwards toward the piano

[20]In addition to the photos given here, excellent photos of released phrases are found in John Thompson's *Modern Course for the Piano, First Grade Book* (Willis Music Co., 1936), p. 16, and in Ruth Slenczynska's book, *Music at Your Fingertips* (Cornerstone Library, 1961), p. 34.

and lifting at the same time). Arrows are helpful in depicting this motion (Ex. 6:14).

Ex. 6:14. Two-note slur.

The lifting of the wrist is the same at the end of a two-note slur or any phrase. When a longer phrase mark is used, it is helpful to relate the group of notes under the phrase sign to a vocal line. If sung, a breath would be taken on the last note of the phrase. At the piano, the hand lifts, the legato line is broken, and the "breath" is accomplished.

Numerous exercises for slurring can be devised by the teacher (Ex. 6:15). The first note of the slur should be slightly louder and the last note should be slightly softer. The student may be told to "float off" on the last note of a slurred group. Teach the young student to make a break in the sound from the slur ending to the first note of the next slur.

Ex. 6:15. Slurring exercises.

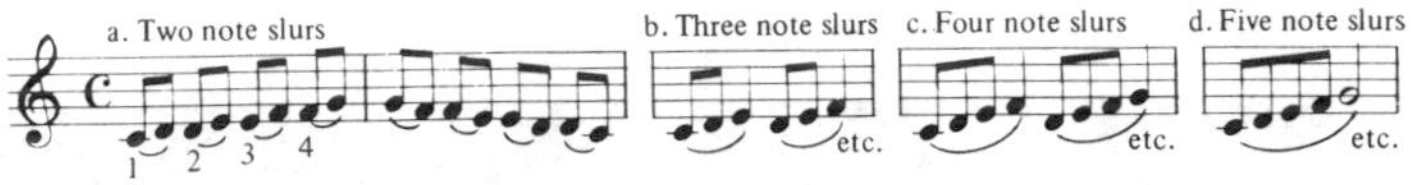

Many first year solos contain a variety of touches–staccato, legato, and slurred groups. For thorough comprehension, direct the student to *say aloud* the hand motions used in the composition (Ex. 6:16). Say "up" for staccato, "down" for long notes or phrases, and "off" for phrase endings. Verbalizing music symbols and transferring them into hand motions is the most effective means of getting the student to reproduce the exact representation of the printed page. This technique is so important that it should be continued over a period of time until the student plays naturally what he sees.

Ex. 6:16. Saying hand motions aloud.[21]

[21]Example from *Little Dog Running Down the Street,* sheet music solo by Jane Smisor Bastien (General Words and Music Co., 1968).

For additional samples of elementary slur exercises see: *Technic Lessons, Level 1* by James Bastien (Kjos West, 1976), pages 11, 19, 25; *A Dozen A Day, Preparatory Book* by Edna Mae Burnam (Willis Music Co., 1957), pages 28-29; and *Piano Technic, Book 1* by Marion McArtor (Summy-Birchard Co., 1954), pages 6-7.

Turning the Thumb Under or Crossing Over the Thumb

Scale playing requires agility in turning the thumb under or crossing another finger over the thumb. Preparation in this process, before actually playing scales, is extremely beneficial.

There are many different opinions among teachers regarding the best time to begin teaching the scales in a serious way. This author is in general agreement with Gát who states: "If the pupil has already mastered small pentachord pieces to the point of sight-reading them he may begin to practice scales."[22] He further states that most pupils are only ready to begin the *correct* study of scales at about the middle of the second year.[23]

Although the actual study of scales and their complexities may be delayed, a beginner can be exposed to scale preparation within the first year of lessons. In the beginning this may be just turning the thumb under first one finger, then another (Ex. 6:17). The thumb should be turned under smoothly without twisting the hand and arm out of shape (Ill. 6:8).[24]

Ill. 6:8. Correct hand position for a thumb crossing.

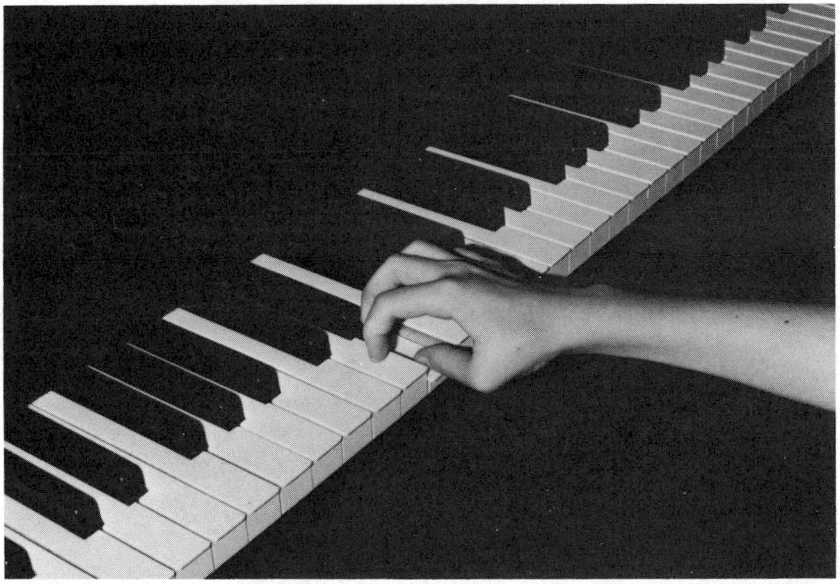

[22]Gát, *op. cit.,* p. 273.

[23]Some teachers prefer to expose students to the sound of the complete scale having them play tetrachord scales, scales divided between the hands (see William Gillock's *Piano All the Way, Level Two,* Willis Music Co., p. 21).

[24]In addition to the illustration given here, two excellent photos of turning the thumb under and crossing over the thumb may be seen in Lillie H. Phillipp's book, *Piano Study, Application and Technique* (New York: MCA Music, 1969), p. 5.

When the student first begins to turn the thumb under, he may start by turning under the second finger (Ex. 6:17). The next step is to turn the thumb under 3, and finally turn under 4. Turning the thumb under 3 and 4 is especially helpful, because this will prepare the student for scale playing.

Ex. 6:17. Thumb under exercise.[25]

Directions:

Practice first hands separately, then together. Turn the thumb under smoothly. Play legato.

Crossing a finger over the thumb is just as important as turning the thumb under (Ex. 6:18). The crossing should be made as smoothly as possible.

Ex. 6:18. Exercise for crossing over the thumb.

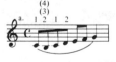

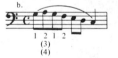

For additional samples of elementary thumb exercises see: *Technic Lessons, Level 1* by James Bastien (Kjos West, 1976), pages 13, 28; *A Dozen A Day, Preparatory Book* by Edna Mae Burnam (Willis Music Co., 1957), pages 9 and 17; and *Piano Technic, Book 1* by Marion McArtor (Summy-Birchard Co., 1954), pages 38-39.

[25] Example from *Magic Finger Technique, Book 1*, p. 16.

Chromatic Scale

Since playing the chromatic scale requires a contracted hand position, it is useful in developing a broad technical background, and it gives relief to the five-finger position. It not only aids in technical development, but it also aids in reading accidentals. How many times have you experienced teaching a first year piece titled something like "The Buzzing Bee"? Usually the student is thrown by the little chromatic passages which contain a number of accidentals. By reading the chromatic scale and practicing it ahead of time, it will not be formidable when encountered in first year literature.

Chromatic exercises may be devised by the teacher similar to Ex. 6:19. The chromatic scale is begun with just a few notes, and each time it is repeated, a higher note is added. In this manner the student is learning to play up and down with equal facility.

Ex. 6:19. Chromatic exercise.[26]

Directions:

Practice first hands separately, then together. Watch the fingering! Say the finger numbers aloud.

For additional samples of elementary chromatic exercises see: *Technic Lessons, Level 1* by James Bastien, page 29; *A Dozen A Day, Preparatory Book* by Edna Mae Burnam, page 22; and *Piano Technic, Book 1* by Marion McArtor, pages 32-34.

Double Notes

Although first year students will not need a great deal of drill on double notes, a few passages containing legato thirds will be found in some of the music studied (Ex. 6:20).

Ex. 6:20. Passage containing right hand double notes.[27]

[26]Example from *Magic Finger Technique, Book 1*, p. 20.

[27]Example from *Next Door Neighbors* by Irene Young (available only in *Five-Finger Music)* (Summy-Birchard Co., 1962)

Similar problems occur between playing single legato notes and playing double legato notes—connecting the fingers without blurring. It takes time and patience to apply the legato touch correctly to two notes; the student's tendency is to disconnect the tones. Double note exercises should be devised by the teacher to give the student experience playing them prior to use in first year pieces (Ex. 6:21).

Ex. 6:21. Double note exercise.[28]

Directions:

Curve fingers. Play legato. Change from one third to another as smoothly as possible.

When practicing double thirds, the student should play the first two notes clearly with the other fingers raised (Ill. 6:9a); if the other fingers are not raised sufficiently, they might play accidentally. It is important to release the first two notes as soon as the next two notes are played (Ill. 6:9b) so there will not be a blur in the legato line.

Ill. 6:9a. Double thirds: first two fingers.

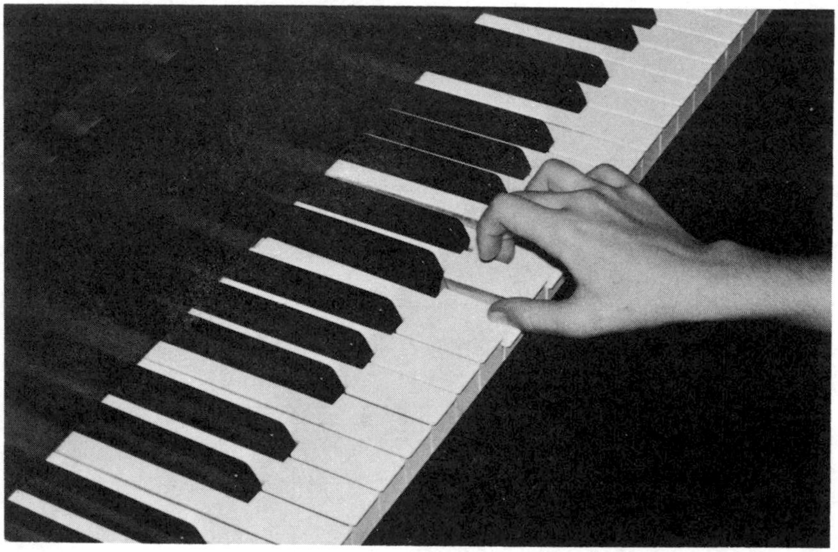

[28]Example from *Magic Finger Technique, Book 1*, p. 22.

Ill. 6:9b. Double thirds: second two fingers.

For additional samples of elementary double note exercises see: *Technic Lessons, Level 1* by James Bastien, page 31; *A Dozen A Day, Preparatory Book* by Edna Mae Burnam, page 30; and *Piano Technic, Book 1* by Marion McArtor, page 21.

Summary of First Year Technique

The job of the teacher is to establish correct fundamentals from the beginning. Too often the first year is approached in a careless way because it is not considered important. On the contrary, beginning instruction will leave lasting impressions, good or bad. Generally, it is difficult to overcome a bad beginning.

It must be conceded that most beginners will not make the concert stage; the majority are merely studying for enjoyment. However, while studying, they may as well play correctly. Often in the beginning it is difficult to tell if a student is really talented. Sometimes a real spark will show up later. Therefore, it is an injustice to let the less talented student do more or less what he pleases. This background would seriously handicap him if he should decide to make music a career. The skilled teacher will strive to improve all students, gifted or otherwise. Technique is an important aspect of piano playing, and it should be developed correctly from the beginning.

Technique is just one part of the music program; it should not be the focal point of lessons. The beginner wants to make music; he does not want to *work* at the piano playing Hanon and scales for two years until he is "ready" to play music.

The technique presented in this chapter is basic and relates directly to first year literature. Each item can be incorporated into lessons as an approach to the piano rather than as drudgery. The teacher should strive to be creative and invent studies as they are needed. It is well worth the effort to establish a basic approach for the beginner which will serve him in whatever direction he chooses to follow.

The basic criteria for a well-trained, knowledgeable student is: Does he *understand* what he is doing? How often have you witnessed a pupil's fine technical performance of an advanced work only to later discover that (1) he did not know the key of the piece, (2) he did not understand the harmonic changes, and (3) he had no understanding of the structure of the composition. This is analogous to a person who can pronounce and read French beautifully, but who does not know the meaning of the words and has no understanding of what was read. To avoid this kind of "unthinking" approach to music study, the teacher must teach theory from the beginning as an integral part of the music program. "All good teaching will present theory, harmony and counterpoint from the earliest stage."[29]

Teachers frequently complain that there is not sufficient time to teach theory in a weekly thirty minute private lesson. It is true that it is easier to cover if an extra class theory lesson can be scheduled each week in addition to the private lesson. However, if only private lessons are given, written theory assignments can be given, and the teacher can check these in a few minutes during the lesson.

A suggested first year theory program is outlined in capsule form near the end of this chapter (see: Diagram of First Year Materials). From this outline it can be seen that the main items include:

1. Major 5-finger positions and major tonic chords
2. Dominant seventh chords (inverted positions)
3. Intervals (unaltered scale tone intervals)
4. The order of sharps and flats
5. Major key signatures
6. Minor 5-finger positions and minor tonic chords
7. Subdominant chords (inverted position)

Major Five-finger Positions and Major Tonic Chords

The major keys can be divided into four "position-related" groups according to their tonic chords (Ex. 6:22). The student should memorize the pattern of black and white keys that comprise each group.

Ex. 6:22. Four major key groups.

Group I: Keys of C, G, F

The Group I keys have *all white keys in their tonic chords.* F is underlined because it is the unusual key in this group. The 5-finger position in F has a *black key* under the *4th finger* in the *right hand,* and under the *2nd finger* in the *left hand.*

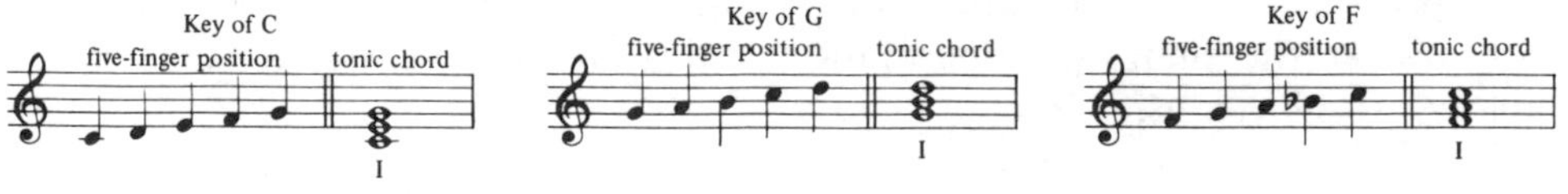

[29] Vera Wills and Ande Manners, *A Parent's Guide to Music Lessons* (New York: Harper & Row, 1967), p. 22.

Group II: Keys of D, A, E

The Group II Keys have a *black key under the middle finger* and *white keys on either side* in their tonic chords. E is underlined because it is the unusual key in this group. The 5-finger position in E has *two black keys* under the *2nd* and *3rd fingers* in the *right hand*, and under the *3rd* and *4th fingers* in the *left hand.*

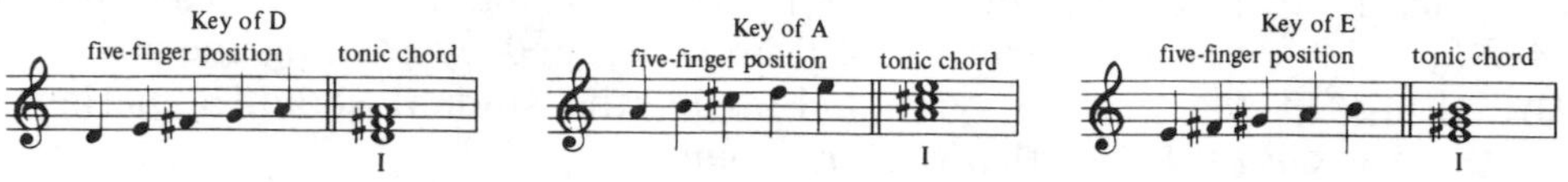

Group III: Keys of Db, Ab, Eb

The Group III Keys have a *white key under the middle finger* and *black keys on either side* in their tonic chords. Eb is underlined because it is the unusual key in this group. The 5-finger position in Eb has *two white keys* under the *2nd* and *3rd fingers* in the *right hand,* and under the *3rd* and *4th fingers* in the *left hand.*

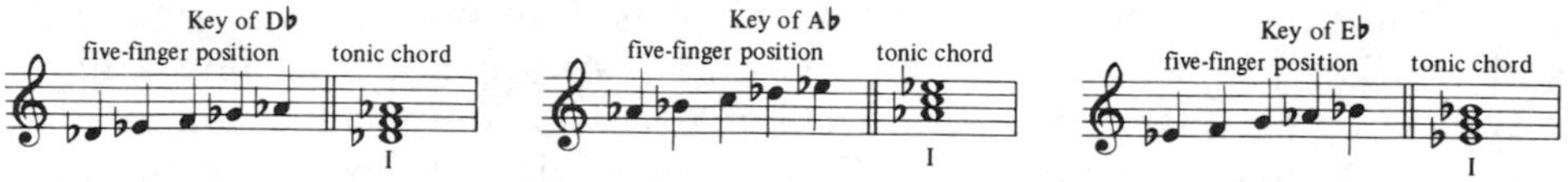

Group IV: Keys of Gb,Bb,B

The Group IV Keys are each unusual. Each key must be learned separately.

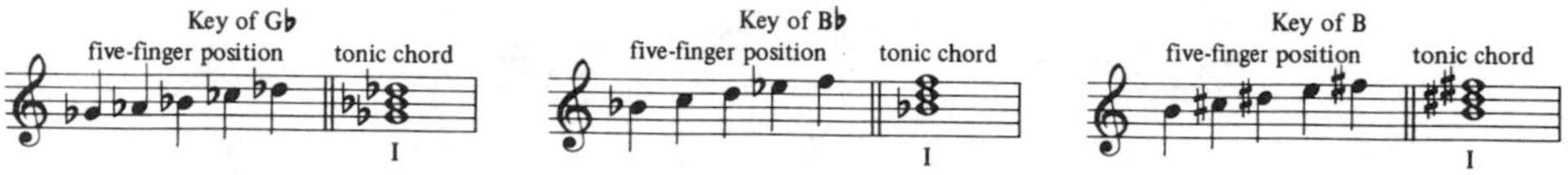

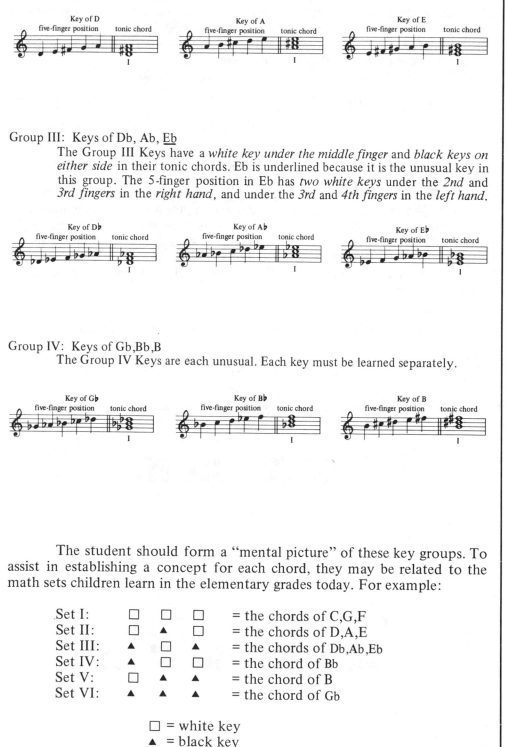

The student should form a "mental picture" of these key groups. To assist in establishing a concept for each chord, they may be related to the math sets children learn in the elementary grades today. For example:

Set I:	□	□	□	= the chords of C,G,F
Set II:	□	▲	□	= the chords of D,A,E
Set III:	▲	□	▲	= the chords of Db,Ab,Eb
Set IV:	▲	□	□	= the chord of Bb
Set V:	□	▲	▲	= the chord of B
Set VI:	▲	▲	▲	= the chord of Gb

□ = white key
▲ = black key

The chords should be learned at the keyboard by "shape" according to the pattern of black and white keys. The tactile sense should be developed to the point where the student can form a mental picture of the chords and "find" them on the piano with his eyes closed. In addition to the tactile sense, the student should be taught to recognize chords aurally and visually. Instruct the student to listen carefully to each chord and sing the notes up and down (1-3-5, 5-3-1). Visual recognition will be developed by relating the shape of the chord to the printed symbol. Finally, the student should experience writing the chords for further reinforcement.

Dominant Seventh Chords

A number of melodies may be harmonized with I and V7 chords: "Lightly Row," "Mary Had a Little Lamb," etc. Within the first year students can learn a number of accompaniment patterns to harmonize simple melodies.

The dominant seventh chord is easily played on the piano in inverted position, V^6_5 (Ex. 6:23). It is not necessary to give an elaborate explanation to a child how this chord is constructed: it is built on the fifth tone of the scale (either major or minor), and it consists of a major triad plus a minor seventh. This explanation is correct, but it is too complicated and cumbersome for a child to comprehend. Simply relate this new chord to the tonic chords already learned.

Ex. 6:23. The V7 chord.[30]

To form a V (five) 7 chord, begin with a I chord position, then:

L.H. Keep 1 the same.
Play 2 (in the five-finger position).
Move 5 DOWN the NEAREST key. (The nearest key may be either black or white.)

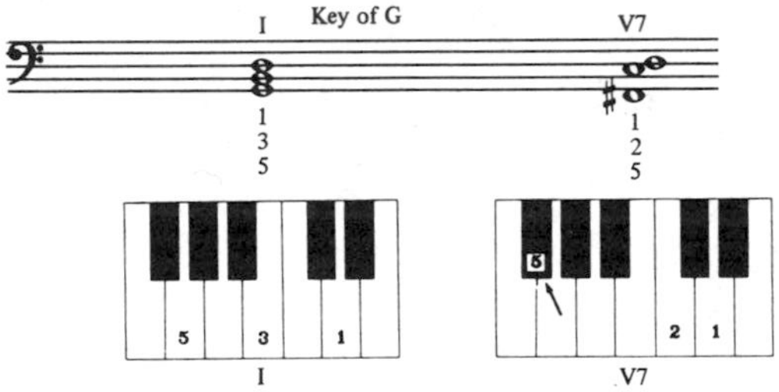

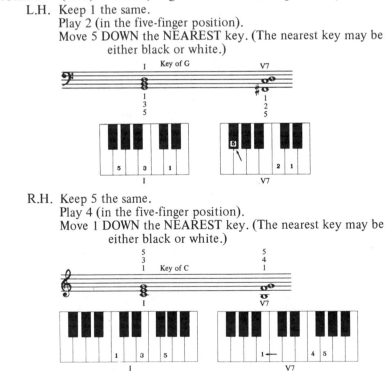

R.H. Keep 5 the same.
Play 4 (in the five-finger position).
Move 1 DOWN the NEAREST key. (The nearest key may be either black or white.)

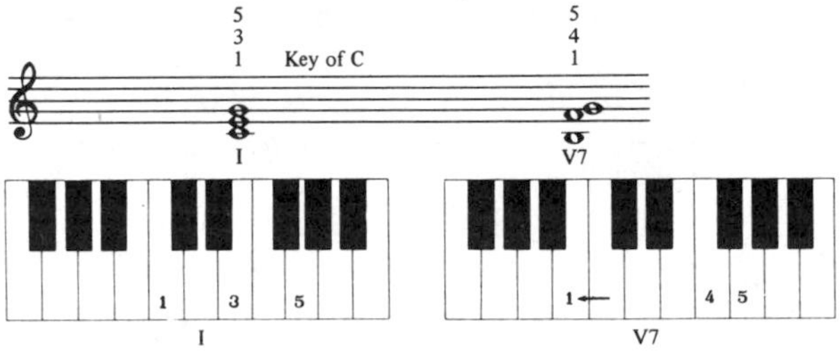

[30]Example from *Multi-Key Reading* by Jane Smisor Bastien (General Words and Music Co., 1970), p. 15.

After explaining the formation of the V7 chord in simple terms, direct the student to practice chord progressions following these directions:

Find the correct position.
Do not look at your fingers.
Play each new chord by "feel" rather than looking at your hands.

1. Play I V7 V7 I in the L.H. – Keys of C,G,F
2. Play I V7 I V7 in the R.H. – Keys of (same as above or others)
3. (Choose other patterns: I V7 I V7 I V7 I, etc.)

By practicing chord progressions without looking down at the hands, the student will be able to read melody and harmony pieces without hunting for the notes.

Most average age beginners have no trouble reaching the V^6_5 chord. However, if the student is a young beginner who has very small hands, the chord may be played with only two notes (Ex. 6:24).

Ex. 6:24. Alternate version of the V7 chord.

Intervals[31]

Since intervals form the basis for most theoretical study, it is important that students understand them clearly. In the beginning the terminology may be steps and skips rather than seconds and thirds. However, within the first year students can be taught unaltered scale tone intervals through the octave.

Intervals can be explained to a child using simple terminology:

An INTERVAL is the difference in pitch between two tones. MELODIC intervals are played separately:  HARMONIC intervals are played together:  [32]

Relate intervals to both the staff and the musical alphabet (Ex. 6:25). At first just work with intervals through the fifth; later, add sixths, sevenths, and octaves.

[31]Although too difficult for the beginner, an interesting book on intervals is *Intervals in Action* by Eula Ashworth Lindfors (Brodt Music Co., 1969), and *From Here to There* by Carolyn Bull (Carl Fischer, Inc., 1972).

[32]From *Multi-Key Reading*, p. 12.

Ex. 6:25. Intervals of 2nds, 3rds, 4ths, 5ths.[33]

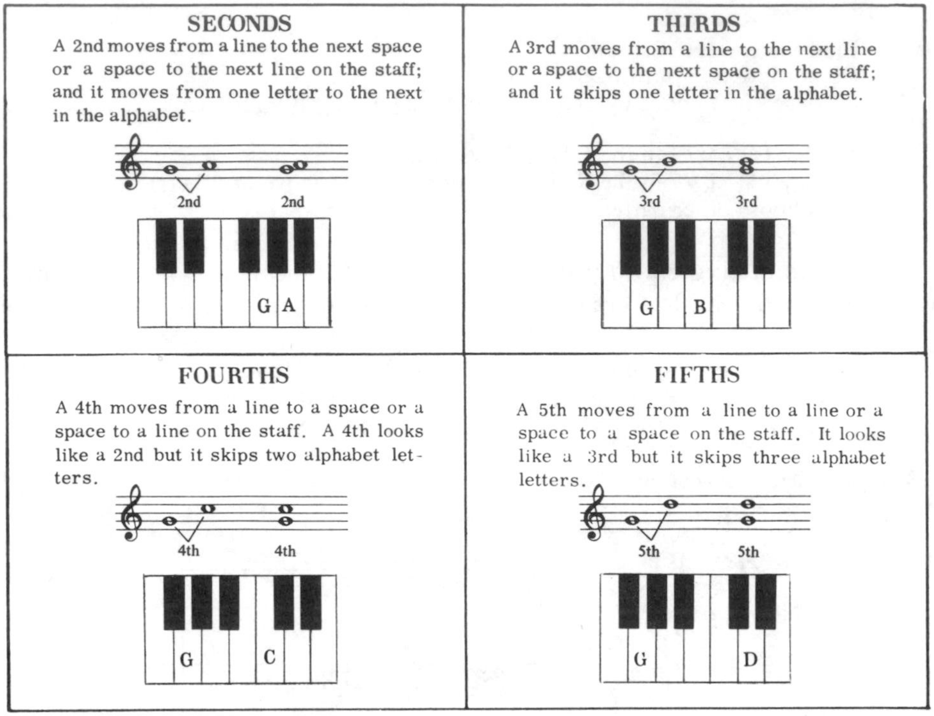

It is important to incorporate ear training drills when teaching intervals. First have the student play and sing intervals at the keyboard (sing: 1-3, 1-5, etc.); next have him try to recognize intervals played by the teacher. Use familiar songs for interval recognition: the first two notes of "I've Been Working on the Railroad," for a fourth; the first two notes of "My Bonnie Lies Over the Ocean," for a sixth, etc.

Flash cards are useful when teaching intervals. They can be made or purchased (see: *Music Flashcards* by Jane Smisor Bastien, General Words and Music Co., 1969). Students may work with flash cards at home and also in both private and class lessons.

The Order of Sharps and Flats

The order of sharps and flats (Ex. 6:26) should be taught in preparation for naming key signatures. Older method books often present a few key signatures first without providing the student with the reasoning process to figure out key signatures. To eliminate confusion, it is advisable to teach the sequence of the sharps and flats first, then teach key signatures.

Ex. 6:26. The order of sharps and flats.

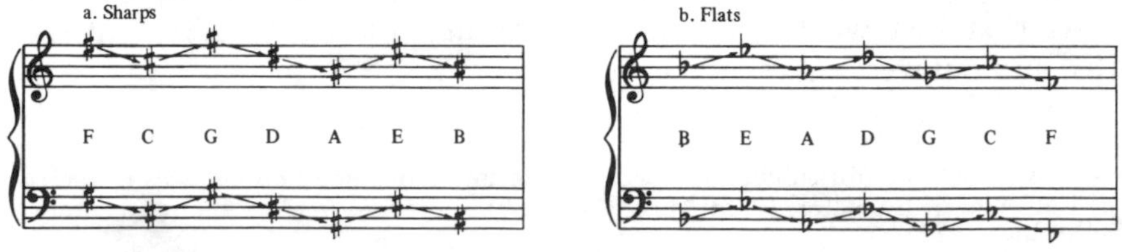

[33] *Ibid.*

To begin, have the student *write* the order of sharps several times a day for homework (use blank music paper). Instruct him to copy the order exactly as shown in Ex. 6:26; write in the arrows and letter names. The order of sharps (and flats) can be learned more easily if the student works on one clef at a time: treble clef, first week; bass clef, second week. After dividing the presentation in this manner, review can be assigned to include both clefs. The order of sharps (and flats) should be memorized.

When learning the flats, point out that the sequence uses the same letters as sharps, but in reverse; they are printed *backwards* (sharps: F,C,G,D,A,E,B; flats: B,E,A,D,G,C,F). Also point out that the first four flats spell the word "bead."

In addition to writing the sequence of sharps and flats, have the student *say* them in rhythm: sharps–F,C,G,D (pause) A,E,B; flats–B,E,A,D (pause) G,C,F. By repeating them over and over, the student will learn this sequence somewhat by ear.

Another aid to learning the order of sharps and flats is to *play* them on the keyboard; use both hands in the following manner:

Play upwards for sharps–	sharps:	F#	—	C#	—	G#	—	
	hands:	r.h.	—	l.h.	—	r.h.		- etc.
Play downwards for flats–	flats:	Bb	—	Eb	—	Ab	—	
	hands:	l.h.	—	r.h.	—	l.h.		- etc.

Playing the order of sharps and flats will give substance to the written work and assist in the general learning process. Also the student will hear what the sharps and flats sound like played in sequence.

Major Key Signatures

The ability to recognize major key signatures is especially important for first year students who are using a multi-key method.[34] Students using a middle C method will probably be playing in just three keys (C,G,F) for at least the first year. Information about keys and key signatures may be presented at an appropriate time at the teacher's discretion.

The logical sequence is to teach the order of sharps first (Ex. 6:26a), then teach sharp key signatures (Ex. 6:27). Next teach the order of flats (Ex. 6:26b), then teach flat key signatures (Ex. 6:28).

Point out that the *key signature* at the beginning of each staff tells: (1) the notes to be sharped (or flatted) throughout the entire piece, and (2) the main key of the piece.

Ex. 6:27. Rules for sharp key signatures.[35]

1. Look at the last sharp to the right: 

D Major
2. Go UP to the next letter in the musical alphabet (a half step), this is the name of the Major key.

[34]One recent multi-key publication presents both major and minor key signatures at the same time: see William Gillock's *Piano All the Way, Level 3* (Willis Music Co., 1969).

[35]Example from *Multi-Key Reading,* p. 18.

After learning the rules for figuring out sharp key signatures, have the student identify several examples, both in the music studied, and on blank music paper. Make up some for him to do. Use the same procedure for teaching flat key signatures.

Ex. 6:28. Rules for flat key signatures.[36]

1. Look at the next-to-the-last flat: 

2. The name of this letter is the name of the Major key.
3. Exceptions:

Key of F (one flat only)

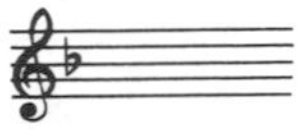

Key of C (no sharps or flats)

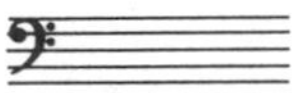

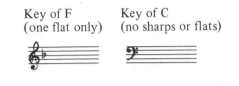

Key signature flash cards are useful for drills both at home and at the lesson. These may be made by the teacher or student or may be purchased from a number of sources, see: *Music Flashcards* by Jane Smisor Bastien, General Words and Music Co.; *Key Signatures* by Robert Pace, Lee Roberts Music Publications/G. Schirmer; *Music Flash Cards, Series 3* by Ted Ross, Hansen Music Corp.; others.

Minor Five-finger Positions and Minor Chords

A number of familiar and folk songs are written in minor mode: "The Erie Canal," "Minka," etc. Also songs written in major can be reharmonized in minor: "Mary Had a Little Lamb" (changed to "Mary Lost Her Little Lamb" in minor).

Minor positions and chords can be related to the Major keys already learned (Ex. 6:29). To form a minor 5-finger position or a minor chord, begin with a Major position and move the middle finger DOWN the nearest key (one half step). The nearest key may be either black or white.

Ex. 6:29. Minor positions and chords.

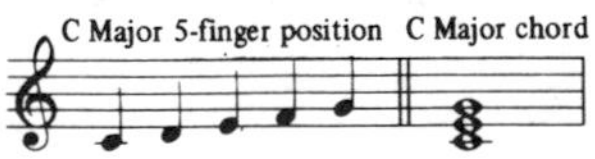

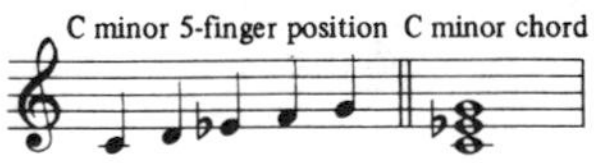

Have the student practice parallel Major and minor chords in various rhythms (Ex. 6:30). When changing chords the student should not have to look down at the keyboard. He should form a mental picture of the chord shape and arrange his fingers accordingly.

[36]Example from *Multi-Key Reading*, p. 34.

Ex. 6:30. Playing Major and minor chords.

Each new phase of theory should be accompanied by ear training drills. Use ear training games to distinguish between Major and minor tonality. At first have the student sing the tones while you play minor positions or chords. Emphasize the minor third. Next have the student listen to a chord and tell if it is Major or minor. Finally, play several chords in a row (M m m M) all in the same key, and have the student tell what was played. Later, play the same pattern, but change the first tone of each chord (CM Am Gm EM).

Each new phase of theory should be put to practical use through creative work. This is analogous to children learning spelling words and then using them in sentences. For example, when working with Major and minor tonality, suggest titles which imply these two sounds (Ex. 6:31). Have students make up pieces from the titles given. It is not necessary for first year students to notate the pieces, as this may be too cumbersome for them. The pieces can be "created" at home and played for either the private or class lesson.

Ex. 6:31. Examples of first year student pieces.

A number of familiar melodies may be harmonized with just three chords (I, IV, V7): "On Top of Old Smoky," "Yankee Doodle," "Lavender's Blue," etc. Young students enjoy playing familiar songs, and at the same time they are learning the subdominant chord and expanding their harmonic vocabulary.

The subdominant chord is easily played on the piano in inverted position (IV^6_4). Relate this chord to the tonic chords already learned (Ex. 6:32).

Ex. 6:32. The IV chord.[37]

To form a IV chord, begin with a I chord position, then:

L.H. Keep 5 the same.
Play 2 (in the five-finger position).
Move 1 UP a WHOLE STEP.

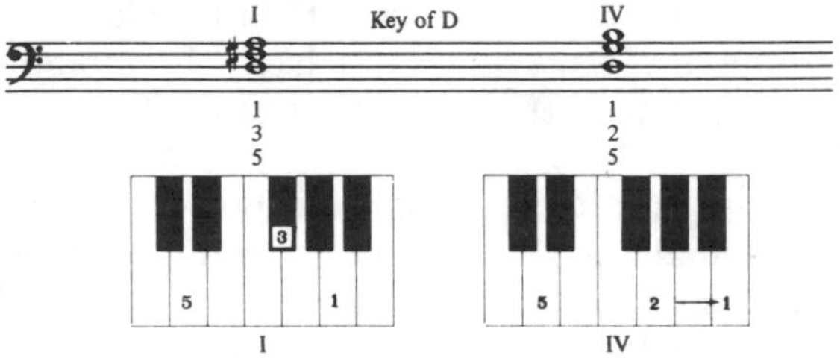

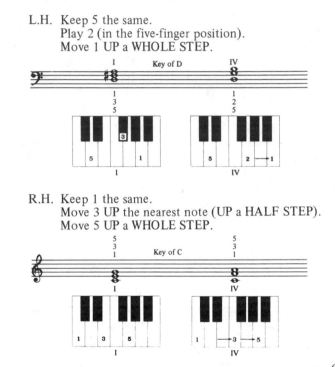

R.H. Keep 1 the same.
Move 3 UP the nearest note (UP a HALF STEP).
Move 5 UP a WHOLE STEP.

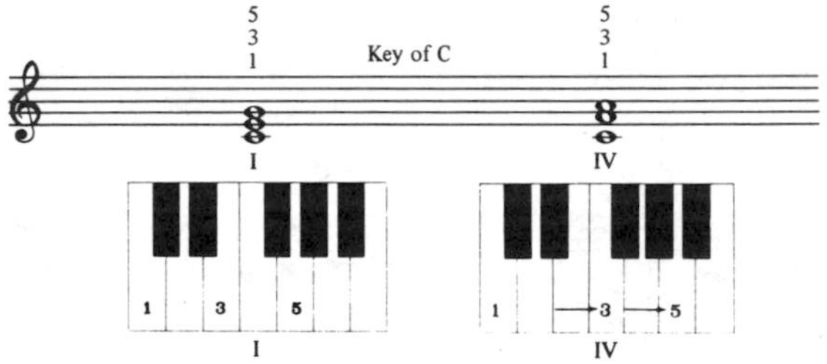

One common error occurs often when playing the IV^6_4 chord in the left hand: students are apt to play fingers 1-3-5 (incorrect) rather than 1-2-5 (correct). The reason for this tendency perhaps is because of the emphasis on tonic triads in root position. Students are accustomed to playing the 1-3-5 fingering, and it is difficult for them to change to another fingering.

Once you have gone over the explanation of the subdominant chord and its proper fingering, suggest some chord progressions to be practiced at home. The logical sequence is:

1. I IV I (Choose the keys in which these are to be played.)
2. I IV I V7 I
3. I IV V7 I

The chord progressions should be played by "feel," not by looking down at the keyboard. If practiced in this manner the student will not have to stop and find each chord when it appears in his music.

[37]Example from *Multi-Key Reading*, p. 31.

Theory and keyboard harmony should be interwoven as a combination of both playing and written work during the first year of lessons. This practical functional background will lay the foundation for more complicated elements yet to come. Students will have the materials needed to improvise, compose little pieces, and analyze music studied. Most importantly, the theory background will form a basis for musical understanding. This basic comprehension will aid the general learning process and will assist in memorization. If the student can analyze his music in terms of tonality, intervals, and chords (or chordal outlines), he will have a broad comprehensive view of the music he is learning. It is for this goal that we must strive.

Diagram of First Year Materials

A student's musical program must be planned in such a way that certain elements will have been covered by the end of the first year. Public school teachers make lesson plans to fulfill this purpose, and college teachers frequently write syllabi. Too often, however, piano lessons are approached in an improvised manner without much overall organization. The teacher should know what will be covered in a year's time. Realistic goals should be listed which average first year students can obtain.

The first year program contains many new concepts. Since drill and review are essential for assimilation of new concepts, the teacher must plan ahead so that new items are spaced evenly apart to allow time for absorption. The beginner should not be hit with a whirlwind series of new concepts at each lesson. The teacher should plan on reviewing old material and present only one or two new items each week. This will take planning and goal defining on the teacher's part.

The following diagram (Ex. 6:33) lists objectives for first year students and is intended only as a general guide based on the nine month school year. Certainly it will not relate to all beginners month for month. Some students will need more time to assimilate each group of keys, rather than learning all twelve at once. Therefore, the purpose of this outline is to organize basic information in the approximate order given to provide a general picture of a thorough music program. The teacher may present parts of this program at a slower progression and fill in other parts later. The main objective would be to cover these materials at some rate of speed, not omitting portions during the elementary stages of instruction.

Ex. 6:33. Diagram of first year materials.

	REPERTOIRE	RHYTHM	TECHNIQUE	KEYBOARD HARMONY
Division I **Sep. - Oct.**	5-finger melodies in all 12 Major positions in pre-staffed notation combination of folk songs and original melodies		Correct hand position curved fingers legato touch Major tonic chords for shaping hands	Playing Major tonic chords in all 12 keys playing V^6_5 chords in all 12 keys
Division II **Nov. - Dec.**	Single line melodies divided between hands (notated) some note against note playing some melody and chord playing supplementary reading: Christmas collection		Exercises in 5-finger positions for: legato and staccato touch balance between hands	Playing minor tonic chords in all 12 keys harmonizing melodies using I, V_7 chords (also i, V_7 in minor)
Division III **Jan. - Feb.**	More complicated melodies with chordal accompaniments (I, V_7 - also I, IV, V_7) extended melodies including 6ths, 7ths, 8ves		Phrasing exercises (down-up wrist motion) exercises for turning over the thumb or thumb under (scale preparation) one octave chromatic scale (contracted hand position)	Playing IV^6_4 chords in all 12 Major keys
Division IV **Mar., April, May**	Melodies with various reaches melodies crossing hands melodies in extended registers melodies crossing thumb under or turning over the thumb		Double 3rd exercises some Major and minor scale playing (teacher's discretion)	Harmonizing melodies with I, IV, V_7 chords

THEORY	EAR TRAINING	NEW ELEMENTS IN ASSIGNMENT
Learning about: 1. major triads 2. steps and skips (2nds and 3rds) 3. transposing	Matching tones using the three black keys matching tones in 5-finger positions	Learn alphabet letters (A-G) forward and backward learn names of keys on keyboard begin to learn note names (use note flash cards) count aloud while playing (quarter, half note, etc.)
Writing and recognizing intervals: 2nds, 3rds, 4ths, 5ths writing the order of sharps and flats identifying Major sharp key Signatures identifying Major flat key Signatures	Recognizing Major and minor triads singing Major and minor triads recognizing I and V_7 chord progressions (Major keys) recognizing intervals (through the fifth) singing intervals	Sing note names aloud while playing play minor 5-finger positions read melodies using intervals through the fifth
Writing Major and minor chords writing Major key Signatures writing and recognizing intervals of 6ths, 7ths, 8ves	Matching tones using melody and harmony playing question and answer phrases (student listens to the question phrase and plays an answer phrase) recognizing and singing intervals through the octave	Read melodies with extended reaches 6ths, 7ths, 8ves work for tone control (dynamics) work for touch control
Writing IV and V_7 chords	Recognizing various chord progressions (I, IV, V_7)	Move around the keyboard (shifting hand positions)

The beginner's musical program should be designed to include a variety of materials. Although method books provide basic information, they are progressive by nature, and if used without supplementary materials, the student will arrive at a higher level too soon. Also, variety is essential to keep the student's interest. "To work for a long time with only a single book, and a single solo, is, as a rule, not enough to maintain interest."[38]

The method book used will present a predetermined approach. If it is based on five-finger positions, then supplementary books should be chosen that move about the keyboard. If the method book is a middle C course, then multi-key reading should be provided from other books. It will not help the student to give him three method books by different authors if the approach is exactly the same in each course. Rather, the student will benefit from different approaches to fill gaps in the basic method book. Even though a course may state that it is "complete" in itself, this is very seldom (if ever) true. It will not "break the methodology" to use supplemental materials which are different from those in the method series the student is using. Rather, it will strengthen the music program and give the student a broad-based background instead of one which is unnecessarily limited and confined to one approach. An intelligent selection of supplementary books and solos will provide the student with complete materials and will give him a variety of reading experiences.

Not only are there hundreds of first year books and solos available, but new ones are constantly being written. The busy teacher often is not able to keep up with this deluge. However, the interested teacher can learn about new materials from piano workshops or from the new issue file in a good sheet music department of a music store. Also, reviews in *Clavier, Piano Quarterly* and other journals assist in keeping the teacher informed.

The supplementary books and solos included in this chapter were culled from the many published. They include old as well as newer publications. The lists were not intended to be inclusive and extensive. Rather, the materials were selected and condensed to provide general guides.

BOOKS

Agay, Denes Folk Tunes and Folk Dances from Many Lands, Vol. A Witmark (1961)

The arrangements in this collection vary in difficulty from about mid-first year to late first year. Some of the accompanying styles are note against note, others use melody and harmony. The folk songs include those which are both familiar and unfamiliar and utilize a variety of keys and moods.

Agay, Denes The Joy of First-Year Piano Yorktown (1972)

Designed for the dual purpose of both a beginning middle C method and a first-year repertoire album, this eighty page volume contains an abundance of original pieces as well as arranged folk tunes and a few pieces by other composers. After the preliminary stages, the majority of the pieces are in two-voice style. A variety of styles and moods is offered primarily within the confines of 5-finger positions.

[38]Beulah Varner Bennett, *Piano Classes for Everyone* (New York: Philosophical Library, Inc., 1969), p. 39.

Agay, Denes The Young Pianist's First Book Witmark (1966)

Fundamentals of note reading for beginning first year students are presented in this book in quasi-method form. Although the reading centers around middle C, the music includes more elements than is usually offered in middle C readers. The book is useful for supplementary reading assignments for students of average ability.

Agay, Denes (ed.) Very Easy Piano Pieces for Children Heritage (no publication date given)

The elementary pieces in this 64 page collection are arranged progressively. Among others, composers Alt, Burnam, Dittenhaver, Richter, and Scher are represented. Almost all the selections are in C, a few are in G and F. Although most of the pieces are rather lackluster recital fare, as a whole they are useful for supplementary sight-reading.

(American composers) The Barnyard Book of Wild Beasts Schroeder & Gunther/ Associated (1969)

Previously printed only in sheet music form, these eleven first year pieces are about animals which are not necessarily wild. In addition to rabbits, frogs, elephants, etc., there are also domestics in the menagerie (puppies, cats, etc.). These pieces written by specialists Nevin, Wilson, Robinson, Glover, Garrow, and Davis, will surely have strong appeal for beginners. Teacher will recognize such favorites as "Pony Go 'Round" by Glover and "The Greedy Alligator" by Garrow.

Bastien, James Playtime at the Piano, Book 1 GWM Co. (1967)

The compositions in this 32 page volume consist of original pieces, folksong arrangements, and easier works by master composers. The pieces are designed to provide supplementary reading at the elementary level. The compositions range in difficulty from mid-first year to late first year.

Bastien, Jane Smisor Bastien Favorites, Level 1 GWM Co. (1976)

This collection of fourteen previously published piano solos includes such favorites as "The Sleepy Alligator" and "Carnival Cha Cha." An attractive first year solo book for study, recital, or early audition. (Each solo is available in sheet music.)

Bastien, Jane Smisor Folk Tunes for Fun GWM Co. (1967)

The arrangements are written for young first year students and are mostly single line melodies divided between the hands.

Bastien, Jane Smisor Piano Solos, Level 1 Kjos West (1976)

Original pieces and folk tunes comprise this attractive collection of easy supplementary first year pieces.

Bastien, Jane Smisor Rock 'n Blues for Fun GWM Co. (1973)

An easy collection of recreational pieces for enjoyment.

Bastien, Jane Smisor Walt Disney Favorites GWM Co. (1969)

Seven longtime favorites comprise this 16 page collection of Disney songs. The arrangements are designed for young beginners.

Butler, Jack Piano Magic Windsor Press (1970)

All six solos in this collection use the pedal which may be held down to the end in each. Youngsters like to use the pedal (if they can reach down that far), and used in this uncomplicated way, young students will "sound big." The pieces are easy, about mid-first year level.

Cobb, Hazel All Over the Keyboard Belwin-Mills (1962)

This book is similar to an earlier publication, *This Way to Music*. Directional reading is stressed from nine given notes—five C's and four G's. The book complements any method book and gives the student a reading range of about four octaves.

Cobb, Hazel This Way to Music Belwin-Mills (1946)

The book follows a plan for teaching beginners an extended reading range by presenting five C's and four G's. Lateral reading from these nine known notes is employed. Reading is done by direction either up or down, by steps or skips from these nine notes. The book is especially useful as a supplementary reader to acquaint students with a broad keyboard range.

(collection) Five-Finger Music Summy-Birchard (1976)

This 64 page supplementary collection contains four previous publications for the beginning student. Irene Young's *Next Door Neighbors* (1962) consists of easy pieces in two parts which begin in C and progress up the white keys to B (accidentals are used in place of key signatures). John LaMontaine's *Copycats* (1957) are written in canonic form. Alec Rowley's *Sketches* (1958) are written in both Major and minor tonalities. Louise Curcio's *Small Pieces* (1957) are written mostly on the white keys.

(collection) Playtime, Parts A-C Summy-Birchard (1976)

These three 16 page books contain supplementary solos, many with optional accompaniment. The original music is by various composers such as Dittenhaver, George, Kraehenbuehl, and McArtor; in addition, some folk tune arrangements are included. Generally first year level, some in *Part C* are early second year level.

(collection) Summy Piano Solo Package, No. 101 Summy-Birchard (1976)

Contained are thirteen previously published solos by various composers (Burnam, Stecher, Sher, Holst, others) available now only in this volume. Useful teaching comments are provided by Sister Rita Simo. The level of difficulty is first year or early second year.

George, Jon Kaleidoscope Solos, Book 1 Alfred (1973)

An abundance of well-written, imaginative solos is found in this five-book series. *Book 1* introduces the student to simple notation, rhythm, sharps-flats (no key signatures). The 5-finger melodies are divided between the hands. Some teacher duet parts are included.

George, Jon Musical Moments, Books 1 & 2 Schmitt Publications (1972)

Elementary reading material for young beginners, some with optional teacher accompaniment.

Gillock, William Accent on Solos, Level 1 Willis (1971)

These imaginative pieces are the first in the series of *Accent on Solos* which comes in three levels. The pieces are melodically inventive and will appeal to first year students.

Gillock, William Big Note Solos Willis (1970)

The ten solos contained in this collection include a variety of styles and moods, and are just the right level for average first year students.

Gillock, William Folk Songs and Rhythmic Dances Willis (1969)

Designed to be used with Gillock's *Piano All the Way, Level Two*, the arrangements in this collection are written in all major and minor tonalities. The music is simple and appealing. The harmonizations are limited to I and V7 chords.

Gillock, William (ed.) Solo Repertoire, Early Elementary 1 Willis (1966)

This 32 page collection contains a wide variety of literature by such composers as Kabalevsky, Glover, Bartók, Thompson, and many others. The pieces range in difficulty from mid-first year to late first year.

Glover, David Carr Five Finger Boogie Belwin-Mills (1955)

This longtime favorite has five solos strictly for fun.

Glover, David Carr Recital Tidbits, Book 1 Schroeder & Gunther/Associated (1953)

The eight original solos in this collection are about mid-first year to late first year difficulty. The compositions cover a wide note range and are useful for better than average readers.

Glover, David, and Louise Garrow Piano Repertoire, Level 1 Belwin-Mills (1967)

Folk tunes and original pieces comprise this attractive collection of supplementary first year pieces.

Johnson, Thomas A. Beginners Tunes Hinrichsen/Peters (1964)

This elementary book is the first in a reading series called *Read and Play*. The book consists of 75 one-line reading studies. It is especially useful for students who need a great deal of practice reading single line melodies over a period of time.

Last, Joan The First Concert Oxford (1950)

This eleven page collection of twelve pieces is not quite typical of Last's best style; however, the volume is attractive and is useful for supplementary assignments. The pieces vary in difficulty from early to late first year levels.

Lindo, Sylvia Easy Solos for Piano Oxford (1968)

The mostly five-finger pieces in this excellent collection provide mid to late first year experiences in reading some single line melodies, some two-voice melodies, some melodies with simple harmony, and some unison melodies in "easy" keys (primarily C,G,F).

Nevin, Mark Tunes You Like, Book 1 Schroeder & Gunther/Associated (1953)

Easy arrangements of familiar tunes comprise this longtime favorite collection.

Olson, Lynn Freeman Further Along C. Fischer (1973)

The eight pieces in this 16 page collection are written for the beginning student, however, the title implies late first year rather than early first year. The music contains a wide keyboard range, some accidentals, and a variety of moods. Imaginative music for children.

Olson, Lynn Freeman Near the Beginning C. Fischer (1971)

As indicated in the title, these pieces are constructed for the first year student, and are technically very easy. Musically, however, the pieces are sophisticated and stress line, phrasing, and linear texture.

Olson, Lynn Freeman Our Small World Schmitt Publications (1969)

Designed especially for young beginners, these 13 little solos sound quite full when played together with the duet accompaniments. The words by Georgia Garlid are immediately appealing.

Richter, Ada Songs I Can Play Witmark/Warner Bros. Publications (1950)

The arrangements of children's favorites are useful for supplementary reading assignments. The arrangements are easy (about mid-first year) and lie well under the hands.

Stecher, Melvin, Norman Horowitz and Claire Gordon Playing to Learn, Books 1 & 2 G. Schirmer (1965)

These two books include solos and duets for young beginners. The music is simple and uncluttered and musically appealing.

Waxman, Donald Introductory Pageant Galaxy (1958)

Consisting of mostly single-voiced pieces in five-finger positions, this easy first year book is well written for young children. The compositions are imaginative and musically inventive.

Wozniak, Franciszek Musical Miniatures Polskie Wydawnictwo Muzyczne/Marks

There is so much excellent domestic teaching music available that one does not need a great number of foreign publications. However, this 93 page collection is so attractive, both in the colored illustrations and the imaginative music, that it is worth using for special students. The music is much easier in the beginning of the book.

Zepp, Arthur Little Songs & Solos Pro Art (1965)

The pieces in this collection include both original and familiar melodies and some duets. The pieces become progressively more difficult and reach late first year level at the end of the book.

SOLOS

EARLY FIRST YEAR LEVEL

Alt, Hansi The Parade Oxford (1964)

C major - 4/4 - In march time. Mostly single line melody divided between the hands in the middle C position. Left hand harmonic seconds provide a snappy drum-like effect for the prelude and postlude. The art work by Dianne Weiss on the outside cover and inside first page is very attractive.

Bastien, James Circus Parade Kjos West (1976)

C major - 4/4 - Strict march time. Using only quarter and half notes this piece states a jaunty melody divided between the hands in the middle C hand position. The beginning and ending are comprised of minor seconds, suggesting drum beats. Especially for boys.

Bastien, Jane Smisor Balloons for Sales Kjos West (1976)

C major - 4/4 - Happily. Mostly single line melody divided between the hands using only quarter, half, and whole notes. The B section has harmonic intervals of seconds and thirds in the right hand. Words tell the story.

Bastien, Jane Smisor The Cat at Night GWM Co. (1971)

F major - 4/4 - Moderately fast. A legato melody in the F position comprises the A section. The B section has some staccato minor seconds in the right hand for the "meow" effect. An easy first solo. (Included in *Bastien Favorites, Level 1.)*

Bastien, Jane Smisor Chinatown GWM Co. (1968)

A minor - 4/4 - Moderately. An easy first solo using alternating legato and staccato touch in the right hand accompanied by open fifths in the left hand. Pedal is used in the last measure. (Included in *Bastien Favorites, Level 1.)*

Bastien, Jane Smisor The Sleepy Alligator GWM Co. (1971)

C major - 4/4 - Moderato. Hand crossings; two-note slurs; shifting hand positions; balance of melody and accompaniment. An easy first solo. (Included in *Bastien Favorites, Level 1.)*

Burnam, Edna Mae The Friendly Spider Willis (1974)

Aeolian mode - 4/4 - Medium fast. Words and music depict a spider crawling on the wall. The B section uses the pentatonic scale ascending up the keyboard. Mostly single line melody.

Garrow, Louise Here Comes the Band Belwin-Mills (1967)

C major - 4/4 - March time. An easy first solo (primer level) in the C 5-finger position. Legato and staccato touch; some note against note passages.

Garrow, Louise The Little Frog Belwin-Mills (1969)

F major - 4/4 - Merrily. Mostly single line melody; a few note against note passages; legato and staccato touch; 8ve sign in the last two measures.

Garrow, Louise The Swinging Bear Schroeder & Gunther/Associated (1963)

G major - 3/4 - With a swinging rhythm. G 5-finger position throughout; some two-voice style writing in several measures; nice melodic line generally.

Glover, David Carr Pony Go 'Round Schroeder & Gunther/Associated (1963)

G major - 3/4 - Moderately. An attractive easy waltz for young beginners. Left hand staccatos; pedal in the last four measures.

Glover, David Carr Yo Ho! The Sailor's Song Belwin-Mills (1969)

C major - 4/4 - With a sturdy beat. A single note 5-finger position piece for young beginners. Especially for boys.

Olson, Lynn Freeman Early in the Morning and **Faraway Drums C. Fischer (1976)**

These two pieces are written in 4/4 meter, the first is marked Cheerfully, the second, Mysteriously. Both pieces cover a wide keyboard range. *Early in the Morning* is written in single notes, *Faraway Drums* has left hand open fifths for the drum beats.

Richter, Ada Our School Band Boston Music Co. (1969)

C major - 4/4 - Moderato. An easy first solo all in the C 5-finger position. Melody is accompanied by the I and V7 chords. Mostly legato touch; staccato is used in the B section.

Suddards, Elizabeth Mister Woof Witmark (1958)

F major - 4/4 - Moderato. A simple melody accompanied by I and V7 chords; middle section uses 5-finger scales in C, F and G. An attractive first solo for young beginners.

Werder, Richard H. The Drum McLaughlin & Reilly (1965)

C major - 4/4 - March-like. A single line melody piece in the C 5-finger position. Some I and V7 chords. An elementary first solo for young beginners.

Wilson, Samuel Attic Ghost Schroeder & Gunther/Associated (1960)

E minor - 4/4 - Moderately. Single line melody divided between the hands; legato and staccato touch; some accents.

MID-FIRST YEAR LEVEL

Bastien, Jane Smisor Have You Seen? GWM Co. (1968)

E minor - 4/4 - Quietly. The two-note slurs throughout make this a good teaching piece for phrasing (drop-lift hand motions). The glissando at the end is optional. (Included in *Bastien Favorites, Level 1.)*

Bastien, Jane Smisor Little Dog Running Down the Street GWM Co. (1968)

C major - 4/4 - Moderately. Mostly single line melody divided between the hands using alternating staccato and legato passages. Some note against note portions. The piece is written mostly in two treble clefs. (Included in *Bastien Favorites, Level 1.)*

Bastien, Jane Smisor Marching to School GWM Co. (1971)

C major - 4/4 - Steady march tempo. Legato and staccato touch; some two-note slurs; brief changes of hand positions; contrasting dynamics. An easy mid-first year solo. (Included in *Bastien Favorites, Level 1.)*

Frost, Bernice Beaded Moccasins J. Fischer/Belwin (1956)

A minor - 4/4 - Moderato. Staccato and legato touch; two-note slurs; shifting hand positions; pedal in two measures. An easy mid-first year solo.

Garrow, Louise At the Trading Post Belwin-Mills (1969)

C major - 4/4 - Moderately. Moving 5-finger positions; staccato and legato combinations; slurred groups. Uses catchy, rock-like rhythms. A good piece for teaching shifting hand positions.

Gillock, William The Prowling Pussy Cat (© assigned to) Willis (1966)

C minor - 4/4 - Stealthily. Primarily staccato touch; two-note slurs; accents. The B section uses the whole tone scale with pedal throughout. A cute, well-written solo for study and recital.

Glover, David Carr Our School Band Belwin-Mills (1967)

F major - 4/4 - Lively. Alternating staccato and legato touch; two-note slurs; some shifts of hand positions. A good piece for teaching phrasing (down-up wrist motions). Especially for boys.

Nevin, Mark Loop the Loop Schroeder & Gunther/Associated (1950)

C major - 3/4 - Moderato. This arpeggio piece is always a hit with students. Teaching features are: legato touch, crossing hands, and balance of melody and accompaniment.

Scher, William The Timid Little Bee Elkan-Vogel (1966)

A minor - 4/4 - Andante con moto. Mostly single line melody with a few minor seconds for color. Contains a variety of staccato and legato passages. An easy mid-first year solo.

Agay, Denes Parade of the Clowns Sam Fox (1959)

C major - ₵ - Lively, with humor. A wonderful plaintive left hand melody is the outstanding feature of this well-written teaching piece. Teaching features include: two-note slurs, accents, and contrasting dynamics. An excellent solo for teaching phrasing (down-up wrist motions). (Available in *Finger Swingers.)*

Bastien, Jane Smisor Wise Old Owl GWM Co. (1967)

C minor - ₵ - Moderately. Legato and staccato combinations; two-note slurs; balance of melody and accompaniment; shifting 5-finger positions; pedal in the last measure. (Included in *Bastien Favorites, Level 2.)*

Bishop, Dorothy Oriental Story C. Fischer (1976)

(pentatonic) - 4/4 - Moderately. A graceful well-written piece using the pentatonic sounds in oriental music. Several tonalities (hand position shifts) and irregular phrase lengths add color and variety. Written in two-voice style.

Burnam, Edna Mae A Haunted House Willis (1973)

A minor - 4/4 - Very Spooky! Words and music depict a ghostly scene. The mood is set by an introduction comprised of parallel fourths in the bass. Melody-chord, thumb crossings, and hand position shifts are the main teaching features. Good study and recital piece.

Carter, Buenta Bouncing the Ball Summy-Birchard (1949)

C major - 4/4 - Gaily, not too fast. An excellent piece for teaching hand motions (staccatos which must be prepared ahead). Other teaching features are: some two-note slurs, pedal, hand crossings. An attractive study and recital solo. (Available only in *Summy Piano Solo Package No. 102.)*

Fletcher, Lelia Echo Canyon Pow-wow Montgomery (1968)

D minor - 4/4 - Con moto, with marked rhythm. Great steady beat in Indian war dance style (open fifths and minor sixths in the left hand). Teaching features are: two-note slurs, hand crossings, and balance of melody and accompaniment (don't let the left hand overpower the right hand!).

Garrow, Louise My New Bike Schroeder & Gunther/Associated (1959)

C major - 6/8 - Allegro. ABA form. C major and minor 5-finger positions are used for the A section; G major 5-finger positions for the B section. Nice phrasing, melodic line, and attractive words make this an effective teaching piece.

Gillock, William Fog at Sea Willis (1975)

(whole-tone scale) - 3/4 - Andante. Cluster and single notes create an eerie atmosphere in this short mood piece using the whole-tone scale beginning and ending on G-flat.

Noona, Walter and Carol Cat and Mouse Heritage (1973)

G minor - 4/4 - Fast. Contrasting dynamics employed in 5-finger positions (left hand, loud; right hand, soft) constitute the main teaching features of this imaginative solo. Phrasing, legato and staccato touch, and hand position shifts are additional teaching features.

Noona, Walter and Carol The Speedy Little Taxi Heritage (1973)

D major - 4/4 - Fast, of course! Mostly staccato touch, minor seconds for effect, and a few chord clusters constitute the main composition/teaching features of this solo.

Ricker, Earl Little Roguish Clown Lee Roberts/Schirmer (1965)

C major - 4/4 - Lively. Mostly single line melody using staccato touch. Some unexpected rhythms and a few minor seconds put a touch of spice in this joking little solo.

Stecher, Melvin, Norman Horowitz, and Claire Gordon Little Caballero G. Schirmer (1969)

C major - 4/4 - Cheerfully. Staccato thirds in the right hand bounce along through the piece creating an appealing effect both melodically and rhythmically. For better than average students.

Stecher, Melvin, Norman Horowitz, and Claire Gordon Mexican Border Town G. Schirmer (1975)

A minor - 3/4 - Rather lively. Single line melodies divided between the hands using staccato-legato touches evoke the flavor and spirit of castanets in a fiesta setting. Mostly quarter and eighth notes.

Stecher, Melvin, Norman Horowitz, and Claire Gordon Under the Big Top Summy-Birchard (1967)

C major - 4/4 - With spirit. Although mostly single line melody divided between the hands, this solo is more difficult than it looks. Teaching features are: legato and staccato touch; rapidly shifting hand positions. (Available only in *Summy Piano Solo Package No. 101.)*

Wagness, Bernard March of Victory Oliver Ditson Presser (1938)

F major - 4/4 - (no tempo indicated). A longtime favorite. Wonderful for teaching staccato and legato-staccato combinations. A time-tested winner excellent for study or recital.

FOR DISCUSSION AND ASSIGNMENT

1. When first teaching beginners do you favor a pre-reading period? Discuss pros and cons of this approach.
2. List several approaches that will aid in teaching students to read musical notation.
3. If possible use a beginning student (students) to demonstrate the following technical items: hand position, arm drops, legato and staccato touch, balance of melody and accompaniment, down-up wrist motion, turning the thumb under, and double notes. Which items do you consider most important? Why? List other first year technical considerations you consider important.
4. Would you (do you) include theory as a part of piano lessons? Why is it important?
5. At a music store make a survey of first year supplementary books and solos. Present five books and five solos other than those listed in this chapter, and tell why they would be useful for first year students.
6. From your experience examining first year literature, compose a first year solo; point out the teaching features.
7. Outline a first year program in these three areas: (1) reading, (2) technique, and (3) theory.

FOR FURTHER READING[39]

Bolton, Hetty. *On Teaching the Piano.* London: Novello and Co. Ltd., 1954. This brief 93 page volume is worth reading in its entirety. Chapter 4, "Teaching the Beginner," is of special interest.

Gát, József. *The Technique of Piano Playing.* London: Collet's Holdings Ltd., 1965. Although written for advanced students, the section called "Notes on Teaching the Technical Problems of Beginners" contains valuable information.

Last, Joan. *The Young Pianist,* 2nd Edition, London: Oxford University Press, 1972. This book contains the most useful information on teaching young students. It should be read in its entirety.

[39] There are very few books written on teaching beginners. Most books on piano pedagogy either present general philosophy (not much practical information) or are on a more advanced level.

Second Year Students 7

In this chapter second year students are considered to be those who began lessons as average age beginners (seven to eleven) and have received either nine months of instruction (one school year), or a school year plus some summer instruction.

Beginners are confronted with numerous concepts which demand application and perseverance. Such elements as notation, rhythm, beginning technique and theory are all new, and the student must wrestle with these basics for a period of time until they are learned.

Most second year students are over the hurdles of absolute basics, and they will be ready for new and interesting repertoire, easy pop music, and expanded technical and theoretical concepts. Although they are still developing basic skills at the elementary level, they have the advantage over beginners of moving into more interesting areas of musicianship.

One of the problems in teaching second year students is that after the first bloom of newness and freshness has worn off, a routine soon is established between lessons, practice, parents, and teacher which frequently results in diminishing student enthusiasm. Parents should be forewarned of this pattern which occurs with almost clock-like regularity, and they should be advised to be understanding and help their child over this hurdle. However, if sufficient practice is maintained resulting in progress, students continue to be interested and excited about continuing piano lessons, but with somewhat less eagerness than when they began.

In addition to diminished enthusiasm for lessons and practice, each successive grade in school produces increased homework and increased demands for time from outside activities. Even third grade children (eight years old) often have heavy demands made on them. They try to squeeze in play time, practice time, time for homework, and other extracurricular activities. This often can produce rebellion over the piano lesson, especially if there are conflicts. However, if the young pupil's interest is maintained, he will be motivated sufficiently to want to continue lessons, and he will find time for practice.

Second year lessons should be considered as a continuation and extension of work begun in the first year. Even though the teacher would like to go right on from where a pupil left off for the summer vacation, it is not practical to do so. No matter if the summer vacation was two weeks or three months, some elements of first year materials will have become a little hazy after the interruption. This being the case, is it advisable to take any time off during the summer? Yes! Nowadays even youngsters are worked and pressured; and they, like adults, need a change of pace and a chance to breathe a little when they can do things that are less taxing mentally.

Review and review drills are an essential part of learning. New concepts must be reinforced with sufficient practice and application. As review is necessary for general learning, it is essential for the resumption of lessons after even a short recess during the summer. Therefore, notes, key signatures, chords, etc., should be reviewed and checked for a few weeks to make certain that students understand what has been taught previously before beginning new concepts.

The continuation of an effective musical program should include and correlate the four major areas of concentration begun during the first year of lessons: (1) repertoire, (2) technique, (3) theory, and (4) sight-reading.

Second Year Repertoire

It is quite difficult to state categorically the exact repertoire level for each student, because factors such as age, ability, amount of practice, interest, encouragement from parents, competition from peers, etc., play an important part in determining the student's musical level. Most average or better second year students will be ready for easy classical repertoire near the end of the second year of lessons. However, younger students, or those of less ability, may not be ready for serious literature until the third year of lessons.

There is no need to rush into music by the master composers just for the sake of getting there. Often a student would be much better prepared to begin easy sonatinas, Bach minuets, etc., if he would study pre-literature pieces for most of the second year. Examples might include *Piano Literature, Book 1* arranged by David Kraehenbuehl in the Frances Clark Library (Summy-Birchard Co.), or *Playtime at the Piano, Book 2* by James Bastien (General Words and Music Co.). The pieces in these collections are mostly arrangements of folk songs that contain many of the musical problems found in music by master composers, but not the technical complexities.

Too many teachers assign difficult music too soon; they do not allow their pupils to develop naturally and gradually from level to level with sufficient material at each level for reinforcement. The result of assigning difficult music too soon is a general breakdown in the natural development process. Often a student will be given a composition such as Bach's *Minuet in G* early in the second year (or even in the first year), and he will spend months on the piece trying to perfect the complexities of two-voice counterpoint with which he is not ready to cope at this time. Difficult music can be learned at an early time, but at the sacrifice of learning a great deal of progressive, graded material which would insure a solid background in reading and general learning comprehension, and not just a kind of rote learning. Rote teaching at this level is not advisable, and teachers should shy away entirely from "pushing the students' fingers down" and spoon feeding them pieces note by note. If a student is ready for pieces by master composers, he should be able to figure them out mostly on his own, and not be led on, coached all the way by the teacher.

Suggestions in this chapter as to repertoire, sight-reading, etc., are purposely designed for average students who comprise the majority of the teacher's class. Therefore, recommendations for literature will be viewed realistically, keeping in mind the purpose intended. Pupils of extraordinary talent are rare, and it is not practical to design materials just for them. Often it is better to underestimate materials than to overestimate. If a student is studying material that is too easy, it is very simple to assign slightly more difficult literature. However, once difficult repertoire has been assigned, problems arise when the teacher realizes the mistake and tries to backtrack.

It generally takes about two full years of lessons to build a solid background to the point where a student would be able to play most of the pieces contained in easy classical collections. Therefore, repertoire such as elementary sonatinas, easy repertoire collections, etc., will be more extensively discussed in Chapter 8, "Third Year Students." However, as a guide to the type of literature that might be accessible to some second year students, three collections are suggested which contain representative works.

Bastien, Jane Smisor (ed.) Piano Literature, Vol. 1 GWM Co. (1966)
Contains easier pieces by Bach, Spindler, Mozart, Beethoven, Schumann, Kabalevsky, Shostakovich, and Bartók.

Diller-Quaile Second Solo Book Schirmer (1919)
Contains a combination of folk tune arrangements and easier classics.

Goss, Louise (ed.) (Frances Clark Library) Contemporary Piano Literature, Bk. 1 Summy-Birchard (1955)
Contains easier pieces by Tcherepnin, Bartók, Kabalevsky, Tansman, and Kraehenbuehl.

The *Contemporary Piano Literature* collection contains easier material than either the Diller-Quaile or the Bastien collection, but it is comprised of contemporary music exclusively. It is difficult to find original literature that is very easy and quite accessible to second year students from the Baroque, Classical, and Romantic periods. Many of the compositions from these periods were not necessarily written *for* children, but were written by young geniuses such as Mozart and Beethoven who composed little pieces when they were youngsters. Therefore, some of the compositions expressly written for young children, like those of Bartók and Kabalevsky, actually are more accessible for young students than those written by composers from earlier periods.

Practice Suggestions for Second Year Repertoire

The performance of easy classical music by youngsters sounds most convincing when the students have developed basic techniques sufficiently to present these works as the composers intended them to sound. The mechanics of hand coordination, phrasing, delineation of linear line, gradation of dynamics, etc., must be at a sufficient level to render these pieces convincingly. Only with careful and correct practice will students begin to develop the equipment that is necessary for projecting the style and mood when performing these miniature master works.

A few general practice suggestions are:

1. Hands separate practice
2. Slow practice
3. Paying careful attention to the correct fingering
4. Using the correct hand motions needed for the phrasing
5. Tapping one hand like a metronome while playing the other hand
6. Using a metronome while practicing

Contemporary Collections

The word "contemporary" is used here mainly to designate recent composers, most of whom do not write in modern styles (twelve-tone music, use of dissonance, etc.).

There are a number of collections by composers of educational piano music that contain suitable music for study and performance that are slightly less difficult than works in easy classical collections. Below are some suggested second year teaching collections written by composers who are merely recent, plus a few works written in modern styles.

Alt, Hansi The Ocean Oxford (1967)

This collection contains ten appealing, well-written little pieces of about early to mid-second year level.

Bastien, James Playtime at the Piano, Books 1 & 2 GWM Co. (1968)

Both volumes contain easy pre-literature pieces designed to prepare students for more difficult literature to follow. The compositions consist of original compositions, folk song arrangements, and a few of the easiest works by master composers.

Bastien, Jane Smisor Bastien Favorites, Level 2 GWM Co. (1976)

This volume contains thirteen previously published piano solos. A variety of keys, styles and moods are used. (Each solo is available in sheet music.)

Brant, Ada Contra Punts Elkan-Vogel/Presser (1953)

More like studies, these short little pieces are excellent first experiences in two-voice counterpoint on an elementary level.

Clark, Mary Elizabeth (ed.) Contempo 1 (1972), Contempos in Crimson (1972), Contempos in Jade (1972), Contempos in Orchid (1973), Contempos in Sapphire (1973) Myklas

This series is designed to introduce the young pianist to twentieth-century idioms such as modes, polytonality, whole-tone, twelve tone, clusters, ostinato, etc. *Contempo 1* contains a brief informative text for each compositional device with a musical example. New idioms are described as used in succeeding books. The music is by various new composers. Generally, the level of difficulty ranges from early second year to third year (some are more difficult).

(collection) Summy Piano Solo Package, No. 201 Summy-Birchard (1976)

Contained are thirteen previously published solos by various composers (Alt, Bentley, Burnam, Brodsky, Gillock, Olson, Stecher, others) available now only in this volume. Useful teaching comments are provided by Sister Rita Simo. The level of difficulty is second year or early third year.

George, Jon A Day in the Jungle Summy-Birchard (1968)

Twelve little pieces comprise this sixteen page collection of imaginative, one-page pieces. The teaching features of the compositions are described in the contents. A superior set of elementary descriptive pieces, tastefully illustrated and annotated by the composer.

George, Jon Kaleidoscope Solos, Books 2 & 3 Alfred (1973-1974)

The pieces in these books include such teaching features as hand extension, contractions, crossings, and some hand position shifts. The pieces are written mostly in two voices. Attractive music for sophisticated students. *Book 2* is about early second year level, *Book 3* is late second year.

Gillock, William Accent on Solos, Levels 2 & 3 Willis (1969)

Both volumes contain well-written original solos. Baroque style is represented in both the "Gavotte" and "Musette" in the *Level 2* book. Sonatina style is represented in "Sliding in the Snow," and Classical style is represented in "The Queen's Minuet" in the *Level 3* book.

Grove, Roger Light Blue Summy-Birchard (1973)

Seven two-page pieces comprise this sixteen page collection of mildly jazzy pieces. Although some syncopations are used, the music is more atmospheric than upbeat jazz or pop style.

Last, Joan Cats Oxford (1964)

Joan Last has written extensively for children and produced some excellent music—*Cats* is a good example of her style. Written in suite form as ten little piano solos, this collection contains imaginative, attractive music of about late second year level. Some excellent teaching features throughout are: phrasing, explicit use of the pedal, quickly changing positions and registers on the keyboard, and a variety of styles and moods. Attractive illustrations enhance this choice collection of educational music.

Last, Joan Country Outing Oxford (1967)

Fifteen little piano pieces are contained in this volume which offer a variety of styles and moods and are excellent for teaching phrasing, dynamics, touch, etc.

Noona, Walter and Carol The Contemporary Performer, Level 2 Heritage (1975)

This series (four books) is designed to introduce youngsters to idioms of twentieth-century style such as modes, polyrhythms, clusters, polytonalities, twelve-tone rows, and ostinato patterns. The information about the compositional devices is concise and informative.

Olson, Lynn Freeman Menagerie Oxford (1963)

Six little pieces are contained in this well-written collection which are of general second year level difficulty. All the animals in the menagerie are wild: porcupine, crocodile, bear, etc. Clever illustrations enhance the imaginative music.

Poe, John Robert Animal World C. Fischer (1976)

This little collection contains nine solos about two domestic animals (cat, poodle) and seven wild animals—some exotic ("Russian Bear," "Himalyian Moth" for example). The music, covering a wide keyboard range, is imaginatively written in a mildly contemporary vein incorporating some clusters, whole tone scale, and unusual accidentals. The attractive art enhances this volume of pieces ranging in difficulty from about late first year through late second year.

Waxman, Donald First Folk Song Pageant Galaxy (1958)

The entire *Pageant* series (including the *Introductory Pageant, First Year Pageant, Second Year Pageant,* and *Second Folk Song Pageant*) contains imaginative, tastefully written music. Although titled *First Folk Song Pageant,* the music is more difficult than "first" implies—about late second year level.

Second Year Technique

Second year students usually have developed individual finger coordination sufficiently to allow concentration on hand coordination drills. Phrasing, dynamic shadings, balance between hands, etc., now can be studied in more depth. Students need to be more aware of the correct hand motions needed in playing pre-literature pieces during the early part of the second year, and some of the easier classics toward the end of the second year.

Technique should not merely be based on "finger wiggler drills" and scales. Phrasing technique, hand motions, chords, etc., also should be studied and technical drills should be constructed based on these and other concepts.

Even though some of the following eight points were begun during the first year of lessons, they all deserve serious attention during the second year and years to follow.

1. Phrasing
2. Legato and staccato combined
3. Balance between hands
4. Dynamic shadings
5. Part playing
6. Scales
7. Triads and inversions
8. Alberti bass

Phrasing

Good phrasing habits do not come easily and naturally, even to gifted students. Teachers constantly must show pupils how to drop on the beginning of a phrase and lift the wrist at the conclusion of the phrase. This will result in a musical sound which is more like breathing in singing. Two books which give ample explanations about phrasing and numerous little pieces for practice are *Technic Tales* (Books 1 and 2) by Louise Robyn (Oliver Ditson Co., originally published in 1928). These are old books and the illustrations seem old-fashioned today, but there are many good ideas about phrasing and hand motions in them which will be of special interest to teachers.

Phrasing is best taught by beginning with short slurred groupings (Ex. 7:1). As discussed in the previous chapter, it is advisable to instruct students to employ a "down-up" wrist movement, the down movement being on the first note (usually a strong beat), and the up movement on the last note (often a weak beat).

Ex. 7:1. Phrasing exercises.

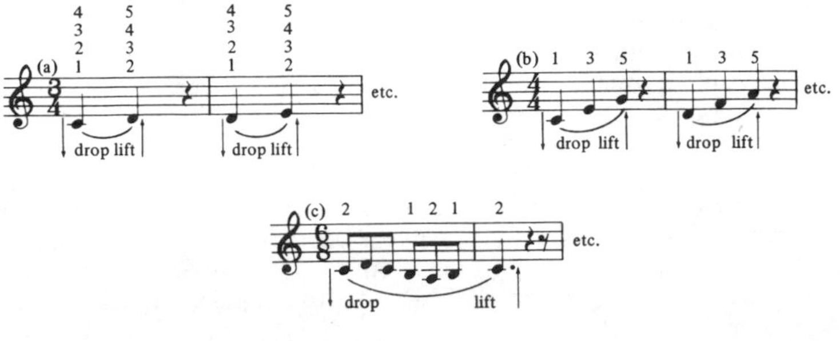

Second year students will encounter a variety of phrases which will include a combination of slurred and staccato groups (Ex. 7:2). It is helpful to design little studies for practicing these combinations.

Ex. 7:2. Exercise for slur and staccato groups.

As indicated in Ex. 7:2 the student should "say" the phrasing aloud: "down-up" for slurs, and "up" for all staccato notes. By saying the phrasing aloud the student will become aware of the correct hand motion for each effect.

The first line of William Gillock's *Dance of the Toys* is given here (Ex. 7:3) to demonstrate slurred groupings alternating between hands. Because of the complexity of hand motions and coordination problems in this piece, the level of difficulty is about late second year or third year. Compositions of this nature serve as excellent pre-literature studies for teaching various aspects of piano technique. Teachers should assign a number of pieces like this before and even during the time standard piano literature is being studied.

Ex. 7:3. Gillock: *Dance of the Toys*[1]

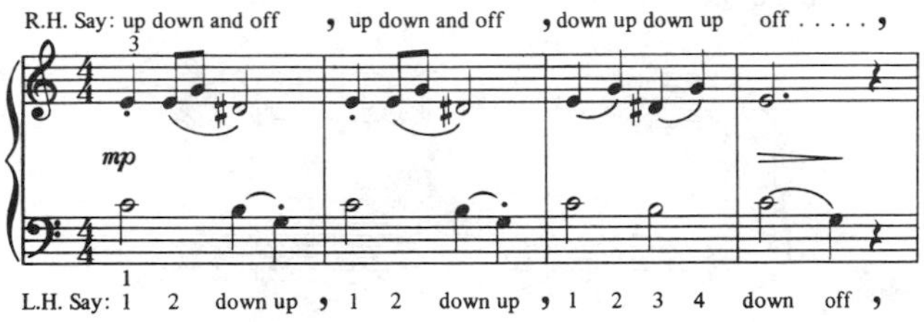

In this piece (Ex. 7:3), as in most compositions of this complexity, each hand should be studied independently (hands separately). By saying the phrasing in each hand the student can begin to acquire the necessary skills and feeling for the correct interpretation of these fundamentals. Notice in the left hand suggestions that it is possible to combine some counting with phrasing (down-up) and intersperse these. Be sure the student phrases (lifts) *both* hands *together* at the end of the first, second, and fourth measures as indicated by the commas. The release of both hands should be simultaneous just like the individual voices in a choir.

[1]Excerpt from *Accent on Solos, Level Three* by William Gillock (Willis Music Co., 1969), p. 12. Used by permission.

Legato and Staccato Combined

The ability to play one hand staccato and the other legato simultaneously (Ex. 7:4) becomes increasingly more important for the correct performance of both pre-literature pieces and some of the easier classical pieces. The main difficulty for students when first combining these two touches is coordination. Both hands "want" to do the same thing at the same time, and each hand must be trained to function independently.

Ex. 7:4. Exercise for the combination of legato and staccato touch.

Balance Between Hands

Even though begun in the first year, this type of hand coordination requires a sufficient time period to develop, and should be studied for at least two years. Most compositions are comprised of some type of melody and accompaniment, or two-voice counterpoint which requires stressing one hand and playing the other softer. The main difficulty for combining "loud and soft" is coordination. Little studies (Ex. 7:5) designed for balance of tone will benefit students and will prepare them for this situation when it is encountered in their music.

Ex. 7:5. Exercise for balance between hands.

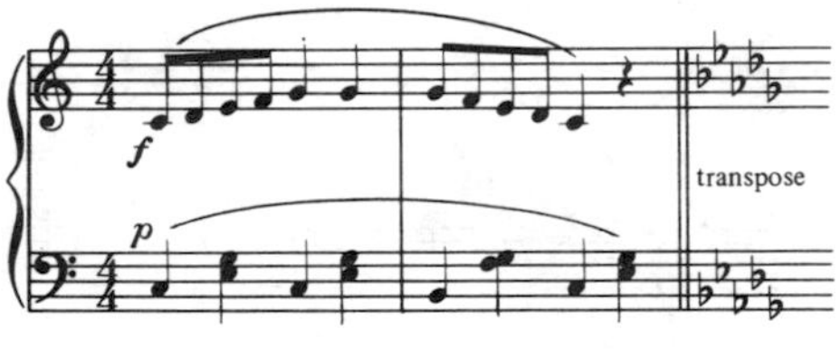

Dynamic Shadings

First year students do not generally have sufficient control over their fingers to warrant a great deal of emphasis on shaping melodies using more sophisticated dynamic colorings. However, within the second year some work should be done to create a more singing line and include dynamic shadings. In addition to the repertoire and sight-reading material studied, which will include increasingly more sophisticated dynamic shadings, a few exercises may be devised for crescendos and decrescendos within a phrase (Ex. 7:6).

Ex. 7:6. Exercises for crescendos and decrescendos.

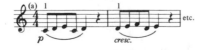

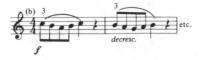

The four points discussed thus far (phrasing, legato and staccato, balance between hands, and dynamic shadings) are clearly evident in a composition like the Spindler *Sonatina* (Ex. 7:7). The melody contains legato and staccato groups, and it must "sing" over the accompaniment (balance). Because the melody is a sequence (repeated melodic motive), it should become slightly louder as it ascends (dynamic shading). It is important to point out these teaching features to students *before* they begin to practice the piece, as this will help to avoid one week of incorrect practice. If carefully adhered to, the correct application of these four teaching points will produce a musical sounding performance.

Ex. 7:7. Spindler: *Sonatina, Op. 157, No. 1*[2]

Part Playing

The ability to hold one finger down while playing others in the same hand (Ex. 7:8) is difficult for students at first, but with some preparatory drills, the difficulties can be overcome. Second year literature frequently contains passages requiring application of this technique.

Ex. 7:8. Part playing.

In both studies (Ex. 7:8) the proper phrasing (down-up wrist motion) should be employed, and both parts should be released at the same time on the fourth count rests with an upward wrist motion.

Numerous second and third year pieces require the mechanics of holding one finger while playing others in the same hand; the following example (Ex. 7:9) is typical. The F in the right hand must be sustained while

[2]Excerpt from *Piano Literature, Vol. 1*, edited by Jane Smisor Bastien (General Words and Music Co., 1966), p. 10.

Ex. 7:9. Sher: *Garden in the Sea*[3]

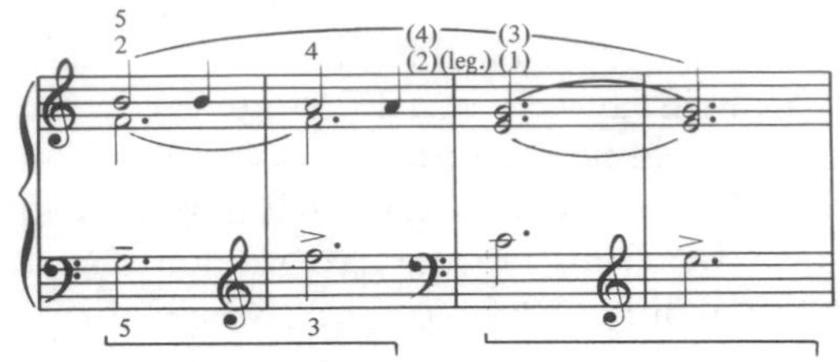

playing from B to A in the first two measures. Also when proceeding from the second measure to the third measure the right hand fingers $\frac{4}{2}$ must connect to $\frac{3}{1}$ without lifting. These two problems can be solved with concentration and practice.

Scales

During the first year of lessons scale playing is minimal for most students. The reason is because few, if any scale passages are used in first year literature. However, most teachers would probably agree that some exposure to scale patterns will benefit first year students—some one or two octave scales, tetrachord scales, etc. Although scale presentation is highly individual and subjective among teachers, it is logical to conclude that the problem of scales as a technique is more easily handled in the second year. This is especially true of parallel scale playing which requires control and coordination.

Unfortunately too many teachers have used scale playing for the *only* source of technique. While it is true that scale study is beneficial for evenness of fingers and for finger control, it is by no means the only aspect of technic. "Technical training is more than just working at scales and finger exercises. It should include practice for *pianissimo* and *fortissimo, crescendo* and *diminuendo*, every variety of tone quality, and also phrasing difficulties."[4]

The two basic problems encountered in scale playing are (1) turning the thumb under or crossing over the thumb, and (2) memorizing the fingering patterns used in parallel motion.

Some thumb under exercises have already been given in Chapter 6; two more are offered here which are slightly more difficult.

Ex. 7:10. Scale preparation exercises.

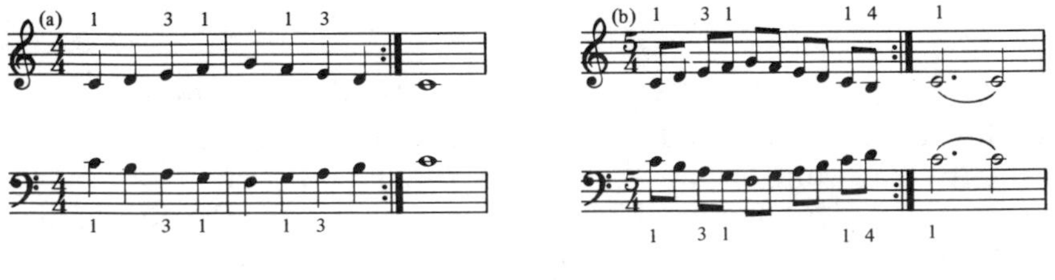

[3]Excerpt from *Garden in the Sea* by William Scher (Elkan-Vogel Co., 1966). Used by permission.

[4]Hetty Bolton, *On Teaching the Piano* (London: Novello and Co. Ltd., 1954), p. 61.

The correct scale fingering for each scale should be learned from the beginning. There is no need to dwell on the exact fingerings because the readers of this book already know the correct fingering sequences. However, there are two viewpoints on scale fingerings:

1. Key of C, r.h.: 1-2-3-1-2-3-4-5
   l.h.: 5-4-3-2-1-3-2-1

2. Key of C, r.h.: 1-2-3-1-2-3-4-1
   l.h.: 1-4-3-2-1-3-2-1

In the first way the little finger is used in the traditional manner represented in the majority of books on scale fingering. In the second way the little finger is not used but is substituted by the thumb, the reason being preparation for playing more than one octave. Several recent books on scale fingerings suggest the little finger substitute: see *Keyboard Scale Fingerings* by J. Parker Nicholson (private publication: Nicholson Music Studios, 337 West 5th St., Scottsdale, Arizona 85251). For an interesting study and history of scales and scale fingering, see *Handbook of Musical Scales* by Lucien Hut and Jody Rhoads Anderson (Missoula, Montana: Mountain Press Publishing Co., 1974: 287 W. Front St., Missoula, Montana 59801). While little finger substitutes may be helpful for students to play scales two octaves or more, generally they are not used this way in compositions, and it appears awkward and mechanical to play them in this manner.

Scale fingerings should be memorized and teachers may or may not use a published book on scales as they see fit. However, for teachers who have grown tired of writing out scales and fingerings in students' notebooks, a few scale books are suggested here which are suitable for second or third year students.

Bastien, James Major Scales & Pieces, Minor Scales & Pieces GWM Co. (1966)
Included are all major and minor scales with related exercises and a piece in each key. Late second or early third year level.

Brimhall, John Encyclopedia of Scales and Arpeggios Hansen (1968)
Included are all major and minor scales (harmonic and melodic), all arpeggios, chromatic scale, modal scales, and diminished seventh chords.

Clark, Mary, and David Carr Glover Write & Play Major Scales, Write & Play Minor Scales Belwin-Mills (1967)
Students write their own fingerings on the blank keyboards and on the blank music paper provided for each scale.

Glover, David Carr Scale Book Schroeder & Gunther/Associated (1964)
Included are all major and minor scales (natural, harmonic, melodic), triads and inversions, and cadence chords.

Hirshberg, David Scales & Chords are Fun Book 1, Major Musichord (1948)
Included are all major scales and a piece in each scale key; about late second or early third year level.

Triads and Inversions

Like scales, chord studies serve two purposes, technical and theoretical. Chord drills are an important part of a student's technical program, because chord playing aids in developing a good hand position, shaping the fingers, and developing a general facility for playing in more than one key at a time.

During the first year students will have learned major and minor triads in root position, dominant seventh chords (V $^6_5$), and subdominant chords (IV $^6_4$). Sometimes near the end of the second year of lessons students may be taught triads and inversions (Ex. 7:11), probably just major and minor triads. The correct fingering is especially important when teaching inversions of chords; students will want to play the same fingers for the root position and the inversions as well. To make them aware of changing fingers, it is helpful to circle the fingering in each hand which is unusual. It is also helpful to teach the chords in both block and broken style.

Ex. 7:11. Chords and inversions.[5]

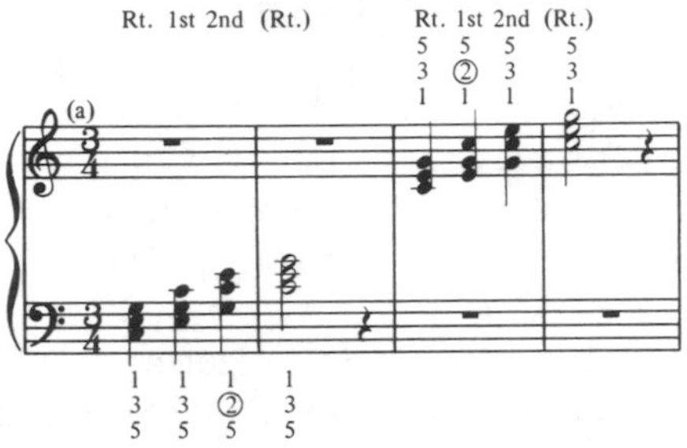

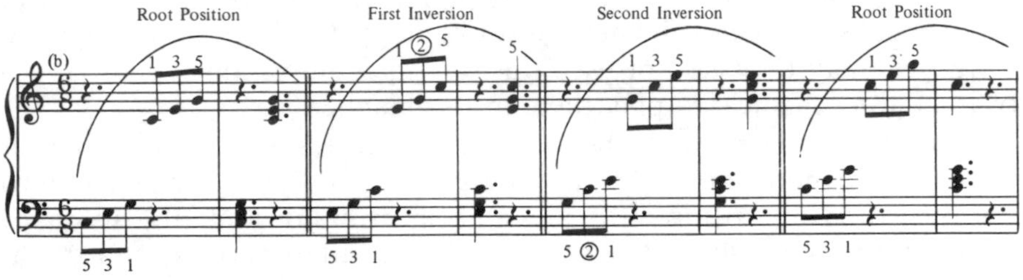

Triads and inversions should be studied *both* ascending and descending. Frequently students will be able to play the chords ascending, but often they will have lost the mental picture of the chord they are inverting, and they will not be able to come back down.

One general fault of practicing these chords is the natural inclination to "hunt" for each successive note of the chord. The chords should not be "discovered" by trial and error using the "hunt and peck" method. A strong mental picture of the correct fingering should be established to form an anticipated feeling for successive chords in the pattern.

Since fingering is an important aspect when learning triads and inversions, sufficient drill should be assigned so that in time the correct fingering will become automatic. It is helpful to have the student say aloud the fingering for the middle note of the chords, as this is the finger that will be changed in the inversions:

r.h. 3-2-3-3
l.h. 3-3-2-3

The student should learn all twelve major (and minor) triads and inversions. However, these are more easily learned if only one group of keys is assigned per week:

[5]Example from *Magic Finger Technique, Book 3* by James Bastien (General Words and Music Co., 1966), pp. 6 & 7.

Example:

(first week) Learn the triads and inversions of C,G,F both up and down, hands separately. Memorize the correct fingering. Practice all chords five times a day in each hand.

(second week) Learn the triads and inversions of D,A,E, etc.

Be specific in your directions to the students and you will get results. Remember that the word *practice* means *repetition;* remind your students of this from time to time, and spell out how many times you want each item repeated.

Alberti Bass

In the first year students have learned some blocked and broken chords; in the second year, the Alberti bass pattern may be studied in preparation for sonatinas and various teaching pieces that use this style accompaniment (Glover's *Ach! My Little Foreign Car,* for example). The coordination involved in playing the pattern can be developed more easily if the student has a mental picture of the figure; play the figure for the student and describe the pattern verbally: "bottom, top, middle, top," etc. Assign exercises using this pattern (Ex. 7:12) to be practiced in all keys. Divide the presentation by groups of keys as suggested for learning triads and inversions.

Ex. 7:12. Alberti bass studies.[6]

Directions: 1. Say the words: "bottom, top, middle, top" for the notes in the left hand.
2. Note the change in position for the V7 chords.
3. Learn to play the Alberti bass in all keys.

[6]Example from *Magic Finger Technique, Book 3*, p. 22.

Suggested Technique Books

In addition to any exercises the teacher might invent for individual drill, a few books are suggested here which would be beneficial for second (or third) year students.

Bastien, James Magic Finger Technique, Books 2 & 3 GWM Co. (1966)
These two books contain short exercises in pure technique in all keys developing phrasing, legato and staccato, balance between hands, chords and inversions, trills, scales, double notes, chromatics, and Alberti bass.

Bastien, James Technic Lessons, Levels 2 & 3 Kjos West (1976)
These books contain a combination of short exercises and studies in various keys developing scales, chords, crossing hands, chromatics, double notes, finger extension, phrasing, legato-staccato touches, and incorporate various rhythms.

Burnam, Edna-Mae A Dozen a Day, Books 1 & 2 Willis (1950)
These two books provide a good representation of short exercises for the development of legato, staccato, double notes, crossings, scales, repeated notes, chromatics, and some phrasing. The exercises are only written in C, but the author suggests transposition in the preface.

Last, Joan Freedom Technique, Book 1 Oxford (1971)
The brief studies in this twelve page volume provide a variety of experiences designed to promote ease of movement over the keyboard. The exercises stress such areas as rotary patterns, slurred groups, arm weight, scale preparation, scales, arpeggios, chromatic scale, and one pedal exercise. Each example is purposely short to allow several to be played in each practice session.

McArtor, Marion (Clark Library) Piano Technic, Books 1 & 2 Summy-Birchard (1954)
Written as short, one-page compositions, these studies are based on positions of the hand: five-finger positions, extended positions, crossings, chords and broken chords, thirds, and part playing. *Book 2* is at least late second or third year level.

Summary of Second Year Technique

As viewed in the preceding eight points, technique is an amalgamation of a number of skills which form a suitable background enabling students to perform piano literature in a musical fashion. When problems are encountered in the student's music, the teacher should invent little exercises to overcome these difficulties. In this creative manner individual exercises can be tailored to fit specific needs. By taking a broad view of technique, the teacher can instill a wide variety of background skills which will serve the student in whatever course he chooses to follow.

Second Year Theory

In the previous chapter the importance of including theory and keyboard harmony as an integral part of piano lessons was discussed. Students must understand what they are doing regarding various phases of theory—key, harmonic structure, etc. The teacher constantly must strive to make students musically literate in every aspect of music.

Theory and keyboard harmony may be included in the private lesson, or it may be taught in a class. In any case it is vital for the teacher to find time to include this important aspect of music. It is the teacher's duty to offer a complete music program which will provide students with a comprehensive background.

The second year theory program is a continuation of items already begun. Review in the beginning of the second year is essential to reestablish concepts started in the first year.

New theoretical inclusions in the second year are:

1. Subdominant minor chords (inverted position)
2. Augmented chords
3. Diminished chords
4. Writing major scales

Subdominant Minor Chords

Melodies were previously harmonized with major I, IV, and V7 chords. Minor melodies may also be harmonized with i, iv, and V7 chords. Students have already learned minor tonic chords and dominant seventh chords (which are the same for major and minor), so the only new chord in the progression is the iv chord in minor (Ex. 7:13). The purpose of learning this new chord is for functional usage in minor tonalities. It is more practical for students to learn to *play* this chord in all minor keys than it is for them to learn to write the chord.

Direct the student to practice the progression i, iv, i (Ex. 7:13). After he has learned the progression, assign i, iv, i, V7, i. Each progression should be learned in one group of keys at a time: *i.e.,* first week in the keys of C,G,F; second week in the keys of D,A,E; third week in the keys of Db,Ab,Eb,; fourth week in the keys of Gb,Bb,B. In this manner there will be sufficient time for thorough comprehension.

Ex. 7:13. The iv Chord in Minor.[7]

To form a iv chord in minor begin with a minor chord position, then follow the rules below:

LEFT HAND

1. Keep the 5th finger the same.
2. Play 2 (in the five finger position).
3. Move 1 up a half step.

RIGHT HAND

1. Keep 1 the same.
2. Move 3 up a whole step.
3. Move 5 up a half step.

Example:

Example:

An example of melodies harmonized with minor iv chords is given here (Ex. 7:14) to show how this chord may be applied to keyboard harmony.

[7]Example from *Book 3 Writing* by Jane Smisor Bastien (General Words and Music Co., 1964), p. 7.

Ex. 7:14. Harmonizing minor melodies using the iv chord.[8]

Augmented Chords

An augmented triad consists of a major third and an augmented fifth. However, since youngsters have not yet been taught chromatically altered intervals, an easier explanation for children is: The word AUGMENT means to make *larger. Raise* the top note (5th) of a *major* triad ½ step to form an augmented chord (Ex. 7:15).

Ex. 7:15 Augmented triad.

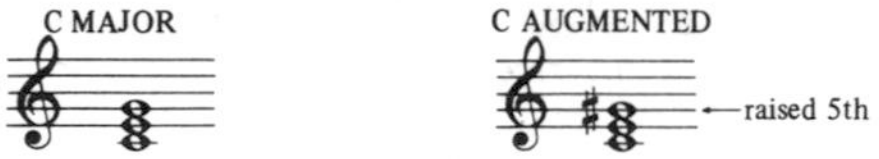

Instruct students to practice the progression: Major, Augmented, Augmented, Major, hands separately in the groups of keys (C,G,F; D,A,E; Db,Ab,Eb; Gb,Bb,B):

Diminished Chords

A diminished triad consists of a minor third and a diminished fifth. An easier explanation for children is: The word DIMINISH means to make *smaller. Lower* the top note (5th) of a *minor* triad ½ step to form a diminished chord (Ex. 7:16).

[8]Example from *Book 3 Writing*, p. 7.

Ex. 7:16. Diminished triad.

Instruct students to practice the progression: minor, diminished, diminished, minor, hands separately in the groups of keys:

After practicing augmented chords related to major, and diminished chords related to minor, all four chords may be combined in the following progression:

Writing Major Scales

Sometime during the second year of lessons students may be taught the pattern of whole and half steps that comprise the major scale (Ex. 7:17). Following the pattern of whole and half steps students may construct the scales and learn to play them with the correct fingering.

Scales may be explained to children in the following manner: The major scale (from the word meaning ladder) uses seven different letters of the musical alphabet. However, because the scale begins and ends on the same letter, there are actually *eight* tones altogether. These tones always appear in a regular pattern of whole steps and half steps. The half steps are between 3 and 4, and 7 and 8; all other steps are whole steps.

Ex. 7:17. The pattern for all major scales.[9]

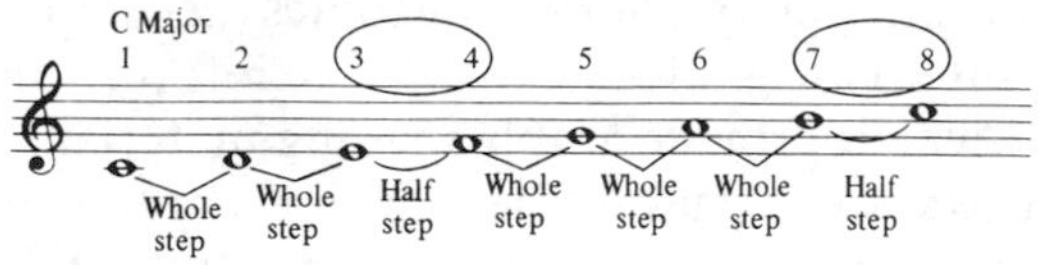

Theory Texts

Like piano courses there are numerous theory books on the market; in fact almost every recent piano course has an accompanying set of theory books. In addition to theory books designed to be used with piano courses there are a number of separate theory books published at various levels. Three sample titles selected at random are:

Barrett, Meredith (pen name for Mary Elizabeth Clark), *Theory Papers, Levels 1-4*. (Edward Schuberth & Co., 1970).

Brimhall, John, *Theory Notebook, Books 1-3* (Charles Hansen Music Corp., 1968).

McIntosh, Edith, *Theory and Musicianship, Books 1-3* (Carl Fischer, Inc., 1956).

[9]Example from *Major Scales and Pieces* by James Bastien (General Words and Music Co., 1966), p. 3.

Although all three of these theory texts have merit, some considerable, the main emphasis appears to be given to written theory exercises. The written studies in these books are commendable. However, since keyboard harmony is essential for pianists (even youngsters), theory books which include considerable playing are to be highly recommended, especially for children. Recommended theory courses which stress keyboard harmony are:

Bastien, James, *Theory Lessons, Levels Primer-4* (Kjos West)
Bastien, Jane Smisor, *Writing, Books 1-6* (General Words and Music Co.).
Kraehenbuehl, David, *Keyboard Theory, Books 1-6* (Summy-Birchard Co.).
Pace, Robert, *Skills and Drills, Books 1-6* (Lee Roberts Music Publications, Inc./G. Schirmer).

Summary of Second Year Theory

The four new concepts introduced during the second year theory program constitute a minimum amount of new materials. Depending on the student's age and ability, other items that could be studied include: writing triads and inversions, and studying some altered intervals (minor third, minor sixth, augmented fifth, and diminished fifth). However, it is more practical to wait until the third year to teach these written concepts.

Second Year Sight-Reading

A reading program should be devised for each student based on a reasonable level which is slightly below the repertoire level. One should not assign second year students music such as the little pieces from the *Anna Magdalena Notebook* for general sight-reading. At the second year level, these pieces are too difficult for that purpose; they are not meant for casual study.[10]

A distinction should be drawn between suitable repertoire for serious study and realistic sight-reading material. Most piano courses are designed around a basic reading program which is progressive by necessity. Often the rate of progression in piano courses becomes accelerated too fast which defeats the basic intent of graded reading. Therefore, supplementary books should be assigned which provide ample reading material at a given level.

Several books are suggested here which contain practical sight-reading material on the second year level for average students.

Adams, Bret *Play Folk Music for Pleasure* Schroeder & Gunther
Agay, Denes *Fun with Sight-Reading, Vol. A* Witmark/Warner Bros. Music
Bastien, James *Playtime at the Piano, Books 1 & 2* GWM Co.
Bastien, James *Sight Reading, Levels 1 & 2* Kjos West
Bastien, Jane Smisor *More Folk Tunes for Fun* GWM Co.
Cobb, Hazel *A Mid-Term Reader* Belwin-Mills
Cobb, Hazel *First Solo Book* Belwin-Mills
Dittenhaver, Sarah Louise, and Marion McArtor *Tune Time, Part B* Summy-Birchard

[10]There is a collection by Fanny Waterman and Marion Harwood called *Second Year Piano Lessons* published by MCA. This volume includes such compositions as the *F Major Scherzo* by Haydn, *Prelude in C* from Book 1 of the *Well Tempered Clavier* by Bach, the *Gavotte en Rondeau* by d'Andrieu, among others. One wonders how the authors can justify such material for less than very gifted students, at the second year level. This collection, excellent though it may be, is excessively demanding as second year pieces, and of course it would be ludicrous for sight-reading purposes.

Gillock, William (ed.) *Solo Repertoire, Early Elementary* Willis
Glover, David and Louise Garrow *Piano Repertoire, Level 2* Belwin-Mills
Johnson, Thomas *Hands Together* Hinrichsen/Peters
Kraehenbuehl, David *Piano Literature, Book 1* Summy-Birchard
Nevin, Mark *Tunes You Like, Books 2 & 3* Schroeder & Gunther
Rozin, Albert *Miniatunes* Schroeder & Gunther
Stecher, Melvin, Norman Horowitz and Claire Gordon *Playing to Learn, Book 2* G. Schirmer
Steiner, Ralph *Fun Time at the Piano* Pro Art
Thomas, Helen Thompson *First Moments at the Piano, Book 2* Presser
Waxman, Donald *First Folk Song Pageant* Galaxy

In addition to supplementary books for sight-reading at various levels, sight-reading flash cards may be made by the teacher either for use in individual lessons or in class lessons (Ex. 7:18). Short musical phrase flash cards are most effective for drill in instant recall.

Ex. 7:18. Musical phrase flash card.

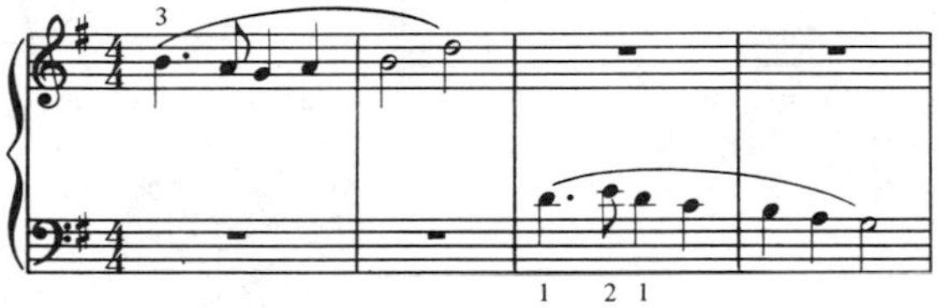

As the card is held up the student should quickly perceive (1) the clef signs, key signature, meter signature; (2) the correct position on the keyboard for both hands; (3) the rhythm (the note values may be tapped before beginning to play); (4) any changes in hand position which might occur (crossing 2 over 1 in the left hand, third measure in Ex. 7:18). While playing the student should say the counts aloud (or sing note names), and look far enough ahead to keep going in tempo, and he should play straight through without stopping.

A series of musical phrase flash cards may be made by the teacher which become gradually more difficult in melody, rhythm, and harmony. This drill works very effectively in a class presentation. Have one student play a drill and the others observe closely to see if the student playing made any mistakes. The student who reads perfectly (correct notes, rhythm, phrasing, fingering, etc.) gets to keep the card; the student who has the most correct cards wins the game. The teacher should not hesitate to create and invent either private or class aids for various purposes.[11]

Diagram of Second Year Materials

Second year material should be planned to introduce the student to new elements while at the same time providing review drills for reinforcement. New items should be spaced evenly to allow time for absorption.

The following diagram (Ex. 7:19) lists objectives for second year students and is intended as a general guide based on the nine-month school year.

[11]For an informative article on sight-reading, see "Sight Reading in the Piano Class" by Dorothy Bishop, *Clavier*, Vol. III, No. 1 (January-February, 1964).

Ex. 7:19. Diagram of second year materials.

	REPERTOIRE	RHYTHM	TECHNIQUE	KEYBOARD HARMONY
Division I **Sep. - Oct.**	General review of previous materials review pieces with waltz bass broken chord bass	Review previous rhythms	Review all 5-finger patterns; make exercises for: 1. phrasing (two-note slur) 2. legato and staccato 3. balance between hands	Review I, IV, V_7 chords review harmonizing melodies with these chords
Division II **Nov. - Dec.**	Assign pieces using note against note style	Triplets: 	Dynamic shadings; make exercises for touch and tone control continuation of chromatic scale continuation of double notes begin exercises in part playing continuation and development of scale preparation drills (crossing over the thumb and turning the thumb under)	Play the iv_4^6 chord in minor harmonize and improvize in minor using i, IV, V7, i harmonize melodies using waltz bass, broken chord bass
Division III **Jan. - Feb.**	Easy literature: Bartók, Kabalevsky, etc. Collections: (examples) *Piano Lit., Vol. 1*, Bastien (ed.) *Contemporary Piano Lit., Book 1*, Clark (ed.)	   	Scales: major and harmonic minor, two octaves h.s. and together triads and inversions: major and minor Alberti bass	Play augmented triads (root position) play diminished triads harmonize melodies using Alberti bass
Division IV **Mar., April, May**	Easy Sonatinas: (examples) *First Sonatina*, Bastien *Sonatina Album*, Cobb	Syncopated rhythms:  		

THEORY	EAR TRAINING	NEW ELEMENTS IN ASSIGNMENT
Review note names (use note flash cards) review order of sharps and flats review major key signatures (use flash cards) review intervals (use flash cards) review writing major and minor chords	Review first year materials: 1. matching tones 2. question and answer phrases 3. singing major and minor triads 4. singing intervals 5. identifying I, IV, V_7 progression 6. identifying major and minor chords	Start new repertoire, new solos, etc.
	Identify i, IV, V_7 chord progression in minor keys give question and answer phrases in minor keys	Begin playing pieces that cross fingers over or turn the thumb under assign pieces with block chords moving around concentrate on subtle dynamics: crescendo, decrescendo
Write augmented and diminished triads write major scales; learn the pattern of whole and half steps used recognize inversions of triads (use flash cards)	Question and answer phrases using different style basses identify augmented and diminished chords	Begin playing pieces with scale passages concentrate on tempo, using a metronome and give metronome markings for home practice
	Recognize triads and inversions	

DUET COLLECTIONS

Bastien, Jane Smisor *Duets for Fun, Book 1* GWM Co.
Campbell, Henry *First Piano Duets* J. Fischer/Belwin
Cobb, Hazel *Playing Together* Flammer
Garrow, Louise *Tunes You Like for Two* Schroeder & Gunther
George, Jon *Kaleidoscope Duets, Books 1 & 2* Alfred
George, Jon *Two at One Piano, Book 1* Summy-Birchard
Glover, David Carr, and Louise Garrow *Piano Duets, Level 1* Belwin-Mills
Johnson, Thomas *You and I* Hinrichsen/Peters
Last, Joan *Two and a Piano, Sets 1-3* Oxford
Pace, Robert *Duets for Piano, Sets 1 & 2* Lee Roberts/Schirmer
Stecher, Horowitz, Gordon *The Pleasure of Your Company, Books 1 & 2* G. Schirmer

SOLOS

EARLY SECOND YEAR LEVEL

Anson, George Spook on the Stairs Willis (1972)

A minor - 4/4 - Stealthily, unhurried. An ostinato bass sets the background for right hand patterns on the white and black keys creating some bi-tonal harmonies in this contemporary sounding piece.

Bastien, Jane Smisor A First Sonatina GWM Co. (1972)

Consisting of three short movements, this sonatina is purposely written on the easiest possible level (late first year, or early to mid-second year). The first movement, *Moderately,* uses 5-finger positions, contrasting touches, and easy hand position changes. The second movement, "Song," states a simple melody first in the right hand, then in the left hand. The third movement, "Gigue," employes modal sounds (lowered leading tone). A number of 5-finger positions are used, especially for the B section. The Gigue is brought to a conclusion by a dramatic use of the whole tone scale in the lower register of the piano. As a whole, the music is attractive and bright and on a realistic level to be called "first."

Bastien, Jane Smisor Parakeets in Birdland GWM Co. (1965)

G major - 4/4 - Lightly. The main feature of this solo is "position playing;" the student must constantly prepare ahead for new hand positions. Staccato and legato combinations are used throughout. Various 5-finger positions are used for the B section. Some I and V7 chords are used sparsely. This piece is easier than it sounds, and it may be easily memorized by analyzing the chordal outlines. (Included in *Bastien Favorites, Level 2.)*

Bishop, Dorothy Hoe Down C. Fischer (1961)

G major - 4/4 - Briskly. A very attractive, strongly rhythmic, square dance piece incorporating the following teaching features: legato-staccato combinations, shifts of hand positions, syncopation (♪♩.𝅗𝅥), and balance of melody and accompaniment.

Dittenhaver, Sarah Louise Fast Train at Night Schroeder & Gunther/Associated (1964)

D minor - 3/4 - Rather fast, with energy and excitement. A nice melodic line, shifting hand positions, some two-voice style writing, and exacting phrasing comprise the main teaching features of this first-rate study and recital solo. Words are given for all but the introduction and postlude.

Elaine, Sister M. March of the Indians J. Fischer/Belwin (1966)

D minor - 4/4 - Martial. Left hand staccato broken fifths form a strong rhythmic background for the legato right hand melody. The melody encompasses a range of an octave, and if the student cannot reach the notes legato, they may be played slightly separated to accommodate small hands. Especially for boys.

Frackenpohl, Arthur Sharp Four Lee Roberts/Schirmer (1965)

G major - 2/2 - Moderately fast. The main melodic feature of this teaching piece is the use of C # (raised fourth) throughout. Teaching features include: staccato and legato touch, two-note slurs, and accents.

George, Jon Turtle Talk Summy-Birchard (1969)

G major - 4/4 - Deliberately. Slurs are the main teaching feature in this well-written solo. Clever words about a turtle that doesn't talk add interest and create a nice effect. This piece is more effective for teaching purposes than for recital. (Available only in *Playtime, Part B.)*

Gillock, William The Glass Slipper Willis (1970)

C major - 3/4 - In waltz time. The typical waltz-style piece made trite over years of use becomes a lyrical, expressive teaching piece by Gillock. The plaintive left hand melody sings in the A section in two-note slurs. The right hand takes over in the B section and makes a nice contrast not only in register but in phrase length. The codetta contains an interesting arrangement of the chromatic scale divided between the hands. An excellent piece to teach balance of melody and accompaniment. (Included in *Big Note Solos.)*

Holst, Marie Seuel Black Pirates Summy-Birchard (1939)

D minor - 4/4 - Boisterously and with much accent. Strong march-like rhythms in the left hand form a background for the legato right hand melody. Teaching features include: legato-staccato combinations, two-note slurs, some shifting hand positions. Especially for boys. (Available only in *Singing Keys, Omnibus.)*

King, Patricia W. A Sad Thing Lee Roberts/Schirmer (1970)

Dorian mode - 3/4 - Slowly. Beginning in the D minor hand position, the modal tonality is effected by the C and B naturals. A singing legato melody is the main feature in this melancholy piece. Two-voice style is used throughout. Some changes of hand positions occur.

Maclachlan, Robin T. Ghost Dance Schroeder & Gunther/Associated (1938)

A minor - 4/4 - Misterioso. This "old favorite" includes the following teaching features: staccato and legato touch, two-note slurs, hand crossings, some changes of hand positions. Chordal accompaniment is provided by the i iv V7 chords in minor.

Noona, Walter and Carol Sailing in the Bay! Heritage (1973)

Db major - 2/4 - Smoothly. Five-finger positions are used in Db, D and B. Pedal is used to help create a flowing, lilting effect. Words enhance the music.

Olson, Lynn Freeman Silver Bugles C. Fischer (1972)

C major - 4/4 - Bright and detached. Repeated notes in both hands create the bugle fanfare throughout. Single, double and triple notes pile up to build the crescendo in the B section. A simple, well-written elementary solo for study and recital.

Stevens, Everett The Funny Eskimo C. Fischer (1956)

A minor - 4/4 - Smoothly, not fast. A beautifully written melodic piece emphasizing touch and color. Excellent for teaching balance of melody and accompaniment and slurred phrases.

Stevens, Everett Told at Dusk C. Fischer (1960)

C major - 3/4 - Moving gracefully. The left hand states the melody using slurs of varying lengths. In the B section the melody moves to the right hand. Balance of melody and accompaniment is an important feature of this sensitive solo. Especially for a musical student with a good feeling for melodic line of better than average ability.

Bastien, Jane Smisor Run-Away Balloon GWM Co. (1968)

F major - 3/4 - Smoothly. Comprised mainly of F major and Db major chordal outlines, this solo incorporates the following teaching features: hand crossings, shifts of hand positions, mostly legato touch. (Available in *Bastien Favorites, Level 2.)*

Bishop, Dorothy Dance of Long Ago C. Fischer (1957)

G major - 4/4 - Slow and graceful. Written in imitative classical style, this musical solo mainly features slurred groups. The entire piece is written in two-voice style. Several shifts of hand positions are used.

Erb, Mae-Aileen Whiz! Goes the Train! Flammer (1964)

C major - 2/4 - Allegro. The motion of the train is effected by steady eighth note figures. The right hand plays staccato double notes and the left hand plays moving legato notes; the staccato-legato combinations are a good study for coordinating both hands.

Frackenpohl, Arthur March On! and **Parade Lee Roberts/Schirmer (1963)**

Both one-page solos are in C major and are written in strict march time. "March On!" uses a simple melodic line and a single note accompaniment. "Parade" is slightly more difficult (late second year level) employing syncopations, quickly changing positions, and a broken chord bass. Both solos are bright sounding, well-written pieces.

Garrow, Louise Agent 402 Belwin-Mills (1968)

C minor - 4/4 - Misterioso. Melodic and harmonic effects include: left hand 5-finger C minor position with a raised fourth, a number of minor chords in the right hand, some in first inversion. All accidentals are written in (the C minor key signature is not used). An effective "spooky" piece which maintains suspense throughout.

George, Jon Frontier Town Summy-Birchard (1969)

D major - ₵ - Robustly. A bright-sounding, well-written piece employing modal effects, off-beat accents, and incorporating a wide keyboard range. Especially for boys. An effective recital solo. (Available only in *Supplementary Solos.*)

Gillock, William Happy Holiday Willis (1966)

G major - 4/4 - Happily. Composed mostly in two-voice style, this jaunty solo incorporates changing hand positions, slurs, some whole tone scale passages, and pedal.

Glover, David Carr Saucer Men Belwin-Mills (1967)

C major - 4/4 - Sturdy beat. The main composition features of this attractive march are shifting triads and the use of the whole tone scale. An effective study and recital solo.

Grove, Roger Boogie Brigade Belwin-Mills (1971)

C major - 4/4 - Not too fast. Teaching features include right hand broken chords, hand position shifts, legato-staccato touches, and two-note slurs. Especially for boys.

Nevin, Mark Jogging Marks (1969)

F major - C - Moderato. More like an etude than a recital solo, this piece is excellent for teaching legato-staccato combinations and balance of tone.

Noona, Walter and Carol The Broken-Down Merry-Go-Round Heritage (1973)

E major - 6/4 - Moderato. A harmonic minor second in the left hand establishes the broken effect in waltz-like meter. Some meter changes (5/4, 6/4, 3/4, etc.) also create an unsteady, broken effect. Rhythmic interest is gained by adherence to the accents.

Olson, Lynn Freeman Secret Mission C. Fischer (1970)

C major - 4/4 - Sinister, but swingy. Comprised mainly of melody accompanied by open fifths, this attractive solo is effective for study and recital. Strong rhythmic verve is maintained throughout and syncopated rhythms are featured. Especially for boys.

Ricker, Earl A Distant Bell, A Deserted Cottage Lee Roberts/Schirmer (1965)

A Distant Bell, the first solo in this two-piece set, is in D minor. The left hand tolls the bell by repeating the pedal point note A; sometimes the bell (A) is heard in the right hand. An effective, well-written solo.

A Deserted Cottage is in the E tonality and has a strong phrygian flavor through the use of shifting left hand triads, all on the white keys. Some meter changes are used: 4/4, 5/4, 3/4.

Senter, Gina Pirate's Den Schroeder & Gunther/Associated (1961)

C minor - 4/4 - Real sneaky. Called a study in accidentals (no key signature is used), this little solo has nice teaching features: contrasting touches, phrase groupings, shifting registers. Mostly two-voice style composition. Good for both study and recital.

Scher, William Cossacks Witmark (1960)

A minor - ¢ - Moderato. An effective teaching piece which lies well under the hands (mostly 5-finger positions). Coordination is a problem for students due to the diverse phrase groupings between hands. For that reason it is better suited to pupils of better than average ability.

Skaggs, Hazel Ghazrian A Little Invention Boston Music Co. (1964)

C major - 3/4 - (no tempo indicated). A good study piece incorporating the following teaching features: voicing imitative melodies, crossing over the thumb, sequential patterns, contrasting dynamics. This type of piece is better suited for study than recital.

Stevens, Everett Comanche R.D. Row Music Co./Boston Music Co. (1965)

Dorian mode - 4/4 - With rhythmic insistance. A nice piece for those students who have difficulty with memorization: recurring left hand open fifths are used throughout. Right hand patterns include finger crossings, and well-written phrase structures. Especially for boys.

LATE SECOND YEAR LEVEL

Bastien, James Mexican Fiesta GWM Co. (1972)

A minor - 2/4 - Brightly. The introduction and postlude establish the bright festive mood of the occasion. The main portion of the piece (*Moderately* in 6/8 meter) sings a plaintive song accompanied by left hand triads. The composition sounds more difficult than it is. An effective recital solo.

Bastien, Jane Smisor Poodles Prancing GWM Co. (1965)

F major - 4/4 - Strict march time. This spirited solo incorporates the following teaching features: rapidly shifting hand positions, hand crossings, slurs, legato and staccato combinations. An attractive study and recital solo.

Bostelmann, Ida The Busy Bee Marks (1960)

C major - C - Vivace. More like an etude than a recital solo, this piece is an excellent study in the use of the chromatic scale.

Clark, Thelma Chipmunk's Lullaby Summy-Birchard (1957)

D minor - 3/4 - Softly. This piece features a nice melody line with a quiet legato accompaniment. An excellent piece to teach part playing, as the left hand has two voices, one stationary and one moving (on the third and fourth lines). A fine slow study piece for a child with better than average musical feeling. (Available only in *Summy Piano Solo Package, No. 101.*)

Cobb, Hazel Sonatina in C Major Belwin-Mills (1950)

Consisting of three short movements, this piece is an effective first sonatina. The first movement is easier than either the second ("Minuet") or third ("Rondino") movements.

Dittenhaver, Sarah Louise Wind in the Pines Schroeder & Gunther/Associated (1964)

A minor - 2/4 - With beauty. A lovely slow teaching piece requiring good balancing of tone, singing legato line, and musical imagination. Although not for the average child, this is a perfect choice for a student with better than average talent. The legato double notes are difficult in the last line and will require extra practice.

Dungan, Olive The Balky Mule Boosey (1956)

C major - 4/4 - Fast and gaily. This attractive, spirited solo uses the Alberti bass, hand crossings, and accents effectively. The B section (lines four and five) may be taught without rearranging the hands. A good study and recital solo.

Ezell, Helen Ingle Peasant Dance C. Fischer (1976)

A minor - 4/4 - Lively. Bouncy rhythms, accents, and staccato touch provide materials to evoke a folk dance flavor. The main teaching feature is the interval of a sixth used considerably.

Frackenpohl, Arthur Gliding Lee Roberts/Schirmer (1963)

D tonality - 3/4 - Smoothly. Rapidly shifting triads (major and minor) are featured in this well-written solo. The left hand keeps a steady pattern (stretching to a sixth) which is repeated in several locations. A useful piece for analyzing major and minor chords.

Glover, David Carr Ach! My Little Foreign Car Hansen (1960)

F major - 4/4 - Very slow. This cute solo incorporates Alberti bass, minor seconds (for the "beep-beep" effect), and appropriate words. The total effect is stunning and always effective in recital.

Glover, David Carr Flags on Parade Belwin-Mills (1969)

C major - 4/4 - Snappy march time. Another of Glover's many marches which are especially effective for boys. Parallel triads, shifting hand positions, repeated (changing) fingers, and parallel fifths are incorporated in this jaunty, crisp solo. Attractive for both study and recital.

Glover, David Carr March of the Fleas Belwin-Mills (1971)

C major - 4/4 - Briskly. Teaching features include parallel triads, shifting hand positions, and interlocking alternating hands. Minor seconds add color. Useful for study and recital.

Grove, Roger Pageants Belwin-Mills (1973)

C major - 4/4 - Briskly. This spirited march evokes the mood of a regal processional. The melody is accompanied by quickly changing triads in a variety of keys. Teaching features include: varieties of touch, balance of melody and accompaniment, and shifting hand positions. Especially for boys.

Grove, Roger The Tireless Traveler Willis (1972)

D minor - 4/4 - Andante, with expression. Hand crossings, balance of melody and accompaniment, and syncopated pedal are the main teaching features. Intervals of fifths in both hands combine to form seventh and eleventh chords. Especially for an older beginner.

King, Patricia W. Jumpin' and Comin' Down the River Lee Roberts/Schirmer (1970)

Jumpin', the first solo in this two-piece set, uses shifting 5-finger positions which begin in E major and gradually work to an A major ending. Staccatos and syncopated off-beat accents are the main features.

Comin' Down the River is in C major, but it also uses shifting 5-finger positions in a variety of keys (positions). Right hand syncopations and left hand moving triads are the main features.

MacKown, Marjorie The Broken Rocking Horse Oxford (1964)

D minor - 6/8 - Moderato. An unusual tonal effect is created in this imaginatively written solo by the use of B natural. Teaching features include: two-note slurs, crossing over the thumb in the left hand (twelfth measure), and controlled dynamics, mostly *piano*.

Nevin, Mark Tango Bongo Mills/Belwin (1961)

A minor - 4/4 - Moderato. A good study and recital piece which has immediate student appeal. Teaching features include: dotted and syncopated rhythms, scale passages, repeated notes (changing fingers), and some chords.

Olson, Lynn Freeman Midnight Express C. Fischer (1964)

G major - 4/4 - Chugging. Moving 5-finger positions, contrasting touches, and balance of tone are the main teaching features in this outstanding solo. Tone painting is evident in the imitation of turning wheels and whistle toots. An attractive, spirited little solo effective for both study and recital.

Sher, William Dream of the Tin Soldier Belwin-Mills (1968)

A tonality - 4/4 - Andante. A nice modal flavor (aeolian mode) is effectively used in this slow march through the use of descending fifths in the left hand. Teaching features include: varieties of touch, three-note slurs, shifting hand positions. Some two-voice style writing is used in the last line. An imaginative piece with an unusual flavor.

Sher, William Garden in the Sea Elkan-Vogel (1966)

C major - 3/4 - Andante con moto. A nice tonal flavor is effected by the use of the raised fourth and lowered sixth. The pedal is an important feature and is used to create atmosphere. Teaching features include: singing legato line, balance of melody and accompaniment, and part playing (on the second page, second line).

Stecher, Melvin, Norman Horowitz and Claire Gordon Waggin' Train G. Schirmer (1969)

Bb major - 4/4 - With spirit. This train jogs along creating a nice lilting effect through the use of a legato melody over a rumbling staccato left hand. The combination of these two touches is the central teaching feature.

Stevens, Everett Parade of the Penguins Flammer (1952)

C major - C - In strict march time, but somewhat awkwardly. Teaching features include: staccato left hand (moving double notes), staccato and legato combinations between hands, right hand scale figure (G scale with F natural), two-note slurs, and changing hand positions.

FOR DISCUSSION AND ASSIGNMENT

1. Discuss your philosophy concerning repertoire versus sight-reading. At the second year level, which do you consider more important? Why?
2. If possible use a second year student (students) to demonstrate the following technical items: phrasing, legato and staccato combinations, balance between hands, dynamic shadings, part playing, scales, triads and inversions, and Alberti bass. Which items do you consider most important? Why? List other second year technical considerations.
3. How much theory is necessary for second year students? Should it be taught along with the private lesson, or apart from the private lesson? Why?
4. At a music store make a survey of second year supplementary books and solos. Present five books and five solos other than those listed in this chapter, and tell why they would be useful for second year students.
5. From your experience examining second year literature, compose a second year solo; point out the teaching features.
6. Outline a second year program in these three areas: (1) repertoire, (2) technique, and (3) theory.

Third Year Students 8

In this chapter third year students are considered to be those who began lessons as average age beginners (seven to eleven) and have received either two nine month periods of instruction (two school years), or two school years plus some summer instruction.

It generally takes about two full years for students of average ability to build a solid foundation in reading and playing skills. During this period they will be acquiring the necessary facility to play music by master composers. Therefore, considering the first two years as an apprentice period, the real advantage for third year students is to have the ability to study and perform piano repertoire which is apart from the type of music found in most beginning methods. Students at this level now are ready to embark on challenging and stimulating repertoire.

In teaching students at this level, one should carefully consider this group's age. If they began lessons at the age of nine or ten, now they would be pre-adolescents (about eleven or twelve). They are no longer young children. They have had lessons for two years and perhaps are not as eager and cooperative as they were in the beginning. Although this happens often, the key to continued interest on the part of pre-adolescent students is in the creativity and expertise of the teacher. New incentives will have to be provided to interest and motivate students in moving ahead at this juncture. Auditions, contests, recitals, and group participation may help to provide motivation during this period.

Pre-adolescence and adolescence may be difficult for students. In addition to psychological and physiological adjustments, there are also social adjustments to be made. "Should I drop piano lessons and devote more time to football, basketball, baseball, track, and swimming?" "Should I continue taking lessons, but only practice a little so I can give more time to Girl Scouts, ballet, horseback riding, and tennis?" These and similar questions will arise at this critical point in music study. There remains little free time after school for piano practice because of homework, T.V., telephone calls, etc. Students and parents will have to decide if it is worth it to continue piano lessons.

Parents should be forewarned that they will need to provide a great deal of encouragement to entice their children to continue to take lessons and to find sufficient time for practice. The repertoire in the third year is more difficult, compositions are longer and more involved, and it will be necessary to practice more. During the first year about thirty or forty minutes a day generally was enough practice time; during the second year about forty-five minutes was adequate; but now in the third year, approximately one hour of practice will be required to make sufficient progress.

In addition to competition from outside activities and finding enough time for practice, students of this age become increasingly more aware of acceptance from peer groups. Is it sissy for John to be practicing the piano when he could be out playing football? Is it square for Mary to be playing Bach minuets when her friends are "turned on" by the latest pop album? Each new year brings an increased awareness of what the "in" thing is at that moment from among one's peers. Realizing the force for conformity, teachers should make an effort to provide students with a balanced program of classical and pop music. The pop music may be studied as recreational music which may be played for friends.

The third year is a critical point in a student's career, but if his interest is maintained, he will be motivated to continue lessons and will move ahead and continue to make progress.

THIRD YEAR MUSIC PROGRAM

In a continuous program of study the materials covered in successive years will gradually broaden and expand and become progressively more complex. The key to successful learning is to pace the rate of advancement gradually. Some students may require further drill at the same level before proceeding to more complex material. Others may be quick to catch on, and they can be pushed ahead faster than the rate at which average students normally progress. The gulf between those who remain at the same level and those who progress at an accelerated rate widens and becomes more pronounced for each year of study.

Although students vary so widely in ability that no fixed rules can be made as to who will play what when, a general program will be outlined in this chapter for *average* third year students. Again, like the previous two chapters, the four major areas of concentration in the general music program include: repertoire, technique, theory, and sight-reading.

Third Year Repertoire

Before discussing repertoire possibilities, it should be understood that not *all* third year students will be ready for music by master composers. Young beginners especially may not be sufficiently prepared to begin the complexities of easy Bach music or sonatina literature until late third year or early fourth year. If young beginners started lessons at the age of six or seven, now they would be only eight or nine. Usually young beginners make slow progress compared to older beginners of nine or ten. Some students are generally "slow" and need more time mastering the mechanics of reading and technique. A student who has not been pushed too fast, who has acquired a broad-based background, will be prepared to execute the complexities of music by master composers in due time, at *his* pace, not at the pace prescribed by the teacher.

When a student is ready for literature by master composers, there is a wealth of fine material available for study and performance. In addition to the standard repertoire by master composers from the seventeenth, eighteenth, and nineteenth centuries, there is an abundance of outstanding music written for this level by twentieth century composers.

Should the music selected for assignment be in its original state as the composer wrote it, an arrangement, or an edition? Arranged works have recently come under fire from music educators who are becoming concerned with teaching original literature rather than music arranged for the piano. The author had an amusing experience concerning arrangements that is worth repeating. A young girl who had lessons for about three years came requesting lessons as a transfer student, and when asked what she would like to play for her audition she responded: "I have a Mozart Symphony, a Haydn Symphony, and Schubert's *Serenade*." Although all these compositions are delightful, her teacher was remiss for not assigning a balanced program of piano repertoire and some arranged works. Arrangements may be used for sight-reading material and for familiarizing students with general music literature, but with the extensive piano repertoire available to this level student, it would seem ludicrous to neglect the obvious and assign arrangements exclusively.

The controversy over urtext publications versus editions seems too pedantic to worry about for third year students. One can purchase Bach's complete *Little Notebook for Anna Magdalena* (Kalmus) which is very interesting, but since it includes such a wide variety of levels (Partitas, little Minuets, Polonaises, etc.), it would not be a suitable collection for an eleven- or twelve-year-old. In addition to being somewhat esoteric as a student's study book, urtext publications of Baroque works often contain no tempo indications, dynamics, fingering, or phrasing. Therefore, if the teacher feels the need to use unedited music, he must be prepared to edit the music himself for his students, which can take up a great deal of unnecessary lesson time.

There are numerous good editions of individual composer works (all Bach, all Schumann, etc.) as well as a number of fine editions of collected works by several composers. Generally the level of difficulty varies widely in collections of works by individual composers. It would appear to be more practical for teaching purposes to buy one volume that contains graded works by several composers. Why buy a Bach book, a Schumann book, and a Kabalevsky book when you can get graded works by these composers and many others in one volume? Separate books are unnecessarily expensive for students. Collections, on the other hand, are less expensive, and they provide a wide variety of music on one level.

There has been a concern recently over the simplification or omission of ornaments in Baroque music (especially the music by Bach). Willard Palmer, an outstanding editor, realistically states in the Foreword to his fine edition of *Selections from Anna Magdalena's Notebook*:

> Some teachers may prefer to have the student learn these selections without the ornaments so the pieces fall more easily into the student's grade level. There is no objection to this, and if the ornaments can be added later, this practice may result in a more thorough understanding of the functions of baroque ornamentation, which was not only to embellish but to add interesting dissonances and harmonic interest.

It is, of course, equally acceptable to retain the simpler ornaments and omit the more difficult ones.[1]

Palmer's suggestions are practical and realistic. The ornaments should be played correctly if they are used.[2] However, for third year students with limited technical ability, they may be omitted and learned later. Bach's *Minuet in G* is generally too difficult for young students played as indicated with mordents and trills. For older students with good facility, the ornaments may be learned as part of the piece. Discretion should be used by the teacher in the use of ornaments.

Repertoire Collections

There are several collections of easy classics that are suitable for study and performance which contain graded literature on a realistic level. A few titles chosen from among the many available include:

Ackerman, Gloria (ed. - compiler) Piano Guide for Second-Year Students, Piano Guide for Third-Year Students Belwin-Mills (1975)

This series (four books) is designed to fulfill requirements of The American Scholarship Association's annual competition. Each book contains an assignment guide, practice hints, selected four-period repertoire, sight-reading and technic suggestions, other activities, and lists of required and supplementary teaching materials by various publishers. The level of difficulty of the repertoire in the Second-Year Guide is either late second year or third year for students of average ability.

Agay, Denes (ed.) Easy Classics to Moderns Consolidated Music Publishers (1956)

This collection of 142 compositions contains piano literature dating from the second half of the seventeenth century to the present time. The compositions range in difficulty from easy level (late second year, or early third year) to medium level (fourth year and beyond).

Agay, Denes (ed.) From Bach to Bartók, Volume A Witmark/Warner Bros. Publications (1960)

Volume A in THE YOUNG PIANIST'S LIBRARY represents the easiest grading of original works by master composers. All pieces are in their original form with the exception of a few helpful editorial additions. Nice biographical sketches accompany this tasteful twenty-four page collection. Along with standard fare (*Minuet in G* by Bach, *Soldier's March* by Schumann, etc.), are some fresh, less seen and heard pieces by famous composers.

Anson, George (ed.) Survey of Piano Literature, Book 1–Early Keyboard Music; Book 2–The Romantic Composers; Book 3–The Contemporary Scene Elkan-Vogel/Presser (1960)

All three short twenty page volumes are tastefully selected and edited. Most of the music in these collections is accessible to average or better late third year students (and beyond).

[1] Willard Palmer, ed., *Bach: Selections from Anna Magdalena's Notebook* (Alfred Music Co., Inc., 1969), p. 4. Reprinted by permission.

[2] Consult Willard Palmer's realization of the ornaments in the preface to all his Bach editions.

Bastien, Jane Smisor (ed.) Piano Literature, Vols. 1 & 2 GWM Co. (1966)

Volume 1 may be given to better than average late second year students, but a number of the pieces are more suited to general third year level. This thirty-two page collection contains short pieces by Bach, Spindler, Mozart, Beethoven, Schumann, Kabalevsky, Shostakovich, and Bartók. *Volume 2* contains pieces at about late third year level and beyond; included are works by the following composers: Bach, Clementi, Beethoven, Schumann, Kabalevsky, Rebikoff, and Bartók.

Goss, Louise (ed.) (Clark Library) Piano Literature, Books 2 & 3 Summy-Birchard (1954)

Both books contain literature from the seventeenth, eighteenth, and nineteenth centuries. *Book 2* is a thirty-two page collection of pieces at about third year level and includes compositions by Bach, Mozart, Haydn, Beethoven, and Schumann. *Book 3* is a forty page collection of pieces at late third year level (and beyond) and includes compositions by Bach, Haydn, Clementi, Beethoven, Schubert, Schumann, and Tchaikovsky.

Zeitlin, Poldi, and David Goldberger (eds.) The Solo Book I and II Consolidated (1961)

Both short thirty-two page volumes contain an excellent cross-section of compositions by composers from the baroque to the contemporary periods. The music in both volumes is graded: *Book 1* is easy (early third year level), and *Book 2* is slightly more difficult (mid to late third year level).

If collections are used, should a large volume be given like Agay's *Easy Classics to Moderns* or should short volumes be given like the Anson, Bastien, Clark, or Zeitlin literature series? Large volumes contain a great deal of literature (160 pages in the Agay collection), and this bulk would benefit students of better than average ability who need more material on a week to week basis. The question is, however, how many of these compositions will students of average ability be able to learn, even in an entire year's period? It is doubtful that average students will need a great amount of music from a single collection.

Too often teachers fall into the one-book syndrome in which they assign music from a single volume for a period of a year or two. Students like to receive new books, new compositions from a variety of composers, and if they are stuck in one book too long, they eventually bog down. Like the prospect of climbing Mount Everest, the sheer task of some day completing a large volume looms as an Olympian obstacle.

An alternative to collections is single-composer volumes. A few of the newer series include: *Easiest Piano Selections* (Bach, Bartók, Kabalevsky, Schumann, etc.) published by the Alfred Publishing Co. (1976); *My First Book of Classics* (Beethoven, Haydn, Mozart, etc.) edited by John Brimhall, published by Charles Hansen (1976); and *Young Pianist's Guide to* (Bach, Bartók, Kabalevsky, etc.) edited by Ylda Novik, published by Studio P/R (1976).

The main drawback to single-composer volumes is the expense. To play music by several composers, the student must purchase a book for each composer. In addition, frequently the music in single-composer volumes progresses considerably in difficulty, from very easy to several grades higher. Therefore, although the single-composer volumes are quite appealing in format and content, when first playing easy classics it would seem to serve the student better to play a variety of music, well-graded, like those contained in collections, rather than playing numerous pieces by one or two composers.

Jazz Collections

One further consideration about third year literature should be discussed–should jazz (blues, pop, rock, country-western, ragtime, etc.) be given as a regular part of lesson? Yes! Most students in this age group will be overjoyed at the prospect of playing some pop compositions. Nothing will motivate and stimulate students as much as being able to perform a pop piece for their peers. This style is a language which communicates to them, one which includes them as a part of today's contemporary world. In addition to giving them a vehicle with which to communicate, jazz and pop styles have some excellent educational features: syncopation, intricate rhythms, cross accents, etc. Pop music does wonders for improving rhythm.

Again, teachers must realize that they are not preparing their entire class of students for Carnegie Hall debuts. The music program should be an amalgamation of various styles which will best serve the interest of students, not merely the teachers' interests.

The popular field is so large that it would be impossible to list enough titles to cover the field in even surface fashion. However, a few representative volumes of pop music are suggested here which contain music at about the third year level.

Bastien, James   Country, Western 'n Folk, Book 1   GWM Co. (1974)

This sixteen page volume contains easy original country-western pieces and country folk-tune arrangements at the third year level.

Bastien, James (arr.)   Scott Joplin Favorites   GWM Co. (1975)

Although the ragtime craze has abated somewhat since the Movie *The Sting* began a revival of rag, the timeless quality of these pieces will appeal to students year after year. Included are arrangements of "The Entertainer," "Ragtime Dance," "Maple Leaf Rag," and "Bethena." (Both "The Entertainer" and "Maple Leaf Rag" are also published in sheet music form.) Late second or early third year for average students.

Bastien, Jane Smisor   Pop, Rock 'n Blues, Books 1-3   GWM Co. (1971)

Each book contains compositions designed to introduce the student to the styles and sounds of today's music. *Book 1* is easy (second year level); *Book 2* is slightly more difficult (early third year level); *Book 3* is about late third year level and beyond.

Garrow, Louise   Boogie and Blues   Schroeder & Gunther (1966)

Although boogie is a bit passe these days, this is a good collection for students of average ability. The pieces are on a realistic level and are not complex rhythmically, which is often the case with pop music of today. The level of difficulty is about early third year for average students, about late third year for slow students.

Glover, David Carr   Jazz (etc.) on 88, Level 3   Belwin-Mills (1975)

Seven pieces in various styles (boogie, blues, rag) are contained in this sixteen page collection. The level of difficulty is generally third year.

Grove, Roger Jazz About GWM Co. (1975)

Seven attractive pieces in jazz, boogie and blues styles comprise this sixteen page collection. The music is bright, spirited and appealing.

Grove, Roger The Riches of Rag Summy-Birchard (1976)

Seven two-page original rags comprise this sixteen page volume. The music is suitably syncopated, all are in ABA form. Generally third year level, or slightly beyond.

King, Sanford I'm Playing Ragtime C. Fischer (1975)

Twelve one-page originals with real rag style flavor are contained in this sixteen page collection. Mostly two-part style writing is used. Syncopations abound in these well-written, catchy pieces. About late second or third year level.

Olson, Lynn Freeman Rock Me Easy C. Fischer (1972)

Syncopation abounds in the attractive seven solos in this collection of rock pieces. Generally third year level.

Stecher, Melvin, Norman Horowitz, and Claire Gordon Rock with Jazz, Books 1-5 G. Schirmer (1969)

These five short volumes contain attractive solos redolent of today's pop sounds–mostly blues and rock. *Book 1* is easy (about late second year); *Books 2-5* are about third year level and beyond.

Contemporary Collections

There are numerous collections of compositions by composers now writing educational piano music. Often these compositions do not sound "contemporary" (twelve-tone style, use of dissonance, etc.). However, the composition of the music has been fairly recent as opposed to music written in the nineteenth century and before. Compositions by William Gillock, Everett Stevens, Joan Last, and others, often are written in imitative styles (modal, seventeenth-century, etc.), and although the music is recent, the sound is not in a contemporary idiom. The following list contains a cross-section of composers who are merely recent, plus works by composers who write in modern styles.

Agay, Denes Seven Piano Pieces Schirmer (1969)

Among these attractive solos is the popular "Dancing Leaves" which is about early third year level. Six other solos of varying difficulty are also included in this collection; No. 7, "Dance Scherzo" is much more difficult than any of the others.

Anson, George (ed.) Bartók, Book 1 Willis (1960)

This twenty-four page volume contains selected works from the many Bartók wrote for children. The edition is first-rate–easy to read, well-spaced on the page, and includes helpful fingering and pedal suggestions by the editor.

Anson, George (ed.) Kabalevsky, Book 1 Willis (1960)

Like the Bartók collection, this volume contains selected works for children. The same excellent editorial features are seen in this volume.

Anson, George New Directions Willis (1961)

New sounds explored include: polytonality, tone-clusters, twelve-tone row, and experimental harmonies. The sampling of styles would assist students and teachers in a better understanding of music of today. For a better than average late third (early fourth) year student interested in learning about new compositional techniques.

Anson, George (ed.) Survey of Piano Literature, Book 3–The Contemporary Scene Elkan-Vogel/Presser (1960)

This is a choice twenty page collection of contemporary favorites excellently edited. Composers include: Bartók, Kabalevsky, Stravinsky, Shostakovich, Phillips, Ornstein, and Persichetti. The pieces at the beginning of the book are easier than the "Capriccio" and "Berceuse" by Persichetti at the end of the collection.

Bartók, Béla The First Term at the Piano Boosey (1950)

A number of the easier pieces in the beginning of the book appear in other collections. The eighteen compositions in this volume range from easy (first year level) to intermediate level. Since the grading is not consistent, the teacher would have to choose a few pieces for study.

Bartók, Béla Young People at the Piano, Books 1 & 2 Boosey (1952, 1967)

The selected works in these two twelve-page volumes are generally about third year level. *Book 2* is more difficult (early intermediate level).

Bastien, Jane and James Bastien Favorites, Levels 3 & 4 GWM Co. (1976)

These volumes contain previously published piano solos in a variety of keys, styles and moods. The level of difficulty is third year and beyond. (Each solo is available in sheet music.)

Clark, Frances, and Louise Goss (eds.) Contemporary Piano Literature, Book 2 Summy-Birchard (1955)

This twenty-eight page volume contains standard contemporary music by Bartók, Kabalevsky, and Shostakovich, as well as some excellent compositions commissioned for this series by composers Siegmeister, Tansman, and Tcherepnin.

(collection) Summy Piano Solo Package, No. 301 Summy-Birchard (1976)

Contained are twelve previously published solos by various composers (Bentley, Cobb, Gillock, Glover, others) available now only in this volume. Useful teaching comments are provided by Jane Knourek. The level of difficulty is third year and beyond.

Dello Joio, Norman Suite for the Young Marks (1964)

This superb collection of ten imaginative one-page pieces rates at the top of the scale in contemporary educational music. Dello Joio, Pulitzer Prize winning American composer, has created a set of miniature masterpieces full of melodic invention, rhythmic verve, color and flair. All the pieces contain special mildly contemporary flavors, and some are specific in didactic devices: "Invention" uses major and minor triadic melodies; "A Sad Tale" uses an ostinato bass. Favorites are "Bagatelle" (staccato touch), "Small Fry" (wonderfully jazzy), and "Little Brother" (staccato and syncopated cross accents). A favorite since its publication, this superior collection is a must for teachers who have not yet discovered it. The compositions are about late third year level (some fourth year).

Frackenpohl, Arthur Circus Parade Oxford (1960)

On a level appropriate for either late second or third year students, these appealing thirteen short compositions are of excellent quality. Imaginative, clever illustrations enhance this fine set of teaching pieces.

George, Jon A Day in the Forest Summy-Birchard (1973)

Consisting of eight pleasant vignettes seen on a country outing, these imaginative pieces are sure to capture the fancy of a sophisticated youngster. Mood and atmosphere dominates throughout evidenced in such descriptive titles as "Forest Dawn," "The Old Hermit," and "Twilight Descends."

George, Jon Kaleidoscope Solos, Books 4 & 5 Alfred (1974)

Sophisticated musical problems employed in the pieces involve such teaching devices as sustained and moving voices in one hand, complex rhythms, irregular meter, asymmetrical phrase lengths, and chromaticism. Colorful and appealing music for the student with above average ability. *Book 4* is mid to late third year, *Book 5* is late third year and beyond.

George, Jon Medieval Pageant Oxford (1972)

The eight fresh, attractive pieces in this brief thirteen page volume create a marvelous atmosphere of "once upon a time" and delve into the story-book land of long ago. Modes and ostinatos used in the pieces maintain a strong medieval flavor. A brief "Fanfare" is the curtain raiser for the ensuing "Processional" which is followed by "The Troubador Sings" and "The Jester Performs." The concluding three pieces are in suite form consisting of "Branle, Air, and Gigge." Great music for a sophisticated imaginative child.

Gianneo, Luis Seven Children's Pieces Southern Music Co., N.Y. (1947)

This is an excellent set of imaginative pieces at about late third or fourth year levels. Favorites are No. 4 "Little Hat," No. 5 "Tango," No. 6 "Small Drum," and No. 7 "Rustic Dance." Catchy syncopated rhythms and characteristic Latin flavors are happily present in most of the pieces.

Gillock, William Accent on Rhythm and Style Willis (1962)

Flare and taste is shown in this superb twenty page collection of seven original compositions. Covering four style eras (Baroque, Classical, Romantic, and Modern), there are imitative pieces from each period. Favorites are "Sonatina" (three movements written in Classical style) and "Spanish Gypsies" (written in Modern style). Discussions of the four style periods add to this impressive volume. The level of difficulty is generally about third year, some are fourth year level.

Gillock, William Fanfare Summy-Birchard (1957)

Written as little suites in imitative Baroque style, this collection is a gem. Descriptive titles, imaginative music, and a variety of moods are found throughout. The level of difficulty is about mid to late third year (or beyond for younger or slower students). A superior collection of tastefully written music.

Goldberger, David (ed.) Kabalevsky for the Young Pianist Schroeder & Gunther/ Associated (1974)

This collection contains mostly selections from *Op. 27* and *39*, and also includes "Seven Variations on the Ukrainian Folksong, Op. 51, No. 4." The level of difficulty is third year and beyond.

Goldstein, Kern, Larimer, Ross, Weiss (eds.) Contemporary Collection, Nos. 1 & 2 Summy-Birchard (1963)

Both volumes contain a cross-section of contemporary music. The first book is easy (second year level or early third year); the second book is about third year level (and beyond).

Grey, Donald Fun at the Fair Boosey (1932)

This attractive collection of fourteen pieces is written in miniature suite form. The music is imaginative and describes fair scenes: "A Dancing Horse," "Acrobats," etc. The level is not difficult, about early to mid-third year (late second year for older beginners).

Hinson, Maurice, and David Carr Glover Contemporary Piano Repertoire Belwin-Mills (1971)

Included in this well-edited collection are standard compositions by Kabalevsky, Rebikov, Bartók, and Gretchaninoff. Attractive biographical sketches are also included.

Kabalevsky, Dimitri Fifteen Children's Pieces, Opus 27, Book 1 MCA, Kalmus, Larrabee, others

This collection contains the famous "Toccatina," and "Sonatina" which are more fourth year level than third. However, a number of the other pieces in the collection are easier, and could be assigned to average or better third year students.

Kabalevsky, Dimitri 24 Pieces for Children, Opus 30 Alfred Music Co., MCA, Schirmer, Kalmus, others

Some of these well-known pieces are accessible to third year students. Many of the easier compositions appear in anthology collections.

Kraehenbuehl, David Calendar Scenes Schmitt Publications (1966)

The compositions in this collection are based on twelve-tone rows. The music appears easy (second year level), but may be given to young third year students (early third year). An excellent introduction to twelve-tone music.

Lombardo, Robert Twelve Contemporary Pieces for Children Peer International (1966)

The compositions in this collection are written in contrapuntal style and employ some of the technics used by contemporary composers. Thus, the purpose is to acquaint the student with contemporary sounds. All the pieces are appealing melodically. No fingering is given, and since some of the writing is a bit unpianistic, the teacher will have to write in the fingering. The level of difficulty is about late third year; the two pieces at the end of the book (Nos. 11 & 12) are *much* more difficult.

Noona, Walter and Carol The Contemporary Performer, Level 3 Heritage (1975)

This series (four books) is designed to introduce youngsters to idioms of twentieth-century style such as modes, polyrhythms, clusters, polytonalities, twelve-tone rows, and ostinato patterns. The information about the compositional devices is concise and informative.

Novik, Ylda (ed.) Young Pianist's Guide to Bartók Studio P/R (1976)

Sixteen of Bartók's easiest pieces comprise this volume and include a number of less frequently taught pieces from the wealth of folk-derived compositions he wrote for youngsters. Attractive photos, informative texts, and a recording of the pieces make this a very useful volume.

Novik, Ylda (ed.) Young Pianist's Guide to Kabalevsky Studio P/R (1976)

Fourteen of Kabalevsky's easiest pieces comprise this volume and include such favorites as "Toccatina" and "Sonatina." Attractive photos, informative texts, and a recording of the pieces make this a very useful volume.

Palmer, Willard (ed.) Béla Bartók, Selected Children's Pieces Alfred Music Co. (1971)

This collection of easy works has been compiled from the following sources: *The First Term at the Piano, For Children,* and *Ten Easy Pieces.* A few of the first pieces in the book could be played by late second year students; however, the collection is generally third year level with the exception of "Evening in the Country" which is more difficult (intermediate level).

Persichetti, Vincent Little Piano Book Elkan-Vogel/Presser (1954)

This little volume of fourteen pieces contains representative contemporary styles that may serve as preparations for larger works. The music looks easy, but the level of difficulty is at least mid to late third year level (and beyond for younger or slower students). The writing is first-rate, and this volume has been a standard contemporary collection since its publication.

Raphling, Sam Five Forecasts for Piano MCA (1965)

These five short one-page sketches all project the weather: "Windy," "Rainy," "Stormy," "Cloudy," and "Sunny." No key signatures are used and many accidentals are written in. The music is imaginative and descriptive and immediately appealing.

Rowley, Alec Five Miniature Preludes and Fugues Chester/Belwin (1946)

Only rarely does one come across such a delightful collection of exceptional pieces. These fine contrapuntal study pieces have great merit, and they are valuable for practice in bringing out voices in either hand. They are a fine introduction to the complexities of contrapuntal style on a realistic level.

Russell, Olive Nelson The Littlest Inventions Willis (1961)

Written as studies in imitative contrapuntal style, these six one-page works offer the student an opportunity for study and analysis of two-voice music without being too difficult. The level of difficulty is about late third year (or beyond).

Stevens, Everett Piano Scenes Presser (1966)

This collection is comprised of seven well-written pieces each with descriptive titles. All the pieces are about mid to late third year level; the last two, "Autumn Fields" and "White Heather," are more difficult (early intermediate).

Szávai, Magda, and Lili Veszprémi (eds.) Piano Music for Beginners Editio Musica/Boosey (1969)

From Hungary comes this attractive sixty page volume which contains a cross-section of literature from various periods. Some of the composers represented are Purcell, Handel, Bach, Mozart, Haydn, Beethoven, and Schumann. About half the book is devoted to music by contemporary Hungarian composers. The title is misleading; most of the compositions are at least *late* third year (many are intermediate level). The attractive illustrations add color and interest.

Vovk, Ivan Sketches Shawnee Press (1971)

The fourteen one-page compositions in this collection are excellently written. Numerous teaching points are included in these imaginative pieces. A first-rate collection.

Waxman, Donald First Recital Pageant Galaxy (1962)

The word "first" in this title is misleading. The excellent compositions contained in the sixteen page book are at least mid to late third year level (and beyond). The writing is first-rate and is suitable for both study and recital. Two duets are also included.

Weybright, June Mildly Contemporary, Books 1 & 2 Belwin-Mills (1964)

These two books offer a variety of compositions featuring such contemporary devices as tone-clusters, bi-tonality, modality, parallel fourths and fifths, and experimental harmonies.

Zeitlin, Poldi, and David Goldberger (eds.) Russian Music, Book 2 MCA (1967)

This is the second book in a six-book series. The series is divided into three grades—elementary, intermediate and advanced—with two levels in each grade. All six books contain first-rate music by contemporary Russian composers, as well as some compositions by such standard composers as Glinka, Tchaikovsky, Prokofiev, Kabalevsky, and others. Several duets are included in each volume.

Sonatina Collections

Although some late second year students may have already played an easy sonatina, generally, easy sonatinas are first given sometime within the third year of lessons. The word "easy" on sonatina collections often is misleading. Sonatinas by Clementi and Kuhlau (and others) usually are more intermediate level than easy, and these frequently appear in first sonatina collections.

There are numerous first sonatina collections available. The following list represents some of the easiest collections from among the many published. Although some of the sonatinas in the following collections could be played by better than average late second year students (or older beginners), the level of the majority of the pieces is definitely third year and up; therefore, they are listed here and not in the previous chapter.

Agay, Denes (ed.) Sonatinas, Volume A Witmark/Warner Bros. Publications (1960)

Mr. Agay is the composer, arranger and editor of *The Young Pianist's Library* which includes twelve series of books, each containing three levels (ABC). Volume A in the entire library represents the easiest level in each series. *Sonatinas, Volume A* consists of eleven sonatinas by composers of all periods.

Composers represented in this thirty-two page collection include: André (only the first movement of the *C Major Sonatina* is given); Biehl, *Sonatina Op. 57, No. 1* (The first movement of this sonatina is very easy and could be played by a second year student.); Clementi, *C Major, Op. 36, No. 1;* Duncombe (only the first movement is given); Beethoven, *G Major Sonatina;* Agay (a very attractive original work); Koehler; Latour; Salutrinskaya; and Schmitt. As a whole, this collection includes a nice cross-section of sonatinas by composers from many periods.

Anson, George (ed.) The Sonata Sampler, Book 1 Willis (1960)

Included in this well-edited thirty-two page volume are representative sonatinas from the four eras of music: Baroque (a Scarlatti sonata which is more difficult than the other compositions in the collection); Classic (the famous Clementi *C Major, Op. 36, No. 1);* Early Romantic (the standard Beethoven *G Major Sonatina);* Late Romantic (Lichner, *C Major, Op. 4, No. 1);* Contemporary (Salutrinskaya–the same sonatina as in the Agay edition). An excellent discussion of sonata form and information about the composers adds to this fine collection.

Bastien, James (ed.) Sonatina Favorites, Book 1 GWM Co. (1977)

Sonatina Favorites is a three-book series containing a representative sampling of sonatinas by various composers. An explanation of sonatina form is provided, and themes are identified in the sonatinas. *Book 1* (32 pages) contains sonatinas by Duncombe, James Bastien *(Sonatina in Classic Style)* Attwood, Spindler, Beethoven *(Sonatina in G Major)*, Lynes, and Clementi *(Op. 36, No. 1)*.

Cobb, Hazel Sonatina Album Belwin-Mills (1959)

Miss Cobb has an affinity tor writing first-rate little versions of classic sounding sonatinas on a realistic level. This sixteen page collection of four sonatinas (three movements each) is just the right level for a first sonatina collection for third year students.

Gillock, William Accent on Analytical Sonatinas Willis (1964)

There is little doubt that William Gillock is one of the best writers of educational piano music; this superb volume is exemplary of his fine style. First-rate melodic invention, logical phrasings, appropriate dynamics, and authentic imitative classic style dominate this twenty-four page collection of three original sonatinas. These works are excellent study pieces to bridge the gap between easy level sonatinas and those of more complexity.

Palmer, Willard (ed.) The First Sonatina Book Alfred Music Co. (1971)

This thirty-two page collection consists of six sonatinas exclusively of classic sound and style. Composers represented are: Latour, Wanhal, Haslinger, Beethoven *(G Major Sonatina),* Clementi *(C Major, Op. 36, No. 1),* and Pleyel. The compositions by Wanhal, Haslinger, and Pleyel are rather trite, uninteresting works. Although called a "first" book, most of the selections are beyond that stage and are more early intermediate level. As a whole, this collection is more difficult than the Agay edition.

Rowley, Alec (ed.) Early English Sonatinas Boosey (no publication date given)

The seven sonatinas in this thirty-two page collection are by infrequently heard composers and are a welcome diversion from the usual fare one ordinarily encounters. The level of difficulty ranges from late third year up. The composers include: Attwood (same *G Major Sonatina* found in the Zeitlin and Goldberger collection), Duncombe (the first in the book–an attractive easy sonatina), Hook, Camidge, Jones, and Wilton.

Zeitlin, Poldi, and David Goldberger (eds.) The Sonatina Book I Consolidated (1961)

Zeitlin and Goldberger are the arrangers and editors of *The CMP Library* which includes six series of books, each containing three levels. This volume is the easiest in the sonatina series and is about late third year level and up. Composers include: André, Attwood, Beethoven (*G Major Sonatina*), Biehl, Gurlitt, Kabalevsky (not a sonatina, but the *Variations on a Russian Folk Song, Op. 51, No. 1*), Köhler, Krieger, and Scarlatti.

Sonatina literature is replete with rich resources for pianistic development. Phrasing, balancing of tone, scales, graded dynamics, mood and tempo constitute basic elements for consideration. In addition to technical considerations, form and style are two aspects for study.

Most elementary sonatinas stem from the classical period (1750-1830), or are written in imitative classical style. The sonatina form is basically that of a diminutive sonata, and the study of sonatinas will acquaint the student with the general musical form and style that are characteristic of the classical sonata.

Sonatina Form

A sonatina usually has three movements (sometimes two) of contrasting moods and tempos. The first movement is comprised of the *sonatina form* which usually contains two themes:

Sonatinas in major keys

First section
1. A theme (tonic key)
2. B theme (dominant key)

Second section
1. transition back to tonic (brief development)
2. A theme (tonic key)
3. B theme (tonic key)
4. (optional) codetta (tonic key)

For an example of model sonatina form, consult the first movement of Clementi's *Sonatina in C, Op. 36, No. 1*:

First section
1. A theme (measures 1-8 in C major)
2. B theme (measures 9-15 in G major)

Second section
1. transition–brief development of the A theme (measures 16-23)
2. A theme (measures 24-31 in C major)
3. B theme (measures 32-38 in C major)

Third Year Technique

Third year students arrive at a juncture between elementary and intermediate levels. Concentration on technique at this point will enable students to bridge the gap between the first two years spent learning fundamentals and the fourth year (intermediate level). The transition will be made smoothly if playing ability can be developed sufficiently to meet new challenges in repertoire.

The following five areas may be considered at this time for serious study:

1. Finger patterns
   a. Hand position shifts
   b. Finger crossings
   c. Broken chord patterns
   d. Legato double note patterns
   e. Arpeggio preparation
2. Finger independence studies
3. Forearm rotation
4. Pedaling
5. Technique studies
   a. Exercises
   b. Etudes

Finger Patterns[3]

Early elementary piano music (first year, and part of the second year) is based essentially on 5-finger patterns. Within that context there is little room for error in choice of fingering. However, even in simple music, the teacher must make sure that good "finger-conscious" habits are formed from the beginning. Good fingering is a matter of habit, and the early years are when most habits are formed—good or bad.

Terms such as muscular reflex, kinesthetic reflex, and muscular habit may all be applied to fingering keyboard patterns. Whether the student responds correctly to a variety of patterns (hand shifts, finger crossings, extended and contracted positions, etc.) will depend largely on his reflexes which should have been trained to meet a variety of keyboard patterns.

As the student's music becomes more complicated, it is essential to choose the correct fingering to solve the problem. The student should not be "left to his own devices" in choosing fingering, for he will almost invariably choose awkward, unpianistic fingerings. The teacher must lead the student to the correct choice, and in many instances support the choice of fingering with reasons why (especially for older students who tend to question).

Hand Position Shifts

A shift from one hand position to another is one of the most basic keyboard patterns. First and second year pieces require hand position shifts with increasing degrees, and by the third year this method of operation is standard fare. The teacher should point out new positions so students will learn to think ahead and perceive shifts *before* they occur.

[3]For an interesting discussion on fingering, see *The Art of Fingering in Piano Playing* by Julien Musafia (MCA Music, 1971).

The first four measures of Bach's *Minuet in G* (Ex. 8:1) contains one hand shift which is a representative example of this type of keyboard pattern. The student should be taught to *span the notes* of the first two measures (G 5-finger position), move to the next position, and span the notes in a row that begin on C (measure 3, C 5-finger position with a raised fourth).

Ex. 8:1. Bach: ***Minuet in G***

Be specific in your directions. Use an arrow indicating a hand position change (Ex. 8:2), or circle the finger that begins a new hand position (or both).

Ex. 8:2. Clementi: ***Sonatina, Op. 36, No. 1***

Measures 16 and 17

Preparing a hand motion ahead is another essential closely related to simply shifting a position. While one hand plays, the other hand must prepare ahead and *be ready to play* (Ex. 8:3). Often students hesitate at the end of

Ex. 8:3. Clementi: ***Sonatina, Op. 36, No. 1***

Measures 8 and 9

the eighth measure in the Clementi *Sonatina* because the left hand was not prepared ahead. It must be ready to play by the time measure 9 is reached. This is an essential aspect of piano playing and should be *taught* as a part of basic techniques.

By giving constant attention to hand position shifts and preparing ahead, students will become aware of these basics which will aid them in reading and memorizing. "Position playing" is an important element of piano playing, and it should be taught within the first three years of lessons.

Students will be confronted more frequently with scale type passages in the third year of lessons. In the previous chapter two exercises for scale preparation were given (Examples 7:10a and 7:10b). These exercises served as basic studies in turning the thumb under a finger or crossing a finger over the thumb. Scale preparation exercises and scales themselves will prepare students physically for this basic keyboard pattern. However, in reading music, students must be taught to *look ahead* and perceive necessary finger crossing *before* they occur.

The sixth measure of Bach's *Minuet in G* (Ex. 8:4) contains a representative example of a finger crossing in a descending figure. The tenth

Ex. 8:4. Bach: *Minuet in G*

Measures 5-8

measure of Clementi's *C Major Sonatina* (Ex. 8:5) contains a representative example of a finger crossing in an ascending figure.

Ex. 8:5. Clementi: *Sonatina, Op. 36, No. 1*

Measures 9 and 10

It is advisable to have the student look through an entire piece and circle all the places where finger crossings occur. By repeatedly pointing out these patterns the student will become aware of finger crossings and will learn to make the correct adjustments. The correct decisions for finger patterns should become second nature.

Broken Chord Patterns

Easy sonatina literature contains a variety of broken chord patterns In the previous chapter two preparatory Alberti bass exercises were given (Examples 7:12a and 7:12b). These should be studied *before* playing music with figures of this type.

Measures 5 and 6 of Beethoven's *Sonatina in G* (Ex. 8:6) contain representative examples of Alberti bass figures. The key to the fingering of

Ex. 8:6. Beethoven: *Sonatina in G*

Measures 5 and 6

such broken chord figures lies in the shape of the blocked chords. It is advisable to have the student play each chord as a whole to discover the correct fingering and also to determine the names of the chords. A unit of notes (chordal group) should be perceived as a whole rather than individual notes in a series. Both reading and memory will be improved by careful analyzation.

A legato line can easily be broken by using incorrect fingering. The following passage (Ex. 8:7) contains both incorrect and correct fingerings which may serve as representative examples.

Ex. 8:7. Beethoven: *Sonatina in G: Romanze*

Measures 5 and 6

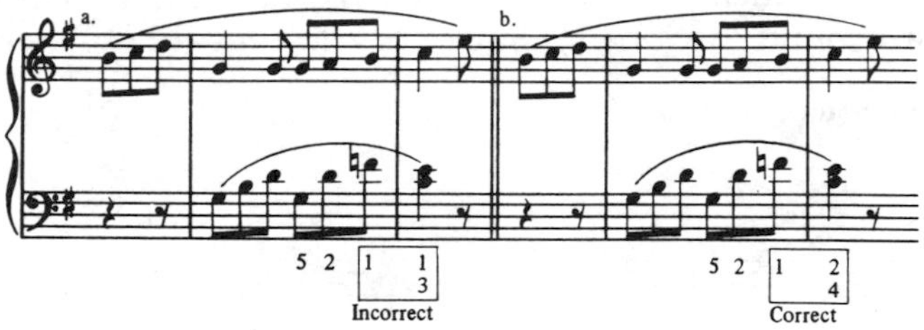

Legato Double Note Patterns

In double note passages the legato effect is dependent upon connecting one or more of the notes in the figure. If both notes move by step, both notes can be connected (Ex. 8:8). However, if only one note moves by

Ex. 8:8. Beethoven: *Sonatina in G*

step and the other is repeated (Ex. 8:9), only the *moving* note can be made

Ex. 8:9. Beethoven: *Sonatina in G*

Measures 3 and 4

to sound legato. Since the latter figure is more difficult to execute (Ex. 8:9), studies should be devised to work on this pattern (Ex. 8:10). The coordination required in holding one finger down while moving another in the same

Ex. 8:10. Double note exercise.

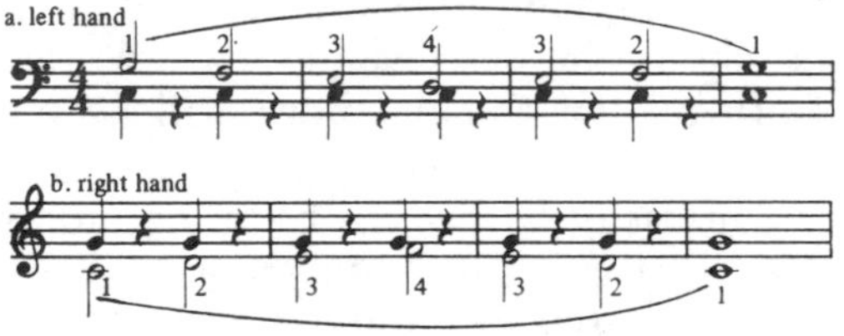

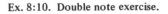

hand is difficult for students; but with sufficient drill, the difficulties can be overcome.

Chords in a cadence passage frequently require holding one note to effect the legato sound (Ex. 8:11). Since it is not possible to create a legato

Ex. 8:11. Connecting notes of a chord.

connection from moving the thumb, or repeating a note, the legato is dependent entirely on the note that moves stepwise. In the first example (Ex. 8:11a) the second finger in the dominant seventh chord must be held and connected to the third finger in the tonic chord. In the second example (Ex. 8:11b) the fourth finger in the dominant seventh chord must be held and connected to the fifth finger in the tonic chord. These figures should be practiced in a variety of keys as exercises.

Arpeggio Preparation

Students probably will have experienced playing arpeggio figures hand over hand style within the first two years and will be acquainted with the sound. However, it is unlikely that arpeggios will have been played with one hand alone during that time. Arpeggios are merely broken chords which require extended reaches, and young students (six, seven, eight) often do not have large enough hands to span the notes in a four-note broken chord figure. However, sometime within the third year (or early fourth year) it is likely that a broken chord figure will be encountered within one hand (Ex. 8:12).

Ex. 8:12. Bach: *Minuet in G*

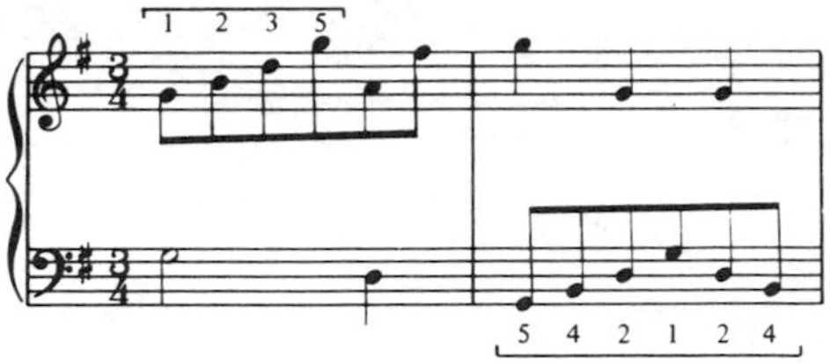

Exercises can be devised for the extended reaches required in broken chord figures (Ex. 8:13). It is important to use the *correct fingering* for

Ex. 8:13. Arpeggio preparation exercises.

arpeggio figures; the fingering is based on the shape of the chord. The general rule for either blocked or broken chords is:

Right Hand

When there is an interval of a *fourth* between the top two notes, use the *third* finger for the third note of the chord:

When there is an interval of a *third* between the top two notes, use the *fourth* finger for the third tone of the chord:

Left Hand

When there is an interval of a *fourth* between the bottom two notes, use the *third* finger for the second tone of the chord:

When there is an interval of a *third* between the bottom two notes, use the *fourth* finger for the second tone of the chord:

Although most average third year students will not be confronted with two-octave arpeggios in their music, it is helpful to give preliminary exercises as preparatory drills (Ex. 8:14). These may be given to students whose fingers are long enough to turn the thumb under without straining.

Ex. 8:14. Preparatory arpeggio exercises.

Finger Independence Studies

In the previous chapter examples of *part playing* were shown (Examples 7:8 and 7:9); these served as preliminary finger independence studies. Finger coordination and control becomes more demanding in the third and fourth years of lessons, and exercises may be devised to meet these new challenges.

Finger independence studies can be given to students when there is sufficient technical control over single line melodies. The following exercises demonstrate various patterns that may be assigned.[4]

Ex. 8:15. Exercises for finger independence.[5]

a. (Hold down all fingers except the one playing.)

b.

c. (Hold down fingers 1 and 2 throughout.)

d.

[4]For an excellent presentation of finger independence studies, see Hazel Cobb's *Technique Builders* (Belwin-Mills, 1964), p. 42.

[5]Examples from *Magic Finger Technique, Book 3* by James Bastien (General Words and Music Co., 1966), pp. 8 and 9.

During the first two years of lessons students are learning basic finger coordination used in legato and staccato touch, and also they are beginning to learn how to phrase slurred groups (down-up wrist motion). Forearm rotation requires a different motion than the preceding considerations. Rotation may be taught when basic control and coordination has been assimilated–sometime within the third year or early in the fourth year.

The rotary movement may be explained to the student by demonstrating how one turns a door handle: the forearm rotates (turns) either left or right (Ill. 8:1). Make sure that *only* the forearm rotates; the upper arm

Ill. 8:1. Rotary movements.

a. Left

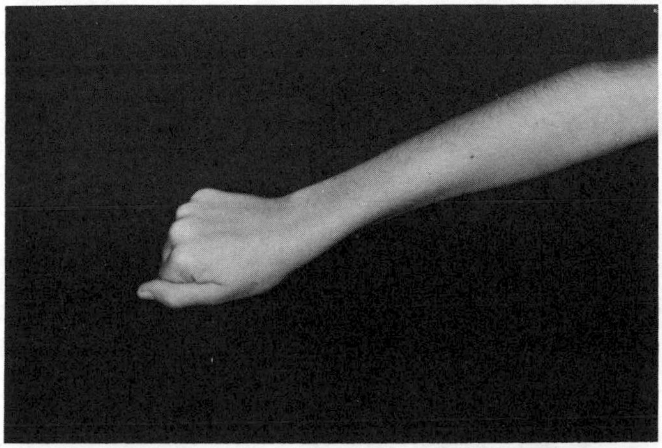

b. Right

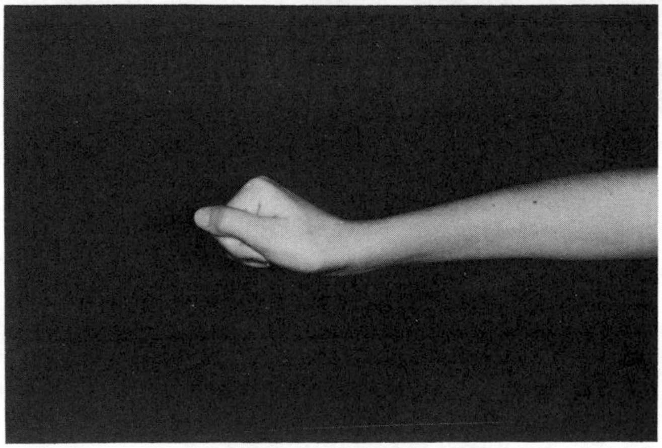

should not wave about. Also explain to the student that the forearm will rotate in the direction of the next note to be played (Ill. 8:2).

Ill. 8:2. Rotation at the keyboard.

a. Left

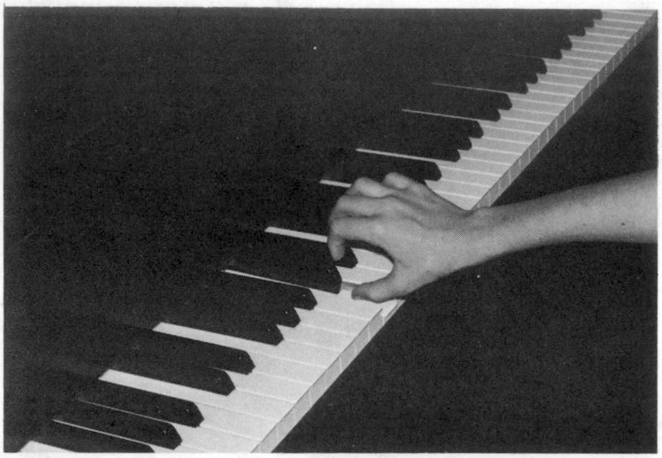

b. Right

At first arrows may be drawn in the music to indicate the direction in which to turn (Ex. 8:16).

Ex. 8:16. Diagram of forearm rotation.

The rotary movement is used whenever notes in a series move back and forth: Alberti bass, broken octaves (sevenths, sixths, fifths, fourths, thirds, seconds), trills, etc.[6] The following exercise (Ex. 8:17) may serve as an introductory study in forearm rotation.

Ex. 8:17. Forearm rotation exercises.

[6] An excellent description and explanation of rotation is given in József Gát's *The Technique of Piano Playing* (London: Collet's Holdings Ltd., 1965), pp. 170-176.

Pedaling

The pedals are rarely used in beginning lessons. Most young children cannot reach the ground with their feet, and thus it is more practical to teach the correct use of the pedals when the physical capabilities are present.

Although youngsters may not be able to reach the pedal without almost standing up, generally they love the pedal and are fascinated by the sound. The sustaining pedal may be used within the first two years for effects. However, it should not be used indiscriminately, even for fun; there is no need to promote a bad habit. The pedal may be used at the end of a piece, with chords, hand over hand arpeggios, etc. In that way the child's eagerness to use the pedal will be satisfied without letting "anything go."

Explain to the child what happens when the foot presses the pedal (right pedal). Let the child look into the piano and see the dampers lift from the strings. In this way the pupil will understand what the pedal does and why the sound is produced. Do not refer to the sustaining pedal as the "loud pedal." By showing the student what the pedal does he can understand why it should be called *sustaining pedal* or *damper pedal.*

The correct use of the pedal may be taught about late second year or early third year—whenever the child's foot is able to reach the pedal with the heel on the floor while at the same time remaining seated in the correct position at the piano (Ill. 8:3).

Ill. 8:3. Position of the foot on the pedal.

a. Incorrect

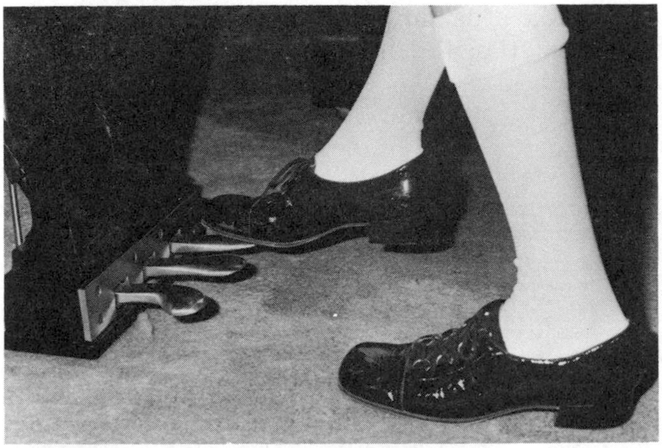

b. Correct

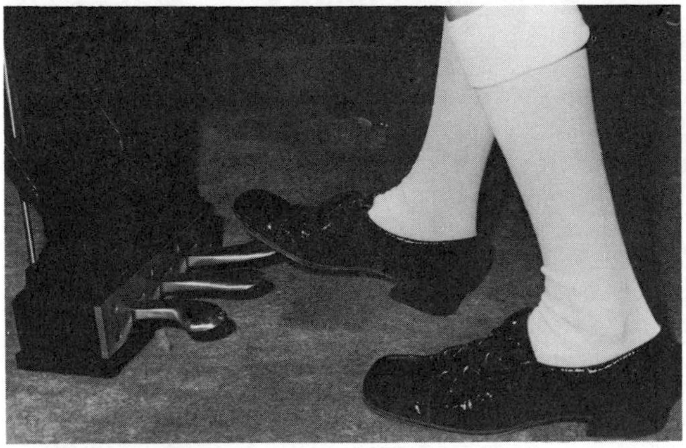

At first the sustaining pedal will be used in a simple way to connect notes of a chord for a certain effect (Ex. 8:18).

Ex. 8:18. Bastien: ***Tumbling***

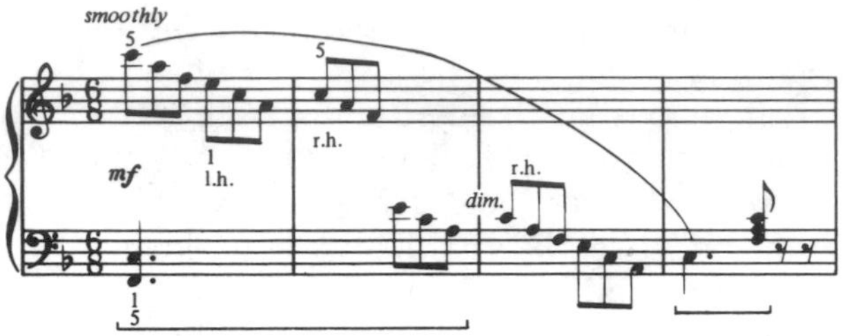

After the basic use of the pedal has been experienced for a period of time, *syncopated pedaling* may be taught. Syncopated pedaling requires an exacting coordination between hands and foot: this type of pedaling is difficult for students and should not be taught too early. However, it is one of the most essential elements of good playing and should be explained carefully when presented.

Explain to the student that the syncopated pedal (or legato pedal) is effected by a change of pedal on the beat (or with each new change of harmony) in the following manner: Push the sustaining pedal down with the first note at the same time (Ex. 8:19). Thereafter, play the key and release the pedal on the beat, then push the pedal down again after the key has been played using a steady, even rhythm. (Use the third finger of either hand.)

Ex. 8:19. Syncopated pedal.

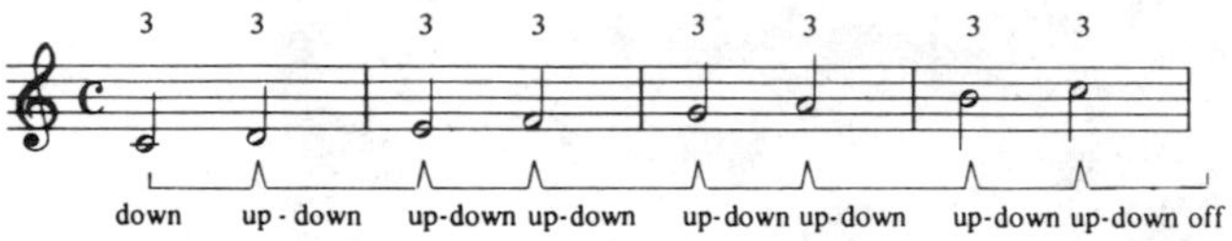

If the student has difficulty in changing the pedal after the beat, it is helpful to use a rhythmic presentation (Ex. 8:20). The arrows describe exactly when to depress the pedal. The pedal will be changed evenly, allowing time for harmonic change.

Ex. 8:20. Rhythmic syncopated pedal.

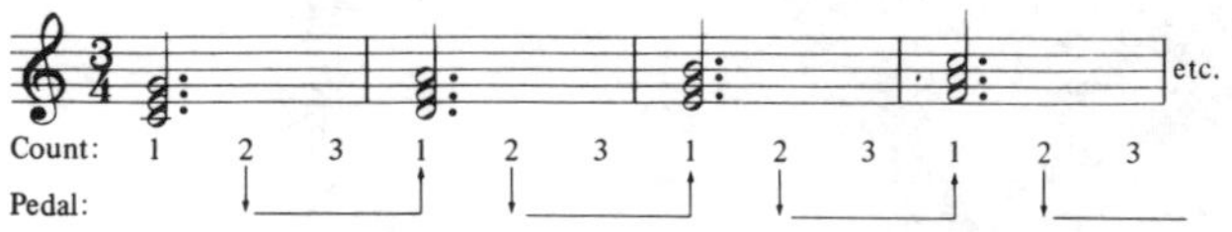

For books on elementary uses of the pedals, see: *Pedal Pushers* by George Anson (Willis, 1966); *Introduction to Pedalling* by Joan Last (Galliard/Galaxy, 1963); *Start Pedalling*! by Sade C. Styron and Everett Stevens (Summy-Birchard, 1964); and *Principles of Pedaling* by Leo Podolsky, June Davison, and Ardella Schaub (Boosey & Hawkes, 1966).

Technique is largely a matter of teacher preference. Some teachers give Hanon to all first year beginners like vitamin pills, others treat Hanon like the plague and never teach it. Some teachers prefer to give scales to beginners, others prefer to wait until some fundamentals have been learned. Hanon, Schmitt, Czerny, Beringer, Pischna, Philipp, and numerous others have written volumes of exercises. Some teachers prefer to give some of these along the way, others do not. The whole realm of technique and emphasis given to it is left essentially to the teacher.

How will the student benefit from exercises and studies? Is technique the ability to play loud and fast? Is it designed to make weak fingers strong? Is it accomplished by playing scales and arpeggios? Is it necessary for students who only want to play for fun? These are some of the questions concerning technique that should be given some serious consideration.

The entire matter of exercises versus pieces should be considered. If the beginner gets his start only through technical exercises, his playing will probably sound mechanical and uninteresting. However, a student who has only played pieces may sound musical but may be lacking in control and agility. A happy compromise can be made by dividing the lesson and practice time into several areas to include both pieces and technique, as well as sight-reading and theory. This composite program will help produce students who are well-rounded musically. Technique is important even for students who are just playing for fun; they will benefit from learning such basic patterns as scales, chords, arpeggios, and the like.

In addition to exercises and studies, technique patterns may be made from difficult passages in the music. A passage may be transposed to a number of keys, the rhythm may be changed stressing certain notes, certain fingers in the passage may be accented, etc. Many teachers prefer this type of study work eschewing mere "finger-wigglers" such as Schmitt, Beringer, Hanon, and the like.

Musical qualities should always take precedence—tone, line, balancing of melody and accompaniment, phrasing, etc. are all necessary components of a technique program. "Every tone resulting from expedient movements will be useful and will help to develop his [the pupil's] technique. Everything he plays will assist him in creating movement associations corresponding to musical interrelations and in acquiring mastery over his arms and fingers."[7]

Study books abound with profusion. The teacher may select a variety of books designed for either pure or applied technique. The following list contains representative books which are approximately third year level or approaching early intermediate level.

HANON STUDIES

Bastien, James (ed.) First Hanon Studies Kjos West (1976)

This twenty-four page volume contains the first twenty studies written in eighth notes, one octave apart. Practice suggestions are provided on the first two pages for varying the touch, phrasing, rhythm, tempo, dynamics, and key. Easy, may be given sooner than the third year.

[7]Gát, *op. cit.*, p. 276.

Brimhall, John Hanon Through the Keys Hansen (1970)

This volume contains twenty-four Hanon exercises with two studies in each of the twelve major keys, arranged in the order of the circle of fifths.

Ferté, Armand The Young Pianist Virtuoso Schott (1963)

Thirty-seven Hanon studies comprise this volume, as well as all major, minor, and chromatic scales.

Thompson, John The Hanon Studies, Books 1 & 2 Willis (1937)

Basic touches of legato and staccato, as well as musical considerations of phrasing are incorporated into these arranged versions of the Hanon studies.

EXERCISE BOOKS

Anson, George The Shape of Things Willis (1966)

This book is especially helpful for the teacher (and student) who needs quick reference to scale fingerings, chord and arpeggio fingerings, and selected explanations of various patterns. More explanations and hints are given in the book than actual playing. The organization and content of this excellent thirty-two page volume is logical, practical, and useful.

Bastien, James Magic Finger Technique, Books 2 & 3 GWM Co. (1966)

These two books in this three-book series include exercises in all keys in the following areas: phrasing, legato and staccato touch combined, balance between hands, chromatic scale exercises, finger independence exercises, chords and inversions, scales, double note exercises, Alberti bass patterns, and wrist staccato exercises.

Bastien, James Technic Lessons, Level 4 Kjos West (1976)

The short exercises and studies develop technic in various keys for scales, pedaling, chords and inversions, finger independence, wrist staccato, trills, double notes, Alberti bass, and incorporate various rhythms.

Brimhall, John (ed.) Beringer: Daily Pianoforte Exercises Hansen (1970)

The selected exercises in this book are divided into four parts: Part I—5-finger studies, hand stationary; Part II—5-finger studies, progressive hand movement; Part III—scale studies; Part IV—chord and arpeggio studies. The first part of the book (exercises 1-25) is easy enough for third year students. The patterns are based on major, minor, and diminished chord shapes.

Burnam, Edna-Mae A Dozen a Day, Books 2 & 3 Willis (1953, 1956)

The patterns in these two books include: exercises in extended positions, chords, chromatic scale patterns, arpeggio patterns, double notes, scales, and studies for legato and staccato touch.

(collection) The Early Virtuoso Summy-Birchard (1974)

Included in this sixty-four page collection are pre-Hanon type exercises by Robert J. Ring, selected studies from *Op. 599, Bk. 1* by Czerny, and *Secondo Scales* by Hansi Alt (for pupil and teacher). These previously published separate small volumes are combined here in this large collection and provide various technical activities at about the third year level (some are easier, some of the Czerny studies approach early intermediate level).

Last, Joan Freedom Technique, Book 1 Oxford (1971)

The distinguished British pedagogue has compiled a three-book series of technical exercises (patterns) ranging from early third year through upper intermediate level and beyond. The studies are short, mostly one-line, covering a variety of technical procedures. The beginning exercises in *Book 1* can be given to a late second year student, but the level of the book is generally third year. Included are exercises for rotation, slurs, scale preparation, chords and inversions, major and minor scales, arpeggios, chromatic scales, and elementary pedal exercises. The examples are designed to promote ease of movement over the keyboard as well as provide elementary experiences in typical keyboard patterns. Explanations throughout are direct and to the point.

Maier, Guy and Herbert Bradshaw Thinking Fingers, Volume 2 Belwin-Mills (1954)
Included in this forty-eight page volume are exercises for the chromatic scale, thumb passing under held tones, major scales, harmonic minor scales, broken chords, and arpeggios. Explicit directions are given for practicing.

ETUDE BOOKS

Bastien, James Major Scales and Pieces, Minor Scales and Pieces GWM Co. (1967)
Both books contain original and arranged etudes at approximately third year level; some of the pieces in the minor book approach early intermediate level.

Czerny, Carl The Little Pianist, Op. 823, Book 1 Schirmer (1902)
For Czerny enthusiasts this thirty-two page collection contains little study pieces at about late second and third year levels.

Germer, Heinrich, and H. W. Nicholl (eds.) Czerny: Selected Piano Studies, Vol. 1 Boston Music Co. (1944)
Comprised of fifty small studies for the upper elementary level, and thirty-two studies for the early intermediate level, this 101 page collection contains a representative cross-section of the many studies Czerny wrote.

Gillock, William Accent on Majors Willis (1964)
White key major scales are presented and a piece in each key is provided.

Gillock, William Accent on Majors and Minors Willis (1963)
Parallel major and minor scales are presented and a piece is provided in each key. Only the white key scales are used. The music is slightly more difficult than the previous book, approaching early intermediate level toward the end of the book.

Glover, David Carr Tuneful Technic, Book 1 Hansen (1961)
Some of the etudes in this thirty-two page collection are by Glover, others are by Biehl, Czerny, Gurlitt, Heller, etc. Scales, chromatic scales, double notes, chords, and various other aspects of technic are interwoven into these study pieces.

Hirschberg, David Technic is Fun, Preparatory Book and **Book 1 Musicord (1948, 1941)**
The *Preparatory Book* contains arranged etudes at approximately late second year or early third year levels. *Book 1* is about right for average third year students. The arrangements in both books are based on studies by Berens, Bertini, Czerny, Diabelli, Gurlitt, Köhler, and others.

Kasschau, Howard (ed.) 106 Greatest Piano Studies, 2 Vols. Schirmer (1961)
Both volumes include drills, exercises, and etudes arranged in progressive order. *Volume 1* (nos. 1-62) is about the right level for average third year students; it contains selected works by such etude composers as Bertini, Burgmüller, Clementi, Czerny, Gurlitt, Heller, and many others. *Volume 2* is more difficult, about early intermediate level.

McArtor, Marion (Clark Library) Piano Technic, Books 1 & 2 Summy-Birchard (1954, 1955)
The studies in these books (and others in the series) are written according to a planned program for developing facility and control. The short etudes are based on the following patterns: 5-finger patterns, extended and contracted patterns, scale patterns, slurred groups, arpeggio patterns, and chord patterns.

In the previous two chapters the importance of including theory and keyboard harmony was stressed. The main function of a theory program is for the basic understanding of harmonic materials in the student's repertoire. The student should be able to discern chordal outlines, chordal progressions, interval relationships, key, etc. The teacher must constantly strive to make the student musically literate in every aspect of music.

Recognition of basic harmonic patterns is helpful in sight-reading, learning new music, and in memorizing. One of the common omissions in piano teaching is theory, and students often have difficulty in memorizing simply because they do not understand what they are playing. They play a piece over and over without comprehension until motor reflex takes over and the piece is finally learned. This type of "learning" should be avoided. Through a systematic theory program students will learn basic fundamentals which will benefit all aspects of their study.

The third year theory program is a continuation of items already begun. Review in the beginning of the third year is essential to reestablish concepts started in the first two years. Continued work on intervals, key signatures, chords (major, minor, augmented, diminished), scales, and analyzing progressions should be reviewed throughout the third year. If class theory is offered, more emphasis should be given to ensemble playing, sight-reading, and creative work. There will be fewer new elements learned in the third year because many fundamentals have been presented so far, and these should be reviewed thoroughly for comprehension.

New theoretical inclusions in the third year are:

1. Building scales with tetrachords
2. Naming scale degrees
3. Writing and playing triads of the scale
4. Writing triads and inversions
5. Creating question and answer phrases

Building Scales With Tetrachords

Although writing major scales was presented briefly in the previous chapter, the third year student may be taught a more comprehensive explanation of scale formation. Teaching the tetrachord formation of the scales is traditional and provides the student with the basis for forming all the scales.

The word "tetra" comes from the Greek meaning four, or having four parts. Tetrachords that comprise the major scale may be explained in the following manner:

> Every scale may be divided into two equal parts called tetrachords. Each tetrachord (a group of four notes), has the same intervals, namely a half step between 3 and 4 of each group of notes and whole steps between the other tones (Ex. 8:21). The tetrachords are separated by a whole step.[8]

[8]From *Book 5 Writing* by Jane Smisor Bastien (GWM Co., 1971), p. 4.

Ex. 8:21. Tetrachord formation.

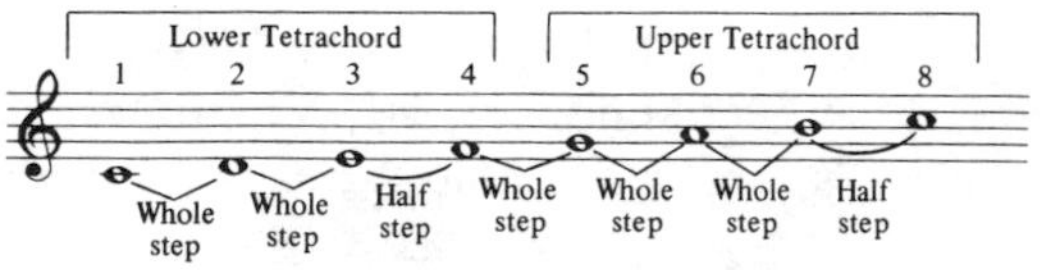

Students may build new scales by adding a new tetrachord to an upper tetrachord of the previous scale (Ex. 8:22). All the major scales may be constructed in this manner.

Provide the student with blank music paper for writing the scales. This work may also be done at the lesson on a blackboard or music slate.

Ex. 8:22. Building scales with tetrachords.[9]

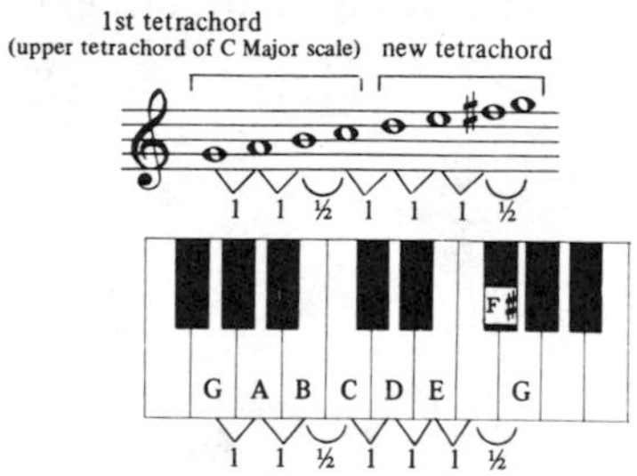

Naming Scale Degrees

The scale degree names, tonic, sub-dominant, dominant, may have already been learned. However, the student may now learn all the names and their relationships within the scale (Ex. 8:23).

Ex. 8:23. Scale degree names.[10]

Scale degrees are also referred to by the following names;

I. Tonic (the key-note)
II. Supertonic (one step above the tonic)
III. Mediant (halfway from tonic to dominant)
IV. Subdominant (as far below the tonic as the dominant is above it)
V. Dominant (a major or "dominant" element in the key)
VI. Submediant (halfway down from tonic to subdominant)
VII. Leading tone (has a melodic tendency towards tonic)

[9]Example from *Book 5 Writing*, p. 5.

[10]Example from *Book 5 Writing*, p. 11.

Triads of the Scale

Explain to the student that triads may be built on each tone of the scale. The pattern is I, IV, V, Major; II, III, VI, minor; and VII diminished (Ex. 8:24). Three chords, the I, IV, and V, are the *principal chords* in the key.

Ex. 8:24. Triads of the scale.[11]

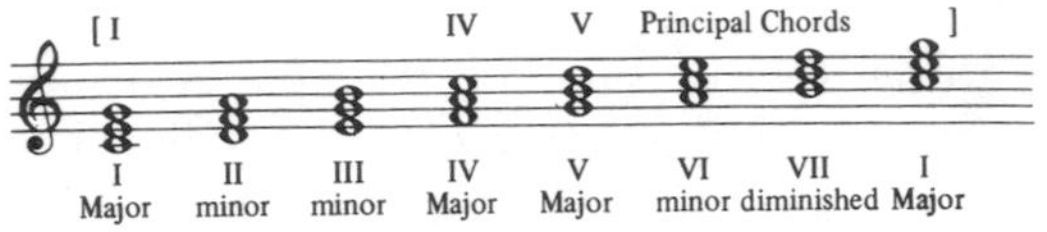

Direct the student to write a number of triads on scale steps, and write in the name of each chord. Have the student practice playing the triads in each key.[12]

Writing Triads and Inversions

In the previous chapter triads and inversions were listed under technique. It would be sufficient for (late) second year students to play these chords. In the third year, however, a more comprehensive explanation of triads and inversions can be given. Students can learn to write Major, minor, augmented and diminished triads and inversions.

Explain to the student that the three notes of a triad are called the root, third and fifth:

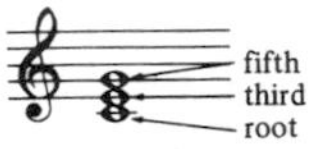

The root, the lowest note, is the name of the chord. When the root is moved to the top or middle of the chord, the chord is called an *inversion* because the position of the notes have been changed (Ex. 8:25).

Ex. 8:25. Major triad and inversions.[13]

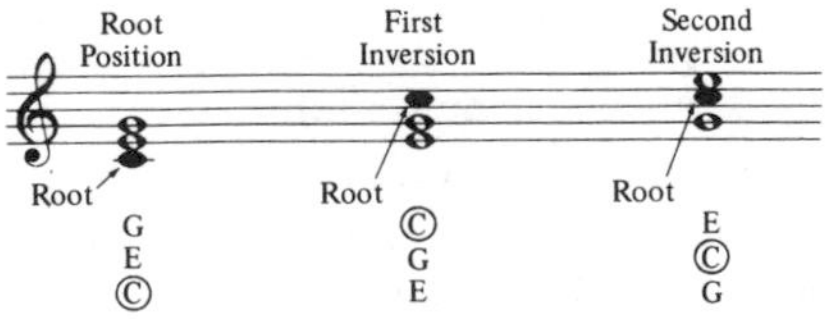

[11] *Ibid*

[12] For an interesting book which provides many ideas for harmonizing melodies with triads, see *Tricks with Triads* by Don Fornuto (Lee Roberts Music Publications, Inc./Schirmer, 1970).

[13] Example from *Book 5 Writing*, p. 16.

When analyzing inversions of triads, it is helpful to notice which two notes of the chords are close together. (1) *First Inversion Triads* have the bottom two notes close together (a third apart); the *top note* is the *keynote.* (2) *Second Inversion Triads* have the top two notes close together (a third apart); the *middle note* is the *keynote.*

Direct students to write a variety of triads and inversions (Major, minor, augmented and diminished). Also have them analyze all inversions in their music.

Creating Question and Answer Phrases

Question phrases played by the teacher and answer phrases played by the student form structured improvisation patterns. This form of improvisation should be taught from the beginning. At first the question phrase may be no more than an ascending five-finger scale answered by a descending five-finger scale. An example of an elementary question and answer pattern is:

Question: 1-2-3-4-5-5-5
Answer: 5-4-3-2-1-1-1

From this simple beginning the process can be expanded to phrases which contain a variety of intervals, chords, and various bass patterns.[14]

At the third year level a triad bass pattern makes an excellent background for simple melodies in march style (Ex. 8:26). After practicing

Ex. 8:26. Triad bass accompaniment.[15]

the left hand alone, the student is ready to improvise melodies above the bass pattern.

The following presentation (Ex. 8:27) describes in detailed form how question and answer phrases may be constructed in march style.

Ex. 8:27. Creating a march (question and answer phrases).[16]

1. Complete the following melody. The four measure phrase given is the "question." Notice that it ends on a note other than the key note or tonic. The "answer" *must* end on the key note. You create the "answer" following these suggestions;

[14]For a thorough presentation of question and answer drills, see Robert Pace's *Skills and Drills, Books 1-6* (Lee Roberts Music Publications, Inc./Schirmer).

[15]Example from *Book 5 Writing*, p. 19.

[16]*Ibid.*

(a) The notes in measures 5 and 6 should be a repetition of those in measures 1 and 2.
(b) The rhythm in the "answer" should be similar to that used in the "question."
(c) Measure 8 should end on the key note.

2. Harmonize the melody using the triad bass.
3. Improvise your own marches using this pattern.

Third Year Sight-Reading

In the previous chapter a suggestion was given to assign material for reading at an easier level than the repertoire level. A distinction should be made between repertoire for serious study and realistic material for reading.

All the technical elements studied so far will be put to use in reading: hand position shifts, finger crossings, broken chord patterns, triads and inversions, etc. The student constantly must look ahead and perceive new shapes and patterns. Reading skills can be developed with persistent effort. William Newman states:

> Reading notes rapidly presents much the same problems as reading words rapidly. We are helped in prose by seeing combinations of letters as syllables, combinations of syllables as words, even combinations of words as whole phrases. Similarly we are helped in music, always depending on the extent of our intuitive and intellectual command of harmony, by seeing combinations of tones as chords and combinations of chords as familiar progressions.[17]

Reading by chord shapes and finger patterns is essential. However, reading is dependent largely on recognition of rhythm patterns. A good reader may "fake" the notes but keep the rhythm going. To assist third year students in becoming rhythm conscious, the teacher might assign *Basic Timing for the Pianist* by Allan Small (Claire Music Co., Inc., 1970). This book presents 105 short rhythmic patterns.[18]

[17]William S. Newman, *The Pianist's Problems* (New York: Harper & Row, 1950), p. 21. Reprinted by permission.

[18]Another book which examines the spectrum of rhythm patterns is *Rhythmic Training* by Robert Starer (MCA Music, Inc., 1969). This book would be especially useful for the teacher or an advanced student.

For an informative discourse on sight-reading, see Sidney Lawrence's *A Guide to Remedial Sightreading for the Piano Student* (New York: Workshop Music Teaching Publications, Inc., 1964). Numerous corrective suggestions are given in this excellent book.

Although almost anything at the right level can be used for reading, several books are suggested here which contain practical sight-reading material at approximately the third year level.

Agay, Denes *Fun With Sight-Reading, Volume B* Witmark/Warner Bros. Publications
Alt, Hansi *Afternoons* Presser
Anson, George *Ten Tunes for Ten Fingers* Elkan-Vogel/Presser
Bartók, Béla *Mikrokosmos, Volumes 1 & 2* Boosey
Bastien, James *Sight Reading, Level 3* Kjos West
Bull, Carolyn *From Here to There* C. Fischer
DeCesare, Ruth *Piano Games* Marks
Deutsch, Leonhard *For Sight Reading, Book 1* Heritage
Diller-Quaile *Second Solo Book* Schirmer
Dumm, Robert *Making Music* Schroeder & Gunther
Goldberger, David (ed.) *The Folk Song Book, III* Consolidated
Johnson, Thomas A. *Moving Forward* Hinrichsen/Peters
Last, Joan *At the Keyboard, Book 3* Oxford
Richter, Ada *Folk Songs of Today* Witmark/Warner Bros. Publications
Royal Conservatory of Music of Toronto Grade II Frederick Harris Music Co.
Steward, Margaret *Folk Music of Brazil* Montgomery
Westmoreland, John and Marvin Kahn *Discovering the Keyboard, Book 3* Mills/Belwin
Zeitlin, Poldi and David Goldberger *Russian Music, Books 1 & 2* MCA

THIRD YEAR SUPPLEMENTARY MATERIALS

DUET COLLECTIONS

Agay, Denes *Broadway Classics, Vol. B* Witmark/Warner Bros.
Bastien, Jane Smisor *Duets For Fun, Book 2* GWM Co.
Bishop, Dorothy *A Folk Holiday* C. Fischer
George, Jon *Kaleidoscope Duets, Books 3 & 4* Alfred
George, Jon *Two at One Piano, Books 2 & 3* Summy-Birchard
Glover, David Carr, and Louise Garrow *Piano Duets, Levels 2 & 3* Belwin-Mills
Grove, Roger *Couples Only* Summy-Birchard
Johnson, Thomas A. *Together We Play* Hinrichsen/Peters
Rollino, Joseph, and Paul Sheftel *Fesitvities* C. Fischer

Schaum, Wesley *Tunes for Two, Book 2* Schaum Publications
Stecher, Horowitz, Gordon *The Pleasure of Your Company, Book 3* G. Schirmer
Zaninelli, Luigi *A Lexicon of Beasties* (for student and teacher) Shawnee
Zeitlin, Poldi, and David Goldberger (eds.) *Duet Book I* Consolidated

SOLOS

EARLY THIRD YEAR SOLOS

Agay, Denes Dancing Leaves G. Schirmer (1961)

A minor (modal flavor) - 3/4 - Lively and lightly. A flowing, cantabile melody is divided between the hands requiring sensitivity and control. This first-rate teaching piece incorporates such teaching features as shifting hand positions, pedal, crossing hands, and staccato triads.

Bastien, James Rock Festival GWM Co. (1973)

C major - 4/4 - Fast rock beat. The melody is accompanied by open fifths. Off-beat accents are used in the B section. Effective recital fare. Strictly for fun. (Included in *Bastien Favorites, Level 3.)*

Bastien, Jane Smisor Little Grey Burro GWM Co. (1973)

D major - ₵ - Moderately. A syncopated melody sings over a steady staccato bass. Balance of melody and accompaniment is the main teaching feature. A most attractive study and recital solo. (Included in *Bastien Favorites, Level 4.)*

Bastien, Jane Smisor Tumbling GWM Co. (1968)

Hand over hand arpeggios, plus elementary basic use of legato pedal are the main teaching features of this effective solo. This piece sounds more difficult than it is. (Included in *Bastien Favorites, Level 3.)*

Brodsky, Michael It's Raining Summy-Birchard (1960)

F major - C - Allegretto. Staccato-legato combinations constitute the essence of this well-written solo. (Available only in *Summy Piano Solo Package, No. 201.)*

Cobb, Hazel Pomp and Pageantry Willis (1938)

G major - C - Majestically. This old-timer is still effective given to the right student. It is a big sounding chord piece written on four staves. An analysis of the piece and practice suggestions are given on the inside cover by John Thompson.

George, Jon Students' Choice, Set 2 Summy-Birchard (1970)

Five well-written solos comprise this brief folio written in suite form. Favorites are "Troubadour's Song," "Dumka," and "Knight's Tale." Most of the compositions are about the same level, although, "Knight's Tale" is more difficult than the others. Imaginative music for musical students.

MacLachlan, T. Robin Yellow Butterfly Boston Music Co. (1928)

G major - 4/4 - Not too fast. Nice melody line, phrasing, and dynamics are found in this antediluvian solo written in pre-sonatina style. Excellent teaching hints are given on the first page showing blocked hand position outlines for the entire piece.

Nevin, Mark Tarantella Schroeder & Gunther/Associated (1953)

G major - 6/8 - Lively. An excellent piece for teaching hand coordination—two-note slurs in the right hand against legato single notes in the left hand. The piece lies well under the hand, but the choice of fingering is not the most economical. Try fingering the left hand first four measure phrase this way: 4,3,2,1,3,2,3,5.

Olson, Lynn Freeman **Festival in Aragon** **C. Fischer (1973)**

E major tonality - 3/4 - Vigorously fast. Although labeled an "intermediate piano solo" on the cover, the level of difficulty appears to be either late second or early third year. It is essentially a 5-finger piece which utilizes hand position shifts, legato-staccato touches, and is written in melody and accompaniment (open fifths) style. A suggestive Spanish flavor permeates throughout.

Stecher, Melvin, Norman Horowitz, and Claire Gordon **I am From Siam** **G. Schirmer (1969)**

C major - 4/4 - Lively. This brisk march uses characteristic staccato fourths and fifths for Oriental color. The left hand keeps a steady rhythmic beat throughout.

Stevens, Everett **White Clouds** **C. Fischer (1955)**

G major - 3/4 - Moderato molto calmato. An attractive flowing piece incorporating the following teaching features: crossing hands, pedal, and graded dynamics. This graceful piece is more suited for girls than boys.

MID-THIRD YEAR LEVEL

Anson, George **The Platinum Pup** **Willis (1971)**

C major - 4/4 - Unhurried. Doggie barks (minor seconds) are heard frequently in this cute solo about a day in the life of a pup. Crisp staccatos, staccato-legato combinations, and balance of melody and accompaniment are the main teaching features.

Balough, Erno **Conversation** **Boosey (1966)**

B minor - 4/4 - Andante. Written in two treble clefs throughout, this is a study piece for reading two-voice melodies in imitative style. More suited for study than recital.

Bastien, James **Fifth Avenue Poodle** **GWM Co. (1972)**

C major - 4/4 - Strict march tempo. Moving left hand triads set the march beat while the right hand plays a melody containing a variety of slurred groups. An effective study and recital solo. (Included in *Bastien Favorites, Level 4.)*

Bastien, Jane Smisor **Chinese Tea Party** **GWM Co. (1967)**

C major - 4/4 - Brightly. Written in march style, this attractive solo features left hand staccato parallel fourths, rapidly shifting hand positions, and elementary use of the pedal. An effective recital solo. (Included in *Bastien Favorites, Level 4.)*

Bastien, Jane Smisor **March of the Troll Dolls** **GWM Co. (1967)**

C major - 4/4 - Strict march time. A steady rhythmic bass sets the background for this precise march. Teaching features include: staccato and legato combinations, shifts of hand positions, grace note in the last measure. (Included in *Bastien Favorites, Level 4.)*

Bastien, Jane Smisor **Space Explorers** **GWM Co. (1968)**

F minor - 6/8 - Moderato, alla marcia. Parallel triads set the mood of adventure and expectation. An interesting tonal effect is created by the use of the Neapolitan chord (Gb major) which is used in almost every measure in the A section. Especially for boys.

Bastien, Jane Smisor **Village Square** **GWM Co. (1973)**

C major - ¢ - Fast. This spirited square dance piece contains these teaching features: slurred groups, staccato and legato touches, and rapidly shifting hand positions. A recital winner. (Included in *Bastien Favorites, Level 4.)*

Bishop, Dorothy Song of the Wind C. Fischer (1963)

G major - 2/4 - With motion. An attractive singing melody is accompanied by broken chord figures in the left hand. Practice each hand alone: shape the melody in phrases and shade it dynamically as indicated (follow the natural rise and fall of the line); play the left hand first as block chords to establish the feeling for each shape and to establish the correct fingering.

Bostelmann, Ida The Little Orchestra Boston Music Co. (1962)

C major - C - Allegro. Characterized by symmetrical phrase patterns typical of classic style, this attractive teaching piece is useful as a representative style piece. Shifting hand positions, phrasing, and contrasting dynamics are the main teaching features.

Brodsky, Michael Calypso Party Elkan-Vogel/Presser (1966)

D major - ₵ - Moderato con ritmo. Syncopated rhythm (♩ ♫♩♩♩♩) is the central feature of this study and recital favorite. Direct the student to practice the right hand alone to establish the correct hand motions for the phrasing. Observe the fingering carefully.

Chagy, John Jazz Tarantella Marks (1967)

A minor - 6/8 - Vivace. The A section sounds typically tarantellaish until the "take-off" on the third line (G7, F#7, F7, E7, Am). A catchy kid-pleaser.

Cobb, Hazel The King's Guard Belwin-Mills (1957)

G major - 4/4 - With spirit. A snappy march incorporating staccatos, triplets, dotted rhythms, and double thirds. The legato double thirds in the right hand are often problematic for average children. Similar patterns can be constructed as exercises to develop the coordination necessary to play double thirds.

Elaine, Sister M. Modal Picture C. Fischer (1961)

Phrygian mode - 3/4 - Moderato. A nice melodic line is projected in this well-written solo. Scale-like finger crossings and shifts in hand positions are the main teaching features. Although the piece does not look difficult, it is tricky to memorize.

Erb, Mae-Aileen Whirling Dancers Witmark/Warner Bros. Publications (1958)

A minor - 6/8 - Presto. A spritely tarantella with running eighth notes. The presto tempo is a challenge

Gillock, William Carnival in Rio Willis (1969)

G major - 2/4 - Tempo di Samba. Using only the barest harmonies (tonic and dominant), Gillock has created one of the best student-pleasers in print. Nice melodic line, excellent phrasing, and fine dynamic contrasts mark the superlative Gillock style. An excellent study and recital solo. (Second piano accompaniment available, Willis, 1976.)

Gillock, William Flamenco Willis (1968)

C minor - 3/8 - Intensely rhythmic. Intense rhythmic drive and a beautiful singing melody in the B section are combined into a student favorite.

Green, Harold Bellman Indian Summer Schroeder & Gunther/Associated (1970)

Bb minor - 3/4 - Andante. This piece contains a plaintive, lyric falling theme characteristic of summer's close. A singing legato touch is used throughout. Pay special attention to balance of melody and accompaniment and the use of the pedal (don't blur). For sensitive young musicians.

MacLachlan, Robin T. Sunny Jim Schroeder & Gunther/Associated (1948)

G major - C - Allegro ma non troppo. The central teaching feature of this catchy solo is rapidly shifting hand positions. An attractive study and recital solo.

Martino, Russ Chili Bean MCA (1965)

C major - 4/4 - Lively. Written in calypso style using syncopations and modal harmonies, this attractive recital solo has been a favorite since its publication. Popular with boys.

Nevin, Mark Mechanical Men Schroeder & Gunther/Associated (1943)

G minor - 4/4 - Strict march time. The central teaching feature of this snappy march is the repeated dotted rhythm figure in the right hand (♪. ♬ ♪. ♬). An effective recital solo. Especially for boys.

Olson, Lynn Freeman Olé! Summy-Birchard (1965)

F minor - 6/8 - Broadly. The Latin atmosphere in this well-written solo is immediately appealing. The melody which contains frequent syncopations flows above a simple bass pattern constructed of parallel fifths. Basic use of the pedal is incorporated throughout most of the piece. (Available only in *Summy Piano Solo Package, No. 201.)*

Raymond, Joseph March on the White Keys J. Fischer/Belwin (1957)

C major - C - Tempo di marcia. This attractive study and recital solo written entirely on the white keys contains such teaching features as moving left hand staccato thirds, slurs, some first and second inversion triads. Popular with boys.

Rowley, Alec Miniature Prelude and Fugue Chester (1946)

C major - 4/4 - Allegretto & Moderato. This solo is an extract from a superb collection titled *Five Miniature Preludes and Fugues*; it is the first in the collection. This composition could be given to average or better students as a first experience in Baroque style. Voicing of linear lines is the dominant teaching feature.

Russell, Olive Nelson Mariachi Band Summy-Birchard (1964)

G major - 3/4 - Lively tempo. An effective teaching piece incorporating legato double thirds, syncopation, and slurred sixths. (Available only in *Summy Piano Solo Package, No. 301.)*

Storr, Sherman Chant of the Bird Woman Presser (1967)

Dorian mode - 2/2 - Mysteriously. Simple plaintive melodies and some nice linear two-voice counterpoint are interwoven effectively in this unusual solo. Correct phrasing and voicing of melodies (balance of tone) are most important to perform this piece convincingly. For a student with better than average musical feeling.

Taylor, Edna Bells in the Night C. Fischer (1960)

A minor - ₵ - Slowly. A nice pedal study piece for the average student. Slow changing chords gently toll in a pensive manner.

LATE THIRD YEAR LEVEL

Bastien, Jane Smisor July 4th Square Dance GWM Co. (1965)

C major - 4/4 - Vigorously. This catchy solo, well-played, is a hit on any recital program. Teaching features include shifting hand positions, staccato jump-bass, syncopation, and a variety of slurred groups. (Included in *Bastien Favorites, Level 4.)*

Burnam, Edna Mae Pastel Desert Colors Willis (1968)

Modal (phrygian) - 4/4 - Moderato. This solo is from a collection of four pieces called *Desert Poem Tones*; it is number two in the group. A nice mood is created by using impressionistic sounds (parallel fifths) and pedal effects.

Carre, John F. Arab Dance Sam Fox (1963)

A minor - 2/4 - Allegro. For students with better than average facility, this is an effective piece. Running sixteenth notes and dotted rhythms comprise the basic patterns of the dance.

Cobb, Hazel Sonatina in A minor Belwin-Mills (1950)

Comprised of three movements, this sonatina of medium difficulty is written in imitative classical style. The first movement, *Allegro con spirito*, uses a variety of shifting patterns which lie nicely under the hands. The second movement, *Andante,* is a song piece in three part (ABA) form. The last movement, *Allegro,* is a spirited rondo.

Coburn, William Frolicky Rollicky Wind Summy-Birchard (1939)

A minor - 2/4 - Molto Allegro. An old study and recital favorite incorporating rapid sixteenth notes, glissandi, and program suggestions. An imaginative, fun piece. (Available only in *Singing Keys Omnibus* and *Cream of the Crop*.)

Dittenhaver, Sarah Louise Sunrise Canter Marks (1961)

G major - ₵ - Allegro. This engaging, spirited march contains the following teaching features: short slurred groups, scale passages, and shifting chord patterns. The left hand melody must be balanced against the right hand chords. An attractive study and recital solo.

Elaine, Sister M. Triads on Parade J. Fischer/Belwin (1961)

C major - 4/4 - In march style. Written in ABA form this excellent four-page solo contains the following teaching features: diatonic triads, staccato-legato combinations, phrase groupings, and balancing of tone. Two very nice compositional effects are created by the use of the whole tone scale in the A section, and the singing melody against legato diatonic triads in the B section. Major, minor, diminished, augmented triads in root position are used throughout. A first-rate study and recital solo.

Gillock, William Valse Triste Willis (1969)

F minor - 3/4 - Lento. A languid melody combined with chromatic harmony make this an effective mood piece reminiscent of Chopin.

Gillock William Yo-Yo Tricks Schroeder & Gunther/Associated (1959)

G major - 4/4 - Moderately fast. Written in pre-sonatina style, this attractive study and recital solo contains the following teaching features: scales, chords (to be balanced against the melody), shifting hand positions, and contrasting dynamics.

Glover, David Carr Little Lead General Summy-Birchard (1951)

C major - C - M.M ♩ = 120. A snappy march especially appealing to boys. The introduction and postlude use rapidly shifting root positions chords. The main portion of the piece uses mostly first inversion triads. (Available only in *Summy Piano Solo Package, No. 301.)*

Glover, David Carr The Plastic Soldier Hansen (1956)

F major - ₵ - Lively. A catchy march especially appealing to boys. Crisp staccatos, shifting chords, controlled dynamics and tempo are the main teaching features.

Green, Harold Bellman Thar She Blows! Willis (1968)

C tonality - 4/4 - Allegro. A boisterous, rollicking mood is created by a catchy melody accompanied by open fifths. Teaching features include rapidly shifting hand positions, finger crossings, and staccato-legato combinations. An excellent study and recital piece. Especially for boys.

Green, Ray Polka Sonatinas, Nos. 1-3; Song Sonatina; March Sonatina; Cowboy Sonatina; Square Dance Sonatina American Music Ed. (early 1960's)

The seven varied sonatinas are catchy, pleasant sounding works in a semipopular style. Attractive recital and study pieces at about the late third and fourth year levels.

Gretchaninoff, Alexander (William Gillock, ed.)   The Seven Dwarfs   Willis (1969)

F major - 4/4 - Happily. Composed entirely in two treble clefs, this catchy solo is a sure-fire teaching piece. Staccato-legato combinations and contrasting dynamics are the central teaching elements. An excellent study and recital solo.

Griffis, Elliot   For a Broken Doll   Composers Press (1960)

A minor - 3/4 - Mournfully. Because of the exquisite linear melodic line of the well-written solo, it requires a student (girl) of much better than average musicality to perform it effectively. Subtle phrasing, rubato, and balance of tone are required.

/e, Roger   March   Belwin (1969)

D major - 4/4 - Deliberate. Using unexpected accidentals this mildly contemporary, spirited piece creates an unusual effect. Right hand stretches and staccatos are the salient teaching features.

n, Lynn Freeman   Rather Blue   G. Schirmer (1965)

G major - ₵ - Slowly and steadily. This slow blues piece creates a dirge-like effect which is immediately appealing. An excellent piece for teaching syncopated pedal (the pedal must be used *after* the left hand notes to avoid blurring). Either a late third year piece or an early intermediate piece.

Persichetti, Vincent   Parades, Op. 57   Elkan-Vogel/Presser (1955)

Comprised of three short movements, *Parades* is of superior quality and has been standard teaching fare since its publication. The first movement, "March," has a driving force effected by accents, lively triads, and a persistent steady bass in quarter notes. The second movement, "Canter," is a serene, graceful piece with a lilting melody accompanied by a staccato bass. The last movement, "Pomp," is a rollicking, intense procession in 3/4 time. The three short pieces played as a suite are effective recital fare.

Scher, William   Cat Chasing Mouse   Witmark/Warner Bros. Music (1960)

A minor - 2/4 - Vivace. A toccata-like piece constructed entirely of unceasing eighth notes. This attractive solo is difficult for students to get straight through without getting stuck along the way. For students of better than average ability with good facility.

Scher, William   Fanfare   Presser (1963)

G major - 2/4 - Like a march. The difficulty in this piece lies in the left hand. The descending and ascending legato line is musically effective, but difficult to play (and memorize). The total effect, with bugle calls in the right and a lively bass part, is excellent. For students with better than average ability. Especially for boys.

Stevens, Everett   Trail of the Covered Wagon   C. Fischer (1970)

G major - ₵ - Moving along smoothly. An ostinato "Western bass" accompanies the rather tame melody. Scale passages, nice phrasing, and sparse pedaling are the outstanding teaching features of the mellow solo.

Storr, Sherman   Back Country Ballad   J. Fischer/Belwin (1964)

A tonality - 4/4 - Lackadaisically. Permeated with folksy flavor, this smoothly flowing song piece is immediately appealing. Each hand takes a turn in singing the folk style tune. Tonal balance is necessary for a good performance of this well-written piece.

Storr, Sherman   In the Engine Room   Schmitt Publications (1975)

C tonality - ₵ - Mechanically. An ostinato bass is the background for a "blurp-blurp" right hand effect with various chords (and some single notes). Numerous accidentals are used. A reach of a seventh is required. Especially for boys.

Storr, Sherman   Runaway Roan   Boston (1963)

G major - ₵ - With spirit. A bouncy bass is the background for the melody containing staccatos and irregular slurred groups. Two-voice style is used throughout. Mildly contemporary sounds (some mixolydian effects) are used. Difficult to memorize. For talented students.

Storr, Sherman Tonto Trail Presser (1966)

G tonality (mixolydian) - 4/4 - At a leisurely pace. The melody alternates between hands accompanied by bouncing thirds. Balance of melody and accompaniment is the dominant teaching feature. Interesting mildly contemporary harmonic effects are used. For musical students.

Weise, Damon Runaway Pablo C. Fischer (1976)

(F # Major - modal flavor) - 4/4 - Moving. Syncopated, rock-type rhythms are used effectively in this block-chord, broken-chord piece. The chordal pattern used frequently is Bm, AM, GM, F#M. A well-written kid pleaser.

FOR DISCUSSION AND ASSIGNMENT

1. Discuss your philosophy concerning repertoire collections. Do you favor one composer volumes (all Bach, Kabalevsky, etc.)? Do you favor multi-composer collections? What is your view concerning the size of multi-composer volumes?
2. Would you use an edition or an urtext edition for third year students? Why?
3. Should pop music be given to youngsters? Why, or why not?
4. What teaching purpose is served by assigning sonatinas?
5. If possible use a third year student (students) to demonstrate the following technical items: finger patterns (various types described in this chapter), finger independence studies, forearm rotation, and syncopated pedaling. Which items do you consider most important? Why? List other third year technical considerations.
6. In addition to the theory items discussed in this chapter, what others would you include for third year students?
7. At a music store make a survey of third year repertoire books and solos. Present five books and five solos other than those listed in this chapter, and tell why they would be useful for third year students.
8. From your experience examining third year literature, compose a third year solo; point out the teaching features.

FOR FURTHER READING

Hodges, Sister Mabelle L. *A Catalogue of Representative Teaching Materials for Piano Since 1900.* Chicago: De Paul University Press, 1970. This 108 page graded survey is divided into the following areas: courses, anthologies, composer collections, solos, and sonatinas. Brief imaginative annotations accompany all areas. This survey is a one-of-a-kind, and is a useful reference source.

Kern, Alice M., and Helen Titus. *The Teacher's Guidebook to Piano Literature.* Ann Arbor, Mich.: J.W. Edwards, Publishers, Inc., 1955. This 151 page volume contains a graded listing of repertoire materials listed chronologically by levels. The book is the most complete of its kind available, and is a valuable reference source for the teacher. A revised, up-to-date edition would be welcome.

Miller, Marguerite, and Frances Wallingford. *Piano Teaching Materials,* Third Edition. Wichita, Kansas: Wichita State University (order from the authors), 1975. This fifty-two page syllabus was designed to be used in the authors' pedagogy classes. Selected materials are presented in various categories which include methods, workbooks, technique books, repertoire collections, and ensemble music. Although the music is not graded, the teacher will find many useful references.

Intermediate Students 9

In the learning sequence, the intermediate level is generally reached after about three years of lessons. This level is evidenced by the playing of piano literature rather than arranged tunes often presented in method books. Music such as sonatinas, Bach *Two-Part Inventions*, Kabalevsky's *Toccatina*, etc., all denote intermediate level.

The age of the student playing intermediate music will vary according to the time when he began lessons, his ability, and rate of progress. However, the intermediate student generally is between eleven and fourteen years of age.

Within the intermediate grade music there is a wide range of levels. Intermediate contest and audition music is frequently qualified by such terms as *early intermediate, intermediate,* and *upper intermediate*. This degree of latitude within the intermediate period indicates that most students will advance slowly through the period. The time span for average students is about three years.

One of the problems in teaching the intermediate student is to keep all levels of musicianship moving ahead at a similar pace. When the transition from method book pieces to piano literature has been made, the tendency often is to concentrate on a few compositions and neglect other teaching elements. This could soon lead to a deficiency in one of the basic musicianship areas.

One such area is technique. New demands will be made upon the student from the music he is studying. The study of repertoire alone probably will not be sufficient for the student to develop his playing skills to meet the increasingly difficult demands of the music. The intermediate student must maintain a balanced program of study to insure gradual progress in all musicianship areas.

The rate of advancement during the intermediate period should be carefully regulated by the teacher. Sometimes the student should be pushed ahead by giving him slightly more difficult music which will promote adequate development. But the reverse is more often true. Frequently there is an inclination for the teacher to push the student too fast through this stage of development. The teacher may reach for material that is too difficult for the student to perform musically and technically. This often leads to frustration and a sense of defeat. Rather than discouraging the student and perhaps causing him to lose interest, he should be given time to develop his playing level at a realistic rate. Hurrying through this period will probably leave him with a number of deficiencies such as reading, fingering, technique, etc.

One of the main problems confronting intermediate students is the demands made on their time from outside activities. Cheerleading, ballet, sports practice, and the like, will take increased amounts of time away from piano practice. If conflicts become too pressing, a number may become piano drop outs. Usually the less interested or gifted are the first to go. If their musical ability is modest, the demands of practice is the straw that breaks the camel's back. Those who find it necessary to quit should be allowed to do so without recriminations from either the parents or the teacher.

Parents can aid in keeping the student practicing and accomplishing at this crucial stage. Encouragement from interested parents usually produces a positive effect. The reverse is also true. Forcing can have an extremely adverse effect. The parents should avoid such a threatening situation as "If you don't practice the piano you can't go to baseball practice today!" Students taking lessons at this level are usually interested in music or they would have stopped before. Encouraging an interested student will add fuel to the fire, but forcing an uninterested student generally does not produce successful results.

The successful teacher will provide a variety of activities to hold the intermediate student's interest. Class participation, piano parties, contests, auditions, ensemble participation, recitals, and the like, will provide incentives. A balanced program of both classical and "pop" music will often stimulate the student and keep him moving through this period. The teacher should be understanding if practice is irregular or if the student's attitude about study and performance is not as keen as before. The adolescent may be going through a stage which is trying to him. However, the teacher can bolster his confidence by complimenting him on such things as an outstanding amount of practice during the week, or excellent accomplishment in one or more areas. The teacher must be aware of the student's mood at this point; encouragement often helps to dispel the gloom which may creep into the lesson.

The intermediate student can be guided through this period successfully if the teacher keeps his needs and goals in proper perspective. Time must be given for development, and the teacher may have to hang on for awhile before pushing ahead. This point is crucial in the student's development. He must make it through this stage to realize his ultimate potential in the higher spheres of piano playing.

INTERMEDIATE MUSIC PROGRAM

The intermediate music program is a continuation of materials begun during the early years of study. Although emphasis will focus on literature, a broad-based program must be maintained to insure continued development in all musicianship phases.

Students at this level vary widely in aptitude and interest, and it is impossible to outline a program that will serve the needs of all students.

However, the general information in this chapter is intended for students of average ability. Four areas of study will be outlined: repertoire, technique, theory, and sight-reading.

Intermediate Repertoire

The intermediate repertoire is generally divided into three levels: early intermediate (for about fourth year students), intermediate (slightly more difficult–late fourth year or fifth year), and upper intermediate (more difficult, approaching the advanced level–about fifth or sixth year). Since the intermediate area covers a wide range, it is necessary to discuss repertoire in these three divisions.

Before discussing repertoire possibilities, consideration will be given to two areas: (1) material for study versus material for performance, and (2) editions versus arrangements.

Study and performance materials are not necessarily the same. A student should be given performance material that is realistic for his ability, both musically and technically. It is not necessary for the student to perform a piece merely because he has worked on it for several months. The piece may do a great deal to develop a weakness in his playing, but he may not yet be capable of performing it convincingly. For example, a student with small hands may be given a large chord piece to help develop his stretch, but as a recital solo, it may be his undoing.

Frequently in contests one hears a sonatina movement played by a student who does not yet have the technical capabilities to perform the piece effectively: the tempo is too slow (or too fast), the runs are not even, or the character and mood of the piece is not evident in the student's performance. His teacher should have chosen a contest piece in a category below which would serve him better in performance.

As to the choice of edition, the teacher should be discriminating in choosing suitable literature. As discussed in the previous chapter, arrangements may be useful for sight-reading material; also arrangements may serve a purpose of familiarizing the student with a variety of music. However, at the intermediate level there are numerous original compositions which will develop the student's playing better than a steady diet of arranged works.

The many collections of classical literature that are available can be surveyed at a good music store. Most of the newer volumes are logically edited with simple editorial suggestions. Some of the older collections of Baroque music are apt to be heavily edited with elaborate phrasing, pedaling, dynamics, etc. The teacher can easily select good editions from the many available.

Repertoire Collections

There are numerous collections of classics available which contain graded literature at the intermediate level. A few titles chosen from among the many available include:

Agay, Denes (ed.) Classics to Moderns in the Intermediate Grades Consolidated (1962)
This 160 page volume contains representative selections from the Baroque

through the Contemporary periods. The compositions provide a range of difficulty levels within the intermediate grades.

Agay, Denes (ed.) The Joy of Baroque (1974); The Joy of Classics (1965); The Joy of Romantic Piano, 2 bks. (1976-1977) Yorktown Music Press

These books (eighty pages each) contain interesting intermediate piano works, many of which are unfamiliar. The music in *The Joy of Baroque* collection is limited to that period. The music in *The Joy of Classics* collection contains a cross-section of composers from the Baroque through the Romantic period. *The Joy of Romantic Piano* contains works mostly by infrequently taught composers (Arensky, Moscheles, Rimsky-Korsakov, Maykapar, Bizet, etc.).

Anthony, George Walter (ed.) Easy Keyboard Music, Purcell to Shostakovich Presser (1967)

The 117 piano pieces in this 164 page volume provide a sufficient sampling of music from four eras at the intermediate level. The music is nicely edited and spaced on the page. The brief notes about the composers are interesting and informative as are the illustrations and information about keyboard instruments in the back of the book. This book is also available in three smaller volumes (1969).

Bastien, James (ed.) Piano Literature, Vol. 3 For the Intermediate Grades GWM Co. (1968)

A cross-section of music from the Baroque, Classical, Romantic, and Contemporary periods is represented by composers Bach (three inventions), Kirnberger, Haydn, Clementi, Beethoven, Kuhlau (two sonatinas), Schubert, Burgmüller, Heller, Ellmenreich (*Spinning Song*), Spindler, Tchaikovsky, Grieg (*Elfin Dance, Puck, Sailor's Song*), Schumann, Rebikoff, Kabalevsky (*Sonatina, Op. 27, No. 11,* and *Toccatina*), Khachaturian, and Bartók (*Evening in the Country*). Much of the music in this seventy-two page volume is familiar to teachers and students. The level of difficulty ranges from early intermediate to upper intermediate.

Brisman, Heskel (ed.) Baroque Dynamite (1975), Classical Classics (1975) Alfred Music Co.

A fine selection of well-edited music is contained in these two volumes. The brief comments on the composers and music are interesting and informative. Major and lesser composers are represented in each book providing a broad spectrum of the period.

Castle, Joseph (ed.) Baroque Piano Styles (1974), Classical Piano Styles (1975) Mel Bay

These two volumes (forty-eight pages each) contain infrequently taught works. Approximate grade levels are given in the index. Three arrangements appear in the Classical Period book. The brief comments about the composers or music are interesting and informative. The other books in this series (Romantic Period, Impressionist Period, Twentieth Century Period) contain slightly more difficult music—upper intermediate to early advanced.

Goss, Louise (ed.) (Clark Library) Piano Literature, Books 4a, 4b; 5a, 5b Summy (1957)

All four books contain representative works from the seventeenth, eighteenth, and nineteenth centuries. Composers include Bach, Scarlatti, Handel, Haydn, Mozart, Beethoven, Schubert, Schumann, Tchaikovsky, and Grieg. Notes on the composers add interest. The level of difficulty ranges from early intermediate to upper intermediate (and beyond).

Lucktenberg, George, and David Carr Glover (eds.) Piano Repertoire Belwin-Mills (1971)

Selected works by Handel, Haydn, Chopin and Schubert comprise this thirty-two page volume. The music provides a brief sampling of intermediate materials. Stories about the composers add interest.

Waterman, Fanny, and Marion Harewood (eds.) The Young Pianist's Repertoire Faber Music Ltd. (1969)

This forty-two page volume contains representative works from composers

Purcell, Rameau, Leopold Mozart, Bach, Handel, Czerny, Beethoven, Tchaikovsky, Schumann, Shostakovich, and others. Most of the pieces are unfamiliar and make a nice diversion from standard fare.

Editions

Even at the intermediate level the music from the four historical eras (Baroque, Classical, Romantic, Contemporary) is so vast that the discussion of editions can only be dealt with in cursory manner in this book. The main problem with editions lies in music from the Baroque era, especially the music of Bach. Bach left most of his keyboard music unedited as to tempo, phrasing, and dynamics. Ornamentation too has been a problem in Baroque music. Therefore, the teacher should make an effort to use reliable editions *especially* in music from this period.

The two most frequently studied works by Bach at the intermediate level are the *Twelve Little Preludes* and the *Two-Part Inventions.* A brief discussion of each is listed for consideration.

Twelve Little Preludes: Three recent editions of this work are worthy of consideration as study volumes. The first by the Willis Music Company (1964) is edited by George Anson; he provides exacting ornamental realizations and judicious fingerings in his sparsely edited version. The second by the Alfred Music Company (1971) is edited by Willard Palmer, and is titled *18 Short Preludes* (six others are included). Palmer's edition provides an excellent discussion of ornamentation as well as an authentic representation of the music as the composer left it; editorial suggestions are in light grey print. The third by Wiener Urtext Edition/Presser (1973) is edited by Walther Dehnhard, and is titled *Little Preludes and Fughettas.* This edition is tastefully done with minimal editorial additions. Whatever edition is selected, these preludes present many technical and musical problems at the intermediate level, and they are a superb introduction to the more complex and demanding Bach works.

Two-Part Inventions: The popularity of the Inventions has led to a profusion of editions. The teacher should compare several of these to discover which one(s) would best suit the needs of students. The editions for consideration are those by publishers Alfred Music Company, Henle, Peters, Kalmus/Belwin, Kjos, Wiener Urtext Edition, and Willis. It is also interesting to consult the original version which can be easily obtained in both the Lee Pocket Scores (Belwin-Mills) and from the Dover reprint series.

Of the editions, two that stand out as being definitive in every way are the editions by Willard Palmer (Alfred Music Company, 1968), and by Joseph Banowetz (General Words and Music Co./Kjos, 1974). Included in both editions is an informative Preface which lists information about the Inventions, ornamentation, and other useful information. Editorial suggestions are printed in light grey (Palmer) and in light red (Banowetz).

The Henle edition, edited by Walther Lampe, is a fine version in clear, easy to read print. The Peters edition, edited by Landshoff has been a standard first-rate version for some time. Likewise the Kalmus edition, edited by Han Bischoff, has been used frequently in this country as a standard text. The Wiener Urtext Edition, edited by Erwin Ratz, has clear print, no phrase markings, and sometimes awkward fingering. The Willis publication, edited by George Anson, presents a definitive version with simple, direct, concise editorial suggestions—primarily realization of ornamentation and fingering.

From the Classical period the intermediate student will be most involved in sonatina literature. It is important to choose reliable editions—ones that are not over-edited. Editions published around the turn of the century frequently tend to place staccato marks at the ends of phrases. In most cases composers did not put these marks in their music. If taken literally, the student will jump off phrase endings in a broken manner rather than releasing the phrase endings smoothly. The teacher can scratch out staccato marks if such an edition is used, but it is simpler to use an edition by Henle, Peters, or Schott.

Editions of Romantic and Contemporary music present much less of a problem. Most of the composers from these periods wrote their interpretive indications for the performer to follow. Therefore, prime consideration should be given to editions of Baroque and Classical music—especially music from the Baroque period.

Sonatina Collections

Intermediate sonatinas abound with profusion. Muzio Clementi (1752-1832) and Friedrich Kuhlau (1786-1832) are two old masters who stand out as being the most significant composers of student sonatinas. Other composers include John Dussek (1761-1812), Anton Diabelli (1781-1858), Cornelius Gurlitt (1820-1901), and Heinrich Lichner (1829-1898). The sonatinas by these composers are readily available by Peters, Schirmer, Kalmus and other publishers.

Although Clementi was a prolific composer who wrote approximately sixty-four piano sonatas and other serious works, he is best remembered for his didactic works: the set of studies called *Gradus ad Parnassum*, and his many sonatinas. The sonatinas are listed as *Opus 36* (six sonatinas), *Opus 37* (three sonatinas), and *Opus 38* (three sonatinas). Because of the easy grade level (early intermediate), *Opus 36* is the most frequently studied of the group; it contains the immensely popular C major sonatina, *Opus 36, No. 1.*

The sonatinas by Kuhlau are less played than those of Clementi, but they are of comparable quality. The best known Kuhlau sonatinas are *Opus 20* (three sonatinas), *Opus 55* (six sonatinas), and *Opus 88* (two sonatinas).

In addition to individual composer sonatina volumes (all Clementi, etc.) there are numerous sonatina collections available. Sonatinas are also found in editions of collected works. Editions by Denes Agay, George Anson, Irl Allison, Jane and James Bastien, Frances Clark, David Goldberger, Leo Podolsky, Poldi Zeitlin, and others in this country contain a sampling of the better known sonatinas.

The complete array of sonatina literature may be seen in a fine sheet music department. For general reference, a few volumes of sonatina collections are given here which contain representative works.

Agay, Denes (ed.) The Joy of Sonatinas Yorktown (1972)

The nineteen works contained in this eighty page volume present a sampling of sonatinas from the Classic through Contemporary periods. The book contains two original works by Agay. It is difficult to classify this volume because of the two levels of music within the book. The first half of the book contains sonatinas at about the third year level; the second half contains intermediate level sonatinas by composers Latour, Gurlitt, Beethoven, Kuhlau, Benda, Mozart, and others.

Anson, George (ed.) The Sonata Sampler, Books 2 & 3 Willis (1960, 1962)

Each volume provides four-period literature and an explanation of sonata/sonatina form. *Book 2* contains works by Scarlatti, Haydn *(C Major)*, Kuhlau *(Op. 55, No. 1)*, Gurlitt, and Kabalevsky *(Op. 27, No. 12)*. *Book 3* contains mostly sonatas which can be played by upper level intermediate students. Included are works by Mozart *(C Major Sonata)*, Beethoven *(Op. 49, No. 2)*, Schumann, and Kabalevsky *(Op. 13, No. 1)*.

Bastien, James (ed.) Sonatina Favorites, Books 2 & 3 GWM Co. (1977)

Sonatina Favorites is a three-book series containing a representative sampling of sonatinas by various composers. An explanation of sonatina form is provided, and themes are identified in the sonatinas. *Book 2* contains sonatinas by Haslinger, Lichner *(Op. 66, No. 1)*, Beethoven *(F Major)*, Clementi *(Op. 36, No. 2)*, and Bastien *(Sonatina in Romantic Style)*. *Book 3* contains works by Clementi, Kuhlau, and Bastien *(Sonatina in Contemporary Style)*. The level of difficulty ranges from early intermediate to upper intermediate.

Frey, Martin (ed.) The New Sonatina Book, Book 1 Schott (edition 2511)

This ninety-six page volume contains an excellent cross-section of sonatinas by such composers as Tobias Haslinger, Jakob Schmitt, Johann André, Clementi, Kuhlau, Dussek, and others. The pieces are arranged in order of difficulty and range in levels from early intermediate to upper intermediate and beyond.

Köhler, Louis, and Ludwig Klee (eds.) Sonatina Album Schirmer (1893)

Sonatinas by Clementi, Kuhlau, and Dussek are presented in this 133 page volume. Some sonatas and other pieces are also found in this collection. The sonatinas edited by Ludwig Klee are over-edited and unnecessarily fussy. The level of the works in the book is intermediate until page 61. The remainder of the book (sonatas and assorted pieces) goes beyond the intermediate level in difficulty.

Köhler, Louis and Adolf Ruthardt (eds.) Sonatina Album, Vol. 1 & 2 Peters (edition 1233a and 1233b)

These two large volumes (130 pages, volume 1; 116 pages, volume 2) contain most of the standard sonatina literature by such composers as Kuhlau, Clementi, Dussek, Diabelli, and others. The music is well-spaced on the page and well-edited. The level of difficulty ranges from early intermediate to upper intermediate and beyond.

Although collections provide standard sonatina literature, there are many fine intermediate sonatinas published either in small volumes or as individual sheet music. The following list contains a representative number of these.

Agay, Denes Sonatina No. 3 Sam Fox (1962)

This three-movement work is written in a mildly contemporary style similar to Kabalevsky. The first movement, *Allegro giocoso,* is an exciting, spirited piece that gains momentum throughout. The second movement, *Andante delicato,* is a stately song piece. The last movement, *Allegro con brio*, is a spirited rondo which is the most difficult of the three movements. Upper intermediate level.

Agay, Denes Sonatina Toccata Boosey (1964)

This whimsical, dashing one-movement piece creates a perpetual motion effect by the rapid eighth notes which run throughout. Rhythmic variety is achieved by the melodic line which is composed in various phrase lengths. Teaching features include balance of melody and accompaniment, varieties of touch, and an even, steady beat throughout. Intermediate level.

Bastien, James Sonatina in Classic Style, Sonatina in Romantic Style, Sonatina in Contemporary Style GWM Co. (1977)

Each sonatina has three contrasting movements. The first movement of *Sonatina in Classic Style,* marked *Allegro moderato,* is useful for teaching phrasing, balance of melody and accompaniment, and rhythmic precision. The second movement, *Arioso,* sings a plaintive melody above a simple accompaniment. The third movement, *Rondo,* is in 6/8 meter and uses running eighth and sixteenth notes. Early intermediate level.

The first movement of *Sonatina in Romantic Style,* marked *Allegro moderato,* features a lyric melody for the A section, and a (not quite so romantic) march-like melody for the B section and closing section. The second movement, *Interlude,* sings a plaintive melody with legato accompaniment. The third movement, *Rondo,* is spirited and rhythmic in A-B-A-Coda form. Intermediate level.

The first movment of *Sonatina in Contemporary Style*, marked *Allegro con brio,* begins and ends in the E tonality. The repeated notes must be crisp, played with good facility. The second movement, *Canzonetta,* sings a Flamenco melody for the A section and has a recitative-like effect in the B section. The third movement, *Tarantella,* is the most difficult requiring clarity and evenness in the running notes and the ability to sustain the energetic pulsation throughout. Upper intermediate level.

Bentley, Bernice Benson Sonatina in D Major Witmark (1961)

Written in late eighteenth-century style, this three-movement work features nice melodic lines, expressive phrasing, and graded dynamics. Intermediate level.

Clark, Mary Elizabeth (ed.) Sonatinas from Myklas, Vols. 1 & 2; Second Piano Parts for Sonatinas, Vols. 1 & 2 Myklas (1977)

These two volumes (forty-eight pages each) contain new sonatinas by various composers. Most are written in imitative classic style, others are somewhat romantic or contemporary sounding. All have three movements. The second piano parts (separate publications) provide useful ensemble opportunities. *Volume 1* is early intermediate level; *Volume 2* is intermediate level.

Faith, Richard Three Sonatinas Schirmer (1971)

Although rather bland these one-page movement sonatinas have some nice moments. The *Sonatina No. 3* is more interesting than the others. Early intermediate level.

Gillock, William Sonatina in Classic Style Willis (1959)

Excellent melodic invention, pulsating rhythms, and a fine imitative Classic style have made this a long time study, recital, and contest favorite. The first movement, *Allegro deciso,* is effective for teaching phrasing, balance of tone, scales, and rhythmic precision. The second movement, *Andante con espressione,* features written out turns in the melody line. The last movement, *Allegro vivace*, is a spirited rondo comprising scales, terraced dynamics, and inventive melodic lines. All three movements are concise and beautifully crafted. Intermediate level.

Glover, David Carr Virginia Sonatina, No. 3 Schroeder & Gunther/Associated (1954)

This attractive three-movement sonatina has been a teaching favorite since its publication. The first movement, *Allegro*, features a singing melody line accompanied by chords. The second movement, *Moderato*, is a lyric song piece only sixteen measures long. The last movement, *Scherzo*, is written in 6/8 meter and features running scale passages. Early intermediate level.

Kabalevsky, Dmitri Sonatina Opus 13, No. 1 MCA, Kalmus, others

Kabalevsky's prolific student works are among the most useful teaching material; this sonatina is one of his best known and most frequently performed works. The first movement, *Allegro assai e lusingando*, requires articulation and clarity to present a convincing performance; it is comprised of irregular phrase lengths which must be phrased carefully as indicated. The second movement, *Andantino*, requires careful balance of melody and accompaniment. The last movement, *Presto*, is a running toccata-like piece in 9/8 meter reminiscent of a gigue. The problems of articulation and clarity are present in all movements, and facilty and control are required for a convincing performance. Upper intermediate level.

Schaum, John (ed.) American Sonatinas Schaum Publications (1963)

Composers of the six original sonatinas in this collection include Holst, Engelmann, Lynes, Porter, Armstrong, and Shackley. Each sonatina is prefaced by brief biographical comments accompanied by an artist's sketch of the composer. The form of each sonatina is indicated. The sonatinas are arranged in approximate order of difficulty. Early intermediate to intermediate levels.

Storr, Sherman Sonatine Brodt Music Co. (1964)

Nice melodic line and unusual harmonies make this three-movement work a colorful teaching piece. The first movement, *Allegro giusto,* is somewhat monothematic using sequence patterns in a rather baroque manner. The second movement, *Sarabande,* is a nice interlude between the first and last movements. The third movement, *Tarantella,* is the most difficult employing relentless eighth notes and numerous accidentals. Upper intermediate level (or beyond).

Contemporary Collections

Contemporary collections (volumes of twentieth-century music) frequently contain standard works by such composers as Bartók, Kabalevsky, Tansman, Prokofieff and Stravinsky. In addition to these, hundreds of individual volumes by contemporary composers are available at the intermediate level. The array can be seen at a fine music store; recent publications will be found in the new issue file.

Not all contemporary (living or recent) composers write in a contemporary idiom (twelve-tone style, tone-clusters, use of dissonance, etc.). Some recent composers prefer to use imitative styles rather than write "far out" music, especially if intended for educational purposes. For example, William Gillock's *Lyric Preludes* is written in the style of the Romantic period.

The following list contains a cross-section of contemporary composers. Most of the music is at least mildly contemporary sounding; some of it is written in imitative styles. The list is not intended to be extensive; it merely provides a representative sampling of some of the less frequently taught music by contemporary composers.

Agay, Denes Petit Trianon Suite Schirmer (1974)

Ten pieces on eighteenth century style dance melodies are contained in this sixteen page collection. Attractive music in imitative style which may be used in place of music by old masters. Excellent study and audition material. Early intermediate to intermediate levels.

Bacon, Ernst Maple-Sugaring Lawson-Gould/Schirmer (1964)

The ten pieces in this collection are a combination of arranged folk tunes and original compositions. Such tunes as "Lavender's Blue," and "In and Out the Window" are cleverly arranged in "folksy" fashion. Intermediate level.

Bartók, Béla For Children Boosey, Schirmer, others

This volume consists of eighty-five pieces based on Hungarian and Slavonic children's folk songs. The music is purposely written without octaves and is graded from about late second year through the early advanced level. Many of the pieces appear in collections.

Bloch, Ernest Enfantines C. Fischer (1934)

The ten pieces in this volume rank among the best children's music. The music is on the sophisticated side stressing mood, color, and imagination. Favorites are "Lullaby," "Joyous March," and "Teasing." Intermediate to upper intermediate levels.

Casella, Alfredo Children's Pieces Universal Edition/Presser (1921)

The eleven mildly contemporary pieces in this volume are well-written and attractive. Several are written in etude form suggesting that these pieces are better suited as study pieces rather than as recital repertoire. Intermediate to upper intermediate levels.

Clark, Frances, and Louis Goss (eds.) Contemporary Piano Literature, Books 3 & 4 Summy-Birchard (1957)

These two volumes contain standard contemporary music by Gretchaninoff, Kabalevsky, Bartók, Prokofieff, and Stravinsky, as well as some excellent compositions commissioned for this series by composers Tcherepnin, Scott, Moore, and Finney. *Book 3* is about early intermediate level; *Book 4* is about intermediate level.

Clark, Mary Elizabeth (ed.) Contempo 2 Myklas (1974)

This book is a sequel to *Contempo 1* (1972). The new twentieth-century idioms introduced include new modes, Japanese scale, and pandiatonic. Previously introduced idioms are not explained, but reference is made to *Contempo 1* where explanations are given. Intermediate to upper intermediate levels.

Clark, Mary Elizabeth (ed.) In the Mode Myklas (1974)

Twelve pieces comprise this volume of pieces by various new composers. The pieces are based on the seven modes which are briefly described on the last two pages of the book. Two duets are included. Intermediate to upper intermediate levels.

(collection) Summy Piano Solo Package, Nos. 401, 501 Summy-Birchard (1976)

These two volumes contain previously published solos by various composers (Bentley, Gillock, Stecher, Tansman, others) available now only in this collection. Useful teaching comments are provided by Jane Knourek. The level of difficulty is intermediate and beyond.

(collection) The Young Pianist's Anthology of Modern Music Associated (1972)

The forty-two pieces by twenty-three composers provide an excellent cross-section of contemporary music by composers from Bartók to Tansman. Although only one often used piece (Kabalevsky's *Toccatina)* is to be found in this sixty-eight page volume, the teacher and student will soon find most of these works appealing and accessible. A superb reference volume. Mostly intermediate to upper intermediate levels.

Copland, Cowell, *et al* Masters of Our Day C. Fischer (1943)

Represented in this forty-eight page volume are composers Aaron Copland, Henry Cowell, Isadore Freed, Howard Hanson, Darius Milhaud, Douglas Moore, Roger Sessions, Deems Taylor, Randall Thompson, and Virgil Thomson. The music is no longer of our day, as it was composed at least twenty years ago. Although the composers are well known, many of the compositions lack color. However, several excellent works are contained in this volume: "Jeneral Jerry's Jolly Jugglers" by Freed, "Grievin' Annie" by Moore, and "March" by Sessions. All the pieces are also published separately. The music spans a wide range of intermediate levels.

Creston, Paul Five Little Dances Op 24 Schirmer (1946)

This little suite of mildly contemporary pieces is appealing in style and mood.

The music is melodic and is attractive to both children and older beginners. Intermediate level.

Dello Joio, Norman Diversions Marks (1975)

The five beautifully written pieces in this collection are of varying styles and difficulty levels. The "Preludio" opens the suite using linear style and pedal point effects. "Arietta" is a lovely song using a singing melody over a constant pedal point bass. "Caccia" is a bright animated dance-style piece using catchy rhythms and fanfare melodies. "Choral" develops from a single line melody into two voices, and ends with four voices. "Giga" is a rollicking dance, starting with thin texture and building to a stunning finish. Mostly upper intermediate level or early advanced.

Dello Joio, Norman Lyric Pieces for the Young Marks (1971)

The distinguished American composer has created a sequel to his popular *Suite for the Young. Lyric Pieces for the Young*, however, does not have the immediate appeal and spontaneity of the earlier collections. Included in this volume are six pieces; the favorite is Number 2, "Prayer of the Matador." Upper intermediate level.

Diemer, Emma Lou Sound Pictures Boosey (1971)

Comprised of ten one-page pieces, this collection explores the realm of contemporary music using such devices as tone-clusters, parallel fourths and fifths, pedal effects, and glissando effects. These sound samplings would give students and teachers a better understanding of music of today. This collection may be given to better than average children or older beginners who are interested in learning about new compositional techniques. Early intermediate level.

Faith, Richard Four Cameos Shawnee Press (1971)

The four short pieces in this brief volume are titled "Waltz," "Toccatina," "Lullaby," and "Rondina." The music is expressive and imaginative in a mildly contemporary style. Early intermediate level.

Fennimore, Joseph Bits and Pieces Marks (1970)

These three pieces consist of varying styles: "Canon and Canon," "Bit of Blues," and "Dance of the Dinosaurs" (fourths and fifths). The music is effective, but it is more difficult for students than it looks. Early intermediate level.

Giasson, Paul A Canadian Childhood Generaly Music Publishing Co./Boston (1968)

Comprised of six pieces in suite form, this charming collection contains some delightful music. With the exception of the last piece, "Summer Storm," which is difficult, the demands are more interpretive than technical. The music is light and fresh in a semipopular style. Upper intermediate level.

Gillock, William Lyric Preludes in Romantic Style Summy-Birchard (1958)

In the same manner as *Fanfare* (written in Baroque style), these preludes serve as an introduction to the Romantic period. The mostly one-page compositions explore the twelve major and minor keys using parallel relationships. The music is colorful and imaginative and has been a teaching favorite since its publication. Intermediate to upper intermediate levels.

Gretchaninoff, Alexander (ed. by Denes Agay) Children's Album Op. 98 MCA (1967)

This delightful collection contains fifteen one-page solos. Although Gretchaninoff died in 1956, his piano music for students is written mostly in a romantic style. Accomplished musicianship prevails throughout this collection. Lovely melodies, a variety of styles and moods, and fanciful titles make this volume excellent teaching fare. Most of the individual pieces appear in other collections by a variety of publishers—for example, "In the Little Meadow" (page 7) in this collection appears in both solo form edited by William Gillock (called *The Seven Dwarfs,* Willis Music Company), and in his *Solo Repertoire* series (Volume 4, page 18). Early intermediate level.

Gretchaninoff, Alexander Five Miniatures for Piano Op. 196 Marks (1954)

These lovely children's pieces are titled "Etude," "Mazurka," "Little Rhapsody," "Insistence," and "Ballad." Several may be played as a group on a recital program. Intermediate level.

Gretchaninoff, Alexander The Grandfather's Book Op. 119 Kalmus

Seventeen well-written children's pieces comprise this collection. All are short, one-page or less in length. A variety of keys, meters, and moods are contained in this expressive music. Intermediate level.

Joachim, Otto 12 Twelve Tone Pieces for Children BMI Canada (1961)

Often composers of twelve-tone music try to create something strictly didactic, frequently with very little appeal to children. Fortunately this is not the case with these compositions. The mostly one-page pieces are based on such descriptive titles as "Plastic Soldier," "King Neptune," "Snowy Morning," etc. The notation naturally contains numerous accidentals, but it is not too complex for children. This volume is especially useful for teaching the older beginner. Intermediate level.

Kabalevsky, Dmitri Four Rondos Op. 60 MCA (1960)

This is a superb collection of four contrasting pieces that have been favorites since their publication. Each depicts a different mood and presents various pianistic problems. No. 1, "Rondo-March," is written in 6ths and 3rds in the right hand and uses dotted rhythms; it is the most difficult of the four. No. 2, "Rondo-Song," is a gracious *Allegretto* requiring a light, elegant touch. No. 3, "Rondo-Song," requires a singing tone and much expressions. No. 4, "Rondo-Toccata," is the show piece of the group employing various forms of staccato; it is a driving, virile, exciting solo. This collection is an absolute teaching must. Intermediate to upper intermediate levels.

Khachaturian, Aram Adventures of Ivan Leeds/MCA (1948)

These imaginative eight pieces evoke a fantasy land atmosphere. The story evolves around Ivan who sings (No. 1), can't go out today (No. 2), gets ill (No. 3), goes to a party (No. 4), is very busy (No. 5, etude-like), is with Natasha (No. 6), rides a hobbyhorse (No. 7), and hears an exotic tale of strange lands (No. 8). The music is melodic, attractive, and of superior quality. Intermediate to upper intermediate levels.

Laburda, Jiri 10 Short Dances and Airs for Piano Presser (1976)

Written in imitative eighteenth-century style, these one-page pieces consist of an aria, berceuse, romance and these dances: march, waltz (two), gavotte, minuet, polka, and galop. These mostly two-voice pieces provide a nice change from frequently taught Bach, Handel *(et al)* literature. Late third year to early intermediate levels.

Last, Joan Down to the Sea Oxford (1957)

Five imaginative seascapes comprise this little volume. The suggestive titles are "Circling Gulls," "Song of a Sea Shell," "Island Church," "Boats at Anchor," and "Sea Spray." The pieces make effective teaching material for touch, tone color, and uncomplicated uses of the pedal. Early intermediate to intermediate levels.

Muczynski, Robert Diversions Op. 23 Schirmer (1970)

This eleven page collection of nine solos is easier than the *Six Preludes* (Op. 6), but they are also written in the same superlative style. Favorites are Numbers 5 and 9 which have wonderful syncopated, jazzy beats. The entire collection is excellent teaching material. Intermediate level.

Nakada, Yoshineo Japanese Festival MCA (1956)

From Japan comes this excellent collection of seventeen varied pieces. Both European and Japanese styles are employed in these engaging pieces. The level of difficulty progresses from about late second year to early intermediate. The sure-fire hit is "Etude Allegro" requiring forearm rotation technic. For students with good technic this makes a stunning recital solo.

Noona, Walter and Carol The Contemporary Performer, Level 4 Heritage (1975)

This series (four books) is designed to introduce youngsters to idioms of twentieth-century style such as modes, polyrhythms, clusters, polytonalities, twelve-tone rows, and ostinato patterns. The information about the compositional devices is concise and informative.

Palmer, Willard Baroque Folk Alfred Music Co. (1969)

The music in this inventive collection is for fun. Fifteen familiar melodies are arranged in Baroque style. A brief explanation of each form (invention, allemande, courante, etc.) is given at the beginning of each piece. The music is both instructive and pleasant. Intermediate to upper intermediate levels.

Poulenc, Francis Villageoises Salabert (1933)

In this delightful collection of six children's pieces even the titles are charming:

I *Valse Trolienne* (reminiscent of Schubert's *Ländler*)
II *Staccato* (a haunting, fast, jaunty melody)
III *Rustique* (a beautiful tune, fast and gay)
IV *Polka* (full of staccatos and accents)
V *Petite Rondo* (a spirited, rhythmic three-measure melody repeated four times)
VI *Coda* (a reprise incorporating melodies from the other movements)

For those who have not used this collection before, they are a joy. Intermediate level.

Ramsier, Paul Pied Piper Boosey (1964)

Fantasy land is portrayed in several of the seven imaginative pieces in this volume: "Road to Hamelin," "A Magic Spell," and "Silver Forest." The music is charming, melodic, and attractive. Early intermediate level.

Sauter, Maya Piano Music for One Hand Alone Pelikan Edition 794 (1971)

For the student who is out of commission with one hand (sprained finger, broken arm, etc.), this twenty-six page volume is a god-send. It is also useful for general reading using one clef. Intermediate level.

Serocki, Kazimierz The Gnomes Polskie Wydawnictwo Muzyczne/Marks (1954)

From Poland comes this attractive little collection of seven children's pieces. The music is inventive and melodic and makes suitable reading, study, and performance material. Early intermediate level.

Sheftel, Paul Interludes C. Fischer (1974)

Eighteen pieces in various moods and styles comprise this collection. The music is based on repetitive keyboard patterns such as chords and arpeggios, and is generally full sounding, some requiring large reaches, implying use with older students. Early intermediate to upper intermediate levels.

Starer, Robert Sketches in Color, Set 1 MCA/Belwin (1964)

A big favorite since its publication, these seven contemporary style prints are extraordinarily well written. All are purposely didactic and feature contemporary writing devices linked with their titles: "Purple" polytonality; "Shades of Blue" diatonic melody against a moving bass in parallel fifths; "Black and White" juxtaposes the pentatonic scale of the black keys to the diatonic scale of the white keys; "Bright Orange" employs parallel harmony and jazz syncopation; "Grey" uses a twelve-tone row; "Pink" is tonal but moves away from the tonal center until the last six bars; "Crimson" uses Bartókish divisions of 7/8 meter (1,2,3,4, - 1,2,3). Although contemporary, these pieces are by no means esoteric, and average or better students find them most appealing. Early intermediate to intermediate levels. *Set 2* (1973) is more difficult and is not as appealing.

Stevens, Everett Six Modal Miniatures O. Ditson/Presser (1957)

With the current interest in modes used in rock music, this volume should be of special interest. The modes are explained in the foreword and used in each of the six original pieces. The music is tastefully written and immediately appealing. This is a superior collection of well-written music. Early intermediate to intermediate levels.

Stoker, Richard A Poet's Notebook Leeds Music Ltd. (1969)

The six short pieces in this collection are a nice introduction to mildly contemporary music. There is just enough dissonance, meter change, etc., to make this simple music interesting. Intermediate level.

Taylor, Colin Whimsies Boosey (1961)

The four well-written pieces in this collection offer a variety of styles, moods, and technical problems. No. 1 (*Con brio*) is a spritely dance in 3/4 meter; No. 2 (*Allegretto*) is a quick firefly-type piece and is the most difficult in the collection; No. 3 (*Andante con moto*) is a study in repeated notes; No. 4 (*Andante tranquillo*) is an expressive song piece. Intermediate level.

Turina, Joaquin Miniaturas Schott (1930)

Eight descriptive pieces comprise this collection. The music has a Spanish flavor with impressionistic effect. Upper intermediate level.

Waxman, Donald A Christmas Pageant Galaxy (1975)

This forty-eight page volume contains arrangements of carols in various styles. A few are for piano solo, most are duet arrangements, and some are accompaniments only with treble parts (for recorder, flute, etc.). In addition to standard carols, the last part of the book offers arrangements of music for the Christmas festivities by Bach, Corelli, Handel, and others. A tasteful collection of well-arranged music for the Christmas season at about the early intermediate level.

Wilson, Samuel Leaves From My Notebook Willis (1965)

Published posthumously, this brief volume of nine solos is a fond remembrance to a talented composer. Expressive, poignant melodies abound in a quasi-romantic style. Touches of pedal highlight special harmonies. Imaginative music for a musical child. Early intermediate level.

Zeitlin, Poldi, and David Goldberger (eds.) Russian Music, Book 3 MCA (1967)

The best known piece in the book is Kabalevsky's *Sonatina* in A minor. The other compositions are less known and are by a cross-section of Russian composers. Four duets are included. Early intermediate to intermediate levels.

Jazz Collections

Students of today usually enjoy a balanced diet of classical and pop music. Intermediate students especially need a boost to keep them practicing and coming to lessons, and pop music often works wonders.

By suggesting pop music, the author is not advocating "social piano lessons" in which the student comes to the lesson with little or no practice and "sight-reads" a few pop pieces. This would be advocating a watered down program to which few (if any) should subscribe. However, the intermediate student especially needs added incentives, and a few pop selections added to his regular program of study may give him the spark he needs at the moment.

The student's sense of rhythm frequently is improved by studying pop music. The music contains syncopations and other intricate rhythms. Once these rhythms have been learned, the student often carries over this knowledge to his other music.

Not all students want to study pop music; a few will elect to stick with classical music and forego the popular idiom. That is the student's prerogative, and the teacher should respect the student's preference. However, most average students will either request some pop music or be pleased that some is assigned.

The popular field is so immense that it would be impossible to provide a list which contains even a fraction of the material available. Therefore, the few following suggestions are merely samplings of some suitable jazz (pop, rock, blues, country-western, ragtime, etc.) selections for the intermediate pianist which may be used as a general guide.

Agay, Denes The Joy of Jazz Yorktown (1964)

The arranged works of such well-known jazz buffs as "Fats" Waller, Dizzy Gillespie, Thelonious Monk, plus a good selection of original music by Gerald Martin, Dave Martin, and Denes Agay make this an attractive collection for the intermediate pianist. Chord symbols are given for every piece thus providing an impetus for using the music in a combo. Intermediate to upper intermediate levels.

Bastien, James Country, Western 'n Folk, Book 2 GWM Co. (1974)

This sixteen page volume contains original country western pieces and country folk-tune arrangements. The snappy arrangement of "Turkey in the Straw" makes a good recital number. Early intermediate to intermediate levels.

Bastien, Jane Smisor Pop, Rock 'n Blues, Book 3 GWM Co. (1971)

The music in this volume is designed to introduce the student to the styles and sounds of today's music. Dotted rhythms and syncopations are found in most of the pieces. Early intermediate level.

Brimhall, John Exercises in Rhythm Hansen (1968)

By now most piano teachers, and especially their students, have discovered Brimhall's numerous arrangements of current pop hits. However, this forty-eight page collection strikes a different chord, and focuses in on how to play such current, rather recent, and distant rhythm styles as Bossa Nova, Blues, Boogie, Samba, Rock, Fox-Trot, Twist, Waltz, Beguine, and others. Excellent clear descriptions of each rhythm style and an exercise reinforcing the description are presented before playing an original piece utilizing the particular rhythm. A record accompanies the volume which has a combo playing each rhythm style for "you-do-it" participation. Intermediate level.

Brimhall, John Piano Blues Hansen (1975)

After a brief description of the stock twelve-bar blues, various blues styles are presented with a piece for each style. The level of difficulty ranges from early intermediate (or easier) to upper intermediate.

Brubeck, Dave Jazz Impressions of New York Groton/Marks (1964)

Twelve original compositions comprise this fine collection. All but the first have chord symbols. One has lyrics by Garson Kanin. Upper intermediate level.

Brubeck, Dave Themes from Eurasia Shawnee (1970)

The seven attractive pieces in this collection were used in a recording by the Dave Brubeck Quartet. The pieces are immediately appealing and display a wealth of melodic and harmonic ideas. Chord symbols are provided and are useful if students want to form a small combo (guitar, bass, and drums). Upper intermediate level.

Burns, Betty, and Jackie Graham You Do It, Book 3 GWM Co. (1972)

Intended as music for improvisation, this volume provides lead-sheet type melodies with chord symbols. Explanations about intervals and chords are included. A variety of styles is represented. Intermediate level.

Clarke, Lucia Jazz and all That! Set 1 Myklas (1976)

Twelve solos and one duet comprise this collection of original mostly blues and jazz pieces. Intermediate to upper intermediate levels.

Gillock, William New Orleans Jazz Styles Willis (1965)

A long-time resident of New Orleans, Gillock writes with authority in a variety of blues and jazz styles that can still be heard on Bourbon Street (and others) in the French Quarter. The five well-written style prints in this volume are immediately appealing to teen-agers. The rhythms are tricky and require a student with a feel for this style of music. Intermediate to upper intermediate levels.

Gillock, William More New Orleans Jazz Styles Willis (1966)

The popularity of the first book provided the incentive to write this sequel. Five selections are offered which are slightly more difficult than the first volume. Upper intermediate level.

Gordon, Louis Introduction to the Art of Rock Belwin-Mills (1971)

These ten pieces contain the essence of the rock feeling in rhythm, harmony, and melody. Syncopation is the featured element in nearly every piece. Intermediate to upper intermediate levels.

Gordon, Louis Jazz for Junior Marks (1964)

Excellent jazz styles are featured in this little volume. Special favorites are "Deep Roots," "Blues in C Minor," and "Quiet Scene." The others in the collection are more difficult. Intermediate to upper intermediate levels.

Gordon, Louis Junior Jazz Marks (1961)

This book was written before *Jazz for Junior*, and the music is slightly easier. Early intermediate to intermediate levels.

Hayward, Lou Three Short Piano Pieces Presser (1973)

The title of each piece indicates the popular idiom: "A Bossa Nova," "A Blues," and "A Jazz Waltz." The music is well written and may be used to introduce the student to a variety of rhythms such as syncopated, off-beat, etc.

Hinson, Maurice, and David Carr Glover An Adventure in Ragtime Belwin-Mills (1975)

With the exception of the first piece by Glover, all others are by Scott Joplin. The last piece is an arrangement of Joplin's *The Cascades* in duet form. The music is bright sounding and well arranged for the intermediate student. The text surveys the ragtime scene and adds interest to this thirty-two page collection of six Joplin rags.

Kasschau, Howard 25 Ventures in Rock, Western and Blues G. Schirmer (1976)

Dotted rhythms and syncopations are the featured rhythms in these pop pieces in various styles. Mostly early intermediate level.

Konowitz, Bert The Complete Rock Piano Method Alfred (1972)

For rock devotees this ninety-six page volume is a must. "Dig on" to rock techniques (accents, rhythm patterns, blue scales and modes, etc.), improvisation "licks," and direct application in an abundance of Konowitz solos. Some duets are provided.

Konowitz, Bert Jazz for Piano, Books 1 & 2 Lee Roberts/Schirmer (1962)

These two instructive books are first-rate collections in the jazz idiom. Basic jazz rhythm patterns, "blue notes," chord patterns, seventh chords, and much more, are combined into an educational sequence leading to improvisation. The music sounds a bit didactic and slightly passé in the current rock-pop scene, but the music provides an educational experience in jazz styles. Intermediate to upper intermediate levels.

Kraehenbuehl, David (Clark Library) Jazz & Blues, Books 4,5,6 Summy-Birchard (1963)

Although the music sounds a bit dated (boogie) and does not contain the pop-rock styles of today, these books offer an excellent selection of well-written original music which will appeal to the teen-ager. Early intermediate to upper intermediate levels. (*Book 4* is now incorporated in *Supplementary Solos.*)

Metis, Frank Rock Modes & Moods Marks (1970)

Metis has evidenced an affinity for the pop scene in this first-rate collection of seven solos. The introductory pages explain modality used in rock music and also explain such divergent styles as Hard Rock, Acid Rock, Psychedelic Rock, Folk Rock, and Soul Music. Most of the pieces in the collection are on the difficult side (about upper intermediate), but both "Blues Explosion" and "Happy to be Home" are easier.

Noona, Walter, and David Carr Glover An Adventure in Jazz, Books 1,2,3,4 Belwin-Mills (1972)

These four thirty-two-page volumes contain an historical survey of jazz through music in various style periods. Informative texts are included which give background information. A quiz pertaining to the text is given at the back of the books. Suggestions for use of rhythm instruments are given. A duet is found at the conclusion of each book. Early intermediate to upper intermediate levels.

Olson/Bianchi/Blickenstaff Something Light, Levels 3,4,5 C. Fischer (1975)

This series contains a potpourri of styles such as blues, boogie, western, rock, arrangements of familiar tunes, and includes some pieces by other composers. Early intermediate to intermediate levels.

Smith, Hale Faces of Jazz Marks (1968)

Syncopations, swingy rhythms, altered chords, chromatic harmony, and a nice contemporary jazz flavor mark these twelve first-rate style pieces. Titles such as "Pooty's Blues," "Off-Beat Shorty," and "Blooz," are descriptive captions that are sure to make a hit with the young teen set. Although labled "for the intermediate pianist," they are a bit on the tough side, but just right for a student with an unusually good sense of rhythm and a feel for jazz. Intermediate to upper intermediate levels.

Intermediate Technique

The intermediate student will be playing music which requires an adequate technique to perform convincingly. Intermediate literature contains such problems as scale passages in sonatinas; trills in the Bach *Inventions*; and arpeggios, quick-changing chords, and double notes in assorted pieces. The student must be prepared to meet these challenges.

Even though the intermediate student may be just taking lessons for fun, not as an intended profession, he will profit from some technical emphasis. The teacher may create exercises for special problems which can be practiced in a minimum amount of time; or the teacher may select a technique book like Joan Last's *Freedom Technique* (Oxford, 1971) which provides short patterns that can be practiced a few minutes at a time. The exclusive study of literature will not be sufficient to develop the student's playing; a balanced study program must be maintained to meet his needs.

The talented student especially needs an expanded technique. He may be considering music as a profession, and he should become proficient by the time he enters college. As a general rule, talented students should spend a minimum of a quarter of the practice period on technique. Thus, if a student practices two hours a day, he would spend thirty minutes on technique.

The intermediate student usually spends several years at this level before progressing to the advanced stage. Therefore, the technique suggestions in this chapter do not apply to any specific year, but are intended as general guides during this time.

Only a few *new* technical concepts will be introduced to the intermediate student. Scale patterns, chords, double notes, etc., will have been encountered before. The new areas will probably be trills and arpeggios. Old concepts will be reconsidered in an expanded view, while concurrently the student will be introduced to new techniques. The following six areas are presented as a general guide for intermediate technical consideration.

1. Scales
2. Arpeggios
3. Chords
4. Double notes
5. Trills
6. Technique studies

Scales

Scale study is subjective. The time at which scales are presented is governed by teacher preference. During the early years, some teachers prefer to introduce tetrachord scales divided between the hands; others prefer to teach two octave scales from the beginning. In any case, most teachers present some scale work during the early years, so the subject of scales will not be new to the intermediate pianist.

The four measure excerpt from Kuhlau's *Sonatina, Op. 55, No. 1,* (Ex. 9:1) is typical of intermediate scale passages.

Ex. 9:1. Kuhlau: *Sonatina, Opus 55, No. 1*

Measures 31 - 34

These runs must be played evenly and smoothly with a good rhythmic pulse, while at the same time shading the dynamics accordingly. To prepare for this type of figure, the student should practice scales independent of literature.

Numerous scale patterns may be devised by the teacher for the student to practice. Scales may be practiced in one, two, three, or four octave spans; parallel and contrary motion may be used; and various rhythm patterns may be incorporated. The following exercises provide representative patterns for practice.

Ex. 9:2a. Two octave scale pattern: parallel motion.

Ex. 9:2b. Three octave scale pattern: parallel motion.

Ex. 9:2c. Four octave scale pattern: parallel and contrary motion.

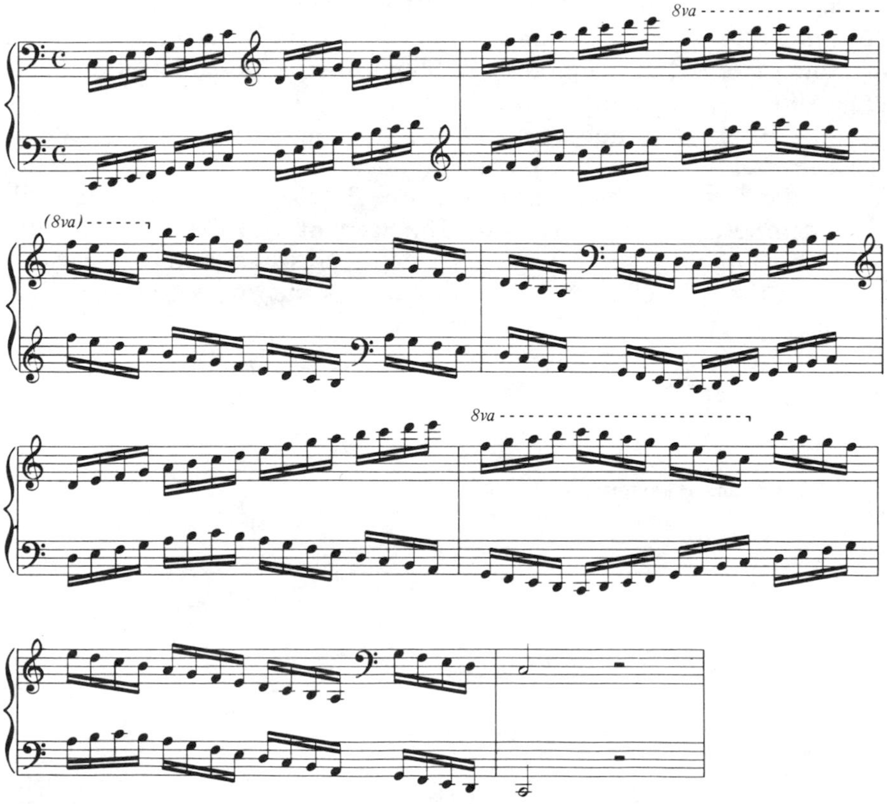

Ex. 9:2d. Contrary motion scale pattern: two against one rhythm.

Ex. 9:2e. Contrary motion scale pattern: two against one rhythm.

The two octave pattern (Ex. 9:2a) is a basic one which probably will have been learned within the first few years of lessons for some scales. The intermediate student should be able to play all scales (major and minor) two octaves, parallel motion. The three octave pattern (Ex. 9:2b) provides an opportunity to play scales in triplets. The four octave pattern (Ex. 9:2c) incorporates the symmetry of contrary motion while developing a feeling for a large keyboard span. This pattern is an excellent one and should be learned by serious students for all scales. The two against one patterns (Examples 9:2d and 9:2e) provide rhythmic variety which aid in developing coordination. These five patterns are only samplings of scale possibilities; the creative teacher should devise others.

Scales should not be practiced unimaginatively. The teacher can suggest several ways of varying scale practice which will aid the student. For example, facility in running passages will be developed by practicing scales at various tempos, from slow to fast. The student will develop a feeling for graded dynamics by practicing scales with crescendos and decrescendos. Likewise, various touches and rhythm patterns incorporated into scale practice will be helpful.

For touch, scales may be practiced all legato; all staccato; one hand legato, the other staccato (Ex. 9:3); or all legato, one hand louder than the

Ex. 9:3. Staccato and legato touch combined.

other for balance of tone (Ex. 9:4). Rhythmic effects may be produced by

Ex. 9:4. Balance of tone.

displacement of the beat through the use of accents (Ex. 9:5); dotted

Ex. 9:5. Off-beat accents.

rhythms may be used (Ex. 9:6); or alternating fingers may be used (Ex. 9:7).

Ex. 9:6. Dotted rhythms.

Ex. 9:7. Alternating fingers.

These suggestions, and others offered by the teacher, will make scales more interesting and help relieve the monotony of scale practice.

Arpeggios

The intermediate pianist should practice arpeggios in preparation for literature containing these figures. A good example of this figure is found in Beethoven's *Für Elise* (Ex. 9:8). Students often have difficulty in this passage playing the arpeggio smoothly. A break in the legato tone often is heard in student performances between fingers 3-1 in the right hand. This is the inherent problem in playing arpeggios; the thumb must turn under smoothly to create the legato effect. Students who are only seven, eight, or nine years old probably will not be able to play arpeggios in this manner, because their fingers are too short and their hands are too small. However, the intermediate student has a bigger reach, and he can now begin to practice arpeggios seriously.

Ex. 9:8. Beethoven: *Für Elise*

Measures 77-79

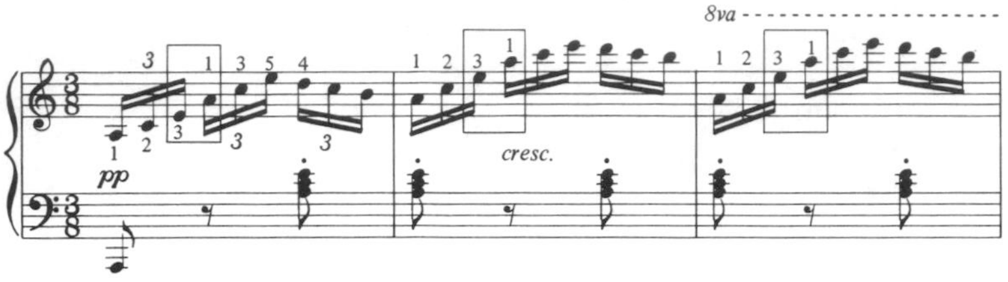

In Chapter 8 some preparatory arpeggio exercises were suggested (Ex. 8:14). It is helpful for younger students (third year students) to practice these preparatory drills before assigning the full arpeggio. Additional preparatory drills are given here for further practice (Ex. 9:9).

Ex. 9:9. Preparatory arpeggio exercises.

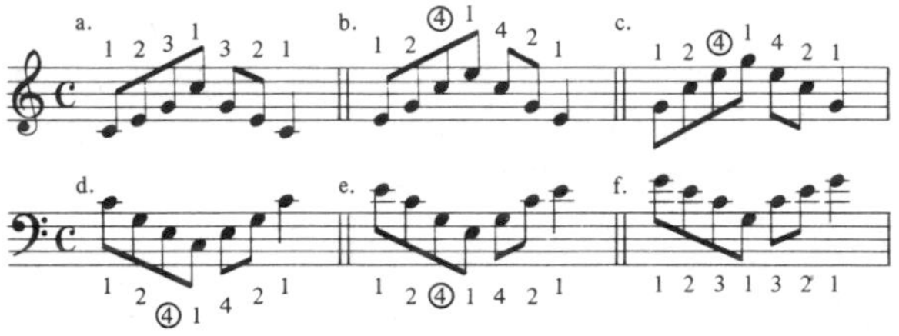

The intermediate pianist should learn all arpeggios at least two octaves in root position and the other inversions (Ex. 9:10).Both major and

Ex. 9:10. Two octave arpeggios.

minor arpeggios should be studied. The fourth finger is circled because students frequently play 3 instead of 4. For a complete presentation of patterns and fingerings, see Walter Macfarren's *Scale and Arpeggio Manual* (Schirmer).

The four octave arpeggio (Ex. 9:11) may be learned by serious students. The rhythm is optional; the pattern may be played either as triplets

Ex. 9:11. Four octave arpeggio.

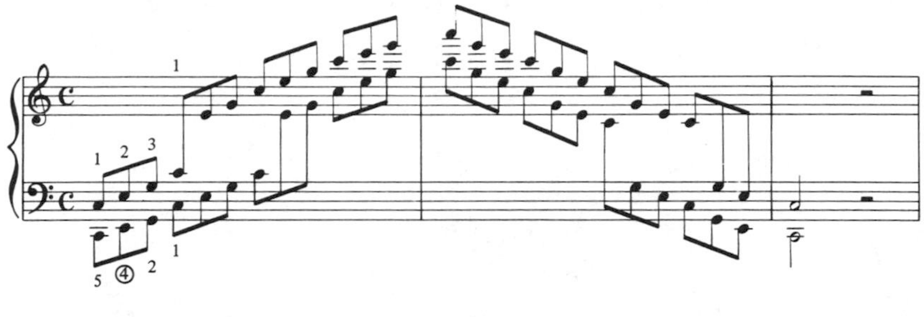

or as four eighth notes. In addition to the root position given here, inversions may also be learned. Also, contrary motion can be incorporated by using the pattern shown in Ex. 9:2c: four octaves up, back down, two octaves up, contrary motion apart, contrary motion together, then back down and end.

Chords

Generally, chord playing is not considered as important a technique as scales and arpeggios. However, chord facility will become increasingly demanding for the intermediate pianist. Intermediate literature such as Kabalevsky's *Toccatina,* Heller's *Avalanche,* Schumann's *Norse Song*, and Grieg's *Sailor's Song* all contain quick-changing chords. The student would benefit from practicing quick-changing chords as preparation for this and other intermediate literature.

Kabalevsky's *Toccatina* is a frequently taught early intermediate piece (Ex. 9:12). It is an excellent study in rapidly changing first inversion triads. Grieg's *Sailor's Song* is an upper intermediate student favorite which

Ex. 9:12. Kabalevsky: *Toccatina, Opus 27, No. 7*

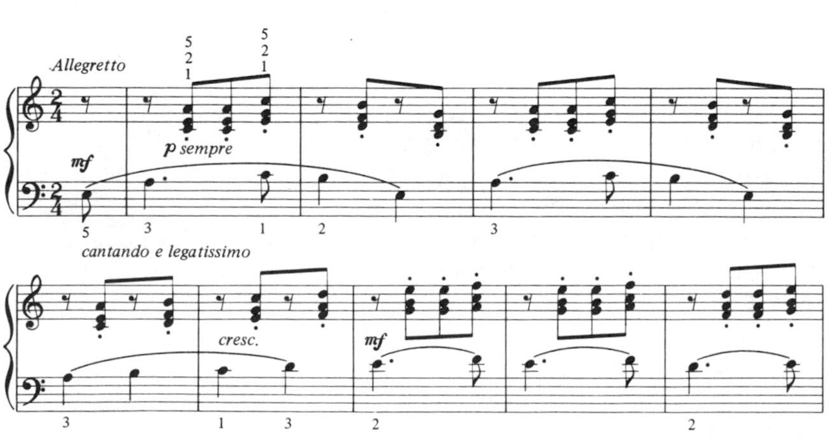

contains some awkward chord changes and large reaches (Ex. 9:13). The Kabalevsky and Grieg pieces are representative examples of intermediate

Ex. 9:13. Grieg: *Sailor's Song, Opus 68, No. 1*

chord pieces which may be used for models to design chord studies.

The student probably has been introduced to triads and inversions prior to the intermediate grades. However, it is now important to be fluent with all positions, both major and minor (as noted in the complete Kabalevsky and Grieg pieces). It is helpful to learn each inversion as an individual unit, isolated from the pattern of root position, first inversion, second inversion. Have the student learn the first inversion triads in a series (Ex. 9:14); once these are learned, exercises can be related to this pattern. The

Ex. 9:14. Major first inversion triads.

inversions should be practiced with both hands, first each hand alone, then together. The inversions should be memorized, so that the student can devote his full attention to using these chords in exercises; he should not have to stop to figure out each chord.

The following patterns (Ex. 9:15) provide varied rhythmic experiences using the inversions. The student's hand(s) should move rapidly from one octave to the next, and be in position over the keys ready to play without losing time. These studies are helpful to build the student's fluency with rapidly changing chords.

Once the major first inversion triads have been learned, have the student learn the minor inversions (Ex. 9:16). The same exercises (Ex. 9:15)

Ex. 9:15. First inversion triad patterns.

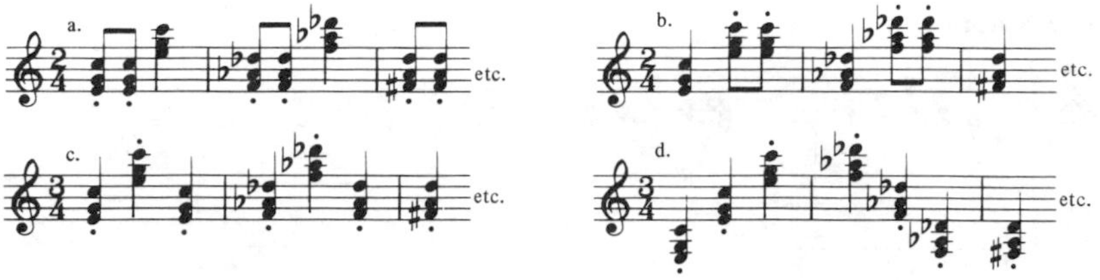

Ex. 9:16. Minor first inversion triads.

may be played in minor.

Second inversion triads should also be learned, both major and minor (Ex. 9:17). The same exercises (Ex. 9:15) may be applied to second

Ex. 9:17. Second inversion triads.

inversion triads.

When the triads and inversions were first introduced (probably late second year or sometime during the third year) it was not necessary to play them fast, but merely to learn the correct fingering and become familiar with the pattern. Now, however, an expanded concept may be applied to these chords to increase the student's facility (Ex. 9:18). The student should practice this pattern in all keys, both major and minor. At first have the student practice the pattern slowly; increase the tempo on each repetition.

Various rhythms may be incorporated in triad and inversion practice (Ex. 9:19). The ones given here require quick reflexes to get from one chord to another. The student must anticipate each new position so there will be no delay in finding the quickly changing chords. Minor chords should also be practiced in this manner. Additional rhythm patterns may be suggested by the teacher.

Ex. 9:18. Triad and inversion pattern.

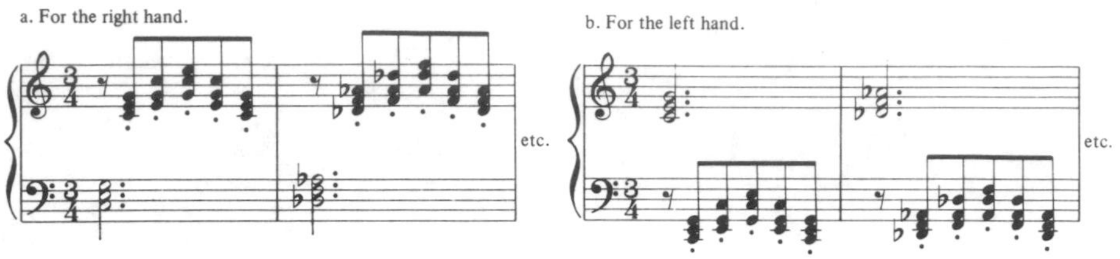

Ex. 9:19. Triad and inversion rhythm patterns.

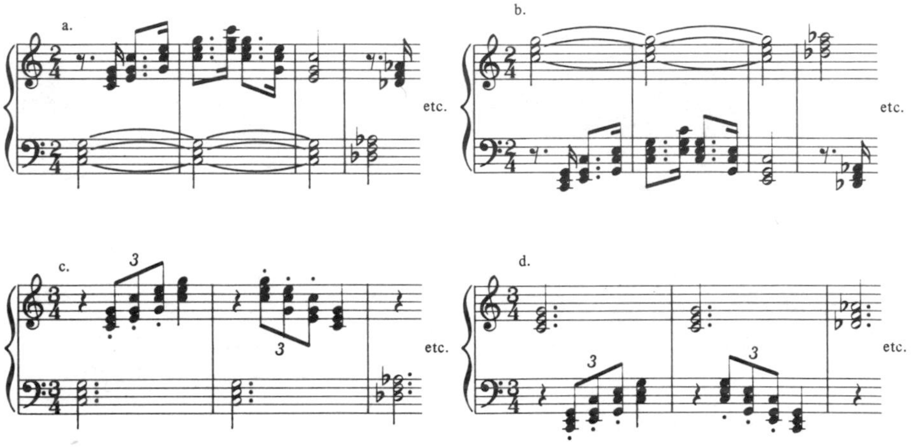

Diminished seventh chords will become more frequently used in intermediate literature. Therefore, it is helpful for the student to practice all twelve chords (Ex. 9:20). These chords should be *memorized*. Have the

Ex. 9:20. Diminished seventh chords.

student practice these chords first with one hand, then the other, and then both hands together. Point out that diminished chords are spelled by alphabet skips which form a series of minor thirds—thus the use of double flats in some of the spellings. Once the diminished sevenths have been learned, have the student use them in patterns similar to those suggested for first inversion triads (Ex. 9:21).

Ex. 9:21. Diminished seventh chord patterns.

Once the root position diminished sevenths have been thoroughly learned, have the student practice the inversions of these chords (Ex. 9:22).

Ex. 9:22. Diminished seventh chord inversions.

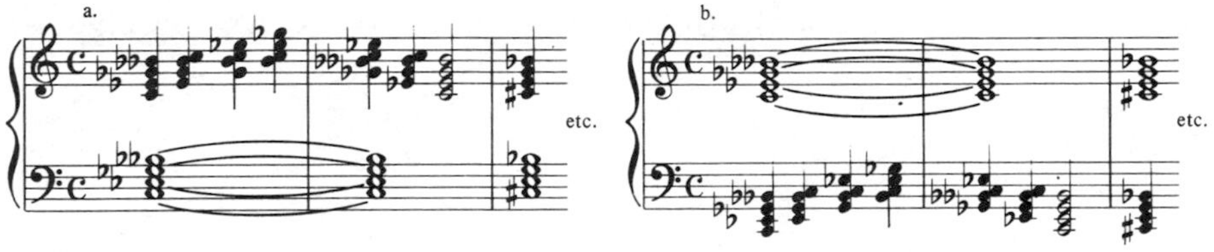

Rhythm patterns may be added to the inversions of diminished seventh chords similar to those suggested for triads and inversions (Ex. 9:19).

The following series of dominant seventh chords (Ex. 9:23) should be learned from memory in all positions. The fingering for these chords

Ex. 9:23. Dominant seventh chords in all positions.

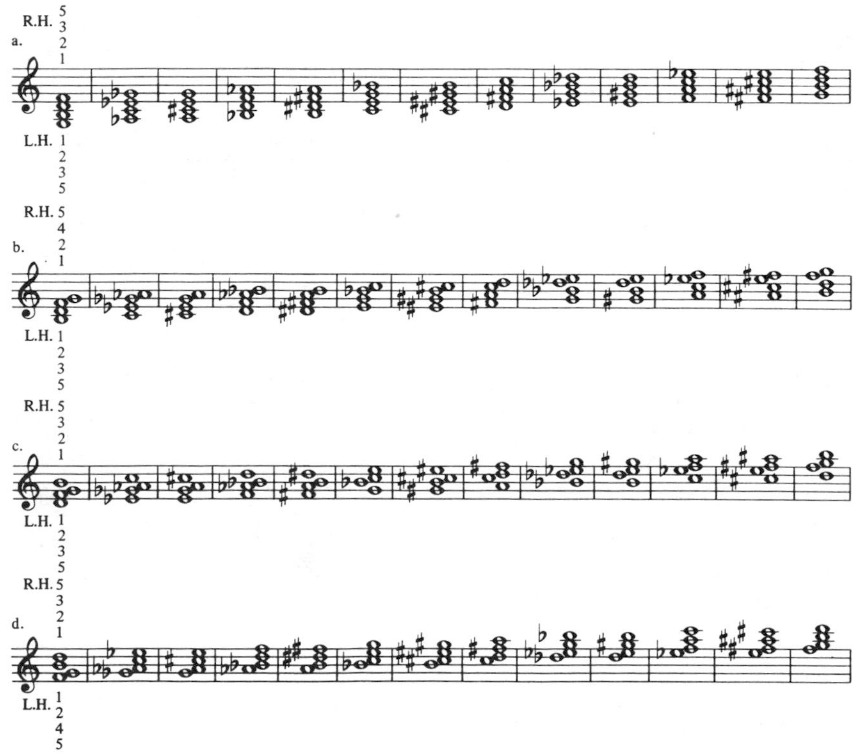

depends to some extent on the span of the hand. The right hand should play 1-2-4-5 in the second position (the left hand may also play this fingering); the left hand should play 5-4-2-1 in the fourth position (the right hand may also play this fingering). Chord drills may be devised similar to those already described (Ex. 9:15). In addition the student should practice the dominant sevenths and their inversions as shown in Example 9:22.

Extensive drill on chords during the intermediate years will provide the student with a solid background. Not only will he be able to play the standard chords, but he will also be able to analyze his music with the knowledge gained from practicing basic chords such as inversions of triads, diminished sevenths and their inversions, and dominant sevenths and their inversions.

Double Notes

Intermediate music such as Beethoven's *Minuet in G* (Ex. 9:24) contains some difficult double thirds and double sixths. Any teacher who

Ex. 9:24. Beethoven: *Minuet in G*

has taught this piece knows how students usually struggle over these double note passages. If no previous experience has been given, it is understandable that these passages will be difficult. Therefore, as preparation for this piece (and others like it), it is helpful to give some double note work.

Double thirds probably will have been introduced during the first few years of lessons. However, the student now needs expanded drills for practice. The following exercises are offered for consideration (Ex. 9:25).

Ex. 9:25. Double third exercises.

Have the student practice these exercises hands separately, then together. On each repetition increase the tempo from slow to fast. Play with a good firm tone.

Double sixths usually fall into the category of advanced technique. However, some drill can be given to the intermediate student. The first exercise presented (Ex. 9:26a) is based on the sixths in the Beethoven

Ex. 9:26. Double sixth exercises.

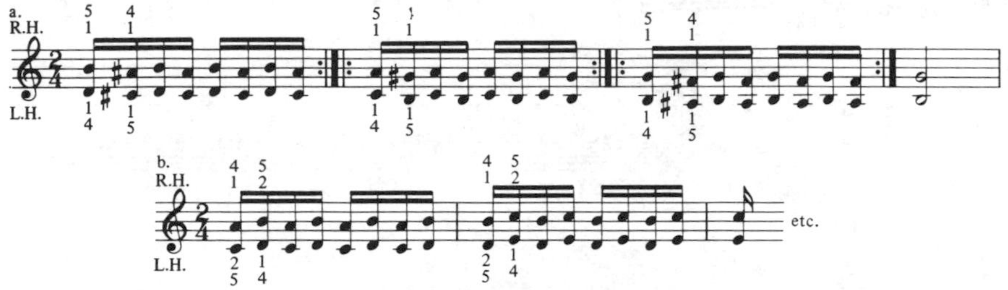

Minuet in G. Even students with small hands will be able to play this because the thumb slides up and down in half steps. The next exercise (Ex. 9:26b) should only be given to students who have big reaches as there is a large stretch between fingers 2-5. These two studies provide a basic introduction to the problem of playing double sixths. The teacher may assign others as necessary.

Trills

Trills are an essential part of piano playing, but often no preparation is given to the student for this technique. He is expected to be able to produce them when needed—for example in Bach's *Two-Part Invention No. 4* (Ex. 9:27). The technique for playing trills can be developed, and trill exercises should be practiced apart from literature in the same manner as scales and arpeggios.

A trill may be just a few notes or many notes extending over several measures (as in the Invention No. 4). One of the commonly used short trills is found in the Bach works (Ex. 9:28). This trill is always started on the

Ex. 9:27. Bach: *Two-Part Invention number 4*

upper note and therefore has at least four notes in its realization. (This sign

Ex. 9:28. Bach trill sign.

is used interchangeably to indicate a long or short trill; the number of repercussions in the trill is determined by the tempo and the note value.) This symbol is used in the first two measures of the *Two-Part Invention Number 1* (Ex. 9:29). The following exercise (Ex. 9:30) serves as a prepara-

Ex. 9:29. Bach: *Two-Part Invention Number 1*

tory drill for Bach's trill symbol. The choice of fingering is determined by

Ex. 9:30. Preparatory trill.

the position of the notes before and after the trill, the tempo, and the particular preference of the student. Pairs of fingers such as 3-2, 2-1, or 3-1 are usually used in trills. Although the student should practice trills with these finger combinations, he will probably use the one that suits him best in performance.

The trill with a *termination* (suffix) is commonly used by many composers. Bach either wrote out this figure or used a sign added to the trill symbol (Ex. 9:31). The termination consists of two notes added to the trill;

Ex. 9:31. Trill with termination.

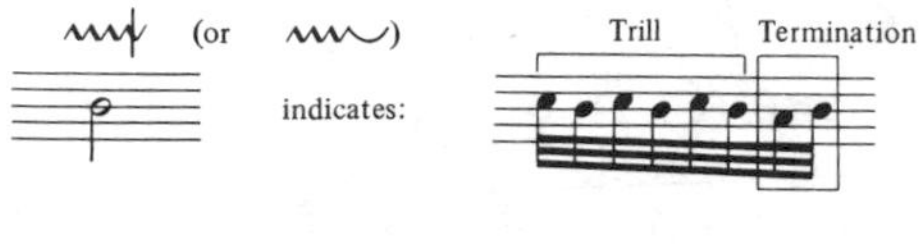

these should be played at the same speed as the trill. Haydn, Mozart, Beethoven, and other composers frequently used a *tr* sign with the termination indicated, instead of the Bach symbol. The following exercise (Ex. 9:32) may be practiced as a preparatory drill for this particular trill.

Ex. 9:32. Trill with termination exercise.

The trill with a *prefix* from *below* is also commonly found in Baroque music (especially in the Bach works) as well as other composers later on. Bach used a symbol for this figure (Ex. 9:33) which is found frequently in both the *Short Preludes* and the *Two-Part Inventions.*

Ex. 9:33. Trill with prefix from below.

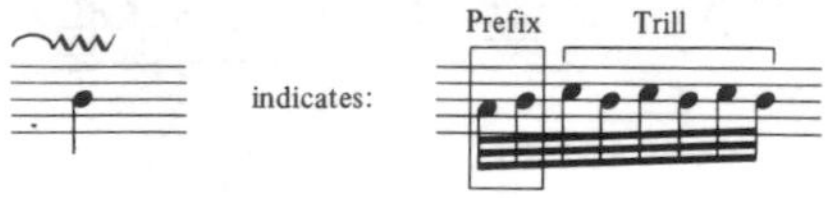

The prefix consists of two notes *below* the actual trill. An exercise may be given to the student similar to Example 9:32; begin on C, and go up the keyboard.

The trill with *prefix* from *above* is commonly used in Bach's music (Ex. 9:34). This figure may also be used in an exercise similar to Example 9:32; begin on C, and go up the keyboard.

Ex. 9:34. Trill with prefix from above.

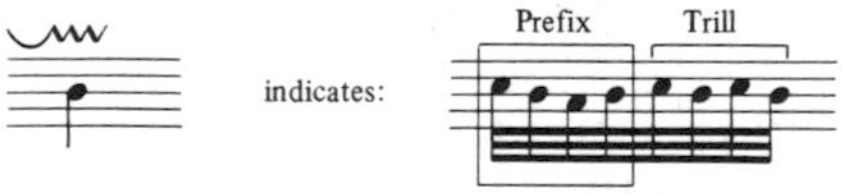

It is important for the student to *understand* the preceding trill symbols and be able to play them correctly when indicated in intermediate literature. As an aid to understanding, the teacher should invent exercises based on these problem spots. In this manner not only will the problems be solved, but the student will have a better understanding of the examples involved.

Some additional trill exercises are offered for the intermediate student to practice. The teacher may suggest others.

In the first exercise (Ex. 9:35) the trill should be practiced with the three finger combinations suggested; others may be assigned by the teacher. The second exercise (Ex. 9:36) provides trill experience for all fingers, even 4-5 which is seldom used in context. The third exercise (Ex. 9:37) follows

Ex. 9:35. Trill with pairs of fingers.

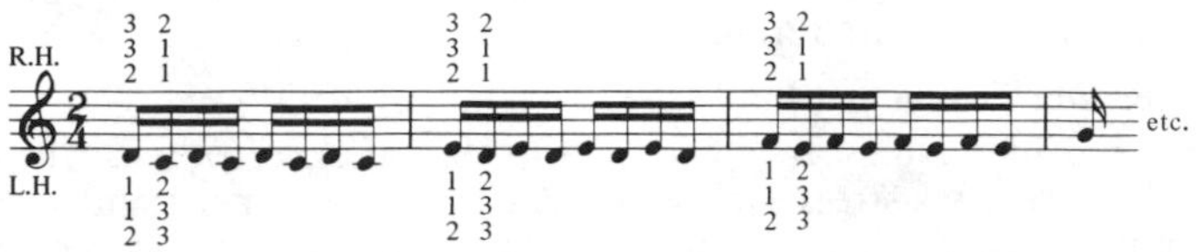

Ex. 9:36. Trill with all fingers.

Ex. 9:37. Chromatic trill.

the chromatic scale fingering (3 on all the black keys; 1 on the white keys, except those adjacent: E-F and B-C which are played with 1-2, right hand, and 2-1, left hand). These three exercises provide varied experiences in fingering combinations which are frequently used in trills.

Technique Studies

The following list contains a representative cross-sampling of intermediate technique books. Some of the books contain exercises, others feature etudes; some of the books contain varied experiences with both exercises and etudes. Exercises usually are brief patterns which can be practiced in a limited amount of time. Etudes are more like pieces which require more practice time. Etudes serve a dual purpose of developing reading as well as technique. It is helpful to assign a combination of exercises and etudes, as this usually produces excellent results.

EXERCISE BOOKS

Aiken, Kenneth Modern Technic Willis (1948)

The word "modern" in the title does not mean contemporary devices (polytonal, etc.), it means a departure from the usual fare of exclusive scale and arpeggio practice. Chords are the featured items in this book. In addition, some drills are provided for repeated note studies, trill studies, phrasing studies, and octave work. The intermediate student will benefit from the chord emphasis in this volume.

Burnam, Edna-Mae A Dozen a Day, Book 4 Willis (1964)

This volume covers a variety of technical exercises such as scales, arpeggios, chords, trills, repeated notes, thirds, sixths, etc. The level of difficulty ranges from early intermediate through upper intermediate.

Last, Joan Freedom Technique, Books 2 & 3 Oxford (1971)

Book 2 provides a number of excellent keyboard experiences at the intermediate level. The exercises stress such items as chords for arm weight, rotation, thirds, scale turns, broken chords, agility studies, repeated note studies, part playing, chromatic and diatonic sequences, expansion studies, and a variety of rhythm patterns. The examples are designed to promote ease of movement over the keyboard. Explanations throughout are direct and to the point.

Book 3 is more difficult (at least upper intermediate level), and provides exercises which can serve to bridge the gap between the upper intermediate level and the more formidable books written for talented students. Included are exercises for arm weight, rotation, wide skips, lateral movement for smooth thumb turns in arpeggios, double thirds, contractions and expansions, chord sequences, chromatic passages, broken octaves, slurs, rhythmic groupings, repeated notes, trill preparations studies, and octave studies. For serious students, this is a fine collection of keyboard patterns which are direct and to the point.

Philipp, Isidor Exercices de Tenues Marks (1944)

These studies are designed to develop balance of finger strength and are built on diminished seventh chords. The exercises may be assigned to students with large hands, as these studies stretch the fingers. The text is written in both French and English.

Pischna, Johann (Bernard Wolff, ed.) The Little Pischna Schirmer (1908)

The exercises in this volume are similar to the more difficult *60 Progressive Technical Studies* in that they are mostly 5-finger drills which are transposed through all the keys. Many of the exercises have holding fingers while other fingers in the same hand move. Also included are various scales, thirds, sixths, and arpeggios.

Pischna, Johann 60 Progressive Technical Studies Schirmer (1904)

This has been a standard technic collection for many years. The studies which feature trills, scales, chords, and arpeggios, are useful for serious students of better than average ability. The level is at least upper intermediate and beyond.

ETUDE BOOKS

Bastien, James (ed.) Czerny and Hanon GWM Co. (1970)

Included in this collection are twenty Czerny studies and the first twenty Hanon exercises. The Czerny studies range in difficulty from early intermediate to intermediate levels.

Burgmüller, Johann Friedrich 25 Progressive Pieces, Opus 100 Alfred Music Co., Schirmer, others

These etudes serve the dual function of providing easy grade studies and reading material. The pieces range in difficulty from early intermediate to intermediate levels.

Czerny, Carl The School of Velocity, Opus 299 Alfred Music Co., Schirmer, Kalmus, others

Scales, arpeggios, and various other techniques are incorporated in these well-known studies. Intermediate to upper intermediate levels.

Dring, Madeleine Twelve Pieces in the Form of Studies Josef Weinberger/Marks (1966)

From England comes this masterful collection of original studies. Some are reminiscent of Czerny on a level below Opus 299. Incorporated are the following technical features: scale passages, double thirds, chords, phrasing, repeated notes, chromatic scale, and broken chords and arpeggios. Most of these miniature etudes are quite musical and imaginative. All lie well under the hand, and with the exception of "The Young Willow" which has difficult double thirds, the studies are on a realistic level—about early to mid-intermediate levels.

Emonts, Fritz Polyphonic Piano-Playing, Books 1 & 2 Schott (Bk. 1, 1965; Bk. 2, 1968)

The problems of reading and playing two or more independent voices correctly are difficult for students. These two books deal directly with the problems and help to overcome the coordination difficulties involved. *Book 1* is restricted to two-part writing. By way of introduction the first group of exercises uses an ostinato in one hand and a melody in the other. The second group deals with the archetype of polyphony, the canon. In addition to original exercises, an excellent selection of extracts is offered by Orff (duets), Hindemith (duets), Kirnberger, Handel, W. F. Bach, J. S. Bach, and others. A number of first-rate preparatory exercises are given in the back of the book (pages 27-30).

Book 2 deals more directly with literature *per se.* After a few pages of preliminary exercises in silent finger changes and playing two parts in one hand, the rest of the book (pages 11-33) contains numerous pieces by master composers for application of principles learned. The music in this book is more difficult than the first book, about upper intermediate level and beyond.

Hirschberg, David Technic is Fun, Books 2,3,4 Musichord (1943-45)

Etudes by Biehl, Concone, Czerny, Heller, Köhler, Spindler, Streabbog, and others comprise these three volumes. Most of the studies are arranged by Hirschberg. Technique such as scales, repeated notes, trills, wrist staccato, etc. is incorporated into these short etudes. The illustrations date the books.

Kraehenbuehl, David (Clark Library) Piano Technic, Books 4 & 5 Summy-Birchard (1960)

These two books are divided into four sections: 5-finger positions, scale crossings, extensions, and arpeggio crossings. The exercises are written in etude style. The music is mildly contemporary and adds flavor to what might have been routine drills. The writing is imaginative and is accessible to students from mid- to upper intermediate levels.

Waxman, Donald Fifty Etudes, Books 1-4 Galaxy (1976)

For the teacher who has become weary of Burgmüller, Czerny, *et al*, these studies provide welcome relief. The etudes are spread throughout four books in progressive order of difficulty. The purpose of each etude is labeled, such as interlocking scales, repeated notes, broken thirds, etc. Some of the etudes have contemporary sounds and effects. The first two books are at the intermediate and upper intermediate levels, the remaining two are much more difficult.

Intermediate Theory

The purpose of including theory as a basic ingredient of the music program is to make the student musically literate. He should be able to analyze his music regarding chordal structure, key, interval relationships, etc. This knowledge will aid him in reading, memorizing, and in performance.

The intermediate student should continue to review materials learned previously. Basic intervals, key signatures, chords (major, minor, augmented, diminished), scales, inversions of triads and other elements of theory should be continued. If class theory is offered, there will be an opportunity for ensemble playing, keyboard harmony, sight-reading, ear training, dictation, and creative work.

New theoretical inclusions during the intermediate years are:

1. Recognizing relative major and minor key signatures
2. Writing minor key signatures

3. Writing minor scales
4. Learning chromatically altered intervals
5. Playing and writing seventh chords
6. Learning to modulate

Recognizing Relative Major and Minor Key Signatures

Relative major and minor key signatures may be explained in the following manner:[1]

> Every major key has a relative minor key. The two keys have the *same* key signature. Thus, every key signature has two possible keys to which it may refer: either the major key or its relative minor. The *sound* of the piece actually determines whether the piece is major or minor.[2]

Explain to the student that there are several methods of determining the minor key (Ex. 9:38). To avoid confusion, have the student choose one

Ex. 9:38. Methods of determining minor key signatures.

1. Count UP to the sixth tone of the Major scale; that tone is the name of the relative minor key.

2. Think DOWN three half steps on the keyboard to find the relative minor key. End TWO alphabet letters below the Major key note.

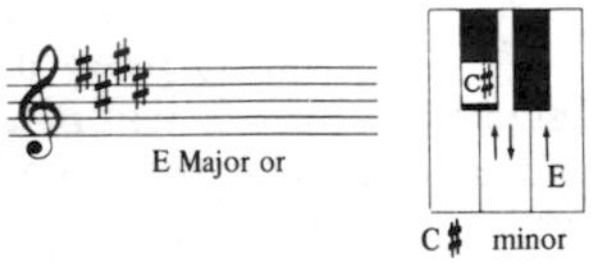

3. Think DOWN an alphabet SKIP from the Major key note. Check the key signature to see if this note is sharped or flatted. If so, add the corresponding sharp or flat to the name of the relative minor key.

of these three methods which is easiest for him, and use that procedure for determining the minor key name. Provide the student with a number of key signatures (in a theory book, ditto sheet, etc.), and have him write the relative major and minor key names.

[1]The information on discerning major or minor keys is not difficult to teach; some teachers prefer to teach it prior to the early intermediate level (fourth year).

[2]From *Book 6 Writing* by Jane Smisor Bastien (General Words and Music Co., 1971), p. 7.

Writing Minor Key Signatures

Since minor and major key signatures are related, it is helpful for the student to think of both of these when writing minor key signatures. Have the student draw or think of a minor chord (Ex. 9:39), the middle note is

Ex. 9:39. Relating major and minor key names to minor triads.

the major key name, and the bottom note is the minor key name. This quick reference will enable the student to relate the minor key to the major already learned. The student may begin writing minor key signatures in this manner. Provide exercises for the student to complete.

Writing Minor Scales

Before writing minor scales, it is helpful to explain the three forms of

Ex. 9:40. The three forms of minor scales.[3]

A minor scale is derived from its RELATIVE Major scale. It is termed relative because both scales share the same key signature. The minor scale is built on the sixth step of the Major scale, and this form of minor is called NATURAL or PURE minor.

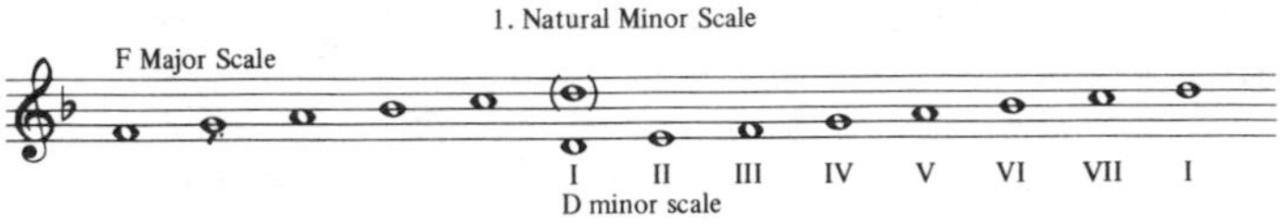

The HARMONIC MINOR SCALE is the most frequently used of the three forms of minor. This scale uses the same notes as the natural minor scale with the exception of the seventh degree of the scale. This change of one note cannot be written into the key signature, but will always appear in the scale as an accidental. To construct the harmonic minor scale, *raise the seventh degree of the scale one half step*.

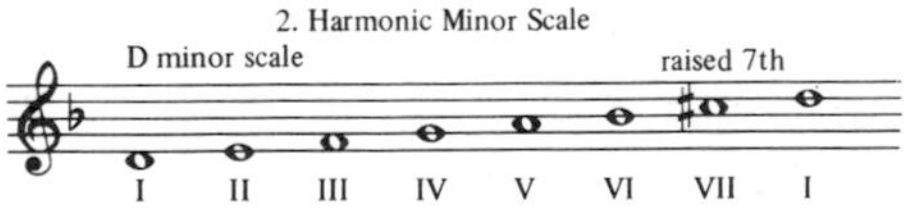

The MELODIC MINOR SCALE is the next most frequently used of the minor scales. This scale consists of two parts; one form of the scale is used ascending and another is used descending. To construct the melodic minor scale, *raise the sixth and seventh degrees of the scale one half step ascending, and lower the sixth and seventh degrees descending*.

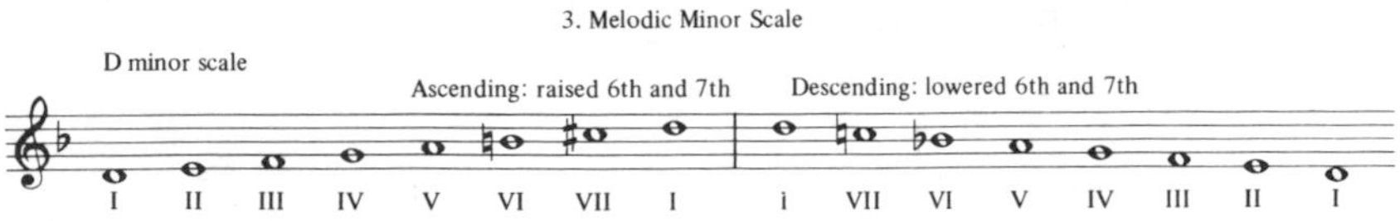

[3]Example from *Book 6, Writing*, p. 11.

minor scales and the major and minor relationships (Ex. 9:40). Have the student write minor scales on blank music paper. The harmonic minor scale should be stressed more than the other two.

Chromatically Altered Intervals

Scale tone intervals will have been learned before; these are either major or perfect intervals. There are three simple rules for altering scale tone intervals (Ex. 9:41):

1. Major intervals become minor by lowering the top note one half step.
2. Perfect intervals become diminished by lowering the top note one half step.
3. Perfect intervals become augmented by raising the top note one half step.

Ex. 9:41. Chromatically altered intervals.[4]

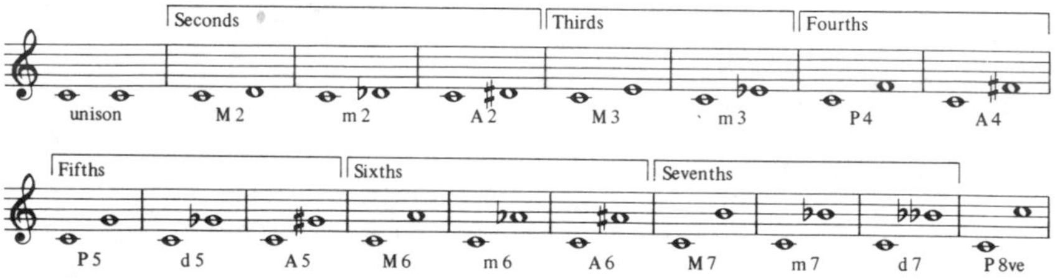

Point out to the student that several intervals have the same sound but are spelled differently:

Augmented second – minor third
Augmented fourth – diminished fifth
Augmented fifth – minor sixth
Augmented sixth – minor seventh

Provide the student with intervals for identification (in a theory book, ditto sheets, etc.). In addition, have the student identify all altered intervals in his music.

Seventh Chords

Because of a limited reach, young students play the dominant seventh chord in inverted position (V^6_5). Now with an expanded stretch, they will be able to play root position seventh chords.

The formation of root position seventh chords may be explained as a chord with four tones: a root, third, fifth, and a seventh (Ex. 9:42). It is called a seventh chord because in root position, the interval from the lowest to the highest note forms an interval of a seventh.

Ex. 9:42. Formation of seventh chords in root position.

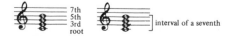

[4]Example from *Book 6 Writing*, p. 19.

There are five basic kinds of seventh chords (Ex. 9:43). They may be easily identified by their triad plus their seventh.

Ex. 9:43. Five kinds of seventh chords.[5]

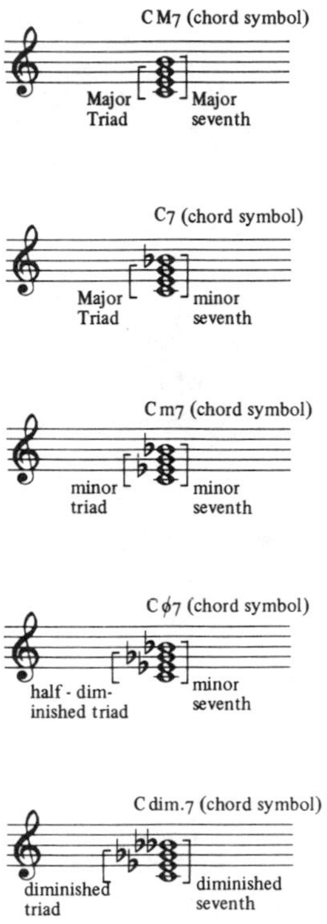

The student should practice the seventh chords in a five-chord sequence (Ex. 9:44); this pattern should be transposed to all other keys. In addition, have the student write this pattern on blank music paper.

Ex. 9:44. Seventh chord pattern.

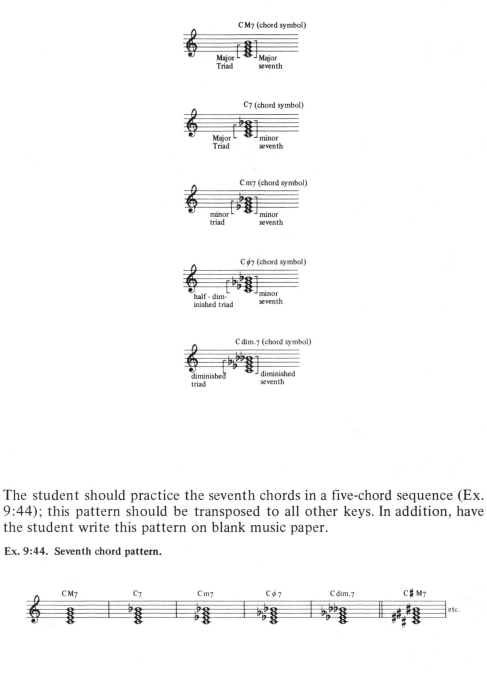

Have the student practice and write seventh chords of the scale (Ex. 9:45) in all keys. Explain the various types of seventh chords built on scale

[5]Example from *Book 6 Writing,* p. 27.

Ex. 9:45. Seventh chords of the major scale.

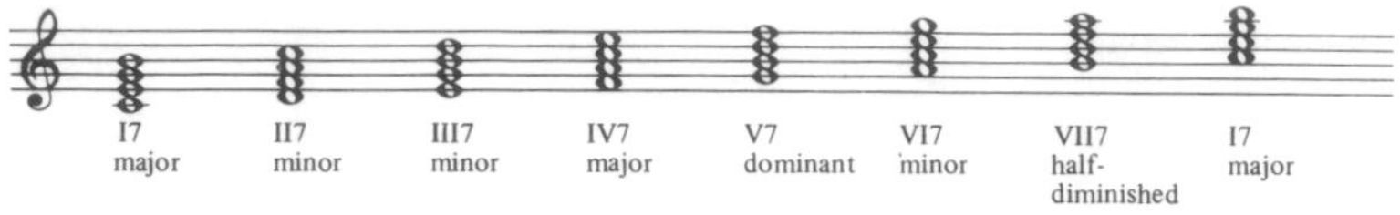

tones (major, minor, minor, major, dominant, minor, half-diminished, major).

Modulation

The abandoning of one tonality and establishing a new one is called modulation. This is often effected by playing the dominant of the new key and resolving to the new key. Dominants such as these are called *secondary dominants.* The chord symbols remains the same for secondary dominants: D7, C7, etc. The Roman numerals, however, frequently are used in relation to the new key: V7 of V (modulation to the key of the dominant); V7 of IV (modulation to the key of the subdominant).[6] Modulations to both the dominant and subdominant are quite common (Ex. 9:46). The student should understand this process and be able to play this type of modulation in all keys.

Ex. 9:46. Modulation to the dominant and subdominant.[7]

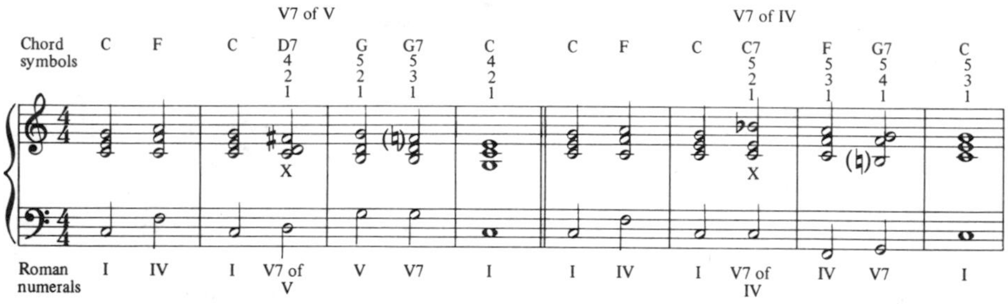

Few theory books for pre-college students provide opportunities for modulation. The intermediate student would benefit from the functional usage of modulation provided in Robert Pace's *Skills and Drills, Books 4* and *5* (Lee Roberts Music Publications, Inc., 1962).

[6] Robert Pace refers to secondary dominants as IIx7 chords; See *Skills and Drills, Book 4* (Lee Roberts Music Publications, Inc., 1962).

[7] Example from *Beginning Piano for Adults* by James Bastien (General Words and Music Co., 1968), p. 124.

DUET COLLECTIONS

Agay, Denes *Broadway Classics, Volumes B & C* Witmark/Warner Bros. Publications

Agay, Denes (arr.) *Joplin-Ragtime Classics* Marks

Bacon, Ernst *Sassafras* Lawson-Gould/Schirmer

Bradley, Richard (arr.) *Bradley's Double Joy* Columbia Publications

Brimhall, John (arr.) *The Rage is Recital Duets* Hansen

Clark, Mary E. *Three German Dances* Myklas

Dello Joio, Norman *Family Album* Marks

Dring, Madeleine *Three for Two* Josef Weinberger/Marks

Eckard, Walter (ed.) *44 Original Piano Duets* Presser

Gretchaninoff, Alexander *Gretchaninoff Album for Four Hands* Schott

Johnson, Thomas *Melody-Making for Two* Hinrichsen/Peters

Lambert, Constant *Trois Pieces Negres* Oxford

Olson/Bianchi/Blickenstaff *Ensemble, Levels 3,4,5* C. Fischer

Martin, Gerald *Jazz Duets* Yorktown

Martin, Hazel *Tune Time for Two* Belwin-Mills

McClenny, Anne, and Maurice Hinson (eds.) *Duets of Early American Music* Belwin-Mills

Pinto, Octavio *Scenas Infantis* Schirmer

Rollino, Joseph, and Paul Sheftel *Further Festivities* C. Fischer

Zeitlin, Poldi, and David Goldberger (eds.) *The Duet Book, II and III* Consolidated

Zeitlin, Poldi, and David Goldberger (eds.) *Easy Original Piano Duets (Volume 23, Music for Millions Series)* Consolidated

Zeitlin, Poldi, and David Goldberger (eds.) *Easy Piano Duets of the 19th Century* Schroeder & Gunther

SOLOS

EARLY INTERMEDIATE

Agay, Denes Soldiers' Hoe-Down Boosey (1964)

C major - 2/4 - Lively, with vigor. Several technical problems are featured in this driving, catchy solo: syncopation, varied touches alternating between the hands, and exacting off-beat accents.

Bastien, James Holiday Serenade GWM Co. (1972)

C major - ₵ - Strict march tempo. The main purpose of this solo is to teach first inversion triads. The entire piece uses first inversion triads, first in the right hand in the A section, then in both hands in the B section.

Bentley, Bernice Benson Piccola Tarantella Summy (1944)

E minor - 6/8 - Spirited. This solo is written in a sonatina-like style and contains the following teaching features: slurred groups, legato-staccato combinations, and balance of tone. (Available only in *For Me and My Piano, Book 3.)*

Brandt, Dorothea Little Donkey in the Snow J. Fischer/Belwin (1964)

G major - 2/4 - Moderato. Coordination between hands is required in the legato-staccato combinations in this imaginative musical portrait. Rhythmic variety is obtained by syncopations and dotted rhythms.

Butler, Jack Flight Willis (1968)

G major - 2/4 - Allegro. This solo is from a series of ten pieces called *Lyrical Sketches. Flight* features three-note slurs, rapidly shifting positions, and requires control in playing the sixteenth note figures evenly. No dynamics are given. The piece is more like an etude than a recital solo.

Chagy, John Desert Scene Presser (1966)

D tonality (melodic minor scale) - 6/4 - Andante. An ostinato bass and a flute-like melody are woven into an unusual, somewhat exotic sounding piece. A hypnotic effect is created by the persistent bass pattern which is repeated without variance throughout. Tone color and balance are the important teaching features.

Dittenhaver, Sarah Louise At the County Fair Witmark (1964)

G major - ₵ - Gay and jaunty. This energetic solo is just right for a student with some flair in his playing. The phrase structure and melodic contours in this piece make it an excellent one for study. Although the pedal is used sparsely, it is tricky; be careful with measures 16 and 28 (use a syncopated pedal).

Finlayson, Walter Alan Little White Burro Boosey (1956)

G major - 4/4 - Brightly. Called a "study for left hand staccato" by the composer, this attractive piece is more like an etude than a recital solo. In addition to the left hand staccatos, the right hand plays a series of legato double thirds.

Freed, Isadore Jeneral Jerry's Jolly Jugglers C. Fischer (1941)

G major - 6/8 - Alla marcia. This spirited, humorous solo makes an interesting study in syncopation. It is first-rate educational music for a student with good coordination who is willing to work hard to achieve the exacting rhythm and phrasing.

Gillock, William Blue Mood Willis (1973)

C minor - 4/4 - Moderately slowly. Dotted and syncopated rhythms dominate this effective blues piece. The B section contains some very tricky syncopated rhythm patterns. Interesting, colorful harmonies throughout.

Gillock, William Festive Piece Willis (1959)

D minor - ₵ - Con moto. Written in imitative early Classical style, this well-written solo is excellent for teaching touch, balance of melody and accompaniment, phrasing, and contrasting dynamics.

Gillock, William Holiday in Spain Schroeder & Gunther/Associated (1961)

E tonality - 3/4 - Danza, intensely rhythmic. Full of excitement and flavor redolent of castanets, guitars, and flashing boots, this solo is a real knock-out played by a student with spirit and relatively good technique.

Glover, David Carr Just Call Me Butch Mills/Belwin (1955)

C major - C - In a cocky manner. Dotted rhythms, crisp staccato chords, and some syncopations set the stage for this jaunty march. Especially for boys.

Last, Joan Miniature Dance Suite Oxford (1961)

The suite consists of four short one-page movements: Allemande, Minuet, Gavotte, and Gigue. The pieces make an excellent introduction to dance forms on an easy level.

Olson, Lynn Brief Encounter C. Fischer (1972)

C major - 6/8 - Con moto. The pedal binds together notes divided between the hands forming broken chords. Teaching features include clarity of pedal changes, evenness in running notes, and balance of tone. A pleasant sounding mood piece requiring little technical demands.

Olson, Lynn Freeman Spanish Serenade Summy-Birchard (1966)

A minor - 6/8 - Slowly and very smoothly. The main feature of this teaching piece is the use of right hand legato thirds. The left hand keeps a steady pulse while the right hand plays a syncopated melody suggestive of a slow dance. (Available only in *Supplementary Solos.*)

Reiser, Violet In Sunny Spain Willis (1973)

G minor - C - Moderato. Syncopated rhythms, legato-staccato touches, and double notes are the main composition/teaching features of this pleasant sounding piece. Requires a large reach (swing-tenths throughout).

Ricker, Earl Hero's March Lee Roberts/Schirmer (1965)

C major - 4/4 - In march time. This contemporary march has a nice bright, snappy sound and is effective played by a better than average student. The piece features rapidly changing thirds in root position, descending (chromatic) staccato double thirds, and dotted rhythms throughout.

Scher, William Phantom Rider C. Fischer (1974)

G minor - 2/4 - Allegro. This etude-like piece has running sixteenth notes which require steady, well-controlled fingers. An effective recital solo.

Scher, William Polonaise Romantique Pro Art (1971)

A minor - 3/4 - Moderato. The characteristic polonaise rhythm creates a spirited background for the nicely phrased melody. This is a good choice for students of average ability.

Storr, Sherman Elysian Suite J. Fischer/Belwin (1967)

Three solos are contained in this folio entitled "Triton," "Endymion," and "Daedalus." Each is based on a highly imaginative Greek poem, and the music is cast in a modal flavor. "Triton" is the easiest of the group, and is written mostly in two-voice style. "Endymion" uses broken arpeggios divided between the hands. "Daedalus" is written in 5/4 meter and changes to 4/4, 3/4, and 6/4; it is the least pianistic of the three, but is highly effective and dramatic.

Weybright, June Braziliana Belwin (1954)

F major - 2/4 - Moderato. Syncopated rhythm () is the central teaching feature of this engaging solo. This student pleaser is also published in a two piano arrangement by the composer.

INTERMEDIATE

Agay, Denes Three Recital Dances Presser (1956)

The dances are "Parade Polka," "Waltz Serenade," and "Mardi Gras Bolero." Mild dissonances, sparkling rhythms, and catchy tunes are present in all three solos. The special student favorite is "Mardi Gras Bolero."

Agay, Denes Two Bagatelles MCA (1965)

These two solos are most effective when played together as a pair. The first, *Andante delicato*, is a brief three-line pastorale incorporating a legato singing line right hand over a sustained left hand. The second, *Allegretto energico*, is a spritely scherzo-like piece employing grace notes, staccatos, and changing meters.

Bach, J. S. (ed. by Hans Barth) Allemande in A Minor Mills-Belwin (1954)

A minor - C - Andante. This is an effective, melodic piece requiring control in running notes, even touch, and the correct balance between melody and accompaniment. The use of sequence phrases makes this an excellent study piece in terraced dynamics.

Boykin, Helen Seafoam Schroeder & Gunther/Associated (1947)

G major - 4/4 - Andantino. The prominent teaching features of this effective solo are even right hand running notes, balance of left hand melody to the right hand figure, and the correct use of the pedal.

Butler, Jack Baroque Suite in D Minor Willis (1969)

Three movements comprise this effective, well-written suite in imitative Baroque style. The first, "Sarabande," is in 4/4 meter and, therefore, is unfortunately titled, as sarabandes are usually in 3/4 meter. The music, however, is excellent, with nice melodic lines and appropriate phrase structure. The second, "Aria," is a poignant song piece with simple accompaniment. The third, "Gigue," is a rollicking, bright-sounding piece in 6/8 meter. All three movements make effective recital material—especially the Gigue.

Ferrell, Billie Outer Space Boston (1964)

Twelve-tone row - 3/4 - Slow, with feeling. Although the twelve-tone technique is used, the tonality in the left hand chords centers around F minor. The melody is lyric, in song style. The rhythm on the first page is a flowing waltz; on the second page there are several meter changes. Some four-note chords are used requiring stretches.

Finlayson, Walter A Song of Bells Boston (1969)

C major - 5/4 - Andante moderato. The ring of bells is heard in both sustained right hand chords and sustained pedal points in the left hand. Numerous interesting harmonic effects are created by pedaled effects.

Gillock, William Command Performance Summy-Birchard (1956)

F major - 4/4 - Con moto. Teaching features of this excellent solo are contrasting touches, numerous phrase lifts, and some scale passages. The piece is written in imitative Classical style. (Available only in the *Gillock Collection* and *Summy Piano Solo Package, No. 401*.)

Gillock, William Pin Wheels Summy-Birchard (1946)

F major - 2/4 - Presto. This is a typical perpetual motion type composition requiring very good fast fingers. Running sixteenth note scale patterns and some hand crossings are used to create an exciting, driving piece. For students with better than average facility. (Available only in the *Gillock Collection* and *Summy Piano Solo Package, No. 501.)*

Kern, Carl Wilhelm The Clown, Opus 192, No. 1 Oliver Ditson (1911)

F major - 2/4 - Allegro. Called a "Humoresque" this playful, sparkling solo is an excellent study piece for creating a mood; imaginative directions are given throughout. Although written some time ago, the music still seems fresh and bright today.

Kern, Carl Wilhelm The Juggler, Opus 192, No. 6 Oliver Ditson (1911)

A minor - 6/8 - Andante. Somewhat resembling Schumann's *Noveletten* on a miniature scale, this old favorite has many nice teaching features. Clear passage work, proper voicing, and balancing of tone are required for a successful performance.

Konowitz, Bert Surf Swing Lee Roberts/Schirmer (1966)

D major - 4/4 - Moderato. This piece is strictly for fun. It is written in jazz style with some "rock" effects.

Kraehenbuehl, David Elegy Summy-Birchard (1969)

C minor - ₵ - Largo espressivo. The teaching features of this slow chorale-style solo include syncopated pedal, voicing of the top note in the chords, and balance of melody and accompaniment in the B section. (Available only in *Supplementary Solos*.)

Lane, Richard The Penguin C. Fischer (1968)

C minor - ₵ - Moderato. This student pleaser features subtle jazz sounds in good taste. Rhythmic control is a basic requirement; the dotted figures and the triplet quarter note figures must be played correctly and "felt" to create a convincing performance. This one is especially for fun. (Included in *Something Light, Level 5.)*

Rozin, Albert Toccatina Boston Music Co. (1961)

E minor - 2/4 - Animated. Alternating staccato notes run continuously throughout this breathless etude-like solo. Dedicated to William Scher, *Toccatina* is reminiscent of Scher's *Cat Chasing Mouse.*

Russell, Olive Nelson Chili Peppers Summy-Birchard (1963)

C major - 4/4 - Rumba tempo. The typical rumba rhythm used in this piece is characterized by an anticipation of the second beat, resulting in a 1-2-3, 1-2-3, 1-2 distribution of the 8 eighth notes per measure. Rhythm is the dominant feature, and precise control of the eighth notes in alternating hands is required. The music is in a semipopular style. (Available only in *Summy Piano Solo Package, No. 501.)*

Scher, William Gypsy Holiday Willis (1974)

E minor - 2/4 - Lively. This snappy folk dance piece features syncopations, running sixteenth notes, and a rhythmic bass.

Scher, William Madrid C. Fischer (1961)

A minor - 3/4 - Allegretto con moto. Syncopations, attractive Latin melodies, and a lively accompaniment are combined into a pleasant repertoire piece for enjoyment.

Schytté, Ludvig Witches' Revels Danse des Sorcieres Boston Music Co. (1950)

A minor - 6/8 - Allegro agitato. Schytté (1848-1909) wrote a number of teaching pieces in a style similar to Mendelssohn and Schumann. This three-page solo appears quite easy at first glance, but the difficulty lies in sustaining the legato line while playing staccato accompaniments in the same hand at the same time. It is an excellent piece for teaching singing legato melody against a subordinated accompaniment.

Stecher/Horowitz/Gordon The Terrain of Spain Summy- Birchard (1967)

D minor - 4/4 - Con spirito. A spirited introduction sets the mood for this sparkling fiesta-like piece. Teaching features include: balance of melody and accompaniment, Alberti bass, grace note, and shifting hand positions. An effective recital solo. (Available only in *Summy Piano Solo Package, No. 401.)*

Taylor, Richard Rain-Covered Carousel C. Fischer (1973)

(begins and ends in A tonality) - 3/4 - Moderato. A lyric melody sings above broken triads in many keys. Excellent phrase structure in this lilting mood study. Especially for students with multi-key background.

Turina, Joaquin Cadena de Seguidillas Oxford (1927)

C major - 3/4 - Allegro vivo. This simple lilting piece evokes an impression of guitars strumming to Spanish dancers. Because of the numerous accidentals, the piece is difficult for students to read at first.

Villa-Lobos, Heitor The Story of Caipirinha Peer International (1954)

From a group of six pieces for children comes this charming two-page solo; it is No. 6 in the series. Brazilian folk tunes and the use of folk inflections in the harmonic, melodic and rhythmic fabric of the music are immediately apparent. Other solos in this group published by Peer International are *The Right Hand has a Rose, My Mother Used to Lullaby Me Like This, Little Country Girl, The Little White Dress,* and *Sacy.*

UPPER INTERMEDIATE

Agay, Denes (transcriber) Concertino Barocco on Themes by Handel Schirmer (1975)

Written in concerto grosso style this attractive work has spirited first and last movements and a melodic second movement. For a student with adequate technique, this is an excellent recital piece, well transcribed for piano solo. The level of difficulty approaches early advanced.

Agay, Denes Serenata Burlesca Boosey (1968)

G major - 3/8 - Allegro scherzando. For students of better than average ability this is a rewarding, challenging, effective piece. It is highly chromatic and contains running eighth notes throughout. The difficulty lies in sustaining the mood of the piece for an unusually long seven pages. Memorization is difficult in this one.

Allen, Gilbert Lament Summy-Birchard (1959)

Eb major - C - Slow, with feeling. This slow blues dirge is sure to be a hit with teen-agers. The style is quite similar to Gershwin. The student must have a big reach to span the chords, octaves, and extended reaches easily. (Available only in *Summy Piano Solo Package, No. 501.)*

Alt, Hansi March Oxford (1971)

C minor - 4/4 - Allegretto. The harmonic texture of this well-written solo creates suspense and provides an imposing background for the tuneful melody. Octaves, and octave stretches abound. The scale in double thirds on the last page is a challenge.

Bastien, James (arr.) Jesu, Joy of Man's Desiring (Bach) GWM Co. (1977)

G major - Andante, flowing. Bach's lovely Choral from the *Cantata No. 147* has a timeless, majestic quality and has been a favorite of concert pianists. This arrangement maintains the simple melodic flow over the recurring bass.

Bastien, James (arr.) Toccata in D Minor (Bach) GWM Co. (1977)

Bach's *Toccato and Fugue in D Minor* for organ is one of his most famous compositions. This arrangement maintains the drama of the toccata in a pianistic version.

Bastien, James Variations on a Theme by Paganini GWM Co. (1977)

The six variations on this well-known theme contain varied technical passages such as running sixteenth notes, chords, and double notes. Each variation has a definitive style and mood. Variation Five is a slow blues; Variation Six incorporates a stunning finale. A showy recital or contest piece.

Bauer, Raymond The Dandy Lion Willis (1962)

C major - 4/4 - Moderately, not too fast. This solo is a gay pictorial representation of the King of Beasts full of growls, heroic promenades and even sly shenanigans. On the difficult side, this piece is highly effective played by a student with better than average ability.

Brussels, Iris Two Preludes MCA Music (1963)

These are two attractive solos which are quite different in style and mood. The first is a lovely flowing piece with a left hand melody and a right hand sixteenth note accompaniment. The second is quite fast and capricious with sharp staccatos in both hands.

Chagy, John Etude Romantique Pembroke/C. Fischer (1974)

F-sharp minor - 4/4 - Allegretto cantabile. A lyric melody sings above running sixteenth notes in the right hand. Evenness and balance of tone are required for a successful performance. An excellent study piece.

Chagy, John Sicilienne and Rigaudon Summy-Birchard (1963)

These two contrasting dance movements are excellent for teaching form and style. The *Sicilienne* is a lilting dance (6/8 meter) employing a singing melody line above a simple bass. The *Rigaudon* is a spirited dance (2/4 meter) containing some written-out trills, sequence phrases, and contains a variety of touches. This is effective material when both movements are played as a pair.

Debussy, Claude Le Petit Nègre Alphonse Leduc (1934)

C major - 2/4 - Allegro giusto. This lovely whimsical piece features syncopated melodic effects to create the dance-like character implied by the title; it is a long-time student favorite.

Donato, Anthony The Rock Crusher J. Fischer/Belwin (1960)

E (minor) tonality - 3/4 - Briskly, with precision. Full of cross accents and unexpected syncopations, this effective contemporary sounding piece is rhythmically challenging. For better than average students.

Eckstein, Maxwell Rhapsodie Boston Music Co. (1943)

A minor - C - Moderato. Written in Hungarian Rhapsodie style, this miniature version is a favorite with young teen-agers of average ability; they will love every kernel of well-ground corn.

Gillock, William Etude in E Minor Willis (1973)

E minor - 2/4 - Allegro moderato. Double notes are used expressively throughout. This piece looks easier than it is.

Harvey, Paul Rumba Toccata Ricordi (1961)

C major - 2/4 - Presto agitato, con ritmo. This spritely two-page composition is written mostly on one clef (using divided hands) and lasts a brief fifty-five seconds. The rumba rhythm *(1-2-3-4; 1-2-3-4)* is maintained throughout. Facility for fast repeated notes and a keen sense of rhythm are essential for a sparkling performance of this first-rate study and recital solo.

Hovhaness, Alan Mystic Flute Peters (1940)

D minor - 7/8 - ♪ =200. The Oriental effect in the melody is created by the tones D, Eb, F#, G, A, Bb, C#, D which produces an Eastern, "snake-charming" sound. Most of the phrases are grouped into two measures. Because of the numerous repetitions of the melody, each time with variations, the piece is difficult to memorize. Few technical problems are encountered with the exception of the embellishments which must be played evenly and clearly.

Kasschau, Howard Dances Sad and Gay Schirmer (1968)

The three contrasting solos in this folio are immediately appealing. The first, *Vivace*, is a light, scherzo-like piece featuring fast changing hand positions. The second, *Andantino*, is a pensive, lyrical song piece in 5/4 meter. The last, *Allegro*, contains rapid scale passages in 6/8 meter. All three pieces make effective audition and recital material.

Martino, Russ Hanky-Panky MCA (1965)

F major - 2/2 - Bright swing. For the student who may need a change to rekindle interest, this jazz piece may be just the answer. Syncopations and seventh chords abound. Strictly for fun.

Pickles, Arthur Cap and Bells Curwen & Sons/Schirmer (1954)

G major - 3/8 - Vivace ma grazioso. Although this piece does not look difficult it has built in problems—one of which is maintaining the momentum throughout. The composition resembles a Mendelssohn scherzo. Quick shifts of hand positions, balance of melody and accompaniment, clarity in all running notes, and shaping the phrases are the dominant teaching features.

Stevens, Everett Homage to Ravel C. Fischer (1971)

C major - 3/4 - In the manner of a Minuet, but not too slowly. This piece evokes the nostalgia and poignancy of Ravel's style (*Pavane*, others). It is an attractive musical portrait requiring control in balancing the melody and accompaniment. Exacting pedaling must be carefully executed. Irregular patterns and extensive use of altered tones makes this one difficult to memorize.

Villa-Lobos, Heitor The Toy Wheel Peer International (1955)

F major - 2/4 - Moderato. Villa-Lobos has written prolifically for children. This piece is from a group of six children's pieces; it is No. 4 in the group. Brazilian folk tunes and the use of folk inflections in the harmonic, melodic, and rhythmic fabric of the music are immediately apparent. Cross accents add rhythmic interest. Other solos in this group published by Peer International are *Put Your Little Foot Out, The Carranquinha Mode, The Three Little Caballeros, Garibaldi Went to Mass,* and *Let Us All Go to Dance.*

Ward-Steinman, David Improvisations on Children's Songs Lee Roberts/Schirmer (1967)

Consisting of arrangements on *Twinkle, Twinkle Little Star, Happy Birthday to You,* and *Frère Jacques,* this set offers some unusual harmonic versions of these well-known tunes. The difficulties lie not in technical problems but in reading and learning the complex harmonizations. The setting of *Frère Jacques* is the most difficult and challenging of the three.

FOR DISCUSSION AND ASSIGNMENT

1. Would you assign repertoire anthologies or individual composer volumes? Why?
2. How important are editions for intermediate students?
3. Does pop music have a place in the music program?
4. If possible use an intermediate student (students) to demonstrate the following technical items: a variety of scale patterns, arpeggio patterns, chord drills, double note drills, and a variety of trill exercises. Which items do you consider most important? Why? List other technical considerations.
5. In addition to the theory items discussed in this chapter, what others would you include for intermediate students?
6. At a music store make a survey of intermediate repertoire books and solos. Present five books and five solos other than those listed in this chapter, and tell why they would be useful for intermediate students.
7. From your experience examining intermediate literature, compose an intermediate solo; point out the teaching features.

FOR FURTHER READING

Consult the books suggested at the end of Chapter 8.

Part Three

Special Subjects

Class Piano for College Piano Minors 10

THE PURPOSE OF CLASS PIANO FOR PIANO MINORS

Most music schools adhere to the dictum that every music student, regardless of his major field of study, should receive keyboard instruction as a basic component of the total music program. With increased enrollments, the feasibility of private piano lessons has decreased markedly, and the trend toward group instruction rather than individual lessons at the minor level has become more prevalent during the past several years.

The move toward class piano is justified in more ways than for merely financial reasons. Group instruction provides the basis for many facets of learning. Unlike the private student who receives specific direction from the instructor, the class student often learns by imitating his peers. The class student usually tends to be more self-reliant and is often forced to solve problems for himself rather than rely entirely on the instructor to do the work for him. If classes are conducted by a skilled teacher, competition among class students tends to be keen, and the students' preparation usually is more deliberate and conscientious. The class student is afforded an opportunity to experience principles of ensemble playing in a fuller capacity than in the private lesson. Group spirit and group dynamics are important factors in motivation while learning elementary skills. Since piano study is a requirement, not an elective, group enthusiasm may play an important role in bridging the gap between those who enjoy the new experience of learning to play the piano, and those who regard it only as a burden.

The primary function of the class piano program is to provide the non-keyboard music major with functional keyboard skills. The ability to sight-read, score-read, harmonize, transpose, and improvise will best serve the practical needs of choir and instrumental directors and general music teachers. In addition, the class piano program may strengthen and unify other areas of college study, such as relating keyboard harmony to theory, and piano literature to music history. Group instruction serves as a laboratory where various components may be pulled together and used to deepen musical understanding.

In the past, individual instruction relied almost exclusively on the perfection of piano playing *per se*, and primary emphasis was given to the study of repertoire and technic. While these important areas should not be forsaken entirely in favor of functional skills, a combination of "traditional" and "functional" instruction will provide a solid keyboard program for the piano minor.

James Lyke[1] reports an interesting thesis project done by William Richards which surveyed class piano curricula.[2] The project's purpose was to construct a program from the results of the survey which would reflect the most desirable keyboard skills. Richards sent a questionnaire to two groups, class piano teachers and music education instructors, which contained a rating scale listing the following twenty keyboard musicianship items: transposition, playing by ear, repertoire study, score reduction (vocal), improvisation, technical development, sight-reading, accompanying, harmonization of melodies, patriotic songs, score reduction (instrumental), critical listening, development of style concepts, playing before others, chord progressions, ensemble playing, realization of figured bass, modulation, memorization, and analysis (melody, harmony, form). In responding to these items both groups reported that such skills as the ability to play by ear, play chord progressions, analyze music, transpose, and improvise were more important than figured-bass playing or memorization. However, it is interesting to note that while repertoire study was considered important by the class piano teacher, music education instructors placed this item at the end of the scale.

The problem of providing a comprehensive program for the piano minor is compounded by several internal factors within the music department. Perhaps the most serious problem confronting group instruction is the selection of the teacher. The accomplished pianist often is not prepared to teach class piano. Lack of training, lack of interest in the program, and lack of imagination and creativity in the instructor too often undermine the goals of group instruction. An additional problem is the "board" exam or jury system which functions in most music departments to aid teachers in grading students enrolled in both major and minor instruction. It is easier to prepare the class piano student to play five or six repertoire selections and some scales than to devote a great deal of class time to functional skills which may not make an immediate "show" at the examination. However, too many safeguards are inherent in the jury procedure to abandon it as the basis for applied music credit. To be comprehensive the examination should cover representative phases of group instruction rather than a limited area.

Minor piano students generally receive a maximum of two years of instruction in most colleges. Within this limited period students must achieve a degree of proficiency in areas such as improvisation, harmonization, sight-reading, etc. Emphasis and time allotted to these areas will vary from school to school and will be dependent largely upon the instructor. Unfortunately, the class piano program will not realistically be able to provide a comprehensive background for all the students enrolled. Too often the program is spread thin by trying to serve the needs of other departments within the college. In a comprehensive study of class piano programs, Marcelle Vernazza concluded that: "The purposes and intentions of the

[1] James Lyke, "What Should our Piano Minors Study?" *Music Educators Journal,* (December, 1969).

[2] William Henry Richards, "Trends of Class Piano Instruction, 1815-1962," (unpublished thesis, The Conservatory of Music, University of Kansas City, 1962).

piano courses have been confused by the demands made upon them by the whole [music] department. The inherent breadth of the subject, with its tendency to overlap into other subjects, makes it difficult to define its limitations."[3]

Finally, the class piano curriculum should be constructed to best suit the needs of the students. Piano teachers and music educators in the college should devise a program based on practical piano study. Emphasis should be given to basic objectives rather than exclusive concentration on one area, such as repertoire. Syllabi and proficiency examinations should reflect a comprehensive view including all important phases of musicianship.

Recently, college educators have been concerned about the carry over from one class to another. A new philosophy of education is evolving to combat this situation. Comprehensive Musicianship (CMP) is a philosophy which is concerned with providing students with a broad base in all classes from which they can draw meaningful conclusions. This philosophy is easily applicable to the class piano situation. Theory, keyboard harmony, and improvisation are incorporated into the piano class. Style, structure, form and content can be analyzed in the pieces studied. The instructor can encourage the class members to compose piano pieces (either solos, duets, or multiple piano arrangements) in representative styles using characteristic materials (twelve-tone row, whole tone scale, etc.). Thus, viewed in a broad spectrum, the class piano program should aid the student in musical concepts not only at the keyboard, but in the ability to draw meaningful connections in all areas of musicianship.

EQUIPMENT AND FACILITIES[4]

Class piano generally is taught in an area termed "the piano laboratory." The piano lab consists mainly of multiple pianos, either conventional or electronic. Other items often housed in the lab include blackboards and a variety of audio-visual equipment. Unfortunately, ideal uniform teaching situations cannot always be assured. The choice of piano models and number of pianos contained in the teaching area will be influenced directly by factors such as budget limitations, teacher preference, size and shape of the classroom, other uses of the room, and other considerations.

The size of the room should be sufficient to comfortably house 12 pianos, electric or conventional; blackboard space over half the wall area; storage space for class materials; and enough room for visual aids such as an overhead projector and screen. In addition, adequate lighting, soundproofing, and appropriate decor is important for creating a pleasant atmosphere in which to work.

[3]Marcelle Vernazza, "Basic Piano Instruction in the College," *American Music Teacher*, Vol. XVI, No. 6 (June-July, 1967), p. 45.

[4]For an informative discussion on equipment and facilities, see *Teaching Piano in Classroom and Studio* (Music Educators National Conference, 1967), Appendix C, "Equipping the Piano Classroom."

For class use the conventional piano has given way to the electronic piano. Electronic piano installations have become widespread in colleges recently. No matter what make or model is selected, the electronic piano is ideal for classroom use. Too often college piano teachers are overly concerned with the tone, touch, and action of the electronic model rather than considering the many possibilities for its use in the classroom.

Electronic piano installations take up less space, are less expensive, and generally serve the class piano situation better than conventional pianos. Noise and confusion are kept to a minimum, and more efficient use of teaching time is possible. Teacher to student, student to student communications, audio aids, and ensemble arrangements can be employed easily on the electronic pianos. While the electronic piano is a useful teaching device, it does not replace the conventional piano. Its purpose is for classroom use rather than as a vehicle for performance. Therefore, at least one conventional piano should be kept in the classroom for periodic performances.

The electronic piano serves a wide range of purposes. Through the communications center at the control piano, the instructor may speak to one or all of the students in the class. Most manufacturers offer units ranging from small groups of four to six student pianos, up to a full complement of twenty-four. Instruction to one or all students may be carried on personally or with programmed tapes or recordings. Different activities may be carried on for selected students without disturbing others in the group. Individual or group instruction may be taught. Beginning and advanced students may practice at the same time without disturbing each other. By means of tape systems, students can record their own performances and keep track of their progress. Students may practice ensemble music in combination with others in the class, or they may have ensemble situations created for them with the aid of record series such as "Music Minus One" or "Analytical Performance."

Manufacturers of Electronic Pianos

A majority of college music departments now have electronic piano laboratories or are in the process of acquiring them. However, some schools have not yet purchased electronic pianos. Therefore, the following data may serve as a guide in selecting models: manufacturers, components, size, keyboard range, tone producing mechanisms, and other information as provided by the various companies.

The four leading manufacturers of electronic piano laboratories presently are Wurlitzer, Baldwin, Rhodes, and Musitronic. The four systems offer many of the same features: all have earphones for individual instruction, a communication center, audio aids which may be adapted to the student or teacher piano; student pianos up to a maximum of 24; and all offer possibilities for combinations of pianos in various ensemble arrangements. However, there are variances in the four models regarding keyboard range, tuning, height, size, weight, etc. A brief description and photo of each model is given for purposes of comparison.

The Wurlitzer Electronic Piano (Ill. 10:1) is manufactured in DeKalb,

Illinois. Specifications include:[5]

Keyboard	64 keys, note range from A to C
Dimensions	Height 32-1/8" Depth 18-9/16" Keyboard height 25-3/4" Width 40"
Weight	130 pounds
Action	Simulated grand piano type; control stroke dynamics, action weight, ring time and let-off similar to a conventional piano.
Hammers	3-ply maple covered with mothproofed felt.
Tone Source	Sandvik Swedish steel reeds; the stroke of the hammer causes a reed to vibrate in a polarized electrostatic field.
Tuning	Tuning not required.
Power	40 watts; operates from 117-volt, 50/60 cycle AC.
Amplification	Solid state.

Ill. 10:1. Wurlitzer Electronic Pianos.[6]

[5]Information furnished by Werleins for Music (Wurlitzer dealer), New Orleans, Louisiana.

[6]Photo of the Wurlitzer lab at the National Music Camp, Interlochen, Michigan. Nancy Stephenson, instructor.

The Baldwin Electropiano (Ill. 10:2) is manufactured in Cincinnati, Ohio. Specifications include:[7]

Keyboard	Full 88-note keyboard; 64-note pianos are also available.
Dimensions	Height 17-1/2" Width 56" (44" for the 64-note model)
Action	Regular piano action: hammers strike strings, and dampers damp strings like a conventional piano.
Tuning	Because strings are used, tuning is required just like a conventional piano.

Ill. 10:2. Baldwin Electropianos. Courtesy of the Baldwin Piano Company.

The Rhodes Electronic Piano (Ill. 10:3) is manufactured in Fullerton, California under the label of CBS Musical Instruments, a division of Columbia Broadcasting System, Inc. Specifications include:[8]

Keyboard	Six-octaves, 73 keys, note range from E to E
Dimensions	Height 34" Width 46" Depth 23"
Weight	214 pounds
Action	Simulated grand piano type.
Tone Source	A specially patented tuning fork.
Power Requirements	177-volts AC, utilizing a three-wire grounded system.
Amplification	Solid state transistorized system.

[7]Information furnished by Mitchell's Piano Company (Baldwin dealer), New Orleans, Louisiana.

[8]Information furnished by CBS Musical Instruments, Fullerton, California.

Ill. 10:3. Rhodes Electronic Pianos. Courtesy of CBS Musical Instruments.

Musitronic, Inc., of Owatonna, Minnesota, is the manufacturer of keyboard systems, accessories, and materials for the complete school and studio program. These include electronic piano labs, a portable six keyboard unit, a keyboard resource center, and an intonation trainer. Specifications for the Musitronic Electronic Piano Model PK 301B (Ill. 10:4) include:[9]

Keyboard	Range, 68 notes, F-9 to C-76 of a conventional 88 key piano
Dimensions	Height 31" Width 40" Depth 19"
Weight	75 pounds
Action	True piano touch sensitivity; dynamics, ring time and weight of depression is similar to that of a conventional piano.
Tone Production	A high octave tone generating system provides reliable performance and absolute stable pitch; crystal controlled – no need for tuning.
Power Requirements	110V AC 50-60hz
Amplification	Twin amplification system – 40 watts
Speakers	Two heavy duty 10" speakers
Pedals	Both damper and sustain pedals
Voicings	Piano, harpsichord, and celeste

Placement of Pianos in the Classroom

The arrangement of the pianos in the classroom is an important factor in group teaching. Although there are several possibilities for

[9]Information furnished by Musitronic, Inc., Owatonna, Minnesota.

Ill. 10:4. Musitronic Electronic Piano. Courtesy of Musitronic, Inc.

positioning student pianos, two are commonly used: (1) arranged horizontally across the room with students facing the front of the room toward the instructor (Ill. 10:1); and (2) arranged vertically in rows with pianos back to back in front of the instructor (Ill. 10:5).

Arranged horizontally with students and teacher facing each other, it is not possible for the instructor to see the students' hands unless he leaves his place and moves about the room. Arranged vertically, however, the instructor can easily look down the rows with minimal movement. After viewing many class piano situations around the country, Marcelle Vernazza reports that "In this kind of arrangement [vertical] the teacher can easily see all of the keyboards from one end of the row. The students can see the teacher by looking to the side. Also, the teacher has easy access to each instrument."[10]

Several practical purposes are served by being able to view the students' hands: (1) hand positions may be corrected, (2) fingering may be corrected, (3) the proper location of hands at the keyboard (correct octave) may be easily corrected. Therefore, the vertical arrangement is recommended for efficient classroom procedure.

[10]Marcelle Vernazza, "Basic Piano Instruction in the College," *American Music Teacher*, Vol. XVI, No. 6 (June-July, 1967), p. 18.

Ill. 10:5. Vertical arrangement of classroom pianos.

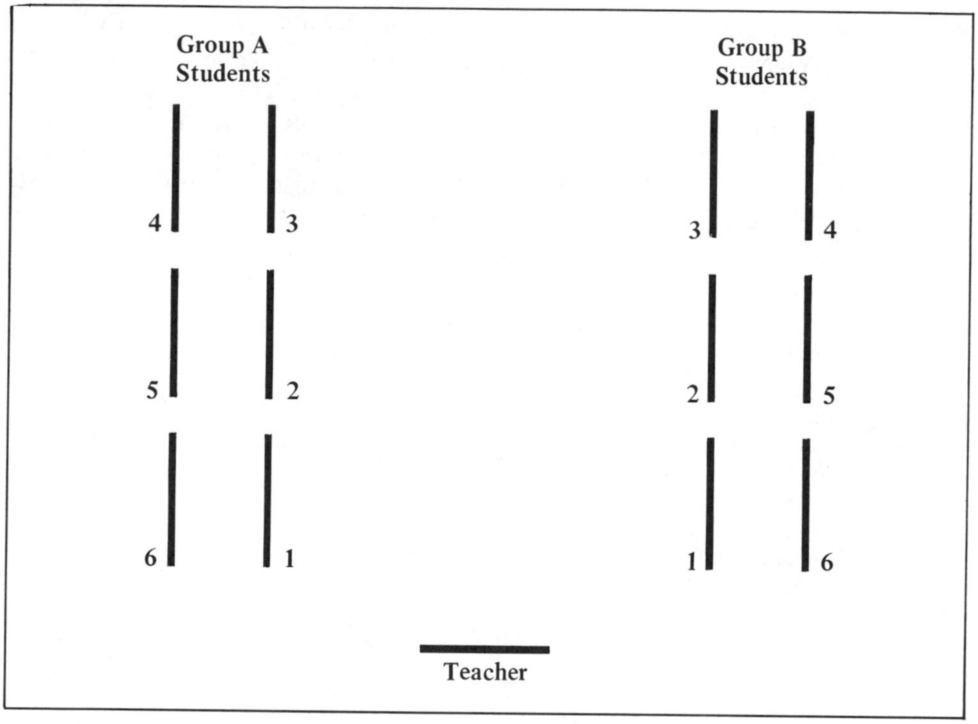

ORGANIZATION OF CLASSES

Levels of Instruction

In teaching college piano minors, problems often arise as to previous training. Some students have had piano instruction, some are beginners, and some are self-taught. With such divergent levels how can group instruction be effectively accomplished?

Consider a freshman piano minor class of thirty students. Twenty are beginners and ten have had previous instruction. The beginners can be easily separated into two sections of ten each, according to ability. Placement tests are advisable before making up the two sections. The remaining ten students will have to be tested before teacher assignments can be made. If several students have had previous piano instruction for about the same time, these can be grouped together into a small class (perhaps three to five students). The remaining students who do not fit into one of these categories may be given private lessons, either from the piano staff or from graduate assistants.

Size of Enrollment

Class size often is determined by the level of instruction, the physical size of the classroom, and teacher preference. Although it is difficult to measure results in terms of class enrollment, small classes appear to achieve better results than large classes.

It is possible to teach a large number of students in a group piano lab; we have already seen that electronic piano manufacturers offer units of up to twenty-four student pianos per classroom. While it is more efficient economically on a cost accounting basis to teach as many students as possible with one instructor, pedagogically, it is not the most effective teaching procedure. A group should contain enough students to create a "group atmosphere," and at the same time remain small enough to allow individual instruction. Helene Robinson suggests that "The recommended maximum enrollment should be ten for the first year class, six for the second year, and fewer for more advanced classes."[11]

A recent study was made on class size by E. L. Lancaster in which the following results were reported:[12]

1. Maximum number of students in any first year section	24
Mean maximum	10.5
2. Maximum number of students in any second year section	24
Mean maximum	9.7
1. Estimate of ideal first year class size - mean	8.6
2. Estimate of ideal second year class size - mean	8.1

The report disclosed that private colleges were more likely to use private instruction rather than class piano; also, those offering class piano tended to have smaller classes and were more apt to use the standard acoustic pianos than an electronic lab.

On the other hand, public colleges and universities maintained the largest class piano sections. On the average, the maximum section size was estimated at thirteen to fourteen students, while nine was judged to be the ideal section size.

Scheduling of Lessons

For effective learning, an ideal teaching arrangement is to schedule daily classes for each section of class piano. Most college music departments offer theory and ensemble classes (band, chorus, etc.) on a daily basis, but only a few music departments are presently scheduling class piano in this manner. Unfortunately, several factors stand in the way of this procedure: the frequency with which the piano lab is used, the number of students to be provided with group instruction, and the amount of teacher time available.

An alternative to daily instruction is an arrangement of two fifty minute class periods per week. For substantial progress, additional classes can be scheduled during the week with student assistants supervising these practice sessions. If additional class time cannot be scheduled, a private

[11] *Teaching Piano in Classroom and Studio*, edited by Helene Robinson and Richard L. Jarvis (Washington: Music Educators National Conference, 1967), p. 120.

[12] E. L. Lancaster, *Survey of Colleges Offering Class Piano* (Palatine, Illinois: William Rainey Harper College), Office of Planning & Development, John A. Lucas, Director: Research Report Series Volume III, No. II, December 17, 1971.

lesson can be arranged with a student assistant to provide individual help with special problems.

Because minor piano instruction is required, students often are not motivated to practice sufficiently to make substantial progress. The student is mostly concerned with his major instrument. Piano study often is approached in the same manner as other minor instruments (woodwinds, brass, or percussion classes) which may require only minimal outside practice. Therefore, the more piano classes that can be scheduled, the better, for these may be the main source of practice.

TWO YEAR CLASS PIANO CURRICULUM

A brief curriculum outline is offered as a guide for planning course sequence. The program is designed for college piano minors and covers four semesters, starting with beginning instruction and proceeding to progressively advanced levels. Four main areas are outlined: sight-reading, technique, repertoire, and functional skills. The areas are not necessarily arranged in order of importance, but constitute a balanced program designed for progress.

FIRST SEMESTER

SIGHT-READING

Be able to read elementary compositions in a variety of keys and meters from the first portion of any beginning college piano text; the style will probably be single line melody, unison melody, or melody with simple accompaniment.

TECHNIQUE

General Considerations

Establish a good hand position.
Establish the basis for correct fingering.
Provide 5-finger (or other) exercises to aid finger coordination.
Explain and use legato and staccato touch.
Explain and use wrist motions for slurred grouping and longer phrases.
Explain balance of melody and accompaniment and work for the correct sound.

Scales

Practice 5-finger scales in all keys, major and minor.
(Optional) Practice tetrachord scales in all keys.

Chords

Play I, IV, and V chords in blocked style in all keys, major and minor.

Arpeggios

Play all major and minor root position triads hand-over-hand style.

Piano Literature

(For beginners, the first semester usually is a keyboard orientation period devoted to learning technical skills to enable the student to play the piano. It is, therefore, unrealistic to devote the majority of the class time to the learning and memorizing of a number of literature pieces such as Bach's *Minuet in G.*) In addition to such study pieces as Bartók's *Mikrokosmos, Vol. 1,* easy literature pieces (five to ten) may be studied and learned at the teacher's discretion such as those by Kabalevsky (*First Dance, A Little Joke,* etc.) and others by Bartók (easier selections from *The First Term at the Piano,* etc.). Literature studied should be analyzed in terms of form (AB, ABA, phrase structure, sequence patterns, etc.), chord structure, and stylistic features.

The music should be harmonically elementary enough for first semester students to comprehend (few, if any modulations).

Ensemble Literature

(Ensemble experience should be incorporated almost from the beginning. First experiences may be no more than having half the class play the right hand part, the other half play the left hand part.) In class, practice and perform some easy duets or easy multiple piano arrangements (see the materials list at the end of this chapter).

FUNCTIONAL SKILLS

Improvisation

Create simple melodies over ostinato basses showing a knowledge of period structure (repetition and contrast).

Complete "answer" phrases to the "questions" played by the instructor; the melodies may be harmonized with primary chords (I, IV, V, or V7).

Transposition

Transpose up or down a whole step (or more) selections from the first portion of any beginning piano text.

Harmonization

Harmonize simple melodies containing I and V chords, or I, IV, V chords, such as "Long, Long Ago," or "On Top of Old Smoky."

SECOND SEMESTER

SIGHT-READING

Demonstrate reading proficiency in easy compositions that require a variety of keyboard patterns such as shifts in hand positions, finger extensions and contractions, and crossing fingers. The compositions should be melody and accompaniment and two-voice style.

TECHNIQUE

General Considerations

Combine staccato and legato touch.

Provide continued finger exercises, now out of 5-finger positions: finger crossings, finger extensions and contractions, etc.

Scales

Play all major scales and harmonic minor scales one octave, hands together. Some scales may be learned two octaves, hand together (those beginning on the white keys).

Learn the chromatic scale fingering and play the scale one or two octaves.

(Optional) Learn the melodic minor scales.

Chords

Play triads of the scale.

Play triads and inversions (especially major, minor, and dominant seventh chords), in both blocked and broken forms.

Arpeggios

Play all major and minor triads and inversions hand-over-hand style.

REPERTOIRE

Piano Literature

Study and perform a minimum number of compositions comparable to the level of difficulty of *The Fifers* by Jean Dandrieu, easier *German Dances* by Haydn, some of the easier selections from Bartók's *Mikrokosmos, Vol. 2*, or some of the easier selections from the *Anna Magdelana Notebook* by Bach.

Ensemble Literature

Continue the study and performance of easy duets and multiple piano arrangements.

Study and perform ensemble music comparable to the level of difficulty of the easier selections from Cleveland Page's *Ensemble Music for Group Piano.*

FUNCTIONAL SKILLS

Improvisation

Create melodies employing both primary and secondary chords of the scale.

Transposition

Transpose a number of arranged tunes such as "My Bonnie," or "Polly Wolly Doodle," similar to the level of difficulty of the arrangements found in Bastien's *Beginning Piano for Adults,* pages 88 and 89.

Harmonization

Learn progressions such as I, ii6, I $^6_4$, V, I and harmonize melodies such as "The Battle Hymn of the Republic," or "America."

THIRD SEMESTER

SIGHT-READING

Continue reading progressively difficult compositions. Include easy vocal and instrumental score reading.

Read, in steady rhythm, music comparable to any of the material found in Deutsch's *For Sight Reading, Book 1.*

TECHNIQUE

General Considerations

Continue emphasis on fingering patterns and chord shapes; provide progressively difficult exercises containing a variety of patterns. Require more sophisticated performance of literature with appropriate balance of melody and accompaniment and dynamic shadings.

Scales

Continue practicing all major and harmonic minor scales two or more octaves hands together.

Practice some of the melodic minor scales two octaves hands together.

Chords

Play seventh chords of the scale in root position, both blocked and broken style.

Play dominant seventh and diminished seventh chords in a variety of ways: blocked, broken, and arpeggio style.

Arpeggios

Play root position chords hands separately two or more octaves; include major, minor, augmented, diminished seventh, and dominant seventh chord arpeggios.

REPERTOIRE

Piano Literature

Begin early level intermediate piano literature comparable to the difficulty of *Arabesque* and *Ballade* by Burgmüller, *Toccatina* by Kabalevsky, or easy sonatinas such as *Sonatina, Opus 157, No. 1* by Fritz Spindler.

Ensemble Literature

Continue duets, multiple piano arrangements and introduce some

easy two piano music such as compositions found in *Ensemble Music for Group Piano* by James Lyke.
Accompany individual members of the piano class in vocal and instrumental solos selected from early grade collections used in public school music books.

FUNCTIONAL SKILLS

Improvisation

Play melodies and harmonic patterns in a variety of phrase structures to include binary and ternary forms. The harmony should include modulations to the dominant and sub-dominant keys.

Transposition

Transpose up or down either a half or whole step music comparable to the difficulty of some of the songs, hymns, and excerpts from easier piano literature found in Winifred Chastek's *Keyboard Skills.*

Harmonization

Use secondary dominants and modulate to closely related keys (V of V, and V of IV mostly). Harmonize such melodies as "Jingle Bells," "Home on the Range," "All Through the Night," etc.

FOURTH SEMESTER

SIGHT-READING

Demonstrate proficiency in reading accompaniments such as those found in presently used school texts.
Be able to read one or more parts of choral or instrumental literature.

TECHNIQUE

General Considerations

Require more fluency in tempos of performed works.
Continue to perfect the performance of scales, chords, and arpeggios.
(Optional) Hanon, Czerny, or other related technical studies may be given at the teacher's discretion.

REPERTOIRE

Piano Literature

Study and perform intermediate piano literature comparable to the difficulty of sonatinas by Clementi and Kuhlau.

Ensemble Literature

Continue duets, multiple piano arrangements and two piano compositions.

Accompany members of the piano class in vocal and instrumental solos.

FUNCTIONAL SKILLS

Improvisation

Continue creating short pieces that modulate to closely related keys.

Transposition

Practice transposing easier arrangements of songs in public school music texts.

Harmonization

Continue harmonizing melodies that employ modulations.
Harmonize major scales with the following suggested progressions:
Ascending: I, V, I, V^4_3, I_6, IV, V7, I; Descending I, iii, IV, I_6, ii_6, I^6_4, V7, I.

Sample Piano Proficiency Examination

Although piano minor requirements vary from school to school regarding the proficiency level for Bachelor of Music and Bachelor of Music Education (vocal or instrumental) majors, the following sample examination is offered as a general guide for all secondary piano students.

PROFICIENCY EXAMINATION REQUIREMENTS FOR THE PIANO MINOR

(To be given at the end of the Sophomore year)

PURPOSE: To administer a composite examination of the keyboard requirements set for all piano minors as stipulated by the piano faculty. The exam will be of fifteen minutes duration and will cover examples from the specific items listed below. Failure to pass the proficiency exam means that the student must continue to take the exam in succeeding semesters until it is passed.

KEYBOARD SKILLS: The student will be expected to demonstrate proficiencies in the areas of reading, performance, technique, and related functional skills. The following items are considered minimal levels.

REQUIREMENTS:

1. *Sight-Reading Ability*
   a. Works of comparable difficulty:

   Bartók, Béla *Mikrokosmos, Vol. 2* Boosey & Hawkes
   Bastien, James and Jane Smisor Bastien *Beginning Piano for Adults* (selected pages from Units 12, 13, and Section IV) GWM Co.
   Deutsch, Leonhard *For Sight Reading* Heritage

Johnson, Thomas *Hands Together* Hinrichsen/Peters
Stevens, Everett *Six Modal Miniatures* Oliver Ditson

b. An accompaniment to a composition from the student's Major instrument (instrumental or vocal accompaniment).

2. *Performance Level (memory optional)*
   a. A solo.
   Repertoire of comparable difficulty:

Bach, J. S. *Little Preludes* Alfred Music Co., others
Bastien, James (ed.) *Piano Literature for the Intermediate Grades* GWM Co.
Clementi, Muzio *Sonatinas*
Kuhlau, Friedrich *Sonatinas* Schirmer, others
Schumann, Robert *Album for the Young* Alfred Music Co., others

b. Two patriotic songs: "America," and "The Star Spangled Banner." Music may be used if necessary.

3. *Technique*
   a. Scales
   The student will demonstrate good fingerings for all major and minor scales, two octaves, in parallel motion.

   b. Chords
   The student will demonstrate a knowledge of triads of the scale, and major, minor, diminished, augmented triads. Knowledge of triads and inversions will be demonstrated. The following seventh chords will be played: major, minor, half-diminished, diminished, and dominant seventh chords.

   c. Arpeggios
   Major, minor, diminished seventh, and dominant seventh arpeggios will be played either with one hand alone or two hands together for two octaves.

4. *Functional Skills*
   a. Accompaniment improvisations of comparable difficulty:

Beginning Piano for Adults (Units 14 & 15) Bastien GWM Co.
Popular lead sheets such as "Love is Blue," etc.
Public School Songs Texts such as *The American Singer,* American Book Co; *Making Music Your Own,* Silver Burdett, etc.

   b. Transposition
   The student will transpose a simple accompaniment or song at sight.

   c. Chord Progressions
   The student will play the progressions I, IV, I_4^6, V7, I in all major and minor keys, and I, VI, IV, ii, I_4^6, V7, I in all major keys.

BRIEF SURVEY OF CLASS PIANO TEXTS AND SUPPLEMENTARY MATERIALS

During the past decade an abundance of class materials has been produced. Texts, ensemble collections, and multiple piano arrangements are now available which are specifically written for the piano class. Because many of these materials have been published recently, a general survey is provided to give an indication of the purpose of the publication as well as the level for which it was written.

TEXTS

Bastien, James and Jane S. Bastien Beginning Piano for Adults Park Ridge, Illinois: General Words and Music Co., (1968)

Designed primarily for students at the college level, either music major (piano minor) or non-music major, this 212 page volume is comprised of four main sections. Section I, *Pre-reading,* is written in pre-staffed notation and is designed for keyboard orientation, and incorporates all twelve major 5-finger patterns, tonic chords, and dominant seventh chords. Section II, *Reading,* contains graded reading material and a variety of exercises for pianistic development. Section III, *Functional Piano,* contains a variety of "lead-sheet" melodies for harmonic improvisation. Section IV, *Piano Literature, Technique and Style,* is a continuation of the first two sections and provides an abundant selection of original piano literature and related exercises. The book is flexible and may be used for a two year period with supplement.

Duckworth, Guy Keyboard Musicianship New York: The Free Press/Macmillan Co., (1970)

Designed primarily for music majors (piano minors), this 261 page volume offers an innovative, contemporary approach to teaching class piano. Based largely on folk material, the compositions are set in a variety of keys and modes. Special emphasis is given to such functional skills as playing by ear, improvising, transposing, and creating traditional and contemporary homophonic and polyphonic accompaniments. Because of the improvisatory emphasis, a great deal of teacher-student creativity is essential in the correct presentation of the material. This book bears the same title as an earlier publication by Elisabeth Hartline and James Lyke which is unnecessarily confusing.

Foxley, William M. and Barbara R. Lowe Piano Study Guide and Workbook Provo, Utah: Brigham Young University Press, (1975)

This comprehensive volume (310 pages) provides the student with valuable insights into theory, and numerous written exercises are included. Beginning music, single-line melodies for harmonization, some duets, and works at varying grade levels by master composers are also included. A portion of the book contains interesting contemporary music based on modes, and various contemporary devices.

Geissmar, Else Invitation to Music, Second Edition, Revised Kenmore, Wash.: Puget Music Publications, Inc., (1972)

Designed for beginners this sixty-four page book may be used for music majors or non-music majors. Materials include: 5-finger melodies in many keys; transposition; tetrachords; key signatures; I, IV, V7 chords; inversions of chords; intervals; major scales; and some modal scales. Arranged folk music and easy music by well-known composers comprise the main study materials. Some duets are included.

Leach, John R. Functional Piano for the Teacher Englewood Cliffs, N.J.: Prentice-Hall, Inc., (1968)

Designed as a text to prepare the undergraduate student in elementary school music, this 163 page volume is comprised mainly of melodies with simple accompaniment. Most of the tunes are selected from folk repertoire and from traditional melodies of many nationalities.

Lowder, Jerry Basic Piano Skills Worthington, Ohio: Charles A. Jones Publishing Co. (Wadsworth Publishing Co.), (1975)

This 198 page volume is designed primarily for college music majors to develop skills in sightreading, transposition, harmonization, improvisation, and analysis. The book is divided into seven chapters: (1) Keyboard orientation, (2) Key signatures, intervals, scales, (3) Triads, chords, I-V7-I chord progression, (4) Harmonization of melodies, (5) Improvisation, (6) Four-voice texture, (7) Patriotic songs and piano repertoire. Numerous folk tunes are used. The text is clear and informative.

Lyke, James, Elisabeth Hartline, and Ron Elliston Keyboard Musicianship, Books 1 & 2 Champaign, Illinois: Stipes Publishing Co., (1974)

Book 1 is an outgrowth of an earlier publication (1964) by Elisabeth Hartline. This present 200 page volume has been expanded into an effective, comprehensive book. Realistic first year goals for beginning class piano students are set by the authors in the areas of performance, technique, sight-reading, improvisation, and keyboard harmony. Some ensemble music is included. *Book 2* is designed for second year class use. This 243 page volume is divded into five main sections: Section One is devoted to melodies for harmonization with various chord patterns (secondary dominants, substitute chords, etc.); Section Two consists of patriotic songs, hymns, Christmas music, and community songs for study and transposition; Section Three is devoted to various technical drills; Section Four consists of various improvisatory studies, many of which are jazz patterns; Section Five is comprised of piano literature from all periods. This substantial volume contains a wealth of developmental materials more than sufficient for sophomore piano minor requirements.

Mach, Elyse Contemporary Class Piano New York: Harcourt Brace Jovanovich, Inc., (1976)

Designed for college students this 250 page volume contains six units: (1) Keyboard basics, (2) Using the 5-finger pattern, (3) Playing pieces with easy accompaniments, (4) Exploring tonality and atonality, (5) Using chord symbols with folk and popular melodies, and (6) Twenty-five piano classics. Some ensemble material is included. The text is clear and informative.

McLain, Margaret Starr Class Piano Bloomington: Indiana University Press, (1974)

Designed as a utilitarian multi-purpose course for music majors (piano minors), this 284 page volume incorporates basic keyboard skills, improvisation, and a panoramic view of theory and keyboard harmony. Voluminous text dominates the book and tends to take precedence over the actual playing presentations. However, a great deal of useful information is imparted in this lengthy volume, especially in the area of theory.

Pace, Robert Piano for Classroom Music, 2nd Edition Englewood Cliffs, N.J.: Prentice-Hall, Inc., (1971)

Basic musical components for the elementary classroom teacher are systematically presented in this new edition. The 123 page book includes a comprehensive view of melody and harmony in all keys, creative work, theoretical and formal structures, and a wide selection of arranged tunes. This new edition of the 1956 original uses larger, readable print.

Page, Cleveland The Laboratory Piano Course, Books 1 & 2 New York: Harper & Row, (1975, 1976)

Designed for class instruction, *Book 1* (132 pages) consists mainly of ensemble material for beginners (piano minors). The book is divided into four parts: Part One – pentachords in two-part texture; Part Two – extended position, position changes in two-part texture; Part Three – scales, arpeggios, triads, pedal (two- and three-part texture); Part Four – more difficult rhythms, greater independence of hands in two-, three-, and four-part texture. The music is primarily arranged folk songs from many countries, spirituals, and some pieces by master composers. *Book 2* is designed for second year piano classes and contains primarily piano literature by master composers with emphasis on perfecting performance capabilities. An instructor's manual is available for each book.

Robinson, Helene Basic Piano for Adults Belmont, Calif.: Wadsworth Publishing Co., Inc., (1964)

Included in this 108 page volume are pieces for reading and playing, exercises for an acquisition of basic skills, some explanation of fundamentals of music theory and structure, and some written exercises. Designed for beginners, music or non-music majors, the book begins with rote 5-finger pieces. However, the material becomes rapidly more difficult. Much of the literature in the last part of the book is at the intermediate level (excerpt from Bartók's *Evening in the Country,* Schubert's *Waltz in B-flat*, etc.). The text throughout is informative and clearly stated.

___________. Intermediate Piano for Adults, Volumes 1 & 2 Belmont, Calif.: Wadsworth Publishing Co., Inc., (1970)

An abundance of excellent materials is provided in these two books, suitable for general second year use. Materials include: four-period intermediate level repertoire, keyboard harmony exercises, developmental studies using a variety of functional skills, ensemble literature, and technique drills.

___________. Piano Skills for Everyday Belmont, Calif.: Wadsworth Publishing Co., Inc., (1977)

This book is designed primarily for music majors who are not piano majors. Emphasis is on the development of pianistic techniques, musical playing, and functional skills – transposing, harmonizing, improvising, reading vocal and instrumental scores of two to four lines, contemporary idioms, and accompaniments. Sight reading develops sequentially at the piano, as basic vocabulary patterns are presented, used, and reviewed.

Sheftel, Paul Exploring Music Fundamentals New York: Holt, Rinehart and Winston, Inc., (1970)

This 263 page volume is cast in a contemporary spirit and is primarily concerned with the development of sight-reading skills; however, some functional skills are included. The author has relied solely on piano arrangements of songs and folk songs; no standard piano literature is included. The collection of folk materials has been selected from the series, *Exploring Music*, by the same publisher. Thorough explanation about elements of music such as rhythm, scales, tempo, chords, and other general musical information, make this an attractive collection of fresh material for the education oriented music student.

Squire, Russel N., and Virginia R. Mountney Class Piano for Adult Beginners, 2nd Edition Englewood Cliffs, N. J.: Prentice-Hall, Inc., (1971)

Comprised of standard piano compositions, excerpts from larger piano works, technical studies, folk melodies, and ensemble literature, this 173 page volume provides ample material for at least one year of study. Key selection throughout the book is limited primarily to C,G,F. The progression of advancement is rapid, and the materials from page 50 on are immediately more difficult.

Starr, William and Constance Starr Basic Piano Technique for the Classroom Teacher

Patterned in simple melody-accompaniment song style, this 122 page volume adequately develops function skills for the classroom teacher. Five-finger positions mostly in C,G,F comprise elements for a basic beginning. Chording throughout is limited primarily to I, IV, and V. Some four-part playing is included.

Vernazza, Marcelle and Leonora J. Young Basic Materials for the Piano Student, 2nd Edition Dubuque, Iowa: Wm. C. Brown Co., (1972)

This present edition has been expanded to 176 pages. The book contains a variety of keyboard materials designed as an aid to elementary theory classes, as an enrichment for students studying more than one instrument, and as a special study for advanced pianists whose previous instruction has been limited to keyboard literature. Scales, modes, arpeggios, keyboard harmony, "lead-sheet" melodies and arranged literature comprise the main features of the book.

Zimmerman, Alex, Russell Hayton, and Dorothy Priesing Basic Piano for the College Student Dubuque, Iowa: Wm. C. Brown Co., (1969)

Designed as a college text to assist in improving the proficiency of music students preparing to become school music teachers, this 146 page volume is divided into six playing sections and includes the following materials: Section II, Techniques; Section III, Keyboard Harmony; Section VII, Ensembles. A great deal of emphasis is given to keyboard harmony and functional playing. The authors state in the preface that this volume is designed for the first year of college piano study, and taken literally, the material on the whole appears to be extraordinarily difficult for one year of study. Numerous keyboard skills are assumed by the authors: notation of both clefs is immediately used without explanation; four-part harmony and figured bass is used early in the book without explanation; various keys and key signatures are used without any explanation; and transposition is suggested without explanation. It must be assumed that the instructor would explain these various musical aspects. The progression of the difficulty of material is questionable, and many of the arrangements are pianistically awkward. However, many excellent features appear in this book such as four-part open score reading, and a nice collection of literature, especially the chorale-style pieces in Section V.

SUPPLEMENTARY BOOKS

Agay, Denes (ed.) Easy Classics to Moderns (Volume 17, Music for Millions Series.) New York: Consolidated Music Publishers, Inc. (1967)

This well-edited volume contains numerous elementary to early intermediate compositions by composers from four eras of music.

Anthony, George Walter (ed.) Easy Keyboard Music: Purcell to Shostakovich (Focus on Music, No. 4) Bryn Mawr, Penn.: Theodore Presser Co., (1967)

This volume contains many less known compositions suitable for reading and study at about late first year or second year level.

Bartók, Béla Mikrokosmos, Volumes 1-3 New York: Boosey and Hawkes, (1940).

Written mostly in 5-finger positions, *Volume 1* contains numerous modal melodies suitable for first year reading. *Volumes 2* and *3* consist of attractive compositions utilizing twentieth century compositional devices at about late first year and second year levels.

Bastien, James (ed.) Czerny and Hanon Park Ridge, Illinois: General Words and Music Co., (1970)

Twenty of the easier Czerny studies and the first twenty Hanon exercises comprise this volume. This collection is useful for students interested in becoming technically proficient. The studies are about second year level.

____________. Piano Literature for the Intermediate Grades (Volume 3) Park Ridge, Illinois: General Words and Music Co., (1968)

A wide style variety of piano literature is contained in this collection. Compositions such as Kabalevsky's *Toccatina*, sonatinas by Kuhlau and Clementi, and three Bach inventions make this a useful second year volume.

Bastien, James Sight Reading, Levels 1-4 San Diego: Kjos West, (1976)

These four thirty-two page books are equally useful for children or adults. Materials consist of short four- to eight-measure reading studies in various keys. Included are reading studies incorporating scale melodies, chords, inversions, pedal, hand position shifts, and other keyboard hand skills.

Bastien, Jane Smisor Pop, Rock 'n Blues, Books 2 & 3 Park Ridge, Illinois: General Words and Music Co., (1971)

Although designed for younger students, these books are also useful for supplementary assignment for piano minor classes. *Book 2* is easily accessible for first year students; *Book 3* is more difficult, about second year level.

Bishop, Dorothy Chords in Action New York: Carl Fischer, Inc., 1956

The book develops an understanding of chords which are applied to harmonizing melodies at the keyboard. Mostly folk melodies are used. The book is written for training classroom teachers, piano minors, keyboard theory classes, or may be used as supplementary functional material for the private student.

____________. A Folk Holiday (Piano Duets) New York: Carl Fischer, Inc., (1959)

Consisting of fourteen duets on folk songs and dances, this collection is useful for ensemble assignments of medium difficulty (about late first year or early second year level). Folk songs such as "Greensleeves," "Minka," and "Night Herding Song" are appealing to piano minors.

Brimhall, John Instant Chord Solos, Issues 1 & 2 Miami: Charles Hansen, (1976)

These two books contain lead-line melodies for you-do-it bass improvisations. The chords are shown on keyboards in the positions to be used.

Brubeck, Dave Themes from Eurasia Delaware Water Gap, Penn.: Shawnee Press, Inc., (1970)

Mostly second year level, this attractive collection of original pieces is immediately appealing to class piano students. Chord symbols are provided and are useful if students want to form a small combo (guitar, bass, and drums).

Burns, Betty, and Jackie Graham You Do It, Jazz, Rock, Pop, and Blues, Books 1-7 Park Ridge, Illinois: General Words and Music Co., (1972)

The single line melodies in these seven books provide an opportunity for harmonization in a variety of styles and for developing functional skills.

Chastek, Winifred Keyboard Skills Belmont, California: Wadsworth Publishing Co., Inc., (1967)

Designed for general keyboard lab classes, this 215 page text develops four important functional skills: sight-reading, transposition, harmonization, and improvisation. Although not a beginning text, the book is suitable for mid-first year through second year assignment.

(collection) 1001 Jumbo Song Book Miami: Charles Hansen

This giant "fake book" contains almost everyone's favorite song. Great material for improvising.

Contemporary Collection No. 1 Edited by Goldstein-Kern-Larimer-Ross-Weiss Evanston, Illinois: Summy-Birchard Co., (1963)

This easy first year collection contains excellent material by today's leading composers.

Deutsch, Leonhard For Sight Reading, Book 1 New York: Heritage Music Publishers, (1950)

Two-voice melodies and a variety of other styles comprise this volume devoted to developing reading skills.

Diemer, Emma Lou Sound Pictures New York: Boosey & Hawkes, (1971)

This attractive collection of contemporary styles is immediately appealing and is suitable for either first or second year assignment.

Dring, Madeline Twelve Pieces in the Form of Studies New York: Marks Music Corp., (1966)

This collection contains melodic etudes at about early intermediate level suitable for better than average students who need more demanding material. About second year level.

Finney, Ross Lee 32 Piano Games New York: C.F. Peters Corp., (1969)

The experimental pieces in this collection are appealing to college piano minors because of their use of such contemporary devices as tone clusters, free rhythms, atonal melodies, etc. The pieces are more for fun than for serious study pieces. First or second year levels.

Frackenpohl, Arthur Harmonization at the Piano, 2nd Edition Dubuque, Iowa: Wm. C. Brown, Co., (1970)

This volume contains numerous materials for assignments in harmonization and improvisation at about the second year level.

Gordon, Louis Introduction to the Art of Rock Melville, New York: Belwin-Mills Publishing Corp., (1971)

The original pieces in this volume introduce the student to various styles of rock music. About second year level.

____________. Jazz for Junior New York: Edward B. Marks Music Corp., (1964)

Excellent jazz styles are featured in this little volume on about second year level.

____________. Junior Jazz New York: Edward B. Marks Music Corp., (1961)

Easier than the preceding book, this volume is suitable for first year assignment.

Hopkins, Antony For Talented Beginners, Books 1 & 2 London: Oxford University Press, (1963)

Because of the appropriate title, these two books are effective supplementary reading collections. *Book 1* is suitable for first year students; *Book 2* is second year level.

Kern, Alice Harmonization-Transposition at the Keyboard Evanston, Illinois: Summy-Birchard Co., (1963)

Numerous folk materials provided the basis for functional harmonizations in this volume. Only a few hints are given (no chord symbols) to the student who must create his own basses for the melodies.

Lewis, Pat A Rockin' Little Tale Lee Roberts, Inc./Schirmer, (1971)

Four little variations are written on a simple rock tune. The student is asked to improvise portions of some of the variations. The music is very easy, first year level.

____________. Rock Lisa Lee Roberts, Inc./Schirmer, (1971)

The tune "Lisa Jane" is set in rock style. Blues patterns and rock rhythms are explained and used. The music is easy, first year level.

Lyke, James (ed.) Ensemble Music for Group Piano, Books 1 & 2, 3rd Edition Revised Champaign, Illinois: Stipes Publishing Co., (1976)

Although much of the material is quite difficult for class piano, some of the duets and two piano selections are accessible for good second year students.

Mack, Glenn Adventures in Improvisation at the Keyboard Evanston, Illinois: Summy-Birchard, (1970)

Basic materials are explained and used as examples for free improvisation. Materials include improvising on white and black keys, harmonizing melodies, improvising in dance rhythms, and others. The book may be used for either first or second year classes.

____________. Adventures in Modes and Keys Evanston, Illinois: Summy-Birchard, (1973)

The short mostly two-line reading pieces incorporate modes, various scales, and polytonality. Explanations about specific musical or compositional devices precede each piece. The music is about intermediate level and can be used for second year classes.

Metis, Frank Rock Modes and Moods New York: Marks Music Corp., (1970)

Metis has evidenced an affinity for the pop scene in this first-rate collection of seven solos. The first four introductory pages explain modality used in rock music and also explain such divergent rock styles as Hard Rock, Acid Rock, Psychedelic Rock, Folk Rock, and Soul Music. Most of the pieces in the collection are difficult, but both "Blues Explosion" and "Happy to be Home" are accessible to second year students.

Page, Cleveland L. Ensemble Music for Group Piano Cincinnati: Canyon Press, Inc., (1970)

This unique 104 page collection contains numerous multi-piano experiences. Directions are provided for combinations, improvisations, and musical considerations. The book begins at the first year level and becomes progressively more difficult.

Palmer, Willard A. Baroque Folk New York: Alfred Music Co., Inc., (1969)

This book provides familiar melodies arranged in such baroque styles as two-part inventions, suites, gavotte, passacaglia, etc. The level of difficulty is about second year.

Peltz, William Basic Keyboard Skills, 2nd Edition Revised by Richard D. Osborne Boston: Allyn and Bacon, Inc., (1968)

The purpose of the book is to provide functional keyboard studies and keyboard harmony drills. The book is not a beginning text and is better suited for second year students.

Swain, Alan Four-Way Keyboard System, Books 1-3 Glenview, Illinois: Creative Music, (1969)

An interesting eye-ear-hand approach to playing jazz at the piano is developed in these books through the use of specific voicing of seventh, ninth, eleventh, and thirteenth chords. Attractive sounds are achieved.

Zeitlin, Poldi, and David Goldberger (eds.). Russian Music, Books 1-6 New York: MCA Music, (1967)

These books are useful for supplementary reading and study assignments. *Book 1* is first year level; succeeding books become progressively more difficult.

MULTIPLE PIANO PUBLICATIONS

Balkin, Alfred Six for Eight (four parts), Piano Quartette Series Park Ridge, Illinois: General Words and Music Co., (1971)

Six short compositions for four pianos, eight hands are contained in this folio. Several compositions are jazz oriented. Directions for performance, combinations, and improvisation are given in the preface. About first year level.

Bastien, Jane Smisor Christmas Carols for Multiple Pianos (four parts) Park Ridge, Illinois: General Words and Music Co., (1971)

The four parts are bass, melody, harmony, and fill-in. The arrangements may be played on four individual pianos or two pianos, eight hands. The four carols contained in this collection are easy, first year level.

Clark, Mary Elizabeth Folk 1 (three and six parts) Carlstadt, N.J.: Lewis Music Publishing Co., Inc., (1971)

Consisting of six arranged folk songs for keyboard ensemble classes, these easy first year arrangements are a welcome addition to the growing repertoire of class piano materials. The collection includes trio and sextet arrangements of favorites such as "The Lonesome Road" and "Charlie is My Darling."

____________. Kum Ba Ya and Scarborough Fair (six parts) Carlstadt, N.J.: Lewis Music Publishing Co., Inc., (1971)

These two sextet arrangements come together in a set which includes individual parts and full score. The arrangements are easy enough for a good first year class or may serve as remedial reading for second year. The arrangements incorporate a variety of keys and modes.

____________. Sweetly Sings the Donkey (four parts) Boulder, Colorado: Myklas Press, (1975)

Arranged as a round, this folk song can be used in the first year or as supplementary reading for second year students.

DePue, Wallace 16 Pawns (four parts), Piano Quartette Series Park Ridge, Illinois: General Words and Music Co., (1971)

This contemporary ensemble piece uses freely used accidentals, 5/4 meter, and syncopated rhythms effectively. Written on a difficult level, it may be given to an advanced piano class.

Gunther, Phyllis Chester (four parts) Melville, New York: Belwin-Mills, (1975)

William Billings' (1764-1800) *Chester* is arranged for easy reading, about first year level.

____________. Early American Suite (four parts) Melville, New York: Belwin-Mills, (1975)

This arrangement of James Hewitt's (1770-1827) Suite has three movements: "Washington March," "Fitzjames," and "Rondo." The music is lively, arranged for about late first year classes or as supplementary reading for second year students.

____________. Patriotic Medley (four parts) Melville, New York: Belwin-Mills, (1975)

The medley consists of the "Battle Hymn of the Republic," "Yankee Doodle," and "America the Beautiful." Arranged for good late first year classes or as supplementary reading for second year students.

Lucktenberg, George Bach for Piano Ensemble (four parts) Melville, New York: Belwin-Mills, (1971)

The collection consists of seven pieces from the *Anna Magdalena Notebook* arranged for multiple ensemble keyboard groups. The arrangements may be performed with from two to four pianists at two pianos, or on four pianos, one player to a part. The compositions are tastefully arranged for either late first year classes or as supplementary reading for second year students.

Metis, Frank Africasian Affair (four parts) Pittsburgh: Volkwein Bros., Inc., (1970)

This arrangement and those succeeding are designed for an assemblage of two, three, or four keyboard instruments; for class use, each of four students may have his own part. The four parts are rhythm, melody, background, and fill-in. The instructions for other combinations, either by the use of tape recorders or the combination of less than four players, are given in the preface of each score. The level of *Africasian Affair* is difficult and is advisable only for advanced piano classes.

____________. Easy Pop/Rock Sketches (four parts) New York: Marks Music Corp., (1970)

This little collection of nine eight-bar tunelets is great for experiencing contemporary pop sounds at an easy level, about late first year.

____________. Easy Together (four parts) New York: Marks Music Corp., (1970)

The arrangements in this collection are similar to *Easy Pop/Rock Sketches*, but they are a little longer and slightly more difficult, about second year level.

____________. Happiness Hill (four parts) Pittsburgh: Volkwein Bros., Inc., (1970)

This arranged original solo is of medium difficulty, about first year level.

____________. Ode to Joy (four parts) New York: Marks Music Corp., (1970)

This arrangement on the famous theme from Beethoven's *Ninth Symphony* is about second year level.

____________. Parisian Polka (four parts) Pittsburgh: Volkwein Bros., Inc., (1970)

Second year level.

____________. Scarborough Fair (four parts) New York: Marks Music Corp., (1970)

Late first or second year level.

____________. Wicked World Waltz (four parts) Pittsburgh: Volkwein Bros., Inc., (1970)

Difficult, for advanced piano classes.

____________. You're a Grand Old Flag (four parts) New York: Marks Music Corp., (1970)

Late first year or second year level.

Page, Cleveland L. Ensemble Music for Group Piano Cincinnati: Canyon Press Inc., (1970)

See above, "supplementary books."

Vandall, Robert **Amazing Grace (6 parts), Cindy (6 parts), Five Will Get You Four (5 parts), Greensleeves (4 parts), Scarborough Fair (6 parts), Shenandoah (6 parts), Silent Night (5 parts), Sleep, Baby, Sleep (6 parts), Theme and Six Variations on "Skip to My Lou" (6 parts)** **Park Ridge, Illinois: General Words and Music Co., (1977)**

Published separately, these piano ensembles are flexible and may be played by one person on a part (as indicated in the fingering) for first year students, or by one person playing more than one part for students with more ability. The part writing is imaginative and intricate making full sounding ensembles out of accessible material. The only original piece is *Five Will Get You Four*; the others are arrangements of well-known tunes.

FOR DISCUSSION AND ASSIGNMENT

1. What is the consensus at your school regarding class instruction? Is it enthusiastically endorsed as an effective means of teaching piano minors, or are private lessons favored? What is your view?
2. If class instruction is offered for piano minors, observe several of the sessions and report on the following: number of each section; type of equipment used; the type of instruction offered (repertoire, technique, functional skills, etc.); and the effectiveness of the instructor.

FOR FURTHER READING

BOOKS

Lyke, James. "An Investigation of Class Piano Programs in the Six State Universities and Recommendations for Their Improvements," (unpublished doctoral dissertation), Northern Colorado University, 1968.

Mehr, Norman. *Group Piano Teaching.* Evanston, Illinois: Summy-Birchard Co., 1965. From his vast background in the field, Mr. Mehr discusses general features of group teaching and offers directions for presentation of rote songs, rhythm, harmony and analysis of form in the class situation. The information presented in the book may be applied to all levels of group instruction.

Rast, Lawrence R. "A Survey and Evaluation of Piano Requirements for Students Enrolled in Programs of Teacher-Training in Elementary Education at Selected Colleges and Universities in the State of Illinois," (unpublished doctoral dissertation), Northwestern University, Evanston, Illinois, 1964.

Richards, William Henry. "Trends of Piano Class Instruction 1815-1962," (unpublished doctoral dissertation), University of Kansas City, 1962.

Robinson, Helene, and Richard L. Jarvis, eds. *Teaching Piano in Classroom and Studio.* Washington: Music Educators National Conference, 1967. Consisting of a collection of nineteen outstanding articles by nationally known music educators, this 176 page volume is a valuable reference source. The book stresses class teaching and creative theory. Chapter XIX deals specifically with college piano classes.

ARTICLES[13]

Buchanan, Gillian. "Skills of Piano Performance in the Preparation of Music Educators," *Journal of Research in Music Education,* Vol. XII (Summer, 1964).

Lancaster, E. L. "Selecting Material for Piano Classes," (two parts), *Clavier,* Vol. XVI, Nos. 3 and 4 (March and April, 1977).

Lyke, James B. "What Should Our Piano Minors Study?" *Music Educators Journal,* Vol. 56, No. 4 (December, 1969).

Owens, Janet Russell. "Piano or Musicianship?" *Clavier,* Vol. VI, No. 8 (November, 1967).

Rast, Lawrence. "Functional Piano for Tomorrow's Educators," *Music Journal,* Vol. XXVI, No. 2 (February, 1968).

Vernazza, Marcelle. "Basic Piano Instructions in the College," *American Music Teacher,* Vol. XVI, No. 6 (June-July, 1967).

[13]Only a few articles are suggested here from the many available. As an example of numerous articles on the subject, one magazine (*Clavier*, Vol. X, No. 1, January, 1971) lists an index of articles on group teaching numbering forty-eight.

11 Keeping Abreast of New Publications

Today numerous new piano publications bombard teachers who become deluged with the onslaught. Methods, teaching pieces, suites, collections, editions, arrangements, exercises, theory materials, and pop music are continually jumping off the presses of numerous publishers (domestic and foreign) and hitting the market like a *blitzkrieg.* From this massive outpouring of materials, how can the teacher become knowledgeable about new publications?

Many teachers don't, they merely play ostrich, hiding their heads from new materials, and use the tried and true. This will give them a feeling of safety and comfort, but it will not broaden their range and scope. Doctors, accountants, and lawyers must keep apprised of new happenings, so too must the piano teacher.

There are several main sources available to the teacher which will assist in providing information about new materials:

1. reviews in music journals
2. publishers' ads in music journals
3. piano workshops
4. music store(s)
5. teacher organization reference copies
6. publishers' catalogs

Teaching without a music journal is like driving a car without a road map. Every profession has a journal, and music is no exception. A subscription to *Clavier, The Piano Quarterly,* the *Robert Dumm Piano Review,* or others will provide valuable information about new music through reviews. Almost all new piano music is reviewed by George Anson in Clavier, especially elementary teaching materials which are not covered as well in other journals. In addition to magazine subscriptions, some new music is reviewed in journals sent to members of organizations such as the Music Teachers National Association (the *American Music Teacher* magazine) and the National Guild of Piano Teachers *(Guild Notes).* However, the reviews in these two journals usually are limited in the number of materials reviewed.

Of course music must be heard, and only limited knowledge about a piece can be given in a review. Nevertheless, valuable general information can be gained through a review. From a review one usually can gain knowledge about grading, the style, and possibly the price, along with additional positive or negative remarks. A composer whose music you like will catch your eye from a review, and you will be encouraged to try his latest effort. Or a new composer's work will be extolled by the reviewer, and you will be moved out of curiosity to try it. Reading reviews is a must, for without this effort, new works will not be brought to your attention.

Publishers place ads of their new issues in music journals. Frequently a special introductory price is offered to teachers to entice them to purchase new music at a discount. Although you are buying a product unseen and unheard, you can rely somewhat on composers of merit and feel confident that their new work will have some of the qualities you liked in previous publications.

Piano workshops provide an excellent opportunity to become familiar with new music. Sometimes workshops are specifically designed to present new music by all publishers, such as the Schmitt Clinic (Minneapolis) and the Midwest Keyboard Festival (Chicago). Both these clinics take place in the summer over several days, and new music is performed and recommended.

Often colleges sponsor workshops in which one or more clinicians will discuss various aspects of teaching and playing, and frequently a session will be given on new music. Sometimes those workshops are offered for credit.

Numerous music stores sponsor workshops (usually free) to area teachers. These are usually given by a composer introducing his new materials. Especially new beginning teaching methods are introduced to a community in this manner. A few hours spent with a composer will acquaint you with numerous materials of which some were probably unfamiliar. In addition to learning about this composer's new music, if you are teaching some of his works, you will have an opportunity to ask questions you might have regarding those works. To be informed of area workshops sponsored by music stores, make sure your name is on their mailing lists. If you move to a new town, give your name and address to the local music stores so you will be informed about workshops.

Most of the larger music stores subscribe to new issues from the various publishers. Often these stores have a new issue file for you to browse through. In addition, some music stores have news letters or catalogs which feature new issues. Unfortunately, the smaller store often is limited financially from receiving new publications from many publishers, and teachers in these communities are handicapped in learning about new music from their music store. If this is the case, a periodic trip to a larger city which has a large music store would be advantageous.

Many local teacher organizations are encouraging publishers to send them their new publications to be kept on file for their members to survey. Even if these materials must be purchased, the expense is kept to a minimum by assessing members a small yearly fee. The publications may be stored in a library, club room, or a teacher's house. The works can be graded and filed and can serve as a most useful source of becoming acquainted with new music by actual examination of the music. In addition, if a college nearby has a piano pedagogy program, you might be able to survey their reference materials.

All publishers have catalogs. By writing to each publisher you can receive the latest one in which attention usually is called to new works. These catalogs are an excellent source of information and are too often not utilized by teachers.

From the foregoing it can be surmised that it is not too difficult to keep up with new materials if some effort is put forth. It is the teacher's responsibility to learn about new materials and to try some of them. Trying a new method or a new teaching piece or collection will add a new dimension to your teaching and will help to keep you current with new publications.

Contests and Festivals for the Young Pianist

12

by Charles Braswell

Charles Braswell received his training in piano from North Texas State University and the American Conservatory of Music, Chicago. He received his training in music therapy from the University of Kansas and the Menninger Clinic. Mr. Braswell is the immediate past-president of the National Association for Music Therapy and an associate editor of the *Journal of Music Therapy*. He is a member of the Board of Directors, New Orleans Music Teacher's Association, and a member of the Board of Examiners for music credit, State of Louisiana. Mr. Braswell is Professor of Piano and Chairman of the Department of Music Therapy at Loyola University, New Orleans.

Each year thousands of young American pianists are evaluated, congratulated and, occasionally, chastised. The name of the musical game may be called a contest, student rally, audition, examination, or festival, according to the locale and sponsoring organization. It is easy to understand why students participate. There are prizes to be won, and opportunity to participate in an exciting event, and perhaps a trip to a nearby city or university is included.

At times it is less easy to understand why teachers enroll students in competitions. A considerable amount of work is involved in the preparation of contest pieces. The teacher often is vulnerable to performance and theory examinations which may reveal teaching deficiencies. At best there is the inevitable comparison of students and, by inference, teachers by means of a variety of rating systems. Whatever the difficulties, the festival concept is a growing one.

The intent here is to provide a clear, if abbreviated, picture of the contest scene. Included will be an overview of the organizations conducting auditions; the values and difficulties encountered at auditions as perceived by officials, teachers, and judges; objectives of auditions as listed by the major organizations; which students are eligible and how much it costs; the judges—their habits, good and bad; the teacher who brings students; types of auditions or contests and repertoire required for each; types of ratings and rating forms; and, finally, some suggestions for the preparation of students for the ordeal.

CONTEST ORGANIZATIONS

There are numerous local, state, and national organizations which sponsor contests and auditions. For this survey, four national organizations were chosen: (1) the Music Teachers National Association (MTNA); (2) the National Guild of Piano Teachers (the Guild); (3) the National Federation of Music Clubs (the Federation); and, (4) the Music Educators National Conference (MENC). From the numerous MTNA state organizations, the Minnesota Music Teachers Association (MMTA) was chosen for survey because of its highly structured examination systems in theory and piano performance. Another MTNA affiliate, the Florida Music Teachers Association (FMTA) was consulted concerning its program of judges training. The Louisiana Music Educators Association (LMEA) was selected as the representative for MENC for two reasons: (1) its State-wide program of piano auditions; and (2) the author's experience in judging for LMEA events. One local organization, the New Orleans Music Teachers Association (NOMTA), is cited for its program of private teacher certification. A systematic survey is presented for MMTA, the Guild, the Federation, and LMEA. Supplementary data are presented from FMTA and NOMTA.

Four publications were utilized as sources:

Piano-Theory Examination Syllabus, published by the Minnesota Music Teachers Association, affiliated with the Music Teachers National Association, in cooperation with music departments of the colleges and universities in the State of Minnesota. Minneapolis, 1970.

The Guild Syllabus, National Guild of Piano Teachers, Teacher Division of the American College of Musicians. Austin, Texas, 1965.

Junior Festivals Bulletin, National Federation of Music Clubs, Junior Division. Chicago, 1970.

The Louisiana Musician, Official Handbook Edition, published by the Louisiana Music Educators Association, Inc., affiliated with the Music Educators National Conference and the Music Section of the Louisiana Teachers Association. Volume 37, No. 1, September, 1971.

In addition to these publications, a quantity of supplementary materials were provided by several individuals. These included, Mrs. Loretta Hotard, faculty member at Nicholls State University, Thibodaux, Louisiana; Mrs. Louise Guhl, President of the Minnesota Music Teachers Association; Mrs. Ethel Hascall, Administrative Secretary of MMTA; Mrs. Ruth Seale, Chairman, New Orleans Division, National Federation of Music Clubs; and Mrs. Natalie Adcock, an officer of the Florida Music Teachers Association. These individuals were kind enough to send rating forms, information concerning student fees, etc. In addition, they were generous with their time in interviews, either in person or by telephone.

PROS AND CONS

The competitive aspects of festivals or auditions have resulted in criticisms of the entire system by some judges and teachers. Some organizations make a sincere attempt to minimize these problems. The Federation states that

> Festival entrants do not compete against each other, but are rated on individual merits. Thus NFMC Festivals are designed for the average student who seriously applies himself to his music as well as for those who are exceptionally talented.

The Guild makes a similar provision:

> . . . the basic aim of the Piano Guild, U.S.A., through its National Guild of Piano Teachers . . . has been to establish definite goals and awards for piano pupils of all grades from the earliest beginners to artistic adult performers—goals for the slow pupils as well as the gifted. These goals are attainable through the measurement of individual merit and not in competitive elimination contests.

However, competition is such an integral part of our culture that students attending festivals ordinarily expect to compete. Possibly a majority of teachers ascribe to the same view. Children tend to be realists and they seldom are impressed by generalities. Perhaps the idea of performance evaluated by some standard or goal of excellence is too abstract for the young mind.

Musicians who advocate periodic formal evaluations for young students list some of the following criteria as reasons:

1. *Motivation*. Students tend to work with increased interest and to

practice more when they receive periodic evaluations from qualified individuals other than their teachers.

2. *Goals*. The presence of goals objectified in the form of ratings, certificates, the passing of "grades" or levels, medals, cups, or plaques signify continuity and progress to students.

3. *Performance experience*. Students receive experience in coping with problems of performance under pressure of unfamiliar surroundings and a critical audience.

4. *Communication*. At festivals there are numbers of young pianists brought together in a formal manner for the purpose of evaluating their musical or performance expertise. Proponents believe that this type of structured experience may lead to the realization that others are working toward similar goals. Such experiences may reduce feelings of isolation and aloneness that sometimes may occur in young pianists studying in private studios.

5. *Systematic musical growth*. Audition divisions, classes, or levels for students in conjunction with graded repertoire recommended or required by organizations such as the Guild, the Federation, and MMTA allow students opportunities to progress musically in an orderly manner. MMTA states that its

> . . . Examination System will provide a means by which educational institutions can sanction or certify private study in music, give standards by which student achievement can be evaluated and recognized, give guidance for parents in their efforts to select a qualified teacher for their children, assist new music graduates in establishing curriculum guidelines for their private teaching studios.

6. *Teacher improvement*. Words can obscure many realities. Piano teachers who enter students regularly in auditions are submitting their teaching expertise for criticism even more than are their students submitting themselves for evaluation. Teachers become "typed" or graded on their ability very quickly. An individual student might have a poor day and receive a low rating, but the teacher who enters ten or more students (and this is a conservative number) has no defense against a high percentage of unfavorable ratings. In such a case her teaching techniques may need modification, she may need additional education, or both. Another possibility is that she might have some type of personality defect that prevents her from relating effectively to students. Whatever the situation, if the audition is effectively organized to meet her needs, the teacher can learn, contest by contest, experience by experience, and improve her teaching techniques significantly.

CONTEST OBJECTIVES

It is possible to judge something about the scope and professional procedures of musical organizations by the objectives that they list. The stated objectives of LMEA, the Federation, and the Guild are listed below.

> The purpose of the Louisiana Music Educators Association, Inc. is to develop the educational, cultural and recreational values of music through approved professional activities within the established framework of national, state, local and private educational organizations. This association seeks to

provide enriched musical opportunities for children and youth, encourage student participation in music, stimulate the quality of instruction and advance the cause of music as an integral part of general education.

The National Federation of Music Clubs has established its program of Junior Festivals to encourage and promote interest among students through the age of 18. With the highest standard of musical achievement as a goal, the Festivals offer an immediate objective toward which the student may work, and an opportunity to receive a rating on the degree of accomplishment achieved. Festival entrants do not compete against each other, but are rated on individual merits. Thus NFMC Festivals are designed for the average student who seriously applies himself to his music as well as for those who are exceptionally talented.

The surest means of including [*sic*] pupils to practice and progress is to stimulate their interest by placing goals and awards before them. Therefore, the basic aim of the Piano Guild, U.S.A., through its National Guild of Piano Teachers . . . has been to establish definite goals and awards for piano pupils of all grades from the earliest beginners to artistic adult performers–goals for the slow pupil as well as the gifted. These goals are attainable through the measurement of individual merit and not in competitive elimination contests. These goals give to music study a definite plan, and prevent aimless drifting. Our entire system of academic education recognizes this need for goals, and provides such milestones of measurements of progress in the goals of examinations, of passing to higher grades and of graduating . . .

STUDENT ELIGIBILITY AND FEES

Young pianists entering auditions or festivals sponsored by the Guild, LMEA and MMTA are required to study with teachers affiliated with these organizations. The Federation, however, requires the following: "An entrant must be under nineteen years of age as of March 1 of the Festival year; must be affiliated with NFMC as a member of an *Active* Federated Junior Club, a member of the Junior Section of a Federated Senior Club, or a Junior Special member, *in good standing* . . . "

Membership, and audition, examination, or festival fees for young pianists vary widely. LMEA does not offer membership in the association to students below the college level; however, pre-college students may enter auditions. Festival fees include $2.00 for the piano solo event, and $2.00 for the piano sight reading event.

MMTA requires students to pay according to their level of accomplishment as well as the type of event entered. Piano examination fees are as follows.

Levels I and II	$ 4.00
Levels III and IV	5.00
Levels V and VI	6.00
Levels VII and VIII	7.00
Level IX	10.00
Level X	12.00
Level XI	15.00

Theory Examination Fees:

Levels I and II	2.00
Levels III and IV	3.00
Level V	4.00

Original compositions submitted:

each entry	2.00

The Guild offers a somewhat complex set of membership requirements and fees for students. As stated earlier, to enter a Guild audition the student must study with a teacher affiliated with the Guild. Student membership then is determined by the type of audition he requests. Fees are determined in the same manner. Types of membership and fees are listed below:

Pledge Member's Certificate (one piece memorized, with scale and cadence). This type of member does not receive a fraternity pin.	$ 3.25
Local Member's Certificate and Fraternity Pin. This membership is awarded students who are passed by a Guild judge on a program of two or three compositions plus a musicianship test.	$ 4.00
District Member's Certificate and Fraternity Pin. This membership is awarded the student who plays a program of four to six pieces plus a musicianship test, and the audition is passed by a judge.	$ 4.75
State Member's Certificate and Fraternity Pin. This membership is awarded to the student who performs a seven to nine composition program, a musicianship test, and is passed by a judge.	$ 5.50
National Member's Certificate and Fraternity Pin. This is awarded the student playing an audition of 10 to 14 compositions plus the musicianship test. The student must achieve a judge's rating of 91 to achieve the next level.	$ 6.75 to 7.75
International Member's Certificate and Fraternity Pin. This student is approved by a judge with a score of 95 or better on a performance of 15-20 compositions plus a musicianship test.	$ 8.75
Hobbyist Certificate and Fraternity Pin. For students who do not memorize their compositions. Five to eight pieces required.	$ 5.25

Membership in the Federation is achieved when the student enrolls for an audition. Each student is charged with a basic fee of $1.25 which goes to the state Gold Cup chairman. In addition, the Division chairman may charge an additional fee to help defray local expenses. For example, a student entering a Federation audition sponsored by the New Orleans division pays three dollars and fifty cents:

$ 1.25	to the State chairman
1.25	to the Gold Cup chairman
1.00	to the local chairman

THE JUDGES

The majority of adjudicators for local and regional competitions are recruited from the piano faculties of nearby colleges and universities. This is standard practice and a fairly safe procedure for the sponsoring organization. A number of advantages are apparent:

1. The judges work cheaply. College music faculty are not lavishly paid, and most are willing to earn extra compensation. Fees range from a

minimum of $25.00 per day (for local festivals) to a maximum of around $300.00 for more prestigious events (regional and national contests). Often travel, food and lodging expenses are added to the fee.

2. The presence of a faculty judge lends credibility to the proceedings.

3. Teachers enrolling students tend to accept faculty judges. Occasionally there is dissatisfaction with individual ratings, but few teachers protest to the extent that could be expected if the judges were considered as peers.

However, there are disadvantages. The teaching of young pianists is a distinct profession with its own methodology and problems. The successful teacher of children either has received instruction in this field during his college career, or he has learned through experience. Few college or university piano instructors have had specific training equipping them to deal with young students, and fewer have had experience in teaching beginners.

American colleges and universities can assume some responsibility for the situation. The highest status accorded to students in these institutions belongs to the performer, usually the superior pianist, vocalist, or string player. Less status is given to the future teacher or educator. Blame is not implied. Rather, it is a situation that will require insight on the part of the university music community and a realigning of values. The fact is that few individuals will make a living as performers. Therefore, the thrust of many music departments is unrealistic, at best.

The Selection of Judges

Festival officials sometimes choose judges who by training or temperament are not the most competent individuals for the job. Nor is the obvious alternative overly attractive. Judgements by peers can create many problems. The most promising solutions are:

1. The utilization of elementary piano teachers of repute who work outside the region. LMEA requires the following for district festivals:

> It shall be the responsibility of the respective Festival chairmen to determine the number of and to secure adjudicators for the various events, keeping in mind the desirability of securing adjudicators who are presently engaged in teaching in the field in which they are asked to adjudicate.

For State instrumental festivals, LMEA states that,

> Judges will be selected from out-of-state directors who are prominent in their respective fields. At least one judge shall be currently engaged in junior or senior high teaching.

The Guild makes a similar provision: "Guild examiners are pianist-teachers of wide experience who possess a thorough understanding of the average pupil." The Federation is less specific:

> As early as possible the DISTRICT CHAIRMAN engages a hall with two good pianos; and also 1, 2, or 3 competent Judges for each section of Events (Piano, Voice, Strings, etc.) in which she has Entries. She should select Judges who are unacquainted with the Entrants . . . Judges' fees and Festival expense should be determined by each State according to its individual needs.

2. Officials could recruit individuals who have achieved a reputation as authors in the field. These would include composers of pedagogical materials for the young pianist.

3. Finally, a good choice would be college or university instructors who are recognized child specialists; that is, those who teach courses in elementary and intermediate piano pedagogy.

The suggestions listed above are not mutually exclusive. It is possible that one individual could have qualifications in more than one area. Nor should the piano faculty member who teaches advanced college pupils be systematically excluded. If the individual proves knowledgeable in the elementary and intermediate areas, and if he is sympathetic to problems encountered by the young performer, he should be asked to return. Difficulties appear to occur most often when festival officials equate status with competence. Perhaps it would be best if officials followed loosely the system adopted by the Guild; that is, systematically develop state and district lists of judges who possess the external qualifications necessary for the job, and who have proved during a trial period to be acceptable to students, teachers, and officials. If such a list were published and made available to officials, some communication problems could be avoided. The Florida Music Teachers Association has solved the adjudication problem by inaugurating training for judges. An apprentice judge must adjudicate under supervision of a trained judge for a certain period of time before he or she is accepted by the Association.

Another excellent procedure would involve the publishing of an explicit set of instructions for judges. These would outline the procedures involved, the type of rating system employed, a description of the classes or divisions under which students perform (elementary I, elementary II, etc.), and suggestions for judges about how to treat students and teachers. This method is not foolproof. Judges can and often do ignore instructions. However, the virtue of this procedure is that it avoids the formal evaluation of judges by contest or festival officials.

Judges' Qualifications

The qualifications of a good judge or adjudicator may be summarized as follows:

1. Knowledge of repertoire appropriate to the students he will hear.

2. The ability to recognize and evaluate properly stages of musical growth. Specific factors might include repertoire, technique, texture and phrasing, and musicianship.

3. Some knowledge of the psychology of young pianists, and experience in dealing with their problems. Of particular importance is the ability to make a criticism in a positive manner. The young pianist should leave an audition feeling that the judge appreciated his preparation (or lack of it). He also should feel motivated to work harder for the next event.

Ethics for Judges

A consideration crucial to the success of any audition or festival is that of ethics. In the context used here, ethical behavior simply is a way of getting along with those around you with a minimum of conflict and with a maximum of benefit to all involved. As often presented, ethical considerations read a little like a club litany. The ones listed below are simple and explicit.

1. The judge should never imply in any manner that the performer's teacher is a poor one. At times this requires some verbal dexterity. It is mandatory that the judge be supportive of the teacher as well as the student.

2. When criticisms are made, they should be concrete ones, and they should deal with specific elements of performance rather than supposed deficiencies in learning.

3. The judge should be interested, and show it, in every performance. This holds true for the poor performance as well as the superior one; the first year student as well as the more advanced.

4. When there is more than one adjudicator for an audition, the judge should make certain that his ratings are a product of his own experience and expertise, rather than a result of consultation with another judge.

5. The judge should never solicit students for himself, another teacher, or an institution. Nor should he make any type of disparaging remark concerning any organization, institution, or individual. This consideration is easily violated. For example, a judge on the rating form may state that he does not approve of or like the performer's choice of music or the edition. If the music was chosen by the sponsoring organization the remark is inappropriate. If the music was chosen by the teacher, this implies a criticism of the teacher. Suggestions for different literature may be made to the teacher.

6. The quality of performance by any individual student, or the performance capabilities of a group of students belonging to a teacher should not be disclosed except to festival officials, the student, or the teacher involved.

7. "Giving a lesson" should be avoided by the judge unless the student is auditioning privately, and unless the teacher gives permission.

Judging Procedures

The procedure that the judge follows during the audition will be determined by the structure of the festival. If the simulated performance procedure is followed (the student performs on a stage and the judge is in the audience), the judge will have little contact with the student. However, if the audition is a private one the following suggestions may obtain:

1. The judge should be supportive to the student. He should make some type of welcoming remark, and allow the student time to position himself at the piano properly and to relax for a moment before beginning the audition.

2. The judge should give some verbal indication to the student after the performance on the type of rating to expect. The remark, "That was an excellent performance" would lead the student to expect a high rating. On the other hand, "You had a few memory problems," spoken in a friendly and positive manner, might indicate to the student to expect a lower rating. Such a procedure is meaningful to the student because it prepares him for his rating. In addition it gives the student an opportunity to inform his teacher, parents, and peers that he either did or did not do well, thereby preventing embarrassment when the ratings are posted.

3. On the rating forms the judge always should offer some encour-

agement to the student, no matter how inadequate the performance.

4. Remarks inscribed on the rating form should be explicit, not conceptual. The rating forms will be read by students, and they should be comprehensive and legible.

5. The judge should request that the piano be placed in a position allowing full view by the judge of the keyboard and pedals, but so that the student cannot see him during the performance.

6. The judge should make an effort to be as quiet and attentive as possible during the performance. He should do as little as possible to distract the student.

7. The judge should keep his schedule up to date. A slow judge is appreciated by no one–students, teachers, or officials. The situation here is somewhat anomalous. The judge is expected to be attentive and supportive, as well as audition a student and write a full evaluation, all within five to eight minutes. This can be accomplished by following the "look, listen, and write" method. By the time three or four measures are completed, the judge will know something about the student's posture, hand position, wrist action, pedaling (if it is used), tempo, and rhythm. A few measures more will reveal pluses or minuses in the areas of texture (staccato-legato), balance, phrasing, and dynamics. A common mistake is for the judge to wait until the student has completed his performance to write the evaluation. Most schedules will not allow enough time for this. Therefore, the judge either loses more time as the day progresses, or he compensates by writing shorter evaluations, or both. Both alternatives involve a disservice to the student and to the festival. Perhaps a solution would be longer judging periods for each student. This is not likely to occur. Participants in piano festivals are increasing not decreasing. Each judge will have to find his own method of dealing with the problem. By following the procedure outlined above the judge has ample time to greet the student, observe and listen to the performance, write a full evaluation, give some indication to the student about his quality of performance, and offer a few words of encouragement.

8. The judge should study the audition or festival rules carefully. Many auditions have rather complicated classifications for students–several classes of elementary, intermediate, etc. If these distinctions are not apparent to the judge he can do students a severe disservice.

9. If the information is not given on the rating form, the judge may ask the student how long he has studied, and how long he has been with his present teacher. Too many officials allow students who have studied for a number of years to enroll in an elementary division thereby increasing their chances for a high rating.

Role of the Teacher During Auditions

One problem often faced by judges is the role of the teacher during the audition or examination. Some officials do not allow teachers to be present when their students are performing. Others allow the judge to decide the issue. MMTA, for example, states that "No person other than the student and Examiner will be allowed in the examination room." The Guild makes a similar provision:

> The Auditions are conducted privately and on the order of conservatory tests and examinations. However, parents and other pupils may be permitted to

attend at the discretion of the teacher, judge or Chairman, but not in the same room.

However, the Guild states that, "Each teacher entering pupils shall receive from the judge a sealed confidential opinion in which may be given detailed suggestions not possible to write upon student report cards, if desired, or deemed advisable by [the] judge."

From personal experience, it appears that a majority of judges prefer that the teacher not be present. However, there are reasons important enough to advance a contrary opinion. Except for students, teachers are the most important members of the festival conglomerate—more important than officials and judges.

Students come to auditions to learn and to objectify a half-year or year's work. Most teachers also come to learn. The teacher can learn as much or more from hearing her students perform and listening to the judge's comments than from reading rating sheets. Also, mistakes in communication are common enough to pose significant problems for judges and officials. When the teacher hears and sees her students perform, she is not forced to rely upon the student's account of the experience. Several types of misunderstandings can occur. For example, in a very "live" room, correct pedaling can appear to be blurred and proper phrasing may not be heard. A seat or bench that is too low or too high (a common occurrence) may wreck havoc with wrist action, hand position, and pedal dexterity, particularly for the very young pianist. In sight reading events often the bench is too low or the music rack too high (particularly if a grand piano is used) for the young musician to see properly. But the most common reason for bruised feelings is the edited account of performances given by students. Most of these difficulties could be avoided if the teacher were present.

However, there are dangers. Some teachers insist upon describing each student in detail before the audition. Others make comments during the performance. Still others distract or embarrass students by overprotective behavior. These problems can be resolved if the judge, in a kind manner, explains to the teacher what he will and will not allow during the audition.

THE TEACHERS

As stated earlier, the teacher is the paramount link in the contest chain. There may be a dearth of students, judges may prove to be incompetent, officials may plan badly, and the festival goes on. But without the support of a significant number of teachers no festival can occur.

At this time there is no national policy that establishes even minimum requirements for the piano teacher. She may have studied two years as a child, or she may have performed with some frequency in the major concert halls. But as the situation stands now, for a parent shopping about for a teacher, there is no guarantee of competence. The medical doctor completes a number of years of specialized training, appears before a medical board, and is licensed to practice. National standards also may apply to the plumber, psychologist, medical technician, and a host of other professionals. Unfortunately there is no apprenticeship, degree requirement, or any other standard applied on a systematic basis to private piano teachers. The only guideline available to parents is the teacher's local reputation, and this may be the least reliable criterion of all.

Several national, state, regional, and local organizations have made attempts to regulate the practice of piano teaching. While such attempts are valuable and should be encouraged, at best they may be described as "stop-gap" measures until national norms are established and enforced.

Teacher Qualifications

The problem of teacher qualifications has been dealt with in various ways. MMTA instituted a certification plan in 1960. Teachers are grouped into three categories according to their training and years of teaching experience.

> I GRADUATE ACCREDITED MEMBERSHIP for teachers with an accredited Master's degree, or its equivalent, and at least five years of teaching experience.
>
> II ACCREDITED MEMBERSHIP for teachers with an accredited Bachelor's degree, or its equivalent, and at least five years of teaching experience.
>
> III ASSOCIATE MEMBERSHIP for teachers with or without an accredited degree, and less than five years of teaching experience.
>
> Those members in Category III are not fully certified until they have completed one of the programs outlined by the Certification Committee. A candidate for full certification must complete his program for advancement in seven years from his initial application to MMTA.

MMTA's *Professional Policies Manual* (1969) further states that "Parents should not hesitate to ask the prospective teacher of their choice to show them his or her certification and current membership in MMTA."

Neither the Federation nor LMEA list requirements for piano teachers belonging to their organizations. Certification for teachers belonging to the Guild is accomplished in the following manner:

> To be certified by the American College of Musicians (that is, to be granted the Certificate of Approval from ACM) please submit to Certification Committee, American College of Musicians . . . twenty-five report cards or stubs of students who have achieved national or international membership in the National Fraternity of Student Musicians with a minimum (14 or more C's than A's) of 95 per cent during the past five years . . . Those granted this award may so designate by "Certified by the American College of Musicians" in their publicity.
>
> After receiving the approval certificate the first time, only 5 nationals yearly with a minimum of 14 more C's than A's will be needed for renewal.

In addition, the Guild offers seven types or grades of diplomas to teachers (as well as pupils). These are:

1. High School Diploma in Social Music
2. High School Diploma
3. Freshman Collegiate Diploma
4. Sophomore Collegiate Diploma
5. Junior Collegiate Diploma
6. Senior Collegiate Diploma
7. Artist Diploma

An example of one local organization's attempt to raise levels of professional competence is listed below. These requirements were taken from the *Directory* of the New Orleans Music Teachers Association (1971-72).

> Applicants for membership in the Association may qualify for active membership by fulfilling one of the following sets of conditions:
>
> 1. Applications will be accepted from those holding Music Degrees from an accredited college or conservatory of music.
>
> 2. Persons not holding music degrees, but who have studied music in an accredited college or conservatory may qualify for active membership by presenting evidence of:
>
> a) 20 semester hours credit (or its equivalent) in the major instrument and
>
> b) one year (or its equivalent) of pedagogies and/or methods.
>
> 3. Persons not holding a music degree, or who have not received training from an accredited college or conservatory sufficient to fulfill either of the above categories, may qualify for active membership by:
>
> a) passing a written examination and
>
> b) performing for a committee. The committee may, at its discretion, accept a past program (or other evidence of competence) from the artist-teacher, in lieu of the performance examination.

The qualifications of a good teacher are a subject of concern to parents and students. However, it is not always easy to present a formula. It seems that today's piano teacher is a combination of music mentor, psychotherapist, family counselor, businesswoman, child psychologist, and public relations expert. Deficiencies in any of these areas can lead to problems for teachers and students alike. It seems that a peculiar combination of skills, temperament, and motivation is necessary for success. Piano teaching requires an individual who is a good musician and pianist (not necessarily of performance calibre), and an outgoing or other-motivated person. The successful teacher will have the conviction that her work is exciting, challenging, and important. As a last ingredient, the teacher must be creative and possess the capacity to study, learn, and experiment.

CLASSES OR DIVISIONS, EVENTS, AND REQUIRED REPERTOIRE

LMEA allows the young pianist to compete in three areas: piano solo, piano ensemble, and sight reading. The latter event is optional for those competing in solo performance. The playing of two compositions is required for both solo and ensemble performance, one from the classical or pre-classical periods, and one from any subsequent period. No specific literature or repertoire is recommended. The classification or division system utilized by LMEA is simple. The student is categorized by the number of years he has studied. Therefore, Division I denotes one year of study. LMEA publishes the following criteria to determine the sight-reading level:

READING LEVEL I

1. Note recognition on flash cards
2. I, V7, I
3. Pieces in five finger positions, alternating hands

4. No notes shorter than eighth notes

READING LEVEL II

1. I, V7, IV, I in all keys
2. Scales in tetrachords or one octave, hands separately in all keys
3. Accompany melodies with above chords
4. Meters: 2/4, 3/4, 4/4, 6/8

READING LEVEL III

1. I, IV, V7, I in root position
2. Contrapuntal reading
3. Scales, one octave minimum, hands together, all keys
4. Triplets, dotted eighths, and sixteenth notes
5. Pieces on Level II

READING LEVEL IV

1. I, VI, IV, II_6 I^6_4, V7, I in root position in all keys
2. Accompany melodies with above chords
3. Scales, minimum of two octaves, hands together, all keys
4. Pieces on Level III

READING LEVEL V

1. I, II_7 (secondary dominant), V7, I in all keys
2. Accompany melodies with the above chords
3. Scales, four octaves, hands together in all keys, moderate tempo
4. Pieces on Level IV

READING LEVEL VI

1. Modulations (to dominant and/or sub-dominant)
2. Compound and simple meters
3. Scales, four octaves, hands together in all keys, rapid tempo
4. Simple and compound meters in the reading material

While the student enters what is termed a sight-reading event, in actuality he or she is competing in a well-structured theory event.

The Federation offers a number of events for the young pianist: piano solo, piano ensemble, piano concerto, hymn playing, musicianship (theory), sight-reading, musical improvisation, and original composition. Students entering the piano solo event are required to perform one composition by an American composer from a required list, plus one composition (selected by the student) "from works of representative non-American composers of the Baroque, Classic, Romantic, or modern Periods." An exception is provided for the very young beginner. All piano ensemble events call for the playing of two compositions, one listed in the Festival Bulletin, and one of the student's choice. Required repertoire for performance events are listed in the Bulletin. The classes or divisions for piano solo, and two representative required compositions for each division are listed below:

Special Class Older Beginners: (10 years of age, or over; less than one year of study . . .)
Dittenhaver: Wind in the Pines
Frost: In a Space Ship

Pre-Primary Class (to age 7, not more than seven months instruction)
Butler: All About Fun
Glover: Henry the Cat

Primary Class I
Bastien: Little Dog Running Down a Street
Garrow: The Little Frog

Primary Class II
Bastien: Chinatown
Garrow: March of the Astronauts

Primary Class III
Alt: Waves
Jesse: Over the Hills in a Sleigh

Primary Class IV
Alt: Cat on the Window Sill
Erb: Rodeo Riders

Elementary Class I
Anson: Space Flight
Carre: Tumbling Clowns

Elementary Class II
Alt: Snow
Scher: Busy Butterflies

Elementary Class III
Anderson: Hopping and Running
Kramer: Plaintive Air

Elementary Class IV
Agay: Two Bagatelles
Butler: Barcarolle (*Lyrical Sketches*)

Medium Class
Gillock: Castanets
Noel: Pantomime

Moderately Difficult I
Brussels: A Dancing Butterfly
Lindfors: Musings

Moderately Difficult II
Bauer: Dandy-Lion
Callahan: Sea Mist

Moderately Difficult III
Alt: The Bee Hive
Gillock: Last Spring

Difficult Class I
Brussels: Two Preludes (either one)
Mackie: Aria

Difficult Class II
Agay: Sonatina Hungarica
Sister M. Elaine: Gay Senorita

Very Difficult Class I
Dohnanyi: A Dedication
Mokrjs: Valcik

Very Difficult Class II
Babin: Sonatina No. 2
Rieti: Contrasts for Piano

Musically Advanced Class I
MacDowell: From a Wandering Iceberg (*Sea Pieces*)
Schramm: Vertical Construction

Musically Advanced Class II
Balogh: Debate
Griffes: Clouds, or Vale of Dreams

The Guild's auditions are structured in such a way that young students may enter under a variety of achievement plans. Students may receive pledge, local, district, state, or national certificates according to the number of memorized pieces played at the audition. For young pianists who do not memorize their music, a hobbyist certificate is available. A social music certificate is awarded to the student who, among other requirements, performs hymns, patriotic, folk, college, and popular music. Bach medals and sonata medals may be awarded for specialized work in these areas. The length of time allowed students at Guild auditions may vary according to the level of the student, and the division or class in which he is entered. For short programs the examiner hears all of the compositions presented. For longer programs, one-half plus one of the compositions are heard. Diploma candidates are allowed one hour for examinations. Students are classified according to their performance ability rather than by age or length of time studied. Classification levels are given below:

> ELEMENTARY A, B, C, and D, from the earliest beginning until the pupil is able to play little Bach dances and the easiest sonatinas of Clementi or other composers . . . A pupil may be classed elem. A-B-C- or D through one to three or more years and still be classed prep. D on high school graduation.
>
> INTERMEDIATE A, B, C, D, E, and F, from the above until the pupil is ready to begin Bach inventions and the easy sonatas by Haydn, Mozart and Beethoven . . .
>
> PREPARATORY A, B, C, and D, when the pupil is playing Bach inventions, Partitas, Suites, Preludes and Fugues, and the above sonatas . . .
>
> COLLEGIATE A, B, C, and D, when the pupil is playing preludes and fugues from the *Well Tempered Clavichord*, Beethoven Sonatas, Chopin Etudes, etc . . .
>
> ARTIST, when the pupil is able to present a twenty piece program of advanced difficulty . . .
>
> INTERMEDIATE AND PREPARATORY SPECIAL may be used to classify young pupils of exceptional gifts and talents, who should remain in these classifications until becoming high school seniors. They may then be classified Preparatory D and become candidates for the high school Diploma.

Repertoire for auditions is listed in a "Suggested Literature Chart" contained in the *Syllabus*. For the earlier divisions no specific literature is listed. Instead, students and teachers are referred to compositions contained in the *Irl Allison Library* (thirty-three volumes), published by The Willis Music Co.

Piano levels or divisions for MMTA are given elsewhere in this chapter (Types of Ratings and Rating Forms). Three types of events are available to students: theory examinations, piano examinations, and original composition competitions. The composition event is optional. However, students wishing to be examined in piano are required to pass a theory examination. Held separately, theory examinations are offered in November and February, and piano examinations in November and May or June. The Association lists recommended editions for the following composers: Bach, Beethoven, Brahms, Chopin, Haydn, Mozart, Schumann, and Schubert. A real service is performed for the teacher by a list of editions that are *not* recommended because of distortions or misrepresentations. MMTA's *Piano-Theory Examination Syllabus* lists technique, sight reading, studies, and pieces required for examination. The second section of the volume lists a remarkably complete theory examination for the various levels. Because of space limitations, representative technique and repertoire requirements for levels I, II, III, and V are listed below.

LEVEL I: TECHNIQUE

a) The Five-Note (Pentachord) Pattern: Play in all major and minor keys, legato, hands together. Finish each pattern with the tonic triad.
b) The Five-Note (Pentachord) Pattern: Play in all major and minor keys, each hand alone, in two-note slurs . . .

Sight Reading

a) Play a simple tune in five-finger position, using half and quarter notes. The first phrase will be for the right hand in the treble clef and the second for the left hand in the bass clef.
b) Clap, or play on a single note, a rhythm example. [the] Example will use 2/4, 3/4, 4/4 meter with the following note values and their equivalent rests . . . [whole, dotted half, half, quarter, eighth]

Studies

Play two selections, with contrasting objectives, from the Level I studies published by MMTA . . .

PIECES (one piece required from Level A and one from Level B)

A: Bacon: Doodlebug (from *My World*)
Olson: The Sandpiper (from *Menagerie*)

B: Bartók: *First Term at the Piano* (no. 6)
Kuhl: Theme with Variations (from *Solo Book I*)

LEVEL II: TECHNIQUE

To be played from memory, ascending and descending, at a moderate tempo, with firm, even touch.

a) Any three major and one harmonic minor scale (of own choice), one octave, legato, each hand alone. Finish each scale with the tonic triad . . .
b) In the same keys, the tonic triad, root positions and inversions, one octave, each hand alone, solid and sustained . . .
c) In the same keys, the tonic triad arpeggiated through four octaves, crossing hands . . . with emphasis on smoothness and evenness. A Triple rhythm should be implied.
d) The Five-Note (Pentachord) Pattern: Play in all major and minor keys, hands together, with one hand legato, the other detached. Finish each pattern with the tonic triad, solid . . .

Theory

Level I or a higher level of the MMTA Theory Test must be passed before a certificate will be issued . . .

Oral Questions

Student may be asked to translate markings in the pieces played and to identify the key and meter of the piece.

Sight Reading

a) Play a short melody consisting of half and quarter notes, divided between the hands, with hands together at the cadence, similar to early work in most beginning methods. Brief, silent examination of the example will be allowed before playing.
b) Clap, or play on a single note, a rhythm example. Note values and rests will be the same as Level I. Tied notes will be used at this level.

Studies

Play two selections, with contrasting objectives, from the Level II studies published by MMTA . . .

PIECES (one required from each list)

A: Bach, J. S.: Chorale in C; Song in F (from *Four Centuries of Keyboard Music,* Book I)
Türk: Joke (from *Forty-Nine Pieces for Children*, Book II)

B: Dello Joio: *Suite for the Young* (Nos. 1, 2, 3)
Stravinsky, S.: Evening Star (from *Piano Music for Children*, Book II)

LEVEL III: TECHNIQUE

To be played from memory, ascending and descending, in keys designated, with firm, even tone and logical fingering. Indicated tempi should be regarded as minimum although the Examiner will stress rhythmic precision and control over speed.

Scales: D, E, F, B Major and parallel Harmonic Minors; each hand alone, two octaves, legato and detached; Quarter = MM 88 in eighth notes.

Chords: D, E, F, B, Major and Minor: root position and inversions, each hand alone . . . ; Quarter = MM 60 in half notes.

Arpeggios: Any three keys of own choice; each hand alone, two octaves, legato; moderate tempo.

The Five-Note (Pentachord) Pattern: in all major and minor keys at a moderate tempo with touches in the two hands as follows and reversed: [combinations of staccato and legato, and legato and slurs are given]

Pedal: Playing the chord formula I-IV-V7-I in either hand and in any key, the student demonstrates basic pedal usage by depressing the pedal *after* the chord has been sounded, releasing it precisely with the sounding of the next chord.

Theory

Level I of the MMTA Theory Test must be passed before a certificate will be issued . . .

Oral Questions

Simple questions may be asked on the pieces played covering such points as key, meter, markings, style (for example: Minuets are in triple time, Gavottes in duple).

Sight Reading

a) Play a short passage, using the two hands and written in half and quarter notes. Passage will be in the five-finger position and easier than a level I piece . . .
b) Clap, or play on a single note, a rhythm example. This example may include all the meter and note values used in Level II with the addition of

[sixteenth] . . . notes. 6/8 meter may be used with the following note values and their equivalent rests:

Studies

Play two, with contrasting objectives, from the Level III studies published by MMTA . . .

PIECES (one required from each list)

A: Bach J. S.: Musette in D
Mozart, L: Entree (from *Notebook for Wolfgang*)

B: Haydn: *German Dances* (any two)
Kullak: Cradle Song

C: Chopin: German Song
Dello Joio: A Sad Tale (from *Suite for the Young*)

LEVEL V: TECHNIQUE

To be played from memory, ascending and descending, in keys designated, with firm, even tone and logical fingering, indicated tempi should be regarded as minimum, although examiner will stress rhythmic precision and control over speed.

Scales: D, G, A Flat, B Flat Major and Parallel harmonic Minor; Hands together, two octaves, legato and detached; Quarter = MM 100 in eighth notes. D and G melodic Minor; hands together, two octaves, legato and detached. G and B Flat Major, contrary motion, two octaves, legato.

Tonic Triads: Above major and minor keys; root position and inversions, hands together . . . Quarter = MM 100 in eighth notes.

Theory

Level II or a higher level of the MMTA. Theory Test must be passed before a certificate will be issued . . .

Oral Questions

As in Level IV

Sight Reading

a) A short passage will be given about equal in difficulty to a level II piece. Brief silent examination (ca. 30 seconds) of the example will be allowed before playing.

Studies

Play two, with contrasting objectives, selected from the Level V studies published by MMTA . . .

Essay

Student will submit to the Examiner a previously prepared essay, not to exceed 200 words in length, based on the composer whose music he plays from List A. Material should include biographical facts, historical period he represents, common musical forms used by him.

PIECES

A: Bach, J. S.: Minuet (from *French Suite, E Major*)
Purcell: Jig in G Minor (*Piano Classics,* Vol. I, Mirovitch)

B: Beethoven: Sonatina in F (either movement)
Diabelli: Sonatina Book III (CMP) (first or third movement)

C: Bloch: Joyous March (*Enfantines*)
Prokofieff: Morning (*Music for Children*)

Memorization

Memorization of compositions performed is required or highly encouraged by the four organizations. Memorization is required by the Federation. LMEA states that "All vocal and piano soloists will be required to perform from memory or be rated one division lower." The Guild expects all performers to play by memory except in the Hobbyist Division. MMTA has the following requirements: "Full credit for Memory is awarded only when all the pieces are memorized. Pieces (those from lettered lists) may or may not be memorized but extra points will be given for successful memorization of one or more. Level XI program must be memorized."

Types of Ratings and Rating Forms

As stated earlier, both the Federation and the Guild have made attempts to reduce the competitive aspects of piano auditions. MMTA holds one competitive examination per year, and one non-competitive. LMEA lists no policy in the matter.

The Guild presents a system whereby three levels of performance success are possible within more than forty separate criteria. A check (√) in the "C" column indicates special commendation. A check in the "A" column indicates that some error has occurred or that the category needs more attention. A middle column is left unchecked, indicating that the performance in that area (in the absence of a "C" or "A") is "Satisfactory for Ability, Age, and Time Studied." Most of the Guild awards and achievement levels require a certain number of "C's" in excess of "A's" awarded by a Guild judge. The *Syllabus* states that, "The average pupil's ability, not the unusually gifted, form the basis of rating." The rating categories or criteria are as follows:

ACCURACY: Time Values
Correct Notes
Rests
Tempo Indications
Marks of Expression

TONE QUALITY: Warmth
Vitality
Legato-Blending
Singing Tone
Sensitivity

TECHNIQUE: Clean-Cut
Arm and Wrist Ease
Fingering
Fluency
Velocity
Command of Touches

RHYTHM: Accent
Steadiness of Beat
Continuity – Momentum
Flexibility

MATURITY IN MEMORY

PHRASING: Slurs
- Proper Grouping
- Rise and Fall – Melody Line
- Range of Shading
- Finesse in Endings

DYNAMICS: Contrast

PEDAL: Well-Timed
- Legato Connection
- Avoidance of Blurs
- Additional Pedal Effects
- Use of Soft Pedal

INTERPRETATION: Style
- Balance – Melody and Accompaniment
- Structural Design
- Clearness of Voices
- Nuances
- Climaxes
- Feeling – Imagination

REPERTOIRE: Classic
- Romantic and Modern

IRREDUCIBLE MINIMUM MUSICIANSHIP TEST
- Added Phases

The indication that the student has passed or failed is signified by whether or not the judge signs the certificate. A space is provided to the left of the rating form for any additional comments the judge wishes to make. The form also allows space for a listing of the compositions performed. For convenience, the compositions are listed in the order in which they are performed. The types of certificates given by the Guild are discussed in an earlier section (Student Eligibility and Fees). The Guild's ratings are listed below.

FAMILY CIRCLE RATING

More A than C Checks	Below 85%

16 more A's than C's constitute not passing, meaning below 70 on a liberal basis.

ROOM CIRCLE RATING

No more C than A Checks	85%
1 more C than A Checks	86% Good
2 more C's than A's	87%
3 more C's than A's	88%
4 more C's than A's	89%
5 more C's than A's	90% Good Plus
6 more C's than A's	91%

SCHOOL CIRCLE RATING

7 more C's than A's	91½%
8 more C's than A's	92% Excellent
10 more C's than A's	93%

CITYWIDE CIRCLE RATING

11 more C's than A's	93½% Excellent Plus
12-13 more C's than A's	94%
14-17 more C's than A's	95% Superior Minus
18-21 more C's than A's	96% Superior
22-27 more C's than A's	97%

CRITICS' CIRCLE RATING
(For Top-Talents only)

28 more C's than A's	98% Superior Plus
36 more C's than A's	99% Superior Plus
44 (or more) more C's than A's	99% Superior Plus

MMTA publishes three sets of rating forms for piano performance. All are presented in duplicate and require a ball-point pen to insure that the copy is properly marked. The form for piano levels I, II, III, and IV are on conventional size letter paper; the forms for levels V, VI, and VII; VIII, IX, and X are on legal size paper. Ratings are assigned on a pre-determined point system; a certain number of points are listed as "maximum" and "obtained" for each category. The categories for each division, and maximum points are listed below:

PIANO LEVELS I, II, III, IV

1. TECHNICAL REQUIREMENTS
   Scales, Chords and Arpeggios (15 maximum points)
2. PERFORMANCE (PIECES AND STUDIES)
   Accuracy: Notation, Time Values and General Adherence to Text (25 maximum points)

   MUSICIANSHIP: Style, Phrasing, Rhythm, Tone Quality, Pedalling, Oral Questions on Repertoire (40 maximum points)

   MEMORY (Pieces only) (8 maximum points)
3. SIGHT READING PIECES (7 maximum points)
   RHYTHM PATTERNS (5 maximum points)

The total points obtained are tabulated, and three categories of attainment are indicated: Pass, 60-69; Excellent, 70-79; and Distinction, 80-100. A generous space is left at the bottom of the form for the examiner's report. There is enough difference in the forms for levels V and VI, and VII, VIII, IX and X to require a separate listing for each.

PIANO LEVELS V, VI

1. TECHNICAL REQUIREMENTS: Scales, Chords and Arpeggios (15 maximum points)
2. PERFORMANCE (PIECES AND STUDIES): Accuracy, Notation, Time Values and General Adherence to Text (25 maximum points)

   MUSICIANSHIP: Style, Phrasing, Rhythm, Tone Quality, Pedalling, Oral Questions on Repertoire (37 maximum points)
3. SIGHT READING PIECES (7 maximum points)

Again, the total points are tabulated. The rating or attainment level is the same as for Levels I, II, III, IV. A considerably more generous space is allowed for the examiner's report.

PIANO LEVELS VII, VIII, IX, X

1. TECHNICAL REQUIREMENTS: Scales, Chords and Arpeggios (10 maximum points)
2. PERFORMANCE (PIECES AND STUDIES): Accuracy, Notation, Time Values and General Adherence to Text (25 maximum points)

   MUSICIANSHIP: Style, Phrasing, Rhythm, Tone Quality, Pedalling, Oral Questions on Repertoire (37 maximum points)

3. SIGHT READING PIECES (7 maximum points)
4. AURAL AWARENESS: Rhythm Patterns (5 maximum points)
   Intervals: (5 maximum points)
5. ESSAY ON COMPOSERS AND HISTORICAL PERIODS (3 maximum points)

MMTA's forms allow the judge or examiner to view performance in broad phases, and to rate on the total *gestalt* presented by the student during the performance. It is interesting to note that 15 maximum points are allowed for technical requirements in piano levels I through VI. Levels VII through X allow only ten maximum points. The performance area remains constant. Musicianship changes slightly from 40 maximum points for levels I - IV, to 37 for V - X. Memory is listed only on the earlier levels. Sight reading is introduced at level V and continues through X. Aural awareness of rhythm patterns and intervals is introduced at level VII, as is an essay on composers and periods.

Evidently the Federation does not publish a uniform rating sheet for piano auditions. It appears that this function is left for the Division or Local chairman. For its annual Piano Tournament, the Federation's New Orleans District publishes a form utilizing the ratings of Superior, Excellent, Satisfactory, and "Needs Improvement." The criteria are as follows:

ACCURACY

TEMPO

RHYTHM
- Steadiness of beat
- Continuity
- Flexibility

PHRASING
- Phrase releases
- Shading
- Melodic line

TONE
- Variety and quality

TECHNIC
- Clear finger work
- Relaxation
- Fluency
- Touches

INTERPRETATION
- Style
- Dynamics
- Pedaling
- Balance of melody and accompaniment

OVERALL MUSICAL EFFECT
- Structure
- Climaxes

POISE AND APPEARANCE

The tournament, with its criteria and ratings described above, is a local effort of the New Orleans Division. This particular function is not monitored by the State or National organization.

LMEA utilizes two forms for piano auditions, one for performance and the other for (sight) reading. A square for the rating or score is provided at the top. Identifying data include the following: the order in which the student appears; the event number; the class or level of entry; date; the student's name, elementary or high school attended, his city, state, and LMEA division; and the selections to be performed. The musical portion of the form includes the following:

> PERFORMER'S TONE: (beauty, control)
>
> TECHNIQUE: (finger dexterity, note accuracy, precision, use of pedals)
>
> INTERPRETATION: (contrast, mood, phrasing, rhythm, style, and tempo)
>
> MUSICAL EFFECT: (artistry, fluency)
>
> OTHER FACTORS: (choice of music, stage presence and appearance)
>
> MEMORIZING

The form for (sight) reading introduces two new factors in the identifying data section: length of study, and the time the student has spent with his present teacher. Three musical criteria are listed: technique, interpretation, and musical effect. On both forms a space is left for the examiner's comments. In its *Official Handbook* (1971), LMEA lists its ratings and offers an explanation for teachers, students, and judges.

> Rating I (Division 1). This division represents the finest conceivable performance for the event and the class of participants being judged; worthy of the distinction of being recognized as among the very best. This rating might be compared to a percentage grade of 95 to 100 . . .
>
> Rating II (Division 2). This rating reflects an unusual performance in many respects but not one worthy of the highest rating due to minor defects. Yet it is a performance of distinctive quality. The rating might be compared to a grade of 87 to 94 . . .
>
> Rating III (Division 3). This rating is awarded for a good performance, but one that is not outstanding. The performance shows accomplishment and marked promise, but it is lacking in one or more essential qualities. The rating might be compared to a grade of 80 to 86 . . .
>
> Rating IV (Division 4). This rating describes a performance that shows some obvious weaknesses. These may reflect handicaps in . . . rehearsal time. The rating is comparable to a grade of 75 to 79 . . .
>
> Rating V (Division 5). This rating indicates a performance which reveals much room for improvement . . .

PREPARATION OF STUDENTS FOR AUDITIONS

After audition dates are set, judges selected, and suggested or required repertoire published, the teacher has the task of preparing students to make as good a showing as possible. If theory and technique requirements are included in the schedule the difficulties are compounded. The first step in the process belongs to the teacher. Before assignments are passed out, it is important that she study the audition requirements and procedures thoroughly. By doing this the teacher can be certain that her preparations are correct and that there will be no embarrassing omissions on the day of the auditions.

Teachers vary in their opinions concerning festivals, in the types of auditions in which they enter students, and on the manner in which they prepare them. Some teachers belong to a single musical organization, and submit their students once a year for examination. Others are "joiners" and may enroll students in four or more events a year (utilizing some of the same pieces for each event). And there is no dearth of opportunities in most metropolitan areas. For example, the following organizations conduct piano auditions in the Greater New Orleans area: Louisiana Music Educators Association (division of Music Educator's National Conference); Louisiana Music Teachers Association (affiliated with Music Teachers National Association); Louisiana State Department of Education; Metairie Music Club; National Catholic Music Educators Association, National Federation of Music Clubs; and the New Orleans Music Teachers Association. In addition to these there are several neighborhood organizations which conduct contests or auditions of various types. If the teacher is so inclined she also may enter students in the annual contests sponsored by the New Orleans Symphony Orchestra, the New Orleans "Pops" Orchestra, the New Orleans Recreation Department (NORD) Orchestra, and annual events sponsored by various universities in the area.

Almost as diverse are the methods teachers employ to prepare students for examination. The bane of judges is the teacher who assigns materials to students in September for examination in February or March. By this method her entire class may achieve high ratings and as a consequence her students have little to show in the way of repertoire and musical progress for the year's work. This practice especially is harmful to the very young pianist. This can be controlled in festivals in which officials keep records on students entering and the music they perform. Otherwise there is no effective defense for the judge or the sponsoring organization.

Other teachers assign audition music early in the school year, allow the students to learn it thoroughly, and then progress to new repertoire. Shortly before the audition date the music is relearned. This procedure has merit. It is ethical, in the best interest of the student, and it is supported by a considerable amount of research.

Perhaps the most important consideration is that the audition or festival can be an important part of the young pianist's education, but only if it is treated as a part of a well structured, planned learning sequence. Therefore, if an audition (or several auditions a year) can be fit into the student's regime of technique, theory, reading, repertoire, and musicianship, it is of value. When the necessity for learning music for festivals interferes with orderly musical growth, students should not be entered. However, if the teacher finds that she is entering very few students in auditions, this could be an indication that her pedagogical techniques are at fault.

Detailed directions aiming at a high level of performance at auditions are not practical within the context of this chapter. Superior performance depends upon sound teaching techniques, and an exposition of these is the aim of this entire volume. However, some suggestions are of practical value. At the elementary and intermediate levels, judges are interested in specifics. These may be organized under the headings of technique, musicianship and style, and aesthetic considerations. From experience, it appears that most judges will give high ratings to an elementary student who is technically proficient for his level, and one who observes the musical and stylistic requirements of the composition. Technically, judges look for posture at the keyboard, hand position, wrist flexibility, finger action, evenness of touch, coordination, pedal dexterity, and facility. The teacher's competence in this area is readily apparent to the judge. These factors cannot be "crammed" for examination. Rather they are the result of lesson by lesson attention by teacher and student.

Musically, the best procedure is to follow the composer's directions explicitly. Elements of style augment the composer's written directions, but the teacher's training will determine her students' expertise in this area. When in doubt consult a good edition. A steady tempo is desirable unless the composer gives other directions. Tempo markings should be followed to the limit of the student's ability. However, it is better to reduce the tempo than to ignore other elements of musicianship. Among the most abused elements of musicianship at festivals are those of texture and phrasing. These particularly are important in music of the pre-Baroque, Baroque, Classical, and early Romantic periods. Correct texture involves the strict observance of staccato-legato, and of rests—a failing by young pianists of epidemic proportions. Phrasing, the "breathing" of a musical line, often is ignored. The judge also will listen carefully for correct balance between the hands, and for the observance of dynamic markings. If the student's technique is flawless and if he observes all musical directions indicated by the composer, this still does not insure a "musical" performance. All these elements need to be fused, to form a *gestalt*. Thus the integration of technique, style and musicianship communicates to the listener that this particular performance is a thing of value. With more complex music performed at advanced levels, the listener may experience an "aesthetic response." But to the teacher or judge interested in young musicians, the same response can be evoked from a superior performance on a much more elementary level.

Teachers tend to attribute the presence or lack of the *gestalt* in students' performance to talent, or the lack of it. Talent has never been adequately defined, if there is such a phenomenon to be defined. On a more practical level, after the student learns the notes, observes the tempo, keeps a steady beat, pays attention to texture, phrasing and dynamics, the teacher then can pay attention to the aesthetic elements of the performance. Much of this may be accomplished by direction during lessons; that is, attention to the contour of phrases, and to more subtle dynamic effects. However, the student will not learn to play musically until he learns to imitate musically. There are explicit factors to the musical art, and these may be learned by direction. However, there is the entire world of musical style, of "musicianship" that probably is learned best by imitation, especially for the young musician.

One of the principal goals of teaching is to encourage students to listen, not only to themselves, but also to others. If the home environment is not amenable to hearing good recordings, provide opportunities for students to hear good music before or after lessons. Specifically for auditions, and after the music has been mastered, students should hear their pieces performed by a good musician. If records are not available (the Federation performs this service for its membership), the teacher can play the compositions. A few sessions of this type can raise ratings from "excellent" to "superior."

In addition to hearing their pieces performed, students should be encouraged to hear their own performances via the tape recorder (at the lesson). The students listen carefully to themselves in play back and are asked to comment on the results. Continuity, rhythm, accuracy, etc. is readily apparent. Sometimes a student does not realize he is doing something incorrectly. Hearing his performance objectively makes him aware of faults and shows the areas in which he needs to improve.

After the music is learned and not more than two weeks before the audition date, a "dress rehearsal" is in order. All of the students can meet and perform. This provides needed practice of playing under pressure. Also, students will recognize the dress rehearsal as the deadline for learning their pieces rather than the later deadline, the audition date. Some teachers utilize the formal rehearsal as a preliminary audition. That is, students who have their music learned and play well at the rehearsal are allowed to go to festival. Unfortunately those who are rejected lose their entrance fee and some degree of status, but by following this procedure the necessity for regular practice and attention to detail is emphasized. In addition this saves the teacher a considerable amount of anxiety during the two weeks before festival. Added benefits are that judges are spared the necessity of giving low ratings, and students are not embarrassed before outsiders.

SUMMARY

Preparing students for auditions need not be a traumatic experience. When the examination is viewed by the teacher and pupils as one factor in the learning sequence, when preparation is orderly and structured, and when a preliminary audition chooses students for the main event, most problems are solved. Through the audition students are helped to recognize the relationship between work and success.

In auditions the competition factor is minimal; since only a rating is given, the student is really competing against himself. However, in a contest the competition aspect is one of the central factors. The main purpose of the contest is to provide incentives for superior performance by such externals as awards, statues, ribbons, etc. However, before entering the contest the student should have a realistic view of his chances, and he should be informed that winning is, to some extent, a matter of luck. Therefore, if he does not realize his highest hopes, he should not feel depressed or rejected but should try harder the next time. Unfortunately, we often find elated winners and despondent losers. Contests must be viewed in their proper perspective, and winning or losing should not be blown up out of proportion.

Finally, a word of caution is in order. The teacher who only sends "superior" students to festivals will not always be pleased with the results. There are too many variables. The usual childhood illnesses will eliminate some contestants, while others will turn in poor performances. A better method is to send those judged to be in the top two categories, or perhaps the top three. Some young pianists rise to the occasion and surprise teachers and peers alike.

The College Preparatory Department

13

by Louise Bianchi

Louise Bianchi received her Bachelor of Music and Master of Music degrees from Southern Methodist University and did advanced study at Teachers College, Columbia University. She is a National Piano Foundation clinician and an adjudicator for the National Guild of Piano Teachers. She is a past president of the Dallas Music Teachers Association and a past member of the Executive Board of the Music Teachers National Association, Southwest Division. Mrs. Bianchi is a professor of piano pedagogy and the founder and Director of the Piano Preparatory Department of the Division of Music at Southern Methodist University, Dallas, Texas.

The training of college piano majors too often centers exclusively on performance. Performance is an important facet of the college program, but emphasis in this area alone will not prepare the average college student for an occupation in music upon graduation. A majority of the graduates will make their livings not from performance but from teaching. This being the case, serious attention should be given to the training of teachers for the home studio and for group instruction in public and private schools. A prerequisite for teacher training is a laboratory situation in which trainees can teach and observe students learning at various levels.

The college piano preparatory department is an ideal training center for future teachers. In addition, the department offers multi-purpose functions in such areas as public service, community relations, and academic stimulation. Moreover, the department usually is able to pay its own way, and in some instances may even be a profitable enterprise for the university.

THE PREPARATORY PROGRAM AT SOUTHERN METHODIST UNIVERSITY

Two important objectives were considered in the creation of the Preparatory Department at Southern Methodist University: (1) instruction could be offered for a selected group of talented pupils who could be a source of future talent for the University; or (2) its function could be to strive for above average results with average students. The latter role seemed more realistic and better suited to serve the Music Department's purpose of providing a pedagogical center for teacher training. It was with this goal in mind that the Piano Preparatory Department of Southern Methodist University was formed.

The Department began in 1965 with one hundred piano students, three full-time teachers, two part-time teachers and two graduate assistants. Subsequently, enrollment has grown to three hundred students, the maximum capacity the program can serve. The program has been self-supporting from the beginning, and it furnishes scholarship funds for an increasing number of graduate students each year.

The Music Division of the School of Fine Arts offers both the Bachelor and Master of Music degrees in piano pedagogy. All undergraduate piano majors are required to take eight hours of pedagogy. Pedagogy majors take three years of pedagogy. Graduate pedagogy majors, in addition to pedagogy classes, have a teaching practicum and a directed studies project. Courses in class piano procedures offer training for teaching both the adult and the younger student. Other courses include fundamentals of teaching, private lesson procedures, and surveys of piano literature for beginning through advanced students.

Through the Preparatory Department piano majors have an opportunity to observe teaching procedures and to follow the learning sequence of children at various levels of advancement. Weekly observation of private and group lessons is required as part of pedagogy courses. By assisting regular staff teachers pedagogy majors gain teaching experience within a clinical structure. The University offers full tuition grants to graduate students for teaching twelve hours weekly, with the requirement that they take two years to complete the degree program.

Organization

The maximum enrollment of three hundred children is maintained each year. Tuition is paid by the semester and payments may be made in one, two, or four installments. Billing is handled by the Preparatory Department's secretary. All income is deposited in the Music Division account. Preparatory Department salaries, scholarship funds, and operating expenses are paid from this account. Personnel of the department includes the Director, assistant director, several full-time teachers, graduate assistants, and a full-time secretary. The Director and assistant director are part of the preparatory teaching staff, and the Director is responsible for the music division pedagogy program.

Instructional Procedures

The Piano Preparatory Department offers instruction to pre-college students of all ages from pre-school through high school. The pre-school program consists of music readiness for four-year-olds and pre-piano study for five-year-olds. Pre-school children attend an hour class once a week in groups of approximately fifteen children per class. Emphasis is placed on rhythmic and singing activities, creative expression, and preparation for music reading.

Children from first grade through junior high school attend combination group and private lessons, meeting for an hour class and a thirty minute private lesson each week. Training includes study in comprehensive musicianship with theory, ear training, and creative activities closely integrated with repertoire for the development of performance skills. Groups for beginners may have as many as twelve students. More advanced groups will have from eight to ten. Senior high school students have forty-five minute private lessons, supplemented by weekly theory classes stressing pre-college theory requirements. All plans are flexible. Closely matched beginners groups may have two group lessons each week, with private or semi-private lessons substituted for one of the group lessons when more time for individual guidance seems advisable. Many well integrated classes continue as groups throughout the high school years with the group lesson curriculum stressing overall musicianship, listening experiences, and advanced technique.

Curriculum

Because of the frequent turnover of graduate assistants, the curriculum for the Department must be carefully evaluated and supervised. Curriculum planning is the responsibility of the Director, with all teachers contributing suggestions for improvement or revision. The Director prepares lesson plans, including a group lesson plan and a private lesson plan for each week. Six or seven weeks of assignments and lesson plans constitute a unit of study. Group lessons are taught by staff teachers with a graduate assistant. Ideally, the student assistant should teach the private lessons of the pupils in the group. The weekly assignment is given at the group lesson and new concepts are presented at that time. The private lesson plan is based on the group presentation and serves as a reinforcement of that lesson. The development of individual technique and the assignment of supplementary materials are the responsibility of the private teacher. A lesson report in the form of a check sheet is given to the group teacher after each private lesson.

Supervision of the Program

The faculty is supervised by the Director, who is responsible for selecting permanent teachers and recommending student assistants for teaching scholarships. Communication between teachers is an important factor in the progress of the student. Monthly planning and evaluation meetings are scheduled for the entire staff, and a weekly meeting time is scheduled for conferences between full-time teachers and graduate assistants. An individual file for each pupil contains registration information, copies of progress reports to parents, a yearly evaluation by his teacher or teachers, and repertoire data. Such records have proved to be invaluable when a student has a change of teacher(s). The group teacher generally has the same students year after year; thus, continuity and smooth transition may be achieved even with the rotation of assistant teachers.

Equipment and Facilities

Basic equipment is furnished by the University. College classrooms are used for preparatory group lessons. There is little conflict because lessons for children are scheduled after school hours, and few Music Division classes are held late in the day. Individual lessons are taught in several practice rooms which have been set aside for the Department's use and in two larger studios. The studios each have a grand piano and an upright. Practice rooms have one studio upright piano. The larger classrooms are furnished with two, four, or six pianos, depending on their purpose as college classrooms. Equipment includes desks with wide arms, which serve to hold simulated keyboards for silent practice; these are made of masonite with plastic black keys and encompass four and a half octaves. All classrooms have ample blackboard space. Tuning of the pianos is charged proportionately to the Music Division and the Piano Preparatory Department. Special equipment, such as the keyboards, seat lifts (of various lengths and thicknesses made of styrofoam covered with self-adhesive paper), and rhythm instruments is purchased by the Preparatory Department. Monthly recitals are held in either the choral room or the concert hall of the music building.

Pre-school classes are held in a large room which is used by the Music Division for chamber music and small ensemble practice. Special low tables and chairs will accommodate up to twenty children at one time. A large wooden keyboard with raised black keys is designed to help children learn note names, steps and skips, and major-minor key patterns. The keyboard, which is comfortable for both stepping and walking, is 6½ feet long, 33 inches wide, and 9 inches high. (See Illustration 5:6 in Chapter 5 for a photo of this keyboard.) Additional equipment includes two pianos, a record player, large size flash cards, and various rhythm instruments.

Parent-Teacher Relationships

Parental support is essential to the success of the student's program.

At Southern Methodist several methods are used to promote beneficial parent-school relationships. A meeting of parents of all beginning students is scheduled approximately six weeks after lessons start. The purpose of the meeting is to inform the parents of immediate and long-range goals, to discuss the advantages of the particular method of instruction being used, and to discuss the parents' and teachers' roles in the child's learning. Practice habits, promptness at lessons, and good practice conditions at home are also discussed. A quiet room, good lighting, a well-tuned piano, and the correct height of the piano bench are important prerequisites for efficient, happy practice periods. These would appear to be unnecessary reminders, but practice conditions at home are often disorganized.

A presentation of the repertoire to be covered during the year may encourage parents who find beginning pieces somewhat dull and repetitious. The scope of the year's work and a planning sequence tend to give parents and students a sense of expectancy and goals for which to strive. Pieces may be demonstrated by teachers or good second year pupils. By outlining the program, by demonstrating some of the compositions, and by initiating a question and answer period, many problems may be solved before they occur.

Parents are invited to at least one class or private lesson each term. Lessons should be conducted much as usual, but the class session should be planned to include representative group activities with every child participating in some phase. Creative work, rhythm activities, reading drill, ensemble playing, practice procedures, and performance could be included. A private lesson might include some discussion and evaluation of accomplishment, but should not put the child in an embarrassing situation.

Progress reports are issued each semester to keep parents informed of the student's accomplishments or deficiencies in the different phases of study. A routine form with categories such as preparation of new pieces, review pieces, theory, technique, written work, and recital preparation may be checked with suitable ratings. A space for teacher comments affords the opportunity for individual suggestions and personal remarks.

Conferences with parents are held whenever the need arises. However, one week of the year designated as conference week will save many hours for the teachers. Parents are notified by mail that the teachers will observe office hours at specified times during the conference week. Parents are requested to make definite appointments. Discussions during this time generally bring fruitful results and help promote closer relationships between the parents, child, and the teachers.

Recitals

An important advantage that the college preparatory department offers piano pupils is the opportunity for frequent public performances. In group teaching situations performance for peers is routine procedure, and acts as an effective aid in eliminating fear of formal recitals. Private pupils who do not have the advantage of playing for a group, may meet in occasional repertoire classes for performance experiences. In addition to individual performances, ensemble programs are encouraged to include both group and private pupils. By providing the Preparatory Department with the usual facilities of the University, the problem of finding a suitable place for frequent recitals is solved. A preparatory department should plan enough recitals so that each student may perform several times during the year. As an aid in giving self-confidence to the performers, and for the overall success of the programs, rehearsals are required for each program. The extra work from both the students and teachers is well worth the effort. At the rehearsal last minute corrections can be made both in performance and stage deportment. Poise and projection will contribute significantly to the enjoyment of the audience.

End of school recitals may use a different format than regular monthly recitals. Demonstration recitals for group students are educational and enjoyable. A combination of two or three different levels of advancement, involving approximately thirty students, presents an interesting learning sequence. The first half of the program may be devoted to demonstrating various keyboard skills, group activities, and short performance pieces which depict the areas of emphasis for a particular year's work. Each group teacher may present his students and give a brief explanation of goals and accomplishments. All children are on stage until the demonstration portion of the program is finished. A more formal recital may follow, with each student performing individually. With good planning and strict rehearsal, this kind of program should not take more than an hour and fifteen minutes. A demonstration recital is interesting to parents and is effective as a means of presenting the department to prospective students and their parents.

Pre-Registration for Continuing Students

Pre-enrollment forms, with a definite due date, are mailed to parents before the end of the spring term. A brief policy statement, a resumé of fees, and a registration calendar may be included. A registration fee, which is deducted from the following year's tuition, is required. Because the S.M.U. Preparatory Department has a limited enrollment, it is necessary to determine as accurately as possible the number of students who will return. When pre-enrollment for continuing students is closed, new students are accepted.

New Students

It is advisable to start new groups of beginners each year. Distribution of students is important to a well rounded department, and incoming graduate assistants need to observe learning processes from all levels. Applications for beginning students should be kept until homogeneous age groups are formed. Interviews for beginners may be scheduled by groups. Tests for pitch recognition, coordination, rhythm and general response to teaching are effective guides for acceptance into the program and for grouping the children.

A transfer student should be interviewed and tested individually to determine how his background relates to the plan of study currently in use in the Preparatory Department. The results of the test will indicate whether or not the student will fit into an existing group. If several transfer students have the same deficiencies, it may be practical to form a remedial group for emphasis on reading, rhythm, theory, or other basic weaknesses. Transfer students with adequate backgrounds may fill groups that have become too small. Others may make better progress in private lessons. In any case, the needs of the individual student are the primary consideration.

The Department and Community Teachers

There are two specific ways in which the preparatory department may be of service to local teachers. The first is the opening of regular theory classes to students of private teachers in the community. Many private teachers do not have the facilities and equipment to offer this special instruction, and they will welcome the opportunity to offer regular theory instruction to their pupils. Another service to teachers is the scheduling of commuter classes. In these classes teachers observe one private lesson and two group lessons at different levels of advancement. Observations should be scheduled on one afternoon of the week, preceded by a resumé of the lesson plans for that day. This is a practical method of providing continuing education for teachers interested in group instructional procedures and newer teaching methods.

SUMMARY

Preparatory Department students have maintained a high level of accomplishment. A well-planned curriculum and practical teaching methods have produced consistent results. Peer relationships, frequent performance opportunities and over-all high standards have contributed to a sense of pride in musical performance and general accomplishment. The success of the department may be measured by the fact that approximately ninety percent of the students return each year.

S.M.U. graduates are entering the teaching profession with a background of practical experience and knowledge gained from participating in a real learning situation. Some have been employed to teach in class piano programs both in elementary schools and in colleges, and some have set up preparatory programs in other colleges. Many of the graduates have opened private studios or operate their own schools. The confidence they have gained from actual teaching experience is a valuable asset in their first professional undertaking.

There is an increasing demand for piano teachers, in the classroom and in the private studio. The college music department has a challenging opportunity to meet this demand by training musicians to a high degree of performance skill and, at the same time, preparing skilled performers to be successful, well-trained teachers—teachers who will go into their profession with confidence and know-how.

FOR FURTHER READING

An interesting survey of preparatory and pedagogy departments was done in 1975 by Stella V. Tatlock of Indiana State University, Terre Haute, Indiana. The survey listed schools offering degrees in piano pedagogy, schools which had a preparatory division, organization of pedagogy courses and preparatory departments, and other pertinent information.

The College Piano Major 14

by Joseph Banowetz

Joseph Banowetz received his musical training from Southern Methodist University, the Juilliard School, the University of Michigan, and graduated *cum laude* from the Vienna State Academy of Music and Dramatic Arts. He has toured as recitalist and orchestral soloist in Europe, the Soviet Union, Mexico, Canada, and the United States, and has also been heard on National Educational Television. An authority on the music of Franz Liszt, his articles have appeared in some of the leading American musical periodicals, and he has several recordings issued for Educo Records—one of which is the complete *Transcendental Etudes*. He is the editor of the *Urtext-Masterclass Editions* and the

Composers-of-Today Editions published by General Words and Music Company. Professor Banowetz has been a guest lecturer in piano for six summers at the National Music Camp, Interlochen, Michigan, and is presently on the keyboard faculty at North Texas State University, Denton, Texas.

The music profession for the pianist is a broad one, with many different avenues available to the prospective university graduate. In spite of the competitive aspects of a music career, there are still great opportunities and rewards of both a personal and professional nature for the properly trained and dedicated individual. Certain areas are growing rapidly, as for instance in the class piano and music therapy specializations, and the private teaching scene shows no signs of slackening. But whatever niche the student eventually finds for himself, personal involvement with an art offering its own unique artistic values and opportunities for self-expression is itself a great challenge and reward.

PRE-COLLEGE PIANO TRAINING

Good pre-college training is vital for the ultimate success of the piano major, for solid habits of technique and study should already have been formed by the time college is entered. Unlike many other disciplines, the performing arts cannot, except perhaps in the case of the vocalist, be pursued to any high degree of proficiency through a late or badly deficient start. Playing an instrument is in some ways similar to excelling professionally in a sport. Although artistic musical performance is at all levels infinitely more involved, still there is a basic set of muscular reflexes and mental patterns that must, in both activities, be established early from a physiological standpoint. This is a difficult fact for the late-starter to realize, and it is especially tragic to see such an individual, deeply in love with music, trying to become a performance major. Without adequate talent or proper early development such efforts sooner or later will prove to be deeply frustrating both professionally and personally.

One of the most valuable pre-college experiences is the senior high school recital which may serve as preparation for both the college entrance audition and the ultimate graduation recital. A typical program might include one or two of the easier preludes and fugues from Bach's *Well-Tempered Clavier*, a Haydn or Mozart sonata, a group of nineteenth-century works of the level of the Chopin waltzes and nocturnes or Schumann's *Fantasy Pieces opus 12*, and perhaps closing with an impressionistic or twentieth-century group of the difficulty of Debussy's *Pour le Piano,*, Copland's *Cat and the Mouse*, or Bartók's *Allegro Barbaro*. Even at this level an effort should have been made on the teacher's part to expose the student to as wide a range of musical periods and styles as possible.

A common error in the pre-college training is the assigning of pieces that are overly difficult both technically and musically. The experienced teacher will develop the student's playing gradually so that proper attention may be given to all areas of musicianship.

The prospective piano major should not only have acquired a degree of competency in performance, but should also be well-grounded in technique (scales, chords, arpeggios, etc.), have a knowledge of theory, and have some knowledge of the literature. Thus, supplied with an adequate pre-college background, the student will be well prepared to meet the demands of the college music department as a piano major.

THE PIANO MAJOR AND DEGREES

There are a number of music programs available to the student desiring a degree with a piano concentration, each offering varying amounts of applied keyboard training. The list of degree titles is long and varied: Bachelor of Music, Bachelor of Music in Applied Music, Bachelor of Music with emphasis in pedagogy, Bachelor of Music Education, Bachelor of Arts with a music concentration, Bachelor of Science in Music, etc. Carried further to the master's and doctoral levels, there are still more ways to list music degrees, all of which may be granted by schools of music, departments of music, colleges of fine arts, colleges of education, schools of fine arts, and so on. Whatever degree program the student chooses to fit his own individual career goals, he should be concerned not only with gaining performance ability on his instrument, but also with acquiring both theoretical and, if possible, practical experience in teaching his specialization. This should be done regardless of the amount of applied keyboard work contained in the degree program.

For the pianist wishing to teach at least some amount of keyboard in either a university or public school situation, only two general types of degrees will in all likelihood be useful as proper credentials and as possible preparation for graduate studies: the Bachelor of Music degree and the Bachelor of Music Education degree. These degrees not only prepare the individual for various employed teaching situations, but also usually well-outfit him for a career in private studio teaching, an area that can offer excellent professional rewards.

The student who obtains a Bachelor of Music degree with a major in piano, and who wishes to go into university teaching, will quickly find upon making job applications little choice but to pursue graduate studies. Few—if indeed any—universities will consider a recent Bachelor of Music graduate for a teaching post, and with the glut of pianists competing for jobs in the teaching field, a masters is absolutely essential to stand even a slight chance of winning a university position. (There are always exceptions to this rule, usually those individuals who have exhibited extraordinary professional achievements, such as concert performers, recording artists, prize winners, etc.) Increasingly, an earned doctorate for the performer, usually the Doctor of Musical Arts degree, is becoming mandatory for successfully competing for the better positions on the university teaching scene. This is especially true in smaller, less sophisticated "emerging" universities where, in an effort to please accrediting agencies and through an at times naive equating of competence with degrees, the percentage of doctorates on the faculty becomes of over-riding importance. The older, more prestige-laden departments and schools of music, as a broad rule, still appear to hire faculty on the basis of demonstrated professional accomplishment in the teaching and performing areas. The young pianist would do well to not only collect degrees, but to endeavor to achieve as much professional concert experience as possible.

The Bachelor of Music Education degree with a heavy keyboard concentration should prove of ever-greater value to the general college-level piano student, for increasingly the public schools at all levels are instigating teaching programs in class piano. For example, the public schools in the cities of Dallas, Texas; Lansing, Michigan; Bethesda, Maryland; Spokane, Washington; Mobile, Alabama; Miami, Florida, and many others, all offer piano programs. Although a person obtaining a Bachelor of Music Education degree will no doubt have to teach other musical subjects, at least part of the public school agenda will probably be devoted to teaching piano in a class situation. Hopefully the keyboard pedagogy classes the student attends will be in part devoted to a discussion and analysis of teaching techniques for the class piano situation. Although the student may desire to ultimately pursue a higher degree, this is usually not mandatory for at least obtaining a first job, as it is in the university job market.

Those electing to specialize in piano pedagogy more heavily than in piano performance can obtain a Bachelor of Music degree stressing this area. Even though this type of program will not have as large a concentration of actual keyboard applied study as the straight Bachelor of Music in piano, it is highly useful to those intending either to carry this type of study through to the graduate level, or to do private studio teaching. Emphasis in this area, especially on the graduate level, can also be instrumental as a means of entering the university teaching scene in a group teaching situation or in a college preparatory department.

KEYBOARD-RELATED COURSE WORK FOR THE PIANO MAJOR

In addition to the usual humanities courses, there are various musical areas with which any well-rounded and informed musician must be acquainted. Familiarity with all periods of music history and music literature outside the immediate specialization are vital for a complete musical culture, as are general theoretical subjects such as theory (or harmony), counterpoint, and composition. All are necessary for a general musical background, and will prove vital for both immediate pursuit of the keyboard specialization, and later for successful teaching.

A number of classes are specifically tailored for the keyboard major. Roughly they can be subdivided into six general areas:

1. Applied keyboard study
2. History of keyboard literature and performance practices
3. Piano pedagogy
4. Accompanying and ensemble performance
5. Functional piano

Applied Study

The applied study of any musical instrument is in a real sense the passing on from generation to generation of an aural tradition which constantly grows and changes. Some subjects, as for instance with many of the sciences, can be adequately formalized and recorded on paper. This is not the case with the elusive performing arts, where a personal teacher-pupil contact is vital. If all performers, teachers, and recordings were eliminated for a full generation, the difficulties in reconstructing performance traditions from reviews, books, music editions, and the like would be staggering, if not impossible. The student should realize that he someday will form a link in this fragile, precious cultural chain, and he should be aware of the importance of this historical tradition when learned from the best available sources.

When the piano major enters college, hopefully already equipped with a good background, further technical development and training should be intensified. The teacher should be able to analyze technical problems, and over an extended period systematically guide the student toward ever greater physical capability at the keyboard. Exercises alone, introduced with the usual arsenal of scales, arpeggios, etc., will not suffice—necessary as these all are. The instructor must also be able to explain *how* to use the playing mechanism, *what* to do with the arm, wrist, and fingers, *how* to produce certain effects, *how* to go about unraveling a technically difficult passage, etc. Unfortunately there is too often at the university level—and for that matter at all levels—the teacher who believes technical development will automatically come simply from going through a tedious ritual of so many finger drills a day. The results are often tragic in terms of lost time, sore muscles, and tight, poor playing. Too often this type of training becomes passed on as a firmly entrenched bad tradition.

In addition to a detailed technical analysis of piano performance, with the corresponding ability to confidently go about learning and performing works of advanced difficulty, the student should receive exposure to a broad range of piano literature. Insight into various styles, an understanding of performance traditions, evaluation of editions, interpretative depth and sensitivity—are all areas which should be explored and developed. The repertory covered should ideally extend from about 1600 to the present, and should not be top-heavy in any one stylistic period. Almost any pianist-teacher will admittedly have certain specialties and preferences, but any weak stylistic area eventually will show up in the student's work, lessening over-all interpretative insight and perspective.

The student should endeavor to learn to make his own interpretative decisions, to be able to gain ever greater technical security and to be able to produce finished results without the teacher's prompting. In short, he should become an artistic entity in his own right. There is something pathetic about the professional student of fifty who still is incapable of functioning independently as a performer—and correspondingly as a teacher—and who is forever auditing master classes in an effort to reach artistic and professional maturity. Hopefully the college experience will, if administered correctly, prepare the student to work independently.

Keyboard Literature and Performance Practices

The college piano major will ideally study and perform works from a large range of styles and periods. But this in itself is not enough, for a wider familiarity with keyboard literature additional to those works actually studied and performed is essential. The piano major should have at least a listening acquaintance of the following:

1. Representative seventeenth and eighteenth century works by such composers as D. Scarlatti, Couperin, Handel, etc.
2. A cross section of J. S. Bach's keyboard works.
3. Familiarity with important sonatas, concertos, and other solo works of Haydn and Mozart.
4. A representative sampling from each of the three periods of the Beethoven sonatas, as well as an acquaintance with the concertos and variations.
5. A cross section of such nineteenth century composers' works as Schubert, Chopin, Schumann, Liszt, Brahms, etc.
6. Familiarity with representative impressionistic works of Debussy and Ravel.
7. An examination of representative pieces of such twentieth century figures as Stravinsky, Bartók, Prokofiev, Copland, Schoenberg, etc.

This is only a start for any serious pianist about to embark into his extremely competitive chosen profession. Most schools give a quick survey course or two in keyboard literature; students cram-memorize a few pages of this or that work for the listening examination, then promptly forget the whole unpleasant business. The pupil should daily be made aware that knowledge of the literature is vital to musical development.

In addition to his own repertory, the student should gain familiarity with symphonies, chamber music, and choral works for genuine interpretative maturity. College survey courses in these areas can only act as an introduction. If the serious piano major avoids exposure-in-depth in these areas, he invites a later artistic crippling as a performer-teacher. All top-rank musicians and teachers have this rich background which aids them in their high artistic attainments.

An awareness of stylistic problems and the history and evolution of performance practices are of great importance. From the Baroque and Classic periods the student should have a knowledge of such areas as ornamentation, old keyboard instruments, and performance practices of the time. This information will be gained largely from books and accounts of the times, and from research done since then. Fortunately, we have available old recordings made on 78 r.p.m.'s of such older generation pianists as Hofmann, Busoni, Schnabel, Rachmaninoff, Godowsky, Cortot, Fischer, Friedman, Lhevinne, Rosenthal, Sauer, and others. (The piano roll transfers are generally misleading and unreliable.) These performances can be compared to those of today for an insight into styles of the time. One notes immediately that their interpretations are different from today's pianists. It should be remembered, however, when listening to recordings of Rosenthal or Sauer, for instance, that these pianists were students of Liszt. If to the unsophisticated ear this style of playing seems at times overly free and mannered, one must take into consideration the fact that these performers represented a fantastically high level of creative artistic individuality often missing in today's young virtuosos. Equally important, these performers were historically close to Chopin, Schumann, and Liszt, and therefore their playing of at least nineteenth century works is historically faithful to the Romantic spirit. By careful and thoughtful examination of style and performance practice, the student can develop his own ability for artistic judgments.

Along with a sense of historical development of performance style, the student should also develop an acquaintance with the history, literature and art of the various period of works studied. Debussy can be more easily understood if one has a knowledge of such French impressionist painters as Monet, Manet, Renoir, and Degas along with a literary knowledge of such figures as Verlaine, Rimbaud, Loüys, Maeterlinck, and others. Liszt's works become more meaningful through a knowledge of such writers as Goethe, Petrarch, and Dante. In short, the student should not isolate performance study from total cultural development. College courses stimulate and introduce, but alone are not a substitute for continued independent intellectual growth. Again, the student must develop and learn for himself.

Piano Pedagogy

Classes in keyboard pedagogy take a variety of approaches which can be geared to teaching the beginner, the intermediate student, the advanced student, or the class and group teaching situation. Needless to say, it is virtually impossible to adequately cover all these categories in one semester. Since discussion of university level teaching demands on the part of the student an already high level of pianistic development, it is best left for a graduate seminar. Therefore, for the college piano major, the study of keyboard pedagogy (learning how to teach) should be confined to pre-college teaching.

The most frequently covered area in the pedagogy class is the beginner, with a close examination of early lesson approaches, teaching methods and techniques, suitable repertoire, and pupil psychology. Class and group instructional techniques should be included here, since these are more and more coming into the national scene at every teaching level. Understanding the mechanics of teaching at the lower levels is especially important, for most piano majors will at some time deal in a large share with the beginning student. It is at this level that good instructional methodology is most important. In the pedagogy class much supervised teaching should be done, each student ideally being assigned one or more test pupils. Audio or video tapings should be used to enable the pedagogy student to gain self-awareness of his actual effectiveness as a teacher. In addition, the student should observe area teachers for background and insight into actual situations.

The pedagogy class should also provide experiences dealing with intermediate students, both in discussion and observation. Within this group the badly taught beginner may be encountered, and ways to correct the most common faults should be discussed by the class. The transfer student will often come from this age group, and the pedagogy class should provide methods of dealing with this special situation.

Finally, the pedagogy class should at least touch upon teaching the advanced pre-college student, the adult beginner, class piano techniques, literature at all levels, technique at all levels, suggestions for practicing, the mechanics of memorization, the recital, the audition and contest, and much more. In short, the pedagogy class should, through discussion, observation and participation, provide a meaningful apprenticeship experience which will form the basis for future independent teaching.

It is difficult to say exactly when college piano pedagogy should first be taught, since the needs of students vary. However, as a broad rule, the junior year seems to be a good choice, for by this time a good applied music foundation should be established, and time is still left before graduation for possible experimentation with private students.

Accompanying and Ensemble Playing

These two areas should be stressed in any college program, both for developing familiarity with important repertory outside the immediate solo keyboard area, and in learning to listen and think more musically. Problems of pedaling, rhythm, subtleties of phrasing, and a host of other musicianship considerations arise in the ensemble situation. Duets, two-piano literature, the large string-keyboard literature, or chamber music with larger groups all have distinctive problems that demand great flexibility and constant attentiveness by the performers.

Accompanying, when well done, must also have the same sense of give and take as found in a good ensemble performance. These elements can, to a certain extent, be taught in the class room, although experience is often the best teacher in this case. The student usually improves in sight reading and overall musicianship through varied accompanying experiences.

Functional Piano

Functional (useful) piano combines several important areas with which the piano major must be familiar: sight reading, keyboard harmony, and improvisation—all the practical areas of musicianship. This course (or courses) is generally taught within the first two years of college. Often the novice college student is deficient in reading and the other abovementioned items.

The ability to read proficiently at sight is a valuable asset for any phase or level of piano study. Classes in sight reading often are little more than supervised reading practice sessions, but when taught properly and with imagination can aid the student in learning sight reading techniques as well as learning how to transpose and to possibly read open scores. Proficient sight playing is a general skill that must be cultivated by the student over a sustained, long period for maximum results. The study and performance of ensemble literature, duets and two-piano music, is also an especially valuable aid in cultivating reading ability. In these experiences the student will learn to "keep going," the basic tenet of good sight reading.

The study of keyboard harmony is highly practical for all levels of piano study. Aural acuity will be heightened by functional harmonization. For anyone using the piano, from the grade school teacher harmonizing simple tunes, to the performer grappling with late Beethoven, a firm sense of harmony in a practical keyboard application is vitally needed. Although somewhat outdated with today's "lead sheet" type chord symbolization usage, an advanced keyboard harmony class will probably include work with figured bass realization. Acquaintance with this harmonization technique is useful, if for no other reason than to understand more fully certain basic style characteristics and performance practices of the Baroque period.

Coupled with a knowledge of keyboard harmony is the ability to improvise. This is especially necessary for the student who will be teaching class piano, or working in a public school situation. The ability to improvise accompaniments to songs, to provide chordal harmony for single-note melodies often found in vocal books used in the public schools, and to be able to play well-known songs by ear are all vital skills. The private studio teacher can also employ these skills in meaningful ways. Today's teacher is offering classes in improvisation, jazz, pop-rock, etc. to young students and teen-agers alike. This special instructional skill may be developed at the college level through the keyboard harmony class. Whatever level of advancement the student will eventually be involved with, the ability to improvise is one which must be developed, and should not be a neglected area in the education of the piano major.

THE ARTIST-TEACHER AND THE COLLEGE PIANO MAJOR

The title "artist-in-residence," "concert pianist-in-residence," "artist-affiliate," or something similar is now a familiar sight in school catalogues. The purpose of the artist-in-residence is to offer study with a professional performer to the students within a university framework. This concept originated in the late 1930's at the University of Wisconsin. Since that time the idea has caught on tremendously, and now many music faculties both large and small, boast their own "artist-in-residence." This may indicate anything from a young artist supplementing a sparse outside concert income by teaching, to the designation of an artist of genuine international reputation and prestige. Depending on whatever understanding has been reached with the officials of the school, this individual may be on campus for any period ranging from a few weeks to the total span of the school year. In some instances the resident artist may frequently be off campus performing concerts, and any or all missed lessons may or may not be made up, depending again on what agreements have previously been made. Sometimes an assistant is used to fill in these lesson gaps. Often the artist-in-residence is expected to give a certain number of local concerts each year. Grants from such sources as the Sears Roebuck foundation may help underwrite artists, usually younger ones "on the way up," for college residency programs generally lasting for a month or two. Local concerts are performed, and master classes, lectures, and private lessons are usually given.

Study with a truly distinguished professional performer active on the concert scene either in the past or immediate present can have great advantages for the student. This is especially true if the pupil is advanced, perhaps already at the graduate level. Aspects of public performance, inside views of the concert profession itself, to say nothing of a highly cosmopolitan and sophisticated musical culture, should all hopefully be made available to students by the ideal artist-in-residence.

Unfortunately, some inherent drawbacks are prevalent in this type of situation. Performing artists can be notoriously bad teachers on occasion, especially for the less advanced pupil who is "less interesting" to the artist-teacher. Very often much of what a highly gifted artist does in actual performance, or has become over long years, is virtually instinctive. Mundane pedagogical drudgery in matters of basic technical analysis and guidance, problems in clearly verbalizing important musical points, a systematic approach to teaching, and the intelligent remedying of a student's pianistic ills, may all be matters which might be ignored by the artist-teacher through inability or lack of desire to communicate on a less advanced level. Some can exhibit blatant favoritism, giving little help to the less advanced, while taking great pains with one or two "stars" in the class. A few are able to do little more than use the "Listen to me play it—now do as I did" approach. Also, the possibility of irregular lessons is a potential difficulty if the artist-teacher has a busy outside concert schedule, especially if the pupil is not advanced enough to work on his own.

When a person has the right insight and personality for inspired teaching, the rewards for the student can be enormous. All in all, great advantages and risks are inherent in this type of pedagogical situation, and no sweeping generalizations regarding desirability or undesirability can be made safely.

TEACHING THE APPLIED PIANO MAJOR IN GROUPS

The noticeable trend toward teaching college level piano in classes has already gained a foothold in California. Although not yet widespread, a number of schools are beginning to teach applied majors in groups. With increasingly difficult budgetary problems facing every university, and with the particularly expensive one-to-one ratio, a total private lesson approach may become a relic of the past. The group system of instruction can have great advantages even for the advanced student. It is in fact little different from the master class approach which has long been a tradition in European state academies and conservatories where private lessons are the exception rather than the rule. In this type of group instruction the number of students can be as high as eight or nine, with classes meeting for one hour periods two or three times a week. Classes are customarily divided into less advanced, intermediate, and advanced classifications. Healthy competition helps to motivate the students, and each can learn from the faults and virtues of the other. An alternative to the "class only" approach is the combination of a half-hour private lesson coupled with a weekly one or two hour group session. As most students find it difficult to adequately prepare a full hour's lesson each week, such an arrangement is in a sense more practical.

For the student particularly interested in keyboard pedagogy a group learning experience can be invaluable for absorbing teaching methods, in analyzing other's pianistic problems, and in being exposed to a wide repertory. This type of university teaching will, as time goes on, no doubt achieve ever greater and widespread acceptance.

IS A SOLO CONCERT CAREER A REALISTIC GOAL?

A heartbreaking aspect of the total music profession is the large number of students, often with great talent and determination, who strive for a concert career, only to ultimately have to come to terms with hard professional realities. The touring performer who can earn a respectable living, after deducting traveling expenses, manager's percentages, publicity expenses, taxes and the like, is a rare being. Following a handful of top drawing names in the Cliburn - Rubinstein - Horowitz league, there is a rapid drop-off a few levels down to the soloist who worries about the next engagement, and who in all likelihood heavily supplements his concert fees by teaching. Even if a younger performer has a couple of good seasons as a result of winning a major international competition, it is all too easy to be displaced by the next new box office sensation, and to quickly drop to relatively few bookings.

Assuming that the young pianist is determined to gamble on a performance career, what steps are open to him? Perhaps the most obvious is that of the international competition, although the winning of a first prize in one of these will not in itself assure an instantaneous career, unless the competition is of the stature of the Queen Elizabeth in Belgium, the Tchaikovsky in Moscow, or the Chopin in Warsaw. Less prestigious but also demanding are contests such as the Busoni (Bolzano, Italy), the Enesco (Bucharest, Romania), the Marguerite Long (Paris), the Leeds (Leeds, England), etc. A win in any of these will bring some cash, good exposure with solo and orchestral engagements for a season or so, but possibly little more. Unless a high prize is won, most of these competitions are fairly useless. And even a first prize can ultimately prove a failure for launching a firm, expanded career if it is not capitalized upon with proper managerial backing. Talent, timing, and luck are vital components.

Several other roads to a solo career exist. The New York debut recital, long a favored means of giving public exposure to the unknown performer, involves a considerable outlay of cash, usually in the vicinity of at least $3,000 if done in a major hall with the proper advance publicity. Ticket sales will of course be nil since the performer is unknown, and the house will be "papered" to gain an audience. Assuming that one of the better known critics can be attracted from the New York Times, what usually results is at best a polite review faintly praising this, and not liking that. To achieve the highly marketable kind of rave review necessary in launching an overnight career takes epitaphs of the most extravagant sort. Of course a career and a reputation can be built slowly, but this takes time, a certain cash outlay over a "dry" period of low paying engagements, and possibly several more personally financed New York recitals after the initial debut.

Auditions for conductors and managers can be arranged through the teacher if this individual has enough national prominence and influence, but unless the young unknown performer is of spectacular ability, managers are usually only interested in booking "name" performers who draw audiences and sell tickets. Recordings also are useful in gaining exposure and building reputations, but unfortunately most major companies are ruthlessly dedicated to selling records, and will not gamble on an unknown name as a rule.

The aspiring pianist should read carefully an annual artist booking directory, such as *Musical America International Directory of the Performing Arts,* noting especially the number of pianists listed in the index. (The 1977 issue has over 400 pianists.) This list is of course only a portion of the serious pianist-performers nation-wide, and when this is all compared with the number of keyboard soloists appearing on the various concert series in any average metropolitan area, grim conclusions are inescapable. The well-known Canadian pianist Glenn Gould has predicted that in twenty years concerts as we know them will be a thing of the past, and will be replaced by recordings, films, or television. This may be a bit alarmist, but without question the percentage of solo recitals has steadily shrunk over the years. This is not the place to explore the numerous and highly complex reasons for this. But the trend shows little signs of reversing itself—a fact that the young aspiring pianist, driven in the direction of a solo concert career, should realistically and honestly face as early as possible.

If, after full recognition of the above facts, the student is still determined to make solo performing a full-time career, he probably does not belong in a multi-purpose university which gives the usual BM or MM degree. He will probably find himself much better off in a highly performance oriented school such as the Curtis Institute in Philadelphia or the Juilliard School in New York, in one of the major European state conservatories, or studying with a well-known concert artist on a private basis. His work will be directed solely toward the concert field. He will need to practice at least six to eight hours a day at this time.[1] Concertos, major works of the solo literature, and chamber music should be explored by the serious pianist. Then, with the right amount of good advice from his teacher, extraordinary talent, and sheer luck, he may be able to get a foothold and a start.

IS A CONCERT ACCOMPANIST CAREER A REALISTIC GOAL?

A field that offers another avenue for the performing pianist is that of professional accompanist. The role of the accompanist—or as it should more often be, partner—can in its own way be as demanding musically, and even technically, as that of the solo performer. The successful concert accompanist must be an excellent sight reader, must be able to transpose vocal accompaniments, must have a first-class keyboard technique in order to handle such "accompaniments" as Schubert's "Erlking" or the Bartók violin and piano duo sonatas, should be able to reduce less complicated orchestral scores at sight, and must be fully conversant with musical styles as divergent as the Bach violin and keyboard sonatas or the Puccini operas.

The place of concert accompanists in the United States historically has been an unfortunate one, for the role of the famous soloist has usually eclipsed that of the pianist. Extremes have sometimes been reached so that on occasion the name of the pianist has been omitted from the program entirely. As a result of "second-billing," accompanists' fees usually are a small fraction of what the singer or instrumentalist receiving "star" billing is paid. Worse, this has affected even the manner of performance, so that in a work such as a Brahms violin and piano duo sonata it is not uncommon to hear the equally important keyboard part dampened down and pushed into the background with subdued dynamics and timid execution. In becoming a professional accompanist the student should be aware of his musical and professional rights, and assert them when possible.

Assuming that the music major has acquired good technical equipment at a reasonably early age, he should prepare for an accompanying career by gaining as much experience and familiarity as possible with all kinds of ensemble and vocal literature. A basic reading and pronunciation knowledge of several languages is helpful, as is an understanding of vocal technique, and of the performance capabilities of various instruments. The accompanist must be a well-rounded musician, for he will be called upon to serve in many areas.

[1] For an insight into the life and work of a concert pianist, see the article in *Clavier* (Vol. XI, No. 8, November, 1972) titled "At Ease with Claudio Arrau." He discusses how as a student he practiced an average of nine hours a day from the time he was about twelve years old.

Professional accompanying is not as difficult to break into as solo playing, assuming a high level of talent and good training exists. If the piano major is studying at a large university, valuable experience can be gained by accompanying lessons in vocal and instrumental studios, playing for opera workshops, accompanying choruses, and performing on numerous recitals for degree candidates. As much as possible the apprentice accompanist should avoid specializing in either the vocal or instrumental area, but should get wide experience in all branches of repertory. Opportunities should be taken to work in the studios of competent artist-teachers, and efforts should be made to play with the best level of performers possible.

If one decides to become a touring accompanist, New York is the logical place to aim for. The apprentice accompanist should try to obtain a job in a voice or instrumental studio of a well-known teacher, or try to obtain a job as a rehearsal pianist for the New York City or Metropolitan Opera companies. From there he can hopefully build a reputation and eventually make contacts with touring artists through the New York City management circuit. During "dry" spells between tours, additional income may be obtained from giving private lessons, coaching, etc.—not an easy life, but many find it a challenging one.

The accompanist, if he is lucky enough to become affiliated with a university large enough to afford one, can become a staff pianist. Usually this brings in a low salary and long hours. He will be expected to accompany a certain number of lessons and recitals. He may be able to charge extra for additional coaching or accompanying sessions given to students. There is a certain security in such a position, even though it normally does not carry professorial rank or tenure.

One further possibility for the professional performer is a position of staff pianist with a major symphony. This entails playing performances of orchestral works, usually twentieth century works, for which a piano part is written. Solo piano concertos are of course excluded. These parts on occasion can be extremely demanding, and often require precise rhythm and a fluent technique—Stravinsky's *Petrouchka* is a good example of what can be expected. When a position becomes available, an audition is generally given to fill the vacancy. Advance preparation with major works using piano is advised. The pay scale varies for the orchestral pianist. Some large symphonies are able to list the pianist as a full-time member in which he receives union scale. However, most average and smaller symphonies hire the pianist "when needed" on a per-job basis—as such, this would not be sufficient to form the sole basis for an income.

THE REWARDS OF THE PRIVATE STUDIO

A career as a private studio teacher cannot be underestimated, for it is in this area that some of the best professional opportunities await the college piano major. There is an immediate need for well-trained, dedicated teachers in communities both large and small. The private teaching field is a growing one. Many teachers now find such a demand for lessons that they have moved to the class approach via the electronic piano. A few especially busy teachers are finding the use of assistants necessary.

The importance of the private teacher has been minimized for too long. Our private teachers have the responsibility of training a wide range of students. Their products, good or bad, supply college music departments. Their amateur trainees often become supporters of concert activities through audience participation. And their work in sponsoring contests, festivals, workshops, etc., is of vital importance to the musical well-being of the community.

Since the private teacher is so vital to the community, one wonders why college and universities often seem oblivious to this fact. Emphasis in most music departments is geared either toward performance, or toward music education (public school teaching, primarily vocal and instrumental). It appears logical that the third element of university musical life, the training of private teachers, should receive an equal emphasis.

The graduating piano major often is hesitant to go into the private teaching field. He fears that he will have a hard time getting started, that he will make a poor living, or that he will "lose face" by turning to private teaching out of necessity. These fears are unfounded. The demand for the private teacher appears to be increasing, not decreasing. If handled properly on a professional basis the private teacher can make a very good living—often better than the college teacher. It is true that it will take awhile to get started; but this is also true for the dentist, lawyer, and other professionals. The beginning teacher's initial problem is gaining a local reputation. [For ideas in building a class, see Chapter 2, "How to Obtain Students."] Because of the severe competition in the performing field, with resulting limited income and the scarcity of college jobs, the graduating piano major would be well-advised to give serious consideration to the private teaching field.

SUMMARY

Entering into the ranks of the professional pianist-teacher requires a number of basic personal traits and inner motivations in order to excel and survive in today's competitive world. First and foremost, some musical talent is vital for anyone intending to become a piano major at the college level. Talent is difficult to describe. In the simplest terms it means an aptitude for learning a particular subject. The prospective piano major must be candidly honest with himself, for without some innate ability any real success in the profession will be difficult. In many music departments an appraisal is given at the end of the sophomore year to determine the plausibility of continuing as a piano major. Although there are always exceptions, anyone who is advised to change majors after a two year trial period should give careful consideration to the evaluation of the professionals. The door to music will not be closed, for one may keep music as a rewarding avocation while pursuing another field.

Once the decision has been made to become a piano major, and all signs point toward career probability in this area, the student should pursue his chosen field in a conscientious, meaningful way. Intellectual discipline is a vital personal trait for the piano major, for heavy demands will be made on his time with classes, practicing, and all the other activities that go into the successful pursuit of a college music degree program. Excluding those rare individuals with enormous instinctive talent but limited aptitude for scholastic studies, a combination of talent and intellect is essential for academic and professional advancement. In addition, perseverance and stability, coupled with personal drive are vital components for success as a piano major.

Finally, in spite of an over-crowding within certain areas of the music profession, there are great opportunities and rewards for the well-prepared and dedicated individual. Few professions contain so many avenues for self-expression, as well as offering the chance to work with others in a meaningful way. Work in the public schools, in the private studio, in music therapy, and even in music related professions such as publishing and instrument selling, are all expanding fields giving a solid income and an important place in the community.

It is impractical to footnote proper credits to the numerous people who have aided with information and advice. I do, however, wish to give special thanks to Mrs. Celia Mae Bryant, past President of the Music Teachers National Association, and Professor of Music at the University of Oklahoma, Robert Gardner of the Hurok Concert Agency, and to Roger Jacobi, President of the National Music Camp and the Interlochen Arts Academy, Interlochen, Michigan.

Reading and Memorization Techniques Leading Toward Peformance

15

by Ylda Novik

Ylda Novik, Hungarian-born pianist, appeared extensively in recitals and workshops both in the United States and abroad. A highly successful teacher, her students were consistent winners in regional and national competitions. She was a contributing critic of the Washington Star, Piano Editor of the American Music Teacher (1968-1972), U.S. Correspondent to the Inter-American Music Bulletin of the Pan American Union, author of innumerable articles, and a faculty member at

George Washington University and Montgomery College in Washington, D.C. She received her training from Arthur Loesser and Beryl Rubinstein at the Cleveland Institute of Music and from Muriel Kerr at the Juilliard School of Music. She published several editions of piano music with the Alfred Music Co. and with Studio P/R. Miss Novik's untimely death in March, 1977 has left a conspicuous void in the music world.

One of the universal issues that confronts teachers concerns the approach to learning and the effects of the learning process on retention (memory) and projection (performance). As a result, many of us who are teachers have undoubtedly found ourselves viewing the student's problems of sight reading, memorization, and performance through totally empathic eyes. How many of us who are performing now, or did in our student days, have agonized and trembled as "judgement day"–*the recital*–approached? How many of us, now that we are teachers, observe our students grappling with the same problems? We must consider how we can improve the first two elements, sight reading and memorization, in order to project the third, performance–to project it more convincingly and with greater security.

Security! Here lies the key to the performance that is enjoyable to the performer and audience alike. We all know that an audience reacts to and sympathetically vibrates with the performer. The listener invariably senses to what degree the performer is involved with the projection of *music* rather than the rendering of notes.

Insecurity at the keyboard, however, is often a psychological matter even when a piece is, by all apparent criteria, thoroughly technically mastered and carefully memorized. No matter how many formulae we give for the mechanical aspects of guaranteeing an unflawed performance, security ultimately stems from the self-confidence of the performer. But what helps him acquire that self-confidence? Perhaps we should say, "Who else helps him acquire that confidence, if not we, his teachers?" In our conscientious efforts to be alert and critical of his lesson preparation, we must never forget to first give him recognition and praise for his accomplishments. We must first indicate our pleasure to the student for his corrections and improvements in performance prior to giving criticism. In this manner we can build self-confidence through stating the positive first.

It has been my experience that, for the most part, the better readers among my students are also those who memorize more securely–and it is secure memorization that permits the performer to concentrate on interpretation and musical effects.

It is my conclusion that the fostering of good reading habits is one of the most critical aspects of teaching–not merely to insure good ensemble capability but to build the basis for artistic solo performance. Reading is the first step in the learning process. From this initial experience the student builds to an eventual performance. When first reading, it is of utmost importance to read accurately. Good reading habits should be fostered; these include correct notes, correct rhythm, the development of acute aural perception, and well-conditioned reflexes. The attendant benefits from accurate reading will result in early recognition of phrases, harmonies, motifs, and a general feel for the over-all concept. These skills will develop as the student becomes more and more convinced of the necessity for accurate reading.

In working with my pupils it became increasingly obvious that the old truism of lasting first impressions is indeed viable. This is where good sight reading is critical to the whole learning process. The mistake learned in the first week of work on a piece is, firstly, difficult to eradicate, and secondly, even if apparently eliminated, far too often returns under the stress of performance to plague the hapless tyro and sometimes even the experienced professional. Our job, therefore, is to convince the student that it is imperative to cultivate correct first-impression learning based upon good reading habits. Taking into consideration neurologists' findings of pattern establishment, it must be recognized that an incorrect initial imprint requires the brain to re-program the entire event in order to "correct" the false impression.

Sight reading skill originates with tactile keyboard familiarity. The student who has acquired conditioned spatial reflexes will not need to look at his hands and will, therefore, keep his eyes on the page—the "first commandment" in sight reading.

This is easy to say, but how does a student acquire these conditioned spatial reflexes? I believe that the most positive approach is to utilize the natural response of the ear which will transmit to the fingers. Fortunately for all concerned, this avenue of "playing by ear," which was once taboo as a means of pianistic learning, has again been reopened. There has been a reversal of the view, prevalent in many teaching circles only a generation ago, that playing by ear was detrimental to sight reading. Today we realize the prime importance of aural perception in the process of learning music.

The noted Japanese violin teacher Shinichi Suzuki, who has trained thousands of young Japanese children in his "ear first, notation later" method, recognized that just as a child first learns speech by imitating his elders, so too could he learn music. Friedrich Wieck, Clara Schumann's father and teacher, postponed the teaching of notes with beginners for about a year, thus devoting the first year to the development of the ear and to the awakening of musical activity. In his book, *The Art of Playing the Harpsichord,* Couperin said: "One should begin in their fingers. It is nearly impossible that, while they are looking at their notes, their fingers should not get out of position, or fumble . . . Besides, memory is developed in learning by heart."[1] (*i.e.*, ear).

Many teachers contend that children with good aural perception, especially those with absolute pitch, pose a problem by their reluctance to play from the page rather than totally by ear. I have found this often to be the case with improperly trained transfer students, but happily never so with

[1] Francois Couperin, *The Art of Playing the Harpsichord* (Wiesbaden: Breitkopf and Härtel, 1933), p.87.

those who began their studies in my class. These children are indeed the ones upon whom I base my contention that the better the readers, the better the memorizers. These youngsters have progressed at a rate that frequently astonishes me, as the combining of all of their avenues of perception are utilized and nurtured from the beginning of their studies.

On a far greater scale, whenever I go to Japan I am continually astonished to hear five- or six-year-old pianists playing Bach Inventions and Partitas, Mozart Sonatas, and similar difficult repertoire—a result of the Japanese method of preparation for piano at the age of three via the avenues of solfege and ear-training.

For others with less good ears, it is doubly advisable that from the onset of lessons ear-finger-keyboard exploration should encompass not merely the narrow range immediately around Middle C, but using short 5-finger pattern melodies, should embrace the entire keyboard from bottom to top and the black keys immediately along with the white. "Hot Cross Buns" and similar tunes, once they have been discovered by ear in any given key, should be played in different keys. The student should be encouraged to sing while he plays, which will further serve to sharpen his ear. This approach, which introduces music by key exploration in a variety of keys rather than just one, is usually referred to as the Multi-Key Approach and is the basis for such piano series as the *Music Through the Piano* series by Jane and James Bastien. The ear is developed as the beginning student is encouraged to reproduce, on every possible place on the piano, the tunes which he has previously learned.

To make the situation more challenging and to reinforce more positively the tactile approach, the teacher might introduce the student to the piano in a Blind Man's Buff fashion. The blindfolded child places his fingers so that they fall at random on the keyboard and from that point plays the tune of his choice. This tactile action is accomplished by the child's learning to orient himself by feeling the landmarks of the twin and triplet black keys. By this means he can determine exactly on what key he is starting and in what key he is playing.

Introduction of major and minor pentachords in all twelve scale degrees commences before note reading (and numerical counting) is taught. The beginner is taught the 5-finger pattern probably on the C major pentachord and then is asked to play it in other places on the keyboard, letting his ear guide him. Rare is the child who does not recognize an intervallic mistake as he produces the pattern. And equally rare is the one who does not immediately search for the key which corresponds to the aural image of the pattern if he makes a mistake.

By thus acquainting the child with the keyboard from the beginning, we are fulfilling his acknowledged reason for coming to us; that is, to play tunes on the piano and to play them, as he was led to believe, even at his very first lesson. It is all well and good to be able to count, clap, sing, and learn note names—all the notational components—but nothing will leave the child as excited at the conclusion of his lesson as actually playing some little piece on the piano. Deprivation of that desired goal can cause a child great disappointment.

As lessons progress and the child has securely learned the pattern, the creative teacher can expand the student's experience aurally and technically by the use of a tape or cassette recorder. Of course the student, in addition to having access to the one in his teacher's studio, must have access to a recorder at home. The teacher then is free to implement ear training during the student's home practice hours by making a tape on which she plays some improvised 5-finger-span tunes. The child listens to the tape at home and tries to play back what he has heard. Once he has succeeded, he transposes the little melodies. These can be very brief two- and four-measure phrases.

Obviously rhythmic-ear as well as pitch-ear training can and should be developed in the initial stages of a child's training by clapping and stepping exercises.[2] Also, benefit is gained by playing a piece on the closed lid to establish rhythmic and physical coordinations without the complexities of playing the notes and rhythm simultaneously. I suggest to the student that he regard playing the piano as the most demanding form of athletic activity, which requires separation of its various components into numerous processes.

After the initial stage of exploring the piano and reading pre-notated melodies in a variety of keys, note reading follows sequentially. It is difficult to say how long a child should "play" the piano before note reading is begun—for some a period of six weeks will suffice, for others a longer period is required. In any case, finger coordination and knowledge of keyboard topography should be thoroughly developed before note reading is presented. The subject of teaching note reading is one which all of us teach in context to our own experiences. The approach we use is based on determining (often by trial and error) what works best for our students. The various and numerous methods of teaching reading are the cornerstones of every course series and therefore a matter of individual preference.

After the child has learned to read notes, transposition of the pieces should follow in the same manner that the ear pieces were transposed. By stressing the directional and intervallic relationship of his little pieces, he can easily replay them in other keys. The experience he has attained in keyboard feel and hearing should give him confidence in sensing his way without looking down at his hands when the printed page is placed before him.

After security is attained in the 5-finger position, exercises for expansion to other intervals (sixths, sevenths and octaves) should be given. The student may also be given exercises for shifting hand positions, leaps, and other out of position situations.

Memorization should come easily to the student who has had sufficient experience in keyboard patterns such as 5-finger melodies, chords, intervals, etc. If he *understands* what he is doing, the memorization process is enhanced greatly. He has acquired the correct eye-hand relationships and in memorizing he will use his listening experience to give him a proper ear-hand relationship.

How else does emphasis on sight reading enhance memorization? For one thing, if the visual image received is uninterrupted, there can be something akin to a continuous recording of this image on the brain. It is said that Artur Rubinstein can literally visualize the page unrolling before him as he plays. If started early enough, this sort of visual recall can be cultivated in the same manner that a great many Hungarian children educated in the Kodály music training program have cultivated tonal memory through developing pitch perception.

A way of creating visual memory in one not endowed with it may be

[2]For the transfer student who has not had the benefit of systematic rhythmic training, remedial work in a book such as Robert Starer's *Rhythmic Training* (MCA Music) is recommended.

achieved in the following way. Ask the student to close the piano, shut his eyes, and play the piece on the lid while attempting to visualize the printed page in the mind's eye. While his eyes are still closed, raise the lid, place his hands on the keys and encourage him to actually play the piece, thus incorporating the keyboard feel which was so carefully cultivated during the reading process. A somewhat costly but unsurpassable extension of the playing-without-sound concept involves using a silent keyboard. I believe that a full silent keyboard is virtually as vital a part of the teacher's equipment as is a tape recorder or metronome. My students are unanimous in extolling the benefit of practicing on my "Silent Steinway." They agree with my experience that the mental processes involved in mentally hearing a page without its being sounded not only acts as an aid to ear development but also to reading. We all feel like virtuosi as we merrily play our music, conjuring up the most flawless and beautiful musical interpretations that we then hope to bring to the sounding keys.

Visual finger memory and kinesthetic reflex are other memory assists. Visualizing the keyboard placement, chordal and cluster groupings are insurance elements. This may seem to be in contradiction to the emphasis I placed on the necessity for cultivating the ability to sight read without looking at the fingers. Actually, it is not, if we recognize that sight reading and memorization are really sequential. After the student has learned the music correctly, he can then profit by watching and knowing where his hands are going on the keyboard.

Although it seems superfluous to mention the importance, or rather, the absolute necessity, of thematic and harmonic analysis, these processes must be a part of the learning methods for every student with every piece he learns. The immediate study of chords is an integral part of the multi-key approach, and it is one of the reasons that students using this approach progress rapidly from the beginning. They are trained to read notes in groups rather than as individual, unrelated splotches on the page.

Ultimately, thinking in harmonically related concepts becomes another acquired learning reflex. How many disasters have you witnessed in festivals, contests, and recitals when a student, obviously oblivious of formal and harmonic principles, took a "wrong turn" and juxtaposed the material of the exposition and recapitulation, playing the given theme in the wrong key, and perhaps not knowing what he was doing that was wrong. There is no total guarantee against slips, but structual awareness is certainly a great security factor; and should the slip occur, it is a reliable aid in finding the way back minus tragedy. I urge my students to write in their thematic and harmonic analyses in each piece they study.

Additional memory safeguards require that each hand be learned separately by memory. Playing the left hand alone while singing the right hand gives the performer an invaluable insurance policy against memory slips. The left hand is generally the hand that plays music which has no real identity of its own. The strong personality of the right hand melody is easily absorbed through the ear, but the somewhat anonymous left hand must be cultivated as an independent entity. Also, being able to start at various key points—sectional guide posts—gives security; should the memory falter, there is a lifeline to grasp somewhere farther on in the score.

Another device I suggest is to ask the student to play mentally through a given number of measures, say four, and then start his playing in the fifth. Stop him and repeat this process until the whole piece has been covered in this manner.

Since confidence means knowing the music and how to project it, the penultimate step before public performance is a conditioning process through a private performance—something akin to a dress rehearsal for a theater group. Students, even the very young ones facing their first recital, and professionals alike, must seek opportunities to simulate stage conditions by playing for audiences in their own homes and those of their friends and teachers until they become accustomed to the variety of performance jitters which is an occupational hazard of the musician.

Our discussion thus far has been confined to the interrelationship between the auditory, the visual, and the kinetic factors in producing a polished performance. However, we must remember that the final element, and perhaps the most elusive, is the aesthetic. Once all the mechanics are assimilated, we must realize that we are dealing with possibly the most personal of the art forms, and that our main goal is to render the silent page with our own unique breath of life as we endeavor to present the composer's message to our listeners.

Ornaments and Embellishments In 18th-Century Keyboard Music

16

by George Lucktenberg

George Lucktenberg studied music at Oberlin College and Ohio State University before receiving degrees from the University of Illinois and Florida State University. He also holds the Artists Diploma from the State Academy of Music in Vienna, Austria. Dr. Lucktenberg was a Fulbright Fellow and received a postdoctoral research fellowship from the Ford Foundation for a year of study of Baroque violin sonata literature at the University of North Carolina. He has appeared in concert as a solo and chamber-music pianist, and is also well known for his second performing specialty, historical keyboard instruments, including the early pianoforte as well as the harpsichord. With his wife, violinist Jerrie Cadek Lucktenberg, he has concertized extensively in duo-recitals. Dr. Lucktenberg's publications include numerous articles and editions of music for both pedagogical and concert use. He has held two vice-presidencies and the presidency of the Southern Division, Music Teachers National Association, and was the founding president of the South Carolina Music Teachers Association. He has been a faculty member at the National Music Camp, Interlochen, Michigan, since 1953. Dr. Lucktenberg is professor of piano and harpsichord and chairman of the keyboard and graduate departments at Converse College, Spartanburg, South Carolina.

INTRODUCTION AND BACKGROUND

> "No one disputes the need for embellishments. This is evident from the great numbers of them everywhere to be found. They are, in fact, indispensable. Consider their many uses: They connect and enliven tones and impart stress and accent; they make music pleasing and awaken our close attention. Expression is heightened by them; let a piece be sad, joyful, or otherwise, and they will lend a fitting assistance. Embellishments provide opportunities for fine performance as well as much of its subject matter. They improve mediocre compositions. Without them the best melody is empty and ineffective, the clearest content clouded."
>
> Carl Philipp Emanuel Bach[1]

Why does this topic cause discomfort among teachers? Why do so many consider it vexing or mystifying? For an excellent reason: everyone is becoming more and more aware of its central importance to satisfactory performance of a literature that occupies so much of our teaching time, even at the elementary levels. Moreover, there often seems to be either too much or too little information given in editions and books designed to help; and it is a complex, many-sided subject, so there is little wonder that widespread confusion may exist.

A little history might be useful. Mankind's urge to decorate his music with "extra" notes, thus subtly varying and "personalizing" it, goes back as far as anyone can trace in any culture. By 1700 in Europe it was already a well-developed but still evolving essential of the Baroque style. During the next one hundred years it became a flexible, diversified art of the utmost refinement which was commented upon extensively by writers and critics of the time.

One cannot, therefore, wish it away. Just playing the notes, ignoring all the odd little signs over and around some of them, would be like having a Christmas tree without a single decoration. Its sturdy branches and bright

[1] From Carl Philipp Emanuel's *Essay on the True Art of Playing Keyboard Instruments*, translated and edited by William J. Mitchell (W. W. Norton & Co., Inc., 1949).

foliage, like the solid counterpoint and rich harmony of the period, would provide some satisfaction; but—it just wouldn't be Christmas. Being unimaginative or too conservative about ornamentation is equally unrewarding. Memorizing three or four standard signs, with the same treatment every time for each, is rather like assembling a coin collection consisting of U.S. pennies from 1965 to the present. It can be done in five minutes, and once it is completed, just what does one really have?

To continue with history: our fascination with the eighteenth century began in the late nineteenth, accelerating rapidly after the Second World War. The majority Romantic view was that eighteenth century music was a bit insipid for the most part, and wanted "modernizing" before it was fit to be heard; in short, they tried to make it sound something like Romantic music in most of the externals of style. These excesses brought about a sharp counter-reaction early in our century, a "purist" approach resulting in insistence by the leaders of the movement upon playing in a bare-bones, "Urtext" way. This is just as lacking in authenticity and proper effect as the prettifying and "souping-up" of the 1830-1900 period.

The warnings and outcries of the purists generated many fine Urtext (*i.e.*, the composer's original score, with nothing added or subtracted) editions, but then the disciplines of conservatory pedants and professional orchestra players, reinforced by their prestige, caused an ironic mishandling of the older style-practice. Their training, admirable for highly-edited late Romantic scores, told them to play exactly what they saw on the page; this is disastrous for eighteenth century interpretation, where notation left much to be added by the performer, particularly in expression and embellishment. Sometimes the composer's score was mainly an outline to be filled in at the discretion of the performer's judgement. Small wonder that the "Urtext"-sort of playing was roundly criticized for being dull; a skilled player from the Baroque or Classic age would have shared that opinion.

Since the 1940's the advent of the LP record and a new generation of specialists in research and performance have fired general public interest in recapturing the whole essence, not just the skeleton or the powdered wigs, of the older styles—the "Baroque Boom," and a search for new values and meanings in the Classicists. We have revived the instruments as well as the performance-practices. Today's sales of recorders, harpsichords, and more exotic members of once-"extinct" families during the past quarter-century must surely gratify the elder statesmen among musicologist-performers of 1900-1940, who sometimes must have felt that they were voices crying in a wilderness. We all owe them a considerable debt, no matter how we may disagree with this or that detail of their conclusions and renditions.

Nonetheless, in the past twenty-five years a very great deal has been learned about eighteenth century ornamentation and made available to the most remote corners of teachingdom through publications, recordings, workshops, etc. In a very condensed way, this chapter will venture a summary of our current perspective on this vital aspect of a great literature.

VARIOUS ORNAMENTS AND EMBELLISHMENTS AND THEIR USAGE

"Embellishments may be divided into two groups: in the first are those which are indicated by conventional signs or a few small notes; in the second are those which lack signs and consist of many short notes."

Carl Philipp Emanuel Bach[2]

To expand upon C. P. E. Bach's statement, in arriving at some system of classification one finds two categories, each with two subtypes:

1. Those which are indicated by the composer himself in original manuscripts or first printings done under his supervision (Urtexts); which may be:
   a) Standardized formulas or conventions indicated by shorthand "signs;" or,
   b) Non-standard, figural passagework either in normal-size or small notes.

and

2. Those which are added later by someone else; which may be:
   a) Added by an editor as part of a printed edition, whether or not he clearly identifies them as not original (he should!); or,
   b) Improvised (with or without some prior planning and practice) on the impulse of the player, without appearing anywhere in the score.

There is, unfortunately, no clear, universally accepted terminology to help us distinguish between types 1a and 1b. It has been proposed that we do away with the confusion of the words "ornament" and "embellishment" (which are now used interchangeably by most people) by calling 1a "ornaments" and 1b "embellishments." It is doubtful, however, that such a uniform usage could be promoted, worthy though the idea may be. One further pairing should be noted: 1a, ornaments with shorthand signs, are primarily identified with the French, particularly with their harpsichord composers; and 1b, small-note free embellishment, with the Italians, particularly their stringed-instrument and vocal writing.

The French, who inherited an ornament tradition from the early Baroque lute school, developed it to the highest state of refinement and taste. Already in 1670 (Chambonnières' *Pièces de Clavecin*) there existed printed tables systematically showing how ornaments should be played. At its peak, ca. 1700-1740, the French practice was widely copied elsewhere in Europe. The famous table of ornaments that J. S. Bach wrote at the beginning of Wilhelm Friedemann's *Little Clavier Book* is essentially that of d'Anglebert (*Pièces de Clavecin*, 1689), one of the many great French keyboardists. This little table (Ill. 15:1) appears in Bach's own hand as he wrote it for his son, and for that reason is an extremely valuable reference source. Since it contains most of the essential French Baroque ornaments it is well worth memorizing. Bach's own treatment of keyboard ornaments is typically and almost totally French. He, of course, knew and was a consummate master of the Italian embellishment style as well. Like other Germans of his time, he probably saw himself as a synthesizer of the two styles, together with his great native northern counterpoint, into a grander art. That he succeeded so well indeed is not necessarily because he was German, however, but because he was Bach.

[2]From Carl Philipp Emanuel's *Essay on the True Art of Playing Keyboard Instruments*, translated and edited by William J. Mitchell (W. W. Norton & Co., Inc., 1949).

Ill. 15:1. Bach's table of ornaments from the *Clavier-Büchlein* of 1720.

The following presentation and discussion of ornamentation is based primarily on Bach's own table (Ill. 15:1). Although this table is remarkably clear for a hand-written, photo re-produced copy, this presentation is intended to illuminate and amplify the original.

The *TRILL*: *t*, *tr*, 〰, 〰〰; (+, x, rare)

is a rapid alternation of the printed note with the half- or whole-step above. It has no set speed or length; it may be short or long, as fast as a doorbell or gently undulating.

Realizations of the trill sign include:

It may have a prefix from below:

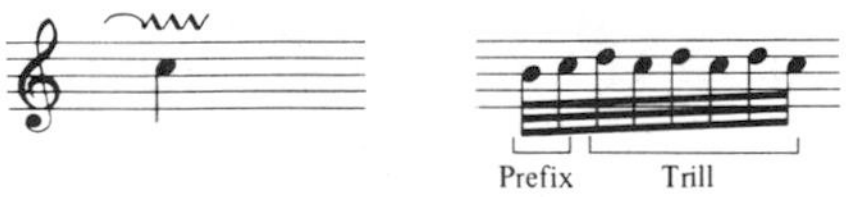

It may have a prefix from above:

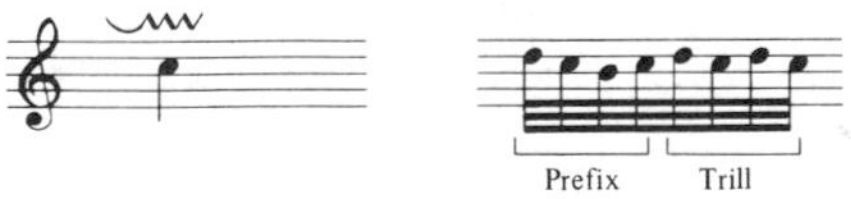

It may also have a suffix:

When no suffix is indicated, the trill can stop on the printed note—*point d'arrêt*, as the French called it:

Or it can take up the whole time of the printed note:

It may also have both a prefix and suffix:

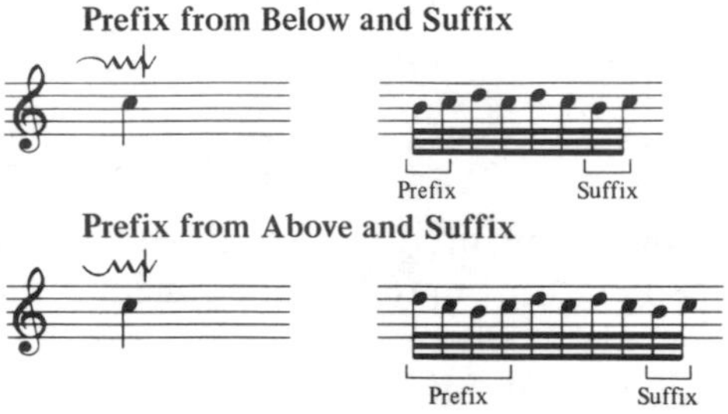

There are two very general rules:

1. Trills, like ninety percent of all eighteenth century ornaments, begin ON THE BEAT—that is, they start where the printed note occurs in time, and not before it; and,

2. They start from ABOVE—not on the printed note. This goes for Haydn, Mozart, and early Beethoven (including most of his "teaching-pieces") as well as for the Baroque. Only one exception can normally be made: when the note preceding the trilling-note is in effect an upper appoggiatura (see ahead), the preceding note being then the upper tone of the trill, it can be tied over into the trill itself. This trill was specifically identified as a PRALLTRILLER by C. P. E. Bach. The French had a convention for this—a slur from the preceding note to the trilled note; J. S. Bach and others often used a "prepared trill" sign:

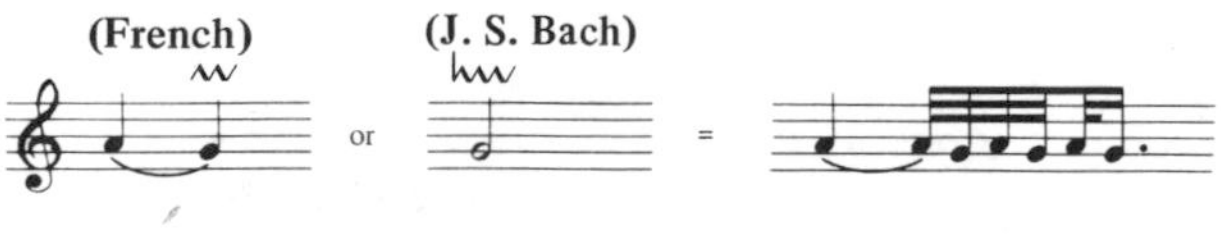

A pedagogical exception may occur in the execution of the trill because the player is not facile enough or not mature enough to handle even the minimum four notes in the basic trill. In the Baroque especially, a quick, single appoggiatura or acciaccatura from above is usually a better choice than the three-note or short "*Schneller*" or snap (C.P.E.'s term once again):

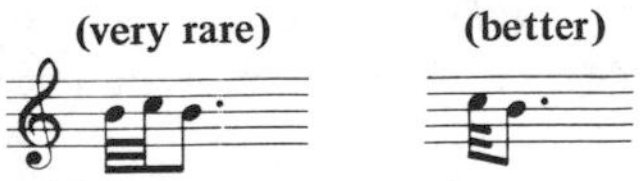

The *MORDENT*: ⁓|⁓, ⊥, ||; ⁓|⁓⁓ (long);) (after, not over, the note)

is a very quick alternation of the printed note with the half- or whole-step below. It starts on the beat as usual, but unlike the trill, the printed note comes first. Normally it consists of only three notes, but occasionally sounds well if prolonged to five, seven, or even more:

Standard Mordent

Long Mordent (Double Mordent)

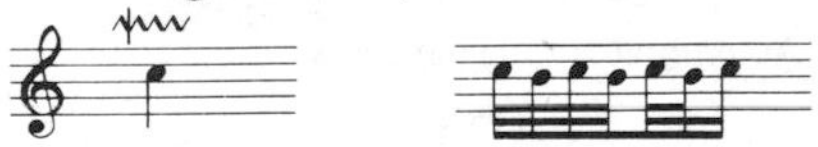

This ornament largely disappeared in the Classic era, although Haydn used a variant of it which was more like a very fast turn:

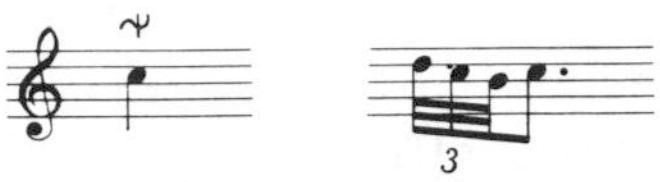

The *TURN*: ∾ (or ∽, rare)

played at varying speeds, starts with the half- or whole-step above the printed note, goes to the printed one next, then a half- or whole-step below, and ends on the printed one:

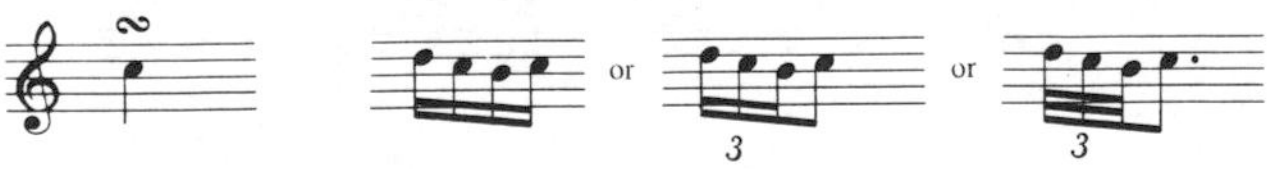

In the Baroque and Classic eras this simple four-note device, at varying speeds, was the sole on-the-beat kind. As far as we can tell, the five-note turn beginning *on* the printed note comes from a later time:

A relative of the unaccented trill described in the exception (Pralltriller) noted above, under TRILL, the unaccented turn occurs when the turn-sign is *between* the notes rather than over them: In this case it is rather

like a group of passing notes, and is unaccented.

The ***APPOGGIATURA***: 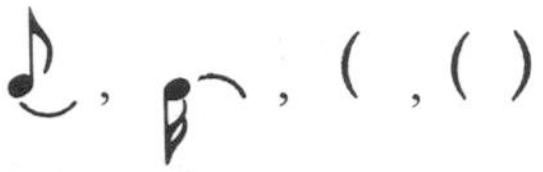 , and  (with a trill)

is an accented note of variable duration a half- or whole-step on either side of the printed note. The appoggiatura (from the Italian verb *appoggiare*, to lean) is a dissonant tone usually occurring on the beat, and normally takes up at least half (sometimes more than half) of the time occupied by the printed note, to which it resolves. It is a particularly expressive, sighing "down-up" or "strong-weak" gesture. Realizations include:

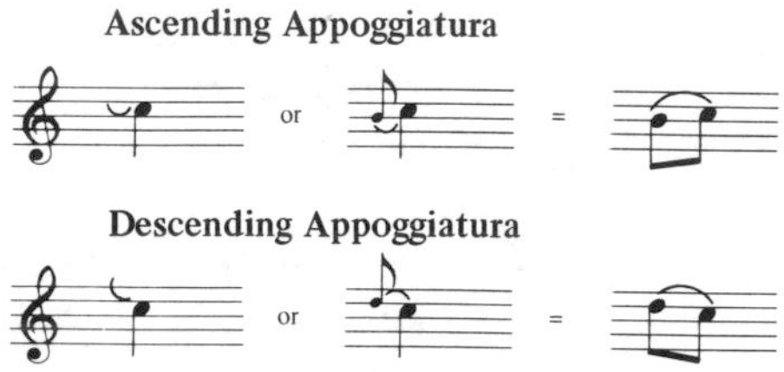

It can preface a trill (see TRILL, again):

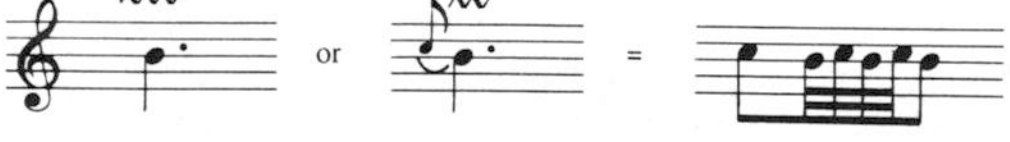

It can also preface a mordent when coming from below:

A much less common variant is the double appoggiatura:

Yet another variant is the passing appoggiatura, an unaccented small note occurring between two notes of a melodic third, usually descending:

The following additional ornaments are not in J. S. Bach's table, but are used in his and other composers' music frequently.

The *SLIDE*: (,) , / , \ , ∾

is another very short note (which, confusingly, the Italians also call acciaccatura), occurring between two notes of a harmonic third (occasionally between a fourth or more):

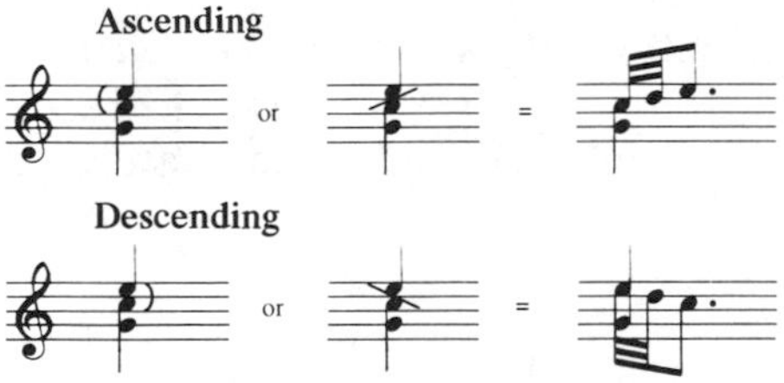

In the previous examples the slide was added to chords. Another commonly used slide, the melodic slide (or German, *Schleifer*), is added to single-line melody:

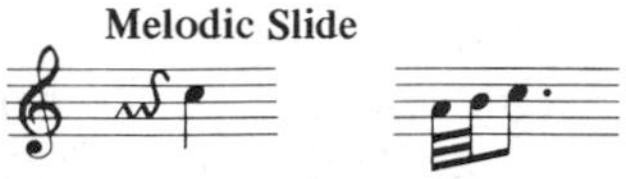

The little notes are released instantly, except perhaps in Scarlatti where the dissonant effect may be prolonged in the "tone-clusters" of which he was fond. In his case, however, they tend to be written out in full with normal-sized notes. This ornament was freely interpolated by Baroque performers, especially in accompaniments, and was probably used far more often than we are now apt to acknowledge in our own playing. Although the practice seems to have died out in the Classic era, it may be added, occasionally, in music up to ca. 1775.

The *ARPEGGIO*: 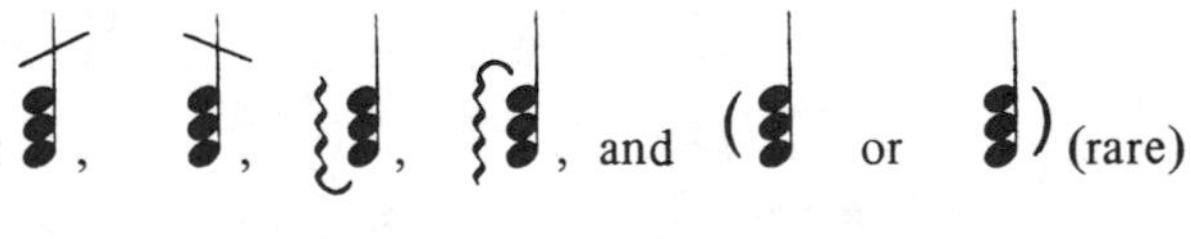

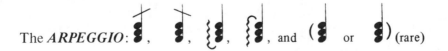

is the practice of playing the notes of a chord with a very slight upward or downward break rather than simultaneously:

Descending

It is another practice that should be present rather more frequently in today's performances of both the Baroque and Classic literature, but especially in the former. It can sometimes also be done at a slower pace, particularly on the last chord of a final cadence, which is often arpeggiated very elaborately, both up and down, with a ritard. All the chord-tones are sustained—held by the fingers, rather than released, as became the custom later on the pianoforte with its sustaining pedal.

The ***ACCIACCATURA***: 

is a very short appoggiatura, usually from below. Its name is derived from the Italian, *acciaccare*, to crush. The two notes are struck almost together, with the acciaccatura being released immediately as if it were marked staccato:

It is used more often in the Classic than the Baroque.

Note: there is insufficient consistency in the manuscripts of any major composers to give us a precise indication of the length of acciaccaturas or appoggiaturas. The notion that  *always* meant appoggiatura (long), and that  *always* meant acciaccatura (short), is absolutely without foundation and must be discarded. Secondly, in determining whether a half- or whole-step is to be used in any of these figures, the ruling principle is that the prevailing tonality must be supported, not negated, by the accidentals used; stay within the key of the moment.

ADDING IMPROVISED ADDITIONAL ORNAMENTATION AND EMBELLISHMENT

"... It is supposed by many that a real good Taste cannot possibly be acquired by any Rules of Art; it being a peculiar Gift of Nature, indulged only to those who have naturally a good Ear: And as most flatter themselves to have this Perfection, hence it happens that he who sings or plays, thinks of nothing so much as to make continually some favourite Passages or Graces, believing that by this Means he shall be thought to be a good Performer, not perceiving that playing in good Taste doth not consist of frequent Passages, but in expressing with Strength and Delicacy the Intention of the Composer."

Francesco Geminiani[3]

[3]From Geminiani's *Treatise of Good Taste in the Art of Musick*, Edited by Donington (Da Capo Press, 1969).

The basic procedure in improvised embellishment is to replace long note-values in melodies with groups of shorter ones, referred to as "diminution" in scholarly terms. In the period 1600-1700 they tended to be written out in long, involved passagework: see the *Fitzwilliam Virginal Book* and works of Frescobaldi for elegant examples. Later, the practice became improvisatory rather than specified in notation by the composers, and during much of the eighteenth century—especially the late Baroque and the Rococo—it was expected of all performers beyond the most elementary level. To what extent it is called for, and indeed, allowable in the Classic works of the mature Haydn, of Mozart, and early Beethoven is much less apparent; but it is clear that its use after 1760 to 1770 is far more restricted than during the first two-thirds of the century.

The Italian violin and vocal school provided the leadership for this kind of embellishment. The slow movements of instrumental sonatas from this period—those of Corelli's (Opus V, 1700) or Handel's (Opus I, 1722) for violin, flute, etc. are excellent examples. They are usually mere outlines upon which the performer must hang tasteful flourishes and passagework of all kinds. Tasteful is the key word. It is necessary for the performer to have both a thorough grounding in eighteenth century counterpoint, and an affinity for the personal idiom of the composer whose works he is playing before the best results can be obtained. Turning an inexperienced student loose without sufficient guidance encourages dilletantism in the bold and confuses the timid. Where can one turn for reliable guidance? Fortunately, eighteenth century masters themselves left us ample amounts of written-out embellishment which we can use as models; and certain very helpful treatises. Of special interest are the varied reprises and "doubles;" these were popular in two-part dance movements and other repeating forms. One plays the first time through as written; on the repeat, extemporized embellishments are added. Some of the finest examples occur in the works of J. S. Bach. Many of his sarabandes have doubles, in which he shows an infinite variety of inspired figuration. The sarabande of the third English Suite is a magnificent demonstration of this art. That he would occasionally embellish even fast movements is evident in the second courante of the first English Suite. Both of these movements are well worth careful study. For contrast, see the ingenuous, simple sarabande of the fourth English Suite; just because Bach provided none, are we to assume that no embellishing of its repeats were intended—after seeing the sarabande of the Third, just preceding? It would seem to be very doubtful.

There are two kinds of performer-added ornaments which can be inserted with a clear conscience by even the least skilled:

1. The cadential trill. At principal cadences, such as the final one in a movement, or the first half of a movement, especially when the melody is:

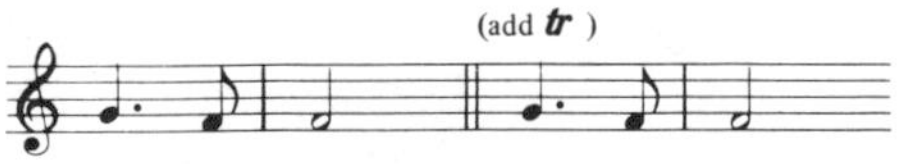

a trill on the first of the notes shown is not only invited, it is virtually mandatory even though not indicated.

2. When a composer has given ornaments for certain notes in the opening statement of a theme—a fugue subject, for example—one may freely

repeat these ornaments any time the identical theme is repeated, even though the ornament-signs may be lacking. Again, one is speaking here mainly of the Baroque; the more explicit notation of the Classicists suggest caution in all such matters.

In the more difficult "free" embellishment of the Italian kind, one can hardly do better than to look to J. S. Bach for yet another example: this time the second movement of his *Italian Concerto*. This is a fully realized sample of an ornate slow movement, typifying the best of that sort of improvising. For a superb specimen from the Classic period, see Mozart's *A-minor Rondo, K. 511*; each time the main thematic elements recur they are subtly and ingeniously varied.

Sources for detailed study are listed at the end of the chapter; there is space here for only a few generalities. One can embellish by adding:

1. Formula-ornaments of the sort usually expressed by conventionalized signs: and
2. Short "filler" notes between skips, of various kinds:
   a) Slides between notes of chords, particularly when arpeggiating.
   b) Filling in the steps between melodic skips with little notes, usually stepwise (diatonically; rarely chromatically)—sometimes even skipwise, usually in thirds, if the interval to be spanned is quite large.
   c) Appoggiaturas, either on the beat or "passing."
3. Imitation—that is, figures which closely or exactly duplicate other material which the composers have previously introduced—when a good opportunity occurs.

In each of these things, the normal procedure is to move from the simple to the complex by gradual stages. And above all, one must strive to preserve a feeling of spontaneity and improvisation, to constantly vary the figuration and not get in a rut with one or another formula, even when everything is carefully planned and practiced. Without taking unnecessary chances, it is useful to make very minor changes from time to time even in live performances, to preserve a sense of immediacy. And finally, it is well to be sparing, rather than lavish, with added material. As in all else in performance, we skate a thin line on thin ice. In this case too little is far better than too much. A good composer, like a good chef, has put some seasoning into his dishes; we may spoil them if we add too many spices at the table!

THE TECHNIQUE OF ORNAMENTATION

"Besides the Graces in general use, such as trills, mordents, appoggiaturas, etc., I have always given my pupils little finger-exercises to play; either passages, or strings of trills or tremolos of various intervals, beginning with the simplest, and on the most natural intervals, and gradually leading them to the quickest and to those most transposed. These little exercises, which cannot be too varied or too multiplied, are, at the same time, material all ready to be put in place, and may prove serviceable on many occasions."

Francois Couperin[4]

"When practicing trills or shakes, only those fingers which are in use should be raised as high as possible. However, as the movement becomes familiar, these

[4]From Couperin's *Art of Playing the Harpsichord* (Breitkopf and Härtel, 1933).

fingers are raised less and less and the considerable movement employed at the outset is finally replaced by a movement which is light and brisk."

Jean-Philippe Rameau[5]

"An ornament badly played is like a smile in a toothless mouth."

Wanda Landowska[6]

The first cardinal principle to be observed is that almost all embellishment consists of numerous quick notes. Particularly on the pianoforte, these should be "little" in loudness as well as in length; they make up in numbers whatever is lacking in volume. Both the speed and the lightness of the notes comprising embellishments invite finger-action alone, unaided by whole-hand or forearm activity. "Light and fast" go together.

Second, most ornaments and embellishments sound best if they are played just a little off-center, or non-symetrically, in time. The Baroque ornament-tables showed the small notes in even, regular sixteenths, thirty-seconds, or sixty-fourths; and the miniature notes of Classic embellishments, which took the place of many older signs, seem equally even and regular. All the best authorities from the eighteenth century, however, agree that they were not intended to be played in a mechanical, clockwork fashion. Playing trills, turns, and other figures in such a way robs them of charm and freedom. Trills in particular rarely need to be measured. It is generally best to allow them to accelerate gradually and consistently until their end. Sometimes they can also start slowly, accelerate, and slow down again toward the end. Short trills, of course, are generally played quite fast, with no attempt to make them conform to any particular time unit or pattern; the same goes for mordents, unless a particularly expressive effect is sought.

Third, they should be a natural and integral part of the melodic line they decorate—not pasted on like gold stars or painted on like lipstick. Every effort must be made to keep them smoothly flowing within the context of the phrase. The "technique" of a fast trill is virtually an involuntary reflex anyway, and that of improvised embellishments more intellectual and emotional than physical, so it is unwise to become too wrapped up in the mechanics of execution to the detriment of musical values.

Finally, a few specific hints may be useful in solving pupil problems:

1. It is rarely advisable to "force" an ornament with power and tension. A relaxed hand and arm will almost invariably yield better results.

2. When the same ornament occurs over and over again, to avoid monotony it is best to slightly alter the way of playing it—timing, dynamics, whatever—in some of its recurrences.

3. When playing very rapid trills on the piano one can hold both keys very slightly "below surface" owing to its sophisticated double-escapement action, thus reducing the time between repercussions of each key. This is, incidentally, a trap for harpsichordists, who must let each key return to its full height to insure a repetition.

4. If a pupil complains of clumsiness in trills and other figures, try

[5]From the essay in Rameau's *Pièces de Clavecin* (Bärenreiter, 1958).

[6]From an article Landowska wrote on interpreting ornaments which now is part of her collected writings in the book, *Landowska on Music*, collected, edited and translated by Denise Restout (Stein and Day, Publishers, 1964).

some less-common fingerings: non-adjacent pairs, for instance—1-3, 2-4, and 3-5. When a slight forearm-rotation "trembling" is added to finger-action, both power and articulation can sometimes be improved. Changing fingers can also help; the handiest combination for the short, four-note trill in the right hand is 3132, and longer trills can be tried with 313231323132 etc. When the lower part of the right hand (thumb and second) is occupied with sustained tones, and an embellishment must be played above it, non-adjacent pairs and rotation are especially useful. An unusual case is:

This fingering is most appropriate when the lower (held tone) is a black key.

SUMMARY

Musical tastes change quite a lot in the course of one hundred years. It is well to remember that the eighteenth century encompassed three distinctly separate, although overlapping, styles: the late Baroque (ca. 1700-1740), the Rococo or "Galant" (ca. 1730-1770), and the Viennese Classic (ca. 1760-1800), each with its own subtle differences and preferences as to embellishment. In this brief discussion it is impossible to cover the gamut of ornamentation with any real depth; the purpose here has been to provide an overview and a guide to basic usages of the times. For a greater insight into periods and styles examine the music of various composers, listen to "experts" interpret the music, and refer to the suggested readings below.

In closing, it must be said that most eighteenth century ornament-playing could be improved by keeping just three basic "ABC's" in mind:

Always Be Careful to—

A. Start from Above on trills and turns,
B. Start on the Beat, not before, and
C. Cling to accented appoggiaturas, holding them long enough and resolving them legatissimo.

FOR FURTHER READING

First, a look at entries in well-known, reputable music dictionaries is useful, such as the Harvard (second edition) and Grove's (fifth edition). Also, there are numerous articles to be found in back issues of magazines such as *Clavier, the American Music Teacher, Piano Quarterly*, and others. Chapters in the following books give specific and more detailed information, as well as general information.

Bach, Carl Philipp Emanuel. *Essay on the True Art of Playing Keyboard Instruments*, translated and edited by William J. Mitchell. New York: W. W. Norton & Co., Inc., 1949. A comprehensive, authentic, highly detailed treatise for musicians concerned with technique, fingering and ornamentation of the time.

Badura-Skoda, Eva and Paul. *Interpreting Mozart on the Keyboard.* London: Barrie and Rockliff, 1962. Included are valuable discussions of phrasing, articulation and ornamentation.

Couperin, Francois. *The Art of Playing the Harpsichord.* Wiesbaden: Brietkopf and Härtel, 1933. The text of this reprint is in French, German and English. First published in 1717, this volume is a definitive reference source on ornamentation and style. This book is now available in a new edition edited by Margery Halford (Port Washington, N.Y.: Alfred Publishing Co., Inc. 1975).

Donington, Robert. *The Interpretation of Early Music.* London: Faber and Faber, 1974. This and the book below are authoritative reference sources.

Donington, Robert. *A Performer's Guide to Baroque Music.* London: Faber and Faber, 1973.

Ferguson, Howard (ed.). *Style and Interpretation (An Anthology of 16th-19th Century Keyboard Music).* London: Oxford University Press, 1964-1966. Four-volume anthology. Each volume contains an invaluable preface with a precise discussion of ornamentation.

Harich-Schneider, Eta. *The Harpsichord: An Introduction to Technique, Style and the Historical Sources.* St. Louis: Concordia Publishing House, 1954. Contains a witty and thought-provoking chapter on ornamentation.

Newman, William S. *Performance Practices in Beethoven's Piano Sonatas.* New York: W.W. Norton & Co., Inc., 1971.

Palmer, Willard A. (ed.). *Bach: 2- and 3-Part Inventions.* Port Washington, New York: Alfred Music Co., Inc., 1968. This edition, like the Ferguson, is provided with a very helpful preface dealing mainly with ornamentation.

Rameau, Jean-Philippe. *Pièces de Clavecin*, edited by Jacobi. Kassel: Bärenreiter, 1958. Contains Rameau's essay on technique and styles.

Tartini, Giuseppe. *Treatise on Ornaments in Music*, edited by Jacobi, translated by Girdlestone. Celle: Moeck, 1961. Offers specific advice on mid-18th-century embellishment practices in the Italian manner.

Editions of Keyboard Music | 17

by Maurice Hinson

Maurice Hinson received his musical training from the University of Florida, The Juilliard School, University of Michigan, and the Conversatoire National in Nancy, France. He is a past president of the Kentucky Music Teachers Association and the Southern Division of the Music Teachers National Association. He has given piano recitals and lectures in many states and in Europe and has written articles for some of the leading American musical periodicals. Hinson is the author of *Keyboard Bibliography,* published by MTNA; *Guide to the Pianist's Repertoire,* published by the Indiana University Press; *The Piano Teachers Source Book*, published by Belwin-Mills; and *The Piano in*

Chamber Ensemble, published by Indiana University Press. An authority in piano literature and early American keyboard literature, he has been a guest-lecturer in piano at the National Music Camp in Interlochen, Michigan for eight summers. Dr. Hinson is professor of piano at the Southern Baptist Theological Seminary, School of Church Music, Louisville, Kentucky.

We are living in a day when many editions of the masterworks are available. A well-informed teacher will try to make available to his students the most authentic and reliable editions of music. The subject of editions is broad and this short discussion can only serve as a brief introduction to the field.

It is necessary to choose a good edition because it is highly desirable to follow as closely as possible the composer's intent. We want to be able to interpret correctly and in an appropriate style what we see on the printed page. Ideally it would be best if we had access to the composer's manuscript, the autograph. This is mainly useful to the scholar but not of so much value to the average teacher, because many autographs contain markings that can only be deciphered by the specialist.

Scholarly and complete editions came into being during the nineteenth century. The Bach-Gesellschaft, first complete edition of the works of Mozart, Beethoven and other major composers, became available during this time as the field of musicology became an accepted discipline. Many of these editions are presently being replaced by more up-to-date scholarship and research. The nineteenth century also produced many "personal" editions, editions that were loaded with a famous performer's interpretations. Many of those editions are still with us today, and it is impossible to distinguish the famous interpreter's markings from those of the composer.

The word "urtext" is seen on numerous masterworks printed today. This word literally means "un-edited" and signifies that the edition is based entirely on the composer's original markings. Few such listed editions can completely justify this claim since some editors have been involved in working with the original manuscript or first editions to bring us a text that is reliably the composer's intention. The use of this word "urtext" does not in itself assure authenticity.

Use the following criteria in judging a good edition:

1. The editor's markings should be clearly differentiated typographically from those of the composer.

2. Judicious choice of fingering can be helpful to the student and the busy teacher who might have to devote valuable lesson time changing unwise editorial fingerings.

3. Sources the editor has used should be identified and their location given; the identification should be complete.

4. Comments by the editor about the music, such as the history, style and interpretation, are desirable.

5. Reference marks are highly desirable. Every fifth, tenth or the first bar of each line should be numbered for ease of reference.

Baroque period. One must be careful in choosing editions from this period because composers generally left the music unedited regarding dynamics, fingering, phrasing, tempo, articulation, and frequently used soprano, alto and tenor clefs. The following considerations are offered for music from this period:

1. Some editing is necessary for all but the most thoroughly prepared teacher. However, too much editing is not desirable.
2. If an urtext version is used, the teacher must be prepared to create the edition for the student which is very time consuming.
3. Henle, Bärenreiter, Peters, Kalmus and Alfred editions are generally recommended for this period.

Classical period. Haydn, Mozart and especially Beethoven left more editorial directions in their scores. Recommended editions for this period are Henle and Vienna Urtext publications (Universal Edition) which have clear, easy to read print, simple editorial markings (frequently explained in footnotes or extensive prefaces), and often include fingerings.

Romantic period. Composers from this period tended to be more specific in their markings, but pedal indications are frequently lacking and must be added by the teacher and/or student. (Pedaling is usually related to the changes of harmony.) Ornaments are more frequently written out during this period. Editions by famous pedagogues and performers appear more and more during this time.

Twentieth century. Most composers from this period mark their music very carefully; some (Bartók) are almost finicky in their effort to indicate even the most minute nuance. New types of notation are used by many contemporary composers; this notation must be intelligently understood if honest performance is to follow.

PRINTED MISTAKES

In spite of all the efforts of a fine editor, mistakes and misreadings sometimes find their way into an edition. One should therefore always have a certain degree of skepticism concerning the absolute degree of accuracy of any printed page. Some of the most common mistakes in printing are: (1) omitted accidentals; (2) incorrect accidentals used; (3) a note on the wrong line or space (e.g., E instead of D or F or G instead of E. This is highly possible in editions that use more than one color in printing); (4) use of incorrect clef; (5) ornament omitted; (6) use of an incorrect ornament; (7) dot of a dotted-note left out; (8) a measure or more omitted; (9) a measure or more duplicated.

If, after repeated playings, a measure or passage does not "feel" or "sound" stylistically correct, the performer should make the necessary "corrections," but only after a plausible explanation based on the above or similar criteria has been carefully arrived at.

RECOMMENDED EDITIONS OF STANDARD COMPOSERS' WORKS

Bach, Johann Sebastian (1685-1750)

The Inventions, Partitas, *Die Clavierbüchlein für Anna Magdelena Bach* and the one for W. F. Bach are the only keyboard works presently available in the Neue Bach-Ausgabe (Bärenreiter); other volumes are forthcoming. Kalmus (Bischoff) offers the complete works, available in separate copies as well as in collections. Peters (Kroll, Landshoff, Sauer, and Bischoff) also publishes the complete works. The editions of the *Well-Tempered Clavier* by Henle (von Irmer and Lampe), Belwin-Mills (Tovey and Samuels), and G. Schirmer (Bischoff) are excellent. The *Two-* and *Three-Part Inventions* are available from Henle (Steiglich and Lampe), Peters (Landshoff), Hansen (E. Fischer), Summy-Birchard (Newman), Alfred Music Co. (W. Palmer), J. Fischer (Friskin), while the *Two-Part Inventions* are available in a fine urtext edition from General Words and Music Company (Banowetz).

Bartók, Béla (1881-1945)

Boosey and Hawkes publish most of the works, including the *Mikrokosmos* and *For Children*. General Words and Music Company (Banowetz) has Vol. I of *For Children* (forty-two pieces) available with a cassette. MCA, Marks, G. Schirmer and Kalmus have smaller lists. Universal also has a fine catalog including the piano concerti.

Beethoven, Ludwig Van (1770-1827)

The most reliable urtext of the sonatas are available in Henle (Wallner), G. Schirmer with preface and notes by Carl Krebs (not von Bülow and Lebert), Dover (Schenker), and from Kalmus. Editions that are fine are Belwin-Mills (Tovey-Craxton), especially for the commentary, Simon and Schuster (Schnabel), Peters (Köhler-Ruthardt), and Peters (Arrau). The variations (urtext) are available in Henle (Schmidt-Görg and Georgii) and Vienna Urtext (Brendel). Vienna Urtext and Henle also have the various pieces (Op. 33 to 129) and Kalmus has the *Six Sonatinas.* Henle publishes all the *Bagatelles* in one volume. Vienna Urtext also has the *Variations on Folksongs,* Op. 105 and 107.

Brahms, Johannes (1833-1897)

Distinguished editions are published by Henle, G. Schirmer (Mandyczewski), and International Music Corporation, Peters (Seeman), Universal (Steuermann), and Kalmus (Sauer). Dover has the solo piano works in three volumes. *The Fifty-one Exercises* are published separately by Kalmus, G. Schirmer, and Ricordi. Vienna Urtext has some of the short pieces (Op. 117, 118, and 119) available. The *Complete Transcriptions, Cadenzas and Exercises* are available from Dover (Mandyczewski).

Chopin, Frédéric Francois (1810-1849)

Highest recommendation goes to Henle, with the Chopin Institute edition (available through Marks) coming in a poor second. A New NATIONAL EDITION from Poland has issued a few volumes but all the comments and reports are in Polish. Well-edited editions but with many differences are the Oxford University Press, Peters (Scholtz), and Augener

(Klindworth, Scharwenka), and Durand (Debussy); Salabert (Cortot) has some volumes with English translations of Cortot's notes but the text is not the most reliable. Vienna Urtext has the Préludes and the Etudes. Alfred has the Préludes (Palmer) and the Etudes, Op. 10 only (Esteban). Special mention should be made of the Norton Critical Score (T. Higgins) of the Préludes. Casella has edited most of the works for Edizioni Curci. The Henle volumes are of special merit for containing both the Fontana versions and the original, when great differences occur.

Debussy, Claude (1862-1918)

Most of the piano music of Debussy is published by Durand, available through Elkan-Vogel. G. Schirmer, C. F. Peters, and Dover have a wide selection. General Word and Music Company has a fine collection of the earlier works (Banowetz). The Dutch publisher Broekmans & Van Poppel has a good selection as well as the State Publishers of Poland, Polskie Wydawnictwo Muzyczne, available through Belwin-Mills.

Handel, Georg Frideric (1685-1759)

The Hallische-Handel edition (Bärenreiter) has five volumes containing the complete solo keyboard works. Vol. I contains the eight "Great" suites, Vol. II has seven suites, a prelude and two Chaconnes; Vol. III contains shorter pieces and the final two volumes contain miscellaneous suites and pieces. Durand (Ropartz) has the complete works in four volumes. Peters (Ruthardt) and Augener also publish the sixteen suites in two volumes and Peters has two other volumes with Lessons, Chaconnes, Pieces, Fugues and Fughettes. Peters also has another complete edition edited by Serouky, in five volumes, more up to date than the Ruthardt. The Kalmus edition lists the sixteen suites in two volumes, and in another volume lists Lecons, Pieces, Grand Fugues and Fughettes. Schott, available through Joseph Boonin publishes Seventy-six Pieces (Fuller-Maitland and Squire). Alfred has an excellent collection of some of the miscellaneous pieces (Lucktenberg).

Haydn, Franz Josef (1732-1809)

Vienna Urtext Edition (Landon, Fussl) and Henle (Feder) publish all sixty-two sonatas (incipits of some lost ones) in three volumes. Peters has forty-nine of the sonatas in five volumes (Martienssen). Kalmus, available through Belwin-Mills, publishes forty-three sonatas in four volumes. Breitkopf and Härtel, available through Associated Music Publishers (Zilcher), publish forty-two sonatas in four volumes. Kalmus and Peters publish other solo works and the sets of variations. The Henle and Vienna Urtext volumes of miscellaneous pieces are excellent.

Liszt, Franz (1811-1886)

Bärenreiter - Editio Musica Budapest (available through Theodore Presser) has all of the *Etudes* (two volumes), *Hungarian Rhapsodies* (two volumes) and the *Années de Pèlerinage* (three volumes). Peters has a broad selection in twelve volumes (Sauer); Salabert has a large selection available (Cortot); G. Schirmer has a large amount (Joseffy and other editors); and Kalmus lists a large amount of representative works. Schott publishes *The Liszt Society Publications* – available now are four volumes of early and late pieces and one volume of Late Piano Works. Some of these are available in the Kalmus edition. General Words and Music Company has a volume (Banowetz) that contains an unusual selection with editorial additions in red print.

MacDowell, Edward (1861-1908)

Hinshaw (Hinson): *Forgotten Fairy Tales,* Op. 4; *Six Fancies,* Op. 7. G. Schirmer: *Tragica Sonata,* Op. 45; *Eroica Sonata,* Op. 50; *Idylls,* Op. 28; *Poems,* Op. 31; *Little Poems,* Op. 32. Breitkopf and Härtel: *Modern Suite,* Op. 12; *Tragica and Eroica Sonatas.* Kalmus: *Etudes,* Op. 39; *12 Virtuoso Studies,* Op. 46; *Sonata No. 3,* Op. 57; *Sonata No. 4,* Op. 59; *Witches Dance; Woodland Sketches,* Op. 51; *Sea Pieces,* Op. 55. C. F. Peters has a collection with works from Opp. 37, 51, 55, 61, 62. Two volumes are available from Schroeder and Gunther that contain a broad selection. Da Capo has one volume that contains Opp. 51, 55, 61, 62.

Mendelssohn, Felix (1809-1847)

Dover has the complete solo works in two volumes. Durand, available through Elkan-Vogel, offers the complete works in nine volumes edited by Maurice Ravel. Augener has the complete works in five volumes edited by Thumer, Pauer and Taylor. Kalmus has the complete works in three volumes. Peters offers the three sonatas, Op. 6, 105, and 106 and also some smaller works. G. Schirmer publishes a representative list including the three sets of variations, Opp. 54, 82, and 83 (Hughes) and smaller works. Henle has a *Selected Works* volume that contains Opp. 7, 35, 54, 106 and a number of the *Songs Without Words.* The *Songs Without Words* are offered by Peters, C. Fischer, Lea, G. Schirmer (Sternberg), and Presser (analytical edition by Percy Goetschius).

Mozart, Wolfgang Amadeus (1756-1791)

Henle (Herttrich) has an outstanding urtext (plus fingering) edition in two volumes of the sonatas. Vienna Urtext also offers a fine urtext in two volumes. Presser has an excellent urtext edition by Broder (unfingered) in one volume. Henle, Vienna Urtext, Peters, and Kalmus have the variations and miscellaneous pieces.

Prokofiev, Serge (1891-1953)

MCA publishes almost everything. Boosey and Hawkes has a few items including *Visions Fugitives,* Op. 22; *Music for Children,* Op. 65; *Two Sonatinas,* Op. 54; and *Tales of Old Grandmother.* Kalmus offers a wide selection. Marks, Associated Music Publishers, and International offer smaller lists.

Scarlatti, Domenico (1685-1757)

The only reliable complete edition (555 sonatas in eleven volumes) is edited by Kenneth Gilbert and published by Heugel (through Presser). G. Schirmer offers sixty sonatas in two volumes excellently edited by Ralph Kirkpatrick. C. F. Peters lists many of the sonatas in three volumes. Other collections are also offered by J. Fischer (Frisken), Mercury (Loesser), Boston, Ricordi (has all of the sonatas edited by Longo), and Kalmus. Also see the Alfred collection with an outstanding discussion of the style, ornaments, etc.

Schubert, Franz (1797-1828)

Henle has the sonatas in three volumes including the incomplete sonatas, completed by the editor Paul Badura-Skoda for practical use. The complete works in five volumes, including fifteen sonatas, is published by Lea Pocket Scores. Breitkopf and Härtel publish the sonatas in three volumes edited by Pauer. Editions of eleven sonatas, dances, impromptus (Op. 90 and 142), various pieces and the *Moments Musicaux*, Op. 94 are offered by Peters and Kalmus. Henle has a fine edition of the impromptus and moments musicaux edited by Walter Gieseking. Vienna Urtext has two volumes of *Complete Dances* and the *Wanderer Fantasy* (Badura-Skoda). Augener has Liszt editions of the dances (Opp. 9, 18, and 33), the *Wanderer Fantasy* and the *Sonata*, Op. 78. Dover reprints all the solo piano music in Vol. 5 of the reprint of the Breitkopf and Härtel 1884-1897 edition.

Schumann, Robert (1810-1856)

Henle has most of the works and is gradually bringing out a complete edition. Breitkopf and Härtel and Kalmus publish the complete piano works in the Clara Schumann edition. Augener also publishes the complete works. Editions by Peters (Sauer) and Salabert (Cortot) are almost complete. Hansen, available through Magnamusic-Baton, has some of the Bischoff edition, one of the earliest and best. Dover has a broad spectrum of the piano works in two volumes. Vienna Urtext has the *Papillons*, Op. 2, *Fantasiestücke*, Op. 12 and the *Kinderszenen*, Op. 15.

MORE COMPOSERS

Albéniz, Isaac (1860-1909)
Union Musical Española (Associated); E. B. Marks

Bach, Carl Philipp Emanuel (1714-1788)
Brietkopf & Härtel (Associated); Peters; International

Barber, Samuel (1910-   )
G. Schirmer

Bloch, Ernest (1880-1959)
G. Schirmer

Chabrier, Emmanuel (1841-1894)
Enoch; International

Clementi, Muzio (1752-1832)
C. F. Peters; G. Schirmer; Alfred

Copland, Aaron (1900-   )
Boosey & Hawkes; Durand; Senart; C. Fischer

Couperin, Francois (1668-1733)
Durand; Heugel; G. Schirmer; Kalmus; Alfred

De Falla, Manuel (1876-1946)
Durand; J. & W. Chester

Dello Joio, Norman (1913-   )
G. Schirmer; C. Fischer; E. B. Marks

Dohnányi, Ernst von (1877-1960)
Doblinger; Universal; E. B. Marks; Kalmus

Dvořák, Antonin (1841-1904)
Artia; C. F. Peters

Faure, Gabriel (1845-1924)
Hamelle; Durand; Heugel; International; Kalmus
Field, John (1782-1837)
G. Schirmer; C. F. Peters; Augener; Kalmus
Finney, Ross Lee (1906-)
C. F. Peters; Boosey & Hawkes; Mercury
Franck, César (1922-1890)
C. F. Peters; Durand; T. Presser; Curci; Kalmus
Gershwin, George (1898-1937)
New World Music (Warner Bros. Publications)
Ginastera, Alberto (1916-)
Durand; Ricordi Americana; C. Fischer; Boosey & Hawkes
Gottschalk, Louis Moreau (1829-1869)
T. Presser; C. Fischer; Kalmus; C. F. Peters
Granados, Enrique (1867-1916)
G. Schirmer; Kalmus; E. B. Marks; International
Gretchaninoff, Alexander (1864-1956)
Schott; Max Eschig
Grieg, Edvard (1843-1907)
C. F. Peters; C. Fischer; G. Schirmer; Kalmus
Griffes, Charles Tomlinson (1884-1920)
G. Schirmer
Hindemith, Paul (1895-1963)
Schott
Honegger, Arthur (1892-1955)
Salabert
Hovhaness, Alan (1911-)
C. F. Peters
Ibert, Jacques (1890-)
Alphonse Leduc
Kabalevsky, Dmitri (1904-)
MCA; C. F. Peters; International; Kalmus
Khachaturian, Aram (1903-)
MCA; Kalmus
Lully, Jean-Baptiste (1632-1687)
Durand
Martinu, Bohuslav (1890-1959)
Boosey & Hawkes; Max Eschig
Moszkowski, Moritz (1854-1925)
C. F. Peters; Augener; G. Schirmer
Muczynski, Robert (1929-)
G. Schirmer
Mussorgsky, Modest (1839-1881)
International; Peters; Kalmus
Persichetti, Vincent (1915-)
Elkan-Vogel
Poulenc, Francis (1899-1963)
J. & W. Chester; Salabert; Durand; Heugel
Rachmaninoff, Sergei (1873-1943)
G. Schirmer; International; Boosey & Hawkes;
Belwin-Mills; Kalmus

Rameau, Jean-Philippe (1683-1764)
Bärenreiter; Durand; Belwin-Mills; International; Kalmus
Ravel, Maurice (1875-1937)
Durand; G. Schirmer; Kalmus
Reinagle, Alexander (1756-1809)
Hinshaw
Saint-Säens, Camille (1835-1921)
Durand
Satie, Eric (1866-1925)
Salabert; Eschig; Associated
Schönberg, Arnold (1874-1951)
Universal; Wilhelm Hansen
Schuman, William (1910-)
Howard Music Co. (G. Schirmer); G. Schirmer; Presser
Scriabin, Alexander (1892-1915)
C. F. Peters; MCA; Alfred; International; Kalmus
Stravinsky, Igor (1882-1971)
Boosey & Hawkes
Tansman, Alexandre (1897-)
Eschig
Tchaikowsky, Peter Ilyich (1840-1893)
C. F. Peters; G. Schirmer; Alfred
Tcherepnin, Alexander (1899-)
G. Schirmer; C. F. Peters; Schott; Durand; E. B. Marks
Toch, Ernst (1887-1964)
Schott
Turina, Joaquín (1882-1949)
Salabert; Eschig; Associated
Villa-Lobos, Heitor (1887-1959)
Consolidated; E. B. Marks; Peer International
Weber, Carl Maria von (1786-1826)
C. F. Peters; Salabert; G. Schirmer
Webern, Anton (1883-1945)
Universal

SUMMARY

One must make a continuous and conscious effort to know what editions are available. The most important question to keep in mind when selecting an edition is: Can I distinguish between the composer's markings and those of the editor? If the answer is no, you should continue to search for such an edition. It may not exist, but you should be unsatisfied with that answer until you have exhausted all possibilities.

Make sure your students know what edition to purchase when you request them to buy music. Price may be a factor, especially in foreign publications, but do not hesitate to specify the edition you think is most valuable.

Build your own library with editions of documented authority.

FOR FURTHER READING

Benton, Rita. "The Problems of Piano Music Editions." *American Music Teacher,* November/December, 1956.

Dexter, Benning, and George Loomis. "Choosing the Best Edition," *Clavier,* 8, September 1969, 50-2.

Emery, Walter. *Editions and Musicians.* London: Novello, 1957.

Ferguson, Howard. *Keyboard Interpretation.* New York and London: Oxford University Press, 1975.

"Guide for Selecting Editions," *Piano Quarterly,* 56, Summer, 1966, 14-36. Compiled by the editors.

Hinson, Maurice. *Guide to the Pianist's Repertoire.* Bloomington: Indiana University Press, 1973.

Meller, Mischa. "Some Critical Comments on Modern Editions of the Piano Classics," *American Music Teacher,* 4, September-October, 1954, 1, 16-17.

Oberdoerffer, Fritz. "Urtext Editions," *American Music Teacher,* 10, July-August, 1961, 2, 15-18.

Serkin, Rudolf. "Some Thoughts on Editions for the Artist Student," in *Comprehensive Guide for Piano Teachers.* New York: The Music Education League, 1963, 94-5.

Part Four

Interviews

An Interview with Rosina Lhevinne

18

by James Bastien

Photo by James Bastien.
Taken outside of her summer home in Aspen, Colorado, 1968.

Rosina Lhevinne—born in Kiev, Russia in 1880—is a legendary figure in the world of music and ranks as one of the great piano teachers of all time. During her remarkable teaching career she has guided to stardom such talents as Van Cliburn, John Browning, Mischa Dichter, and a host of others. Madame Lhevinne's own career began when she graduated from the Moscow Imperial Conservatory in 1898, winning a gold medal. She married Josef Lhevinne, the famous concert pianist, in 1898. She made her debut with the Moscow Symphony Orchestra in 1895, and subsequently toured widely in Europe and the United States. She frequently appeared in two-piano recitals with her husband. She joined the faculty of the Juilliard School of Music in 1925 and also joined the summer faculty of the Aspen Music Festival in 1956. During her teaching career at the Juilliard School, which spanned five decades, Rosina Lhevinne had a spectacular career and produced some of the world's greatest pianists. Madame Lhevinne died on November 9, 1976, in Glendale, California. Thus a great tradition comes to an end, but her influence will live on in the many talented students who were fortunate to have received her inspiration and guidance.

No book on piano teaching would be complete without the personal views of one of the world's great teachers, Rosina Lhevinne. She is a personable, pleasant grande dame whom I found most gracious. She made an appointment for the interview through her secretary, and when I arrived she had just been out for a daily walk and was resting in the living room of her summer home. Her secretary offered us tea, and we had a lovely chat during the better part of two hours in the late afternoon. Before the actual interview began, we had an informal discussion of her childhood training in Russia. Her sense of humor was quite keen. In her reminiscences she jokingly told that when she grew up in Russia it was very unusual for girls to pursue a concert career; she said that after her marriage everyone told her she would be ruined and divorced in a year! She also went on to say that at that time in Russia two-piano teams were rather rare. She discussed the beginnings of her concert career and the first tour she and her husband made in this country in 1906.

At the time of the interview Madame Lhevinne was eighty-eight; she was spry, witty, and offered astute brief answers to the general teaching questions I asked her. Similar questions were asked of Adele Marcus, and it is interesting to compare answers. The interview took place in Madame Lhevinne's summer home in Aspen, Colorado (1968).

What qualities do you find necessary in a student before accepting him for study?

The qualities that I am most concerned about are musicality and sensitivity, this cannot be taught. Technique can be taught—and the Russian school stresses technique, but only as a means to the end—but beyond that there must be an inner feeling for music that transcends the purely mechanical—this must be an inborn quality.

What do students generally lack in their playing and background upon entering college?

You know, we get some fantastic talents at the Juilliard School; sometimes their auditions are really quite amazing. But the thing I notice very often is fingers, fingers, fingers, when I would rather hear music, music, music. However, concern with musical qualities rather than with the mechanical often grows as the student matures and is surrounded with good music day and night.

How would you define a talented student?

Talent to me means a special inner creative ability that is difficult to define. A genuine love for music and the determination to work hard to achieve one's goals also imply talent.

Do you feel that perfect pitch is a must for a pianist?

No. Sometimes it is a detriment because a person may be thrown by the varying pitches of different pianos. However, it is a desirable quality to have.

It has been said that a student's beginning training is so important that it can either "make or break him." How important do you think correct teaching is in the beginning?

I think beginning training is of *great* importance (this is an excellent question). The first teacher (or teachers) is so important because he must instil love, understanding, and interest in music.

How personally involved do you think a teacher should become in his relationship with his students?

To understand the pupil and his needs thoroughly, I must feel very close to him. I can only teach him if I know him personally. You cannot have one formula which will work for all students—what is right for one is not right for another.

Very often a student will work very hard to please his teacher, especially if he has great respect for the teacher. This must certainly be true in your case; what pleases you most in lesson to lesson work with a student?

I am pleased most by individual understanding. Also, I want week to week improvement.

I often hear students practicing in university practice studios. It seems to me that they repeat and repeat, often aimlessly, the same passage over and over again without really much thought and direction. If this is so, how can you teach a student to practice correctly?

Well, first practice does mean repetition, but it should be meaningful, not haphazard. One must practice with one hundred percent concentration and must stop when thoughts wander. If concentration begins to go, run around the block, or anything, but don't continue—only resume practice when you are fresh. I usually tell my students to listen carefully to what you are doing—be your own critic, if it does not sound right to you, find out why and fix it, that is what practice is for.

How do you feel about mental practice away from the keyboard?

I am very much for it. Actually, it should be taught from the beginning—one must first hear the sound, then practice. Reading a score without the piano develops a better understanding of the music; one will be able to think slower in the fast passages. I like to think of the whole page when I am playing—the phrasing, the dynamics, etc. These details should be worked out mentally away from the piano. In this way, a meaningful performance will be given.

Can a student be taught to project in his performances, or is this an inborn quality?

A musical student can improve greatly, but if he does not have it, I don't think he can be taught how to project, because then it would be imitation. In the beginning the student may imitate the teacher in learning how to shape the phrase, how to pedal, etc., but projection of the music for the artist-student must transcend imitation and come from inner feelings that he, the performer, wants to communicate to his audience.

What importance do you give to sight-reading?

I consider it so important that I insist from very early study that students practice a minimum of fifteen minutes a day on sight-reading. By doing some reading each day they will know the repertoire better; then when it comes time to discuss a program, they will have a knowledge of the literature and will already have an idea what interests them most. I teach students to read the melody and bass line; the reading of the top and bottom is so important—the inner parts can be filled in as much as possible. Learning to read in this manner will develop a reading skill and help students to read faster over a period of time. Practice time should be divided into technique, repertoire, and reading; reading should not be neglected.

You have had so many excellent students in your teaching career, and, of course, not all these students became concert artists. Many of them have become important teachers. What do you feel are the most important qualities to become a successful, inspiring teacher?

In my long career at Juilliard (forty-three years) I have had a great number of talented students, but talent alone is not enough to become a great success. Personality is the determining factor in the make-up of a great teacher—as well as being a fine performer. This is a quality that is quite indescribable. To develop and grow musically as an individual one must be constantly reading—not just on music, but one must develop an acquaintance with the other arts, go to museums, lectures, one must travel—all these are a great help to continue the growth and development of the personality. Also, the teacher must be willing to give of himself for the student's good. The teacher must really be interested in teaching, and want to help his students.

Do you think it is a realistic approach for all students studying with you to want to become concert artists?

Definitely not, and this is a great mistake which is made by young pianists. Out of one hundred students, when you ask them what they want to do, nearly all say they want to be concert pianists. Only a few are destined to become great pianists. A much more nobler occupation than concertizing is teaching. By teaching you can pass on the art of piano playing from generation to generation and continue this art forever.

An Interview with Irl Allison

19

by James Bastien

Dr. Irl Allison—born in Valley Mills, Texas in 1896—is an outstanding figure in the field of music education. He is the founder and organizer of the National Guild of Piano Teachers which is now one of the largest organizations of its type with annual participation of approximately 80,000 students. Dr. Allison received the BA degree in 1915 and the MA degree in 1922 from Baylor University. Upon graduation from Baylor, his teaching career began with a private studio in Dallas. His college teaching career includes the position of Dean of Music at Rusk Junior College, Rusk, Texas; Dean of Music at Montezuma Baptist College in New Mexico; and Dean of Music at Hardin-

Simmons University in Abilene, Texas. His piano teachers included Ernest Hutcheson in New York and Percy Grainger in Chicago. Because of his outstanding work in the field of music education, Dr. Allison received honorary doctorates from Southwestern Conservatory, Dallas (1947), Hardin-Simmons University (1949), and from the Houston Conservatory (1953). Dr. Allison has composed numerous compositions including *Through the Years,* and he is the editor-author of a thirty-three volume library titled *The Irl Allison Piano Library.* Through the founding and building of the Guild to national prominence, Dr. Allison's contribution to the field of music is unique and commendable.

Because of the magnitude and scope of the Guild organization which includes 663 chapters, 10,000 teachers, and approximately 80,000 piano students who play upwards of 850,000 memorized pieces annually, I thought that Dr. Allison's personal views on the vision and organization of the Guild would be of special interest to piano teachers throughout the country. Dr. Allison is a deeply religious man whose devotion to the formation and promulgation of the Guild is carried on with great fervor and personal zeal. One sees immediately that he is convinced that students of all levels and abilities need an opportunity to play for an impartial judge, not in a contest in which there are winners and losers, but in an audition in which the student receives a rating.

In 1950 Dr. Allison expanded the auditions to include the National Piano Recording Competition which is an important annual event which offers cash awards and founder's medals to all entrants. In 1958 he carried the Guild concept another step forward by joining Grace Ward Langford in Fort Worth to plan and develop the now world-famous Van Cliburn International Quadrennial Piano Competition which has launched the careers of many young artists.

From its meager beginning at Hardin-Simmons University in 1929, Dr. Allison's personal hand has guided the Guild to the fantastic success which it now has reached. It is this story that I wanted to record. The interview took place in Dr. Allison's lovely home in Austin, in the spring of 1970.

I want to ask you particularly about the formation of the National Guild of Piano Teachers. I noted that the first auditions were held in Abilene, Texas in 1929. How did the idea come to you for the beginning of this tremendous organization?

If you remember about the financial situation of the country at that time, we were facing a depression. It had not yet struck West Texas, but everyone was frightened. Due to the panic of the stock market crash, many college piano students simply stopped studying. I had had one of the largest departments in the State at Hardin-Simmons University prior to that time, and it was growing tremendously. However, beginning in the fall of 1929 we felt an abrupt decrease in enrollment. In order to meet this situation I felt that we should try to interest more students from the city to attend the College. So I started what we called the Junior Piano School at the university in which we combined class work with private teaching. I had a number of advanced students who aided me as teaching assistants.

In this preparatory department that you started, what type of work was done in classes?

I began organizing the piano curriculum so that various elements of musicianship could be taught in class, such as scales, chords, and arpeggios—basically, we taught keyboard technique in a class setting. I prevailed upon the school board to purchase ten Howard (Baldwin) uprights; we converted our small recital hall into a class piano studio. We had two grands on the stage, and ten uprights arranged in wings of five, each immediately in front of the stage. We gave each student a piano—two on the stage, and one at each piano. Besides myself, we always had an assistant in the room to help the children when necessary. I undertook the teaching of these children in this fashion. We advertised in the paper, and we enrolled a class of fifty students. To schedule these students in sections we needed five hours which just exactly filled a week of class lessons. I taught one hour every afternoon. From this experience I developed some very efficient means of teaching student keyboard technique. They learned all their scales, chords, and arpeggios in class.

Did you present programs of any kind to interest other teachers and students?

Yes. We rehearsed materials for our twenty-piano concert at the end of the year. We had students playing duets, trios, etc., with some twelve to twenty pianos going at the same time. This was one of the first piano ensemble presentations in the United States. In preparing for this event we outlined our program carefully that first year, step by step. Throughout the year my purpose was to have about eight or ten numbers that my groups would work up for this concert. Because we had a unique situation, and in order to create enthusiasm for piano playing, we invited students from the area to participate in an all Southwestern Piano Tournament.

Was that the first Guild tournament?

Actually, that first event was the beginning of the national piano playing auditions. At that time I set up goals for our students so that every one had a complete program in repertoire and technique to play for an important examiner. As a point of interest, the first examiner was John Thompson, the author of well-known teaching materials. He was giving a workshop there for teachers, and afterwards he stayed over three days for the auditions. That first event had only forty-six entrants; thirty-three of them were from my own class from the Junior Piano School. Several children came from far away; one child came from Lufkin which is about 400 miles away from Abilene. When Thompson came out of the room that first day, he said "Irl, is this your idea?" When I answered "yes," he said, "This ought to be everywhere—it has all the advantages of a contest but without the disadvantages." This was my purpose: each student was winning some kind of award, and in a sense they were all winners, none were losers. If Thompson thought the student performed his pieces well, with a grade of 90 or above, he was awarded a blue ribbon for each piece he played. The minimum requirement at this first audition was four pieces, the maximum was ten. Even at that time we set up district, state, and national honors. Students would get national honors and receive blue ribbons if they made a grade above 90 on all four pieces; state honors and red ribbons went to those whose grade was from 80 to 90; district honors and white ribbons went to those whose grade was from 70 to 80. In any case, every child came out with a hand full of ribbons.

How did you promote this idea to other areas, out of the state of Texas?

At first it was one teacher telling another. However, when I conceived of having auditions outside of Abilene, I sent out a little booklet stating the rules and regulations. I sent this booklet to various music stores and asked them to send me a list of teachers in their area. The first year I sent out about five hundred booklets. We had auditions patterned after the one in Abilene in seven other Texas cities. The entries were very small that first year. To build interest and numbers of entrants, I tried some unusual methods. To start the Dallas center, for example, I sent twenty-four of my own students to play for the judge up there. Also, during the early years I went out myself and sold the idea house to house, you might say, just like the Fuller brush man. For a period of about eight years I worked very hard at building interest and enthusiasm for these auditions. I visited about one hundred and fifty cities during that time. We moved to California for a year (Los Angeles) from which I traveled to other cities in the area.

Did you organize and set up the centers alone, by yourself?

Yes. I organized the centers myself. During the early years my wife acted as the national secretary helping me greatly in this project.

Did you move to other cities for a period of time other than Los Angeles?

Yes. I went to New York and organized the center there about 1935, and I stayed there for a period of time. I had a great deal of help from one publishing house in particular, Schroeder and Gunther. Edwin L. Gunther knew every teacher there, and his help in soliciting their support was invaluable. I had several works published with Gunther—one in particular, *To a Rosebud*, which had sold eight hundred copies in New York alone which was pretty good at that time! With Mr. Gunther's help we grew slowly; the first year we had one hundred entrants. Fortunately, we had wonderful support from the newspaper. Mr. Gunther knew a man by the name of Edward L. Workheim who specialized in publicizing non-profit educational and religious ventures for the New York papers.

What kind of support did the New York papers give you?

Well, it was really fantastic. We held the first audition in Aeolian Hall which was a very beautiful recital hall on Fifth Avenue. We got it for almost nothing—actually, the space was donated for the audition. This audition caught the fancy of the New York papers, and they gave us good coverage of this event. Our largest direct support from the papers came about through a coincidence. The president of Hardin-Simmons University was Dr. J. D. Sanford, and his son-in-law was none other than the great Stanley Walker who was the editor of the *Times Herald* in New York. When Mr. Walker found out that this project was taking place and had evolved from Hardin-Simmons, he sent his reporters to cover the story. The stories in the papers featured the auditions, but also reported some unusual children who performed. We discovered a prodigy there who was only five at the time; he played the Mozart *C Major Sonata*, among other pieces. We also had a little Negro girl who played eight of her own compositions that were just marvelous. These prodigies were played up in the front pages of some of the leading New York papers, in fact, we got three hundred and twenty-nine articles in the papers that first year! Of course I was amazed at the coverage which was beyond any of my wildest expectations. We had so many reporters that we could hardly handle them. The teachers helped take care of them, and most of them were interviewed at great length. That was the beginning of the New York auditions.

At that time, 1935, how many students did you have audition nationally?

We had about 1700 students from coast to coast in twenty-nine cities.

Were there any other unusual events that led up to this first national audition?

Well, the first miracle was the unbelievable coverage in the New York papers. The second came about through an interesting circumstance. I had a large United States map on my dining room wall in which I had placed stars in 100 cities where I had hoped to set up centers. It was not possible for me to visit all of these cities myself, and I didn't know how this could be accomplished. One evening a father of one of my pupils came over and saw this map. Since his child had played in the auditions in Abilene for several years, he was interested in my project. His name was Mr. Gorman, and he was an auditor for the books of oil men in that area. He asked about the map, and I told him that I would like very much for the auditions to spread to the other cities indicated with stars. He had seen how enthusiastic his daughter, Laurine, was over her ribbons and certificates. (We converted to certificates about the third year.) I told him how John Thompson had given me the idea of setting up centers all over the country based on those given in Abilene. I told him that my only trouble in getting all these started was money. I told him that we needed to send someone to each of these places to organize the project and get the idea planted. He then informed me that he audited the books of seven oil men, and he thought one of these might just provide the money. He said he would speak to Charles L. Kliner in Cisco, Texas, the next Thursday about the idea. When oil was discovered on his land it turned out to be something really fabulous; he soon had seventeen gushing wells which produced an income of six hundred dollars per day! Since Mr. Kliner had only a third grade education, he turned over the management of his money to professionals. Because of his lack of education, Mr. Gorman thought it might be possible that he would be interested in helping an educational project. So Mr. Gorman said he would speak to him about the matter. And he did—in fact, he called me the very next day and said that Mr. Kliner would give me an appointment. So on Sunday afternoon I drove out to see him. He came to the door in his overalls—he said he had been working on the plumbing in the basement. I explained to him what I wanted and he listened very respectfully, but he didn't commit himself in the least. When I went home I told Mrs. Allison that I thought we had wasted our time; I thought Kliner was not the least bit interested in giving support to this project. However, the next day Mr. Gorman called and said that Kliner did indeed like the idea and wondered how much money I would need. I ventured a figure of $4000. He said "You will get your check," and I did have it just a few days later. With that money I was able to find three people to help me. These three people covered three parts of the Nation, and I took the fourth myself. On that meager budget of $4000 we got this program started in twenty-nine cities—that included Boston, Portland, Seattle, New York, Dallas—most of the big centers.

Was that the only backing you received?

Yes, and it turned out to be just as well. After the first year when we had 1700 students audition, I decided that since this project was for the students and for the students' teachers, there should be some way for them to support this program themselves. So the next year we had the first membership dues which were five dollars. We had about one thousand teachers to start. With these dues I was able to reach 150 cities over the next eight years.

You mentioned the benefits for teachers belonging to the Guild; what are they?

First, the audition provides incentives; the teacher can hold up goals to work for. The program can be planned in advance so that the material will be learned in time for the examiner. The student knows that judgement day is coming. Every scale learned, every piece, will have an opportunity to be heard and appraised objectively by an impartial party. It helps increase the student's repertoire. The goal is to learn about ten pieces from memory. Also, the literature to be performed is somewhat specified in that certain selections such as a Bach piece, a sonatina, etc., are required. This not only helps the student in providing a guide to the selection of his repertoire, but it also helps the teacher who may have been indiscriminately choosing material before.

As an example of increased repertoire, one year I had four students who had learned all fifteen *Two-Part Inventions* of Bach. I told my students that we would startle the judge; I told them that no judge coming out here to West Texas would expect to hear this number of pieces played by memory by students twelve to fifteen years of age.

So you can see that the goals are to increase the repertoire, the quality of the repertoire, to upgrade technique, to improve all the aspects of piano playing, and then give the student an opportunity to perform these aspects for a competent judge.

Have you noticed improvements in teaching standards over the years after the Guild came into being?

Very definitely. Actually at that time many teachers had no idea of piano repertoire. We had teachers in Dallas that entered such pieces as *The Black Hawk Waltz* and *The Midnight Fire Alarm*, for example! One of the old dealers in Dallas, Mr. Council, told me that a revolution had been made with the suggested repertoire from the Guild. He said almost no teacher at that time was giving anything like the Bach Inventions, and very few were giving sonatinas. I brought most of the standard repertoire into their teaching through the Guild. A structured program was not even taught in New York City such as outlined in the Guild [a piece from the Baroque, Classical, Romantic, and Contemporary periods].

Where did you get the idea to require a structured program covering four eras of music?

That idea evolved out of my work with Ernest Hutcheson with whom I studied after I graduated from Baylor. Actually my repertoire was limited to sort of flowery, fancy pieces. Hutcheson asked me to play a Two-Part Invention, and I didn't know a one. So he started me on these polyphonic pieces, and until that time I had never played anything polyphonic. Likewise I had not played a Mozart sonata, and he began me on these. In other words my background was limited to certain areas of music, and I saw the need for an expanded, comprehensive survey of four-period literature. When I came back to Texas I vowed that my pupils would never have to go through what I did when I was twenty-four years old!

Did you find actual proof that classical repertoire, so to speak, was gaining in popularity?

Yes. Actually Schirmer made a survey of the sales of the Edwin Hughes *Master Series for the Young*, and discovered that in one year alone sales had increased 20%—not only that, but the years before, there were no increases in sales at all. On the basis of these results, Schirmer gave me ads in our Syllabus for their publications—that was before we had our *Yearbook* or the *Piano Guild Notes*. Then other publishers began giving me page ads for their new publications of classical music for the young. Until that time the Boston Music Company had no such series; Schirmer had only the Hughes editions—after that, all the publishers began publishing classical music for young students.

When you judged in different centers I'm sure you heard some outstanding students who had been well-prepared by their teachers. In this regard, what do you think are the qualities of fine teachers?

Mainly they must be enthusiastic. That is the most important thing in any undertaking. I think all really good musicians are enthusiastic people—the more enthusiasm they have, the better teachers they make. You have to sell classical music to students; they are not born with a love for Bach, Mozart, etc.—the teacher must generate enthusiasm for this music. Most students come into serious music through popular music, as I did. The teacher must generate the feeling that everything that is taught and practiced is really worthwhile.

What would you like to see happen to the continuation of the Guild, and what would you hope for its future?

I would like most of all to see an organized plan for providing concert engagements for our young artists who have been produced through the Guild auditions during the past forty years—for example such artists as James Dick, Ralph Votapek, and Radu Lupu. Artists like these are perfectly groomed and experienced to face the concert stage, and we need more opportunities for these gifted young artists to perform. I have thought of organizing Van Cliburn clubs all over the country for the purpose of presenting young pianists. I would limit it to piano because the Guild is already organized and has the group with which to work. The teachers in these clubs would encourage their pupils to hear the young artists who have been built up through the Guild. Too many young artists are ready to perform but they have no managers.

Would this be your main hope for a new direction for the Guild?

Yes, I would like to give deserving young performers an opportunity to play for appreciative audiences throughout the country sponsored by students and teachers in the Guild organization. I wish I were young enough to take this project on—I think I could make it go!

An Interview with Adele Marcus

20

by James Bastien

Photo by James Bastien.
Taken after a master class session in Aspen, Colorado, 1968.

Adele Marcus, distinguished faculty member of the Juilliard School in New York, is one of the most outstanding piano teachers in the world. Her fantastic teaching capabilities have sprouted such prize-winning students as Byron Janis, Augustin Anievas, Thomas Schumacher, and most recently Horacio Gutierrez who won second prize in the 1970 Tchaikovsky Competition in Moscow. Miss Marcus studied with Josef Lhevinne and Artur Schnabel and was Josef Lhevinne's assistant for seven years. She has given numerous master classes and demonstration lectures in this country and other countries throughout the world. Miss Marcus was on the faculty at the Aspen Music Festival for many summers and has recently been on the summer faculty of the Temple University Festival at Ambler, Pennsylvania. She has represented the United States by serving on international piano juries for such contests as the Marguerite Long contest in Paris and the Munich International Piano Contest in Germany. Adele Marcus is a unique musician with a meteoric career in three fields as a performer-teacher-lecturer and is unparalleled in these capacities.

After seeing Adele Marcus work with students in master classes and seeing her present several demonstration lectures, I realized that because of her remarkable capabilities as a teacher and performer, her personal views would be most valuable. She is an energetic, pleasant, spontaneous woman who inspires her students to amazing achievement. In observing her master classes one realizes that the work there reveals only a small portion of the teaching potential of which she is capable; but even this brief encounter with students often brings remarkable improvement. Of special interest to teachers and students is her presentation of technique which is quite special. Fortunately, her views were recently printed in *Clavier* magazine (Vol. XI, No. 6, September, 1972) as related by Dean Elder. Teachers and students alike will find this discussion extremely informative and helpful.

In this interview Adele Marcus discusses important teaching items that are of interest to teachers of all levels. Similar questions were asked of Madame Lhevinne, and it is interesting to compare answers. The interview took place at Miss Marcus' summer home in Aspen, Colorado (1968).

What qualities do you find necessary in a student before accepting him for study?

In my estimation the most essential quality for a student who is about to embark upon serious study, would be for him to have a genuine emotional response to music. This person must have the capability to penetrate a piece of music and get an appropriate response. Also, the physical equipment is important in that one has to handle the instrument adequately in order to convey the musical message to other people. There must be some degree of proficiency at the piano, and there must be a *desire* to become technically equipped—this is of utmost importance.

What do students generally lack in their playing and background upon entering college?

Often the communicative quality is not present—there is too much moving of the fingers, too much practicing and not enough studying; there is not enough emphasis on the character and mood of the composition. They are working primarily with externals.

How would you define a talented student?

A talented student is one who is thoroughly dedicated and able to enjoy discipline, which means to me, the *love* of work. Also talent means the desire to improve one's standard, not to compete with others, but rather to compete with his or her own standard.

Do you feel that perfect pitch is a must for a pianist?

No, I don't think perfect pitch is a must; it's one of those physical phenomena. However, good relative pitch is very important. It probably is necessary for a string player, a conductor, and only in rare cases for a singer. But I don't think it is necessarily an indication of a great talent—I know many great pianists who do not have perfect pitch.

It has been said that a student's beginning training is so important that it can either "make or break him." How important do you think correct teaching is in the beginning?

Elementary training is of paramount importance. It does not necessarily make or break a student, but any experienced teacher on the advanced level knows immediately when the elementary training has been excellent. It's like the foundation of a house; if the foundation is really solid from the standpoint of musicianship and basic principles of study and practice, then it is much easier to work on an advanced level and the whole structure will not fall apart so easily.

How personally involved do you think a teacher should become in his relationship with his students?

The personal involvement should primarily direct itself toward evaluating the student's potential. If the teacher can create for the pupil an exact image of himself as to his basic potential and the lacking ingredients, then he has involved himself to the extent of taking a long-range view of what possibilities might lie ahead—either as a performing career, or as a teaching-performing career. The teacher can also counsel and guide the student when he needs advice concerning auditions, the much dreaded competitions, or other aspects of his professional world. However, I don't think it is advisable for the teacher to involve himself with the personal matters of the student.

Very often a student will work very hard to please his teacher, especially if he has great respect for the teacher. This must certainly be true in your case, what pleases you most in lesson to lesson work with a student?

The thing which pleases me most is *progress*. This is my basic and initial interest and my ultimate one. I usually tell a student I will work with you as hard as I know how, with all of my integrity and knowledge—I expect you to do the same.

I often hear students practicing in university practice studios. It seems to me that they repeat and repeat, often aimlessly, the same passage over and over again without really much thought and direction. If this is so, how can you teach a student to practice correctly?

This is one of my pet subjects! I think music is the only profession in the world where people practice first and study afterwards. A lawyer would first study, then practice—in medicine the same order would follow. The student often practices too much. While practicing there should be a constant questioning, because to benefit the person there must be a creative approach—practicing must be creative; teaching must be creative; and performing must be creative. One must learn to *study* a score first and find out where the problems are. One cannot successfully solve a problem until he first knows what the problem is. After it has been solved, then one should practice the solution. Regarding repetition, too much repetition of a passage can very easily stifle the imagination. One should only repeat by constantly questioning: "Why am I repeating? Is it for a different fingering, a different nuance, a different phrase, a different pedaling, a different tonal effect?" If one repeats aimlessly, the constant repetition can lull one into a stupor.

How do you feel about mental practice away from the keyboard?

I think it should go on all the time. In visualizing a score, I think a big talent usually lives with a great work—he must think of it constantly. The study away from the piano enhances a certain security, not only in the interpretive concept, but also very often in the memorization. I believe in it one hundred percent!

Do you think even a young student can be taught this type of practice?

Definitely. I always say that a student should learn to "hear" through his eyes and "see" through his ears. In other words when he hears a score, he should be able to visualize how it might look on the printed sheet, and when he sees the printed sheet, he should hear what it might sound like from looking at it.

Do you think that when a student plays a composition he should somehow visualize how it appears on the page?

This is, of course, having a photographic memory, and I think it is one of the four facets of knowing how to memorize. My feeling is that the other three are also very important. I happen to have a photographic memory, most people don't, and many people are afraid of it, because they feel that it is exhausting and nerve-racking, particularly before a performance. In addition to visual memory, one must know the basic harmonic structure of a work. Also, one must be able to hear it to some appreciable extent—if without perfect pitch. Finally, the tactile sense is very important in memorization—being able to anticipate and "feel" patterns on the keyboard. So, the visual or the photographic memory very often goes with an important talent, but other memorization items are also necessary. I believe in visual memory firmly.

Can a student be taught to project in his performances, or is this an inborn quality?

Many students project naturally, but projection goes with wanting to communicate. You cannot project projection, you have to project something, and if you have something vital you want to say, you usually *want* someone to hear it. The art of projection has to do of course with *how* you study, how you are able to listen, not only to what you feel about the music, but what you actually hear coming out of the piano. You feel it subjectively and you hear it objectively as a listener does—then, you are actually projecting.

Would you consider stage deportment one aspect of projection?

Very definitely. The moment you leave the wings and are faced with the public, you are already being evaluated as a person who either belongs to his task, or someone who is totally detached. There is nothing divorced from the making of music when you are involved with it on stage. There is sometimes more meaning in a gesture than all the notes in the world.

Usually teachers are concerned with the perfection of a piece or the perfection of a number of compositions. This effort directed exclusively to one area of musicianship often leads to neglect of another—sight-reading. How do you feel about this?

I think sight-reading is of paramount importance. I like to feel that students can read fluently, not necessarily as fast as possible, but easily, and preferably in depth. I think a certain portion of every day should be devoted to sight-reading. When I find that a student is lacking in this particular ingredient of the whole musical output, I insist that he devote between a half hour to forty-five minutes a day reading something—not especially difficult, but within a given style, over a period of time—so that he can capture a particular style and become acquainted with a composer's works. I believe that reading at sight is a phenomenon with some students—that they read inordinately fast, and that they get over a tremendous amount of material—but it is extremely important to be able to read with *meaning.*

Would your approach to teaching beginners be channeled through sight-reading or playing scales and exercises?

I believe that after fundamentals of hand position and finger coordination have been established it is important to read music from the earliest stage possible. Young children should learn to enjoy their music and not be made to practice scales and exercises as this drudgery will either produce unmusical results or discouragement with music. I was singularly fortunate in having taught children exclusively for ten years. That experience served as a most valuable apprentice period, and I feel that teaching children was the greatest factor in developing me as a teacher.

Would you include some sight-reading work as part of your teaching program, and would you hear sight-reading during the course of your lessons?

Very often if a student has only been able to prepare half of the lesson assignment, I will say, "Let's read through this particular work and let me see what you read into it, and what ideas you will bring forth." I think that one should read, but not just ramble through a lot of material—the reading should be serious. One should really penetrate the score and at the same time one should not only just see one or two things at the same time, but many things: primarily the character, the mood, and the tempo of the work.

You have had so many excellent students in your teaching career, and of course not all these students became concert artists. Many of them have become important teachers. What do you feel are the most important qualities to become a successful, inspiring teacher?

A good teacher does not teach by stereotyped formulas, but rather he summons up all of his creative prowess and directs this toward handling the potential of each student. I do not have any methods; I try to evaluate the total personality. The primary factor in teaching is to take a long-range view of what each student might accomplish and determine what his goals might be. The teacher should discuss with the student how the two of them will go about building a road toward development and rewarding progress.

Do you think it is a realistic approach for all students studying with you to want to become concert artists?

I'm probably renowned for being singularly discouraging about reaching for *only* the performing career. Fortunately we are living in an age where the performer-teacher has come into his own. The demands of becoming a concert artist are severe. I think it is rare indeed to find a person who at a very early age manifests an almost spectacular talent, can carry through with proper training, build a large repertoire, develop excellent nerves, be blessed with an attractive appearance, find a manager, launch a career, and sustain it! These special musicians are very, very far and few between. As we know, these are the peaks, but the peaks are easy to slide down from. Sometimes the musician who is able to achieve a more modest goal, a little less than the highest peaks, usually, and very often, will have a happier life in music. I do not encourage students to become exclusively concert artists. I believe that the teaching field is tremendously rewarding, tremendously creative, and has in recent years become even glamorous.

Do you personally take as much interest in a student that you know will not make a concert career, even if he is very gifted and proficient?

I definitely do. If the student is serious and is willing to work hard, I take an interest, because to me, it means that I am confronted with an individual whose life and livelihood is really important. If it is a young man, especially, he has to live by his work. I usually try to outline a minimum of a four year's course of study, which will bring him to a level, so that at least when he leaves the Juilliard School of Music with any type of degree, he will feel totally equipped to face the professional world.

What do you think teachers can do who have already been teaching for a number of years to upgrade their own work?

I think they should reach out for the understanding of all the new trends in music, even if it is music which does not particularly appeal to them, like avant-garde music, electronic music etc. We must all be conversant with what is going on in the world around us, and we all need to broaden our horizons. Also, I think that all the periodicals are good in the general broadening of the teacher's knowledge, whether it is the *Saturday Review of Literature,* or *Clavier*, or any of the magazines and books on music. I think, however, the personal contact with workshops, with master classes, and with participation in local, state, and national organizations has a very broadening effect. Also, the teacher should not be afraid to expose his own pupils to contests, auditions, and master classes. Certainly, none of us can know all the answers; I think it is very rewarding for the student when he finds that his own teacher's ideas have been upheld by other people. Finally, I advocate that the teacher get back to his instrument and try to practice at least a little each day; actually, he should be able to play up to the level of the music he is teaching. We all need self-involvement, and the teacher must strive for personal attainment for a rewarding and full life.

An Interview with James Dick

by James Bastien

James Dick—hailed by Tass and honored at the White House—was a top prize winner in three of the most prestigious international competitions within a period of eight months: the Tchaikowsky International in Moscow; the Edgar M. Leventritt in New York; and the Busoni in Bolzano, Italy. He was acclaimed first prize winner of the International Recording Competition, sponsored by the National Guild of Piano Teachers and awarded a Fulbright Fellowship to the Royal Academy of Music in London by the Institute of International Education (1963-65). Because of his outstanding achievements, Mr. Dick was elected an Honorary Associate of the Royal Academy by its Board of

Directors in 1968, an honor accorded few non-Britishers. James Dick graduated in 1963 with Special Honors in Piano from the University of Texas where he studied with the late Dalies Frantz. During his Fellowship at the Royal Academy Dick studied privately with the eminent British pianist, Clifford Curzon. Mr. Dick was named one of the "Outstanding Young Men of America" in 1970. He represented the United States as a member of the distinguished jury at the Fourth International Van Cliburn Competition. James Dick has performed more than 300 concerts throughout the United States and Canada. He opened the International Festival of Music in St. Moritz, Switzerland in June, 1973, in addition to concerts in England, France and Italy.

James Dick is an exciting young pianist whose views are of special interest because of his long association as a student of the brilliant teacher, Dalies Frantz. Frantz, himself a noted concert pianist, studied with Vladimir Horowitz in Switzerland and Artur Schnabel in Berlin. Thus, he had a rich background to bring to his students and was one of the most outstanding teachers of his time. James Dick discusses highlights of his association with Frantz, along with highlights of his personal career. This interview took place in Shreveport, Louisiana during the fall of 1972.

How long did you study with Dalies Frantz at the University of Texas?

Five years.

Was there anything seriously lacking in your pre-college training or would you have liked to have come to the University with a more complete background?

Rather than single out what I wish I might have had more of, I believe it should be pointed out that I had remarkably fine teaching on a local level. It began well and continued up to the time I left for the University. I had three teachers; the first evidently started me out very well, because I made good progress. My mother practiced with me for the first four years, which was of great benefit to me as a young boy. It demonstrated her interest in what I was doing and made it a pleasure rather than a task. Parental interest and participation is essential for any family contemplating a musical career for their child.

At what age did you start lessons?

One month before I was six. For about the first four years my mother would sit down with me to see that I was reading the notes correctly and would pay particular attention to the rhythm. She would also play duets with me which interested me enormously. I felt that both my parents were completely behind my work and there was nothing whatever they would do to interfere with my practice. My father would often come in from work very exhausted, as he worked both on a farm and as an auto mechanic. Even so, he encouraged my practice and took genuine pleasure in it. The importance of that kind of interest and help is very clear to me now. Perhaps as a child I did not realize this, but subconsciously I possibly realized that their interest was very important and it inspired me.

How much interest in piano did you have at a young age? Did you ever think you wanted to become a concert pianist?

No. I never thought about that. The main thing was study with my teachers, expanding my repertoire and practicing at the piano. That seemed to be the main goal at the time. My parents took me to all the concerts that came to Hutchinson [Kansas], and I was always thrilled by the artists. They made a tremendous impact on me. And, as my experience grew, my interest heightened.

Did your interest ever wane at any time—when you were a teen-ager, or when you had more activities in high school?

I became very interested in school politics and I thought then that it was an important thing that I must do. I was president of the class in my Junior year and student body president my Senior year. But of course it was only a phase. However, much of that experience in working with committees and organizing activities gave me contact with others who had interests quite different from my own and has proven invaluable in my career today.

How much were you able to practice during your high school years?

What I feel about practicing is not how long, but how much one concentrates during the practice period. This is true for concert artists and students alike. Fortunately, I had the ability to concentrate very well and thoroughly, and I was able to practice less in actual hours than one might think would have been required.

What was the actual time you spent at the piano per day?

As I recall, two hours at the most. I was not always able to have that much time, but I did manage to practice at least an hour and a half because I worked early in the morning. I would have one practice session before school and another forty-five minute session or so afterwards.

How was your repertoire when you came to the University?

Well, my repertoire was good in that I had learned many pieces that I feel increased my musicality, particularly my direction in the romantic works. In other ways I had much work to do when I arrived at the University, particularly in concerto repertoire. Astonishingly, I had only one movement of one concerto when I entered the University of Texas! It has been a blessing in that the so-called "old war horses" are unburdened by any preconceived ideas and are fresh for me.

Were you encouraged to enter contests while in high school?

During my pre-college years I did have the opportunity to enter a number of contests and auditions and this did much to strengthen my repertoire. One in particular was the National Guild of Piano Teachers, which I entered from a very early age. It was an event to which I looked forward, and it brought all the work I had done during the year to a polish—there was focus and culmination to the year's work. The Guild, as you know, is not a competition but an audition in which we knew there would always be a competent judge, and thus it was a learning experience. I also entered other contests and auditions such as the Naftzger Young Artists Award in Wichita, the Kansas Federation of Women's Clubs, the Federation of Music Clubs, and so forth. I believe in contests and auditions from a very early age, as performance experience is crucial to both musicality and technique. Performance experience is the only effective way to prepare a student for the realities of a career.

In your University work with Dalies Frantz, can you describe some of his teaching techniques? Did he play for you, or did he insist you do things a certain way?

Dalies had a remarkable ability to teach music with clarity and to keenly focus on each student's interpretative problems. He was careful to let students have freedom, but in order for them not to become chaotic or erratic musicians without any idea of what makes music breathe and communicate, he gave strict guidelines as well. I feel that students must first imitate someone who has had professional and recognized experience. It is an important and necessary part of learning, especially in the beginning. However, a brilliant teacher, as was Dalies Frantz, shows students that imitation eventually ends and that individual styles and qualities must be asserted. It was a great part of Dalies' teaching to show students that they can find something in music that is their own because of their personal discovery and that they can work toward the realization of that discovery, not as self-expression or subjective gratification only, but as the realization of a well thought-out, intelligent conviction.

He would direct students' attention to rhythm and phrasing, what the music itself said, not pedantically trying to interpret only the printed page, but beginning the arduous task of realizing the composer's intent and meaning. From hearing students at master classes, and judging competitions and tapes, I think that rhythm and the structure of a piece are most often overlooked in performances. This, in addition to an ever-increasing musical sensitivity, was one of the basic things upon which Dalies insisted.

Did he discuss pure technique with you, hand motions, etc?

Dalies was concerned with letting students discover their own solutions to technical problems. However, he would always advise if things were out of place, unnecessary, or needed correcting. Technique without musical sensitivity or poetic instinct does not support the concept of an artist. I believe that technique has built some careers, but has never sustained an artist. Although Dalies was concerned mainly with musical considerations, he still had very disciplined ideas and approaches to technique, yet usually from the music itself. He did stress the importance of flexibility over the entire keyboard. One area he certainly stressed was clearness of articulation in passages.

Did Frantz assign etudes or special pieces for work in clarity?

Yes. There is an E-flat Major Czerny study which he would give to most students for developing clarity. He would frequently give students the Schumann *Toccata* or the *C minor Variations* of Beethoven as a basis for discussing technical ideas. I found the Schumann very difficult when I first came to Dalies.

Were there any exercises per se prescribed?

He was very interested in stretch exercises for fingers at the keyboard; he felt this developed clarity and strength. Dalies was also particular about "being over a note" before it was played. We would do many jump chords in which I would get to the chord before it was actually struck. This was done at great distances, from one end of the keyboard to another. Any exercise that can be devised in that way, getting from one place to the next at a lightning speed, is extremely beneficial. It gives command and ease over the whole keyboard, which a performer must develop.

Did Frantz give any special advice on practicing—to practice a phrase or hands alone, or to play with one hand and conduct the other, anything of that sort?

He felt that rather than arbitrary practice measure by measure, it was better to practice to the end of the phrase or to the beginning of a new phrase. His intention was for his students to always practice within a musical sphere rather than a contrived or arbitrary line.

Regarding practice, did he consider mental practice as important as physical practice?

Definitely, in many ways more so. He emphasized that if something was not clearly conceived in mental practice, it would be performed unclearly. Concept precedes the reality of a performance. I believe this is true of all the arts. That is why in practice the standard for a serious musician must never be how long in time, but rather a disciplined concentration.

How did you develop facility in mental practice?

It is similar to developing physical technique at the piano, by working slowly and painstakingly, one phrase at a time.

Can you actually visualize the notes and fingering on the page?

Yes, to begin with you must visualize it almost basically, and then suddenly it becomes a part of you. You must be able to visualize the notes and actually hear the performance within your mind's ear. The final step in mental practice is to sit away from the keyboard and be able to visualize and experience the same performance that you would actually give in concert. It is difficult to achieve, yet very necessary. Mental practice demands that a performer be completely honest and look deeply within his understanding of a work. I believe that endless rote practice sessions are like a narcotic, to escape. Technique can be approached through such practice, but never musical understanding.

Do you know the music so well that you could actually write it out note for note?

If one wished to use his time in that way, it could be done, yes. However, it would be a situation of not seeing the forest for the trees. I would not advise a student to use mental practice for that purpose, because it could then be harmful for a performance. The performer should be interpreting all the elements together in one entity. How well a performer knows the music mentally plays a vital role in a convincing interpretation of the musical content. However, mental practice is beneficial for the total concept, not notes for notes sake. It provides an indelible blueprint of the entire structure and interpretation of a work.

Did Frantz play portions or complete works for you at a lesson?

Sometimes Dalies would play parts for emphasis to demonstrate certain points. When I came to the University of Texas he was no longer giving concerts, although he had already attained a fantastically acclaimed concert career before coming to Austin. His health was at the point where he could not afford to travel and support the rigors of concert life. It was beyond what his health would allow him to do. It was a great loss for concert audiences. As a teacher, Dalies was a magnificent musician. I remember him coming to class about a month before he died and giving a rare performance of several Beethoven movements—one of the most moving experiences I have ever witnessed.

I have heard that Frantz was a fine musician. In his teaching did he sing phrases for you to demonstrate melodic contours?

I cannot remember that he would sing a specific phrase, but there was always a strong insistence on lyricism in our work, and the intelligent student would be caught up by that.

In your college work were you influenced by what other students were doing?

Happily, there were some magnificent talents at the University when I attended—and in the South in general. I was certainly inspired by competition and the general activity of others engaged in music.

Do you think Frantz took a really personal interest in you and in other of his students?

Definitely. Dalies would never be content to hear the lesson and then go home. He would telephone additional suggestions that he had been thinking about, or he would say: "Let's have another session tomorrow, because I want to see something else in this piece." When I first studied in Austin the music building was closed on Sunday morning, and Dalies would come and personally open the building, lock me in, and then come back to let me out when the time was up. I can fully attest to his inspiring personal interest in all his students.

How much encouragement do you think a teacher should give a student who aspires to concert performance, but lacks the ability?

Frankly, I think there is too much emphasis placed on whether or not a student is capable of developing into a concert artist; this judgement is often premature, and more concerns the student's teaching or lack of it rather than his or her ability. Some teachers equate a concert career with stardom; that is instant commercial success, and they feel it is their duty to discourage all but those who blossom first. Several summers ago a young girl came to me after a concert and asked where she could go to become a concert pianist. That told me much about her outlook and to some extent how she had been trained. One should not dwell on the concert potential and besides, teachers have been wrong. There are stories that both the young Paderewski and Schnabel were told that they would never become pianists. I recall a number of lessons that Dalies gave, and no matter how talented or untalented the student was, he gave of himself in the interest of music. He was solely intent on the music and not whether he was guiding that person to a concert career. He was more interested in how he could shape each student.

Rather than focusing on a career as a performer, don't you think that while students are in college an important aspect of their training would be to study how to teach, since most graduates will be teaching in some capacity or another?

Certainly. Pedagogy classes can be of great help in this direction with a gifted teacher. It is difficult to discover just what one has learned from simply attending such a class. I feel that all students should have some practical experience in teaching before they graduate. Of course, a great insight into teaching comes from what one's own teacher is doing; his style will influence the student and give him guidelines.

Regarding Frantz's personality as a teacher, what was it that influenced you? Was he enthusiastic, energetic, outgoing, etc.?

To know him and the qualities of his character and personality could not help but inspire anyone. When I came to the University his health was in such a state that some would have discounted his ability to teach, but he had magnificent qualities to offer. His concern, passion and enthusiasm for the music itself overcame his physical problems.

Was he able to maintain a cheery attitude with his students even though he was in very bad health?

Not only cheery, but he created a great intellectual excitement.

Dalies was a brilliant mind in so many areas. He was a great reader and thinker, and I feel this transferred to his music and to his students. They knew that his interest was not limited to music alone, but extended to literature, philosophy, drama and so many facets which make the total musician and human being and this inspired everyone who came into contact with him.

When you completed your studies with Frantz, was it his idea for you to continue your studies in Europe or was it your idea?

Dalies felt that after five years of study with him I should have another teacher. Even though I could not disagree with him, I felt that it would be difficult to find a greater musician with whom to study. However, his suggestion to study with Clifford Curzon, the great British pianist, was a marvelous choice. When you reach the level of both my teachers, Mr. Frantz and Mr. Curzon, you really cannot compare them, because they are in another strata of existence. There are simply no comparisons of great artists, they are all singular.

I know that you must have gained much from your work with Mr. Curzon in London. Were there special things that you would care to relate?

I learned many things from Mr. Curzon. Firstly, I was inspired onward. He is a wonderful musician. I believe that some of the greatest performances I have ever attended were those given by him while I was studying at the Royal Academy. He gave me many new insights regarding some of the same ideas that Dalies had given me. They were two different artists approaching the same ends in music, but in different ways. Regarding my experiences in London, I would advise all young persons to study abroad at some time in their lives. It is important to live outside of one's own culture in order to fully appreciate it and that of others.

When you first began your career I know you were given impetus by the contests you entered. What did you find to be of most value in the two major competitions you entered, the Tchaikowsky International in the Soviet Union and the Edgar M. Leventritt in New York?

The opportunity to go to the Soviet Union was obviously an exciting one. Unfortunately, I was ill during most of the time, having two Russian doctors each day giving me penicilin shots. In many ways this was a unique experience—certainly no other contestant was in a position like that! Many times I thought that I must give it up and return home because I saw no chance of achieving what I had hoped and worked for. Nevertheless, I saw it through. As I was confined to the bed with fever, I could not practice as much as I would have liked; however, I was greatly benefited by my long association with mental practice. With the limited ability to practice I was indeed fortunate to go on to the finals and then to receive one of the top prizes. It was terribly exciting to be there to begin with and it was especially inspiring to be able to perform the Tchaikowsky First with Maestro Kondrashin. I think that this was the high point of the Moscow experience.

Regarding the Leventritt, I think that it is, along with the Van Cliburn Competition, one of the most important competitions in the world. It offers finalists an opportunity to perform under Leventritt auspices for as long as three years, throughout the United States and Canada. This opportunity provides the necessary experience for a young artist to perform in a variety of situations—with orchestra, at colleges, and on various concert series. This is essential and vital to anyone who aspires to a concert career. Artists must continually grow musically and no management or recording contract can provide that development for them. Only a constant succession of live performances and study and re-study of the repertoire can do that.

True, there is so little room for the young performer to gain experience before he goes on to bigger and better things, and I am sure that the Leventritt was of tremendous value for you.

Where else can a young performer gain this experience? Most competitions do not provide it sufficiently. A young artist cannot possibly know what he must still discover and learn about the technique of performance unless he has an opportunity to develop this skill over an extended period. I have been named to represent the United States as a member of the jury at the Fourth International Van Cliburn Piano Competition in 1973. I had several meetings with the Competition Board to discuss this same matter. The 1973 Competition will follow the example of the Leventritt and stress concerts for top prize winners. Already over forty performances are promised for the first prize winner. I am happy to have had a part in that decision, for I could certainly speak from my own experience with the Leventritt.

Didn't you perform an incredible number of concerts these past seasons under a variety of circumstances?

Yes. Under the Leventritt sponsorship I performed over a hundred concerts during the 1967-68 season alone. In the past five seasons I have given over three hundred concerts. In addition, I give free performances in public schools in cities where I am engaged for concerts, which I feel to be of the greatest importance. I have performed in prisons, for senior citizens, in state schools and institutions as a public service as well. When my schedule permits, I also give concerts for several charities of particular interest to me, notable the Institution of International Education (IIE), which administers all Fulbright Awards for the U.S. Department of State. It was the IIE that sponsored my Fulbright Fellowship to the Royal Academy and made it possible for me to represent the United States at the Tchaikowsky Competition and the Busoni Competition in Italy. I feel very close to the IIE and their magnificent work.

In addition to concertizing, would you like to teach someday?

Well you know it is not someday. I have been teaching since I was fifteen. When my teacher went on vacation I would sometimes have charge of her class, and I taught several students at home during high school. I have often been asked to take students privately and there are offers from several universities each season. Perhaps that might happen someday. I do not feel that I would be able to fairly devote time to both my career and students under an ordinary conservatory or university arrangement. For that reason I established the James Dick Festival-Institute at Round Top, Texas, which is developed and funded primarily by the James Dick Foundation for the Performing Arts. In 1971 I selected ten students for study with me from throughout the United States for three weeks of intensive work during June and July. In 1972 I accepted fourteen, and I anticipate a similar number for study in 1973.

Why is it that you decided to establish a Festival at Round Top? Why not a larger city?

Round Top is a unique and historic area dating back to the 1830's settled by German and Czech families. The major part of the old village has been restored by the Pioneer Arts Foundation which has given my Foundation a ten year lease on their restoration areas in the summer. The students live in restored homes, I teach in a lovely old theater on Round Top's Henkel Square. We perform open-air concerts on Henkel Square or in the Round Top Association Hall, which can easily accommodate a symphony orchestra. The Pioneer Arts Foundation has also restored a very elegant stone mansion with its original ballroom and painted ceilings. It is planned to use the ballroom for solo concerts, lieder and chamber concerts during the Festival.

Do you offer any unusual performances or performance opportunities for those students attending?

Yes, we try to offer as much variety as possible. During the 1971 Festival I gave the American premiere of Soviet composer Arno Babajanian's *Six Pictures for Piano*, and the students performed two concerts. This past June and July I invited the American composer, Benjamin Lees, to be composer-in-residence. I intend to include a guest composer and an American or world premiere each year. The 1973 Festival will feature the premiere of a new *Nocturne* for piano by Ulysses Kay, and the 1972 Festival commissioned a new work for piano and orchestra from Mr. Lees entitled *Five Etudes for Piano and Orchestra*. The full Houston Symphony will perform on Henkel Square during June and July of 1973 and hopefully other great orchestras and guest conductors will join us in the years to come. The Festival will also include a chamber trio in residence from the San Antonio Symphony as well as guest faculty from other areas of the arts. There will also be an International Young Artists Series featuring top prize winners of the Van Cliburn Competition, the Leventritt, and the International Recording Competition of the National Guild of Piano Teachers. The Festival is built around the students, who are selected on their advancement and major musical potential. They need experience, as we have discussed, and that is what the Festival is really about. I have combined intensive study with myself and others, with performance opportunities. It is a program designed to assist young artists in accomplishing the difficult transition from student life to professional careers.

Then the students working with you will be performing with the Houston Symphony next summer?

Yes, selected students will perform with orchestra, others will perform with the chamber trio and be featured in solo recitals. In that way I will have students performing with recognized professionals, something of enormous value.

When you perform in the United States and abroad and during your annual Festival, you give master classes and listen to many student performances every season. Are there any special deficiencies that you notice?

I would not say deficiencies as such, but rather something that cannot be discovered and realized by students all at once—that is solid rhythmic projection in music. Rhythmic pulsation is a dominant factor in every performance; one notices if it is captivating, and one notices if it is less than so. I also believe that the ability to express musical ideas imaginatively, without being mechanical, is absolutely necessary. Dalies stressed this to me as a student and I stress it today. Mr. Curzon once told me that every performer must have the courage to take chances—even in a performance.

To conclude, do you think that American audiences are gaining or losing as far as participation at concerts?

Definitely gaining. I see this happening on University campuses and in organized concerts in general. As long as people are willing to concentrate on the optimistic aspects of concert going, and not dwell on the pessimistic, enthusiasm for concerts will gain steadily. Music will continue to communicate and speak, whether it be that of four hundred years ago or serious contemporary compositions. Music and its influence will become more and more a part of everyone's life. This will be accomplished, in part, through the selfless contributions of concert performers, young artists and students giving of themselves where the Arts are not always available or recognized. It is through the Arts that civilizations are remembered. It is within the Arts that we must strive to be responsible and significant to future generations.

Appendices

Appendix A
Brief Theory Outline

SCALES

A scale is an arbitrary arrangement of tones in a series of ascending or descending pitches. The various scales may be identified by the number of pitches used and their interval sequences. A scale may have the same tones for both ascending and descending or may have one series of tones ascending and another descending. Scales are constructed with half steps (½ step: the smallest interval in Western music), whole steps (two ½ steps), or with larger intervals (1½ steps). In the scales below ⌣ = ½ step, ∧ = 1½ steps.

COMMONLY USED SCALES

Major (Ionian mode)

Natural minor (Aeolian mode) (Aeolian mode = white keys on the piano starting on A)

Harmonic minor

Melodic minor (Ascending) (Descending)

Dorian mode (Dorian mode = white keys on the piano starting on D)

Phrygian mode (Phrygian mode= white keys on the piano starting on E)

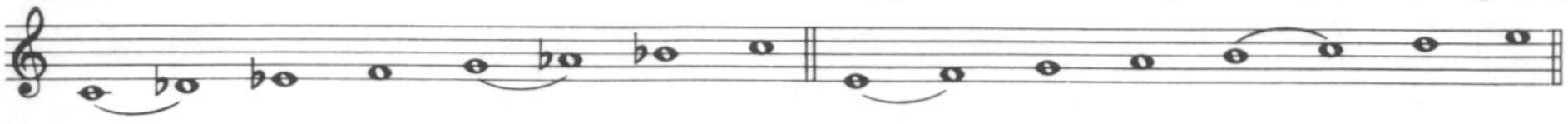

Lydian mode (Lydian mode = white keys on the piano starting on F)

Mixolydian mode (Mixolydian mode=white keys on the piano starting on G)

Pentatonic Whole tone

Chromatic (Ascending) (Descending)

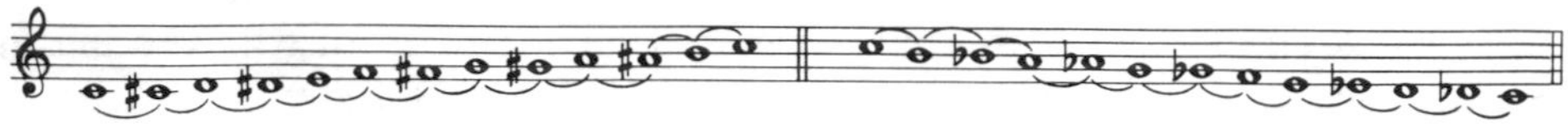

SCALE DEGREE NAMES

It is customary to refer to the scale degrees by Roman numerals:

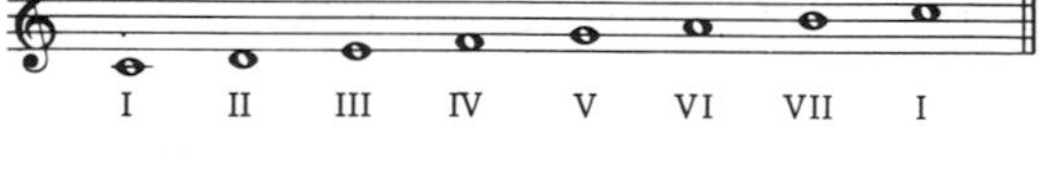

Scale degrees are also referred to by the following names:

I. Tonic (the key-note)
II. Supertonic (one step above the tonic)
III. Mediant (halfway from tonic to dominant)
IV. Subdominant (as far below the tonic as the dominant is above it)
V. Dominant (a major or "dominant" element in the key)
VI. Submediant (halfway down from tonic to subdominant)
VII. Leading tone (has a melodic tendency towards the tonic)

INTERVALS

An interval is the pitch relation or distance between two tones. The various types of intervals are: Major, minor, perfect, augmented, diminished.

MAJOR AND PERFECT INTERVALS

CHROMATICALLY ALTERED INTERVALS

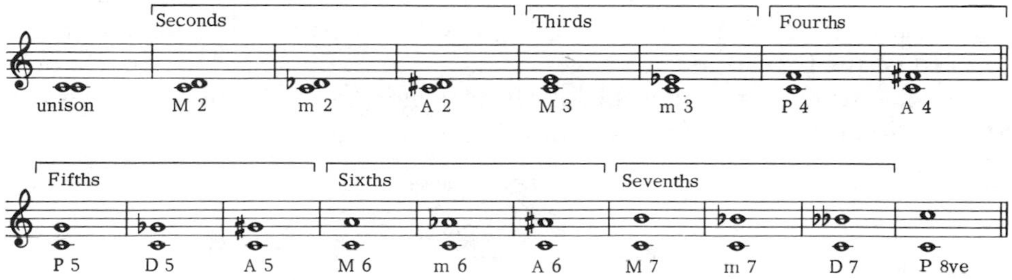

TYPES OF TRIADS

A triad (three-note chord) is formed by superposition of thirds. There are four kinds of triads, classified according to the nature of the intervals formed between the root and the other two tones.

(a) Major triad (Maj.) composed of a major third and perfect fifth
(b) minor triad (min.) composed of a minor third and perfect fifth
(c) augmented triad (aug.) composed of a major third and augmented fifth
(d) diminished triad (dim.) composed of a minor third and diminished fifth

TYPES OF TRIADS WITHIN THE MAJOR SCALE

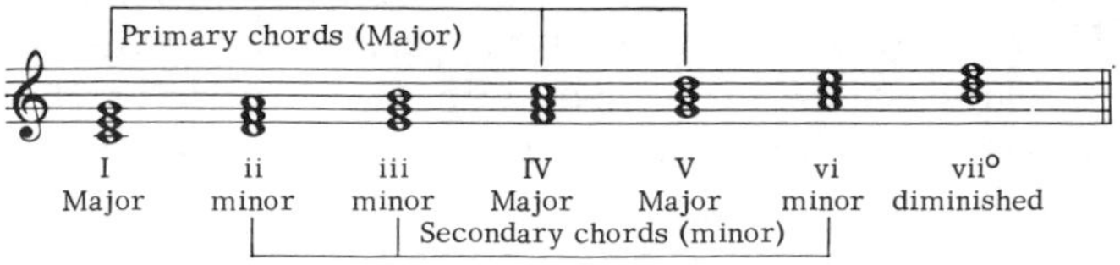

TYPES OF TRIADS WITHIN THE HARMONIC MINOR SCALE

FIRST INVERSION TRIADS

An inversion is a rearrangement of the same tones used in the basic chord (root position chord). Triads in first inversion are called chords of the sixth because of the interval of a sixth between the top and bottom notes. The third of the triad is in the bass.

The figured bass (method of musical shorthand) Arabic numerals for first inversion chords are $^{6}_{3}$, or simply 6, the third being assumed.

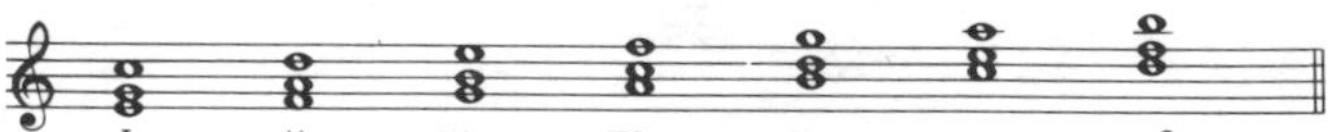

SECOND INVERSION TRIADS

Triads in second inversion are termed six-four chords because of the interval of a sixth between the top and bottom notes and the fourth between the middle and bottom notes. The fifth of the triad is in the bass.

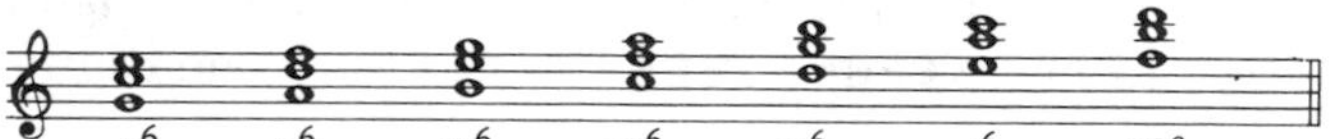

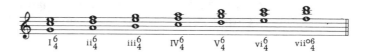

FOUR-PART HARMONY

Four-part harmony is the basis for most music of the eighteenth and nineteenth centuries. This means a vertical construction of four chord tones (one being doubled in triads), and a horizontal movement of four different melodic voices. Voices refers to the standard vocal quartet: soprano, alto, tenor, bass. However the term 'voices' may also refer to instrumental *parts.* The study of harmony is concerned with the principles that govern the vertical and horizontal movement of these four voices (or parts).

CHORDAL DISTRIBUTION IN FOUR-PART HARMONY

Essentially the spacing of tones within chords is either in *close* or *open* structure. When the three upper voices are as close together as possible (soprano and tenor not exceeding an octave apart), the spacing is called close position. Any spacing that exceeds a distance greater than an octave between soprano and tenor is called open position.

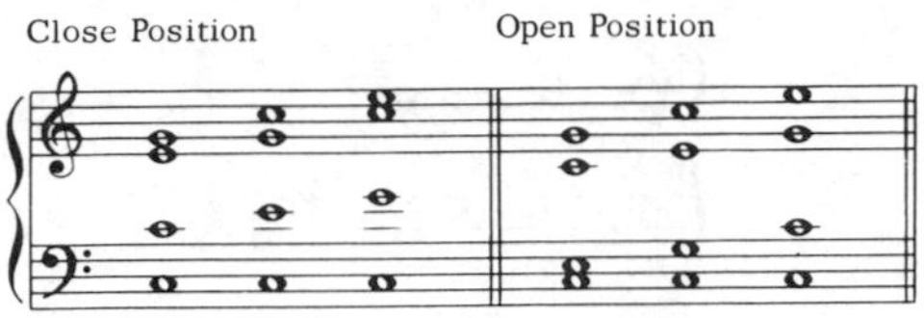

DOUBLINGS

It is obvious that one of the three tones in a triad must be doubled to write four-part harmony. The extra tone is usually obtained by doubling the root in root position chords (as in the examples above). Other rules apply for doublings of first and second inversion chords. (Consult a formal theory text.)

CADENCES

Music is quite analogous to literature because of its essentially linear, horizontal (left to right) motion. The horizontal, melodic movement of music is punctuated by phrases, whereas the vertical (chordal) structure culminates in *cadences* (various points of rest). Below are examples of frequently used cadences.

(a) The *authentic cadence* is comparable to a full stop or a period in punctuation, and consists of a V-I harmonic progression.

(b) The *half cadence* acts like a comma, indicating a partial stop in an unfinished statement. It ends on a V chord, however approached.

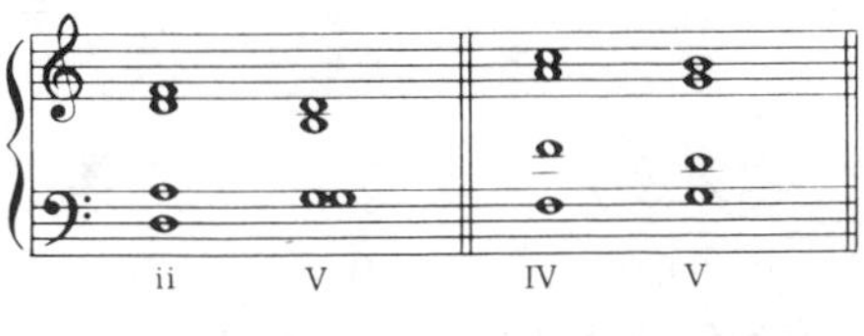

(c) The *plagal cadence* is the next most frequently used progression for a full stop or final repose after the authentic cadence. It is also the "amen" sound used in hymns and consists of a IV-I progression.

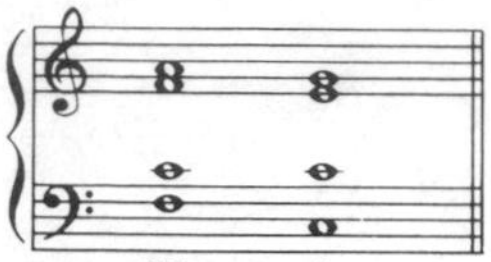

(d) The *deceptive cadence* is a frequent substitute for the authentic cadence. As an alternative to V-I, V-vi (deceptive cadence) is often used.

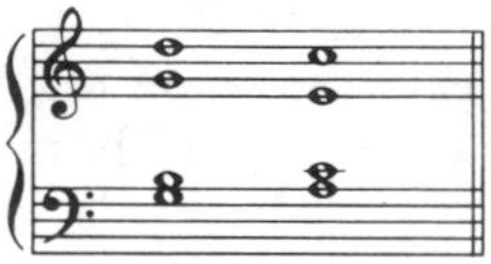

NON-HARMONIC TONES (Non-Chord Tones)

The texture of music is comprised of melodic tones and rhythms which are interwoven. Some of these tones appear as factors of chords and some do not. *Non-harmonic tones* are tones that become foreign to the prevailing harmony during the course of melodic movement. Below are examples of frequently used non-harmonic tones.

(a) A *passing tone* is a dissonant tone (non-chordal tone) interpolated generally between two consonant tones. It usually occurs on a rhythmically weak beat and is approached and left by step without change of direction. The passing tone (or tones) may be either diatonic or chromatic.

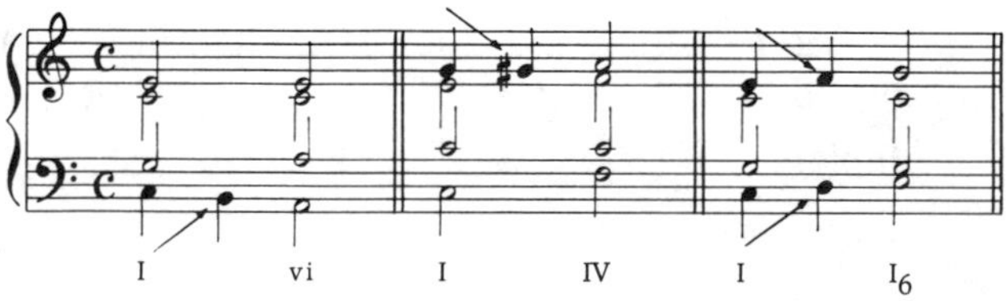

(b) An *auxiliary tone* (also called neighboring tone or embellishment) is a dissonant tone of weak rhythmic value which serves to ornament a stationary tone (either from above or below). It is approached and left by step with change of direction.

(c) An *anticipation,* as its name implies, is an advance sounding of the subsequent tone. It acts as an up-beat to the tone anticipated. It is a dissonant, rhythmically weak tone, usually approached by step, and becomes consonant without moving as the harmony resolves to it.

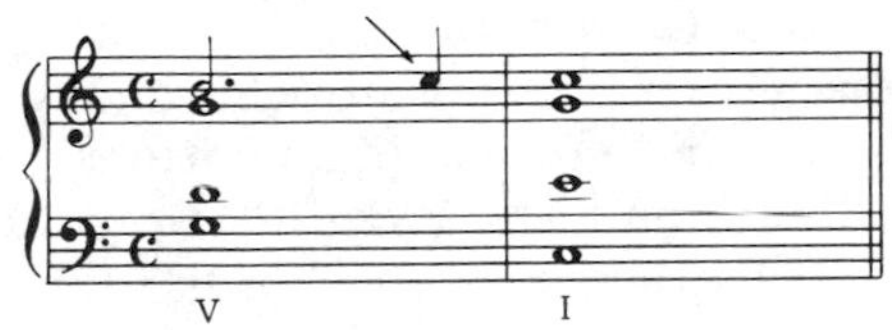

(d) An *escape tone* (or échappée) is a dissonant, rhythmically weak tone, approached by step and left by leap.

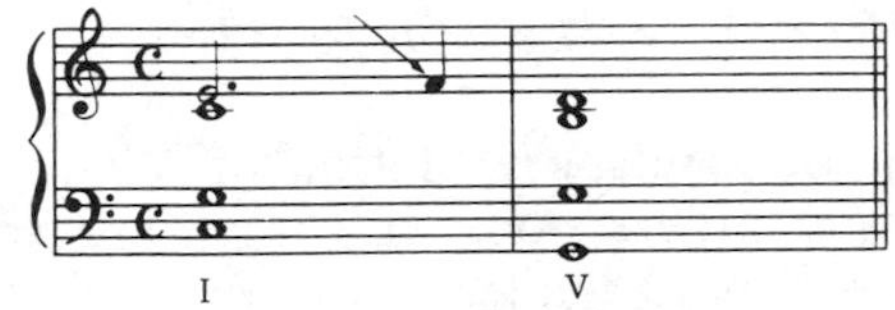

(e) An *appoggiatura* (from the Italian verb *appoggiare*, to lean) is a dissonant tone on a rhythmically strong beat which is usually approached by leap and left by step.

(f) A *suspension* (or retardation) is the prolongation of a chordal tone of which it is a member, into a chord of which it is not a member. The three elements of the suspension are frequently referred to as the *preparation* (consonant tone), *suspension* (dissonant tone on a rhythmically strong beat), and *resolution* (usually by step downward).

SEVENTH CHORDS

A seventh chord (four-note chord) is formed by superposing an interval of a third upon a triad. A seventh chord may be constructed on any scale degree, with or without chromatic alterations. The seventh chord built on the fifth of the scale (dominant seventh) is the most frequently used of the seventh chords. All other seventh chords (non-dominant) are termed *secondary sevenths.*

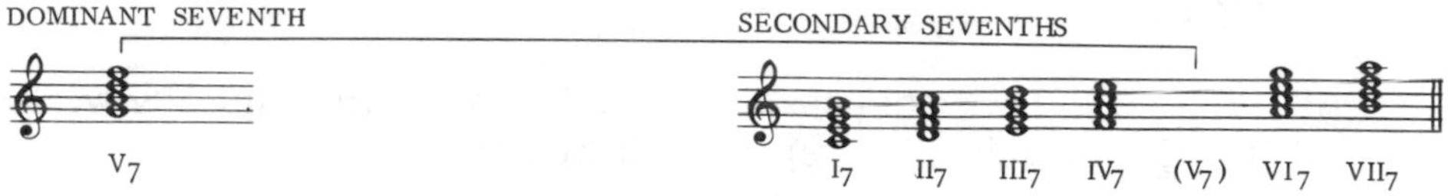

V7-1 PROGRESSION IN FOUR PARTS

The natural (or regular) resolution of V7 to I is one of the most fundamental harmonic progressions in music. The tones of the dominant seventh chord have a natural tendency to resolve to the tonic. The root of the chord resolves up a fourth (or down a fifth); the third of the chord (leading tone) usually ascends to the tonic; the fifth of the chord (having no tendency) descends to the tonic; the seventh resolves downward one scale degree to the third of the tonic chord. This results in an incomplete tonic chord in resolution (three roots and one third).

The *first inversion* of the dominant seventh chord (with the third in the bass) is figured $\text{V}\begin{smallmatrix}6\\5\\3\end{smallmatrix}$; the 3 is often omitted, and the chord is most frequently referred to as $\text{V}\begin{smallmatrix}6\\5\end{smallmatrix}$.

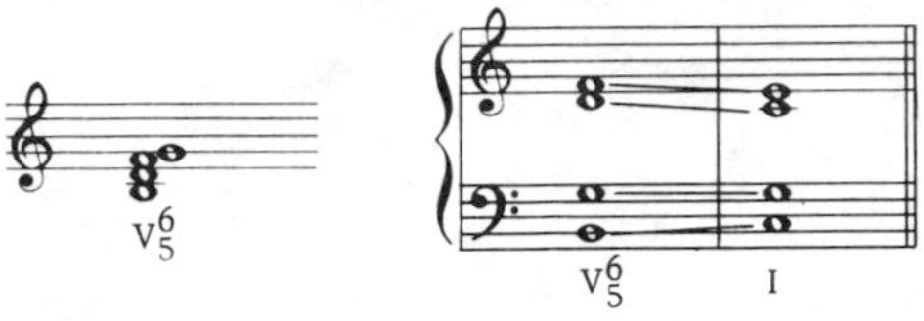

The *second inversion* of the dominant seventh chord (with the fifth in the bass) is figured $\text{V}\begin{smallmatrix}6\\4\\3\end{smallmatrix}$; the 6 is often omitted, and the chord is most frequently referred to as $\text{V}\begin{smallmatrix}4\\3\end{smallmatrix}$.

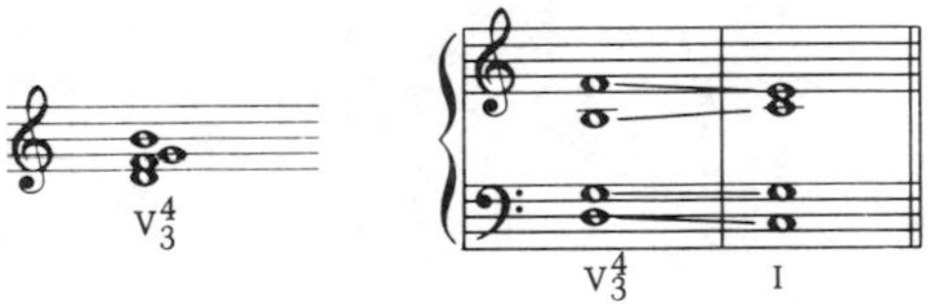

The *third inversion* of the dominant seventh chord (with the seventh in the bass) is figured $\text{V}\begin{smallmatrix}6\\4\\2\end{smallmatrix}$; the 6 is often omitted, and the chord is most frequently referred to as $\text{V}\begin{smallmatrix}4\\2\end{smallmatrix}$, or V_2.

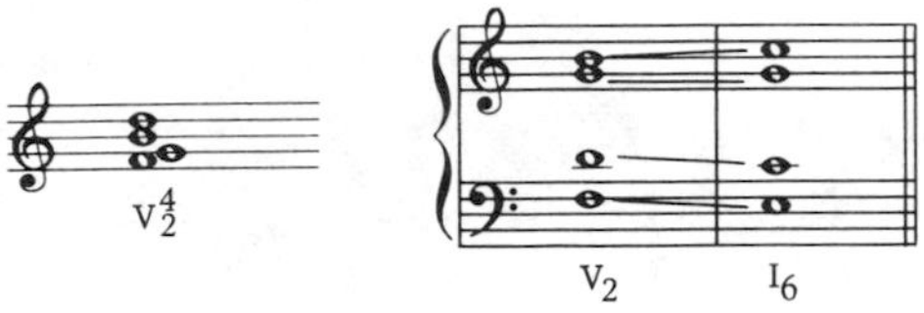

OTHER ASPECTS OF THEORY

Continued theoretical studies would include: irregular resolutions of the V7 chord (and other seventh chords); modulation; diminished seventh chords; ninth, eleventh, thirteenth chords; neapolitan sixth chords; augmented sixth chords; other chromatically altered chords. Consult any of the suggested theory books listed in Appendix B for a listing of theory books.

Appendix B

General Music Reference Books

PIANO

Piano Pedagogy

Ahrens, Cora, and G. D. Atkinson. *For All Piano Teachers.* Oakville, Ontario, Canada: Frederick Harris Music Co., Ltd., 1955.

Bastien, James. *How to Teach Piano Successfully,* 2nd Edition, Revised. Park Ridge, Illinois: General Words and Music Co., 1977. Paper.

Benner, Lora. *Handbook for Piano Teaching.* Schenectady, New York: Benner Publishers, 1975. Paper.

Bennett, Beulah Varner. *Piano Classes for Everyone.* New York: Philosophical Library, Inc., 1969.

Bianchi, Louise Wadley. *The Young Pianist's Training* (thesis published by the author). Dallas: Southern Methodist University, 1963.

Bolton, Hetty. *How to Practice: A Handbook for Pianoforte Students.* London: Elkin & Co., Ltd., 1939.

____________. *On Teaching the Piano.* London: Novello and Company Limited, 1954.

Booth, Victor. *We Piano Teachers,* revised by Adele Franklin. London: Hutchinson University Library, 1971.

Broughton, Julia. *Success in Piano Teaching.* New York: Vantage Press, 1956.

Bruxner, Mervyn. *Mastering the Piano: A Guide for the Amateur.* New York: St. Martin's Press, Inc., 1972.

D'Abreu, Gerald. *Playing the Piano with Confidence: An Analysis of Technique, Interpretation, Memory and Performance.* New York: St. Martin's Press, Inc., 1965.

Deutsch, Leonard. *Piano: Guided Sight-Reading,* 2nd Edition. Chicago: Nelson-Hall Co., 1959.

Diller, Angela. *The Splendor of Music.* New York: G. Schirmer, Inc., 1957.

Edwards, Ruth. *The Compleat Music Teacher.* Los Altos, Calif.: Geron-X, Inc., 1970.

Enoch, Yvonne. *Group Piano-Teaching.* London: Oxford University Press, 1974.

Everhart, Powell. *The Pianist's Art: A Comprehensive Manual on Piano-Playing for the Student and Teacher.* Atlanta: Author, 1958. (962 Myrtle Street, N.E. Atlanta, Ga. 30309).

Gát, József. *The Technique of Piano Playing,* translated by István Kleszky. (Budapest: Covina Publishing Co.), English edition, London: Collet's Holdings, Ltd., 1965. (order from San Francisco: Tri-Ocean, Inc.).

Gibbs, Polly, and Martha Stacy. *Effective Piano Teaching.* Author (Martha Stacy), Oberlin, Ohio: Oberlin College, 1974. Paper.

Glasford, Irene S. *Rhythm, Reason and Response*. Jericho, New York: Exposition Press, Inc., 1970.

Handbook for Piano Teachers. Evanston, Illinois: Summy-Birchard Co., 1958.

Harrison, Sidney. *The Young Person's Guide to Playing the Piano.* London: Faber & Faber, Ltd., 1973.

Hinson, Maurice. *Keyboard Bibliography*, Booklet. Cincinnati: Music Teachers National Association, 1968.

__________. *The Piano Teacher's Source Book*. Melville, New York: Belwin-Mills, 1974. *First Supplement,* 1976.

Hodges, Sister Mabelle L. *A Catalogue of Representative Teaching Materials for Piano Since 1900.* Chicago: De Paul University Press, 1970.

Hope, Eric. *A Handbook of Piano Playing*. Chester Springs, Pa.: Dufour Editions, Inc., 1972.

Kochevitsky, George A. *The Art of Piano Playing: A Scientific Approach.* Evanston, Illinois: Summy-Birchard Co., 1967.

Last, Joan. *Interpretation for the Piano Student.* London: Oxford University Press, 1960.

__________. *The Young Pianist: A New Approach for Teachers and Students,* 2nd Edition. London: Oxford University Press, 1972.

Maier, Guy. *The Piano Teachers Companion.* Melville, New York: Belwin-Mills, 1963.

Mehr, Norman. *Group Piano Teaching.* Evanston, Illinois: Summy-Birchard Co., 1965.

Merrick, Frank. *Practising the Piano.* New York: Dover Publications, Inc., 1965. Paper.

Miller, Marguerite, and Frances Wallingford. *Piano Teaching Materials,* 3rd Edition. Wichita, Kansas: Wichita State University, 1975. Paper.

Musafia, Julien. *The Art of Fingering in Piano Playing.* New York: Music Corporation of America, 1972. Paper.

Neuhaus, Heinrich. *The Art of Piano Playing,* translated by K. A. Leibovitch. New York: Praeger Publishers, 1973.

Newman, William S. *The Pianist's Problems,* 3rd Edition. New York: Harper & Row, Publishers, Inc., 1974.

Pollei, Paul C. *Pedagogical Tips for Piano Teaching.* Provo, Utah: Brigham Young University Press, 1969. Paper.

Riefling, Reimar. *Piano Pedalling,* translated by Kathleen Dale. London: Oxford University Press, 1962.

Robinson, Helene, and Richard L. Jarvis, eds. *Teaching Piano in Classroom and Studio.* Vienna, Virginia: Music Educators National Conference, 1967.

Savler, Roberta, ed. *Selections from the Piano Teacher, 1958-1963.* Evanston, Illinois: Summy-Birchard Co., 1964.

Seroff, Victor. *Common Sense in Piano Study.* New York: Funk & Wagnalls, 1970.

Slenczynska, Ruth. *Music at Your Fingertips,* 2nd Edition, Revised and Enlarged, with Corrections. New York: Da Capo Press, 1974. Paper.

Swenson, Lucile Burnhope. *Discovering the Piano: The Multiple Key Approach.* Bryn Mawr, Pa.: Theodore Presser Company, 1969, 1972.

Terwilliger, Gordon B. *Piano Teacher's Professional Handbook.* Englewood Cliffs, N.J.: Prentice-Hall, Inc., 1965.

Whiteside, Abbey. *Indispensables of Piano Playing.* New York: Charles Scribner's Sons, 1955. 2nd Edition, 1961.

Wolff, Konrad. *The Teaching of Artur Schnabel: A Guide to Interpretation.* New York: Praeger Publishers, 1971.

Piano Literature, History and Style

Abraham, Gerald. *Chopin's Musical Style.* New York: Oxford University Press, 1960. PB.

Apel, Willi. *Masters of the Keyboard.* Cambridge, Mass.: Harvard University Press, 1947.

____________. *The History of Keyboard Music to 1700,* translated and revised by Hans Tischler. Bloomington, Ind.: Indiana University Press, 1972.

Bach, C.P.E. *Essay on the True Art of Playing Keyboard Instruments.* New York: W. W. Norton & Company, Inc., 1948.

Badura-Skoda, Eva and Paul. *Interpreting Mozart on the Keyboard.* New York: St. Martin's Press, Inc., 1962.

Blom, Eric. *Beethoven's Pianoforte Sonatas Discussed.* London: J. M. Dent, 1938. Reprint, New York: Da Capo Press, 1968.

Bodky, Erwin. *The Interpretation of Bach's Keyboard Works.* Cambridge, Mass.: Harvard University Press, 1960.

Butler, Stanley. *Guide to the Best in Contemporary Piano Music: An Annotated List of Graded Solo Piano Music Published Since 1950,* 2 Vols. Metuchen, N.J.: The Scarecrow Press, Inc., 1973.

Caldwell, John. *English Keyboard Music Before the Nineteenth Century.* New York: Praeger Publishers, 1973.

Chang, Frederic Ming, and Albert Faurot. *Team Piano Repertoire.* Metuchen, New Jersey: Scarecrow Press, Inc., 1976.

Dolmetsch, Arnold. *Interpreting Music of the 17th and 18th Centuries.* London: Novello & Co., Ltd., 1949.

Drake, Kenneth. *The Sonatas of Beethoven.* Cincinnati: Music Teachers National Association, 1972.

Emery, Walter. *Bach's Ornaments.* London: Novello & Co., Ltd., 1953.

Evans, Edwin. *Handbook to the Pianoforte Works of Johannes Brahms.* New York: Charles Scribner's Sons, 1936. Reprint, New York: Bert Franklin, 1970.

Faurot, Albert. *Concert Piano Repertoire: a Manual of Solo Literature for Artists and Performers.* Metuchen, New Jersey: Scarecrow Press, Inc., 1974.

Forman, Denis. *Mozart's Concerto Form: the First Movements of the Piano Concertos.* New York: Praeger Publishers, 1972.

Friskin, James, and Irwin Freundlich. *Music for the Piano: A Handbook of Concert and Teaching Material from 1580 to 1952.* New York: Holt, Rinehart and Winston, Inc., 1954. Paperback reprint, New York: Dover Publications, Inc., 1973.

Ganz, Rudolph. *Rudolph Ganz Evaluates Modern Piano Music.* Evanston, Illinois: The Instrumentalist Co., 1968. Paper.

Gillespie, John. *Five Centuries of Keyboard Music.* Belmont, Calif.: Wadsworth Publishing Co., Inc., 1965. Unabridged Republication, New York: Dover Publications, Inc., 1972. Paper.

Hinson, Maurice. *Guide to the Pianist's Repertoire, Vol. 1: Solo Piano.* Bloomington, Indiana: Indiana University Press, 1973.

____________. *Guide to the Pianist's Repertoire, Vol. 2: The Piano in Chamber Ensemble.* Bloomington; Indiana: Indiana University Press, 1977.

Hopkins, Antony. *Talking About (Piano) Sonatas.* New York: International Publications Service, 1972.

Hutcheson, Ernest, and Rudolph Ganz. *The Literature of the Piano,* Revised Edition. New York: Alfred A. Knopf, Inc., 1964.

Iliffe, Frederick. *Analysis of Bach's Forty-Eight Preludes and Fugues,* 2 Vols. London: Novello & Co., Ltd., 1897. Paper.

Kern, Alice, and Helen Titus. *The Teacher's Guidebook to Piano Literature.* Ann Arbor, Michigan: J. W. Edwards Publisher, Inc., 1964.

Kirby, Frank E. *A Short History of Keyboard Music.* New York: The Free Press, 1966.

Kirkpatrick, Ralph. *Domenico Scarlatti.* Princeton, N.J.: Princeton University Press, 1955. Paperback reprint, New York: Apollo Editions, 1968.

Lockwood, Albert. *Notes on the Literature of the Piano.* Ann Arbor: University of Michigan Press, 1949. Reprint, New York: Da Capo Press, 1968.

Lubin, Ernest. *The Piano Duet.* New York: Grossman Publishers, 1970.

Mathews, Denis, ed. *Keyboard Music.* Baltimore: Penguin Books, 1972. PB.

Moldenhauer, Hans. *Duo-Pianism* (out of print, available at libraries). Chicago: Chicago Musical College Press, 1950.

Newman, William S. *A Selected List of Music Recommended for Piano Students: Prefaced and Compiled According to Types, Eras, and Teaching Levels.* Chapel Hill: The University of North Carolina Press, Extension Division, 1953. Brought up to date, 1967.

____________. *Performance Practices in Beethoven's Piano Sonatas.* New York: W. W. Norton & Company, Inc., 1971.

Philipp, Lillie H. *Piano Study: Application and Technique.* New York: MCA Music, 1969. Paper.

Reif, Sister Frances Marie. *A Compendium of Piano Concertos for the Preparatory Student* (thesis). Washington, D.C.: Catholic University, 1973.

Rezits, Joseph, and Gerald Deatsman. *The Pianist's Resource Guide: Piano Music in Print and Literature on the Pianistic Art.* Park Ridge, Illinois: Pallma Music Co./Neil A. Kjos Jr., Publishers, 1974. [2nd edition, Jan. 1978]

Richner, Thomas. *Orientation for Interpreting Mozart's Piano Sonatas.* New York: Bureau of Publications, Teachers College, Columbia University, 1953. Reprint, Rexburg, Idaho: Ricks College Press, 1972.

Searle, Humphrey. *The Music of Liszt.* London: Williams & Norgate, 1954. 2nd Revised Edition, New York: Dover Publications, Inc., 1966.

Strain, Tracey. *Bibliography of Piano Music for the Left Hand Alone* (thesis) Kent, Ohio: Kent State University, 1972.

Suchoff, Benjamin. *Guide to Bartók's Mikrokosmos,* Revised Edition. London: Boosey & Hawkes, 1971.

Thompson, Ellen. *Teaching and Understanding Contemporary Piano Music.* San Diego, Calif.: Kjos West, 1976. Paper.

Walker, Alan, ed. *Franz Liszt: The Man and His Music.* New York: Taplinger Publishing Co., 1970.

____________, ed. *Frédéric Chopin: Profiles of the Man and Musician.* New York: Taplinger Publishing Co., 1967.

Weitzmann, Carl F. *A History of Pianoforte-Playing and Pianoforte-Literature.* New York: G. Schirmer, Inc., 1893. Reprint, New York: Da Capo Press, 1969.

Piano Care

Schmeckel, Carl D. *The Piano Owners Guide.* Sheboygan, Wis.: Apex Piano Publishing, 1971. Paper.

Piano Construction and Design

Bie, Oscar. *A History of the Piano and Piano Players.* New York: Da Capo Press, 1966.

Closson, Ernest. *History of the Piano.* London: Paul Elek, 1947. New Edition, Paul Elek, 1973, revised by Robin Golding.

Dolge, Alfred. *Pianos and Their Makers.* Covina, Calif.: Covina Publishing Co., 1911. Paperback reprint, New York: Dover Publications, Inc., 1972.

Pierce, W. Robert. *Pierce Piano Atlas.* Long Beach, Calif.: Author, 1965. (1880 Termino Avenue, Long Beach, Calif. 90815).

Summer, William Leslie. *The Pianoforte,* Revised Edition. New York: St. Martin's Press, Inc., 1971.

Wier, Albert. *The Piano, Its History, Makers, Players and Music.* London: Longmans, Green, 1940.

Piano Tuning

Stevens, Floyd A. *Complete Course in Professional Piano Tuning, Repair & Rebuilding.* Chicago: Nelson-Hall Co., 1972.

Travis, John W. *Let's Tune Up.* Takoma Park, Md.: Author, 1968. (8012 Carrol Avenue, Takoma Park, Md. 20012).

Pianists

Chasins, Abram. *Speaking of Pianists,* 2nd Edition. New York: Alfred A. Knopf, Inc., 1961.

Gerig, Reginald R. *Famous Pianists and Their Technique.* Washington, D.C.. Robert B. Luce, 1974.

Kaiser, Joachim. *Great Pianists of Our Time,* translated by David Wooldridge and George Unwin. New York: Herder and Herder, 1971.

Loesser, Arthur. *Men, Women, and Pianos.* New York: Simon & Schuster, Inc., 1954.

Schoenberg, Harold C. *Great Pianists From Mozart to the Present.* New York: Simon & Schuster, Inc., 1963.

Piano Periodicals

Clavier (1418 Lake Street, Evanston, Illinois 60204).

The Piano Quarterly. (Box 815, Wilmington, Vermont 05363).

The Robert Dumm Piano Review, bi-yearly. (144 Fleetwood Terrace, Silver Spring, Md. 20910).

DICTIONARIES AND ENCYCLOPEDIAS

Ammer, Christine. *Musician's Handbook of Foreign Terms.* New York: G. Schirmer, Inc., 1971.

Apel, Willi, and Ralph Daniel. *The Harvard Brief Dictionary of Music.* PB. Cambridge, Mass.: Harvard University Press, 1960.

Barlow, Harold, and Sam Morgenstern. *A Dictionary of Musical Themes.* New York: Crown Publishers, 1948.

Clark, Mary Elizabeth. *New Pocket Music Dictionary.* Carlstadt, N.J.: Edward Schuberth & Co., Inc., 1971.

Grove, Sir George, ed. *Grove's Dictionary of Music and Musicians,* 5th Edition, edited by Eric Blom. New York: St. Martin's Press, 1954. 9 Vols.

Hindley, Geoffrey, ed. *The Larousse Encyclopedia of Music.* New York: The World Publishing Co., 1971.

Lee, William. *Music Theory Dictionary.* Miami: Charles Hansen, 1965.

Lloyd, Norman. *The Golden Encyclopedia of Music.* New York: Golden Press, 1968.

Sacher, Jack. *Music A to Z.* New York: Grosset and Dunlap, 1963.

Slominsky, Nicolas, ed. *Baker's Biographical Dictionary of Musicians,* 5th Edition, with 1971 supplement. New York: G. Schirmer, Inc., 1971.

Thompson, Kenneth. *St. Martin's Dictionary of Twentieth-Century Composers 1911-1971.* New York: St. Martin's Press, Inc., 1973.

Thompson, Oscar, ed. *The International Cyclopedia of Music and Musicians,* 9th Edition, edited by Robert Sabin. New York: Dodd, Mead, 1964.

Westrup, J. A., and F. L. Harrison. *The New College Encyclopedia of Music.* New York: W. W. Norton & Co., Inc., 1960.

Westrup, J. A., *et al,* eds. *The New Oxford History of Music.* London: Oxford University Press (1957-). 11 Vols. planned, 4 completed.

INTRODUCTORY BOOKS ON MUSIC

Bernstein, Leonard. *The Joy of Music.* New York: Simon & Schuster, Inc., 1959.

Bockmon, Alan G., and William J. Starr. *Scored for Listening,* 2nd Edition. New York: Harcourt, Brace, Jovanovich, Inc., 1972. Paper.

Brofsky, Howard, and Jeanne Shapiro Bamberger. *The Art of Listening: Developing Musical Perception.* New York: Harper & Row Publishers, Inc., 1969.

Copland, Aaron. *What to Listen for in Music,* Revised Edition. New York: McGraw-Hill Book Co., Inc., 1957.

Crocker, Richard L., and Ann P. Basart. *Listening to Music.* New York: McGraw-Hill Book Co., Inc., 1971.

Gillespie, John. *The Musical Experience,* 2nd Edition. Belmont, Calif.: Wadsworth Publishing Company, Inc., 1973.

Hoffer, Charles R. *The Understanding of Music.* Belmont, Calif.: Wadsworth Publishing Company, Inc., 1967.

Machlis, Joseph. *The Enjoyment of Music,* 3rd Edition. New York: W. W. Norton & Co., Inc., 1970.

Nadeau, Roland, and William Tesson. *Listen.* Boston: Allyn and Bacon, Inc., 1971.

Newman, William. *Understanding Music,* 2nd Edition, Revised and Enlarged. New York: Harper & Row, Publishers, Inc., 1961.

Politoske, Daniel T. *Music.* Englewood Cliffs, N.J.: Prentice-Hall, Inc., 1974.

Wink, Richard, and Lois G. Williams. *Invitation to Listening: An Introduction to Music.* Boston: Houghton Mifflin Co., 1972.Paper.

HISTORIES

General

Borroff, Edith. *Music in Europe and the United States; A History.* Englewood Cliffs, N.J.: Prentice-Hall, Inc., 1971.

Collaer, Paul, and Albert Vander Linden. *Historical Atlas of Music,* translated by Allan Miller. Cleveland: World Publishing Co., 1968.

Gal, Hans, ed. *The Musician's World, Great Composers in Their Letters.* New York: Arco, 1966.

Grout, Donald J. *A History of Western Music.* Revised Edition. New York: W. W. Norton & Co., Inc., 1973.

Lang, Paul H. *Music in Western Civilization.* New York: W. W. Norton & Co., Inc., 1941.

Pincherle, Marc. *An Illustrated History of Music.* London: Macmillan Company, Ltd., 1962.

Siegmeister, Elie. *The New Music Lover's Handbook.* New York: Harvey House, Inc., 1973.

Ulrich, Homer, and Paul Pisk. *A History of Music and Musical Style.* New York: Harcourt, Brace and World, 1963.

Watkin, Harold. *History of Music, An Outline*. New York: Monarch, 1962.

Worner, Karl H. *History of Music: A Book for Study and Reference.* New York: The Free Press, 1973.

Young, Percy M. *A Concise History of Music.* New York: David White, Inc., 1974.

Medieval Period

Reese, Gustave. *Music in the Middle Ages.* New York: W. W. Norton & Co., Inc., 1940.

Seay, Albert. *Music in the Medieval World.* Englewood Cliffs, N.J.: Prentice-Hall, Inc., 1965. Paper.

Baroque Period

Borroff, Edith. *The Music of the Baroque.* Dubuque, Iowa: Wm. C. Brown Co., 1970. Paper.

Bukofzer, Manfred. *Music in the Baroque Era.* New York: W. W. Norton & Co., Inc., 1947.

Newman, William S. *The Sonata in the Baroque Era,* Revised Edition. Chapel Hill: University of North Carolina Press, 1966. Paperback, 3rd Edition, New York: W. W. Norton & Co., Inc., 1972.

Palisca, Claude V. *Baroque Music.* Englewood Cliffs, N.J.: Prentice-Hall, Inc., 1968. Paper.

Classical Period

Landon, Howard Chandler Robbins. *Essays on the Viennese Classical Style: Gluck, Haydn, Mozart, Beethoven.* New York: Macmillan Co., 1970.

_____________, ed. *Studies in Eighteenth-Century Music.* New York: Oxford University Press, 1970.

Newman, William S. *The Sonata in the Classic Era.* Chapel Hill: University of North Carolina Press, 1969. Paperback, 2nd Edition, New York: W. W. Norton & Co., Inc., 1972.

Pauly, Reinhard G. *Music in the Classic Period,* 2nd Edition. Englewood Cliffs, N.J.: Prentice-Hall, Inc., 1973. Paper.

Rosen, Charles. *The Classical Style: Haydn, Mozart, Beethoven.* New York: W. W. Norton & Co., Inc., 1972. Paper.

Romantic Period

Klaus, Kenneth B. *The Romantic Period in Music.* Boston: Allyn and Bacon, Inc., 1970.

Longyear, Rey M. *Nineteenth-Century Romanticism in Music.* Englewood Cliffs, N.J.: Prentice-Hall, Inc., 1969. Paper.

Newman, William S. *The Sonata Since Beethoven.* Chapel Hill: University of North Carolina Press, 1969. Paperback, 2nd Edition, New York: W. W. Norton & Co., Inc., 1972.

Contemporary Period

Austin, William W. *Music in the 20th Century.* New York: W. W. Norton & Co., Inc., 1966.

Deri, Otto. *Exploring Twentieth-Century Music.* New York: Holt, Rinehart and Winston, 1968.

Hansen, Peter S. *An Introduction to Twentieth Century Music,* 3rd Edition. Boston: Allyn and Bacon, Inc., 1971.

Hartog, Howard, ed. *European Music in the Twentieth Century.* New York: F. A. Praeger, 1957. Paper.

Machlis, Joseph. *Introduction to Contemporary Music.* New York: W. W. Norton & Co., Inc., 1961.

Myers, Rollo, ed. *Twentieth Century Music: A Symposium.* New York: Orion Press, 1968.

Salzman, Eric. *Twentieth-Century Music: An Introduction.* Englewood Cliffs, N.J.: Prentice-Hall, Inc., 1967. Paper.

Yates, Peter. *Twentieth Century Music: Its Evolution from the End of the Harmonic Era into the Present Era of Sound.* New York: Minerva Press, 1968. Paper.

Acoustics

Backus, John. *The Acoustical Foundations of Music.* New York: W. W. Norton & Co., Inc., 1969.

Bartholomew, Wilmer. *Acoustics of Music.* Englewood Cliffs, N.J.: Prentice-Hall, Inc., 1942.

Sabine, Wallace C. *Collected Papers on Acoustics.* New York: John Wiley, 1962.

Wood, Alexander. *Acoustics.* New York: Dover Publications, Inc., 1967. Paper.

Counterpoint

Bassett, Leslie. *Manual of 16th Century Counterpoint.* New York: Appleton-Century-Crofts, 1967.

Jeppesen, Knud. *Counterpoint,* translated by Glen Haydon. Englewood Cliffs, N.J.: Prentice-Hall, Inc., 1960.

Mason, Neale. *Essentials of Eighteenth-Century Counterpoint.* Dubuque, Iowa: Wm. C. Brown Co., 1968.

Piston, Walter. *Counterpoint, 18th and 19th Century Styles.* New York: W. W. Norton & Co., Inc., 1947.

Roberts, Stella, and Irwin Fischer. *A Handbook of Modal Counterpoint.* New York: The Free Press, 1967.

Salzer, Felix, and Carl Schacter. *Counterpoint in Composition: The Study of Voice Leading.* New York: McGraw-Hill Book Co., Inc., 1969.

Searle, Humphrey. *Twentieth Century Counterpoint.* London: Ernest Benn, Ltd., 1954.

Ear Training

Ellsworth, Eugene. *Aural Harmony.* Park Ridge, Illinois: General Words and Music Co., 1970.

Horacek, Leo, and Gerald Lefkoff. *Programed Ear Training.* New York: Harcourt, Brace & World, Inc., 1970. 4 Vols.

Thomson, William Ennis, and Richard P. Delone. *Introduction to Ear Training.* Belmont, Calif.: Wadsworth Publishing Co., 1967.

Form

Fontaine, Paul. *Basic Formal Structures in Music.* New York: Appleton-Century-Crofts, 1967.

Walton, Charles W. *Basic Forms in Music.* Port Washington, N.Y.: Alfred Publishing Co., Inc., 1974.

Harmony

Christ, Delone, Kliewer, Rowell, Thomson. *Materials and Structure of Music.* Englewood Cliffs, N.J.: Prentice-Hall, Inc., 1966.

Harder, Paul O. *Harmonic Materials in Tonal Music.* Boston: Allyn and Bacon, Inc., 1968. 2 Vols.

McHose, Allen I. *Basic Principles of the Technique of 18th and 19th Century Composition.* New York: Appleton-Century-Crofts, 1951.

Ottman, Robert. *Elementary Harmony,* 2nd Edition. Englewood Cliffs, N.J.: Prentice-Hall, Inc., 1970.

Piston, Walter. *Harmony,* 3rd Edition. New York: W. W. Norton & Co., Inc., 1962.

Robinson, Raymond C. *Progressive Harmony,* Revised Edition. Boston: Bruce Humphries, 1962.

Introductory Books

Ashford, Theodore H. *Fundamentals of Music.* Dubuque, Iowa: Wm. C. Brown Co., 1969.

Harder, Paul. *Basic Materials in Music Theory.* Boston: Allyn and Bacon, Inc., 1970.

Howard, Bertrand. *Fundamentals of Music Theory.* New York: Harcourt, Brace & World, Inc., 1966.

SPECIAL BOOKS

American Music

Chase, Gilbert. *America's Music,* Revised 2nd Edition. New York: McGraw-Hill Book Co., Inc., 1966.

Barzun, Jacques. *Music in American Life.* Bloomington, Ind.: Indiana University Press, 1956. A Midland PB.

Hitchcock, H. Wiley. *Music in the United States: A Historical Introduction.* Englewood Cliffs, N.J.: Prentice-Hall, Inc., 1969. Paper.

Machlis, Joseph. *American Composers of Our Time.* New York: Thomas Y. Crowell Co., 1963.

Mellers, Wilfrid. *Music in a New Found Land.* New York: Alfred A. Knopf, 1964.

Chamber Music

Ferguson, Donald. *Image and Structure in Chamber Music.* Minneapolis: University of Minnesota Press, 1964.

Ulrich, Homer. *Chamber Music,* 2nd Edition. New York: Columbia University Press, 1966.

Concerto

Young, Percy M. *Concerto.* Boston: Crescendo Publishers, 1968.

Veinus, Abraham. *The Concerto,* Revised Republication. New York: Dover Publications, Inc., 1964.

Conducting

Green, Elizabeth. *The Modern Conductor.* Englewood Cliffs, N.J.: Prentice-Hall, Inc., 1961.

Grosbayne, Benjamin. *Techniques of Modern Orchestral Conducting.* Cambridge, Mass.: Harvard University Press, 1956.

Rudolf, Max. *The Grammar of Conducting.* New York: G. Schirmer, Inc., 1950.

Folk Songs

Boni, Margaret Bradford, ed. *Fireside Book of Folk Songs,* arranged by Norman Lloyd. New York: Simon and Schuster, Inc., 1947. Paper.

Dallin, Leon and Lynn. *Folk Songster.* Dubuque, Iowa: Wm. C. Brown Co., 1967. Paper.

Deutsch, Leonhard, compiler and arranger. *A Treasury of the World's Finest Folk Song,* Revised Edition. New York: Crown Publishers, 1967.

Stevens, Denis, ed. *A History of Song.* London: Hutchinson, 1960.

Harpsichord and Clavichord

Harich-Schneider, Eta. *The Harpsichord.* Kassel: Bärenteiter, 1960.

Hoover, Cynthia A. *Harpsichords and Clavichords.* Washington, D.C.: Smithsonian Institution Press (for sale by the Supt. of Documents, U.S. Government Printing Office), 1969.

Kenyon, Max. *Harpsichord Music.* London: Cassel & Co., Ltd., 1949.

Neupert, Hanns. *Harpsichord Manual: A Historical and Technical Discussion,* translated by F. E. Kirby, 2nd Edition. Kassel: Bärenreiter, 1968. Paper.

Russell, Raymond. *The Harpsichord and Clavichord.* London: Faber and Faber, 1959.

Zuckerman, Wolfgang Joachim. *The Modern Harpsichord: Twentieth-Century Instruments and their Makers.* New York: October House, 1969.

Instruments

Bragard, Roger, and Ferdinand J. de Hen. *Musical Instruments in Art and History,* translated by Bill Hopkins. New York: Viking Press, 1968.

Kendall, Allan. *The World of Musical Instruments.* London: The Hamlyn Publishing Group Ltd., 1972.

Sachs, Curt. *The History of Musical Instruments.* New York: W. W. Norton & Co., Inc., 1940.

Winternitz, Emanuel. *Musical Instruments of the Western World.* New York: McGraw-Hill Books Co., Inc., 1967.

Jazz and Rock

Belz, Carl. *The Story of Rock.* New York: Oxford University Press, 1969.

Brown, Len, and Gary Friedrich. *Encyclopedia of Rock and Roll.* New York: Tower Publications, 1970.

Dankworth, Avril. *Jazz: An Introduction to its Musical Basis.* London: Oxford University Press, 1968.

Eisen, Jonathan, compiler. *The Age of Rock, Sound of the American Cultural Revolution.* New York: Random House, 1969.

Schuller, Gunther. *The History of Jazz, Vol. 1: Early Jazz: Its Roots and Musical Development.* New York: Oxford University Press, 1968.

Stearns, Marshall. *The Story of Jazz.* New York: The New American Library, 1958. A Mentor PB.

Williams, Martin T. *The Jazz Tradition.* New York: Oxford University Press, 1970.

Musical Ability

Fisher, Renee B. *Musical Prodigies: Masters at an Early Age.* New York: Association Press, 1973.

Lehman, Paul Robert. *Tests and Measurements in Music.* Englewood Cliffs, N.J.: Prentice-Hall, Inc., 1968.

Revesz, Gesa. *The Psychology of a Musical Prodigy.* Freeport, N.Y.: Books for Libraries Press, 1970. Reprint of 1925 edition.

Shuter, Rosamund. *The Psychology of Musical Ability.* London: Methuen, 1968.

Music and Art

Fleming, William. *Art, Music and Ideas.* New York: Holt, Rinehart and Winston, 1970.

Janson, H. W., and Joseph Kerman. *A History of Art and Music.* Englewood Cliffs, N.J.: Prentice-Hall, Inc., 1968. PB.

Lesure, Francois. *Music and Art in Society,* translated by Denis and Sheila Stevens. University Park: Pennsylvania State University Press, 1968.

Music Books for Children

Bernstein, Leonard. *Young People's Concerts,* Revised Edition. New York: Simon and Schuster, Inc., 1970.

Britten, Benjamin, and Imogen Holst. *The Wonderful World of Music.* Garden City, N.Y.: Doubleday, 1968.

Davis, Maryilyn K., and Arnold Broido. *Music Dictionary.* Garden City, N.Y.: Doubleday, 1956.

Gass, Irene. *Mozart; Child Wonder, Great Composer.* New York: Lathrop, Lee & Shapard Co., 1970.

Gimpel, Herbert J. *Beethoven Master Composer.* New York: F. Watts, 1970.

Greene, Carla. *Let's Learn about the Orchestra.* Irvington-on-Hudson, N.Y.: Harvey House, 1967.

Reingold, Carmel Berman. *Johann Sebastian Bach; Revolutionary of Music.* New York: F. Watts, 1970.

Wechsberg, Joseph. *The Pantheon Story of Music for Young People.* New York: Pantheon Books, 1968.

Winn, Marie, ed. *The Fireside Book of Children's Songs,* arranged by Allan Miller. New York: Simon and Schuster, Inc., 1966.

Music Careers

Ward, John Owen. *Careers in Music.* New York: H. Z. Walck, 1968.

Music Education

Andrews, Frances M. *Junior High School General Music.* Englewood Cliffs, N.J.: Prentice-Hall, Inc., 1971.

Collins, Thomas C., ed. *Music Education Materials.* Vienna, Virginia: Music Educators National Conference, 1968.

Garretson, Robert L. *Music in Childhood Education.* New York: Appleton-Century-Crofts, 1966.

Glean, Neal E., William B. McBride, and George H. Wilson. *Secondary School Music.* Englewood Cliffs, N.J.: Prentice-Hall, Inc., 1970.

Gordon, Edwin. *The Psychology of Music Teaching.* Englewood Cliffs, N.J.: Prentice-Hall, Inc., 1971.

Hoffer, Charles R. *Teaching Music in the Secondary Schools.* Belmont, Calif.: Wadsworth Publishing Co., Inc., 1964.

Nye, Robert Evans, and Vernice Trousdale Nye. *Essentials of Teaching Elementary School Music.* Englewood Cliffs, N.J.: Prentice-Hall, Inc., 1974.

__________. *Music in the Elementary School,* 3rd Edition. Englewood Cliffs, N.J.: Prentice-Hall, Inc., 1970.

Music Engraving

Ross, Ted. *The Art of Music Engraving and Processing.* Miami: Hansen Books, 1970.

Musicology

Haydon, Glen. *Introduction of Musicology.* Englewood Cliffs, N.J.: Prentice-Hall, Inc., 1941. Unaltered Reprint, Chapel Hill, N.C.: University of North Carolina Press, 1959.

Pruett, James W., compiler. *Studies in Musicology.* Chapel Hill, N.C.: University of North Carolina Press, 1969.

Reese, Gustave, and Robert J. Snow, compilers. *Essays in Musicology, in Honor of Dragan Plamencac on His 70th Birthday.* Pittsburgh: University of Pittsburgh Press, 1969.

Watanabe, Ruth Taiko. *Introduction to Music Research.* Englewood Cliffs, N.J.: Prentice-Hall, Inc., 1967.

Music Therapy

Gaston, Thayer E., ed. *Music in Therapy.* New York: The Macmillan Co., 1968.

Notation

Read, Gardner. *Music Notation,* 2nd Edition. Boston: Allyn and Bacon, Inc., 1969.

Williams, Charles Francis Abdy. *The Story of Notation.* New York: Haskell House Publishers, 1969. Reprint of 1903 edition.

Opera

Austin, William W., compiler. *New Looks at Italian Opera: Essays in Honor of Donald J. Grout.* Ithaca, N.Y.: Cornell University Press, 1968.

Brody, Elaine. *Music in Opera: A Historical Anthology.* Englewood Cliffs, N.J.: Prentice-Hall, Inc., 1970.

Cross, Milton John, and Karl Kohrs. *More Stories of Great Operas.* Garden City, N.Y.: Doubleday and Co., Inc., 1971.

Davidson, Gladys. *The Barns Book of the Opera.* New York: Barnes & Noble, Inc., 1962.

Dent, Edward J. *Opera.* Baltimore, Md.: Penguin Books, 1949. A Pelican PB.

Goldovsky, Boris. *Bringing Opera to Life: Operatic Acting and Stage Direction.* New York: Appleton-Century-Crofts, 1968.

Grout, Donald J. *A Short History of Opera,* 2nd Edition. New York: Columbia University Press, 1965.

Pauly, Reinhard G. *Music and the Theater: An Introduction to Opera.* Englewood Cliffs, N.J.: Prentice-Hall, Inc., 1970.

Peltz, Mary Ellis, ed. *Introduction to Opera,* 2nd Edition. New York: Barnes & Noble, Inc., 1963. Paper.

The Victor Book of the Opera, Revised by Henry W. Simon, 13th Edition. New York: Simon & Schuster, 1968.

Orchestration

Carse, Adam. *The History of Orchestration.* New York: Dover Publications, Inc., 1964. Paper.

Kennan, Kent. *The Technique of Orchestration,* 2nd Edition. Englewood Cliffs, N.J.: Prentice-Hall, Inc., 1970.

Piston, Walter. *Orchestration.* New York: W. W. Norton & Co., Inc., 1955.

Read, Gardner. *Thesaurus of Orchestral Devices.* New York: Greenwood Press, 1969. Reprint of 1953 edition.

Organ

Andersen, Paul Gerhard. *Organ Building and Design,* translated by Joanne Curnutt. New York: Oxford University Press, 1969.

Barnes, William Harrison, and Edward B. Gammons. *Two Centuries of American Organ Building.* Glen Rock, N.J.: J. Fischer, 1970.

Summer, William Leslie. *The Organ,* 3rd Edition. London: MacDonald, 1962.

Parents

Bastien, James. *A Parent's Guide to Piano Lessons.* San Diego, Calif.: Kjos West, 1976. Paper.

Performance

Dart, Thurston. *The Interpretation of Music,* 4th Edition. London: Hutchinson, 1967.

Dorian, Frederick. *The History of Music in Performance.* New York: W. W. Norton & Co., Inc., 1942.

Performing Arts

Ackerman, James, *et al. The Arts on Campus: The Necessity for Change,* edited by Margaret Mohoney with the Assistance of Isabel Moore. Greenwich, Conn.: New York Graphic Society, 1970.

Baumol, William J., and William G. Bowen. *Performing Arts: The Economic Dilemma.* Cambridge, Mass.: The M.I.T. Press, 1968.

Harris, John S. *Government Patronage of the Arts in Great Britain.* Chicago: University of Chicago Press, 1970.

Psychology of Music

Farnsworth, Paul Randolph. *The Social Psychology of Music,* 2nd Edition. Ames, Iowa: Iowa State University Press, 1969.

Lundin, Robert William. *An Objective Psychology of Music,* 2nd Edition. New York: Ronald Press Co., 1967.

Seashore, Carl Emil. *Psychology of Music.* New York: Dover Publication, Inc., 1967. Reprint of 1938 edition.

Stage Deportment

Sorel, Claudette. *Mind Your Musical Manners.* New York: Marks Music Corporation, 1972. Paper.

Symphony

Cuyler, Louise. *The Symphony.* New York: Harcourt Brace Jovanovich, Inc., 1973.

Appendix C
Recommended Music

SOLOS AND COLLECTIONS

Recommended by Jane Smisor Bastien and James Bastien (Workshop List)

ELEMENTARY (1st year)

Bishop *Oriental Story* C. Fischer
Carter *Bouncing the Ball* Summy-Birchard
Garrow *Agent 402* Belwin-Mills
Garrow *At the Trading Post* Belwin-Mills
Garrow *The Little Frog* Belwin-Mills
Glover *Saucer Men* Belwin-Mills
Noona *Cat and Mouse* Heritage
Noona *The Speedy Little Taxi* Heritage
Richter *Our School Band* Boston Music Co.
Scher *The Timid Little Bee* Elkan-Vogel
Stecher, Horowitz, Gordon *Mexican Border Town* Schirmer
Stecher, Horowitz, Gordon *Under the Big Top* Summy-Birchard
Stevens *The Funny Eskimo* C. Fischer
Suddards *Mister Woof* Witmark
Wagness *March of Victory* Oliver Ditson
Werder *The Drum* McLaughlin & Reilly
Wilson *Attic Ghost* Schroeder & Gunther

ADVANCING ELEMENTARY (2nd year)

Agay *Frolic* Schirmer
Dittenhaver *Fast Train at Night* Schroeder & Gunther
Frackenpohl *March On!* and *Parade* Lee Roberts
George *A Day in the Jungle* Summy-Birchard
George *Kaleidoscope Solos, Bks. 1-5* Alfred
Glover *Ach! My Little Foreign Car* Hansen
Glover *Flags on Parade* Belwin-Mills
Karp *The Busy Little Train* Lee Roberts
Last *Cats* Oxford
Noona *Broken Down Merry Go Round* Heritage
Olson *Midnight Express* C. Fischer
Olson *Secret Mission* C. Fischer
Olson *Silver Bugles* C. Fischer

Poe *Animal World* C Fischer
Sochting *The Cuckoo's Call* Willis
Stecher, Horowitz, Gordon *Little Caballero* Schirmer
Stecher, Horowitz, Gordon *Waggin' Train* Schirmer
Stevens *Parade of the Penguins* Harold Flammer

EARLY INTERMEDIATE (approx. 3rd year)

Agay *Dancing Leaves* Schirmer
Brodsky *Calypso Party* Elkan-Vogel
Brodsky *It's Raining* Summy-Birchard
Cobb *Sonatina in C Major* Mills/Belwin
Clementi *I Grandi Classici* Ricordi
Dello Joio *Suite for the Young* Marks
Gianneo *Seven Children's Pieces* Southern, N.Y.
Gillock *Accent on Rhythm and Style* Willis
Gillock *Carnival in Rio* Willis
Gillock *Yo-Yo Tricks* Schroeder & Gunther
Green *Indian Summer* Schroeder & Gunther
Green *Thar She Blows!* Willis
Gretchaninoff *The Seven Dwarfs* Willis
Grove *March* Belwin-Mills
Last *At the Keyboard, Book 3* Oxford
Nevin *Tokyo Toccatina* Belwin-Mills
Persichetti *Parades* Elkan-Vogel
Raymond *March on the White Keys* J. Fischer/Belwin
Rowley *Miniature Preludes & Fugues* Chester
Storr *In the Engine Room* Schmitt
Villa-Lobos *The Toy Wheel* Peer-Southern

INTERMEDIATE (3rd or 4th year)

Agay *Petit Trianon Suite* Schirmer
Agay *Sonatina Toccata* Boosey
Agay *Three Recital Dances* Presser
Anson (ed.) *Survey of Piano Literature, Bks. 1-3* Elkan-Vogel
Bastien/Bach *Jesu, Joy of Man's Desiring* GWM/Kjos
Bastien/Bach *Toccata in D Minor* GWM/Kjos
Bastien *Variations on a Theme by Paganini* GWM/Kjos
Brandt *Little Donkey in the Snow* J. Fischer/Belwin
Elaine, Sister M. *Triads on Parade* J. Fischer/Belwin
Freed *Jeneral Jerry's Jolly Jugglers* C. Fischer
Gillock *Blue Mood* Willis
Gillock *Holiday in Spain* Willis
Glover *Variations on a Minor Theme* Belwin-Mills
Glover *Virginia Sonatina, No. 3* Schroeder & Gunther
Labunski *Four Variations on a Theme of Paganini* C. Fischer
Labuda *10 Short Dances and Airs for Piano* Presser
Last *Down to the Sea* Oxford
Martino *Gospel Meeting* MCA
Nakada *Japanese Festival* MCA
Olson *Rather Blue* Schirmer
Poulenc *Villageoises* Salabert
Ricker *Hero's March* Lee Roberts
Rowley (ed.) *Early English Sonatinas* Boosey
Stecher, Horowitz, Gordon *The Terrain of Spain* Summy-Birchard
Weybright *Braziliana* Belwin-Mills

EARLY ADVANCED (4th, 5th year)

Agay *Concertino on Themes by Handel* Schirmer
Agay *Concerto Barocco* Schirmer
Agay *Serenata Burlesca* Boosey
Agay *Sonatina No. 3* Sam Fox
Allen *Lament* Summy-Birchard
Bilotti *The Firefly* C. Fischer
Brussels *Two Preludes* MCA
Copland *The Cat and the Mouse* Boosey
Gillock *3 Jazz Preludes* Willis
Gillock *Sonatine* Willis
Harvey *Rumba Toccata* Ricordi
Hovhaness *Mystic Flute* Peters
Kabalevsky *Four Rondos* MCA
Kern *The Clown* Oliver Ditson
Kern *The Juggler* Oliver Ditson
Smith *Episodic Suite* Presser
Starer *Sketches in Color, Set 1* MCA
Wigham *Scherzino* Franco Columbo

ADVANCED (5th year up)

Agay *Sonatina Hungarica* MCA
Babin *Sonatina No. 1* MCA
Bartók *Bear Dance* Boosey
Bartók *Sonatina* Boosey
Bartók *Suite, Opus 14* Boosey
Bastien *Toccata* GWM/Kjos
Bernstein *Four Anniversaries* Schirmer
Bloch *Poems of the Sea* Schirmer
Chasins *Rush Hour in Hong Kong* J. Fischer/Belwin
Dello Joio *Suite for Piano* Schirmer
Faith *Finger Paintings* Shawnee Press
Finney *Nostalgic Waltzes* Mercury
Frank *Bagatelle* MCA
Ginastera *Danzas Argentinas* Elkan-Vogel
Ginastera *Rondo on Argentine Folk Song* Boosey
Godard *Le Cavalier Fantastique* Schirmer
Harris *Introduction and Fugato* Willis
Hawes *Toccata* C. Fischer
Hovhaness *Two Ghazelles* Peters
Ibert *Histoires* Alphone Le duc
Kabalevsky *24 Preludes, Opus 38* MCA
Kennan *Three Preludes* Schirmer
Khachaturian *Toccata* MCA, Schirmer, others
Koelling *Hungary* Schirmer, Shawnee, others
Mompou *Cancion Y Danza 6* Marks
Muczynski *Six Preludes* Schirmer
Persichetti *Poems for Piano, 2 Vols.* Elkan-Vogel
Philipp *Feux-Follets* Schirmer
Poulenc *Suite for Piano* Chester
Poulenc *Toccata* Presser
Rachmaninoff *Humoreske* Schirmer, C. Fischer, others
Rorem *Three Barcarolles* Peters
Tauriello *Toccata* Boosey
Tcherepnin *Bagatelles, Opus 5* Schirmer
Toch *Sonatinetta* MCA
Toch *The Juggler* Schott

Recommended by Jane Smisor Bastien and James Bastien (Workshop List)

EASY

Atkinson *Trends for Two* (duets) Schmitt
Bastien *Duets for Fun, Bks. 1 & 2* GWM/Kjos
Campbell *First Piano Duets* J. Fischer/Belwin
Clark, M.E./Mozart *Serenade* Myklas
Cobb *Playing Together* (duet) Flammer
Cobb *Primo Secondo* Summy-Birchard
Garrow *Tunes You Like for Two* (duets) Schroeder & Gunther
George *Kaleidoscope Duets, Bks. 1-3* Alfred
George *Two at One Piano, Bks. 1-3* Summy-Birchard
Glover *Butterscotch & Bagpipes* (2 piano) Hansen
Glover *Clapit Boogie* (duet) Schroeder & Gunther
Glover & Garrow *Piano Duets, Level 1* Belwin-Mills
Johnson *You and I* (duets) Hinrichsen (No. 383)
Karp *Jon Peter Polka* Schmitt
Karp *Sleigh Ride* Schmitt
Last *Two and a Piano, Sets 1-3* Oxford
Olson *The Ash Grove* (duet) C. Fischer
Pace *Duets for Piano* Lee Roberts
Pace *The Farmer Left the Dell* (duet) Lee Roberts
Scher *Hobby Horse* (duet) Pro Art
Stecher, Horowitz, Gordon *The Pleasure of Your Company, Bks. 1-3* (duets) Schirmer
Weybright *Polly Put the Kettle On* (2 piano) Willis
Wilson *Easy for Me* (duets) Boston Music Co.

INTERMEDIATE

Agay *Dance Toccata* (duet) Sam Fox
Agay *Joplin–Ragtime Classics* (duets) Marks
Arensky *Six Recital Pieces* (duets) MCA
Atkinson *Trends for Two* (duets) Schmitt
Bishop *A Folk Holiday* (duets) C. Fischer
Bradley (arr.) *Bradley's Double Joy* (duets) Columbia
Brimhall (arr.) *The Rage is Recital Duets* Hansen
Bruckner *Quadrille* (duets) Heinrichshofen's Verlag
Clark, M.E. *Three Spanish Dances* Myklas
Clarke, L. *Jazz Duet 1* Myklas
Clarke, L. *Jazz Duet 2* Myklas
Dello Joio *Family Album* (duets) Marks
Dittenhaver *Street Fair* (2 piano) Schroeder & Gunther
Dring *Four Duets* Schirmer
Dring *Three for Two* (duets) Marks
Dungan *Dance of the Fleas* (duet) Oliver Ditson
Dungan *Red Nosed Clown* (duet) Presser
Eckard (ed.) *44 Original Piano Duets (Easy to Intermediate Grades)* Presser
George *Kaleidoscope Duets, Bks. 4 & 5* Alfred
Gillock *On a Paris Boulevard* (2 piano) Willis
Gillock *Sidewalk Cafe* (duet) Willis
Gunther/Grieg *Elfin Dance* (duet) Belwin-Mills
Gunther/Kabalevsky *The Horseman* (2 piano) Belwin-Mills
Gunther/Kabalevsky *Sonatina* (duet) Belwin-Mills
Johnson *Melody-Making for Two* (duets) Hinrichsen (No. 885)
Johnson *Together We Play* (duets) Hinrichsen (No. 884)
Lambert *Trois Pieces Negres* (duets) Oxford

Last/Corelli *Sarabanda & Giga* (2 piano) Galaxy
Last/Corelli *Tempo di Gavotta* (2 piano) Galaxy
Martin, G. *Jazz Duets (Recital Notebook Series, No. 10)* Yorktown
Martin, H. *Tune Time for Two* (duets) Belwin-Mills
Marwick and Nagy *Folk Song Duets, Level 2* Screen Gems
McCleary and Hinson (eds.) *Duets of Early American Music* Belwin-Mills
Metis *Pop/Rock Sketches for Piano Duet* Marks
Nagy *Double Exposure* (duet) Lee Roberts
Olson, Bianchi, Blickenstaff *Ensemble, Levels 3-5* C. Fischer
Persichetti *Serenade No. 8* (duet) Elkan-Vogel
Starer *Five Duets for Young Pianists* MCA
Stecher, Horowitz, Gordon *The Pleasure of Your Company, Books 4 & 5* (duets) Schirmer
Stevens *Jo-Jo the Juggler* (2 piano) J. Fischer/Belwin
Weybright *Braziliana* (2 piano) Belwin-Mills
Zeitlin and Goldberger (eds.) *The Duet Book, Bks. 1-3* Consolidated
Zeitlin and Goldberger (eds.) *Easy Piano Duets of the 19th Century* Schroeder & Gunther
Zeitlin and Goldberger (eds.) *Eleven Piano Duets* Schirmer

ADVANCED

Andre *Six Sonatinas* Summy-Birchard
Bach- M. Hess *Jesu, Joy of Man's Desiring* (2 piano) Oxford
Beer (ed.) *Classic Masters Duets* Presser
Benjamin *Jamaican Rumba* (2 piano) Boosey
Bishop/Strauss *Serenade* (2 piano) C. Fischer
(collection) *Classical Album* (duets) Schirmer
(collection) *Classical Duets* Chester
(collection) *Duet Album* Mercury
(collection) *Pianoforte Album #2* (duets) Hinrichsen (388)
Debussy *Petite Suite* (duets) Durand
Dvorák *Slavic Dances, Bks. 1 & 2* (duets) Schirmer
Fauré *Dolly, Opus 5* (duets) International
Gliere *The Wind* (2 piano) Marks
Grieg *Norwegian Dances, Opus 35* (duets) Peters
Hill *Jazz Study No. 1* (2 piano) Schirmer
Poulenc *L'embarquement pour Cythere* (2 piano) Max Eschig
Poulenc *Sonata* (duet or 2 piano) Chester
Ravel *Mother Goose Suite* (duet) Durand
Simmons *Scherzino* (2 piano) J. Fischer/Belwin
Vaughn Williams-H. Foss *Fantasia on Greensleeves* (2 piano) Oxford

FOR TEACHER AND PUPIL

Alt *Secondo Scales* (duets) Summy-Birchard
Dello Joio *Five Images* (duets) Marks
Lubin (ed.) *Teacher and Student* Amsco
Ruthardt *Teacher and Pupil* (duets) Kalmus
Tcherepnin *Exploring the Piano* (duets) Peters
Wilson *12 Fun Tune Duets* Boston Music Co.

BRIEF LIST OF POP MUSIC (COLLECTIONS AND SOLOS)

Recommended by Jane Smisor Bastien and James Bastien (Workshop List)

EASY (1st – 3rd year)

Bastien, J. S. *Pop, Rock 'n Blues, Book 1* GWM/Kjos
Bastien, J. S. *Rock 'n Blues for Fun* GWM/Kjos
Bastien, J. W. *Rock Concert* (solo) GWM/Kjos
Bastien, J. W. *Rock Festival* (solo) GWM/Kjos
Burns & Graham *You Do It, Books 1-3* GWM/Kjos
Chagy *Jazz Tarantella* (solo) Marks/Belwin
Garrow *Boogie and Blues* Schroeder & Gunther
Glover *Jazz, Etc. on 88, Books 1-3* Belwin
Grove *Jazz About* GWM/Kjos
Kasschau *25 Ventures in Rock, Western & Blues* Schirmer
Kraehenbuehl *Jazz and Blues, Books 1-3* Summy-Birchard
Lewis *A Rockin' Little Tale* (solo) Lee Roberts
Lewis *Rock Liza* (solo) Lee Roberts
Martino *Chili Bean* (solo) MCA/Belwin
Mehegan *Jazz Bouree* (solo) Sam Fox
Olson *Rock Me Easy* C. Fischer
Stecher, Horowitz, Gordon *Rock with Jazz, Book 1* Schirmer

INTERMEDIATE (moderately difficult)

Agay *The Joy of Jazz* Yorktown
Baker (compiler) *Sounds of Today, Vol. 1* Warner Bros.
Bastien, J. S. *Final Exam Blues* (solo) GWM/Kjos
Bastien, J. S. *Pop, Rock 'n Blues, Books 2 & 3* GWM/Kjos
Bastien, J. W. *Country, Western 'n Blues, Books 1 & 2* GWM/Kjos
Bastien, J. W. *Gospel* (solo) GWM/Kjos
Bastien, J. W. *Rock Time U. S. A.* (solo) GWM/Kjos
Bastien, J. W. (arr.) *Scott Joplin Favorites* GWM/Kjos
Brimhall *Exercises in Rhythm* Hansen
Brimhall *Piano Blues* Hansen
Brubeck *Jazz Impressions of New York* Marks/Belwin
Brubeck *Themes from Eurasia* Shawnee
Burns & Graham *You Do It, Books 4-7* GWM/Kjos
Chagy *Razz-Ma-Jazz* (solo) Kjos West
Clarke, Lucia *Jazz and all That! Set 1* Myklas
Dennis *Ragtime Piano Styles* Mel Bay
Gillock *Blue Mood* (solo) Willis
Gillock *New Orleans Jazz Styles* Willis
Gillock *More New Orleans Jazz Styles* Willis
Gillock *Still More New Orleans Jazz Styles* Willis
Gillock *Three Jazz Preludes* Willis
Gordon *Introduction to the Art of Rock* Belwin
Gordon *Jazz for Junior* Marks/Belwin
Gordon *Junior Jazz* Marks/Belwin
Grey *Jazz Czerny* Puget Music Pub.
Grey *Jazz Hanon* Puget Music Pub.
Grove *The Riches of Rag* Summy-Birchard
King *I'm Playing Ragtime* C. Fischer
Konowitz *The Complete Rock Piano Method* Alfred
Konowitz *Jazz for Piano, Books 1 & 2* Lee Roberts
Konowitz *Jazz is a Way of Playing* Lee Roberts
Konowitz *Surf Swing* (solo) Lee Roberts
Konowitz *Time Changes* (solo) Lee Roberts
Kraehenbuhl *Jazz and Blues, Books 4-6* Summy-Birchard
Martino *Hanky-Panky* (solo) MCA/Belwin
Metis *Easy Pop Rock Sketches* (4 parts) Marks/Belwin
Metis *Easy Together* (4 parts) Marks/Belwin

Metis *Kids 'n Keyboards* (4 parts) Marks/Belwin
Metis *Rock Modes and Moods* Marks/Belwin
Noona & Glover *An Adventure in Jazz, Books 1-4* Belwin
Olson *Rather Blue* (solo) Schirmer
Olson, Bianchi, Blickenstaff *Something Light, Levels 3-5* C. Fischer
Small (arr.) *Ragtime Piano* Alfred
Smith *Faces of Jazz* Marks/Belwin
Stecher, Horowitz, Gordon *Rock with Jazz, Books 2-5* Schirmer
Thomas (compiler) *Sounds of Today, Vol. 2* Warner Bros.

ADVANCED

Allen *Jazz Impressions* Frank Music
Blake *Sincerely Eubie Blake* Marks/Belwin
Dennis *Blues Piano Styles* Mel Bay
Dennis *Jazz Piano Styles* Mel Bay
Dennis *Pensive Piano Moods* Mel Bay
Dennis *Rock Piano Styles* Mel Bay
Glover & Hinson *An Adventure in Ragtime* Belwin
Morath (compiler) *The Mississippi Valley Rags* Schirmer

TECHNIQUE AT ALL LEVELS

Recommended by James Bastien (Workshop List)

EASY

Bastien, James *Magic Finger Technique, Books 1-3* GWM/Kjos
Bastien, James *Major Scales and Pieces* GWM/Kjos
Bastien, James *Minor Scales and Pieces* GWM/Kjos
Bastien, James *Technic Lessons, Primer–Level 3* Kjos West
Cobb, Hazel *Technique Builders* Mills/Belwin
(collection) *The Early Virtuoso* Summy-Birchard
Last, Joan *Freedom Technique, Book 1* Oxford

INTERMEDIATE

Aiken, Kenneth *Modern Technic* Willis
Bastien, James (ed.) *Czerny and Hanon* GWM/Kjos
Bastien, James *Technic Lessons, Level 4* Kjos West
Dring, Madeline *Twelve Pieces in the Form of Studies* Marks
Last, Joan *Freedom Technique, Book 2* Oxford
Wolff, Bernard (ed.) *The Little Pischna* Schirmer

ADVANCED

Clementi, Muzio ed. by Tausig *Gradus ad Parnassum* Peters, Schirmer, Kalmus, etc.
Czerny, Carl *Art of Finger Dexterity, Opus 740* Schirmer, Kalmus, etc.
Dohnányi, Ernst *Essential Finger Exercises* Marks
Emonts, Friz *Polyphonic Piano Playing,* 2 books Schott (5451-2)
Ganz, Rudolph *Exercises for Piano: Contemporary & Special* Summy-Birchard
Grey, Jerome *Jazz Czerny* Puget Music Publishers
Last, Joan *Freedom Technique, Book 3* Oxford
Macfarren, Walter *Scale & Arpeggio Manual* Schirmer
McDowell, Edward *12 Virtuoso Studies, Opus 46* Associated, Kalmus, etc.
Moscheles, Ignaz *24 Studies, Opus 70* Schirmer
Moszkowski, Moritz *15 Etudes de Virtuosité* Schirmer, Boosey, Kalmus, etc.

Philipp, Isidor *Exercises for Independence of the Fingers,* 2 books Schirmer
Pischna, Johann *Technical Studies* Schirmer, Kalmus, Peters, etc.
Sorel, Claudette *Compendium of Piano Technique* Marks
Waxman, Donald *Fifty Etudes, Books 1-4* Galaxy

CLASS PIANO TEXTS AND SUPPLEMENTARY MATERIALS

Compiled by James Bastien (Workshop List)

TEXTS

Bastien, James and Jane S. Bastien. *Beginning Piano for Adults.* Park Ridge, Illinois: General Words and Music Co., 1968.

Duckworth, Guy. *Keyboard Musicianship.* New York: The Free Press, 1970.

Erlings, Billie. *Comprehensive Keyboard Skills Unit 1.* Tucson, Arizona: Nuove Music, Inc., 1975.

Foxley, William M. and Barbara R. Lowe. *Piano Study Guide and Workbook.* Provo, Utah: Brigham Young University Press, 1975.

Geissmar, Else. *Invitation to Music,* 2nd Edition, Revised. Kenmore, Washington: Puget Music Publications, Inc., 1972.

Leach, John R. *Functional Piano for the Teacher.* Englewood Cliffs, N. J.: Prentice-Hall, Inc., 1968.

Lowder, Jerry. *Basic Piano Skills.* Worthington, Ohio: Charles A. Jones Publishing Co., 1975.

Lyke, James, Elisabeth Hartline, and Ron Elliston. *Keyboard Musicianship, Books 1 & 2.* 2nd Edition. Champaign, Illinois: Stipes Publishing Co., 1974.

Mach, Elyse. *Contemporary Class Piano.* New York: Harcourt Brace Jovanovich, Inc., 1976.

McLain, Margaret Starr. *Class Piano.* Bloomington: Indiana University Press, 1974.

Pace, Robert. *Piano for Classroom Music,* 2nd Edition. Englewood Cliffs, N. J.: Prentice-Hall, Inc., 1971.

Page, Cleveland. *The Laboratory Piano Course, Books 1 & 2.* New York: Harper & Row, 1975, 1976.

Robinson, Helene. *Basic Piano for Adults.* Belmont, Calif.: Wadsworth Publishing Co., Inc., 1964.

____________. *Intermediate Piano for Adults, Volumes 1 & 2.* Belmont, Calif.: Wadsworth Publishing Co., Inc., 1970.

____________. *Piano Skills for Everyday.* Belmont, Calif.: Wadsworth Publishing Co., Inc., 1977.

Sheftel, Paul. *Exploring Music Fundamentals.* New York: Holt, Rinehart and Winston, Inc., 1970.

Squire, Russel N. and Virginia R. Mountney. *Class Piano for Adult Beginners,* 2nd Edition. Englewood Cliffs, N. J.: Prentice-Hall, Inc., 1971.

Starr, William and Constance Starr. *Basic Piano Technique for the Classroom Teacher.* Dubuque, Iowa: Wm. C. Brown Co., 1971.

Vernazza, Marcelle and Leonora J. Young. *Basic Materials for the Piano Student,* 2nd Edition. Dubuque, Iowa: Wm. C. Brown Co., 1972.

Zimmerman, Alex, Russel Hayton, and Dorothy Priesing. *Basic Piano for the College Student.* Dubuque, Iowa: Wm. C. Brown Co., 1969.

SUPPLEMENTARY MATERIALS

Agay, Denes (ed.). *Easy Classics to Moderns,* (Vol. 17, Music for Millions Series). New York: Consolidated Music Publishers, Inc., 1956.

Anthony, George Walter (ed.). *Easy Keyboard Music: Purcell to Shostakovich,* (Focus on Music, No. 4). Bryn Mawr, Penn.: Theodore Presser Co., 1967.

Bartók, Béla. *Mikrokosmos, Volumes 1-3.* New York: Boosey and Hawkes, 1940.

Bastien, James (ed.) *Czerny and Hanon.* Park Ridge, Illinois: General Words and

Music Co., 1970.

____________. (ed.) *Piano Literature for the Intermediate Grades*, (Volume 3). Park Ridge, Illinois: General Words and Music Co., 1968.

____________. (ed.) *Piano Literature for the Early Advanced Grades*, (Volume 4). Park Ridge, Illinois: General Words and Music Co., 1974.

____________. *Sight Reading, Books 1-4.* San Diego, Calif.: Kjos West, 1976.

Bastien, Jane Smisor. *Pop, Rock 'n Blues, Books 2 & 3.* Park Ridge, Illinois: General Words and Music Co., 1971.

Bishop, Dorothy. *Chords in Action*. New York: Carl Fischer, Inc., 1956.

____________. *A Folk Holiday*, (Piano Duets). New York: Carl Fischer, Inc., 1959.

Brimhall, John. *Instant Chord Solos, Issues 1 & 2.* Miami: Charles Hansen, 1976.

Brubeck, Dave. *Themes from Eurasia.* Delaware Water Gap, Penn.: Shawnee Press, Inc., 1970.

Burns, Betty, and Jackie Graham. *You Do It, Jazz, Rock, Pop, and Blues,* Books 1-7. Park Ridge, Illinois: General Words and Music Co., 1972.

Chastek, Winifred. *Keyboard Skills*. Belmont, Calif.: Wadsworth Publishing Co., Inc., 1967.

(collection) *1001 Jumbo Song Book.* Miami: Charles Hansen.

Contemporary Collection, 2 vols. Edited by Goldstein-Kern-Larimer-Ross-Weiss. Evanston, Illinois: Summy-Birchard Co., 1963.

Diemer, Emma Lou. *Sound Pictures*. New York: Boosey & Hawkes, 1971.

Deutsch, Leonhard. *For Sight Reading, Book 1*. New York: Heritage Music Publishers, 1950.

Dring, Madeline. *Twelve Pieces in the Form of Studies.* New York: Marks Music Corp., 1966.

Finney, Ross Lee. *32 Piano Games*. New York: C.F. Peters Corp., 1969.

Frackenpohl, Arthur. *Harmonization at the Piano,* 2nd Edition. Dubuque, Iowa: Wm. C. Brown Co., 1970.

Gordon, Louis. *Introduction to the Art of Rock.* Melville, New York: Belwin-Mills Publishing Corp., 1971.

____________. *Jazz for Junior*. New York: Edward B. Marks Music Corp., 1964.

____________. *Junior Jazz*. New York: Edward B. Marks Music Corp., 1961.

Hopkins, Antony. *For Talented Beginners,* 2 Vols. London: Oxford University Press, 1963.

Kern, Alice. *Harmonization-Transposition at the Keyboard*. Evanston, Illinois: Summy-Birchard Co., 1963.

Lewis, Pat. *A Rockin' Little Tale,* (sheet music). Lee Roberts, Inc., 1971.

____________. *Rock Lisa*, (sheet music). Lee Roberts, Inc., 1971.

Lyke, James (ed.). *Ensemble Music for Group Piano, Books 1 & 2,* 3rd Edition Revised. Champaign, Illinois: Stipes Publishing Co., 1976.

Mack, Glenn. *Adventures in Improvisation at the Keyboard.* Evanston, Illinois: Summy-Birchard, 1973.

____________. *Adventures in Modes and Keys.* Evanston, Illinois: Summy-Birchard, 1973.

Metis, Frank. *Rock Modes and Moods*. New York: Marks Music Corp., 1970.

Page, Cleveland L. *Ensemble Music for Group Piano.* Cincinnati: Canyon Press, Inc., 1970.

Palmer, Willard A. *Baroque Folk*. New York: Alfred Music Co., Inc., 1969.

Peltz, William. *Basic Keyboard Skills,* 2nd Edition Revised by Richard D. Osborne. Boston: Allyn and Bacon, Inc., 1968.

Swain, Alan. *Four-Way Keyboard System, Books 1-3.* Glenview, Illinois: Creative Music, 1969.

Zeitlin, Poldi, and David Goldberger (eds.) *Russian Music,* 6 vols. New York: MCA Music, 1967.

MULTIPLE PIANO PUBLICATIONS

Balkin, Alfred. *Six for Eight* (four parts), Piano Quartette Series. Park Ridge, Illinois: General Words and Music Co., 1971.

Bastien, Jane Smisor. *Christmas Carols for Multiple Pianos* (four parts). Park Ridge, Illinois: General Words and Music Co., 1971.

Clark, Mary Elizabeth. *Folk 1,* (three and six parts). Carlstadt, N.J.: Lewis Music Publishing Co., Inc., 1971.

____________. *Kum Ba Ya* and *Scarborough Fair*, (six parts). Carlstadt, N.J.: Lewis Music Publishing Co., Inc., 1971.

____________. *Sweetly Sings the Donkey* (four parts). Boulder, Colorado: Myklas Press, 1975.

DePue, Wallace. *16 Pawns* (four parts), Piano Quartette Series. Park Ridge, Illinois: General Words and Music Co., 1971.

Gunther, Phyllis. *Chester* (four parts). Melville, New York: Belwin-Mills, 1975.

____________. *Early American Suite* (four parts). Melville, New York: Belwin-Mills, 1975.

____________. *Patriotic Medley* (four parts). Melville, New York: Belwin-Mills, 1975.

Lucktenberg, George. *Bach for Piano Ensemble*, (four parts). Melville, New York: Belwin-Mills, 1971.

Metis, Frank. *Africasian Affair* (four parts). Pittsburgh: Volkwein Bros., Inc., 1970.

____________. *Easy Pop/Rock Sketches* (four parts). New York: Marks Music Corp., 1970.

____________. *Easy Together* (four parts). New York: Marks Music Corp., 1970.

____________. *Festival Fingers* (four parts). New York: Piedmont/Marks Music Corp., 1976.

____________. *Happiness Hill* (four parts). Pittsburgh: Volkwein Bros., Inc., 1970.

____________. *Ode to Joy* (four parts). New York: Marks Music Corp., 1970.

____________. *Parisian Polka* (four parts). Pittsburgh: Volkwein Bros., Inc., 1970.

____________. *Scarborough Fair* (four parts). New York: Marks Music Corp., 1970.

____________. *Wicked World Waltz* (four parts). Pittsburgh: Volkwein Bros., Inc., 1970.

____________. *You're a Grand Old Flag* (four parts). New York: Marks Music Corp., 1970.

Vandall, Robert. *Amazing Grace* (six parts). Park Ridge, Illinois: General Words and Music Co., 1977.

____________. *Cindy* (six parts). Park Ridge, Illinois: General Words and Music Co., 1977.

____________. *Five Will Get You Four* (five parts). Park Ridge, Illinois: Geneneral Words and Music Co., 1977.

____________. *Greensleeves* (four parts). Park Ridge, Illinois: General Words and Music Co., 1977.

____________. *Scarborough Fair* (six parts). Park Ridge, Illinois: General Words and Music Co., 1977.

____________. *Shenandoah* (six parts). Park Ridge, Illinois: General Words and Music Co., 1977.

____________. *Silent Night* (five parts). Park Ridge, Illinois: General Words and Music Co., 1977.

____________. *Sleep, Baby, Sleep* (six parts). Park Ridge, Illinois: General Words and Music Co., 1977.

____________. *Theme and Six Variations on Skip to My Lou* (six parts). Park Ridge, Illinois: General Words and Music Co., 1977.

BRIEF LIST OF MULTI-KEY READING MATERIALS

Compiled by James Bastien (Workshop List)

EARLY ELEMENTARY (1st year)

Bastien, Jane S. *Book 1 Reading* GWM/Kjos
Burrows & Ahern *The Young Explorer at the Piano* Willis
Duckworth, Guy *Keyboard Discoverer* M-F Co.
Gillock, William *Folk Songs & Rhythmic Dances* Willis
Gillock, William *Piano All the Way, Level 2* Willis
Glover, David and Mary E. Clark *Chords and Keys, Level 1* Belwin-Mills
Swenson, Lucile B. *Melody Preludes Through the Keys* Presser
Swenson, Lucile B. *Melody Rhymes Through All the Keys* Presser
Swenson, Lucile B. *More Melody Rhymes Through All the Keys* Presser

ADVANCING ELEMENTARY (2nd or 3rd year)

Anson, George *30 Pieces in 30 Keys, Books 1 & 2* Willis
Bastien, James *Major Scales & Pieces* GWM/Kjos
Bastien, James *Minor Scales & Pieces* GWM/Kjos
Bastien, James *Piano Lessons, Levels 2-4* Kjos West
Bastien, James *Sight Reading, Levels 2-4* Kjos West
Bastien, Jane S. *Books 2 & 3 Reading* GWM/Kjos
Bastien, Jane S. *Multi-Key Reading* GWM/Kjos
Cobb, Hazel *Around the Keys* Summy-Birchard
Cobb, Hazel *Major Miniatures for Piano* Belwin-Mills
Duckworth, Guy *Keyboard Musician* M-F Co.
Gillock, William *Accent on Majors* Willis
Gillock, William *Piano All the Way, Levels 3 & 4* Willis
Glover, David and Mary E. Clark *Chords and Keys, Level 2* Belwin-Mills
Oldenburg, Elizabeth *Miniatures, 30 Short Studies in all Major and Minor Keys* Volkwein Bros.
Pace, Robert *Music for Piano, Books 2 & 3* Lee Roberts
Smith, Hannah *Sight Reading Exercises, Parts 3 & 4* Schroeder & Gunther
Swenson, Lucile B. *Melody Modes and Moods Through All the Keys* Presser
Swenson, Lucile B. *Piano Pieces Through All the Keys* Presser

INTERMEDIATE (4th and 5th year)

Bishop, Dorothy (ed.) *Clementi Preludes* C. Fischer
Cobb, Hazel *Around the Keys Again* Summy-Birchard
Currie, Edward *Twelve Pieces in Related Keys, Books 1 & 2* Willis
Gillock, William *Accent on Black Keys* Willis
Gillock, William *Accent on Majors & Minors* Willis
Gillock, William *Lyric Preludes* Summy-Birchard
Gillock, William *Piano All the Way, Level 4* Willis
Smith, Hannah *Sight Reading Exercises, Parts 5-8* Schroeder & Gunther
Sorel, Claudette *The 24 Magic Keys, Books 1-3* Marks
Wigham, Margaret *Musical Moods in All Keys* Schroeder & Gunther

DIFFICULT 20th CENTURY PIANO MUSIC

Compiled by James Bastien

Barber, Samuel *Excursions; Nocturne; Sonata, Op. 26* Schirmer
Bartók, Béla *Allegro Barbaro; Mikrokosmos, Books 1-6; Rumanian Folk Songs; Sonata; Sonatina; Three Rondos* Boosey & Hawkes
Berg, Alban *Sonata, Op. 1* Universal
Bloch, Ernest *Poems of the Sea,* Schirmer *Sonata* Carisch & Co.
Boulez, Pierre *Three Piano Sonatas* Presser (No. 2) Universal (No. 3)
Carter, Elliott *Sonata (1946)* Mercury Music
Copland, Aaron *Piano Fantasy* Boosey & Hawkes *Passacaglia* Senart/Salabert *Piano Variations; Sonata* Boosey & Hawkes
Creston, Paul *Prelude and Dance* Mercury Music
Dello Joio *Sonata No. 3; Suite for Piano* Schirmer
Ginastera, Alberto *Danzas Argentinas,* Durand *Sonata para Piano* Barry/Boosey & Hawkes
Hindemith, Paul *Ludus Tonalis; Sonata No. 2* Schott
Hovhaness, Alan *Two Ghazals* Peters
Ibert, Jacques *Histoires* Alphonse Le duc
Ives, Charles *Concord Sonata* Arrow Music Press
Kabalevsky, Dmitri *Sonata No. 3; Twenty-Four Preludes, Op. 38* MCA
Khachaturian, Aram *Toccata* MCA
Kirchner, Leon *Sonata* Bomart
Krenek, Ernst *12 Short Piano Pieces, Op. 83* Schirmer
Menotti, Gian Carlo *Ricercare & Toccata* Ricordi
Muczynski, Robert *Six Preludes, Op. 6; Suite for Piano, Op. 13* Schirmer
Persichetti, Vincent *Eight Piano Sonatas; Poems, 2 Vols.* Elkan-Vogel
Poulenc, Francis *Movements Perpetuels; Suite (1920)* J & W Chester *Trois Pieces: Pastorale, Toccata, Hymn* Heugel/Mercury Music
Prokofiev, Serge *9 Piano Sonatas; Suggestion Diabolique; Toccata, Op. 11; Visions Fugitives, Op. 22* MCA
Schoenberg, Arnold *Three Piano Pieces, Op. 11* Universal *Five Piano Pieces, Op. 23* Wilhelm Hansen
Schostakovich Dimitri *24 Preludes, Op. 34; 24 Preludes & Fugues, Op. 87* MCA
Stockhausen, Karlheinz *Klavierstück I-IV* Universal
Stravinsky, Igor *Serenade en la; Sonata* (1924); *Trois Movements de Petrouchka* Boosey & Hawkes
Villa-Lobos, Heitor *Prole do bebe* Marks

SELECTED LIST OF ADVANCED TWO PIANO COMPOSITIONS

Compiled by James Bastien

I. ORIGINAL WORKS

Arensky, Anton *Suite No. 1 for Two Pianos, opus 15* Schirmer or Boosey
Babin, Victor *Six Etudes: Tempo guisto con fuoco, Adagietto cantabile, Veloce, Vivace* (based on Flight of the Bumble Bee), *Quasi una Siciliana, Allegro Molto, dramatico* Universal (Boosey)
Bach, Johann Christian *Sonata for Two Claviers in G major, opus 15, No. 6* Schott or International
Barber, Samuel *Souvenirs, Op. 28* Schirmer
Benjamin, Arthur *Jamaican Rumba* Boosey
Berezowsky, Nicolai *Fantasy, Op. 9* Associated
Bizet, Georges *Children's Games* (the complete four hand version is published by International) Kalmus/Belwin
Bowles, Paul *Sonata for Two Pianos* Schirmer
Brahms, Johannes *Sonata for Two Pianos, opus 34 bis* International *Variations on a Theme by Haydn, opus 56b* Schirmer or Peters

Busoni, Ferruccio *Duettino Concertante, after Mozart* Breitkopf & Härtell
Chopin, Frédéric *Rondo in C major, opus 73* Schirmer or Peters
Clementi, Muzzio *Two Sonatas for Two Pianos, opus 12* and *opus 46* Schirmer
Corigliano, John *Kaleidoscope* Schirmer
Debussy, Claude *En Blanc et Noir; Trois Morceaux* Durand
Dello-Joio, Norman *Aria and Toccata* C. Fischer
Freed, Isadore *Carnival* Presser
Gershwin, George *Second Rhapsody I Got Rhythm* Warner Bros.
Glière, Reinhold *Le Vent, opus 61, No. 24* Marks *Six Original Pieces, opus 41: Prelude, Valse Triste, Chanson, Basso Ostinato, Mazurka* International
Grieg, Edvard *Romanze and Variations, opus 51* Peters
Hill, Edward Burlingame *Jazz Studies, Numbers 1-4* Schirmer
Hindemith, Paul *Sonata for Two Pianos* Associated
Infante, Manuel *Trois danses andalouses: Ritmo, Gracia, Sentimiento* Salabert (Elkan-Vogel)
Khatchaturian, Aram *Suite for Two Pianos: Ostinato, Romance, Fantastic Waltz* Leeds (MCA)
Lees, Benjamin *Sonata for Two Pianos* Boosey
Liszt, Franz *Concerto Pathétique for Two Pianos* (without orchestra) Schirmer or Boosey
Lutoslawski, Witold *Variations on a Theme of Paganini (1941)* Polskie Wydawnictwe Muzyczne (Marks)
Milhaud, Darius *Scaramouche Suite* Salabert (Elkan-Vogel) *Carnaval á la Nouvelle Orleans* Leeds (MCA)
Moschelles, Ignaz *Hommage á Händel, opus 92* Augener, Ltd. (Galaxy)
Mozart, Wolfgang Amadeus *Fugue in C minor, K. 426* Schirmer *Sonata in D major, K. 448* Schirmer or Peters
Pattison, Lee *The Arkansas Traveler* and *Old Fiddler's Tune* Schirmer
Persichetti, Vincent *Sonata, opus 13* Leeds (MCA)
Philipp, Isidor *Caprice* Schirmer
Poulenc, Francis *L'embarquement pour Cythere* Max Eschig *Sonata* (for two pianos or one piano, four hands) Chester *Sonata for Two Pianos (1953)* Max Eschig
Rachmaninoff, Sergei *Russian Rhapsody* Leeds (MCA) *Suite No. 1, opus 5: (Fantaisie), Barcarole, "Oh night, oh love," Tears, Russian Easter,* International or Boosey *Suite No. 2, opus 17: Introduction, Waltz, Romance, Tarantella* International or Boosey
Reger, Max *Variations and Fugue on a Theme by Beethoven, opus 86; Introduction, Passacaglia, and Fugue, opus 96* Bote & Bock (Associated)
Reiger, Wallingford *Variations, Op. 54A* Associated
Rieti, Vittorio *Suite Champetre* Associated *Three Vaudeville Marches* General Music Publishing *Second Avenue Waltzes* Associated *Choral, Variations and Finale* General Music Publishing
Rorem, Ned *Sicilienne* (1950) Peer-Southern
Rubinstein, Beryl *Suite for Two Pianos: Prelude, Canzonetta, Jig, Maska* Schirmer
Saint-Saëns, Camille *Variations on a Theme by Beethoven, opus 35* Schirmer or Durand *Polonaise, opus 77* Durand *Scherzo, opus 87* Durand *Fantasy and Fugue, Chorale, Scherzo, Finale* E.F. Fromont (Elkan-Vogel)
Schumann, Robert *Andante and Variations, opus, 46* Schirmer or Boosey
Shostakovich, Dimitri *Concertino, opus 94* Leeds (MCA)
Simmons, Homer *Alice in Wonderland, Modern Suite: The Duchess, The Gryphon and the Mock Turtle, The Queen of Hearts, The Cheshire Cat, The Dormouse, The Lobster Quadrille; Scherzino* J. Fischer (Belwin)
Starer, Robert *On the Fringes of a Ball* Presser
Stravinsky, Igor *Concerto per Due Pianoforti Soli* Associated *Sonata for Two Pianos* Chappell
Tansman, Alexander *Carnival Suite* Leeds (MCA)

Tcherepnin, Alexander *Rondo for Two Pianos, opus 87a* Peters
Thomson, Virgil *Synthetic Waltzes* Elkan-Vogel
Williams, Ralph Vaughan *Introduction and Fugue* C. Fischer or Oxford

II. A SELECTED LISTING OF ARRANGED WORKS

COMPOSER-TITLE *ARRANGER* *PUBLISHER*

Bach, J.S. *Air in D major* Guy Maier, (J. Fischer/Belwin)
Allegro in G minor Ralph Berkowitz, (Elkan-Vogel)
Jesu, Joy of Man's Desiring Victor Babin, (Boston Music Co.); Myra Hess (Oxford)
Sicilienne Guy Maier, (J. Fischer/Belwin)
Toccata in the Dorian Mode William H. Harris (Novelle)
Trio Sonatas: Third Sonata in D minor, Fourth Sonata in E minor, Fifth Sonata in C major, Sixth Sonata in G major Victor Babin (Boosey)

Bartók, Béla *Five Mikrokosmos for Two Pianos* Béla Bartók (Boosey)

Bizet, Georges *Carmen Fantasy* Abram Chasins (J. Fischer/Belwin)

Brahms, Johannes *Five Waltzes from opus 39* Johannes Brahms (Schirmer)

Cherubini, Luigi *Scherzo in C major* Ralph Berkowitz (Elkan-Vogel)

Copland, Aaron *Billy the Kid* Aaron Copland (Boosey) *Danzon Cubano* Aaron Copland (Boosey)

De Falla, Manuel *Spanish Dance No. 1 from "La Vie Brève"* Stephen Kovacs (Max Eschig/Associated)

Glinka, Michael Ivanovich *The Lark (Romance)* Pierre Luboshutz, (J. Fischer/Belwin)

Godowsky, Leopold *Alt Wien* Leopold Godowsky (Schirmer)

Gottschalk, Louis *Tournament Galop* Phyllis Gunther (Belwin)

Handel, George Friderick *Passacaglia* Pierre Luboshutz (J. Fischer/Belwin)

Moussorgsky, Modest *Coronation Scene* Pierre Luboshutz (J. Fischer/Belwin)

Rachmaninoff, Sergei *Floods of Spring; It's Lovely Here; Vocalise* Victor Babin (Universal/Boosey)

Ravel Maurice *Bolero; La Valse* Maurice Ravel (Durand)

Saint-Saëns, Camille *Danse Macabre, opus 40* Camille Saint-Saëns, (Durand or Marks)

Schumann Robert *Six Etudes in the Form of a Canon, opus 56* Claude Debussy (International)

Strauss, Johann *Fledermaus Fantasy* Abram Chasins (O. Ditson/Presser) *The Bat, A fantasy from "Die Fledermaus"* Pierre Luboshutz (J. Fischer/Belwin)

Strauss, Richard *Serenade* Dorothy Bishop, (C. Fischer)

Stravinksy, Igor *Tango; Three Movements from Petrouchka: 1. Russian Dance, 2. Petrouchka, 3. The Shrove-Tide Fair* Victor Babin (Boosey)

Telemann, Georg Philipp *Fantasia on Themes by Georg Philipp Telemann* Victor Babin (Boosey)

Tchaikowsky, Peter Ilyich *Valse des Fleurs from "Nutcracker"; Waltz from "Eugene Onegin"; Waltz from "Serenade for Strings"; Waltz from "Swan Lake"* Victor Babin, (Boosey)

Williams, Ralph Vaughan *Fantasia on Greensleeves* Hubert Foss (Oxford)

Villa-Lobos, Heitor *Moreninha* Whittemore & Lowe (Associated)

Vivaldi, Antonio *Concerto in A minor* Wendell Nelson (Schirmer)

Weber, Carl Maria von *Invitation to the Dance, opus 65* Felix Weingartener (Boosey) *Rondo* Pierre Luboshutz, (J. Fischer/Belwin)

III. A SELECTED LIST OF TWO PIANO CONCERTI (CHAMBER WORKS INCLUDED)

Babin, Victor *Concerto No. 2 for Two Pianos and Orchestra* Boosey

Bach, Johann Sebastian *Concerto No. 1 in C minor; Concerto No. 2 in C major* Peters

Bartók, Béla *Sonata for Two Pianos and Percussion*, (also exists as a Concerto for Two Pianos with Orchestra) Boosey

Bliss, Arthur *Concerto for Two Pianos and Orchestra* Oxford

Bowles, Paul *Concerto for Two Pianos, Winds and Percussion (or orchestra)* American Music Edition

Diamond, David *Concerto for Two Pianos* Peer-Southern

Harris, Roy *Concerto for Two Pianos and Orchestra*

Lopatnikoff, Nikolai *Concerto for Two Pianos and Orchestra* Leeds (MCA)

Martinu, Bohuslav *Concerto for Two Pianos and Orchestra*

Mozart, Wolfgang Amadeus *Concerto for Two Pianos and Orchestra, F major, K. 242* (transcribed by the composer from the original Concerto for Three Pianos) Schirmer *Concerto for Two Pianos and Orchestra, E flat major, K. 365* Schirmer

Poulenc, Francis *Concerto for Two Pianos and Orchestra* Max Eschig

Reinecke, Carl *Cadenzas to Mozart's Concerto in E flat major, K. 365* International

Saint-Saëns, Camille *Carnival of the Animals* Durand

Williams, Ralph Vaughan *Concerto for Two Pianos and Orchestra*

SELECTED COLLECTIONS FOR THE DEVELOPMENT OF STYLE

Recommended by Louise Bianchi*

BAROQUE

Anthony, George (ed.) *Composers for the Keyboard, Easy Vol. 1; and Intermediate, Vol. 1* Presser

Bartók, Béla *Mikrokosmos, Vols. 1-3* Boosey

Brandt, Ada *Contra Punts* Elkan-Vogel

Butler, Jack *Pageants for Piano* (Processional, Toccata) Windsor

Earle, Eugenia *Conversation Pieces* (Canons) Lee Roberts

Emonts, Fritz (ed.) *Easy Baroque Piano Music* Schott

George, Jon *Mediaeval Pageant* Oxford

Gillock, William *Fanfare* Summy-Birchard

Last, Joan *In Classic Style* Oxford

McGraw, Cameron (ed.) *Four Centuries of Keyboard Music, Book 1* Boston

Palmer, Willard *Baroque Folk* Alfred

Roberts, Kenneth (ed.) *Six Little Fugues* (attributed to Handel) Concordia

CLASSICAL

Anthony, George (ed.) *Composers for the Keyboard, Easy Vol. 1* Presser

CMP Piano Library *The Sonatina Book I, II* Consolidated

Gillock, William *Classic Carnival* Willis

McGraw, Cameron (ed.) *Four Centuries of Keyboard Music, Book 1* Boston

Pace, Robert (ed.) *Recital Series for Piano* Lee Roberts

***Louise Bianchi is Director of the Preparatory Department, Southern Methodist University, Dallas. Used by permission.**

ROMANTIC

Butler, Jack *Pageants for Piano* (Summer Song) Windsor
Franck *Short Pieces* Peters
Gillock, William *Lyric Preludes* Summy-Birchard
Gretchaninoff *Children's Album, Op. 98* MCA
Grieg *Lyric Pieces* Schirmer
Heller *Fifty Selected Studies* Schirmer
Maykapar *Eighteen Selected Pieces* MCA
Mendelssohn *Songs Without Words* Schirmer
Niemann *In Children's Land, Op. 46* Peters
Schumann *Album for the Young* Schirmer
Wilson, Samuel *Leaves from My Notebook* Willis

IMPRESSIONISTIC

Alt, Hansi *The Ocean* Oxford
Bauer, Marion *Summertime Suite* MCA
Bernstein *Birds* Schroeder & Gunther
Butler, Jack *Pageants for Piano* (Clouds at Sunset) Windsor
Clawson, Donald *Adventures in the Park* Marks
Faith, Richard *Finger Paintings* Shawnee Press
George, Jon *A Day in the Forest* Summy-Birchard
Rebikov *Silhouettes, Op. 31* Schirmer
Wilson, Samuel *Leaves from My Notebook* Willis

CONTEMPORARY

Bartók *Mikrokosmos, Vols. 1-3* Boosey
Bartók (ed. Agay) *Ten Easy Pieces for Piano* Leeds/MCA
Frances Clark Library *Contemporary Literature, Bks. 1-6* Summy-Birchard
Clawson, Donald *Adventures in the Park* Marks
Ginastera *Twelve American Preludes* C. Fischer
Pace, Robert (ed.) *Recital Series for Piano* Lee Roberts
Ricker, Earl *Legend of an Ancient Land* Lee Roberts
Starer, Robert *Sketches in Color, Sets 1 & 2* MCA
Tcherepnin *Expressions, Op. 81* Leeds
Verne *City Set* Lee Roberts

GENERAL

Bull, Carolyn *From Here to There* C. Fischer
Casella, Alfredo *Children's Pieces* Universal
Dello Joio *Suite for the Young* Marks
Frackenpohl, Arthur *Circus Parade* Oxford
Furze, Jessie *Town and Country* Marks
Gillock, William *Accent on Rhythm and Style* Willis
Noel, Henri *Drolleries* Galaxy
Olson, Lynn F. *Menagerie* Oxford
Olson/Bianchi/Blickenstaff *Something Light, Books 1-5* C. Fischer
Sheftel, Paul *Interludes* C. Fischer
Tansman, Alexandre *Children at Play* Leeds/MCA
Waxman, Donald *Pageants for Piano* (Second Year Pageant) Galaxy

JAZZ, BLUES AND ROCK

Bastien, Jane S. *Pop, Rock 'n Blues, Books 1-3* GWM/Kjos
Gillock, William *New Orleans Jazz Styles* Willis
Gillock, William *More New Orleans Jazz Styles* Willis
Konowitz, Bert *Jazz for Piano, Books 1 & 2* Lee Roberts
Lewis, Pat *A Rockin Little Tale* Lee Roberts
Lewis, Pat *Rock Liza* Lee Roberts
Olson, Lynn F. *Light and Bright* Schmitt Publications
Olson, Lynn F. *Rock Me Easy* C. Fischer
Stecher, Horowitz, & Gordon *Rock with Jazz, Books 1-5* Schirmer

SELECTED SUITES, PIECES AND COLLECTIONS

Recommended by Dorothy Bishop*

LEVEL 1

Bastien, James *Playtime at the Piano, Book 1* GWM/Kjos
Bastien, James *Sight Reading, Level 1* Kjos West
Bastien, Jane S. *Pop, Rock 'n Blues, Book 1* GWM/Kjos
Bastien, Jane S. *Solos for The Very Young Pianist, Books 1 & 2* GWM/Kjos
George, Jon *Kaleidoscope Solos, Books 1 & 2* Alfred
Glover, David *Chords and Keys, Levels 1 & 2* Belwin-Mills
Grove, Roger *Images* Schroeder & Gunther
McGraw, Cameron *Trip to a Faraway Place* C. Fischer
Olson, Lynn F. *Near the Beginning* C. Fischer
Olson, Lynn F. *Further Along* C. Fischer
Schonthal, Ruth *Miniscules* C. Fischer
Waxman, Donald *First Folk Song Pageant* Galaxy
Weybright, June *Mildly Contemporary, Book 1* Belwin-Mills
Zeitlin/Goldberger (eds.) *The First Solo Book* Consolidated

LEVEL 2

Bastien, James *Playtime at the Piano, Book 2* GWM/Kjos
Bastien, James *Sight Reading, Level 2* Kjos West
Bastien, Jane S. *Multikey Reading* GWM/Kjos
Bastien, Jane S. *Pop, Rock 'n Blues, Book 2* GWM/Kjos
Gillock, William *Accent on Majors and Minors* Willis
Olson, Lynn F. *Menagerie* Oxford
Olson/Bianchi/Blickenstaff *Performance, Level 2, A-C* C. Fischer
Owens, Terry Winter *Confetti* Galaxy
Schonthal, Ruth *Near and Far* C. Fischer
Waxman, Donald *Second Folk Song Pageant* Galaxy

***Dorothy Bishop is widely known as clinician, composer and editor. Professor Bishop teaches at the University of Southern California Community Schools of the Performing Arts where she is a specialist in piano methods. Used by permission.**

LEVELS 3 and 4

Bastien, James (ed.) *Piano Literature, Book 3* GWM/Kjos
Bastien, James *Sight Reading, Levels 3 & 4* Kjos West
Bastien, Jane S. (ed.) *Piano Literature, Book 2* GWM/Kjos
Bastien, Jane S. *Pop, Rock 'n Blues, Book 3* GWM/Kjos
Clark, Frances, Lib. *Contemporary Piano Literature, Books 2 & 3* Summy-Birchard
Clark, Frances, Lib. *Piano Literature of the 18th and 19th Century* Summy-Birchard
Clark, Mary E. *Contempo* (series) Myklas
Clark, Mary E. *In the Mode* Myklas
George, Jon *Six Sonatinas* Alfred
Gillock, William *Accent on Rhythm and Style* Willis
Goldstein (et. al, eds.) *Contemporary Collection, Book 1* Summy-Birchard
Grove, Roger *Contrasts, Books 1 & 2* Schmitt Publications
Hopkins, Anthony *For Talented Beginners, Book 2* Oxford
Olson/Bianchi/Blickenstaff *Repertoire, Levels 3-A, B 4-A,B* C. Fischer
Olson/Bianchi/Blickenstaff *Something Light, Levels 3 & 4* C. Fischer
Palmer, Willard *Baroque Folk* Alfred
Palmer/Lethco *Creating Music at the Piano, Books 3-5* Alfred
Persichetti, Vincent *Little Piano Book* Elkan-Vogel
Rowley, Alec *Little Preludes and Fugues* Chester

SELECTED ENSEMBLE MUSIC FOR GROUP PIANO

Recommended by E. L. Lancaster*

EASY

Agay, Denes (arr.) *The First Duets* Yorktown
Alt, Hansi *The Cat Sat on a Chair of Gold* (multiple pianos) Presser
Barrett, Betsy (arr.) *Two Folk Tunes for Eight Hands at Two Pianos* Schmitt
Bastien, Jane S. *Christmas Carols for Multiple Pianos* GWM/Kjos
Bastien, Jane S. *Duets for Fun, Books 1 & 2* GWM/Kjos
George, Jon *Two at One Piano, Books 1 & 2* Summy-Birchard
Grove, Roger *Couples Only* (duets) Summy-Birchard
Maykapar, Samuel *First Steps, Op. 29* (duets) Leeds/MCA
Stecher, Horowitz, Gordon *The Pleasure of Your Company, Books 1 & 2* (duets) Schirmer

INTERMEDIATE

Beeson, Jack *Round and Round* (duets) Oxford
Bishop, Dorothy *A Folk Holiday* (duets) C. Fischer
Clark, Mary E. (arr.) *Folk 1* (multiple pianos) Lewis Music Co.
Clark, Mary E. (arr.) *Kum Ba Ya* and *Scarborough Fair* Lewis Music Co.
Dello Joio, Norman *Family Album* (duets) Marks
Dello Joio, Norman *Five Images* (duets) Marks
Diabelli, Anton *Pleasures of Youth, Op. 163* (duets) Kalmus/Belwin

***E. L. Lancaster is Coordinator of Group Piano at William Rainey Harper College, Palatine, Illinois. Used by permission.**

Dorolle, Annie (arr.) *Ancient Dances, Books 1 & 2* (duets) Boosey
Dring, Madeleine *Three for Two* (duets) Marks
Dungan, Olive *Dance of the Fleas* (duet) Presser
Eckard, Walter (ed.) *44 Original Piano Duets* Presser
Gillock, William *On a Paris Boulevard* (two pianos) Willis
Gillock, William *Sidewalk Cafe* (duet) Willis
Karp, David *Polly Wolly Swings* (duet) Lee Roberts/Schirmer
Lovell, Joan *Twos and Threes* (duets) Elkin & Co., Ltd.
Lucktenberg, George *Bach for Piano Ensemble* (duets or multiple pianos) Belwin-Mills
Lyke, James *Ensemble Music for Group Piano, Book 1* Stipes Publishing Co.
Metis, Frank *Easy Pop/Rock Sketches* (multiple painos) Piedmont/Marks
Metis, Frank *Easy Together* (multiple pianos) Piedmont/Marks
Metis, Frank *Good 'n' Groovey* (multiple pianos) Piedmont/Marks
Metis, Frank *Kids 'n' Keyboards* (multiple pianos) Piedmont/Marks
Metis, Frank *Pop/Rock Sketches* (duets) Piedmont/Marks
McClenny and Hinson *Duets of Early American Music* Belwin-Mills
Page, Cleveland *Ensemble Music for Group Piano* (multiple pianos) Canyon Press
Pozzoli, Ettore *Ten Little Characteristic Pieces* (duets) Ricordi
Rea, John *12 Single Pieces or 6 Polytonal Duets* Jaymar Music
Starer, Robert *Five Duets for Young Pianists* MCA
Stecher, Horowitz, Gordon *The Pleasure of Your Company, Books 3, 4, 5* (duets) Schirmer
Suchoff, Benjamin *Bartok for 2* (duets) Marks
Tschaikowsky, Peter *Russian Folk Songs* (duets) Peters
Vandall, Robert *Amazing Grace* (multiple pianos) GWM/Kjos
Vandall, Robert *Cindy* (multiple pianos) GWM/Kjos
Vandall, Robert *Five Will Get You Four* (multiple pianos) GWM/Kjos
Vandall, Robert *Greensleeves* (multiple pianos) GWM/Kjos
Vandall, Robert *Scarborough Fair* (multiple pianos) GWM/Kjos
Vandall, Robert *Shenandoah* (multiple pianos) GWM/Kjos
Vandall, Robert *Silent Night* (multiple pianos) GWM/Kjos
Vandall, Robert *Sleep, Baby, Sleep* (multiple pianos) GWM/Kjos
Vandall, Robert *Theme and Six Variations on "Skip to My Lou"* (multiple pianos) GWM/Kjos
Weybright, June *Braziliana* (two pianos) Belwin-Mills
Zeitlin and Goldberger (eds.) *The Duet Books 1, 2, 3* Consolidated
Zeitlin and Goldberger (eds.) *Easy Original Piano Duets* Consolidated

TEACHER-STUDENT DUET COLLECTIONS

Alt, Hansi *Second Scales* (available only in *The Early Virtuoso)* Summy-Birchard
Barens, H. *Melodious Exercises, Op. 62* Kalmus/Belwin
Diabelli, Anton *Melodious Exercises, Op. 149* Kalmus/Belwin
Lubin, Ernest (ed.) *Teacher and Student* Amsco Music Co.
Pozzoli, Ettore *Smiles of Childhood* Belwin-Mills
Ruthardt *Teacher and Pupil* Kalmus/Belwin
Sabol, Mary *Rock and Rhythm Studies for Class Piano* Canyon Press

MATERIALS LIST FROM THE "MUSIC TEACHERS' ASSOCIATION OF CALIFORNIA" *CERTIFICATE OF MERIT SYLLABUS*

Compiled by Clarice Lincoln and David KortKamp*

PREPARATORY LEVEL

Agay, D. *The Joy of First-Year Piano* Yorktown
- Pages 1-39 and:
- Monastery Echos
- Lullaby for a French Doll
- The Bagpipers
- Fiddler's Holiday
- Moonlit Pagoda
- In the Swing

Badings, H. [1]*Arcadia, Bk. 1* Schott
- Basso Ostinato
- Canon (No. 5)
- Canon (No. 8)
- Intermezzo

Bittner, F. *The Creatures Speak* C. Fischer

(Clark, F.) *Contemporary Literature, Bk. 1* Summy-Birchard
- Folk Dance – Tansman

Frost, B. *20th Century Piano Music, Bk. 1A* Belwin-Mills
- Comic
- A Duet
- Across the Meadow
- Stepping Stones

George, J. *Kaleidoscope Solos, Bk. 1* Alfred

George, J. *Musical Moments, Book 1* Schmitt Publications

George, J. *Playtime, Bks. A, B, C* Summy-Birchard

George, J. *Solos for Students, Set 1* Schmitt Publications

George, J. *Two at One Piano, Bks. 1 & 2* Summy-Birchard

Grove, R. *Keynotes* Schmitt Publications

Grove, R. *Ready for Reading – Bks. 1-3* Schmitt Publications

Karp, D. *Solo-ettes* Schmitt Publications

Last, J. *The First Concert* Oxford
- A Peal of Bells
- Creep Quietly
- A Plaintive Pipe Tune
- Swing Hill
- Hobbledehoy
- March of the Shadow Men
- The Pipers Pass By
- True Top Song
- Rock-a-Bye

Last, J. *Fun Fair* Oxford
- Roundabout
- Swing Boats
- Helter Skelter

Noona, W. *The Performer, Phase 2* Heritage
- Blue Monday
- Fierce Rider
- In a Mood
- Inside Out
- Little Jig
- Rocking
- Step Right Up

Olson, L. *Further Along* C. Fischer

Phillips, R. *Je Joue du Piano* M. Combre-Phillippo (Presser)
- Au Indien
- Chanson Triste
- Je Fais Danser les Amis
- Valse

(Sheftel) [2]*Sounds and Shapes, Bks. 1 & 2* International Music Library

Stecher/Horowitz/Gordon *Playing to Learn, Bks. 1 & 2* Schirmer

Waxman, D. *Pageants for Piano, Introductory Bk.* Galaxy

[1]Suitable for older beginners
[2]For teachers who use the International Library

***(Current Materials List (1976-). Used by permission of Clarice Lincoln and the "Music Teachers' Association of California," Gurtha Rodda, President.**

LEVEL 1

Badings, H. [3]*Arcadia, Bk. 1* Schott
- Ballo
- Rondo Finale

Balazs, A. *Fourteen Easy Pieces for Piano* Boosey & Hawkes
- Playing at Soldiers

(Burkhard) *Eight Little Piano Pieces* Barenreiter
- Zweifacher

Butcher, J. *Hana-matsuri (Japanese Flower Festival)* GWM/Kjos
- Happy Little Sumio
- Raining in Japan (at teacher's discretion)
- Fujiama
- Bird in a Tree
- Sayonara, Mitsu

(Clark, F.) *Contemporary Piano Literature, Bk. 1* Summy-Birchard
- Joy and Tears (Tcherepnin)
- March (Tcherepnin)
- Relays (Tcherepnin)
- Marching (Kabalevsky)
- Polka (Kabalevsky)
- Running Along (Kabalevsky)
- Song (Kabalevsky)
- A Little Song (Tansman)
- Bulldozer (Kraehenbuehl)
- Daydreaming (Kraehenbuehl)
- March of the Trolls (Kraehenbuehl)
- Sleeping Beauty (Kraehenbuehl)
- Whistlin' Tune (Kraehenbuehl)
- Dialogue No. 1 (Bartók)

(Clark, F.) *Piano Literature, Bk. 1* Summy-Birchard

(Emonts, F.) *Play with Five Tones* Schott
- Circus March
- Phrygian Melody

(Frost, B.) *20th Century Piano Music, Bk. 1A* Belwin-Mills
- A Little Scherzo (Kabalevsky)
- Comic Dance (McKay)
- Lights and Shadows (Fletcher)
- Serious Story (Kabalevsky)

George, J. *A Day in the Jungle* Summy-Birchard

George, J. *Kaleidoscope Solos, Bk. 2* Alfred

George, J. *Students' Choice, Set 1* Summy-Birchard

(Grey) *Very First Classics* Boosey & Hawkes
- Gavotte in G –Purcell

Grove, R. [3]*Images* Schroeder & Gunther
- Games
- Restless River
- The Happy Wanderer
- The Merry Mountaineer

Grove, R. *Ready for Reading – Book 3* (Preparatory or Level 1 at teacher's discretion) Schmitt Publications

Grove, R. *Sonatina in a* Schmitt Publications

Gurlitt, C. *First Steps of the Young Pianist, Op. 82* Schirmer
- Allegretto

Kabalevsky, D. *24 Pieces for Children, Op. 39* Alfred
- A Little Dance
- A Little Joke
- Funny Event
- Playing
- Song
- Song of Autumn

Kasemets, U. *10 Piano Pieces on Well-Known Songs, Vol. 2* BMI-Canada
- Au clair de la lune

Kraehenbuehl, D. *Calendar Scenes* Schmitt Publications

Kraehenbuehl, D. *Jazz and Blues, Bk. 1* Summy-Birchard

Last, J. *Black and White* Oxford

Last, J. *The First Concert* Oxford
- Drowsing in Sun
- River Song
- Merry Thought

Last, J. *Notes and Notions* Oxford

Last, J. *One a Penny, Two a Penny* Oxford
- We Shall Have Snow All Through the Night

McGraw, C. *Pet Silhouettes, Bk. 1* Presser
- The Little White Mouse

Nelhybel, V. *Kaleidoscope for Young Pianists, Vol. 1* General
- Nos. 41 & 42

[3]Especially appropriate for older beginners

Olson, L. *Near the Beginning* C. Fischer
Japanese Moon

Owens, T. *Confetti* Galaxy
Wondering
Trick or Treat

Pace, R. *Through the Keys* Lee Roberts/Schirmer
A Proclamation
Cowboy Song
Highland Fling
The Cuckoo and the Music Box

Phillips, R. *Je Joue du Piano* M. Combre-Phillippo (Presser)
En Bretagne

Rowley, A. *Sketches* (Available in *Five-Finger Music)* Summy-Birchard

Satie, E. [3]*Menus Propos Enfantins* Eschig
Waltz of the Chocolate Almond Bar
War Song of the Bean King
What the Tulip Princess Said

(Sheftel) [4]*Sounds and Shapes, Bk. 3* International Music Library

Tansman, A. *Happy Time* Leeds/MCA
Arabia
[3]Common Tones
[3]Both Ways
Obsession

Waxman, D. [5]*Pageants for Piano – First Folk Song* Galaxy

Waxman, D. *Pageants for Piano, First Year* Galaxy
Cuckoo on the Branch
Fanfare
Grand March
Peter's Song
Sunday on the Prairie
The Dance of the Spider and the Fly

Young, I. *Next Door Neighbors (*available in *Five-Finger Music)* Summy- Birchard
Swaying

(Zeitlin-Goldberger) *The Solo Book, Vol. 1* Consolidated
The Four Seasons (Turk)

LEVEL 2

(Anson, G.) *Survey of Piano Literature, Bk. 3, The Contemporary Scene* Elkan-Vogel
Little Song (Phillips)
March (Shostakovich)
Song for Spring (Bartók)

(Anthony, G.) *Moments at the Piano* Presser
Song from the Hills (Stevens)
Waltz for a Penny (Watson)

Bach *Notebook for Anna Magdalena Bach* Alfred
Musette in D, p. 10
Menuet in G, p. 20
Menuet in g, p. 22

Bacon, E. *Friends* Colombo
Grace

Balazs, A. *Fourteen Easy Pieces for Piano* Boosey & Hawkes
Questions and Replies
Dance in Front of a Mirror
March
Trudging
Game
Study

(Bastien, J. S.) *Piano Literature, Vol. 1* GWM/Kjos
A Winter Tale (Bartók)
Dance (Kabalevsky)
Ecossaise in G (Beethoven)
March (Shostakovich)
Minuet in F (Mozart)
Minuet in G (Bach)
Minuet in g (Bach)
Quick March (Kabalevsky)
Solders' March (Schumann)
The Lonely Traveler (Bartók)

Bauer, R. *Miniludes* Boston
Great Spirit
Little Miss Muffett
Serenades
The Cowboy's Lament

[3]Especially appropriate for older beginners
[4]For teachers who use the International Library
[5]Later compositions in the collection – Level 2

Brandse, W. *Descriptives* Schmitt Publications
Harlequinade

Carley, L. *Eleven Miniatures* Galaxy
Hoe Down

(Clark, F.) *Contemporary Piano Literature, Bk. 2* Summy-Birchard
Galloping (Kabalevsky)
A Gay Little Story (Kabalevsky)
Quick March (Kabalevsky)
Song of the Dark Woods (Siegmeister)
Street Games (Siegmeister)
Peasant Tune (Tansman)
Chromatics (Tansman)
Melody (Tcherepnin)
To and Fro (Tcherepnin)
Chimes (Tcherepnin)
Two Folk Songs (Bartók)
Children at Play (Bartók)
Folk Dance (Bartók)
March (Shostakovich)
Waltz (Shostakovich)

(Clark, F.) *Piano Literature, Bk. 2* Summy-Birchard

(Clark, M. E.) *Contempos in Crimson* Myklas Press

DeFossez, R. *Three Fragments* Schmitt Publications
Little Goat
Magic Bagpipe

Dello Joio, N. *Suite for the Young* Marks
Little Sister
Mountain Melody

Dittenhaver, S. *My Piano Sketchbook, Part 2* Presser

Frackenpohl, A. *Circus Parade* Oxford
Air for Southpaw

(Fried, I.) *American Music for Distinguished Composers* Presser
Bounce Dance (Corwell)
A Habanera (Fletcher)
Dance Pastorale (McKay)
Lullaby for a Panda (Fine)

(Frost, B.) *20th Century Piano Music, Bk. 1A* Belwin-Mills
Folk Song (Bartók)
Gaiety (Kabalevsky)
The Saddle Trail

George, J. *Solos for Students, Bk. 2* Schmitt Publications

George, J. *Students' Choice, Set 2* Summy-Birchard

Grove, R. *Adventures* Schmitt Publications

Grove, R. [6]*Images* Schroeder & Gunther
Puppet March
Secret Shadows

Gurlitt, C. *Album for the Young, Op. 140* Alfred
The Little Wanderer

Gurlitt, C. *Albumleaves, Op. 101* Schirmer
The Little Northerner

Handel, G. *Twenty Little Dances* Schott
Menuett in d

Kabalevsky, D. *24 Pieces for Children, Op. 39* Alfred
A Fable
Jumping
March
Scherzo

Kraehenbuehl, D. *Jazz and Blues, Bk. 2* Summy-Birchard

Lessard, J. *New Worlds for the Young Pianist, Vol. 1* General
No. 8 Prelude 3

Lombardo, R. *Contemporary Pieces for Children* Peer-Southern
Clowning

Mozart, W. *Mozart at 8* Presser
Country Dance, p. 10
Country Dance, p. 18

Mozart, W. *The Young Mozart* Schott
Allegro K. 3
Menuett in F

Owens, T. *Confetti* Galaxy
Pony Ride
Marching
A Bedtime Story
Dreams
A Song for Spring
The Wishing Well
A Mystery Story

[6] Especially appropriate for older beginners

Persichetti, V. *Little Piano Book* Elkan-Vogel
Fanfare

Pinto, O. *Children's Festival* Schirmer
Menuet

(Poldolsky, L.) *Guild Repertoire – Elem. C.* Summy-Birchard
A Gay Waltz (Gurlitt/Krentzlin)
A Little Story (Schmitt)
Minuet – Bartók
Whirligig – Lemont

Ponce, M. *Twenty Easy Pieces* Peer-Southern
No. 12 Mexican Folk Dance

Scher, W. *Patterns, Bk. 2* Summy-Birchard

(Sheftel) [7] *Sounds and Shapes, Bk. 4* International Library

Siegmeister, E. *American Kaleidoscope* Fox

Stravinsky, S. *Piano Music for Children* Peters
Carefree
Daddy is Home
For the Kid Next Door
Pagoda
Seesaw
Tag
Wandering

Takacs, J. *Fur Mich, Op. 76* Doblinger
Raindrops

Tansman, A. [8] *Happy Time, Bk. 1* Leeds/MCA
Popular Air
Sailors' Dance

Waxman, D. *First Folk Song Pageant* Galaxy
Winter is Coming
There Was a Little Shepherd
Pretty Little Susie
London Bridge
Robin
Two Folk Dances
Coventry Carol

Waxman, D. *Second Folk Song Pageant* Galaxy
The Postillion
Where O Where Has My Little Dog Gone
Cock A Doodle Doo
Scotland's Burning
Goodbye Old Paint
St. Paul's Temple
Hickory Dickory Dock

(Zeitlin/Goldberger) *Russian Music for the Young Pianist, Bk. 1* MCA
Waltz
Etude

(Zeitlin/Goldberger) *The Solo Book, Vol. 2* Consolidated
German Dance in A (Beethoven)

LEVEL 3

Agay, D. *15 Little Pieces On Five-Note Patterns* Boston

(Anson, G.) *Survey of Piano Literature, Bk. 1 Early Keyboard Music* Elkan-Vogel
A Toy (Anonymous)
Minuet (Handel)
Hornpipe (Barrett)
Sonata in C (D. Scarlatti)
Minuet in c (AMB Notebook)
German Dance in C (Haydn)
Rondo in F (Turk)

(Anson, G.) *Survey of Piano Literature, Bk. 3 The Contemporary Scene* Elkan-Vogel
Song for Spring (Bartók)
Playtime (Bartók)

Bach *Notebook for Anna Magdalena Bach* Alfred
Minuet in G, p. 8
Minuet in c, p. 30
Aria in d, p. 6
Polonaise in g, p. 7

Badings, H. *Arcadia, Bk. 2* Schott
Valzer
Elegia
Country Dance

Balazs, A. *Fourteen Easy Pieces for Piano* Boosey & Hawkes
A Little Invention
Arietta

[7] For teachers who use the International Library
[8] Especially appropriate for older beginners

(Bastien, J. S.) *Piano Literature, Vol. 2* GWM/Kjos
- Minuet in F (AMB Notebook)
- Polonaise in g (AMB Notebook, p. 8)
- The Clown (Kabalevsky)
- First Loss (Schumann)
- Playtime (Bartók)
- Hungarian Folk Song (Bartok)

Beethoven, L. *Six German Dances* Kalmus/Belwin
- No. 5 only

Benjamin, A. *Fantasies* Boosey & Hawkes
- [9] Soldiers in the Distance

Bennett, R. *Seven Days A Week* Belwin-Mills

Brandse, W. *Descriptives* Schmitt Publications
- Nocturne
- Valsette
- Romance
- Burlesca

(Clark, F.) *Contemporary Piano Literature, Bk. 3* Summy-Birchard

(Clark, F.) *Piano Literature, Bk. 3* Summy-Birchard

Clementi, M. *Six Sonatinas for Piano* Alfred
- Op. 36, No. 1

De Fossez, R. *Three Fragments* Schmitt Publications
- Bengelese Dancers

Dello Joio, N. *Suite for the Young* Marks
- Little Brother
- A Sad Tale

Diamond, D. *Eight Piano Pieces* Schirmer
- Pease Porridge Hot
- Rock-A-Bye-Baby
- Jack-a-Dandy
- Little Jumping Joan

Fletcher, S. *Street Scenes* Summy-Birchard

Frackenpohl, A. *Circus Parade* Oxford
- Ebony Waltz
- Lullaby
- Jig
- Follow the Leader
- Lydian Tune
- Every Step a Whole

(Frost, B.) *20th Century Piano Music, Bk. 2A* J. Fischer/Belwin
- Windmill (Storr)
- The Cuckoo (Gnessina)
- A Gay Day (Frost)
- Bagatelle (Maykapar)

(Frost, B.) *20th Century Piano Music, Bk. 2B* J. Fischer/Belwin
- A Folk Dance (Bartók)
- Mother's Caress (Gretchaninoff)
- A Happy Fairy Tale (Shostakovich)
- In the Forest (Rebikov)
- Musing (Bartók)

(Frost, B.) *20th Century Piano Music, Bk. 3A* J. Fischer/Belwin
- Cradle Song (Gnessina)
- A Sad Fairy Tale (Shostakovich)
- The Lute Player (Mills)

George, J. *A Day in the Forest* Summy-Birchard

George, J. *Kaleidoscope Solos, Bk. 5* Alfred

George, J. *Student's Choice, Set 3* (available in *Supplementary Solos–Levels 3-4)* Summy-Birchard

Gretchaninoff, A. *Children's Album, Op. 98* MCA
- A Little Fairy Tale
- In the Camp of the Toy Soldier
- Riding on the Stick
- The Toy Soldiers Are Marching
- In the Little Meadow
- A Frightful Story
- Etude
- I Am Big Already

Grove, R. *Contrasts, Set One* Schmitt Publications

Gurlitt, C. *Album for the Young, Op. 140* Alfred
- Morning Song
- In the Garden
- The Little Norwegian
- Scherzo

Haydn, J. *Memories of Old Vienna* Heritage Music
- My Clavichord
- The Palace Guard
- Dance of the Queen's Ladies
- The Journey Home

Haydn, J. *Ten German Dances* Kalmus/Belwin
- No. 4

Holoman, J. *Three Echoes* Presser
- Like a Polish Folk Song
- Almost Classical

[9] For older students

Kabalevsky, D. *24 Pieces for Children, Op. 39* Alfred
- Galop
- Waltz
- A Sad Story
- The Clown
- Slow Waltz

Kraehenbuehl, D. *Jazz and Blues, Bk. 3* (available in *Supplementary Solos – Levels 3-4)* Summy-Birchard

(Lambert, C.) *Classics, Bk. 2* Heritage Music
- German Dance (Haydn)
- Minuetto (Scarlatti)
- Minuet (Bach)
- Minuet (Mozart)

LaMontaine, J. *Copycats, Op. 26* (available in *Five-Finger Music)* Summy-Birchard
- Sing No More It's Time To Dance

Last, J. *Let's Go To the Theater* Oxford

Majorelle, P. *6 Petite Pieces* Presser
- Prelude
- Gavotte
- Valse
- Petit Conte
- Reverie

Mozart, L. *Notebook for Wolfgang* Schott
- Menuet de Sigr. Bach, p. 3
- Menuet in C, p. 5
- Bourree in e, p. 10

Mozart, W. *Mozart at 8* Presser
- Andante, p. 5
- Country Dance, p. 8
- Minuet, p. 11

Owens, T. *Confetti* Galaxy
- Cloudy Skies
- Autumn
- The Clock Shop
- Halloween

(Palmer, W.) *The First Sonatina Book* Alfred
- Sonatina in C (Latour)
- Sonatina in F (Wanhal)

Phillips, R. *Je Joue du Piano* M. Combre-Phillippo (Presser)
- Bibelots
- Fanfare

Pinto, O. *Children's Festival* Schirmer
- Prelude

(Podolsky, L.) *Guild Repertoire, Elem. D* Summy-Birchard
- Daring Horseman (Gurlitt)
- Gavotte (Beach)
- Sailor's Song (Liszt/Coburn)
- Kitten (Michelet)

Price, B. *On The Go* Oxford

Rybicki, F. *Young Modernest* PWM (Boosey & Hawkes)

Schumann, R. *Album for the Young* Alfred
- First Loss
- The Wild Horseman

Siegmeister, E. *American Kaleidoscope* Fox
- The Toy Railroad
- Feeling Easy
- Boogie Rhythm
- Bicycle Wheels

Stevens, E. *Six Modal Miniatures for Piano* Ditson

Taycevic, M. *Lieder von der Mur-Insel (Songs from Murinsel)* Henle
- No. 1 – No. 10

Waxman, D. *Second Folk Song Pageant* Galaxy
- Bosa
- Winter Goodbye
- Skip to My Lou
- Oh, Dear
- Oranges and Lemons
- Three Princesses
- Bohemian Song
- Soup in the Kettle

Waxman, D. *Second Year Pageants* Galaxy
- Mechanical Man
- Bell Song
- The Little Witch
- The Mill Wheel
- Two Flutes
- Two Bassoons
- Indian Fires
- On the Way Home
- Kim's Lullaby
- Kim Awake
- Finale

LEVEL 4

(Anson, G.) *Survey of Piano Literature, Bk. 3 The Contemporary Scene* Elkan-Vogel
- Having Fun

Bach *Notebook for Anna Magdalena Bach* Alfred
- Polonaise in g, p. 38
- Menuet in G, p. 16
- Menuet in d, p. 26
- March in G, p. 24

Bach (Etts) *Beginning to Play Bach* Schroeder & Gunther
- Minuet, p. 21
- March, p. 22

Balazs, A. *Fourteen Easy Pieces* Boosey & Hawkes
- Cantilena
- Leaps

(Bastien, J. S.) *Piano Literature, Vol. 2* GWM/Kjos
- Polonaise in g (Bach)
- Sonatina in F (Beethoven)
- Hunting Song (Schumann)
- Variations on a Russian Folk Song (Kabalevsky)
- Playing Soldiers (Rebikoff)

Brandse, W. *Descriptives* Schmitt Publications
- Berceuse

Beethoven, L. *Allemandes, Waltzes and Songs for Piano* Boston
- Allemandes: Nos. 2, 3, 5
- Scottish Air

Beethoven, L. *Six German Dances* Kalmus/Belwin
- Nos. 1, 2, 4, 6

Beethoven, L. (Etts) *Beginning to Play Beethoven* Schroeder & Gunther
- German Dance
- Three Country Dances

Benjamin, A. *Fantasies* Boosey & Hawkes
- Silent and soft and slow descends the snow

Bennett, R. *Diversions* Universal
- Nos. 1, 2, 4, 6

Bishop, D. *Outdoor Suite* C. Fischer

Boldon, B. *Musically Speaking* Leeds/MCA
- Call From the Hills
- Spring Morning
- Wild Geese Calling

(Clark, F.) *Piano Literature, Bk. 4A* Summy-Birchard

Clementi, M. *Six Sonatinas for Piano* Alfred
- Op. 36, No. 2

Dello Joio, N. *Suite for the Young* Marks
- Invention
- A Sad Tale
- Small Fry

Diamond, D. *Alone at the Piano* Peer-Southern
- all Level 4

(Emonts, F.) *Easy Baroque Piano Music* Schott
- Menuet (Dandrieu)
- Gavotte en Rondeau (Dandrieu)
- Menuett (Handel)
- Sarabande (Corelli)
- Gigue (Bach)
- Gigue (Anonymous)
- Gigue (L. Mozart)
- Quadrille (Anonymous)
- Bourree (Bach)
- Ungarischer Marsch (Anonymous)

Fennimore, J. *Bits and Pieces* Marks
- Canon and Cannon
- Bit of Blues
- Dance of the Dinosaurs

Finney, R. *24 Piano Inventions* Peters
- Crossing Over
- Searching
- Almost Opposite
- Lonesome Song
- Dancing
- Walking

Floyd, C. *Episodes, Vol. 1* Boosey & Hawkes
- First Lyric Piece
- Scherzino
- Ancient Air
- Chorale
- Ballad
- Burletta

Frank, C. *Short Piano Pieces* Peters
Song of the Creuse
Christmas Carol from Anjou

(Frey, M.) *The New Sonatina Book, Bk. 1* Schott
Sonatina (Haslinger)

(Frost, B.) *20th Century Piano Music, Bk. 2A* J. Fischer/Belwin
The Russian Doll (Rebikov)
Grecian Holiday (Frost)
A Waltz in G (Kabalevsky)

Gillock, W. *Accent on Rhythm & Style* Willis

Grove, R. *Contrasts, Set Two* Schmitt Publications

Holoman, J. *Three Echoes* Presser
Somewhat Jazzy

Hovhaness, A. *Mountain Idylls* Associated Music

(Irmer, D.) *Old Masters-Miniatures for Piano* Schirmer
Air (Purcell)
The Well-Mannered Cuckoos (Couperin)
Andante (Bach)
Sad (Telemann)
Impertinence (Handel)
Menuett (Scarlatti)
Allegro (Scarlatti)
Allegretto (Bach)
Gypsy Music (Haydn)
Sicilienne (Schumann)
Melody (Schumann)

Joachim, O. *12 Tone Pieces for Children* BMI Canada

Kabalevsky, D. *5 Sets of Variations, Op. 51* MCA
5 Happy Var. on a Russian Folk Song
Gray Day Var. on a Slovakian Folk Song
7 Good Humored Var. on a Ukranian Folk Song

Kabalevsky, D. *24 Little Pieces, Op. 39* Leeds/MCA
Country Dance
Prelude
Improvisation
Carefree

Koch, F. *Five Memories* C. Fischer

Kraehenbuehl, D. *Jazz and Blues, Bk. 4* (available in *Supplementary Solos – Levels 3-4)* Summy-Birchard

(Lambert, C.) *Recital Classics, Bk. 2* Heritage
Pastorale
The Witch in the Forest (Rebikov)
The Fall of the Leafe (Pierson)
Hunting Jig (Duncombe)
Allegro (Handel)

(Lambert, C.) *Sonatinas, Bk. 1* Heritage
Sonatine
Sonatina in F

Last, J. *The Big Top* Oxford

Mailman, M. *Martha's Vineyard* Presser
Lazy Circles
Short Parade
Walk on the Beach
Inside and Out
Sand Dance

(Motchane, M.) *An Introduction to Pianistic Styles* Bourne
Preludium (Kuhnau)
Minuetto (Scarlatti)
Pavana (Scarlatti)
Sonata (Scarlatti)
Minuet in d (Bach)
Polonaise (Bach)
Minuet in G (Bach)
Menuet (Daquin)
Minuetto (Kirnberger)
Menuet (Kirnberger)
Minuetto (Haydn)
Arietta (Mozart)
Minuet in Canon (Mozart)
Time Passes with Merry Play (Turk)
Tinkering is Part of Busywork (Turk)
The Silly Grasshoppers (Turk)
Butterfingers (Turk)
Melody (Schumann)
Sicilian (Schumann)

Mozart, L. *Notebook for Wolfgang* Schott
Polonaise
Menuet in D, p. 7
Waldhorn (Stuck)
Entree
Schwaben (Tanz)

Mozart, W. *The Young Mozart* Schott
Kontretanz
Menuett

Mozart, W. (Etts) *Beginning to Play Mozart* Schroeder & Gunther
Minuet
Little Song
Allego
Air
Minuet in F
Minuet in C
Minuet in Eb
Country Dance

Muczynski, R. *Fables – Nine Pieces for the Young* Schirmer
Nos. 1, 2, 3, 4, 5, 7, 9

Palfalvi, J. *Four Pieces for Piano* Editio Musica/Boosey & Hawkes
Air

(Palmer, W.) *The First Sonatina Book* Alfred
Sonatina in C (Haslinger)
Sonatina in D (Pleyel)

(Palmer, W.) *Kullak – Album for the Young, Op. 62* Alfred
A Little Story
Sunday Morning
Cradle Song

Perry, N. *Through the Kaleidoscope* Oxford
Elephant Tune
Lullaby
Donkey
Sicilian Dance

Rowley, A. *Aquarelles* Boosey & Hawkes
Ballerina
Cuckoo Fughetta

(Saminsky, Lazare & Freed) *Masters of our Day* C. Fischer
Touches Noires (Milhaud)
Touches Blanches (Milhaud)
Fiddlin' Joe (Moore)
Enchantment (Hanson)
The Irishman Dances (Cowell)

Schloss, J. *23 Pieces for Children in 12 Tone Style* Peer-Southern
Follow the Leader
A Picture
Let's Go
Going Places
Chimes
Feeling Blue
Determination

Schubert, F. *Waltzes* J. Fischer/Belwin
No. 5

Schumann, R. *Album for the Young* Alfred
Melodie
Humming Song
A Little Piece
Sicilienne
The Merry Farmer

(Shaw, B.) *Early Italian Piano Music of the 17th Century* J. Fischer/Belwin
Minuetto (Scarlatti)
Air (Scarlatti)

Shostakovich, D. *Dances of the Dolls* MCA
Hurdy-Gurdy

Siegmeister, E. *The Children's Day for Piano* Leeds/MCA
Sunny Morning
Bedtime Story

Tajcevic, M. *Lieder von der Mur-Insel (Songs from Murinsel)* Henle
Nos. 11, 12, 13

Tansman, A. *Pour les Enfants, Bk. 1* Associated
Old Song
The Doll
The Bouncing Ball
The Dancing Bear
The Fireman
Dream
Conclusion
Valse des Marionnettes

Tansman, A. *Pour les Enfants, Bk. 2* Associated
The Young Swing Pianist
The Dancing Lesson
Arabian Nights

Tchaikovsky, P. *Album for the Young, Op. 39* Schirmer
Morning Prayer
Waltz
The New Doll
Old French Song

Toch, E. *Reflections* Belwin-Mills

(unedited) *Spanish Piano Music for the Young Musician* Boosey & Hawkes
Pavana (Milan)

Waxman, D. *Second Folk Song Pageants* Galaxy
- I Saw Three Ships
- Did You Ever See a Lassie
- Sleep, Little One, Sleep
- The Weasel in the Woods
- The Curious Man
- Bibabutzeman
- Go Round the Village
- Jim Crack Corn
- Three Folk Dances
- Scottish Bag-Pipe March
- Spanish Popular Dance – I Come from Catalona

Wolford, D. *Suite a la Mode* Boosey & Hawkes
- Escapade
- Sadness
- Witches Hoedown
- Falling Snowflakes
- Madame Chatterbox
- March
- To and Fro
- Fanfare
- Shindig

LEVEL 5

Bach, C. P. E. *Short and Easy Piano Pieces* Universal
- No. 1 – Allegro in C
- No. 2 – Arioso in C
- No. 3 – Fantasia in d
- No. 4a – Minuetto I
- No. 4b – Minuetto II
- No. 15a
- No. 15b

Bach, J. S. *Notebook for Anna Magdalena Bach* Alfred
- Menuet in Bb, p. 14
- March in Eb, p. 28

Bach, J. S. *Short Preludes & Fugues* Henle (No. 106)
- Little Preludes for W. F. Bach
  - No. 1 in C – S. V. 924
  - No. 2 in d – S. V. 926
- Six Little Preludes
  - No. 1 in C – S. V. 939

Balazs, A. *Fourteen Easy Pieces* Boosey & Hawkes
- A Sort of Rondo
- Ostinato
- Intermezzo

Bartók, B. *For Children, Vol. 2* Boosey & Hawkes
- Farewell
- Ballad

Bartók, B. *Ten Easy Pieces for Piano* Boosey & Hawkes
- Dedication
- Hungarian Folk Song

Beethoven, L. *Ecossaises and German Dances* Peters
- German Dances, Nos. 1-11

Beethoven, L. *An Introduction to His Piano Works* Alfred
- Variations on a Swiss Song

Benjamin, A. *Fantasies II* Boosey & Hawkes
- A Gay Study

Bennett, R. *Diversions* Universal
- Nos. 3, 5, 7

Berkowitz, S. *12 Easy Blues* Boston

Block, E. *Enfantines* C. Fischer

Boldon, B. *Musically Speaking* Leeds/MCA
- Favourite Pony
- Twilight
- Finger Ballet
- One Summer Day
- The Lonely Island

Casella, A. *Children's Pieces* Universal
- Bolero
- Siciliana
- Minuetto
- Berceuse

(Clark, F.) *Contemporary Literature, Bk. 5* Summy-Birchard

(Clark, F.) *Piano Literature, Bks. 5A-6A* Summy-Birchard
- Prelude in C (Bach)
- Sonatina (Handel)
- Minuet (Handel)
- Sonata in d (Scarlatti)
- Sonata in C (Scarlatti)
- Allegro (C. P. E. Bach)
- Fantasia (C. P. E. Bach)
- Minuet in C (Haydn)

(Clark, F.) *Piano Literature, Bk. 5B* Summy-Birchard

Clementi, M. *Six Sonatinas for Piano* Alfred
- Op. 36, No. 3

Corelli, A. *24 Pieces for the Piano, Vol. 1* Kalmus/Belwin
Sarabande in d - No. 5

Creston, P. *Five Little Dances* Schirmer
Languid Dance
Toy Dance
Pastoral Dance (hand permitting)

Dello Joio, N. *Lyric Pieces for the Young* Marks
Boat Song
Prayer of the Matador
The Village Church

(Emonts, F.) *Easy Baroque Piano Music (5096A)* Schott
Praludium (Kuhnau)
Air und Double (Handel)
Sarabande (Graupner)
Larghetto (Scarlatti)
Sarabande (Bach)

Faith, R. *Finger Paintings* Shawnee
Country Scene
Reflections in a Still Pool
Medieval Gardens
Moonless Night
Celebration
March
In the Meadow
Pipes and Shawms
Ice Palace
End of the Day (also acceptable on Level IV)

Faith, R. *Three Sonatinas* Schirmer

(Farmer, G.) *Airs and Dances* Boosey & Hawkes
Nos. 4, 6, 8, 11, 12, 15, 16, 17

Finney, R. *24 Inventions* Peters
Uncertainty
March
Dawn

Gillock, W. *Three Jazz Preludes* Willis
Blues Prelude

Gretchaninoff, A. *Suite Miniature* Marks
Little Prelude
A New Friendship
Small Complaint
Scherzando
Souvenir

Grieg, E. *Lyrical Pieces, Op. 12* Schirmer
Waltz
Watchman's Song

Handel, G. *A Handel Album* Universal
Nos. 6, 7, 8, 9, 11, 13, 14

Haydn, J. *Six Sonatinas* Alfred
Sonatina in C – H.XVI No. 7

Haydn, J. *12 Short Piano Pieces* Alfred
Nos. 2, 4, 5, 6, 9, 10

Hayward, L. *Three Short Piano Pieces* Presser
A Bossa Nova
A Blues
A Jazz Waltz

Kabalevsky, D. *Ten Children's Pieces* MCA
Cradle Song
The Horseman

Kay, U. *Ten Short Essays* Leeds/MCA
So Gay
Tender Thought
Make Believe
March Song

Kraehenbuehl, D. *Jazz & Blues, Bks, 5 & 6* Summy-Birchard
Rollin' Along
Holiday Bells
Fade Out Boogie
Fire and Ice
Dark Street
Blues Largo
Relaxin'
Weeping Willow
Got the Jitters

Last, J. *Time Twisters* Oxford

Longmire, J. *Vikings of the Sunrise* Galaxy

MacDowell, G. (Anson) *Music by MacDowell* Schroeder & Gunther
To a Wild Rose

Mechem, K. *Whims – 15 Easy Vignettes for Piano* E. C. Schirmer

Mozart, W. *Salzburger Tanzbuchlein* Verlag/Peters
March in D
Menuetto in A, p. 5
Menuetto in D, p. 9
Gavotte Gracieuse, p. 12
Contretanz, p. 13
Menuetto in C, p. 20
Menuetto in Bb, p. 19
Menuetto in D, p. 21

Mozart. W. (Etts) *Beginning to Play Mozart* Schroeder & Gunther
Rondo in F, p. 20
Rondo in D, p. 26
Polonaise, p. 28
Andantino, p. 29
Rondo in C, p. 30

Muczynski, R. *Fables – Nine Pieces for the Young* Schirmer
Nos. 3, 9

Palfalvi, J. *Four Pieces for Piano* Editio Musica/Boosey & Hawkes
Lullaby
March

Peeters, F. *10 Bagatelles* Peters
Menuet
Preghiera
Lied
Air

Perry, N. *Through the Kaleidoscope* Oxford
Russian Serenade
March of the Tin Soldiers

Persichetti, V. *Little Piano Book* Elkan-Vogel
Dialogue
Humoreske
Fanfare
Canon
Epilogue

Persichetti, V. *Piano Sonatinas* Elkan-Vogel
Nos. 4, 5, 6

Pinto, O. *Children's Festival* Schirmer
Little March
Serenade

Prokofieff, S. *Music for Children, Op. 65* MCA
Morning
Promenade
Parade of the Grasshoppers
Waltz

Rea, J. *What You Will* Jaymar (Oxford)

(Saminsky, Lazare & Freed) *Masters of Our Day* C. Fischer
Careful Etta (Moore)
Dance of the Warriors (Hanson)
Grievin' Annie (Moore)
The Bell (Hanson)

Scarlatti, D. *12 Easy Sonatas (Mirovitch)* Marks
Nos. 1, 2, 8, 10

Schubert, F. *Classics of Piano Music* Peters/Hinrichsen
Minuet in F, p. 1
Ecossaises, p. 2
Waltzes – Op. 9

Schumann, R. *Album For the Young, Op. 68* Alfred
Chorale
Little Study
The Reaper's Song
Rustic Song

(Shaw, B.) *Early Italian Piano Music of the 17th Century, Vol. 1* J. Fischer/ Belwin
Air (Pasquini)
Gavotte (Corelli)
Corrente (Frescobaldi)
Sarabande (Zipoli)
Allegretto (Grieco)

Shostakovich, D. *Dances of the Dolls* MCA
Romance
Petite Ballerina
Dance

Siegmeister, E. *The Children's Day* Leeds/MCA
Skipping Rope
On a Golden Afternoon

Tansman, A. *Happy Time, Bk. 3* Leeds/MCA
A la Schumann
Organ
Little Game
Iberian Mood
In Memory of George Gershwin "1925"

Tansman, A. *Pour Les Enfants – Second Set* Associated
The Arithmetic Lesson
Meditation
Solemn Occasion
The Spinning Top
Parade

Tansman, A. *Pour Les Enfants – Third Set* Associated
- Petite Reverie
- Tin Soldiers
- The Old Beggar
- The Music Box

Telemann, G. *Klavierbuchlein* Schott
- Bouree in F, p. 5
- Bouree in A, p. 13
- Moderato in C, p. 21

Toch, E. *Reflections – Op. 86* Belwin-Mills
- Nos. 3, 4, 5

(unedited) *Spanish Piano Music for the Young Musician* Boosey & Hawkes
- Quatro diferencias (Narvaez)

Wolford, D. *Suite a la Mode* Boosey & Hawkes
- Night Shadows
- Lullaby
- Musette
- Quiet Lagoon

LEVEL 6

(Agay, D.) *Anthology of Piano Literature, Vol. 4* Yorktown
- Rondo in a, Op. 60, No. 4 (Kabalevsky)
- March, Op. 65 No. 10 (Prokofieff)
- Moonlight Meadows, Op. 65 No. 12 (Prokofieff)
- Shepherd Playing His Pipe (Rebikoff)
- Two Short Piano Pieces, Op. 19 No. 2 & 4 (Schoenberg)
- Shades of Blue (Starer)
- Bright Orange (Starer)

Bach, C. P. E. *Short Easy Piano Pieces* Universal
- No. 6 in D
- No. 11 in d
- No. 12 in F
- No. 13 in g
- No. 21 in C

Bach, J. S. *18 Short Preludes* Alfred
- 12 Short Preludes
  - No. 3 in c
  - No. 5 in d
  - No. 7 in e
  - No. 8 in F
  - No. 12 in a
- 6 Short Preludes
  - No. 1 in C
  - No. 2 in c
  - No. 3 in d
  - No. 4 in D
  - No. 6 in e

Bach, J. S. *Notebook for Anna Magdalena Bach* Alfred
- Polonaise in g, p. 38
- Polonaise in g, p. 40

Bach, J. S. *Short Preludes and Fugues* Henle (Vol. 106)
- Little Preludes for W. F. Bach
  - No. 3 in F – S. V. 927
- Six Little Preludes
  - No. 1 in C – S. V. 933
  - No. 2 in c – S. V. 934
  - No. 3 in d – S. V. 935
  - No. 4 in D – S. V. 936
  - No. 6 in e – S. V. 938
- Six Little Preludes
  - No. 2 in d – S. V. 940
  - No. 3 in e – S. V. 941
  - No. 4 in a – S. V. 942
  - No. 6 in C – S. V. 999

Bartok, B. *For Children, Vol. 2* Boosey & Hawkes
- Pleasantry, No. 21
- Revelry, No. 22
- Pleasantry II, No. 27
- Song, No. 39

Bartok, B. *Ten Easy Pieces* Boosey & Hawkes
- Evening in the Country
- Bear Dance

(Bastien, J. W.) *Piano Literature, Vol. 3* GWM/Kjos
- Solfeggieto (C. P. E. Bach)
- Fur Elise (Beethoven)
- Minuet in G (Beethoven)
- Sonatina, Op. 55 No. 3 (Khulau)
- Polka (Tchaikovsky)
- Sailor's Song (Grieg)
- Elfin Dance (Grieg)

Bauer, R. *Sonatina in G* C. Fischer

Beethoven, L. *Bagatelles* Henle
- Op. 33, No. 6
- Op. 119, No. 1
- Op. 119, No. 2
- Op. 119, No. 3
- Op. 119, No. 4

Beethoven, L. *An Introduction to His Piano Works* Alfred
Joyful – Sorrowful
Menuet in C
Menuet in G
Menuet in D
Bagatelle – Op. 119, No. 1
Bagatelle – Op. 119, No. 3
Fur Elise
Six Ecossaises
Bagatelle – Op. 119, No. 2
Sonata in G – Op. 49, No. 2

Beethoven, L. *Six Ecossaises and German Dances* Peters
Six Ecossaises

Beethoven, L. *Six Menuetts* Schott (0277)

Beethoven, L. *Two Little Sonatas* Henle (56)
Op. 49, No. 2 in G

Benjamin, A. *Fantasies, Bk. 2* Boosey & Hawkes
Waltz

Bentzon, N. *7 Small Pieces, Op. 3* (For Evaluation student must play at least 3) Wilhelm Hansen

Berkowitz, S. *Four Blues for Lefty* Presser

Bjercke, O. *Romeriks Svite* Norsk Musikksamling (C. F. Peters)
Polonese
Vals
Fandango

Boldon, B. *Musically Speaking* Leeds/MCA
Musically Speaking
A Tree's Winter Story
Celebration Dance

Bull, C. *Music for Haiku* C. Fischer

Casella, A. *Children's Pieces* Universal
Preludio
Valse Diatonique
Giga
Minuetto
Galop Final

Cherny, B. *Pieces for Young Pianists* Jaymar

Chopin, F. *An Introduction to His Piano Works* Alfred
Waltz in a
Album Leaf
Prelude in A, Op. 28, No. 7
Mazurka in g, Op. 67, No. 2
Mazurka in a, Op. 67, No. 4
Mazurka in F, Op. 68, No. 3

(Clark, F.) *Contemporary Piano Literature, Bk. 6* Summy-Birchard

(Clark, F.) *Piano Literature, Bk. 6B* Summy-Birchard

Clementi, M. *Sonatinas* Schirmer
Op. 36, Nos. 4, 5, 6

Corelli, A. *24 Pieces for the Piano, Vol. 1* Kalmus/Belwin
No. 1–Sarabande in e
No. 2–Adagio
No. 3–Corrente in F
No. 6–Sarabande in Bb
No. 8–Adagio in b
No. 9–Largo in D
No. 10–Gavotte in E

Creston, P. *Five Little Dances* Schirmer
Rustic Dance
Festive Dance

(Emonts, F.) *Easy Baroque Music* Schott (5096A)
Rigaudon (Bohm)
Bourree (Graupner)
Air (Purcell)

Faith, R. *Finger Paintings* Shawnee
Long Ago
Spinning

(Farmer, G.) *Airs and Dances* Boosey & Hawkes
Nos. 19, 20

Finney, R. *24 Inventions* Peters
Chatter
Holiday
Playing Ball

(Geiringer, K.) *The Bach Family* Universal
Allegretto (J. C. F. Bach), p. 35
Waltzes (W. F. E. Bach), p. 47
(All 3 for Evaluation)

Gillock, W. *Sonatine in C* Willis

Gillock, W. *Three Jazz Preludes* Willis
- No. 1
- No. 3

Gretchaninoff, A. *Suite Miniature, Op. 202* Marks

Grieg, E. *Lyrical Pieces, Op. 12* Schirmer
- Elfentanz (Elfin Dance)
- Folk Song
- Norwegian Melody
- Albumblatt

Griffis, E. *Letters From a Maine Farm* C. Fischer
- Homage to MacDowell
- A Forgotten Poem

Handel, G. *A Handel Album* Universal
- No. 10 Gavotte
- No. 15 Courante
- No. 16 Gigue

Haydn, F. J. *Sonatinas* Alfred
- H. XVI No. 8 in G
- H. XVI No. 9 in F
- H. XVI No. 11 in G

Haydn, F. J. *12 Short Pieces* Alfred
- Nos. 1, 3

Kabalevsky, D. *Rondos, Op. 60* Leeds/MCA
- No. 2 in D
- No. 3 in g
- No. 4 in a

Kabalevsky, D. *Ten Children's Pieces* MCA
- Snow Flurries
- Quick March
- Fairy Tale
- A Quaint One

Kabalevsky, D. *Variations on an American Folk Song* MCA

Kabalevsky, D. *Variations, Op. 40, No. 1 in D* MCA

Kraehenbuehl, D. *Jazz and Blues, Bks, 5 & 6* Summy-Birchard
- Sittin' Pretty
- Tango Grande
- Doghouse Boogie
- Weeping Willow
- Got the Jitters

MacDowell, E. (Anson) *Music by MacDowell* Schroeder & Gunther
- A Tin Soldier's Love

Maykapar, S. *18 Selected Pieces* MCA
- In the Garden
- Student Piece
- Waltz
- Dewdrops
- The Little Music Box
- The Little Shepherd
- Passing Fancy
- The Moth
- The Blacksmith
- Echo in the Mountain
- Ballad
- Little Story

Menotti, G. *Poemetti* F. Colombo
- Lullaby
- The Bagpipers

Mozart, W. *Little Known Pieces* Kalmus/Belwin
- Marche funebre
- Menuett in Bb
- Courante

Mozart, W. *Salzburger Tanzbuchlein* Verlag/Peters
- Gavotte
- Pantomime

Muczynski, R. *Fables – Nine Pieces for the Young* Schirmer
- Nos. 6, 8

Palflavi, J. *Four Pieces for Piano* Editio Musica/Boosey & Hawkes
- Waltz

Peeters, F. *10 Bagatelles* Peters
- Intrata
- Tarantella
- Valse lente
- Invention
- Tango
- Rondo

Prokofieff, S. *Music for Children, Op. 65* MCA
- Tarantella
- Regrets
- Rain and the Rainbow
- March
- Evening
- Moonlit Meadows

Rameau, J. *The Graded Rameau* Belwin-Mills
- Menuet I & II
- Rigaudon I

Rieti, V. *5 Pieces for Young Pianists* General Music
- Prelude, p. 4
- Valsette, p. 6

(Saminsky, Lazare & Freed) *Masters of our Day* C. Fischer
- A Day Dream (Thompson)
- Song after Sundown (Thompson)
- Little Prelude (Thompson)
- The Harper Minstrel Sings (Cowell)
- March (Sessions)

Scarlatti, D. *12 Easy Scarlatti Sonatas* Belwin
- No. 5 in Bb – L. 97
- No. 6 in d – L. 58

Schubert, F. *Classics of Piano Music – Schubert* Peters
- Two Country Dances, No. 6

Schubert, F. *8 Ecossaises* Henle (529)

Schubert, F. *Waltzes – Set 1* J. Fischer/Belwin (5270)

Schumann, R. *Album for the Young* Alfred
- Folk Song, No. 9
- Little Romance, No. 19
- Untitled, No. 21
- Echoes from the Theater, No. 25
- Mignon, No. 35
- Northern Song, No. 40

Shostakovich, D. *Dances of the Dolls* MCA
- Lyrical Waltz
- Gavotte
- Polka

Siegmeister, E. *The Children's Day* Leeds/MCA
- Playing Clown
- Catching Butterflies

Starer, R. *Sketches in Color, Set 1* MCA
- Purple
- Shades of Blue
- Black and White
- Bright Orange
- Grey
- Pink

Stoker, R. *From An Artist's Sketchbook* Peters

Tansman, A. *Happy Time, Bk. 3* Leeds/MCA
- Night Mood
- Arioso
- Finale

Tansman, A. *Pour Les Enfants, 3rd Set* Associated
- Awakening
- The Warbler
- Rest
- Coquette
- Ping Pong

Taylor, C. *Whimsies, 2nd Set* Boosey & Hawkes
- Nos. 1, 2, 3

Telemann, G. *Klavierbuchlein* Schott (4230)
- Tansfolge III
- Tansfolge IV

Toch, E. *Reflections, Op. 86* Belwin-Mills
- Nos. 1, 2

(unedited) *Spanish Music for the Young Musician* Boosey & Hawkes
- Fabordon y glosas (Cabezon)
- Sonata (Rodriguez)
- Sonata (Casanovas)
- Rondo (Rodriguez)

(unedited) *U. S. A. Vol. 1* Leeds/MCA
- Outdoor Song (McKay)

LEVEL 7

(Agay, D.) *Anthology of Piano Music, Vol. 4* Yorktown
- Prelude, Op. 13 No. 3 (Scriabin)
- Prelude, Op. 11 No. 9 (Scriabin)

Bach, C. P. E. *Short and Easy Piano Pieces* Universal
- No. 8 in A
- No. 9 in g
- No. 10 in Bb
- No. 14 in c
- No. 19 in E

Bach, C. P. E. *Sonatas and Pieces* Peters (4188)
No. 5 in C

Bach, J. S. *18 Short Preludes* Alfred
12 Short Preludes
No. 4 in D, p. 12
No. 6 in d, p. 16
No. 11 in g, p. 25
6 Short Preludes
No. 5 in E, p. 42

Bach, J. S. *Short Preludes and Fugues* Henle (Vol. 106)
Little Preludes for W. F. Bach
No. 4 in g – S. V. 930
No. 6 in D – S. V. 925
Six Little Preludes II
No. 5 in E – S. V. 937
Six Little Preludes III
No. 5 in C – S. V. 943

Bach, J. S. *Two-Part Inventions* Alfred
No. 1 in C

Beethoven, L. *Two Easy Sonatas* Henle (Vol. 56)
Op. 49 No. 1

Bernard, O. *Promenades* Presser
I, II, III

Bovet, J. *Impressions* Magna Music
I through VI

Britten, B. *Waltzes, Op. 3* Schirmer
No. 1

Chopin, F. *Mazurkas* Polish Music Publications
Op. 7 No. 1
Op. 24 No. 1
Op. 67 No. 2
Op. 68 No. 3

Chopin, F. *Preludes, Op. 28* Alfred
No. 4 in e
No. 6 in b
No. 20 in c

Cimarosa, D. *10 Sonatas, Bk. 1* Eschig
No. 11 in Eb

Corelli, A. *24 Pieces for the Piano* Kalmus/Belwin
No. 4 Praludium in g
No. 7 Praludium in E
No. 11 Allegro in D
No. 12 Gigue in A

Delacroix, R. *Esquisses* Presser

Delius, F. *Five Piano Pieces* Boosey & Hawkes
Mazurka
Waltz II

Dello Joio, N. *Diversions* Marks

Gretchaninoff, A. *Three Pieces for Piano, Op. 198* Marks

Grieg, E. *Lyrical Pieces, Op. 12* Schirmer
Arietta

Grieg, E. *Poetic Tone Pictures, Op. 3* Peters
No. 1

Griffis, E. *Letters from a Maine Farm* C. Fischer
The Spider at my Window

Haydn, F. J. *Six Sonatinas* Alfred
H. XVI No. 4 in D
H. XVI No. 10 in C

Hengeveld, G. *Rhythmical and Melodic Pieces* Peters

Kabalevsky, D. *Four Rondos, Op. 60* MCA
No. 1 in Eb

Kabalevsky, D. *Six Preludes and Fugues* Leeds/MCA
No. 1 in G

Kabalevsky, D. *Ten Children's Pieces* MCA
Fleet Fingers

Kabalevsky, D. *Variations, Op. 40* MCA
No. 2 in a

La Montaine, J. *A Child's Picture Book* Broude

MacDowell, E. *Sea Pieces, Op. 55* Kalmus/Belwin
Song

MacDowell, E. *12 Etudes, Op. 39* Boston
Hunting Song
Romance

MacDowell, E. (Anson) *Music by MacDowell* Schroeder & Guenther
Song, Op. 55, No. 5

Maykpar, S. *18 Selected Pieces* MCA
Skating
Toccatina
Polka
Little Fairy Tale

McKay, N. *Four Miniatures* Shawnee
Dance
Lullaby

Menotti, G. *Poemetti* F. Colombo
Giga
Bells at Dawn
The Spinner
The Manger

Mopper, I. *For Today and Tomorrow* Boston

Poulenc, F. *Suite Francaise* Durand
Pavane
Complainte
Sicilienne

Prokofieff, S. *Music for Children, Op. 65* MCA
Tag

Rameau, F. *The Graded Rameau* Belwin-Mills
Tambourin
La Joyeuse
Gigue en Rondeau
La Villageoise

Rieti, V. *5 Pieces for Young Pianists* General Music
Canon
Silly Polka
Tarantella

Rorem, N. *A Quiet Afternoon* Peer-Southern

Scarlatti, D. *12 Easy Sonatas* Belwin-Mills
No. 4 in G – L. 84

Schectmann, S. *Recreations for Piano* MCA

(Schott) *The New Piano Book* Schott (6010/1)
Marsch (Hindemith)
Zei leichte Funftonstucke (Hindemith)
Praludium (Genzmer)
Andante (Genzmer)
Invention (Hessenberg)
Lied (Fortner)
Air (Badings)

Schumann, R. *Album for the Young* Alfred
No. 12 Knecht Ruprecht
No. 13 May Sweet May
No. 15 Spring Song
No. 17 The Little Morning Wanderer
No. 22 Roundelay
No. 23 The Horseman
No. 24 Harvest Song
No. 26 Untitled
No. 28 Remembrance
No. 29 The Stranger
No. 30 Untitled
No. 32 Scheherazade
No. 36 Italian Mariners' Song
No. 37 Sailors' Song
No. 38 Wintertime I

Scriabin, A. *Scriabin Masterpieces* Marks
Prelude Op. 11 No. 9
Prelude Op. 27 No. 2

Scriabin, A. (M. Baylor) *Selected Works* Alfred
Prelude in e, Op. 11 No. 4
Prelude in B, Op. 27 No. 2

Shostakovich, D. *24 Preludes, Bk. 1* Peters
Op. 34, No. 22

Stravinsky, S. *Six Sonatinas* Peters
Nos. 4, 5

Tcherepnin, N. *Dix Pieces Gaies* J & W Chester
I, II, V, VI

(unedited) *Spanish Piano Music for the Young Musician* Boosey & Hawkes
Sonata (Freixaner)
Sonata (Albeniz)

(unedited) *U. S. A. Vol. 1* Leeds/MCA
Prelude (Creston)
Marionette (Still)

Villa-Lobos, H. *Five Pieces on Brazilian Folk Songs* Mercury (A377)

Zbinden, J. *Album Pour Mon Chien* Magna Music
I – Jeux
II – Berceuse

LEVEL 8

(Agay, D.) *Anthology of Piano Literature, Vol. 4* Yorktown
- May Night (Palmgren)
- Carillon (Casella)
- Elegia (Rieti)
- Sonatina in C, Op. 13 No. 1 (Kabalevsky)

Bach, C. P. E. *Short and Easy Piano Pieces* Universal
- No. 5 in a
- No. 7 in b
- No. 17 in Eb
- No. 20 in A
- No. 22 in e

Bach, C. P. E. *Sonatas and Pieces* Peters (4188)
- No. 1 in A
- No. 2 in G
- No. 4 in E

Bach, J. S. *Short Preludes and Fugues* Henle
- Little Preludes for W. F. Bach
  - No. 5 in F – S. V. 928
- Little Fugues and Preludes with Fugues
  - No. 1 in c – S. V. 961
  - No. 4 in G – S. V. 902a

Bach, J. S. *Two-Part Inventions* Alfred
- No. 3 in D
- No. 4 in d
- No. 6 in E
- No. 13 in a
- No. 15 in b

Bartók, B. *Roumanian Folk Dances (6) 1915* Boosey & Hawkes

Beethoven, L. *Bagatelles* Henle
- Op. 33, No. 1
- Op. 33, No. 3
- Op. 33, No. 4

Beethoven, L. *Contra-Dances* Schirmer
- No. 1 in C

Beethoven, L. *Sonatinas (Bonn)* Peters
- No. 1 in Eb
- No. 2 in f

Beethoven, L. *Variations* Henle
- Nel cor piu non mi sento (Paisiello)

Berkeley, L. *Five Short Pieces* J & W Chester

Bernard, O. *Promenades* Presser
- IV

Bovet, J. *Impressions* Magna Music
- VII, VIII

Brahms, J. *Two Sarabandes and Gigues* Peters

Britten, B. *Waltzes, Op. 3* Schirmer
- Nos. 2, 3, 4

Casella, A. *Children's Pieces* Universal
- Carillon

Chopin, F. *Mazurkas* Polish Music Publications
- Op. 6 No. 2
- Op. 7 No. 2
- Op. 67 No. 4
- Op. 68 No. 2

Chopin, F. *Waltzes* Polish Music Publications
- Op. 34 No. 2
- Op. 69 No. 2

Cimarosa, D. *10 Sonatas, Bk. 1* Eschig
- III in Bb
- IV in Bb
- V in Bb
- IX in d

Delius, F. *Five Piano Pieces* Boosey & Hawkes
- Waltz III

(Dobler, C.) *Contemporary Swiss, Bk. I* MCA (Edition Gerig)
- Intermezzo (Burkhard)
- Lullaby (Wendel)
- At Montsouris Park (Miez)
- Piano Piece (Schoeck)
- The Two Gossips (Gagnebin)
- Three Rubes (Ganz)
- Intermezzo (Sturgenegger)
- Cristallisations (Pfieter)
- Vision III (d'Alessandro)

Faith, R. *Night Songs* Shawnee

(Geiringer, K.) *The Bach Family* Universal
- Polonaise (W. F. Bach), p. 24
- Farewell (C. P. E. Bach), p. 26

Grieg, E. *Lyrical Pieces, Op. 43* Schirmer
- Solitary Wanderer
- Little Bird

Grieg, E. *Lyrical Pieces, Op. 54* Schirmer
- March of the Dwarfs
- Notturno
- Scherzo

Grieg, E. *Poetic Tone-Pictures, Op. 3* Peters
- Nos. 2, 4, 5

Griffis, E. *Letters From a Maine Farm* C. Fischer
- The Music Box

Hanson, H. *For the First Time* C. Fischer

Herrarte, M. *Six Sketches for Piano* Elkan-Vogel
- No. 2

Ibert, J. *Histoires* Marks
- The Little White Donkey

Kabalevsky, D. *Six Preludes and Fugues* Leeds/MCA
- No. 2 in C

Kabalevsky, D. *Sonatina in C, Op. 13 No. 1* MCA

Kabalevsky, D. *Sonatina, Op. 13, No. 2* Leeds/MCA

Khachaturian, A. *Sonatina (1959)* MCA

Krenek, E. *Twelve Short Piano Pieces (12 tone)* Schirmer
- Peaceful Mood
- Walking on a Stormy Day
- The Moon Rises
- A Boat, Slowly Sailing
- Glass Figures
- The Sailing Boat Reflected in the Pond

Liszt, F. *Consolations* Schirmer
- No. 1 in E
- No. 4 in Db

MacDowell, E. (Anson) *Music by MacDowell, Bk. 1* Schroeder & Guenther
- The Witch, Op. 38 No. 4
- Villain, Op. 38 No. 6
- Alla Tarantella, Op. 39 No. 2
- Starlight, Op. 55 No. 4
- To a Water Lily, Op. 51 No. 6

MacDowell, E. *Sea Pieces, Op. 55* Kalmus/Belwin
- Starlight

MacDowell, E. *12 Etudes, Op. 39* Boston
- Alla Tarantella
- In the Forest

Martinu, B. *Fables* Boosey & Hawkes

Maykapar, S. *18 Selected Pieces* MCA
- Variations

McKay, N. *Four Miniatures* Shawnee
- March
- Caprice

Mendelssohn, F. *Six Pieces for Children, Op. 72* Schirmer
- No. 1 in G
- No. 2 in Eb
- No. 3 in D

Mendelssohn, F. *Songs Without Words* Schirmer
- Regrets, Op. 19 No. 2
- Confidence, Op. 19 No. 4
- Venetian Boat Song, Op. 19 No. 6
- Consolation, Op. 30 No. 3
- Venetian Boat Song No. 2, Op. 30 No. 6
- Sadness of Soul, Op. 53 No. 4
- Retrospection, Op. 102 No. 2
- Faith, Op. 102 No. 6

Menotti, G. *Poemetti* F. Colombo
- The Book
- The Shepherd
- Nocturne
- The Stranger's Dance
- Winter Wind
- War Song

Mozart, W. *Little Known Pieces* Kalmus/Belwin
- No. 5 Lison dormait

Mozart, W. *Viennese Sonatinas* Peters

Poulenc, F. *Mouvements Perpetuels (1918)* Belwin-Mills

Poulenc, F. *Suite Francaise* Durand
- Petit marche militaire
- Carillon

Rameau, J. *The Graded Rameau* Belwin-Mills
Les Tendres Plaintes

Rieti, V. *Six Short Pieces* Ricordi/Belwin
Preludio
Elegia

Scarlatti, D. *12 Easy Sonatas* Boston
No. 7 in a – L. 93
No. 9 in G – L. 388
No. 11 in D – L. 413
No. 12 in g – L. 386

Schubert, F. *Four Impromptus, Op. 142* Schirmer
No. 2 in Ab

Schumann, R. *Album for the Young* Alfred
No. 27 A Little Canon
No. 31 Song of War
No. 33 Gathering of the Grapes
No. 38 Wintertime II
No. 42 New Year's Eve

Schumann, R. *Bunte Blatter (Colored Leaves)* Kalmus/Belwin
Three Little Pieces, Op. 99
No. 1 in A
No. 3 in E

Schumann, W. *Three Score Set* Schirmer

Scriabin, A. *Scriabin Masterpieces* Marks
Prelude, Op. 11 No. 13
Prelude, Op. 11 No. 15

Scriabin, A. (M. Baylor) *Selected Works* Alfred
Etude in c#, Op. 2, No. 1
Prelude in Gb, Op. 16, No. 3
Prelude in a, Op. 11, No. 2

Shostakovich, D. *24 Preludes, Bk. 1* Peters
Op. 34 No. 3
Op. 34 No. 18
Op. 34 No. 19

Shostakovich, D. *24 Preludes, Bk. 2* Peters
No. 13 in F#
No. 14 in Eb

Stravinsky, S. *Six Sonatinas, Bks. 1 & 2* Peters
Nos. 2, 6

Tcherepnin, A. *Dix Pieces Gaies* J & W Chester
III, IV, VII, VIII, IX

(unedited) *Spanish Piano Music for the Young Musician* Boosey & Hawkes
Due sonate (Soler)
Sonata (Cantallos)
Sonata (Serrano)
Sonata (Ferrer)

(unedited) *U. S. A. Vol 1* Leeds/MCA
Young Prince (Fuleihan)
Moods (Jacobi)
Dancing Leaves (Joseten)

Zbinden, J. *Album Pour Mon Chien* Magna Music
III – Promenade
IV – In Canum Paradiso

LEVEL 9

(Agay, D.) *Anthology of Piano Music, Vol. 4* Yorktown
Poem, Op. 31 No. 2 (Scriabin)
Invenzione (Rieti)
Clowns (Turina)
Prelude, Op. 34 No. 16 (Shostakovich)
Fantastic Dances No. 1, No. 2 (Shostakovich)

Agay, D. *Sonatina No. 3* Fox

Bach, C. P. E. *Sonatas and Pieces* Peters (4188)
No. 6 in Eb
No. 7 in d (Variations on Folie d'Espagne)

Bach, J. S. *French Suites* Henle (71)
No. 4 in Eb – S. V. 815
No. 5 in G – S. V. 816

Bach, J. S. *Little Preludes and Fugues* Henle
Little Fugues and Preludes with Fugues
No. 2 in C – S. V. 952
No. 3 in C – S. V. 953
No. 5 in d – S. V. 899

Bach, J. S. *Two-Part Inventions* Alfred
No. 2 in c
No. 8 in F
No. 9 in f
No. 10 in G
No. 14 in Bb

Bartók, B. *Six Dances in Bulgarian Rhythm* Boosey & Hawkes
Nos. 2, 6

Beethoven, L. *Complete Bagatelles* Henle (158)
No. 5 in Ab

Beethoven, L. *Contra-Dances* Schirmer
No. 2 in Eb
No. 3 in C

Ben-Haim, P. *Five Pieces for Piano, Op. 34* Leeds/MCA
Pastorale
Intermezzo
Canzonetta
Toccata

Britten, B. *Waltzes, Op. 3* Schirmer
No. 5

Chopin, F. *Mazurkas* Polish Music Publications
Op. 24 No. 4
Op. 63 No. 3
Op. 33 No. 4

Chopin, F. *Nocturnes* Polish Music Publications
Op. 15 No. 3
Op. 55 No. 1
Op. 72 No. 1

Chopin, F. *Preludes, Op. 28* Alfred
No. 2 in a
No. 9 in E
No. 13 in F#
No. 14 in eb
No. 15 in Db

Chopin, F. *Waltzes* Polish Music Publications
Op. 64 No. 2

Cimarosa, D. *10 Sonatas, Bk. 1* Eschig
No. 6 in A
No. 7 in c
No. 8 in C
No. 10 in Bb

(collection) *The New Piano Book* Schott (6010/1)
Variationen uber fin baschkirisches Volkslied (Seiber)
Toccatina (Seiber)
Intermezzo (Martinu)

Copland, Aaron *Four Piano Blues* Boosey & Hawkes
Nos. 1, 3

Debussy, C. *Children's Corner* Durand

Delacroix, R. *Ambiance* Presser
Farniente
Far West

Delius, F. *Five Piano Pieces* Boosey & Hawkes
Toccata

Delius, F. *Three Preludes* Oxford
No. 2

(Dobler, C.) *Contemporary Swiss Piano Music, Book I* MCA (Edition Gerig)
Questions–Answers (Vuataz)
Implacable (Moeschinger)
The Little Mirror (Kelterborn)
Loneliness Falling in Drops (Vogel)
Music for Piano in Five Parts (Frischknecht) Nos. 1, 3

Faith, R. *Five Preludes and a Nocturne* Shawnee
Five Preludes

Ferguson, H. *Five Bagatelles* Boosey & Hawkes

(Geiringer, K.) *The Bach Family* Universal
Sonata (J. C. Bach), p. 37

Gershwin, G. *Preludes* New World
No. 2

Grieg, E. *Lyric Pieces, Op. 43* Schirmer
- Papillon
- At Home

Grieg, E. *Poetic Tone-Pictures, Op. 3* Schirmer
- Nos. 3, 6

Griffis, E. *Letters From a Maine Farm* C. Fischer
- The Sunlit Woods
- The Girl on the Farm Below

Hanson, H. *Three Miniatures* C. Fischer
- Lullaby (10ths in L. H.)

Harriess, D. *Four Impromptus* Oxford

Harris, R. *American Ballads* C. Fischer
- Streets of Laredo
- Wayfaring Stranger
- Black is the Color of My True Love's Hair

Herrarte, M. *Six Sketches for Piano* Elkan-Vogel
- Nos. 1, 3, 6

Hovhaness, A. *Two Ghazals, Op. 36* Peters

Jelinek, H. *Twelve-Note Music, Op. 15* Presser

Kabalevsky, D. *Preludes, Op. 38* MCA
- No. 1 in C
- No. 2 in a
- No. 12 in G
- No. 15 in b flat minor
- No. 17 in Ab
- No. 18 in f
- No. 20 in c
- No. 23 in F

Krenek, E. *5 Piano Pieces, Op. 39* Universal

Krenek, E. *Twelve Short Piano Pieces (12 tone)* Schirmer
- Dancing Toys
- Little Chessmen
- Streamliner
- On the High Mountains

Lang, W. *Nachtstimmen* Magna Music
- I, II

Liszt, F. *Consolations* Schirmer
- No. 2 in E
- No. 5 in E

MacDowell, E. *Sea Pieces, Op. 55* Kalmus/Belwin
- To the Sea
- From a Wandering Iceberg
- A. D. MDCXX

MacDowell, E. *Twelve Etudes, Op. 39* Boston
- Idylle
- Intermezzo

Mechem, K. *Suite for Piano* E. C. Schirmer

Mendelssohn, F. *Songs Without Words* Schirmer
- Contemplation, Op. 30 No. 4
- The Brook, Op. 30 No. 5
- Hope, Op. 38 No. 4
- May Breezes, Op. 62 No. 1
- The Shepherd's Complaint, Op. 67 No. 5
- Reverie, Op. 85 No. 1
- The Adieu, Op. 85 No. 2

Mozart, W. *Little Known Pieces* Kalmus/Belwin
- No. 4 Allegro

Mozart, W. *Sonatas* Presser
- K. 280 in F, p. 13
- K. 570 in Bb, p. 283

Pinto, O. *Scenas Infantis* Schirmer

Poulenc, F. *Valse in C* Eschig

Prokofieff, S. *Tales of the Old Grandmother, Op. 31* MCA

Rameau, J. *The Graded Rameau* Belwin-Mills
- La Timide
- Le Rappel des Oiseaus
- La Poule

Rieti, V. *Six Short Pieces* Boston
- Invenzione
- Momento Musicale
- Barcarola

Schubert, F. *Moments Musicaux, Op. 94* Schirmer

Schumann, R. *Album for the Young* Alfred
No. 34 Theme

Schumann, R. *Album-Leaves, Op. 124* Schirmer
No. 2 in a – Leides Ahnung
No. 3 in F – Scherzino
No. 5 in e – Phantasietanz
No. 11 in Bb – Romanze

Schumann, R. *Forest Scenes* Schirmer
Entrance
Wayside Inn

Schumann, R. *Three Sonatas for Young People* Peters
No. 1 in G, Op. 118

Scriabin, A. *Scriabin Masterpieces* Marks
Album Leaf, Op. 45 No. 1
Prelude in Eb, Op. 45 No. 3

Scriabin, A. (M. Baylor) *Selected Works* Alfred
Prelude in b, Op. 11, No. 6
Mazurka, Op. 40, No. 1

Shostakovich *24 Preludes, Bk. 2* Peters
No. 16 in b flat
No. 17 in Ab
No. 23 in F
No. 24 in d

Starer, R. *Five Caprices* Peer-Southern
Nos. 2, 4

Stravinsky, S. *Piano Variations – 1st Series* Peters
Stravinsky, S. *Piano Variations – 2nd Series* Peters
Tauriello, A. *Toccata (1949)* Boosey & Hawkes
Taylor, C. *Whimsies, Second Set* Boosey & Hawkes
No. 4

Tcherepnin, A. *Dix Pieces Gaies* J & W Chester
X

Telemann, G. *Easy Fugues and Short Pieces* International
Telemann, G. *Three Dozen Clavier Fantasies* Barenreiter
Turina, J. *Danses Gitanes, Op. 55* Salabert
Turina, J. *Miniatures* Associated
(unedited) *Spanish Piano Music for the Young Musician* Boosey & Hawkes
Sevilla (Albeniz)

(unedited) *U. S. A., Vol. 1* Leeds/MCA
Sombrero (Bacon)
Improvisation (Piston)
Melody (Recommended for Advanced)

Villa-Lobos, H. *The Three Maries* C. Fischer
Alnitah
Alnilam

Waldon, M. *Reflections in Modern Jazz* Fox
Zbinden, J. *Preludes, Op. 4* Magna Music

MATERIALS LIST FROM THE "MUSIC TEACHERS' ASSOCIATION OF CALIFORNIA" *CERTIFICATE OF MERIT SYLLABUS*

Compiled by Rita Fuszek & Ralph Pierce*

LEVEL 1

Classic/Romantic: Select from these collections.
Very First Classics (Gray) Boosey & Hawkes
The Solo Book, Vol. 1 (Zeitlin-Goldberger) Consolidated
Little Dance Book (Burkhard) Schott
or:
Gurlitt, C. *First Steps, Op. 88* Schirmer

***Previous Materials List (1972–1975). Used by permission of the "Music Teachers' Association of California," Eleanor Dalton, past-President.**

Contemporary: Select from these collections.
Play with Five Tones (Emonts) Schott
Pageants for Piano, Introductory (Waxman) Galaxy
Twentieth Century Piano Music, Vol. 1 (Frost) J. Fischer/Belwin
Contemporary Piano Lit., Vol. 1 (Clark) Summy-Birchard
or:
Badings, Henk *Arcadia, Vol. 1 or 2* Schott
Bartók, Béla *Mikrokosmos, Vol. 1* Boosey & Hawkes
Burkard, Willy *Eight Easy Piano Pieces* Bärenreiter
Kasemets, Udo *Ten Pieces on Well-Known Tunes* BMI-Canada
McGraw, Cameron *Pet Silhouettes, Vol. 1* Presser
Nelhybel, Vaclav *Kaleidoscope, Vol. 1* General
Olson, Lynn F. *Near the Beginning (7)* C. Fischer
Rowley, Alec *Sketches* Summy-Birchard
Satie, Eric *Menu propos Enfantines* Eschig
Tansman, Alexandre *Happy Time, Vol. 1* MCA
Young, Irene H. *Next Door Neighbors (18)* Summy-Birchard

LEVEL 2

Baroque:
Handel, G. F. *Twenty Little Dances* Schott

Classic: Select appropriate period material from the following:

**The Solo Book, Vol. 2* (Zeitlin-Goldberger) Consolidated
**The Sonatina Book, Vol. 1* (Zeitlin-Goldberger) Consolidated
**Piano Literature, Vol. 2* (Clark) Summy-Birchard
or:
Haydn, J. *German Dances* Universal
Mozart, L. *Notebook for Wolfgang* Schott

Romantic:
**Russian Music for Young Pianists, Vol. 1* (Zeitlin-Goldberger) MCA
**Selected Graded Classics, Bk. 2* Mills/Belwin
or:
Gurlitt, C. *Op. 101 Album Leaves* Schirmer
Gurlitt, C. *Op. 140 Album for the Young (20)* Alfred

Contemporary:
First Piano Pageants (Waxman) Galaxy
Contemporary Piano Lit., Vol 2 (Clark) Summy-Birchard
or:
Bacon, Ernst *Friends (8)* Colombo
Bartók, Béla *Mikrokosmos, Vol. 2* Boosey & Hawkes
Carley, Isabel *Eleven Miniatures* Galaxy
Dello-Joio, Norman *Suite for the Young* Marks
Diamond, David *Eight Piano Pieces* Schirmer
Gretchaninoff, A. *Op. 98 Children's Book* Schott
La Montaine, John *Copycats* Summy-Birchard
Lessard, John *New Worlds for Young Pianists, Vol. 1* General
Lombardo, Robert *Contemporary Pieces for Children (12)* Peer
Persichetti, Vincent *Little Piano Book* Elkan-Vogel
Pinto, Octavio *Children's Festival* Schirmer
Ponce, Manuel *Twenty Easy Pieces* Peer
Stravinsky, Soulima *Piano Music, Vol. 1 or 2* Peters
Takacs, Jeno *Op. 76 For Me* Doblinger
Wilder, Alec *Twelve Mosaics* Presser
Kabalevsky *Op. 39 Twenty-four Pieces* Schirmer

*Multi-period collections. Select appropriate composer.

LEVEL 3

Baroque:

Easy Piano Music of the Baroque (Emonts) Schott

Bach, J.S. *First Bach Book* Kalmus
Fischer, J.K.F. *Notebook of J.K.F. Fischer* Schott
Handel, G. F. *A Handel Album* Universal
Muthel *Minuets (12)* Bärenreiter

Classic:

**Airs and Dances, Vol. 1* (Dorelle) Boosey & Hawkes
**Old Masters: Miniatures* (Von Irmer) Schirmer
**Classic Dances* (Zeitlin-Goldberger) Consolidated
**Piano Literature, Vol. 3* (Clark) Summy-Birchard
**Piano Literature, Vol. 2* (Bastien) GWM/Kjos

Clementi, Muzio *Op. 36 Sonatinas* Schirmer
Dittersdorf, Karl *English Dances (20)* Schott
Haydn, Michael *Six Minuets for Piano* Noetzel
Haydn, Joseph *Twelve Easy Pieces* Universal
Mozart, W. A. *The Young Mozart* Schott
Mozart, W. A. *Eight Minuets K. 315a* Henle

Romantic:

**The Solo Book, Vol. 3* (Zeitlin-Goldberger) Consolidated
**The New Sonatina Book-elementary* (Frey) Schott
**Easy Piano Works, Vol. 1* Henle
**Favorite Romantic Pieces* (Watson) Row

Burgmüller *Op. 100 Progressive Studies* Schirmer
Diabelli, A. *Op. 151 Sonatinas* Schirmer
Heller, Stephen *Op. 47 Studies (25)* Schirmer

Contemporary:

American Music, Bk. 1 Presser
Canadian Festival Album, Vol. 1 BMI-C
Badings, Henk *Arcadia, Vol. 3* Schott
Bartók, Béla *For Children, Vol. 1 or 2* Boosey & Hawkes
Bennett, Richard R. *Diversions (8)* Universal
Bloch, Ernst *Enfantines* C. Fischer
Creston, Paul *Op. 24 Five Little Dances* Schirmer
Fussl, K. H. *Five Tones, Five Fingers* Universal
Hovhaness, Alan *Armenian Folk Songs (12)* Peters
Nakada, Yashinao *Japanese Festival (17)* MCA
Poot, Marcel *Bon Voyage (10)* Universal
Stevens, Everett *Modal Miniatures (6)* Ditson
Tansman, Alexandre *For the Children, Vol. 1 or 2* Associated
Toch, Ernst *Op. 59 Ten Studies for Beginners* Schott

LEVEL 4

Baroque:

**Early Italian* (Shaw) J. Fischer/Belwin
**Early French Masters* (Von Irmer) Schirmer

Bach, J. S. *Anna Magdalena Bach Notebook* Kalmus
Handel, G. F. *The Young Pianists: Handel, Vol. 1* Oxford
Krieger, Johann *Collection of Piano Works* Bärenreiter
Türk, D. G. *Easy Pieces for Piano* Schott

*Multi-period collections. Select appropriate composer.

Classic:

**The New Sonatine Book, Vol. 1* (Frey) Schott
**Early American Music* (McClenny-Hinson) Belwin-Mills

Beethoven, L. *Waltzes (15)* Schott
Dussek, J. *Op. 20 Sonatinas* Schirmer
Haydn, J. *Dances and Pieces for Piano* Litolff
Kuhlau, F. *Op. 20 Sonatinas* Schirmer
Mozart, W. A. *Waltzes (12)* Universal

Romantic:

**From Ancient to Modern* (Rowley) Boosey & Hawkes
**Easy Piano Works, Vol. 2*

Franck, Cesar *Eighteen Short Pieces* Peters
Grieg, Edvard *Op. 12 Lyric Pieces* Schirmer
Gurlitt, C. *Op. 131 Studies (24)* Schirmer
Tchaikovsky, Peter *Op. 39 Album for the Young* Schirmer

Contemporary:

The World of Modern Piano Music (Agay) MCA
Masters of Our Day (Freed) C. Fischer
From Bartók to Stravinsky (Emonts) Schott

Bartók, Béla *Mikrokosmos, Vol. 3* Boosey & Hawkes
Bortkiewicz, S. *Op. 54 Marionettes* Associated
Creed, John *Nine Bagatelles* Hinrichson
Diamond, David *Alone at the Piano, Vol. 2* Southern
Floyd, Carlisle *Episodes, Vol. 1* Boosey & Hawkes
Gretchaninoff, A. *Op. 123 Glass Beads* Leeds/MCA
Hindemith, Paul *Little Piano Music, No. 4* Schott
Kabalevsky, Dmitri *Op. 51 Five Sets of Variations* MCA
Kodaly, Zoltan *Children's Dances* Leeds/MCA
Lavry, Marc *Five Country Dances* Leeds/MCA
Paporisz, Yoram *Discoveries at the Piano, Vol. 1* Southern
Muczynski, Robert *Fables (9)* Schirmer
Schloss, Julius *Pieces in 12-tone Style (23)* Peer
Stravinsky, Soulima *Sonatinas (6) Vol. 1 or 2* Peters
Tansman, Alexandre *For the Children, Vol. 3* Eschig

LEVEL 5

Baroque:

Sixteen Masterworks (Kuranda) Universal

Bach, J. S. *Small Preludes (BWV 933-938)* Henle
Scarlatti, D. *Pieces and Sonatas (37) Vol. 1* Mills/Belwin
Türk, D. G. *Little Pieces* Nagel

Classic:

**Dance Music of Three Centuries* (Lambert) Schirmer
**Early Piano Pieces from Sons of Bach to Beethoven* Schott
**The New Sonatina Book, Vol. 2* (Frey) Schott

Bach, C.P.E. *Small and Easy Piano Pieces* Universal
Beethoven, L. *Op. 49 Sonatas, No. 1 or 2* Henle or Schirmer
Haydn, J. *Sonatinas (6)* Schott
Mozart, W. A. *K. 585 Menuettos (12) Vol. 1 or 2* Hinrichson
Paisello, G. *Sonatas (6)* Mills/Belwin

*Multi-period collections. Select appropriate composer.

Romantic:

Easy Piano Music of the Romantics (Emonts) Schott

Gade, Niels *Op. 19 Aquarellen (10)* Peters
Grieg, Edvard *Op. 3 Poetic Tone Pictures* Peters
Mendelssohn, Felix *Op. 72 Children's Pieces (6)* Peters or Schirmer
Schubert, Franz *Viennese Danse Book* Litolff
Schumann, Robert *Op. 68 Album for the Young* Schirmer

Contemporary:

Auric, Georges *Petite Suite* Heugel
Benjamin, Arthur *Fantasies, Set 1 or 2* Rogers
Berry, Wallace *Eight 20th Century Miniatures* C. Fischer
Blacher, Boris *Op. 14 Two Sonatinas* Bote and Bock
Casella, Alfred *Children's Pieces* Universal
Diamond, David *Then and Now (11)* Southern
Diemer, Emma Lou *Sound Pictures (10)* Boosey & Hawkes
Finney, Ross Lee *Inventions (24)* Peters
Fuleihan, Anis *Five Very Short Pieces for Talented Young Bipeds* Southern
Khachaturian, Aram *Adventures of Ivan* MCA
Prokofiev, Serge *Op. 65 Music for Children* Boosey & Hawkes or Schirmer
Schectman, Saul *Recreations for Piano* MCA
Takas, Jeno *Op. 51 Small Sonata* Doblinger
Tansman, Alexandre *The Young at the Piano, Vol. 3* Eschig
Tardos, Bela *Sonatine* Boosey & Hawkes

LEVEL 6

Baroque:

Bach, J. S. *Small Preludes and Fughettas* Henle
Cimarosa, D. *Sonatas Vol. 1 or 2* Eschig
Handel, G. F. *Easier Piano Pieces* Hinrichson
Scarlatti, D. *Pieces and Sonatas, Vol. 2* Mills/Belwin

Classic:

**Piano Classic Collection (8444)* J. Fischer/Belwin
**Easy Classic Variations* Henle
Six Keyboard Sonatas from the Classic Era (Newman) Summy-Birchard
**Piano Music from Two Centuries* Henle

Bach, C.P.E. *Wq 46 Prussian Sonatas (6)* Nagel
Beethoven, L. *Op. 33 or 119 Bagatelles* Henle, others

Romantic:

**Classics to Moderns* (Agay) Consolidated

Gade, Niels *Op. 34 Idyllen* Peters
Gliere, Reinhold *Student Pieces (12)* MCA
Grieg, Edvard *Op. 6 Humoresques (4)* Peters
Heller, Stephen *Op. 45 Studies* Schirmer
Liszt, Franz *Five Discoveries* Curwen
Schubert, Franz *Waltzes, 5 vols.* (ed. by Maier) J. Fischer/Belwin

Contemporary:

The New Piano-Book, Vol 1 Schott
USA, Vol. 1 MCA

Bartók, Béla *Mikrokosmos, Vol. IV* Boosey & Hawkes
Binkerd, Gordon *Piano Miscellany (5)* Boosey & Hawkes

*Multi-period collections. Select appropriate composer.

Delius, Frederick *Preludes (3)* Oxford
Diamond, David *Alone at the Piano, Vol. 3* Southern
Dello-Joio, Norman *Lyric Pieces for the Young (6)* Marks
Gibbs, Alan *Six Characters from Shakespeare* Hinrichson
Harris, Roy *Little Suite* Schirmer
Kabalevsky, Dmitri *Op. 40 Variations* International or MCA
Menotti, Gian Carlo *Poemetti* Ricordi
Tcherepnin, Alexander *Episodes* Heugel
Toch, Ernst *Echos of a Small Town* Associated
Webern, Anton *Kinderstück* C. Fischer

LEVEL 7

Baroque:

Style and Interpretation, Vol. 1 or 2 (Ferguson) Oxford

Handel, G. F. *Piano Book for the Young, Vol. 5* Peters
Soler, Padre A. *Sonatas 4 Vols. (ed. by Marvin)* Mills/Belwin
Telemann, G.P. *Little Fantasias* Schott

Classic:

Beethoven, L. *Variations WoO. 70 or WoO 77* Henle or Peters
Haydn, J. *Variations Hob. XVII:2 in A* Henle or Peters
Haydn, J. *Variations Hob. XVII:3 in Eb* Henle or Peters
Mozart, W. A. *Variations K. V. 179 in C* Henle or Peters
Mozart, W. A. *Variations K. V. 573 in D* Henle or Peters

Romantic:

Chopin, F. *Selected Easy Pieces* Polish/Marks
Chopin, F. *An Introduction to Piano Works* Alfred
Grieg, E. *Op. 54 Lyric Pieces* Schirmer
Liszt, Franz *Christmas Tree, Vol. 1 or 2* Peters
MacDowell, E. *Op. 39 Etudes (12)* Boston or Kalmus
Schubert, F. *Op. 94 Moment Musicaux* Henle, Peters, or Schirmer
Schumann, R. *Op. 124 Album Leaves* Schirmer
Schumann, R. *Op. 68 Album for the Young, Part II* Hartel, Alfred, or Henle

Contemporary:

The New Piano Book, Vol. II Schott

Aitken, Hugh *Three Connected Pieces* Oxford
Bartók, Béla *Rumanian Folk Dances (6)* Boosey & Hawkes
Calabro, Louis *Suite of Seven* Elkan-Vogel
Herrate, Manuel *Six Sketches for Piano* Elkan-Vogel
Ibert, Jacques *Histoires* Leduc
Jelinek, Hans *Op. 15 Twelve Note Music, Vol. 1* Universal
Kevins, Talivaldis *Diversities* Leeds-Canada
Krenek, Ernst *Op. 39 Five Piano Pieces* Universal
La Montaine, John *Op. 10 Twelve Relationships* C. Fischer
Milhaud, Darius *The Household Muse (15)* Elkan-Vogel
Paccagnini, A. *Recreations* Universal
Pitfield, Thomas *Studies on an English Dance Tune* Elkin
Scott, Cyril *Selected Works* Schirmer
Starer, Robert *Five Caprices* Peer
Tjeknavorian, Loris *Op. 7 Sonatine No. 1* Doblinger/Assoc.
Turina, Joaquin *Miniatures* Schott

LEVEL 8

Baroque:

Style and Interpretation, Vol. 1 or 2 (Ferguson) Oxford
Sonatas and Ancient Pieces, Vol. 1 (Nin) Eschig
Elizabethan Virginal Music Universal

Bach, J. S. *French Suites* Henle or Peters
Handel, G. F. *Pieces for Harpsichord, Vol. 1* Schott
Hassler, J. W. *Six Easy Sonatas* Peters
Scarlatti, D. *Sonatas (25) Longo edition* Ricordi

Classic:

Bach, J. C. *Sonatas, Vol. 1 or 2* Peters
Beethoven, L. *Op. 51 Rondos (2)* Henle or Schirmer
Clementi, Muzio *Sonatas* Peters or Schirmer
Haydn, J. *Piano Pieces* Henle
Mozart, W. A. *Rondos K.V.485 D.* Henle or Schirmer

Romantic:

Style and Interpretation, Vol. 3 (Ferguson) Oxford
**Classic Keyboard Music* (Sauer) Universal

Albeniz, I. *Op. 232 Cantos de Espana* UME
Brahms, J. *Sarabandes and Gigues* Peters
Chopin, F. *Op. 28 Preludes* Schirmer, Marks, etc.
Liszt, F. *Pieces for Piano (14)* Marks
Mendelssohn, F. *Songs without Words* Schirmer or Peters
MacDowell *Op. 62 New England Idylls* Schirmer
Schumann, R. *Op. 15 Scenes from Childhood* Schirmer, Henle, etc.
Schubert, F. *Op. 90 or Op. 142 Impromptus* Peters or Henle

Contemporary:

American Composers of Today Marks

Bartók, Béla, *Mikrokosmos Vol. V* Boosey / Hawkes
Bowles, Paul *Six Preludes* Mercury
Cooper, John *Op. 13 Three Bagatelles* Boosey & Hawkes
David, Thomas C. *Bagatelles (5)* Doblinger/Assoc.
Flagello, Nicolas *Three Dances* General
Guarnari, Camaro *Sonatina No. 3* Associated
Kadosa, Pal *Op. 3 Epigrams (8)* Boosey & Hawkes
Schumann, William *Three Score Set* Schirmer
Takacs, Jeno *Toccata* Doblinger/Assoc.
Tjeknavorian, L. *Op. 8 Sonatine No. 1* Doblinger
Toch, Ernst *Op. 31, No. 3 The Juggler* Schott
Turina, Joaquin *Circus Suite* Schott

LEVEL 9

Baroque:

Keyboard Music of Baroque and Rococo, Vol. 1 or 2 (Georgi) MCA
Early Italian Music, Vol. 1 or 2 (Ferguson) Oxford

Bach, J. S. *English Suites* Henle or Peters
Scarlatti, D.* *Sonatas (60) 2 Vols.,* (Kirkpatrick) Schirmer

Classic:

**Classical Piano Sonatas, Vol. 1* Henle
**Classical Piano Sonatas, Vol. 1* Peters (2114a)

*Multi-period collections. Select appropriate composer.

Bach, C.P.E. *Sonatas and Pieces* Peters
Haydn, F. *Sonatas* Henle or Universal
Clementi, Muzio *Sonatas* Peters
Mozart, W. A. *Piano Pieces* Henle

Romantic:

Brahms, J. *Op. 39 Waltzes* Schirmer
Chopin, F. *Waltzes* Schirmer, Marks, Henle
Grieg, E. *Op. 43 Lyric Pieces* Schirmer or Peters
Liszt, F. *Consolations (6)* Schirmer or Peters
MacDowell, E. *Op. 43 Four Little Poems* Schirmer
Schubert, F. *D. 943 Three Pieces* Peters
Schumann, R. *Op. 12 Fantasy Pieces* Henle

Contemporary:

Bartók, Béla *Three Rondos* Boosey & Hawkes
Bernstein, Leonard *Four Anniversaries* Schirmer
Dohnányi, Erno *Op. 11 Rhapsodies (4)* Willis or Doblinger
Faure, G. *Op. 17 Romances sans Paroles* International
Griffes, Charles *Preludes* Peters
Helm, Everett *New Horizons* Schirmer
Hindemith, Paul *Sonata No. 2* Schott
Lloyd, Norman *Episodes for Piano* Elkan-Vogel
Persichetti, V. *Poems for Piano, Vol. 1 or 2* Elkan-Vogel
Poulenc, F. *Impromptus (5)* Chester
Satie, Eric *Piano Music* Eschig
Schoenberg, Arnold *Op. 19 Six Little Pieces* Universal
Shostakovitch, D. *Op. 34 Preludes (24)* MCA
Ulehla, Ludmilla *Preludes (5)* General

LEVEL 10

Baroque:

Keyboard Music of Baroque and Rococo, Vol. 3 (Georgi) Leeds/MCA
Early English Keyboard Music, Vol. 1 or 2 (Ferguson) Oxford
Early French Keyboard Music, Vol. 1 or 2 (Ferguson) Oxford

Bach, J. S. *BWV 919 Fantasy Cm* Henle, Schirmer, Alfred
Bach, J. S. *BWV 802 Four Duets* Henle
Handel, G. F. *Suites* Peters

Classic:

Bach, C.P.E. *Sonatas* (Friskin) Galaxy
Beethoven, L. *Sonatas* Henle or Universal
Haydn, J. F. *Sonatas* Henle, Peters, Universal
Mozart, W. A. *Sonatas* Henle or Peters

Romantic:

Brahms, J. *Op. 117 Intermezzi* Schirmer
Chopin, F. *Nocturnes* Schirmer, Marks, Henle
Field, John *Nocturnes* Schirmer or Peters
Liszt, Franz *The Late Years* Schirmer
Mendelssohn, F. *Op. 14 Andante and Rondo Capriccioso* Schirmer
MacDowell, E. *Op. 46 Virtuoso Etudes (12)* Associated
Schumann, Robert *Op. 28 Three Romances* Henle or Schirmer
Scriabin, A. *Op. 11 Preludes* Marks

Contemporary:

Thirty-six 20th century Piano Pieces Schirmer
Bartók, Béla *Op. 14 Bagatelles* Boosey & Hawkes

Casella, A. *Deux Contrasts* Chester
Castro, Washington *Intermezzi* Southern
Creston, Paul *Op. 38 Preludes (6)* MCA
Dohnányi, E. *Op. 13 Winterreigen* Doblinger/Assoc.
Faure, G. *Op. 84 Eight Short Pieces* International
Ginastera, A. *American Preludes (12)* C. Fischer
Granados, E. *Spanish Dances (12)* International
Griffes, Charles *Album* Schirmer
Ireland, John *The Island Spell* Augener
Kabalevsky, D. *Sonata No. 3* International or MCA
Lees, Benjamin *Three Preludes* Boosey & Hawkes
Pick-Magiagalli, R. *Collogue au Clair de Lune* Ricordi
Poulenc, F. *Album of Six Pieces* Chester
Tcherepnin, A. *Op. 5 Bagatelles* Schirmer
Toch, E. *Op. 85 Three Little Dances* Schott
Travis, Roy *Five Preludes* Presser

SELECTED LIST OF MUSIC FOR ONE PIANO, FOUR HANDS

Compiled and Recommended by Maurice Hinson*

Alkan, Charles *Trois Marches, Op. 40* Editions Costellat
Bach, Johann C. *Sonatas* C. F. Peters
Barber, Samuel *Souvenirs, Op. 28* G. Schirmer
Bennett, Richard R. *Capriccio* Universal
Berkeley, Lennox *Sonatina* Chester
Berners, Lord Gerald T. *Valses Bourgeoises* Chester
Brahms, Johannes *Twenty-One Hungarian Dances* G. Schirmer; C. F. Peters
Bruch, Max *Swedish Dances* Simrock
Bruckner, Anton *Quadrille* Heinrichshofen
Chabrier, Emmanuel *Souvenir de Munich* Costellat
Chopin, Frederic *Variations sur un air national de Moore* E. B. Marks
Clementi, Muzio *Seven Sonatas* Breitkopf and Härtel
Debussy, Claude *March ecossaise* Jobert; Ballade Jobert
Diercks, John *Suite No. 1* Music Corporation of America
Donizetti, Gaetano *Sonatas* E. C. Kirby
Dvorak, Antonin *Slavonic Dances, Op. 46, Op. 72* Simrock; G. Schirmer
Flothuis, Marius *Valses Nobles, Op. 52* (Donemus)
Frid, Geza *Kermesse a Charleroi* Peer-Southern
Gilbert, Henry Franklin *Three American Dances* Boston Music Co.
Godowsky, Leopold *Miniatures* C. Fischer
Gottschalk, Louis M. *La Gallina (The Chicken)* Hinshaw
Haydn, Franz J. *Il Maestro e lo scolare* B. Schott
Helps, Robert *Saccade* C. F. Peters
Hiller, Ferdinand *Operette ohne Text, Op. 106* Augener
Husa, Karel *Eight Czech Dances* B. Schott
Jongen, Joseph *Jeux d'enfants* Centre Belge de Documentation Musicale
Kohn, Karl *Recreations* C. Fischer
Krieger, Edino *Sonata* Peer-Southern
La Montaine, John *Sonata, Op. 25* Elkan-Vogel
MacDowell, Edward *Three Poems, Op. 20* G. Schirmer; *Lunar Pictures, Op. 21* Hainauer
Moszkowski, Moritz *Spanish Dances, Op. 12* C. F. Peters; G. Schirmer
Rachmaninoff, Sergei *Six Pieces for Piano, Four Hands, Op. 11* International Music Co.

***Maurice Hinson is Professor of Piano at the Southern Baptist Theological Seminary, Louisville. Used by permission.**

Reinagle, Alexander *Thirteen Short and Easy Duets* Hinshaw
Reinecke, Carl *Nutcracker and Mouse King, Op. 46* G. Schirmer
Russell, Robert *Places, Op. 9* General Music Publishing Co.
Saint-Saëns, Camille *Pas redouble, Op. 86* G. Schirmer; Durand
Satie, Erik *En Habit de cheval* Rouart; Lerolle
Schickele, Peter *The Civilian Barber* Elkan-Vogel; *Toot Suite, S. 212*, by P.D.Q. Bach Presser
Schmitt, Florent *Musiques Foraines, Op. 23* Hamelle
Tchaikowsky, Peter *Russian Folk Songs* C. F. Peters
Townsend, Douglas *Four Fantasies on American Folk Songs* C. Fischer
Wagner, Richard *Polonaise in D* Breitkopf and Härtel
Woolen, Russell *Sonata for Piano Duo* Peer-Southern
Wourninen, Charles *Making Ends Meet* C. F. Peters

COMPOSITIONS BY AMERICAN COMPOSERS
Selected and Recommended by William Gillock*

PRIMARY I

Bostelmann *How Do You Do Today?* Marks
Erb *Hungry Pussy* Boston Music Co.
Glover *Sugar Cookies* Belwin-Mills
Hollander *Parade* Summy-Birchard
Olson *Silver Bugles* Summy-Birchard
Scher *Merry Little Raindrops from: Music for Advancement, Vol. 1* Hansen

PRIMARY II

Carley *Fox and Geese* Summy-Birchard
Dittenhaver *Fast Train at Night* Schroeder & Gunther
Erb *Whiz Goes the Train* Harold Flammer
Frost *Waltzing Bird* J. Fischer/Belwin
Garrow *Noisy Woodpecker* Belwin-Mills
George *Distant Chimes* Summy-Birchard
Schaum *African Explorer* Willis
Stecher, Horowitz, Gordon *Under the Big Top; Waggin' Train* Schirmer
Stevens *Parade of the Penguins* J. Fischer/Belwin

PRIMARY III

Carter *Bouncing the Ball* Summy-Birchard
Glover *Banjo on My Knee* Belwin-Mills
Nevin *Rickshaw Man* Belwin-Mills
Olson *Pagoda* C. Fischer
Phippeny *Candy Band* Summy-Birchard
Ricker *Little Roguish Clown* Lee Roberts
Seul-Holst *Black Pirates* Summy-Birchard

PRIMARY IV

Agay *Parade of the Clowns* Sam Fox
Beck *Bells of Kyoto* C. Fischer
Glover *Winter Wind* Belwin-Mills
Green *Thar She Blows!* Willis
Kelley *Foreign Agent* Pro Art
Martin *Danish Dancer* Belwin-Mills
Sr. M. Elaine *Modal Picture* C. Fischer
Stevens *After Sundown* O. Ditson

***In compiling this list, Mr. Gillock wishes to acknowledge with gratitude suggestions from the committees on repertoire of the "Junior Pianists Guild of Dallas." The list contains a cross sampling of American composers and purposely omits Gillock and Bastien compositions. Used by permission.**

ELEMENTARY I

Anson *Spinning Top* Belwin-Mills
Beck *Buffoon* C. Fischer
Bentley *Drifting Moon* Summy-Birchard
Burnam *Chimney Smoke* Willis *Whirling Leaves* Summy-Birchard
Martino *Chili Bean* MCA
McCay *Dance in the Meadow* Presser
Olson *Spanish Serenade* C. Fischer
Scher *Flamenco* Summy-Birchard
Stecher, Horowitz, Gordon *The Terrain of Spain* Summy-Birchard
Stevens *A Lively Dance* C. Fischer *White Clouds* O. Ditson
Taylor *Neapolitan Dance* C. Fischer

ELEMENTARY II

Agay *Dancing Leaves* Schirmer
Blake *Somersaults* Willis
Dring *The Soldiers Pass* Marks
Glover *Great Smoky Mountains* Belwin-Mills
Lemont *Rondino* Boston Music Co.
Scher *Cat Chasing Mouse* Witmark *Pedro Dances* Schirmer
Stevens *Six Modal Miniatures* O. Ditson *White Heather* O. Ditson
Taylor *Winter Fairyland* C. Fischer

ELEMENTARY III

Dungan *The Everglades* Boston Music Co.
Frackenpohl *Gliding* Lee Roberts
Goodenough *Gigue* Summy-Birchard
Jesse *La Fiesta* Hansen
MacLachlin *Havana* Schroeder & Gunther
Sr. M. Elaine *Triads on Parade* J. Fischer/Belwin
Watson *Alborada* C. Fischer
Wilson *Sleepy Bayou* C. Fischer
Wolford *Pastels* J. Fischer/Belwin

ELEMENTARY IV

Agay *Soldier's Hoe Down* Boosey & Hawkes
Bentley *Sagebrush Serenade* Summy-Birchard *Toccata* (from *Pagaents*) Windsor Press
Garrow *Hungarian Holiday* Schroeder & Gunther
McGrath *Coasting* C. Fischer
Wilson *Leaves from My Notebook* Willis

MEDIUM

Goeman *Children at Play* World Library
Lane *The Penguin* C. Fischer
Olson *Rather Blue* Schirmer
Richman *Prism* Schirmer
Slifer *Skier's Challenge* Schroeder & Gunther
Wermel *Barcelona Bazaar* Boston Music Co.

MODERATELY DIFFICULT I

Agay *Three Recital Dances* Presser
Berkman *Prelude* Summy-Birchard
Boykin *Poem* Schroeder & Gunther
Brussels *Arabesque* Schirmer
Glover *Three Preludes* Belwin-Mills
Goodrich *Caprice in C* Summy-Birchard
MacDowell *Alla Tarantella* any standard edition
Nevin *Tokyo Toccatina* Belwin-Mills

MODERATELY DIFFICULT II

Bentley *The Restless Sea* Summy-Birchard
Boykin *Soliloquy; Sea Foam; En Bateau* Schroeder & Gunther
Dungan *The Peacock* Belwin-Mills

Goodrich *Novelette* C. Fischer
Scher *Shepherd's Song & Dance* Schirmer
Sr. M. de la Salle *Scherzo* J. Fischer/Belwin

DIFFICULT I

Bilotti *The Firefly* C. Fischer
Harper *La Playa de Malaga* Boston Music Co.
Starer *Sketches in Color* MCA
Verne *Phrigian Tocatta* Willis
Wigham *Rhapsody* Willis
Wright *Windy Weather* Southern Music Co.
Zechwar *In a Boat* C. Fischer

DIFFICULT II

Agay *Dance Scherzo* Schirmer
Dittenhaver *Appalachian Reverie* GWM/Kjos
Gershwin *Prelude No. 2* Warner Bros.
Goemann *Space Flight of the CCL64* World Library
Jacobi *Prelude in E Minor* Shawnee Press
Mason *Legende de Nuit* Belwin-Mills
Wigham *Gay Caprice; Summertime Prelude* Willis

VERY DIFFICULT I

Copland *Cat and Mouse* Elkan-Vogel
Gershwin *Prelude* Warner Bros.
Guion *Harmonica Player* Schirmer
Hovhaness *Mystic Flute* Peters
Kennan *Three Preludes* Schirmer
Kramer *Epilogue* J. Fischer/Belwin
MacDowell *Arabesque; Shadow Dance* any standard edition
Soeurs *Impromptu* Willis
Tcherepnin *Bagatelles* MCA

VERY DIFFICULT II

Boykin *Scherzo in B Minor* Schroeder & Gunther
Bernstein *Four Anniversaries* Schirmer
Bloch *Poems of the Sea* Schirmer
Creston *Prelude and Dance* Schirmer
Rachmaninoff *Humoresque* any standard edition
Rachmaninoff *Waltz in A, Op. 10* any standard edition

MUSICALLY ADVANCED I

Carpenter *Polonaise Americaine* Schirmer
MacDowell *Elfin Dance* any standard edition
Mac Dowell *March Wind* any standard edition
Muczynski *Six Preludes* Schirmer
Persichetti *Poems for Piano* Elkan-Vogel
Rachmaninoff *Polichinelle* any standard edition
Schuman, W. *Three-Score Set* Schirmer
Soeurs *Toccata Breve* Willis

MUSICALLY ADVANCED II

Copland *Passacaglia* Senart/Salabert/Belwin
Dello-Joio *Sonatas 2 & 3* Schirmer
Dohnányi *Rhapsody in C* Marks
Griffes *The White Peacock* Schirmer
MacDowell *Concert Etude* any standard edition
Perl *Toccatina* Schirmer
Toch *The Juggler* Schott

CONTEMPORARY PIANO MUSIC AT THE ELEMENTARY AND INTERMEDIATE LEVELS

Compiled and Recommended by Frances Larimer*

COLLECTIONS

American Composers of Today (23 pieces) Marks
American Music by Distinguished Composers, Vols. 1 & 2 (Isadore Freed) Theodore Presser
Canadian Festival Album, 2 Vols. BMI Canada
Contempo I; Contempo II; Contempos in Crimson; Contempos in Jade (Mary E. Clark) Myklas Press
Contemporary Collection for Piano Students, Revised Ed. (Goldstein, Kern, Larimer, Ross, Weiss) Summy-Birchard
Contemporary Music and the Pianist: A Guidebook of Resources and Materials (Alice Canaday) Alfred Publishing Co.
Contemporary Piano Music –a series of collections of new music from other countries – *Czechoslovakian, Bks.1 & 2; Bulgarian, Bks. 1 & 2; Soviet, Bks. 1 & 2; Yugoslav, Bks. 1 & 2; Greek, Bks. 1 & 2; Swiss, Bks. 1 & 2* (Edition Gerig) Belwin-Mills
In the Mode (Mary E. Clark) Myklas Press
Masters of Our Day (18 solos) C. Fischer
Mosaics: 32 Pieces for Learning Musicianship (Marguerite Miller) Sonos Music Resources, Inc.
Teaching and Understanding Contemporary Piano Music (Ellen Thompson) Kjos West
The Twentieth Century: Anthology of Piano Music, Vol. 4 (Agay) Yorktown Press
U. S. A., Vols 1 & 2 MCA
World of Modern Piano Music (Denes Agay) MCA
The Young Pianist's Anthology of Modern Music Associated Music Publishers

SINGLE COMPOSER COLLECTIONS

Anson, George *New Directions* Willis
Adler, Samuel *Gradus, Bks. 1 & 2* Oxford
Applebaum, Stan *Sound/World* Schroeder & Gunther
Bartók, Bela *For Children, Vols. 1 & 2; Mikrokosmos, Vols. 1-6* Boosey & Hawkes
Bernstein, Seymour *Birds, Bks. 1 & 2* Schroeder & Gunther
Butcher, Jane Elizabeth *Hana-Matsuri – Japanese Flower Festival* GWM/Kjos
Cines, Eugene *Abbreviations* Boosey & Hawkes
Dello Joio, Norman *Suite for the Young; Diversions* Belwin-Mills
Diamond, David *A Private World; Alone at the Piano, Bks. 1-3* Peer-Southern *Eight Piano Pieces* Schirmer
Diemer, Emma Lou *Sound Pictures* Boosey & Hawkes
Faith, Richard *Finger Painting; Travels* Shawnee Press
Finney, Ross Lee *32 Piano Games; 24 Inventions* Peters
Floyd, Carlisle *Episodes, Bks. 1 & 2* Boosey & Hawkes
Heiss, John *Four Short Pieces* Boosey & Hawkes
Hopkins, Antony *For Talented Beginners, Bks. 1 & 2* Oxford
Joachim, Otto *12 Twelve-Tone Pieces* Associated Music Publishers
Kraehenbuehl, David *Calendar Scenes* Schmitt Publications
Kunz, Alfred *Music to Do Things By, Bks. 1 & 3* Waterloo Music (Canada)
Lombardo, Robert *12 Contemporary Pieces for Children* Peer-Southern
Long, Tom *Alea, Music By Chance* Canyon Press
Mack, Glen *Adventures in Modes and Keys* Summy-Birchard
Mageau, Mary Magdalen *Forecasts* Schmitt Publications

***Frances Larimer is an Associate Professor of Piano and Director of Group Piano and Piano Pedagogy at Northwestern University, Evanston, Illinois. Used by permission.**

Mailman, Martin *Martha's Vineyard* Theodore Presser
McCabe, John *Five Bagatelles* Eklin/Galaxy
Muczynski, Robert *Fables* Schirmer
Noona, Walter and Carol *The Contemporary Performer, Phases 1-4* Heritage Press
Pentland, Barbara *Music of Now, Bks. 1-3* Waterloo Music (Canada)
Persichetti, Vincent *Little Piano Book* Elkan-Vogel
Phillips, Burrill *Five Various and Sundry* Elkan-Vogel
Rea, John *What You Will: 12 Single Pieces or 6 Polytonal Duets* Jaymar Publications
Schloss, Julius *23 Pieces in Twelve-Tone Style; 23 Studies in Twelve-Tone Style* Peer-Southern
Shaw, Arnold *Stabiles* Mansion Music Corp.
Sheftel, Paul *Interludes* C. Fischer
Starer, Robert *Sketches in Color, Sets 1 & 2; Seven Vignettes; Preludes* MCA
Stevens, Everett *Modal Miniatures* Oliver Ditson
Stravinsky, Soulima *Piano Music for Children, Bks. 1 & 2* Peters
Weybright, June *Mildly Contemporary, Bks. 1 & 2* Belwin-Mills
Wuensch, Gerhard *12 Glimpses into 20th Century Idioms* Leeds Music (Canada)

Collections from Poland:

Garscia, Janina *Favourite Tunes; Let's Play a Piano Duet, Bks. 1 & 2*
Hundziak, Andrezej *A Circus*
Luciuk, Julius *Children's Improvisations*
Niewiadomska, B. *Miniatures for Piano*
Raube, S. *Little Frogs*
Serocki, K. *Les Gnomes; Small Pieces for Piano*

POP-ROCK-JAZZ-BLUES COLLECTIONS

Adams, Paul *Folk Rock* Belwin-Mills
Bastien, James *Country, Western 'n Folk, Bks. 1 & 2* GWM/Kjos
Bastien, Jane S. *Pop, Rock 'n Blues, Bks. 1-3; Rock 'n Blues for Fun* GWM/Kjos
Brubeck, Dave *Jazz Impressions of New York; Themes from Eurasia* Shawnee Press
Gordon, Louis *Junior Jazz; Jazz Meets Junior* Belwin-Mills
Grove, Roger *Jazz About* GWM/Kjos
Kraehenbuehl, David *Jazz and Blues, Bks. 1-6* Summy-Birchard
Metis, Frank *Rock Modes and Moods* Belwin-Mills
Noona, Walter and David Glover *An Adventure in Jazz, Bks. 1-4* Belwin-Mills
Stecher/Horowitz/Gordon *Rock With Jazz, Bks. 1-5* G. Schirmer
Waldron, Mal *Reflections in Modern Jazz* Sam Fox

PIANO ENSEMBLE

Aitken, Hugh *Four Pieces, Four Hands* Elkan-Vogel
Dello Joio, Norman *Images; Family Album* Belwin-Mills *Stage Parodies* Associated Music Publishers
Metis, Frank *Pop/Rock Sketches for Piano Duet; Easy Pop/Rock Sketches* (multiple pianos); *Easy Together* (multiple pianos); *Good 'n' Groovey* (multiple pianos); *Kids and Keyboards* (multiple pianos) Belwin-Mills
Persichetti, Vincet *Serenade No. 8* Elkan-Vogel
Rollino and Sheftel *Festivities; Further Festivities* C. Fischer
Sabol, Mary *Rock and Rhythm* Canyon Press
Starer, Robert *Five Duets for Young Pianists* MCA
Walton, William *Duets for Children, Bks. 1 & 2* Oxford
Zaninelli, Luigi *Lexicon of Beasties* Shawnee Press

MATERIALS FOR IMPROVISATION

Burns, Betty and Jackie Graham *You Do It, Bks. 1-7* GWM/Kjos
Gray, Jerry *Bluesblues* Mitchell Madison, Inc.
Konowitz, Bert *The Complete Rock Piano Method* Alfred Music Co.
Jazz for Piano, Bks. 1 & 2; Jazz is a Way of Playing Lee Roberts/Schirmer
Lloyd, Ruth and Norman *Creative Keyboard Musicianship* Harper & Row
Mack, Glen *Adventures in Improvisation* Summy-Birchard
McLean, Edwin *Improvisation for the Pianist* Myklas Press
Mehegan, John *The Jazz Pianist, Bks. 1-3* Sam Fox
Metis, Frank *Rhythm Factory* Belwin-Mills
Noona, Walter and Carol *The Improvisor, Phases A-C; Improvisor Projects, Phases A-C* Heritage Press
Swain, Alan *Four-Way Keyboard System, Bks. 1-3* Creative Music

TEEN-AGE TEACHING MATERIALS

Compiled and Recommended by Ylda Novik*

Agay *Mosaics* MCA
Agay *Sonatina No. 3* Sam Fox
Bach (ed. Kalmusor) *Aria Variata Alla Maniere Italiane* Peters
Bach (ed. Palmer) *Fantasia in C Minor* Alfred Music
Barber *Excursions* Schirmer
Bartók *Allegro Barbaro* Boosey & Hawkes
Bartók *Hungarian Peasant Songs (15)* Boosey & Hawkes
Bartók *Rondos, Three* Boosey & Hawkes
Bartók *Rumanian Folk Dances* Boosey & Hawkes
Bartók *Sonatina* Boosey & Hawkes
Bartók *Ten Easy Pieces* Boosey & Hawkes
Bernal *Carteles* Southern Music Publishing Co.
Chopin (ed. Palmer) *Chopin, An Introduction to His Piano Works* Alfred Music
Creston *Five Little Dances* Schirmer
Dello Joio *Suite for Piano* Schirmer
Gershwin *Three Preludes* Warner Bros.
Ginastera *Danzas Argentinas* Elkan-Vogel
Ginastera *Twelve American Preludes, Vol. 1* Carl Fischer
Hovhaness *Macedonian Mountain Dance* Peters
Hovhaness *Mountain Dance No. 2* Peters
Latrobe *Three Sonatas* Boosey & Hawkes
Lavry *Five Country Dances* MCA
Liszt *Five Hungarian Folk Songs* Schirmer
Liszt *Six Consolations* Kalmus
Palmer *Baroque Folk* Alfred Music
Poulenc *Mouvements Perpetuels* J. & W. Chester
Rosza *Berceuse* Associated
B. Rubinstein *Day in the Country* C. Fischer
Santoro *Danzas Brazilieras* Southern Music Publishing Co.
Smith, Hale *Faces of Jazz* Marks
Starer *Sketches in Color* MCA
Starer *Three Israeli Sketches* MCA
Tauriello *Toccata* Boosey & Hawkes
Tcherepnin *Bagatelles* MCA

*Used by permission

RECENTLY PUBLISHED COLLECTIONS FOR THE INTERMEDIATE AND EARLY ADVANCED STUDENT

Selected and Recommended by Jeanne Hansen Weisman*

INTERMEDIATE

Agay (ed.) *The Joy of Baroque* Yorktown
Agay (ed.) *The Joy of Romantic Piano, Bk. 1* Yorktown
Bastien (ed.) *Piano Literature, Vol. 3* GWM/Kjos
Bastien (ed.) *Sonatina Favorites, Bks. 1 & 2* GWM/Kjos
Brisman (ed.) *Baroque Dynamite* Alfred
Brisman (ed.) *Classical Classics* Alfred
(collection) *Easy Keyboard Music from Two Centuries, Vol. 1* Henle
(collection) *Easy Piano Solos by Classical and Romantic Composers, Vol. 1* Henle
(collection) *The Ragtime Current* Marks
(collection) *The Young Pianist's Anthology of Modern Music* Associated
Olson/Bianchi/Blickenstaff (eds.) *Repertoire 5A & 5B* C. Fischer
Palmer (ed.) *The Baroque Era* Alfred
Palmer & Lethco (eds.) *Creating Music at the Piano, Bk. 6* Alfred
Svavai & Veszpremi (eds.) *Album for Piano, Bk. 1* Belwin-Mills
Svavai & Veszpremi (eds.) *Album for Piano, Bk. 2* Belwin-Mills

UPPER INTERMEDIATE

Agay (ed.) *The Joy of Romantic Piano, Bk. 2* Yorktown
Agay (ed.) *Piano Recital, Intermediate to Early Advanced* Amsco
Agay (ed.) *Sonatas: Classics to Moderns* Consolidated
Agay (ed.) *Themes and Variations* Consolidated
Bastien (ed.) *Piano Literature, Vol. 4* GWM/Kjos
Bastien (ed.) *Sonatina Favorites, Bk. 3* GWM/Kjos
Bergenfeld (ed.) *Renaissance to Rock* Amsco
(collection) *Easy Keyboard Music from Two Centuries, Vol. 2* Henle
(collection) *Easy Piano Solos by Classical and Romantic Composers, Vol. 2* Henle
(collection) *Easy Variations for Piano by Baroque and Classical Composers* Henle
(collection) *Selected Piano Sonatas by Classical Composers* Henle
Kuehl (ed.) *An Introduction to the Spanish Keyboard* Alfred

EARLY ADVANCED

Agay (ed.) *The Baroque Period* Yorktown
Agay (ed.) *The Classical Period* Yorktown
Agay (ed.) *The Romantic Period* Yorktown
Agay (ed.) *The Twentieth Century* Yorktown
Blesh (ed.) *Classic Rags, Complete Original Music for 81 Piano Rags* Dover
(collection) *Piano Performance: Modern Pieces for the Young Artist* Amsco
Lubin (ed.) *Beethoven and his Circle* Amsco
Lubin (ed.) *Chopin and his Circle* Amsco
Maitland & Squire (eds.) *The Fitzwilliam Virginal Book, Vols. 1 & 2* Dover

***Jeanne Hansen Weisman teaches piano in suburban Akron, Ohio. She and her husband own and operate a music business (Allegro Enterprises) specializing in classical and instructional piano literature. Used by permission.**

Appendix D
Publishers of Keyboard Music

Acorn Music Press, See – Music Sales Corp.
Alfred Publishing Co., Inc., 15335 Morrison Street, Sherman Oaks, California 91403
American Composers Alliance, 170 West 74th Street, New York, New York 10023
American Music Edition, See – Carl Fischer, Inc.
Amsco Music Publishing, See – Music Sales Corp.
Arrow Music Press, See – Boosey & Hawkes, Inc.
Ashley Publications, Inc., 263 Veterans Blvd., Carlstadt, New Jersey 07072
Associated Music Publishers, Inc., 866 Third Avenue, New York, New York 10022
(distributed by G. Schirmer, Inc.)
Mel Bay Publications, Inc., 107 W. Jefferson, Kirkwood, Missouri 63122
Belmont Music Publishers, P. O. Box 49961, Los Angeles, California 90049
Belwin-Mills Publishing Corp., 25 Deshon Drive, Melville, New York 11746
Benner Publishers, 1739 Randolph Road, Schenectady, New York 12308
Berklee Publishers, 1140 Boylston Street, Boston, Massachusetts 02215
The Big 3 Music Corp., 729 Seventh Avenue, New York, New York 10019
Joseph Boonin, Inc., P. O. Box 2124, South Hackensack, New Jersey 07606
Boosey & Hawkes, Inc., P. O. Box 130, Oceanside, New York 11572
Boston Music Co., 116 Boylston Street, Boston, Massachusetts 02116
Bourne Co., 1212 Avenue of the Americas, New York, New York 10036
Brodt Music Co., 1409 East Independence Blvd., Charlotte, North Carolina 28205
Alexander Broude, Inc., 225 West 57th Street, New York, New York 10019
Broude Brothers, Ltd., 56 West 45th Street, New York, New York 10036
Canyon Press, Inc., P. O. Box 1235, Cincinnati, Ohio 45201
Century Music Publishing Co., See – Ashley Publications, Inc.
Chappell Music Co., 810 Seventh Avenue, New York, New York 10019
(distributed by Theodore Presser Co.)
M. M. Cole Publishing Co., 251 East Grand Avenue, Chicago, Illinois 60611
Franco Colombo, Inc., See – Belwin-Mills Publishing Corp.
Columbia Pictures Publications, 16333 N. W. 54th Avenue, Hialeah, Florida 33014
Composers Press, Inc., See – Seesaw Music Press
Consolidated Music Publishers, Inc., See – Music Sales Corp.
Oliver Ditson Co., See – Theodore Presser Co.
Dover Publications, Inc., 180 Varick Street, New York, New York 10014
Durand, Fis., See – Elkan-Vogel, Inc.
Elkan-Vogel, Inc., See – Theodore Presser Co.
Emerson Music, 265 West Emerson Drive, Melrose, Massachusetts 02176
Carl Fischer, Inc., 62 Cooper Square, New York, New York 10003
J. Fischer and Bro., See – Belwin-Mills Publishing Corp.
Harold Flammer, Inc., See – Shawnee Press, Inc.
Mark Foster Music Co., P. O. Box 4012, Champaign, Illinois 61820
Sam Fox Publishing Co., Inc., See – Carl Fischer, Inc.
Frank Music Corp., 119 West 57th Street, New York, New York 10019
Galaxy Music Corp., 2121 Broadway, New York, New York 10023
General Music Publishing Co., Inc., P. O. Box 267, Hastings-on-Hudson, New York 10706
General Words and Music Co., (GWM), See – Neil A. Kjos Music Company
H. W. Gray Co., Inc., See – Belwin-Mills Publishing Corp.
Hamelle & Cie., See – Theodore Presser Co.
Hansen Publications, Inc., 1842 West Avenue, Miami Beach, Florida 33139
The Frederick Harris Music Co., Limited, 529 Speers Rd., Oakville, Ontario LGK 2G4, Canada
Editio Helios, See – Mark Foster Music Co.
Henmar Press, See – C. F. Peters Corp.
Heritage Music Press, See – Lorenz Industries
Hinrichsen Edition, Ltd., See – C. F. Peters Corp.
Hinshaw Music, Inc., P. O. Box 470, Chapel Hill, North Carolina 27514
The International Music Company, 509 Fifth Avenue, New York, New York 10017
Jean Jobert, See – Theodore Presser Co.
Edwin F. Kalmus, P. O. Box 1007, Opa-Locka, Florida 33054
(distributed by Belwin-Mills)

Kenyon Publications, 17 West 60th Street, New York, New York 10023
Keyboard Publications, Inc., 1346 Chapel Street, New Haven, Connecticut 06511
Neil A. Kjos Music Company, National Order Desk, 4382 Jutland Drive, San Diego, California 92117
Kjos West, See – Neil A. Kjos Music Company
Larrabbee Publications, See – Ashley Publications, Inc.
Lawson-Gould Music Publishers, Inc., See – G. Schirmer, Inc.
Leduc, See – Theodore Presser Co.
Leeds Music Corp., See – MCA Music
Hal Leonard Publishing Corp., 960 E. Mark Street, Winona, Minnesota 55987
Lewis Music Publishing Co., Inc., See – Ashley Publications, Inc.
Lillenas Publishing Co., Box 527, Kansas City, Missouri 64141
Lorenz Industries, 501 East Third Street, Dayton, Ohio 45401
Magnamusic-Baton, 10370 Page Industrial Blvd, St. Louis, Missouri 63132
Edward B. Marks Music Corp., 1790 Broadway, New York, New York 10019
(distributed by Belwin-Mills)
MCA Music, 445 Park Avenue, New York, New York 10022
(distributed by Belwin-Mills)
Mercury Music Corp., See – Theodore Presser Co.
M-F Co., Box 351, Evanston, Illinois 60204
Mills Music, Inc., See – Belwin-Mills Publishing Corp.
Montgomery Music, Inc., Box 157, Niagara Square Station, Buffalo, New York 14202
Musicord Publications, Inc., See – Belwin-Mills Publishing Corp.
Music Publishers Holding Corp., See – Warner Bros. Publications, Inc.
Music Sales Corporation, 33 West 60th Street, New York, New York 10023
Music Treasure Publications, 620 Fort Washington Avenue, No. 1-F, New York, New York, 10040
Myklas Press, P. O. Box 929, Boulder, Colorado 80306
National Keyboard Arts Associates, University Park, Princeton, New Jersey 05840
Novello Publications, Inc., 145 Palisade St., Dobbs Ferry, New York 10522
Oak Publications, See – Music Sales Corp.
Oxford University Press, Inc., 200 Madison Avenue, New York, New York 10016
Peer-Southern Organization, 1740 Broadway, New York, New York 10019
C. F. Peters Corp., 373 Park Avenue South, New York, New York 10016
Piedmont Music Co., Inc., See – Edward B. Marks Music Corp.
Pointer System, See – Hal Leonard Publishing Corp.
Theodore Presser Co., Presser Place, Bryn Mawr, Pennsylvania 19010
Pro Art Publishing, Inc., 469 Union Avenue, Westbury, New York 11590
Providence Music Press, P. O. Box 2362, East Side Station, Providence, Rhode Island 02906
Puget Music Publications, Inc., P. O. Box 471, Kenmore, Washington 98028
Remick Music Corp., See – Warner Bros. Publications, Inc.
Ricordi, See – G. Schirmer, Inc.
Lee Robert Music Publications, Inc., Box 225, Katanah, New York 10536
(distributed by G. Schirmer, Inc.)
R. D. Row, See – Carl Fischer, Inc.
Editions Salabert, 575 Madison Avenue, New York, New York 10022
Schaum Publications, Inc., 2018 East North Avenue, Milwaukee, Wisconsin 53202
E. C. Schirmer Music Company, 112 South Street, Boston, Massachusetts 02111
G. Schirmer, Inc., 866 Third Avenue, New York, New York 10022
Schmitt Publications, 110 North Fifth St., Minneapolis, Minnesota 55403
Schott, See – Joseph Boonin, Inc.
Schroeder & Gunther, See – Associated Music Publishers, Inc.
Edward Schuberth and Co., Inc., See – Ashley Publications, Inc.
Screen Gems-Columbia Publications, See – Columbia Pictures Publications
Seesaw Music Corp., 177 East 87th Street, New York, New York 10028
Shawnee Press, Inc., Delaware Water Gap, Pennsylvania 18327
Sonos Music Resources, Inc., Department CM, 1800 South State, Orem, Utah 84057
Southern Music Company, 1100 Broadway, San Antonio, Texas 78206
Southern Music Publishing Co., See – Peer Southern Organization
Stipes Publishing Co., 10-12 Chester Street, Champaign, Illinois 61820
Studio P/R, Inc., 224 South Lebanon Street, Lebanon, Indiana 46052
Summy-Birchard Co., 1834 Ridge Avenue, Evanston, Illinois 60204
Universal Editions, See – Joseph Boonin, Inc.
The University Society, Inc., 25 Cottage Street, Midland Park, New Jersey 07432
Volkwein Bros., 117 Sandusky, Pittsburgh, Pennsylvania 15212
Warner Bros. Publications, Inc., 75 Rockefeller Plaza, New York, New York 10019
Waterloo Music Company, Ltd., 3 Regina Street, North, Waterloo, Ontario, Canada
Willis Music Co., 7380 Industrial Highway, Florence, Kentucky 41042
M. Witmark and Sons, See – Warner Bros. Publications, Inc.
Yorktown Music Press, Inc., See – Music Sales Corp.

Appendix E

Historical Listing of Concert Pianists

THE PAST GENERATION

Louis Moreau Gottschalk, American (1828-1869)
Anton Rubinstein, Russian (1829-1894)
Amy Fay, American (1844-1928)
Vladimir de Pachmann, Russian (1848-1933)
Ignace Jan Paderewski, Polish (1860-1941)
Moriz Rosenthal, Polish (1862-1946)
Leopold Godowsky, Polish-American (1870-1938)
Sergei Rachmaninoff, Russian (1873-1943)
Josef Lhevinne, Russian-American (1874-1944)
Josef Hofmann, Polish-American (1876-1957)
Alfred Cortot, French (1877-1962)
Ossip Gabrilowitsch, Russian-American (1878-1936)
Wanda Landowska, Polish (1879-1959)
(pianist-harpsichordist)
Artur Schnabel, Austrian (1882-1951)
Wilhelm Backhaus, German (1884-1969)
Edwin Fischer, Swiss (1886-1960)
Myra Hess, English (1890-1966)
Benno Moiseiwitsch, Russian (1890-1963)
Walter Gieseking, German (1895-1956)
Clara Haskil, Rumanian (1895-1960)

THE OLDER GENERATION

Artur Rubinstein, Polish-American (1887-)
José Iturbi, Spanish-American (1895-)
Wilhelm Kempff, German (1895-)
Alexander Brailowsky, Russian (1896-1976)
Guiomar Novaes, Brazilian (1896-)
Robert Casadesus, French (1899-1972)
Cutner Solomon, English (1902-)
Claudio Arrau, Chilian (1903-)
Rudoff Serkin, German-American (1903-)
Vladimir Horowitz, Russian-American (1904-)
Louis Kentner, Hungarian-English (1905-)
Oscar Levant, American (1906-1972)
Clifford Curzon, English (1907-)
Beveridge Webster, American (1908-)
Lili Krauss, Hungarian-American (1908-)
Alexander Uninsky, Russian-American (1910-1972)
Rudolf Firkusny, Czech (1912-)
Hans Richter-Hauser, German (1912-)
Gyorgy Sandor, Hungarian-American (1912-)
Gina Bachauer, Greek (1913-1976)
Witold Malcuzynski, Polish (1914-)
Sviatoslav Richter, Russian (1914-)
Rosalyn Tureck, American (1914-)
Jorge Bolet, Cuban-American (1914-)
Emil Gilels, Russian (1916-)

Dinu Lipatti, Rumanian (1917-1950)
Arturo Benedetti Michelangeli, Italian (1920-)
William Kapell, American (1922-1953)

THE MIDDLE GENERATION

William Masselos, American (1920-)
Grant Johannesen, American (1921-)
Geza-Anda, Hungarian (1921-1976)
Alicia de Larrocha, Spanish (1923-)
Leonard Pennario, American (1924-)
Ruth Slenczynska, American (1925-)
Eugene Istomin, American (1925-)
Julius Katchen, American (1926-1969)
Raymond Lewenthal, American
Theodore Lettvin, American (1926-)
Paul Badura-Skoda, Austrian (1927-)
Jorg Demus, Austrian (1928-)
Leon Fleischer, American (1928-)
Gary Graffman, American (1928-)
Byron Janis, American (1928-)
Alexis Weissenberg, Bulgarian (1929-)
David Bar-Illan, Israeli (1930-)
Friedrich Gulda, Austrian (1930-)
Lazar Berman, Russian (1931-)
Alfred Brendel, Austrian (1931-)
Tamas Vasary, Hungarian (1931-)

THE YOUNGER GENERATION

Ivan Davis, American (1932-)
Glen Gould, Canadian (1932-)
Claudette Sorel, French-American (1932-)
John Browning, American (1933-)
Agustin Aneivas, American (1934-)
Van Cliburn, American (1934-)
Philippe Entremont, French (1934-)
Malcom Frager, American (1935-)
Vladimir Ashkenazy, Russian (1936-)
Coleman Blumfield, American (1938-)
Ilana Vered, Israeli
Michael Ponti, Italian
Ralph Votapek, American (1939-)
Steven Bishop, American (1940-)
James Dick, American (1940-)
Martha Argerich, Argentine (1941)
Daniel Barenboim, Israeli (1942-)
Maurizio Pollini, Italian (1942-)
Aleksander Slobodyanik, Russian (1942-)
John Lill, English (1944-)
Lorin Hollander, American (1944-)
Jean-Bernard Pommier, French (1944-)
Nelson Freire, Brazilian (1944-)
Yevgeny Mogilevsky, Russian (1945-)
Minoru Nojima, Japanese (1945-)
Rafael Orozeo, Spanish (1946-)
Murray Perahia, American (1947-)
Radu Lupu, Rumanian
Andre Watts, American
Mark Westcott, American
Misha Dichter, American (1945-)
Garrick Ohlsson, American (1948-)
Horacio Gutierrez, Cuban-American
Vladimir Viardo, Russian (1950-)

Appendix F
Chronological Listing of Keyboard Composers

BAROQUE PERIOD (1600-1750)

Jean Baptiste Lully, French (1632-1687)
Henry Purcell, English (1658-1695)
Francois Couperin, French (1668-1733)
Georg Philipp Telemann, German (1681-1767)
Jean-Philippe Rameau, French (1683-1764)
Johann Sebastian Bach, German (1685-1750)
Domenico Scarlatti, Italian (1685-1757)
Georg Frideric Handel, German (1685-1759)

CLASSICAL PERIOD (1775-1825)

PRE-CLASSIC KEYBOARD COMPOSERS

Wilhelm Friedemann Bach, German (1710-1784)
Carl Philipp Emanuel Bach, German (1714-1788)
Johann Philipp Kirnberger, German (1721-1783)
Johann Christian Bach, German (1735-1782)

CLASSICAL KEYBOARD COMPOSERS

Joseph Haydn, Austrian (German) (1732-1809)
Muzio Clementi, Italian (1752-1832)
Wolfgang Amadeus Mozart, German (1756-1791)
Daniel Gottlieb Türk, German (1756-1813)
Johann Dussek, Bohemian (1760-1812)
Ludwig van Beethoven, German (1770-1827)
Anton Diabelli, Austrian (1781-1858)
Friedrich Kuhlau, German (1786-1832)

ROMANTIC PERIOD (1800-1900)

Franz Schubert, German (1797-1828)
Friedrich Burgmüller, German (1806-1874)
Felix Mendelssohn, German (1809-1847)
Frédéric Francois Chopin, Polish (1810-1849)
Robert Schumann, German (1810-1856)
Franz Liszt, Hungarian (1811-1886)
Stephen Heller, Hungarian (1813-1888)
Fritz Spindler, German (1817-1905)
Theodor Kullak, German (1818-1882)

Louis Köhler, German (1820-1886)
Cornelius Gurlitt, German (1820-1901)
Cesar Auguste Franck, French (1822-1890)
Louis Moreau Gottschalk, American (1829-1869)
Johannes Brahms, German (1833-1897)
Camille Saint-Säens, French (1835-1921)
Mili Balakirev, Russian (1837-1910)
Modest Mussorgsky, Russian (1839-1881)
Peter Ilyich Tchaikovsky, Russian (1840-1893)
Edvard Grieg, Norwegian (1844-1908)
Gabriel Fauré, French (1845-1924)
Isaac Albeniz, Spanish (1860-1909)
Anton Arensky, Russian (1861-1906)
Vladimir Rebikoff, Russian (1866-1920)

CONTEMPORARY PERIOD (1900-)

Edward MacDowell, American (1861-1908)
Claude Debussy, French (1862-1918)
Alexander Gretchaninoff, Russian (1864-1956)
Erik Satie, French (1866-1925)
Alexander Scriabin, Russian (1872-1915)
Max Reger, German (1873-1916)
Sergei Rachmaninoff, Russian (1873-1943)
Arnold Schoenberg, German (1874-1951)
Maurice Ravel, French (1875-1937)
Manuel de Falla, Spanish (1876-1946)
Ernst von Dohnanyi, Hungarian (1877-1960)
Ernest Bloch, Swiss (1880-1959)
Béla Bartók, Hungarian (1881-1945)
Joaquin Turina, Spanish (1882-1949)
Igor Stravinsky, Russian (1882-1971)
Anton Webern, Austrian (1883-1945)
Alfredo Casella, Italian (1883-1947)
Alban Berg, Austrian (1885-1935)
Heitor Villa-Lobos, Brazilian (1887-1959)
Jacques Ibert, French (1890-1962)
Sergei Prokofieff, Russian (1891-1953)
Darius Milhaud, French (1892-1974)
Paul Hindemith, German (1895-1963)
George Gershwin, American (1898-1937)
Francis Poulenc, French (1899-1963)
Alexander Tcherepnin, Russian (1899-1977)
Aaron Copland, American (1900-)
Ernst Krenek, Austrian (1900-)
Aram Khachaturian, Russian (1903-1978)
Dmitri Kabalevsky, Russian (1904-)
Dmitri Shostakovich, Russian (1906-1975)
Paul Creston, American (1906-)
Ross Lee Finney, American (1906-)
Elliott Carter, American (1908-)
Samuel Barber, American (1910-)
Gian Carlo Menotti, American (1911-)
Norman Dello Joio, American (1913-)
Vincent Persichetti, American (1915-)
David Diamond, American (1915-)
Alberto Ginastera, Argentine (1916-)
Leonard Bernstein, American (1918-)
Ned Rorem, American (1923-)
Robert Starer, American (1924-)
Robert Muczynski, American (1929-)
Stanley Babin, Israeli (1932-)

Appendix G
Brief Dictionary of Musical Terms

TEMPO Indicates rate of speed.

Largo – broadly, very slowly
Lento – slowly
Adagio – slowly, leisurely
Andante – a walking pace, flowing
Andantino – slightly faster than andante
Moderato – moderately
Allegretto – quickly, but not as fast as allegro
Allegro – at a quick pace, lively
Vivace or Vivo – lively
Presto – very fast
Prestissimo – faster than presto

Changing Tempos

Accelerando (*accel.*) to become faster
A tempo – resume original tempo
Mosso – motion
Moto – motion ; (*con moto*) with motion, or quicker
Rallentando (*rall.*) gradually slowing in speed
Ritardando (*rit.*) becoming slower
Ritenuto (*riten.*) immediate slowing

DYNAMICS Pertaining to the volume of sound.

Pianissimo (*pp*) very soft
Piano (*p*) soft
Mezzo piano (*mp*) moderately soft
Mezzo forte (*mf*) moderately loud
Forte (*f*) loud
Fortissimo (*ff*) very loud
Sforzando (*sfz*) strong accent

Changing Dynamics

Crescendo (*cresc.*) growing louder <
Decrescendo (*decresc.*) growing softer >
Diminuendo (*dim., dimin.*) growing softer

STYLE The character of mood of the composition.

Animato – animated, with spirit

Brio – vigor, spirit
Cantabile – singing
Dolce – sweetly
Espressivo (*espress.*) with expression, feeling
Giocoso – humorously
Grazioso – gracefully
Legato (*leg.*) smoothly connected tones
Maestoso – majestically
Marcia – as a march
Portamento – slightly disconnected tones
Scherzando – playfully
Sostenuto – sustained
Staccato (*stacc.*) disconnected tones
Tenuto (*ten.*) held note
Tranquillo – calm, quiet, tranquil

MISCELLANEOUS TERMS

Coda – ending
Con – with
D. C. (*Da Capo*) go to the beginning
D. C. al Fine – repeat from the beginning to the end (Fine)
D. S. (*Dal Segno*) the sign
D. S. al Fine – repeat from the sign to the end (Fine)
Fermata – pause, or hold the note
Fine – the end
Loco – in normal location or pitch register
Meno – less
Molto – much
Non – not
Piu – more
Poco – a little
Poco a poco – little by little, gradually
Sempre – always
Simile – in a similar way
Troppo – too much

NOTES AND RESTS

whole note
half note
quarter note
eighth note
sixteenth note
thirty-second note
grace note – to be played quickly
arpeggiated, or rolled chord

whole rest
half rest
quarter rest
eighth rest
sixteenth rest
thirty-second rest

SIGNS

— sharp

— double sharp

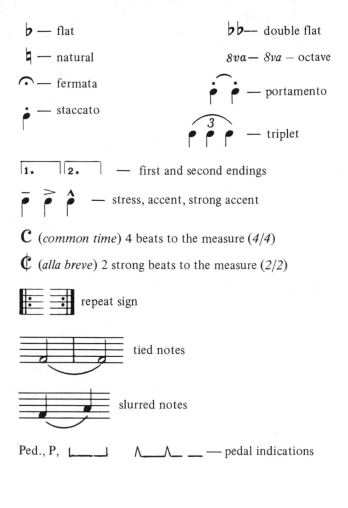

♭ — flat

♭♭— double flat

♮ — natural

8va— *8va* – octave

𝄐 — fermata

 — portamento

 — staccato

 — triplet

 — first and second endings

 — stress, accent, strong accent

𝄴 (*common time*) 4 beats to the measure (*4/4*)

𝄵 (*alla breve*) 2 strong beats to the measure (*2/2*)

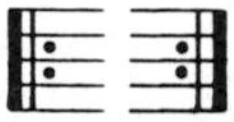 repeat sign

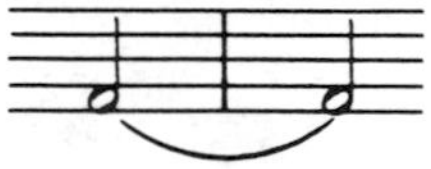 tied notes

 slurred notes

Ped., P,  — pedal indications

Index of Compositions

General Index